HEALING THE MIND

Michael Stone, M.D., is Professor of Clinical
Psychiatry at Columbia College of Physicians &
Surgeons in New York. He is the author of
several books, including *Abnormalities of Personality: Within and Beyond the Realm of Treatment.*

HEALING THE MIND

A History of Psychiatry
from Antiquity to the Present

MICHAEL H. STONE

PIMLICO

Published by Pimlico 1998

2 4 6 8 10 9 7 5 3 1

The photographs on pages 27, 29, 31, 39, 45, 46, 47, 66, 77, 82, 88, 89, 91, 97,
102, 103, 107, 113, 114, 121, 124, 126, 129, 130, 131, 132, 133, 136 and 272
taken by Zindman/Fremont

First published by W.W. Norton & Company, Inc. 1997
Pimlico edition 1998
Random House, 20 Vauxhall Bridge Road,
London SW1V 2SA

Random House Australia (Pty) Limited
20 Alfred Street, Milsons Point, Sydney,
New South Wales 2061, Australia

Random House New Zealand Limited
18 Poland Road, Glenfield,
Auckland 10, New Zealand

Random House South Africa (Pty) Limited
Endulini, 5A Jubilee Road, Parktown 2193, South Africa

Random House UK Limited Reg. No. 954009

A CIP catalogue record for this book
is available from the British Library

ISBN 0-7126-6662-1

Papers used by Random House UK Limited are natural,
recyclable products made from wood grown in sustainable forests.
The manufacturing processes conform to the environmental
regulations of the country of origin

Printed and bound in Great Britain by
CPD, Wales

FOR JOHN GACH

CONTENTS

PREFACE

My interest in the history of psychiatry began some 25 years ago, when I was asked to teach a course on the subject to the residents in training at the New York State Psychiatric Institute. There was an antiquarian section in the Institute library that was helpful in getting me started with the necessary research, but the rare books could not be taken out. In order to have something to show the students, and to give them a more direct "feel" for the old literature, I began purchasing some of the old books of historical importance in our field: Pinel's *Nosographie Philosophique*, Burton's *Anatomy of Melancholy*, Weyer's *De Praestigiis Daemonum* were among the first.

What started out as a hobby soon became—well—something more than a hobby. This evolution can perhaps be best explained by reference to one the old books themselves: the *Medicine of the Passions*, an 1841 monograph by a little-known French alienist, Jean-Baptiste Descuret. There, in a chapter devoted to the various "monomanias," Descuret had this to say about book collectors: "The difference between bibliophilia and bibliomania is that the bibliophile *possesses* books, while those with bibliomania are possessed *by* the books." I leave it to the reader to guess on which side of the line I stand. In the intervening 25 years, I have haunted antiquarian shops in the United States, France, England, Sweden, Germany, Italy, Denmark, and the Netherlands in the never-ending task of "completing" my personal library.

Many book dealers have aided me in this quest: Jeremy Norman in San Francisco, the late Thomas Heller in New York, Rebecca Hardie in London, Franz Siegle in Germany, Alain Brieux in Paris—to mention only a few. But I am most indebted to John Gach of Baltimore, whose stock of rare books on psychiatry and psychology is the largest in the world. A historian of psychiatry in his own right, he has been enormously and unstintingly helpful to me, not only as my main "connection"—for every addict must have his "connection"—but also as one of the few professionals with whom I can discuss the subject and enhance my knowledge of the many writers and the important trends that make up the history of psychiatry. Thanks to my many contacts, but most especially to John Gach, I have by now built up a collection of sufficient size that the "sources" necessary to me in the compilation of this book were, with only two or three exceptions, only a few steps away from my word processor.

I am grateful also to a number of prominent psychiatrists who have sent me historical material or discussed topics of relevance to the history of psychiatry with me. In particular, my thanks go to Dr. Jules Angst of the Burghölzli clinic in Zurich and to Dr. Malcolm Pines in London.

The direct stimulus for this book came from Dr. Allan Tasman, chairman of the psychiatry department at the University of Louisville Medical School. Two years ago Dr. Tasman asked me if I might contribute a chapter on the history of our field to his new textbook of psychiatry: something on the order of 70 pages, he had mentioned. I noticed, by the time I had penned 90 pages, that I was only up to the 16th century. With his indulgence, I went ahead and finished the book into which his "chapter" had grown, and then finally prepared a 70-page précis of this book for him. Dr. Tasman had known of my interest in the history of psychiatry from our days together on the staff at the University of Connecticut Medical Center—though I had not intended to write a book on the subject "until my old age."

As it turns out, old age is not so very far away as I might like to think, and besides, the other English-language texts of Zilboorg and Alexander and Selesnick, both fine in their day, are becoming out of date. It was time for a new "history" and I am grateful to Dr. Tasman for hurrying me along with the mission. Given the dizzying pace of new discoveries and the expansion of psychiatry into all corners of the globe, the next "update" of the history of psychiatry will surely have to be multi-authored. I am well aware that this book is far from a "complete" history, especially in the areas of contemporary psychiatry, with which I am less familiar.

More thanks than I can readily express in words go to Susan Barrows Munro, my editor, for her suggestions and advice on tightening and improving the text, and to my wife Beth, who has sustained me uncomplainingly during the unavoidable incursions into family life that writing a long book necessitates.

PROLOGUE: THE ROLE OF
RELIGION IN HEALING THE MIND

Psychiatry was Religion before it was Psychiatry. Implicit in the opening pages of this book is the fact that in early society, both the understanding of the mind and the healing of its troubles were the province
of religious adepts. In all likelihood, shamans and physicians were later
developments, with the shamans being, in effect, *specialists* within
the domain of religion. Their functions included dispensing advice to
those who were troubled in their personal lives as well as interceding
on behalf of such persons through invocations to the gods. Alongside
these protopsychiatrists were the priests and other religious leaders
entrusted with the task of ensuring group survival and solidarity via
moral instructions and warnings. It seems fair to say that this specialization within the body social must be a reflection of human nature—
of enduring qualities embedded within our species, to be encountered
in all people of all cultures in every epoch.

Religion, among its other functions, addresses our needs both on
the plane of the individual (the domain of the shaman/psychiatrist-
to-be) and on that of the social group (the domain where moral instruction is relevant: How should we behave toward one another?).
In a manner paralleling the evolution of the shaman into the psychiatrist, religious adepts concerned with the group's moral behavior
served as the springboard from which philosophy evolved. This is
especially true of that branch of philosophy concerned primarily with
ethics and morals. Closely related to these themes are a culture's
ideals about raising children. In the writings of Juan Vives we see
how expertise in matters of religion, moral instruction, and pedagogy
can be combined in the same person. In our own day it is common
for persons who are particularly devout in their religious observances

to seek pastoral counseling when seeking help for personal or inter-personal troubles.

To illustrate my point about the importance of religion in the unfolding of our story, I have chosen a number of anecdotes—some ancient, some as fresh as yesterday—drawn from many cultures and many of the major religions.

CHRISTIANITY

The following example is taken from the speech given by Governor Keating of Oklahoma a week after the terrorist bombing of an Oklahoma City federal building, in which almost 200 men, women, and children lost their lives. Governor Keating's address at the memorial service was nonsectarian on the surface yet clearly inspired by a deep Christian faith. Here are some excerpts from his talk reprinted in the April 26, 1995, *New York Times*:

> Today we stand before the world and before our God together, our hearts and our hands linked in a solidarity these criminals can never understand. We stand together in love. . . .
> Through all of this, through the tears, the righteous anger, the soul-rending sorrow, the immeasurable loss, we have sometimes felt alone. But we are never, ever truly alone. We have God and we have each other. . . .
> Today we have our heroes and we have our heroines, saints in gray and blue and whites and khakis—the rescuers and the healers. They have labored long and nobly and they have cried with us. . . .
> And today we have our God. He is not a God of your religion or mine, but of all people in all times. He is a God of love but He is also a God of justice. Today, He assures us, once again, that good is stronger than evil, that love is greater than hate, that each of us is His special child embraced by His father's love. . . . The thousands of us gathered here today are multiplied by God's love, anointed by His gentle mercy. Today we are one with Him and with one another.
> It is right for us to grieve. We have all been touched by this immense tragedy. And our sorrow is part of the healing process. For some of us stricken with intense personal loss, it will be a long and tortured path. For all of us, it is a journey through darkness. But darkness ends in the morning light. That is God's promise, and that is our hope.
> There is a lovely parable of a man who looked back on his life and saw it as an endless series of footprints in the sand. At times

there were two sets of footprints side by side. And he remembered those times as happy times.

At other times, there was only one set of prints—times of sadness and pain. He confronted God. And he asked Him why He had ceased to walk beside him when he most needed that support. Why, he wondered, had God abandoned him, and God answered, "But, my son, those were the times I was carrying you."

He carries us today, cupped gently in his loving hands.

Even as I write this vignette, a year and a half after the event, and after my twentieth or thirtieth reading of Governor Keating's speech, I cannot get through it without tears, though I live two thousand miles from Oklahoma and lost no one in the bombing. The poignancy and wisdom of the Governor's words embody all that is noblest in Christianity and in humankind in general. His was a healing speech, and if psychiatry means *healing of the soul*—whether the individual soul or, as in this instance, the collective soul—then Keating's words were the very essence of psychiatry. Listening to Keating leaves *Listening to Prozac* far, far behind. The Governor's speech should remind us that we are, after all, human, mortal . . . not machines that every so often run out of oil or some other chemical. And there are no chemicals—not Prozac, not Clozaril, not anything to be developed in the 21st century—that will replace a healing speech, a mother's soothing word, a father's reassurance, a religious leader's wisdom, or a psychiatrist's warmly supportive comment or life-unifying interpretation.

BUDDHISM: THE TALE OF THE POPPY SEEDS

The young wife of a wealthy family, Kisagohtami by name, lost her mind in the aftermath of the death of her infant son. Clutching its cold body in her arms, Kisagohtami would wander in the streets, beseeching whomever she encountered to restore health to her "sick" child. The townspeople, having no idea what to do for the crazed soul, would gaze sorrowfully at her for a moment and then walk on past. But a devotee of the Buddha noticed her, and rather than walking past her, suggested to the distraught woman that she go to the abode of the Buddha in Jetavana.

Straightaway, Kisagohtami took herself to the Buddha, carrying the dead infant in her arms. The Buddha, calmly surveying the situation, told her: "Woman! To restore this child, it will require some seeds of the poppy. Go then into the town and get you some four or five seeds. But these poppy seeds—they must come only from the houses of families who have never been touched by Death!"

So the crazed mother went out into the town, asking for the poppy seeds. The seeds themselves would have been easy to obtain—however, there were no such homes whom Death had never touched.

At last, unable to obtain the seeds, Kisagohtami returned to the abode of the Buddha. There in the company of his calm figure, she began to realize the inner meaning of the Buddha's words. As though awakening from a dream, her mind was restored and she buried the cold body of her dead child in a grave. After the burial she returned to the abode of the Buddha and became his disciple. [Author's translation]

In this poignant example of a healing encounter between Gautama Shakyamuni (*Bukkyoh Seiten*, 1966), whom we know as the Buddha, and the distraught mother, genius and compassion are combined in the Buddha's response in such a way as to enable the mother simultaneously to achieve enlightenment (*satori*) and to save face. The Buddha nudges her toward the necessary discovery and acceptance that together would dispel her delusion, yet he does so with consummate gentleness and indirectness. We can understand this as a model of psychotherapy, with its elements of wisdom, empathy, and noble rhetoric—which few who have practiced the art of therapy have reached, let alone surpassed, in the 2,500 years between the time of Buddha and our time.

THE ZEN ROSHI

The story is told of a Zen Buddhist mentor or *roshi* who was once walking along a shallow stream with his disciples. As they came alongside a bamboo bridge, an impatient woman from the minor nobility was shouting angrily at the bridge-tender. It seemed that the bridge had suddenly collapsed, making it impossible for her to get across the stream, unless she were to willing walk in the shallow water, soiling her shoes and her dress. The *roshi* listened briefly to her complaining at the hapless bridge-tender—and then, hoisting her upon his shoulders, waded across the stream and set her down, all clean and dry, on the other side.

Returning to the other shore, the *roshi* then walked on, philosophizing with his disciples. They were aghast and uncomprehending, and interrupted him, saying: "But, *sensei*, why did you carry that woman across the stream? She is nothing but a rude, vain, and arrogant woman, unfit for her high position and undeserving of even a glance from a man of wisdom such as yourself!" This kind of talk kept up for some minutes, as the *roshi* led them on their walk. Finally, turning around to face them, he admonished: "Ah, but *you* are still carrying her."

The time period of this story is unclear; perhaps it dates back a thousand years or so. The story's profundity, both as folk wisdom and as an example of on-the-spot psychotherapy, consists in the difference between the *roshi*'s handling of the "crisis" and that of his disciples.

The *roshi* grasps the situation immediately, solves it efficiently—and promptly forgets about it, returning to his task of teaching philosophy. The disciples were still distracted, obsessively ruminating about the ill-deserving woman.

As with Dante's *Divine Comedy*, this story has meaning on the "anagogic" (leading to a higher level of understanding) level. Therapists working with patients who hold grudges, who complain endlessly about the anniversary present the husband forgot last year, or about the expensive dress the wife bought last fall, can make great use out of the story of the Zen *roshi*. For the master takes care of even unpleasant matters with dispatch and then returns to what is important.

HINDUISM AND THE *BHAGAVAD GITA*

The seeds of the Hindu religion were planted by the Aryan invaders during the first part of the second millennium B.C. (approximately 1600 B.C.). From the standpoint of literature, the religion first found expression in the ecstatic poems of the *Veda*. These in turn influenced the philosophical writings, the *Upanishads*, of the period from 700 to 400 B.C. In the middle of that era Gautama Shakyamuni, the future Buddha, was born in northern India. Although the philosophy that bears his name was strongly influenced by Hinduism—a religion adorned by a pantheon of gods and goddesses—Buddhism is nontheistic (Sargeant, 1979). There are strong similarities between the fundamental message of Hinduism, especially as explicated in the *Bhagavad Gita*, and that of Buddhism. The great poem, the *Bhagavad Gita*, is itself a section of the tremendously long Hindu epic, the *Mahabharata*. The roots of the *Gita* probably go back as far as 800 B.C. and thus antedate the life of Buddha, yet the poem was not written down in the form it has reached us until the second or third century A.D. As such, its final form was apparently modified from the original version—paradoxically, in response to Buddhist lines of thought that had evolved from the earlier Hindu teachings. Buddhism, for example, emphasizes nonviolence (*ahimsa*), a concept adopted in the later version of the *Gita*.

One important parallel between Hinduism and Buddhism is to be found in the *Gita* in an exhortation made by the god Vishnu (in his earthly incarnation as Krishna), speaking to the young warrior Arjuna:

"vita-raga*-bhaya-khrodá//man-maya mam upasritah// bahavo jñana-tapasa//puta mad-bhavam agatah."

"Freed from passion, fear, and anger, clinging only to me,

---

* Raga has also been translated as greed, though its root meaning is that of *color, emotion, passion.*

purified through the penance that comes through wisdom, many have attained my state of being."

Book IV, 10. [Author's translation]

Krishna's advice to Arjuna (the representative of humankind) is similar to a number of key passages in the teachings of Buddha. In the chapter on sin or impurity (in Japanese, *kegara*), it is written:

There are two varieties of sin that cover up and obscure Buddhahood. The first is sin via the intellect; the second is sin associated with the passions [*kanjoh*]. These two sins embrace the whole classification of all possible sins. Spiritual darkness [*mu-myoh*, absence of clarity, ignorance] and lust are capable, on their own, of generating every possible sin . . . and are the sources from which arise three major sins: greed, anger, and foolishness (*musabori, ikari,* and *orokasa* respectively), and the sins related to these: envy, jealousy, deception, extravagance, contempt, insincerity, etc.

[*Bukkyoh Seitan: The Teachings of Buddha, Chap. 4, 1;* Author's translation.]

These passages reflect the prescriptive function of religion or religious philosophy: how human beings should ideally conduct themselves. What, in effect, are the optimal personality or character traits of normal men and women? The Asian religions stress self-abnegation and the suppression of anger. Self-abnegation encompasses the overcoming of desire in its two most common forms: lust and greed. The failure to achieve this freedom from anger, greed, and lust leads to unhappiness, despair, and a great deal else that we would equate with mental "dis-ease"—literally, not being at ease with oneself or with others.

Though there are comparable commandments in Judaism and Christianity, the points of emphasis are different. In the Ten Commandments of the Old Testament greed is condemned in the form of covetousness; lust is condemned in the form of adultery; but anger is not mentioned specifically (though perhaps alluded to in the prohibition against murder), let alone accorded pride of place among the sins. Much later, 13th-century Jewish mystic Moses ben Nachman (*Nachmanides*) singled out anger as the worst evil. Nevertheless, as Scholem noted (1946), the Zohar (the major book of Jewish cabalistic mysticism) places the supreme religious value on continuous attachment or "adhesion" to God, leading to oneness with God and a corresponding loss of preoccupation with the trappings and travails of this world. But this is the same message Krishna wished to impart to Arjuna;

Buddha, to his disciples. The Christian emphasis on humility is a closely related, though not identical, concept.

TWO TALES OF DELUSIONS

Guess Who's Coming to Dinner

A vignette from the 19th century, recorded in John Conolly's 1830 book, *An Inquiry Concerning the Indications of Insanity*, describes a very ingenious method of circumventing the potentially fatal consequences of a delusion. A prince of Bourbon imagined himself to be dead and refused to eat. To prevent him from dying of starvation, he was introduced to two persons who, he was assured, were dead like himself. After some conversation respecting the world of shades, they invited the prince to dine with another distinguished and deceased person, Marshal Tourenne. The prince accepted this polite invitation and they prepared a very hearty dinner. Every day, whilst this fancy prevailed, it was necessary to invite the prince to the table of some ghost of rank and reputation. Yet in the other common affairs of his life, the prince was not incapacitated by attending to his delusions.

The Rooster Conviction

From roughly the same time period comes another story of a deluded prince, this one in a tale told by Rabbi Nachman of Bratzlav. It seems that in a distant land, a prince had lost his mind and imagined himself a rooster. He sought refuge under the table, living there naked, refusing to partake of the royal delicacies served in golden dishes, asking instead for the grain reserved for the roosters. The king was desperate. He had summoned the best physicians, the most famous specialists in the land, but all admitted their incompetence. So did the magicians . . . and the monks, the ascetics, and the miracle-makers; all their interventions had proved fruitless.

One day an unknown sage presented himself at court. "I think that I could heal the prince," he said shyly. "Will you allow me to try?"

The king consented. To the surprise of all present, the sage proceeded to remove his clothes, joined the prince under the table, and began to crow like a rooster!

Suspicious, the prince stopped his crowing to interrogate him: "Who are you and what are you doing here?"

"And you," replied the sage, "who are you and what are you doing here?"

"Can't you see? I am a rooster!"

"Hmm," said the sage, "how very strange to meet you here!"

"Why strange?" asked the prince.

"You mean, you don't see? Really not? You don't see that *I* am a rooster just like you?" exclaimed the sage, feigning surprise.

The two men declared their friendship and swore never to leave each other. And then the sage undertook to cure the prince by using himself as an example. He started by putting on a shirt. The prince couldn't believe his eyes. "Are you crazy?" he gasped. "Are you forgetting who you are? Do you really want to be a man?"

"You know," said the sage in a gentle voice, "you mustn't ever believe that a rooster who dresses like a man ceases to be a rooster." The prince had to agree.

The next day they both dressed in a normal way. When the sage sent for some dishes from the palace kitchen, the prince protested. "Wretch! What are you doing? Are you going to *eat* like them now?"

His friend allayed his fears. "Don't ever think that by eating like men or with men that a rooster ceases to be what he is. You mustn't ever believe that it is enough for a rooster to behave like a man to become human; you can do anything with humans and even for humans and yet remain the rooster you are."

The prince was convinced, and he resumed his life as a prince.

The vignettes of these two princes—the real one of Conolly's book and the fictitious one of Rabbi Nachman's story, both from about two hundred years ago—show a remarkable sensitivity and wisdom in dealing with unmistakably paranoid persons. One of the "healers of the mind" was a physician, the other a religious adept. I include the rabbi's story as "real" in the sense that it must have been a reflection, a distillation, of Nachman's experience with the mentally ill persons he encountered during his years as a religious sage. In both cases we see an instinctive awareness—*intuition* might be a better word—that the hardened convictions of the "psychotic paranoid" (terms that would have been foreign to both Conolly and Nachman) cannot be dented by a frontal assault on the unreasonableness of the deluded thinking. Instead, a roundabout way is needed, one that leads the "patient" inch by inch out of the delusory conviction, and does so in such a way as to spare the person from humiliation. The same premium is put on "saving face" in these two stories as Buddha demonstrated in his approach to the grieving and deluded princess of the Poppy Seed story. We see this same respect for the "crazy" person's thinking in the approach used by the psychoanalytic pioneers who began to work with paranoid or otherwise psychotic patients in the first decades of our waning century. The same recognition is present: that there is a grain of truth in the otherwise deluded idea, which lends a reasonableness to the distortion and establishes a common meeting ground where healer and sufferer can begin to communicate. While our taxonomy has changed considerably, and our understanding of the neurophysiology of mental illness has facilitated unimaginable leaps in treatment since the time of Buddha, our ways of healing the deluded through verbal means, while different perhaps in outward form, have *in their essence changed very little over the past three millennia.*

Healing the Mind

A HISTORY OF PSYCHIATRY

FROM ANTIQUITY

TO THE PRESENT

After the first mention, these citations are abbreviated in the text:

Alexander and Selesnick's *The History of Psychiatry* becomes A. & S.

Beauchesne's *Historie de la psychopathologie* becomes B.

Hunter and Macalpine's *Three Hundred Years of Psychiatry: 1535–1860* becomes H. & M.

Zilboorg's *A History of Medical Psychology* becomes Z.

Unless otherwise noted, all citations to Sigmund Freud can be found in *The Complete Psychological Works of Sigmund Freud*, translated and edited by James Strachey, New York: Norton.

PART I

The Early Period:

1000 B.C.–Fifteenth Century

Chapter 1

A LONG AND WINDING ROAD: FROM OLD TESTAMENT TIMES TO EARLY CHRISTIANITY

As human beings we are social animals dependent upon the group for our welfare and survival. Differences in our genes and in our early developmental experiences combine to bring about impressive variations in our ability to adapt to the group, to the human family in general, and to our surroundings. Since earliest times people within particular communities have noticed that some fraction of their number behave, think, or show emotion in ways that are distinctly odd and maladaptive—and in the extreme cases, even dangerous—in relation to the welfare of the persons themselves or to the group at large. It was this fraction of people, who evidenced behavior that deviated from that of the majority, that was to become the domain of *psychiatry*—which means, literally, the "healing of the mind." Long before the age of sophisticated psychodiagnosis (the past 200 years), a simple vocabulary sprung up to describe the odd and unconventional people within the body social: terms such as "wild," "eccentric," or "mad." Collectively, such persons became known as the "insane" (whose root meaning conveys merely "not healthy"), especially if their behavior was so aberrant as to make living within their own families intolerable.

The *history of psychiatry* is the history of humankind's identification and diagnosis of these abnormalities as well as our efforts to ameliorate, or at least contain, them. This history has no distinct beginning. As far back as our first written records go, there are allusions to people whom the group considered strange, and also to mental phenomena that were regarded as mysterious and even miraculous—such as dreaming, which seemed to partake of the divine. It is highly likely that our ancestors were similarly intrigued by these phenomena long before the age of writing, which, after all, occupies not even the last one percent of our million-year history.

The complexity of modern psychiatry, with its bewildering array of techniques, medications, mechanisms of drug action, and neurotransmitter pathways to understand and commit to memory, may render the history of psychiatry, in the eyes of some practitioners, a useless field of study—at best, a quaint diversion in the midst of one's busy schedule. Not so. Professionals in all the mental health disciplines have a greater need than ever to learn something of this history, for only then do we learn *what has remained constant in human nature throughout the ages,* what, in the nature of men and women, for example, is subject to modification by our interventions, and what is likely to remain highly resistant. Which illnesses (given minor differences in their clinical expression over time) have always been with us? Which are "new"? How did we develop our current nosology? Upon what foundations are contemporary notions of temperament built? How is it we still use terms, such as *hysteria* and *melancholy,* which are based on long-outmoded and discredited theories?

The questions proliferate: What were the historical forces that kept certain patterns of male-female and parent-child relationship alive and valid in one time period, only to appear outrageous and pathological in another? What cultural attitudes kept us blind for millennia to the existence and impact of physical and sexual traumata on children— and what allowed us to open our eyes just in the last few generations? All these issues, which belong to the first reason for learning our history, lead us to the second reason: to grant us a sense of *pride* in having come so far, when compared with our ancestors, in our understanding of the mind and in our ability to treat those who suffer; but more importantly, to teach us *humility.* For who can doubt, once acquainted with our history, that the curative methods we now employ—we, who are "listening to Prozac" at the end of the 20th century, still contemplating with amusement the primitive drugs and treatments used in the 1700s—will not be superseded two centuries hence by methods so much more effective than our own as to make the psychiatrists of the 22nd century scratch their heads in amazement at the barbarity of the treatments we are currently so proud of, and at the pathetic simplicity of our understanding of the brain?

WORD ORIGINS

That we have named this field *psychiatry*—treatment of the soul[1]— stems from ancient ideas about the soul. Mankind has ever been reluc-

---

[1] The Greek is "ψυχη" (psychē) used for mind and soul interchangeably.

tant to contemplate the possibility that death entails our utter decomposition and disappearance. Instead we have postulated the existence of a *soul* or *spirit* that invisibly inhabits us while we are alive, and which then ascends (under favorable circumstances) to a better place upon the death of the body. Notions about the soul are themselves intertwined with the notion of a *self,* which is viewed as the collection of all that characterizes each of us during our lifetime. Related to the primarily religio-philosophical ideas about the soul is the concept of a *mind,* which we nowadays define as the set of all the functions of the brain.

Indo-European Languages

In the Western world, whose languages are predominantly Indo-European in origin, terms denoting these concepts stem from primitive words having to do with *breath* or *smoke*—words, that is, that designate something thin, scarcely visible, and vaporous, which thus accorded well with the emerging ideas about this filmy, mysterious something that constituted our individual, and presumably God-given, essence.

The word *psyche,* for example, comes from a Greek verb *psycho,* which means to breathe, to freshen, and stems from an Indo-European root **bhs* or "breath." *Thymos* (as in our word *dysthymia*) signified passion, courage, and soul in Greek, and is a cognate of the Sanskrit *dhumah* (smoke, vapor) as well as of the Latin *fumus* (smoke)—all stemming from the root **dhu-lis,* meaning dust or smoke. The Greek word for God, *theos,* comes from a similar root, *dhu-esos* (spirit) or *dhous* (soul), from which arose the Slavic word *dusha* (soul).

The word *soul* has a different etymology: It comes from the Old German *saiwalo,* meaning "belonging to the sea." According to ancient Teutonic myths, the sea was the stopping place for the spirit both prior to one's birth and after one's death. From this comes the German word for soul (*Seele*), the German term for mental illness (*Seelenkrankheit*), and the old term for psychiatry (*Seelenheilkunde,* literally, soul healing science).

The early Hindus spoke of a "vital principle" (*prana*), an "immaterial part of man, or one's intellect" (*jiva*), an "animating soul" (*jivatma*), and consciousness (*samjna,* which also means "signal").

Oriental Languages

In the non-Indo-European Orient, the words for *soul* and *spirit* do not stem from root words expressing the concept of breath but rather from the root words for *altar* and *lightning* or *voice of God* (in Chinese *shen²;* in Japanese, *shin)²* or *purity,* as in the Japanese *seishin* (whose two characters for *rice* and *pure* signified refined rice, which came to mean *refined* in general, and then *spirit* and *soul*). In Japanese *psychiatry* is *seishin-byoh-gaku:* the science of illness of the soul. The other Japanese word for *soul, shinrei,* contains the notion of a shaman descended from heaven, as the raindrops. The Chinese distinguished between a superior soul (*ling²-hun²*)—the spiritual essence of the human that ascends to heaven after death—and an inferior or animal soul (*p'e²*), which inheres in the body, returning to earth with the body after death. We will soon see that there is a similarity between these concepts and those of the ancient Greeks, as expressed in the works of Plato and Aristotle.

EARLY TIMES

The soul in all its synonyms and attributes—mind, intellect, awareness, passions—was, whether normal or disordered, very much in the hands of the gods for our distant ancestors. Not surprisingly, its study was the province of religious adepts and philosophers and it was administered to (when needed) by priests and shamans. Until the study of human aberrations entered the realm of medicine in Greece 2,500 years ago, there were only allusions to madness, strange behaviors, unusual (mostly unpleasant) personalities, and to both demonic and divine possession.

For the Israelites of the Old Testament, mysterious dispositions of mind often were manifestations of the divine. In the books of the Old Testament there is a smattering of references to mental illness, but no hint of a nosology. The generic term used was *madness,* with its accompanying attributes of fury and rage. The presumed cause of madness ("shigeon"): possession by evil spirits.

King Saul

In about 1,000 B.C., for example, King Saul grew envious of David, whose reputation after killing Goliath had outstripped his own. In response to the ". . . evil spirit which came upon Saul," Saul tried to kill David (1 Sam. 18:11). Some time later, Saul and his army were defeated by the Philistines, in reaction to which Saul begged his armorbearer to kill him, ". . . lest these uncircumcisèd come and thrust me through and abuse me." When the armor bearer refused, Saul took his own life (1 Sam. 31). (Given the intensity of Saul's homicidal and suicidal feelings, perhaps it is legitimate to suppose he exhibited some kind of mood disorder, in our terms. But whether this is so, let alone

---

² The superscript shen² refers to the standard way of designating the second tone in the Chinese (Mandarin-standard) language. Occasionally, one also sees " ´ " as: shén for tone #2, i.e., the "rising" tone.

how we should best classify it, remains unclear.) A little earlier in the story, David *feigned* madness in order to escape from his capture by the forces of Achish, the king of Gath (1 Sam. 21). Achish pronounced David mad ("Lo, ye see the man is mad: wherefore then have ye brought him to me?") and then released him.

In the beginning of the Book of Samuel, we meet Hannah, who had been bitter and depressed for a long time because she had been unable to conceive. Attempting to lift her depression, her husband Elkanah asked: "Why weepest thou? Why eatest thou not? And why is thy heart grieved? Am I not better to thee than ten sons?" Apparently not, since Hannah's "vegetative signs of depression" (as we would call them) persisted, even as she beseeched the Lord to answer her prayers for a son. Once she finally conceived and bore a son (who would become King Samuel), Hannah became so proud and exuberant ("mine horn is exalted in the Lord; my mouth is enlarged over mine enemies" (1 Sam. 2:1), that she had to be warned not to become arrogant! How would we label Hannah in our current taxonomy? As having dysthymia? Reactive depression? Mild personality disorder? Clearly, her condition was milder than that of Saul, but as to its precise characteristics, and how aberrant in relation to her culture, we cannot say.

Hannah

Far more difficult to assess from a diagnostic standpoint are the Biblical prophets, several of whom (most notably, Jeremiah and Ezekiel) would strike us as "fanatical" and even "paranoid" were they around today. Was Ezekiel in an ecstatic state when he heard the Lord order him to eat bread made with "dung that cometh out of man" in sight of the Israelites, whom God wished to humiliate in this way? Was this a "normal" experience of a special person—or a highly abnormal experience in a paranoid, albeit socially valuable, person? At our distance from the sociocultural forces that shaped such behavior, I believe we had best not attempt to judge it in psychopathological terms. The most we can say with validity is that throughout much of our history certain persons have entered exalted states in which they have performed deeds or expressed ideas that literally reshaped society, sometimes only briefly, sometimes for generations to come. In cultures where it is normal to hear God's voice, to do so does not then constitute "hallucination." Thus we have no way of telling whether religious prophets of long ago were supernormal or "schizophrenic"—or a bit of both.

Ezekiel

THE BEGINNINGS OF A METHODOLOGICAL APPROACH TO MENTAL PHENOMENA

Hindu and Buddhist Teachings

In Hinduism and in its 6th-century B.C. offshoot, Buddhism, mind and body were not conceptually separate. In Buddhist teachings, particularly, the mind is not viewed as a "substance" (*jittai*, literally "nature body") but rather as an "aggregate of causes and conditions" (*Bukkyoh Seiten*, 1966, p. 90)—something mutable, impermanent, composed of atoms that come together for a time, destined to fly apart and then resituate themselves in other objects or creatures. This atomistic view, which was also mirrored in the works of Greek philosophers (such as Eratosthenes), did not lend itself to a theory of the mind built upon notions of stability, predictability, and compartmentalization into categories of normal and abnormal. A hundred years before Hippocrates, however, the Hindu physician Sushruta expressed a view of mental illness that distinguished it, at long last, from demonic possession: He asserted that the causative factors were *strong emotions* and *passions*. Around this time period the concept of soul (*prana*) was divided into three "dispositions," presaging those identified by Plato: *wisdom* (in the brain), *passion* (in the heart), and *crudity* (in the abdomen).

Sushruta

Greek Philosophers and Physicians

Plato (427–347 B.C.) embraced a dualistic theory in which mind and matter were separate phenomena. Soul, which was conceptually commingled with mind, was further subdivided into the rational and irrational aspects. The *rational soul* was immortal, divine, and located in the brain; the *irrational soul* was located in the chest, in close proximity to the seat of anger and audacity in the heart and of hunger and the other carnal passions in the abdomen. Plato, like his Egyptian and Babylonian predecessors, associated strong emotions with a heaving of the chest. The diaphragm (*phren*) was important in this domain, along with the nearby liver and heart. Hence the Latin term *phrenesis* (madness, delirium), and our cognate word *frenzy*. Eventually, *phren* designated the intellectual, as opposed to the passionate, soul (*thymos*).[3]

Plato's psychopathology consisted of various forms of *mad-*

Plato, 427–347 B.C. Courtesy
Corbis-Bettman

[3] Though it would be too great a leap to say Plato "anticipated" Freud, the analogy between the theories of the two great men, separated by two millennia, is compelling. This similarity is, in part, due to the unchanging qualities of human nature. Bennett Simon, psychoanalyst and student of the classics, has captured the many points of comparison in his monograph on the Grecian roots of modern psychiatry (1978). Plato spoke of *eros;* Freud, of *libido.* Both viewed *conflict* as central to understanding the psyche. Plato's concept of rational versus irrational souls corresponds well with Freud's ego and id, respectively. For both, dreams could be understood as the products of an inner battle between wishes and prohibitions. Similarly, there is a close comparison between Plato's

ness—melancholia, mania, and dementia—which occurred when the irrational soul was somehow separated from its rational counterpart. As Zilboorg (1941) noted, this process stemmed from a maldistribution of the *chymoi* or "humours" that reached the organs of the irrational soul. Madness might take the form of abnormal emotions, such as cowardice, sadness, or embarrassment. *Mania* is derived from *mēnis,* which connotes wrath and fury as well as *mental excitement* and *thought.* The Indo-European root **MN* is also the source of such words as *mind, memory,* and *dementia.* For Plato there was both an abnormal variety of mania as rage and a god-inspired variety of revelatory mania, which empowered one to make prophesies. This distinction influenced Christian philosophers centuries later, congenial as it was to the newly evolving religion.

Plato's pupil, Aristotle (342–322 B.C.), contended that the brain condensed vapors that emanated from the heart. This viewpoint endured well into the 18th century, where "vapours" were believed to cause nervous, especially "hysteric," states (Pomme, 1767; Purcell, 1707). Aristotle's characterology, based on the concept of the Golden Mean (and deviations to either side), was expounded in *Nichomachaean Ethics.* Aristotle's pupil, Theophrastus (370–285 B.C.), also developed a characterology. Whereas his teacher was interested primarily in our

Aristotle

Pomme; Purcell

Theophrastus

---

epithymiai (appetites) and Freud's *instinctual drives.* For Plato mental illness was the expression of these primitive appetites clamoring for satisfaction—a notion not unrelated to Freud's view of neurosis as the outgrowth of imbalance in the struggle between reason (ego) and desire (id).

Ideas about the betterment of the human condition and theories of psychological cure were also similar. Plato recommended such measures as coercion, suggestion, exhortation, and promise of reward as tactics promoting control over one's wild, irrational soul. These measures correspond to the supportive aspects of therapy, whose importance Freud recognized, alongside the advantages of psychoanalysis proper. Plato likewise felt there were advantages to a higher form of influence: the dialectic dialogues of the philosopher with his student, whose reasoning powers are thereby improved in such a way as to enhance mastery over the baser desires. If we read *analyst* or *therapist* for philosopher and *patient* for student, the aims and methods of Plato and Freud are quite closely related. As Simon mentions, both theoreticians sought to bring the student/patient into better harmony with self and world, with a lessening of conflict. Plato actually strove for the elimination of conflict, whereas Freud saw conflict as an ineradicable substrate of the psyche—something one could perhaps eventually master, as the charioteer controls his horses (Plato's metaphor from *Phaedrus*), but never altogether extinguish. Plato's goal of rising above, and thus escaping, the realm of conflict has an Eastern ring to it: Compare this with Buddha's goal, enunciated two centuries before Plato, of achieving self-mastery in the conquest of lust, greed, and anger.

Hippocrates, 406–377 B.C.
Courtesy National Library of
Medicine

virtues, Theophrastus was more intrigued by our faults. More a popularizer than a deep thinker, Theophrastus became a famous lecturer (Rusten, 1993).

In contrast to the philosophers just cited, Hippocrates was a physician, a contemporary of Plato, though a generation older (460–377 B.C.). More a systematizer than an innovator, Hippocrates added little to our nosology, relying on the diagnostic catalogue already in place. This consisted primarily of mania, hysteria, paranoia, and (in the later works, and perhaps added by another author) melancholia. Hippocrates, endorsing the scientifically correct notion, enunciated earlier by Anaxagoras (500–428 B.C.), stated that:

> . . . from the brain, and from the brain only, arise our pleasures, joys . . . as well as our sorrows, pain, grief [*dysphrosunē*], and tears. It is the same organ which makes us mad or delirious, inspires us with dread and fear, brings sleeplessness . . . and aimless anxiety.

The theories of Hippocrates incorporated aspects of anatomy, physiology, and temperament. He postulated that temperament arose from varying admixtures of the four humours (earth, air, fire, and water) that accounted for fears (*phoboi*), shame and grief (*lypē*), pleasure (*hēdonē*), and the passions in general. A similar list of elements, by the way, was put forward by the savants of China and Japan: fire, water, wood, metal, and earth.

To the popular four-humour theory, Hippocrates added the notion that during breathing one took "ether," which went first to the brain, where it became separated into a tenuous substance that then found its way into the blood. This *ether* was responsible for movement and sensation. If *phlegm* interfered with this process, the result might be epileptic fits or paralysis. The froth that accumulates during a *grand mal* seizure was taken as evidence of this excess phlegm. In this, as in other nervous system conditions, Hippocrates ignored the nerves in favor of the blood vessels. He also described puerperal insanity and attacked the notion that epilepsy was a "sacred" disease, asserting that it was no more sacred or divinely inspired than any other malady.

Dreams, for Hippocrates, were the province of the soul: "When the body is awake, the soul is its servant and divides her attention among hearing, sight, etc., but when the body is at rest, the soul administers her own household." Dreams had the ability to foretell events. Hippocrates claimed that dreams, "contrary to the acts of the day, showing either struggle or triumph," betoken trouble of some sort. Similarly, "to see the earth as flooded by water signifies disease, as there is excess moisture in the body." The remedy for this was to rid the body of this "excess" moisture via emetics.

Given what he observed to be the remarkable recuperative powers of the body, Hippocrates' general prescription for treatment relied on the idea of giving nature a chance. He subscribed to the prevailing notion that hysteria affected only women, resulted from the womb (*hystēr*) traveling periodically to the brain, and could best be remedied by (early) marriage. Here he hints at a connection between sexual frustration and hysteria, a notion that persisted to the time of Pinel, who, in the 1790s, also advocated early marriage as the cure.

The Greek philosopher Epicurus (342–270 B.C.) belonged to the generation following Theophrastus. His views on the emotions were adumbrated in Aristotle's analysis of the subject: Fear, grief, or anger, for example, is not "merely" irrational if it is directed at persons or situations that *warrant* the emotion, thereby rendering it *rational* (Nussbaum, 1994). An *interpersonal* component was included in Aristotle's understanding of emotion. If one's anger were based on false beliefs (prejudice, for example) or on misunderstanding of another's motives, then it would be *irrational*.

Epicurus

More practical minded than Aristotle, Epicurus wrote: "Just as there is no use in a medical art that does not cast out the sickness of bodies, so too there is no use in philosophy, if it does not throw out suffering from the soul" (Nussbaum, 1994, p. 102). Epicurean philosophy, in contrast to that of Aristotle or of Hippocrates, was more oriented to the *individual*, perhaps due, in part, to Epicurus' rejection of the existence of a hereafter, such that humankind should make the most out of physical life. As Nussbaum (1994) explains, Epicureans prided themselves on the responsiveness of their ethical arguments to particular cases and situations. Usually, the doctor would accomplish the most by means of "moderate discourse." But at times harsher and stronger argument might be necessary—and here Epicurus was talking about psychotherapy, as it was conducted in his era. If a doctor could not wean a patient from some destructive path by using mild suggestions and arguments, a more outspoken, even temporarily wounding, remark may be justified, in order to rescue the patient from some terrible attitude or plan.

We know about the work of Asclepiades (first century A.D.) through the Roman author Caelius Arelianus. For Asclepiades the soul represented the convergence of all the senses.[4] He preferred the term *furor* rather than *insanus* to describe abnormal excitement. Differentiating between *hallucinations* and *delusions*, he taught that a patient who

Asclepiades

[4] The influence of Epicureanism is apparent in Asclepiades' system of thought.

sees an object but who perceives it as something else is deluded, whereas a patient who hears something that cannot be heard by others is hallucinating. (Little was added to this topic until Esquirol in the early 19th century.) Like the Epicureans, Asclepiades focused on the needs of the individual patient, advocating comfortable baths and soothing music as therapeutic measures for mental patients. He argued against the uses of phlebotomy (venesection, bloodletting), of keeping patients in dark dungeons, and of other painful measures that he saw as either useless or harmful. Among such painful measures: the use of the drug *hellebore* (from white lily) for melancholy, as had been advocated by Hippocrates and later by Diascorides (circa 60 A.D.).

In the early years of the first century A.D. we are afforded an example of self-mutilation still viewed as demonic possession. While Jesus and his disciples were in the land of the Gadarenes (Mark 5:1–11), they came upon a wild and untamable man, a hermit perhaps, whose strength was so great that he had broken the chains by which people had tried to bind him. He was seen as possessed of an "unclean spirit" who "always, night and day, was in the mountains and in the tombs, crying and cutting himself with stones." Jesus cured the man by ordering the evil spirit to depart from him. As in the Old Testament, this kind of aberration was not understood in medical terms as a symptom of some condition, but in terms of good and evil and the world of spirits.

Artemidorus of Ephesus

At the end of the first century A.D., Artemidorus of Ephesus compiled a book in which he outlined some 130 common dream symbols (hair, teeth, ants, bread, gladiator fights, sex), appending to each the presumed significance for the dreamer. For nearly two thousand years this book remained the most popularly accepted authority on the understanding of dreams, until the appearance of Freud's *Traumdeutung* [*Interpretation of Dreams*] in 1899. In Pushkin's *Eugene Onegin,* for example, the heroine, Tatyana, has a dramatic dream she tries to decipher by using a dream manual (from Pushkin's time, the 1830s) similar to the one created by Artemidorus (Stone, 1977a).

THE EARLY CHRISTIAN PERIOD

The religious and philosophical forces that had up to this point shaped attitudes toward the mentally ill now began to swing towards those of medicine and the humanities.

Celsus

The Roman encyclopedist, Celsus, writing during the time of Christ, accepted humoural theory, adding that the humours flow more amply during springtime. Hence melancholy and insanity were more common in this season. The emotions themselves could intensify so as to bring on an attack of "black bile disease when there has been prolonged sadness and sleeplessness and fearfulness" (p. 125). Insanity (probably in the form of delirium) could be induced by fever—and cured, as Celsus recognized, by whatever cured the fever. Celsus' recommendations for treatment vary widely from the humane to the harsh. Melancholy could be relieved sometimes by soft music. Exaggerated fears could be set to rest, sometimes, by sensitive handling, as in the case Celsus cites of the (perhaps depressed?) wealthy man who lived in fear of starvation: Those in attendance would announce pretended legacies to him, by way of allaying his anxieties, until he recovered his reason. But Celsus also favored the use of restraints, phlebotomy, clysters (enemas), and in the case of melancholy without fever, induced vomiting. He described patients who had "imagines" (visions, fantasies), which could be of the depressed or "hilarious" (presumably, manic) type: "If it is the mind that deceives the madman, he is best treated by torture, starvation, fetters or flogging"—methods which remained in favor in many quarters for the next 1,800 years.

A generation later, Aretaeus of Cappadocia (30?–90 A.D.) taught that mental disease had its origins in the head or abdomen and that both melancholy and mania were different expressions of the same malady. In his opinion younger people were more prone to mania; older ones, to melancholy. This view comes close to our modern conceptions, but it was not solidly accepted until well into the 19th century. Aretaeus, like Hippocrates, had an interest in the prognostic aspects of the various mental disorders. He departed from humoural theory, however, favoring instead a language that emphasized personality traits. For example, he spoke of manics as being "irritable, violent and given to joy." Aretaeus also described patients as showing a combination of "stupidity, absence (in the sense of unrelatedness) and musing." Conceivably, this clinical picture may have been a "phenotype" of schizophrenia during that era, but the clinical sketch is too scanty to permit any certainty on this point. Aretaeus' perspective may be seen as a presage to contemporary continuum theories of personality, in which abnormal states represent the extremes of otherwise normal attributes.

Aretaeus of Cappadocia

The standard Roman nosology of the time was simply taken over from the Greek authors, with some words kept the same, others translated into Latin. There was *mania* (or the Latin equivalent *furor*) for abnormally excited or irritable states; *melancholia* for depressed states; *vesania* for madness and irrationality (similar to *paranoia,* which also signified abnormality of thought); *amentia,* for those who lacked normal mental function from birth; *dementia* for those who once had, but then lost, normal mentation; and *stultitia,* for those exhibiting mental dullness, idiocy, etc.

Around the time of Aretaeus we find a reference to *bulimia.* But this reference comes from the Talmud (tr. Yoma 8, Mishnah 6), where the condition was recognized as a valid excuse for dispensing with the ob-

bulimia

ligation to fast during Yom Kippur: "If anyone be seized with bulimy, he is to be fed, even unclean things . . . ." The word itself is of Greek origin (*bous,* ox; *limos,* hunger—to have the hunger of an ox) and appears in the works of Aristotle and in Aristophanes' play *Plutus.*

Caelius Aurelianus

In the first half of the second century, a North African physician, Caelius Aurelianus, summarized the various causative factors that might underlie mental illness: abuse of wine, head injury, suppression of the menses, exposure to strong sunlight, superstition, excessive preoccupation with philosophy, glory or money. According to Zilboorg (1941), Aurelianus may have been influenced by the asceticism of the early Christians, insofar as he expressed disgust at sexual perversions and likened the sensuality of the day to "the most malignant and fetid passion of the mind" (p. 85). Not free of superstition himself, he accepted the notion that *incubi* existed: demons who, as their name suggests, lay upon women and seduced them during sleep.

Soranus

It is to Aurelianus, however, that we owe our knowledge of the medical writer Soranus, whose works (circa 100 A.D.) have not survived in the original. Soranus' recommendations for the care of the mentally ill showed an intensely humanistic spirit, which was in accord with the Stoic and Epicurean schools, and far removed from the dry scholasticism of the early Greek writers and the severe asceticism of the early Christians who came after him. Whereas Asclepiades advocated the use of emetics and alcohol, Soranus objected, saying, "How can it occur to the mind of any man to dispel intoxication by intoxication?" (Z., 1941, p. 80). He valued giving service to patients over controlling them. In treating manic patients, for example, he urged the use of a tranquil, lighted room on the ground floor, given that such patients sometimes jump out the window. Tact and discretion were to be employed in directing attention to a patient's faults; sometimes the physician should overlook minor misbehavior, or, at other times, give an explanation of the advantages of proper conduct. Here, Soranus presages the approach of our cognitive/behavioral therapists today. Long before Pinel, Soranus inveighed against restraints. He also recommended talking to patients in their own language: One spoke to a sailor about navigation; to a farmer about the cultivation of his fields.

In the latter half of the second century medicine was dominated by Galen (131–200), who was born Claudius Galenus in the city of Pergamum in what is now Turkey. We actually know something of his psychological makeup, since he spoke of his father as a highly amiable, just, and benevolent man. His mother, in contrast, was bad-tempered and quarrelsome—to the point of biting her maids. Galen resolved at an early age to emulate the qualities of his father and to avoid those of his mother.

Galen, 131–200. Courtesy National Library of Medicine

Galen was a generalist and eclecticist; he studied the doctrines of all the sects and extracted what was useful from each (Z., 1941). He elaborated a theory reminiscent of the 17th century English sensualist psychologists. Galen asserted that *sensation*—hearing, vision, etc.—is the foundation of all our faculties, and that if there is no pain or pleasure, there will be no sensations, and, in Galen's view, no soul. The seat of sensation and therefore of the soul was in the *nerve centers* (a more advanced view than that of Hippocrates), and the brain was the center of psychic functions.

For Galen, the soul was divisible into components: The five senses constituted the *external* soul; the various cognitive abilities (imagination, memory, reasoning/thinking, judgment) the *internal* soul; the *rational* soul was centered in the brain; the *irrational* soul (governing the passions) in the heart and liver. The heart was pictured as embodying *maleness* (energy, aggressiveness); the liver *femaleness* (sensuality, sexual desire). In his *Peri Physikon Dynameon* [*On the Natural Faculties*] Galen categorized temperaments in relation to their origins in the four basic elements, which, in turn, were linked to one of the four humours:

Temperament	Element	Humour
Melancholic	Earth	Black bile
Sanguine [manic]	Air	Blood
Choleric	Fire	Yellow bile
Phlegmatic	Water	Phlegm

In other respects Galen's nosology was similar to that of Aretaeus and the physicians of the period. He concluded that yellow bile was the product of eating food under conditions of excessive heat and was cleared by the biliary vessels; even greater heat led to "black bile," which was supposedly cleared by the spleen. Yellow bile was associated with irritability and rage, a notion preserved to this day in our word *choleric.* Galen did not believe the womb traveled in cases of hysteria, but instead ascribed the latter condition to engorgement or "suffocation" of the uterus. The term *suffocation* was still current in the first English treatise on hysteria—Edward Jorden's *Suffocation of the Mother* (*mother* is a synonym for the uterus) in 1603.

The next 500 years are considered the "Dark Ages" in Western civilization: roughly the time period between the 5th and 11th centuries, from the fall of Rome to the beginnings of the Renaissance. Fortunately, the eclipse of light was not total. Galen's teachings were kept alive by

Avicenna

virtue of their transmission via the Nestorians[5] to Persia, and from there to the 10th-century court of Harun ar Rashid in Baghdad. The path of transmission reached full circle when Greek medical lore passed back into Western Europe a century later, about 1150, thanks to compilations made by an Arab physician, Avicenna. The logical approach of the Greek writers appealed to the medieval scholastic writers within the Catholic Church, including St. Thomas Aquinas.

[5] The Nestorians were a heretical Christian sect founded by Nestorius in 428 in Constantinople. Expelled from Byzantium, the sect migrated to Persia, where they set up a center for medical learning.

Chapter 2

DESCENT INTO DARKNESS: FROM THE MIDDLE AGES TO THE INQUISITION

The philosophy of the early Christian church was in part a reaction against the anarchic sexuality and corruption of the Graeco-Roman world—the world of Nero and Caligula—that ringed the Christians on every side. In place of sexual license and gluttony, the early Christians took pride in abstinence and sparseness of diet—acts of restraint that ordinary people could impose on themselves. To the extent that they succeeded, they could take pride in their self-denial and higher morality. As the influence of the Church grew stronger, Europe experienced a dramatic shift in mentality: Faith became more important than logic. Belief in magic persisted (despite discouragement by the Church) and what had been understood as abnormal mental states based on humoural excesses or anatomical lesions was reformulated in the language of the priests and astrologers. Aberrant mental phenomena were now explained in quasi-moral terms involving references to evil spirits, ghosts, incubi and succubi, and the like.

As time went on, the effects of sexual repression (particularly intense among the celibate clergy and nuns) would erupt in the form of hysterical crises, prolonged (and sometimes feigned) bouts of fasting, the showing of the stigmata, indulgence in acts of self-mortification, and the belief in witchcraft and black magic. Strange behavior in others, unacceptable impulses in oneself, personal shortcomings—especially in the sexual sphere (barrenness, impotence)—were no longer accounted for by science and observation. The mechanism of externalization won the day: These were all the Devil's fault, or the result of one's sins, or due to a witch's hex. Influential Church leaders, such as St. Jerome in the 5th century and Pope Gregory IX in the 6th century, disparaged book-learning. The way to knowledge was through

St. Augustine, 5th century. Courtesy
Corbis-Bettmann

Rhazes

Unhammad

belief; the cure for madness was through the application of holy relics to the head or the exorcism of evil spirits via incantations.

During this same time period (and in a manner strangely parallel to the Buddhist philosophers) St. Augustine (5th century) asserted that sensation is not a physical but a purely mental phenomenon. He assigned memory, will, and intellect to the *superior soul*, which was not dependent on the body; passions and imagination were allocated to the *inferior soul,* which (as in the earlier Chinese conception) died with us.

ARAB AND PERSIAN INFLUENCES

The century between the death of Mohammed and the blocking of the Moorish advance into Western Europe by Charles Martel and his troops in 732 witnessed the rapid expansion of Arab troops over Northern Africa and Spain. In the early 800s the translation into Arabic of Aristotle's works led to a "renaissance" of Greek medicine and thought in the Arab world, one consequence of which was the humane treatment of the insane by Rhazes (860–930), who created a separate wing for the mentally ill in his hospital. As Zilboorg points out, though, the Arabs, like their Christian counterparts, saw their holy books, the source of all authority, as prohibiting dissection, and therefore demurred when it came to dissecting the body. There was less demonology within Arabic medicine but no new discoveries about anatomy. Among the common people, belief in certain spirits (*jinns*) as the responsible agents of mental illness held sway, as is still true in parts of the Moslem world today.

A contemporary of Rhazes, Unhammad, developed a classification of mental illnesses (Z., 1941) consisting of nine major types, each with several subtypes. These included—in addition to melancholia and mania—"febrile delirium" (*souda a tabee*), "manic restlessness" (*janoon,* "crazy" in modern Arabic), "persecutory psychosis" (*kutrib*), "lovesickness with anxiety and depression" (*ishk*), and "disorders of judgment" (*haziyan*), one subtype of which resembled our modern conception of antisocial personality. Unhammad also described a condition he called *murrae souda,* characterized by worrying and doubting along with obsessions and compulsions. The Arab physicians viewed an excessive preoccupation with law or philosophy as the forerunner of this condition. We may take it that, working backwards in time, the obsessive-compulsive disorder ("OCD") of our day had a counterpart in the *folie du doute avec delire de toucher* [doubting mania with touching phobia] of 19th century France and in the much earlier *murrae souda* noted by Unhammad.

Still another contemporary of Rhazes was Isaac Judaeus (855–955), an Egyptian Jewish physician who attended the Fatimid rulers in Tunisia. His was among the first works translated into Latin (in 1080); his comments on melancholy were cited extensively by Robert Burton in his 17th-century volume, *Anatomy of Melancholy* .

Isaac Judaeus

Perhaps the greatest scholar during the "Golden Age" of Islamic science was the Persian-born abu 'Ali al-Husayn ibn Sina (980–1037), whom we know as Avicenna (Arnold & Guillaume, *Legacy of Islam,* 1931). A neo-Platonist, he wrote a voluminous *Canon of Medicine,* a vast medical encyclopedia containing sections on mania and melancholy. Avicenna rejected the notion of spirits (*jinns*) having anything to do with mental illness. More codifier than original thinker, Avicenna's remarks about mania and melancholy were couched in Greek-inspired descriptions of temperament: The melancholic, for example, was described as irritable and exaggeratedly fearful, owing to abnormal temperament.[1]

Avicenna was more than just an encyclopedist. He was also a master diagnostician and a therapist of extraordinary skills. Fady Hajal (1994), in a historical essay on lovesickness, mentions an anecdote related by the Persian poet Nizami-i-Arudi. It chanced that Avicenna was passing through the province of Gurgan in his native Persia, when the king was distressed because one of his young nephews had taken ill. None of the local physicians could cure him. Avicenna was summoned and quickly surmised that lovesickness might be the cause of the young man's condition. Avicenna asked to inspect the patient's urine and then felt his pulse. He asked someone familiar with the region to name aloud all the districts in the city. At the mention of a certain one, the boy's pulse fluttered. Avicenna then asked someone to name all the streets; then all the houses on each street; then all the families residing in those houses. Putting together the names of the places and persons that made the young man's pulse quicken, Avicenna concluded: "The lad is in love with so-and-so at such-and-such an address . . . ." The boy, though greatly ashamed, admitted that Avicenna was correct.

The details of his son's "illness" were then told to the king,

Avicenna (abu 'Ali al-Husayn ibn Sina), 980–1037. **Courtesy National Library of Medicine**

---

[1] Actually, a more complete and modern-sounding description of melancholy was provided by the 10th-century physician Ishaq ibn Amram, who cited the following symptoms: general slowing down, immobility, mutism, sleep troubles, poor appetite, agitation, taciturnity, demoralization, worry, anxiety, sadness, and risk of suicide.

who remarked that the boy and his *innamorata* were cousins, the children of his sisters. Since a marriage was appropriate and favorable in the eyes of the king, this was quickly arranged—to the satisfaction of all, and to the relief of the patient, whose "lovesickness" rapidly subsided.

Avicenna was neither the first nor the last to rely on this ingenious method of reading the pulse to deduce information about patients. As Hajal mentions, the ancient Greeks had hit upon this method; Jacques Ferrand rediscovered it in the 17th century, and Robert Burton alludes to it in his *Anatomy of Melancholy* .

Avenzoar
Averrhoes

The most prominent Islamic physicians in the 12th century were ibn Zuhr (Avenzoar) (d. 1162) and ibn Rushd (Averrhoes) (d. 1198): the former, an aristocratic physician to the Almohad court in Spain; the latter, his disciple and friend, who became a great Aristotelian philosopher in addition to writing some 16 medical works (Arnold & Guillaume, 1931). A rationalist like Avicenna, Avenzoar rejected the idea of demons. Averrhoes also found his way around the thorny issue of religion, which was beginning to encroach upon the scientific spirit of the Islamic savants in the 13th century by postulating *two* truths: one based on religious teaching, the other on rational philosophy! This construction permitted him to examine data that might otherwise contradict the "revealed" truth of religion (Z., 1941).

JEWISH INFLUENCES

Maimonides

Even more free from the restraints of religion than Avenzoar and Averrhoes were the medieval Jewish physicians. The most renowned was Spanish-born Moses ben Maimon, whom we know as Maimonides (1135-1204). He spent most of his life in Cairo, at the court of Saladin, Sultan of Egypt and Syria (Bevan & Singer, 1927). Philosopher and moralist as well, Maimonides wrote extensively on diseases of the soul. Many of his aphorisms and commentaries related to the topic of personality, particularly to the differences between the "good" and the "wicked": "The wicked and the morally perverted imagine that the bad is good and the good is bad" (Goshen, 1967, p. 34). The Aristotelian concept of a Golden Mean was also present. Good deeds, for example, are those that are "equibalanced, maintaining the mean between two equally bad extremes, the *too much* and the *too little*" (Goshen, 1967, p. 35). At the court in Cairo, Maimonides found it necessary to speak in apologetic terms when recommending a bit of wine (and music) as a cure for the sultan's melancholy, given the Koranic injunction against alcohol (Arnold & Guillaume, 1931).

In Spain during the time of Maimonides there was a flourishing group of cabalistic Jewish mystics, who lived side by side with Christian mystics, each influencing the other. This mutual exchange came to a crashing halt with the expulsion of the Jews and the Moors by Ferdinand in the 15th century. A figure of importance (albeit indirect) for psychiatry was 13th-century Jewish mystic Abraham Abulafia of Saragossa, who developed the technique of *k'fitsah* or "skipping": While in a trance-like state (aided by staring at one of the Hebrew letters for long periods of time), the practitioner makes a deliberate effort to skip from one thought to another, until all thoughts leave the plane of the mundane and concentrate on God.

Abraham Abulafi of Saragossa

This technique worked its way down the centuries to serve as a stimulus to Freud's method of *free association* (Stone, 1977a). Abulafia's hypnotic-like state found another application along the way: As they were being burned at the stake in Spain a century after Abulafia, Jewish mystics would practice this self-induced trance state to render themselves insensible to the flames that were beginning to consume them. The induction of ecstatic states, autohypnosis, and the like, especially by religious adepts (such as the Hindus), antedates Abulafia, to say nothing of Mesmer and his followers, and probably dates back to remote antiquity.

CATHOLIC INFLUENCES

In Christian Europe during this long period, concern about the mentally ill was replaced by concern about divine versus evil forces, since it was to devil-possession that mental conditions were largely attributed. This was the case even when humane treatment prevailed, such as in the singular community of Gheel in Belgium. It was to this tiny village, just north of Brussels, that St. Nymphna repaired, an Irish princess who, according to legend, had fled the incestuous advances of her father. She joined a religious order there in the 7th century, after which she cured two persons whose madness was deemed to have stemmed from demonic possession. A church was built in Gheel in the 12th century to honor St. Nymphna, and it became a refuge for the insane. As Esquirol (1838) recounted in his 1822 visit to Gheel, the townspeople eventually took up the practice of sheltering the mentally ill as lodgers in their own homes! The patients were free to come and go as they pleased. The custom persists to this day; for at least seven centuries Gheel has served as a model for the community-based treatment of the severely mentally ill.[2]

St. Nymphna

[2] Only a few modern approaches measure up to this model. For example, in Copenhagen, recuperating schizophrenic adolescents are sent to attend a nearby regular school, but even so, they are housed in an adjacent half-way house (Aarkrog, 1981).

During the millennium following St. Augustine (500–1500), little distinction was made between normal persons who disagreed with certain aspects of the evolving dogma and persons whose non-conformity arose out of mental abnormality. Both groups were generally considered to be guilty of heresy, for which the "treatment" was often punishment. Parallel to this was a tendency to accept, and even to beatify, persons whose departure from expectable behavior was understood by Church authorities as a commendable example of religious devotion. Religious ecstatics—those who fasted beyond ordinary mortal endurance, those who had visions of Mary or Christ, etc.—might find themselves the objects of veneration, whether their actions were prompted by utter sincerity, by cunning, or by frank delusion. This was the case, for example, with the Venerable Lukardis of Oberweimar,[3] a young nun who lived during the 13th century (she died in 1309) who became the first to show the stigmata (Bynum, 1987). She also claimed to have fasted for several months, during which time she was kept alive (she claimed) by drinking from Mary's breast. Even reading between the lines of the *Analecta Bollandiana,* where her story is recorded, it is not easy to discern whether Lukardis was emotionally "balanced" within the context of her culture or whether we would see her as "hysteric." That she was sincere in her faith seems beyond question. Nor can we tell with certainty how long she really went without food or how she was kept alive in the meantime. What is important to glean from this historical vignette is that *cultural* factors determined in a significant way what was considered "mental illness" and what was not, what was correct treatment and what was not.[4]

Venerable Lukardis of Oberweimar

The century of Lukardis also marks a turning point in the attitude towards the *dream.* Before the time of Albertus Magnus (1193–1280), the teacher of Thomas Aquinas, dreams were viewed mostly with suspicion by the Christian community as likely to be the work of the Devil (LeGoff, 1988). After Albertus Magnus' work—*De Somno et Vigilia* [*On Dreaming and Wakefulness*]—dreams began to be understood as related more to medicine and psychology than to matters sacred, prophetic, or profane.

Albertus Magnus

---

[3] An earlier example was that of Princess Margaret of Hungary (1242–1271). As reported by Halmi (1994), her father, King Bela IV, dedicated his daughter to the service of the Lord, in honor of his staving off a Tartar invasion. His daughter, after whom Margitsziget (Isle of Margaret) in Budapest is named, fasted and did other bodily penance to such a degree that she died at the age of 28 from fever and wasting.

[4] For a more complete account of apparitions experienced by the faithful of Spain in the 15th century and the devotions they inspired, see W. A. Christian's monograph (1981).

THE GREAT PLAGUE

The time period between the founding of the first university in 1205 and the outbreak of bubonic plague in 1347 saw the proliferation of universities in Paris, Naples, Heidelberg, Prague, and elsewhere, evidencing a new striving toward independent thought. Honest controversy even erupted between clerics and professors—at times, *heated* controversy—as when the books of Aristotle were burned in public in the early 1200s (Z., 1941). Pope Gregory IX inaugurated the Inquisition in 1233 in an effort to refute the "heretical" works of Aristotle and Averrhoes. Persons whom the Church or the public saw as mentally ill were still feared as creatures tainted by demonic influences, to be cured only through exorcism by a priest or by individual repentance.

Pope Gregory IX and the Inquisition

As for the Great Plague, it is difficult to grasp the magnitude of the devastation it wrought upon much of Europe, or of the impact this sudden depopulation had upon the minds and hearts of those who survived. Europe lost a third to half of its population; some towns were truly "decimated"—i.e., reduced to a tenth of their populations. Not understanding the all-too-mundane cause of the disaster—a rat-borne bacillus—people blamed the Devil, the Jews, or their own "sinfulness." Sometimes people undertook dramatic displays of self-mortification. Hysteric crises involving whole groups took place, as in the case of the "Flagellants" of Hungary, who, in an orgy of self-scourging, took to whipping themselves in public.[5]

Great Plague

Flagellants

It was not a good time for women, either. Many were denounced as witches, held responsible, through their supposed malefactions, for the ever-mounting death-toll. Some clerics described Woman as a "temple built upon a sewer" (Beauchesne, 1993, p. 29). Even so, a few forward steps were taken during this dark time on behalf of the mentally ill: The first asylum in Europe was built in Hamburg in 1375, followed by another in Valencia in 1410, and in London ("Bedlam hospital") not long thereafter.

In the 15th century a number of events paved the way for the mentally ill to be understood as just that—*ill*, rather than devil-possessed. The plague affected Western more than Eastern Europe and contributed indirectly to a weakening of Roman authority and to the Great Schism of 1378–1417. The widespread granting of indulgences, partly to raise funds for the Crusades (which began in 1096 and continued

---

[5] Gottfried (1983) notes that the movement spread across Central Europe in 1348, at first as an ascetic group of men who were not allowed to speak to women. But by 1349 few were left in the movement except vagabonds, and they were condemned by Pope Clement VI. The movement was eradicated by 1350.

*anti-papal reforma-
tory movements*

until the sack of Constantinople by the Turks in 1453), soured many of the faithful and gave rise to the anti-papal reformatory movements of the 15th century, which were further galvanized shortly thereafter when Martin Luther nailed his 95 theses to the door of the Wittenberg church in 1517. The fall of Constantinople led to the flight westward of many Christian scholars who had become familiar with Greek and Latin learning (including medical learning). This fostered a renewal of interest— a renaissance—of scholarship and investigation in the face of Church dogma.

THE INQUISITION

Pope Innocent VIII

Now pockets of intellectual freedom coexisted with pockets of entrenched dogmatism. The consolidation of Spain under Ferdinand and Isabella was bought at the price of expelling or burning the Moors and the Jews. In 1484 Pope Innocent VIII's bull denounced the rising number of Catholics who "abandoned themselves to the Devil" (in the form, oftentimes, of *incubi* and *succubi*) and gave full powers to the Inquisitors to punish to the maximum those who had "strayed." In 1487 two Dominican monks, Heinrich Krämer and James Sprenger, published what became, in effect, a guidebook for the Inquisitors: the *Malleus Maleficarum* [*The Witches' Hammer*]. This volume, whose repugnant and paranoid message is a match for *Mein Kampf,* had as its target half the human race—namely, women. Here are a few extracts:

> All wickedness is but little to the wickedness of a woman. Wherefore St. John Chrysostom says: It is not good to marry. What else is woman but a foe to friendship, an inescapable punishment, a necessary evil, a natural temptation, a delectable detriment, an evil of nature, painted with fair colors! (Part I, Q. 6)

> How is it possible to distinguish whether [impotency] is due to witchcraft or not? Hostiensis gives the answer in his Summa (but this must be publicly preached): When the [virile] member is in no way stirred, and can never perform the act of coition, this is a sign of frigidity of Nature; but when it is stirred and becomes erect, but yet cannot perform, it is a sign of witchcraft. (Part I, Q. 8)

The last decade of the 15th century and the first years of the 16th represent the pinnacle of the Inquisition's destructiveness. Witch-burnings and the torture and death of countless "heretics" culminated in the Church's anti-biologic strictures, which fostered exaggerated fasting, the externalization of unacceptable sexual impulses, and the forced suppression of normal sexual outlets that underlay the beliefs in witchery, the devil, and in the persecution of the unconventional (including the mentally ill) among the populace.

PART II

The Beginnings of Modern Psychiatry: Sixteenth through Nineteenth Centuries

Chapter 3

RUMBLINGS OF REVOLUTION:

THE SIXTEENTH CENTURY

The beginning of the 16th century was marked both by the culmination of the Inquisition and by the reemergence of rational and humanistic thought concerning mental life—a movement spearheaded by philosophers—which set the stage for a more reasoned, empirical, and compassionate treatment of the mentally ill. Hence the irony that 1492 (an easy year for Americans to remember)—a scarce 40 years after Gutenberg's invention of the printing press, a time period coinciding with Ferdinand II's conquest of Granada (which put an end to the Islamic presence in Spain) and the height of the Inquisition—was also the birth-year of the famed Spanish philosopher Juan Luis Vives (1492–1540).

Vives, a convert whose family was killed in the Inquisition, was the author of humanistic writings on the soul, which have established him, in the opinion of many, as the father of modern psychiatry. Although he also wrote about the proper education of children and the duties of spouses, Vives' most influential treatise was the *De Anima et Vita* [*On the Soul and Life*] (1538). His contribution here lay in his demystification of the soul concept. He leaves it to theologians to ponder *what* the soul is in its essence. Of greater relevance to him were the questions: What is the soul *like*? How does it function? He concluded: "*Est ergo anima ipsa artifex, est agens, non aliunde in eo utique corpore vim suam mutuans* [the soul therefore is itself the author, the moving force (behind our functions), drawing its energy not elsewhere than within the body]" (p. 48).

Juan Luis Vives, 1492–1540

Vives then proceeded to outline the soul's functions. The first section of the *De Anima* is devoted to a description of the five senses; the second, to general mental functions; the third, to affects. The categories sketched in Book 2 call to mind

Hartmann's description of the "conflict-free Ego sphere"in his psycho-analytic treatise of 1950. Vives' categories included intelligence, memory, recall (*recordatio*), natural ability or talent, thought (both as reasoning and as contemplation) and the will. To these he added sections on sleep, dreams and habit. Book 3 dealt with the emotions, which he divided into three groups. Among the *positive* emotions were love, lust or desire (*cupiditas* has both connotations), good will, veneration, sympathy/pity, joy (*gaudium*), and pleasure (*laetitia*). The *negative* emotions included displeasure, contempt, anger, hatred, envy, jealousy, indignation, vengeance (*ultio*), and cruelty. Finally, Vives identified the third group, which included sadness, tearfulness, fear, hope, shame and pride (*superbia* connotes the negative aspect of pride, arrogance, rather than the positive aspect).

Vives' compendium was a forerunner of Descartes' *De Passionibus*, in which he developed a hierarchical approach to the emotions in the form of six basic affects from which all others are derived. Freud's pleasure/pain principle is also in this tradition. Vives, incidentally, spent some years attached to the court of the English king, Henry VIII, where Vives' recommendations for the correct upbringing of children were highly valued. Vives was also instrumental in advancing the ideas promulgated by Pico della Mirandola (1463–1494), who taught that "Man" is free to determine his own fate and to realize his own ideal, but that this could only be achieved through education (Alexander & Selesnick, 1966).

Actually, a lesser known commentator, Frenchman Jean Gerson, also wrote of "six basic passions" as early as 1500. These consisted of three "good" and three "bad"emotions: love-lust-desire, and sorrow-hatred-anxiety (*inquietudo,* defined as "fleeing that which is hateful").

The 16th century produced two very colorful figures of relevance to our history. The first of these, the son of a Swiss physician, was Philippe Aureole Theophrastus Bombastus von Hohenheim, known to us as Paracelsus. His years of birth and death (1493–1541) are one later than those of Vives. Though he was appointed city physician in Basel (after curing an ailment of the great Erasmus), there is some question as to whether he completed his medical training. While still a student, he once threw books by Galen and Avicenna into the flames, claiming that "my shoe buckles have more wisdom than those men"(A. & S., 1966, p. 85). His outspoken anti-authoritarianism carried over into his views on witchcraft: He vehemently denounced witch-burners. Paracelsus viewed the mind and body as inseparably intertwined and believed that illnesses of any kind could be cured by medicine. He was one of the first to employ a concept of an "unconscious." For example, in discussing children who swallow strange objects, under the influence of a leader-child who first does so, Paracelsus used the term *ignotans* (unaware/unconscious) in alluding to the children's

Paracelsus

unawareness of the motives behind their imitation.

The second, still more bohemian, figure was Giralomo Cardano (1501–1576), an illegitimate son of a prominent Milanese lawyer. He

From Giralamo Cardano, *Metoposcopia*, 1658.

> (left) "These lines denote a man of wantonness or lewdness. Likewise in a woman: a craving for pleasure; unnatural feelings."
> (center) "Here also the lines bespeak, in a man, a lover of married women, or else, if he himself is married, he might consort with a close relative. He will be lewd or an adulterer."
> (right) "This configuration denotes a man of pronounced viciousness."

at least finished medical school, but was denied a license to practice in Milan because of his illegitimacy. In addition to being a doctor, he was a gambler, mathematician (discovering the laws of probability even as he lost all his money!), and charlatan—proposing in his famous *Metaposcopia* (literally, forehead inspecting) that one's character could be diagnosed just by assessing the arrangement of lines on the forehead. The shibboleth of Cardano's treatment of philosophy—he cures most in whom most believe—presaged the emphasis on the curative powers of *suggestion,* as practiced by the late-Renaissance (and non-medical) cure-worker, Valentine Greatraks (1628–1666), and still later (and more importantly) by Mesmer.

Johann Weyer

For our purposes, the most outstanding physician of the second half of the 16th century was Dutch-born Johann Weyer (1515–1588), pupil of the German humanist physician, Cornelius Agrippa von Nettesheim.

VINCE TE IPSVM.

EFFIGIES IOANNIS WIERI ANNO
ÆTATIS LX.SALVTIS M.D.LXXVI.

Johann Weyer (1515–1588). From the title page of his *De praestigiis daemonum.* 1583. Courtesy of Special Collections of Vassar College Libraries

It was the latter's influential tract on the nobility of women that inspired Weyer to take up the cause of women who were being persecuted as witches. Weyer's magnum opus *De Praestigiis Daemonum* [*The Deceptions of the Devil*] (1564) debunked the *Malleus Maleficarum* and the still active belief in deviltry and witchcraft. Because so much of his practice was devoted to the humane and rational treatment of the mentally ill, Weyer has many modern-day supporters who claim him as the father of modern psychiatry.

A less known but equally important work was Weyer's *De Ira Morbo* [*On the Disease of Anger*] (1577), whose organization is surprisingly modern: definition, causes, signs, effects, and treatment. Weyer describes the kinds of anger associated with melancholy and mania, introducing his thoughts on the dire effects of anger with this comment: "*Iram perturbationum omnium esse atrocissimam, et foecundissimam infinitorum malorum matrem, quae naturam hominis in truculentam commutet feram, manifestum est* [it is obvious that of all disorders, anger is the most dreadful and is the most fertile mother of numberless evils, converting the nature of man into that of a savage beast]"(p. 42). [Author's translation]

Weyer's astuteness as a diagnostician and debunker of hoaxes shines through in another monograph, *De Commentitiis Jejuniis* [*On Feigned Fasting*]. While serving as private physician to the Duke of Cleves (a man with serious depression and a strong family history of psychosis), Weyer was called upon to examine a ten-year-old girl, Barbara Krämers, who was unusually pious in demeanor and who allegedly had gone without food or drink for some six months, not even emptying her bladder or bowels in all that time. Townspeople were coming to the girl's home as though they were witnessing a miracle.

Weyer removed Barbara to his own home for a period of close examination. She came, reluctantly and on crutches, insisting she be accompanied by her sister. This was allowed. Weyer and his wife then proceeded to think up some ingenious ways of testing the veracity of her story. For example, his wife pretended to fall asleep at the breakfast table (where, so far, Barbara had eaten nothing). When Barbara saw that Weyer's wife was "asleep,"she signaled her sister quickly, who handed her a goblet of beer; later, the sister pilfered some rolls from the pantry, which she gave to Barbara when they thought no one was looking. But Weyer had a hole drilled between the basement and kitchen floor, so that his servants could spy on the girl from below (Stone, 1973).

In this way Barbara's deception was discovered. Here was a case, unlike that of the Venerable Lukardis, of feigned "anorexia nervosa"— easily concealed within the cultural context of religious ardor, since there were so many girls who genuinely fasted during that era (Bynum, 1987).[1]

Digging Out from Dogmatism

Toward the end of the 16th century we encounter a number of prominent commentators and physicians who studied mental illness. Rudolf Goeckel, for example, wrote a treatise in 1590 on the means to improve humankind, where the term *psychology* appears for the first time. Spanish physician Juan Huarte y Navarro carried forward the tradition of Vives by conceptually separating psychology and theology. His theories were derived from Galen's; he was concerned with the balance of the four "factors" related to the temperaments: warm, cold, dry, moist. Believing (incorrectly!) that castrated males lost their intelligence and skills, Huarte claimed that the testicles must be the key to temperament in men. In his most widely read book, *Examen de Ingenios* [*The Examination of Men's Wits*] (1575), we find "eugenic" recommendations to parents on how to produce optimal children: a week before the act of generation, the spouses should drink plenty of goat's milk mixed with honey, so that all four elements will be present (cheese/earth, whey/water, butterfat/air, and honey/fire). The child thus begotten will have a fine level of intelligence, memory, and imagination (Stone, 1973).

The "constricted, deadly forehead" of the tyrant, Actiolinus of Padua, resembling that of a lion. *From* Giovanni della Porta, *De Humana Physiognomonia.*

Now that the Church's objections to dissection of the body had begun to lose power, the 16th century became notable for the efforts made in medicine to identify correspondences between diseases and anatomical abnormalities. In this spirit, Italian ophthalmologist Giovanni della Porta (1545–1615) extended his research into the area of abnormal personality. In his *Humana Physiognomonia* [*Human Physiognomy*] there are many engravings of people's heads alongside pictures of the animals they most closely (in della Porta's eyes, at least) resembled. Thus a man who looked leonine presumably possessed the lion's courage and strength of will; someone with goat-like features would be expected to show the lubricity often ascribed to that animal, and so forth. As a pseudoscience, della Porta's physiognomy is not without its charm—but before we dismiss it, we should remember that these efforts constitute the origins of biological psychiatry—of which, more below.

Giovanni della Porta

That the forces *opposing* dissection and its findings (which radically

---

[1] Actually, anorexia nervosa, as we know the syndrome, was not described until 1694, when Richard Morton wrote his treatise on "nervous atrophy," where he drew attention to other features, such as amenorrhea and hyperactivity.

Melanchthon

overturned Galen's assertions concerning the four humours) were still strong is well illustrated by the reaction of the great humanist scholar and reformer, Philip Melanchthon (1497–1560), at the execution of Miguel Servetus (Z., 1941). Melanchthon was delighted! Servetus had discovered the pulmonary circulation of blood—for which anti-Galenic demonstration he was burned at the stake in 1553. As with many great men of this age—which was just digging itself out from the dogmatisms of the past—Melanchthon was at once progressive (as in his *Liber De Anima* [*Book about the Soul*], where he expresses similar ideas about the soul as did Vives) and arch-conservative (as to how the body works).

Felix Plater

Swiss anatomist Felix Plater (1536–1614) was a careful taxonomist of mental illness, for which he used the term *alienation,* which became the norm for the next 200 years. He even spent time in dungeons among mentally ill prisoners, emerging with a system of classification based on the idea that mental disease was a product of *brain damage,* especially if the brain were excessively "dry."(The latter thought reflects his affiliation to Galenic humoural theory.) With his 1602 treatise, the *Praxeos,* he is generally given credit as the first to attempt classification of mental diseases *according to symptoms.*

Plater also believed that *hallucinations* (another general term for mental illness in his time) containing a sexual theme were the work of the Devil.[2] As to therapy, Plater recommended purgatives and, for highly disturbed patients, the use of chains. Still, this is a gentler prescription than the advice of 13th-century Arnold de Villanova (1240–1313), who also described hallucinations, but whose attempt to unify Galenism with devil theory led him to treat mania by incising a cross in the skin of the head, perforating the cranium so that both the demons and the morbid vapors could escape to the outside (A. & S., 1966).

The English Contributors

Reginald Scot

King James

The English made several significant contributions to psychiatry in the late 16th century. In 1584 essayist Reginald Scot (1538-1599) published his *Discoverie of Witchcraft,* whose subtitle establishes his rational stance: "Proving that the Compacts and Contracts of Witches with *Devils and all Infernal Spirits or Familiars,* are but Erroneous Novelties and Imaginary Conceptions." King James, whose commissioned scholars produced the magnificent translation of the Bible, himself wrote a *Demonologie,* adhering to the old views about witches; he also ordered the burning of Scot's books!

[2] *Hallucination* is a term dating back to the time of Cicero. It stems from the Greek word *aluo*—meaning to wander, to be distraught—and initially had no connotations of seeing visions or hearing voices.

Timothy Bright's treatise on "Melancholie" is notable chiefly for its having been read and absorbed by Shakespeare. Bright (1551–1615) accepted Galenic theory, stating: "Black Bile riseth by excessive heate of such parts where it is engendered"(p. 31)—an idea endorsed earlier by Arnold de Villanova, who opined that the devil likes heat, because excess heat facilitates the devil's disruption of the soul along melancholic lines. Shakespeare's works contain 69 allusions to *melancholy;* none to mania. An example from *Twelfth Night* is Viola's reply to the Duke, who is in love with Countess Olivia: ". . . she pin'd in thought, and with a green and yellow melancholy She sat like Patience on a monument"(act 2, scene 4, lines 112–114). *Timothy Bright*

The English Jesuit priest Thomas Wright (1561–1623), whose *Passions of the Mind* appeared in 1601, offered a new classification of the emotions, establishing himself as a "lumper"(even more so than Gerson) rather than a "splitter"(like Vives). Wright insisted that there was only one sensual *appetite* (amounting to one power of the soul) with two *inclinations:* the *concupiscible* (coveting, desiring, wishing) and the *irascible* (anger, invading [similar to our *aggressive*], impugning). This notion resembles our contemporary one of the pleasure/pain principle, where affects are divided into positive and the negative polarities. Wright acknowledged that many feel that "no passion is more sensible knowne unto us than desire or concupiscence, yet . . . I think there is no man that ever perceived himselfe so vehement a desire of anything he loved, as sadness and grief when hee was afflicted with that hee hated"(p. 217). Regarding love as the "fountaine, root and mother of the passions"—even the negative ones—Wright pondered, ". . . who hateth death, but hee which loveth life?"(p. 221). *Thomas Wright*

Chapter 4

FIRM FOUNDATIONS IN EMPIRICISM
AND CLASSIFICATION:
THE SEVENTEENTH CENTURY

Progress in anatomy led to a further weakening of Galenic influence in discussions of etiology, though the humoural terminology persisted (*melancholic, sanguine,* etc.), as it does to this day. The durability of the old terms reflects the stability of certain clinical profiles across the centuries (such as that of vegetative depression/melancholia), even though theories about causation have come and gone.

Perhaps influenced by the tradition of medieval courtly love and the troubadours, a strong interest emerged toward the end of the 16th century in madness brought on by frustrated love. The descriptions of this malady come mostly from the French literature (as might be expected).

Along with the ascending importance of rationalism and observation was another strong interest in "sympathetic magic" and other effects-at-a-distance (Mettler & Mettler, 1947, p. 543). Paracelsus stimulated this interest by proposing that the magnet operated in this mysterious way. The magnet (in the form of the lodestone) was now recommended for cases of choreic spasmodic movements (Tarentism).

Syphilis first surfaced in Europe in the 1500s[1] and was particularly virulent at first. By the 17th century, the infection was milder, now manifesting sometimes as a gradual brain degeneration, and was identified as a form of insanity (general paresis). (The connection between

[1] It is a matter of some debate whether syphilis was brought by Columbus' returning sailors or by African slaves who were brought into Europe (Gottfried, 1983).

syphilis and the spirochete bacteria was not to be made for another two centuries.)

From the 17th century onward, a shift took place in the locus of psychiatric advance: Progress and original thought were confined almost exclusively to nations where a French, English, or Germanic language was the mother tongue—i.e., France, England/America, Germany/Austria/Switzerland/The Netherlands. Spain, perhaps because the Inquisition had expelled so many of her intellectuals or because her armada was defeated in 1588, was henceforth left "out of the loop." Some contributions were still to come from Italy, often high in quality but quantitatively less than what was to emerge from the Northern countries.

FRENCH CONTRIBUTIONS

In a revolutionary yet all but unknown treatise on medicine written in 1618, Charles LePois (1563–1633) stated that the condition of hysteria had nothing to do with the uterus and could occur in men as well as women. This latter possibility was still stoutly denied by Freud's teachers when he asserted the same, some 250 years after LePois. So much had etymology and entrenched beliefs impeded new thought concerning this syndrome!

Charles LePois

Another physician who proved himself able to shuck traditional explanations when they no longer seemed sensible was Jacques Ferrand. In his treatise on lovesickness, *De la Maladie de l'Amour, ou Mélancholie Érotique* [*The Malady of Love and Erotic Melancholy*] (1623), he takes issue with the age-old assertion that the heart is the organ of love. In the condition of "erotic melancholy" (depression provoked by disappointment in love), the trouble comes about *"par le vice du cerveau, lors que l'imagination est depravée"* [by a derangement of the *brain,* for it is the imagination that is depraved] (p. 65). Later he gives an example of a married woman who thought she was afflicted by the *incubus*—but who, after Ferrand cured her, could recognize that this conviction had been the product of a depraved imagination. However, the cure did not involve helping the patient deal more adaptively with the sexual frustration, but rather with the ministration of philters and love potions, using recipes going back to antiquity. Nevertheless, Ferrand's advancement in thinking lay in his realization that the melancholy in these cases was not a matter of "black bile" but of unrequited love (though his cure still involved magical thinking).

Jacques Ferrand

That love, particularly unrequited love, could induce such disequilibrium of the mind was perfectly in keeping with the prevailing ideas of the time concerning the passions. Theologian J. F. Senault (1649), who catalogued eleven important emotions, noted that Plato spoke of four passions that were more violent than all the others: voluptuous-

Réné Descartes, 1596–1650. Courtesy
National Library of Medicine

Nicholas Venette
François Bayle

ness, choler (anger), desire for honor, and fear of death. But hierarchically, voluptuousness (read *lust*) was given first place. Senault's listing included love, hatred; desire, eschewing; hope, despair; audacity, fear; anger; delight and sorrow.

In a somewhat misogynistic tract written toward the end of the century, physician Nicholas Venette asserted that women were keeping alive the belief in *incubi* because it provided them with an excuse when they became pregnant by their lovers instead of by their husbands. Elsewhere Venette likened love to a mild attack of epilepsy, which was also capable of engendering melancholy. According to Venette, dissolute love (*l'amour déréglé*) is the worst plague that can afflict men, causing incurable pangs of jealousy and the foreshortening of life itself—because of the "coldness and dryness" it causes (a Galenic notion)—whereas proper life thrives on "moistness and warmth."

Adding further to the understanding of witchery and the hysterical phenomena that often accompanied it were the observations of François Bayle (1622–1709). He noted that certain women accused of being witches created an atmosphere of contagion around themselves, such that other people began to behave in similar ways: If the "witch" succumbed to spasmodic movements and contortions, suddenly mere witnesses would break into similar attacks. Bayle insisted that neither the supposed witch nor her imitators should be deemed guilty of sorcery or possession by the devil.

The greatest contributions to psychiatry from 17th century France came not from a physician but from the deductive-rationalist philosopher Réné Descartes (1596–1650). Although he gave too much weight to deductive reasoning and too little to direct observation (a fault reminiscent of Aristotle), in the field of emotions his deductions were brilliant. For in a manner more compelling than that of his predecessors, Descartes separated out the *basic* from the *complex* "passions" in a monograph, *Passiones Animae* [*Passions of the Soul*], he wrote just before he died. His notions about the physiological workings of the emotions were admittedly primitive, albeit interesting. For example, Descartes reasoned that since the gland in the middle of the brain (the pineal gland) was solitary, whereas everything else in the brain had bilateral representation, this gland must be the "center of the soul"— the place where the spirit works its effects.

Of the 49 emotions he described in the *Passiones,* six were considered *primary:* admiration, love, hate, desire, joy and sorrow. (Descartes meant *admiration*[2] only in the etymological sense of attracting one's

[2] Our interest is attracted by whatever impinges on our sense organs that seems unusual and surprising. Descartes saw the brain as a center for processing stimuli from our five senses. This view underlay the empiricist ideol-

interest by virtue of novelty.) Other emotions involved combinations of these six. For example, *envy* is a complex emotion composed of *sorrow* (that we do not have something) and *hate* (that someone we deem unworthy does have it). Even more complex is *jealousy*, which pertains to love triangles: There is an admixture of *desire* (for the love-object), *sorrow* (at the loss of this person), and *hate* (toward the rival). Contemporary conceptions of emotion are neatly prefigured in the *Passiones*: Hierarchical classifications of the emotions by de Rivera (1977) and H. Dahl (1978) rely on almost the same "elements" as those identified by Descartes 330 years earlier.[3]

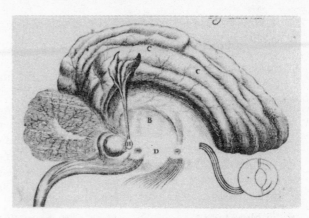

The brain in mid-sagittal section, highlighting the pineal gland, which, because of its singularity and centrality, Descartes believed was the seat of the soul. From Descartes, *De Homine Figuris*, 1662.

GERMAN CONTRIBUTIONS

Dutch- and German-speaking contributors to psychiatry were few in number in this century and made their appearance at its close, their works published just before or just after 1700.

In his *Pathologia Daemonica* (1707) Dutch-born Johann-Caspar Westphal described several nervous maladies (epilepsy, catalepsy, melancholy, and certain skin conditions) that had heretofore been ascribed to witchcraft—specifically to the temptations and powers of the devil—but which "today we recognize as obsessions." Westphal defined witchcraft as an "intense power and action of the imagination directed at the body of another [person]." Writing still in Latin (use of local languages did not become widespread in scientific Europe until the mid-1700s), he used the term *fascinatiô* for witchcraft, from which we get our word *fascination.* The origin of the word is, well, fascinating. It is derived from the Greek *baskanon* or amulet. *Fascinus* was a deity in the form of a phallus, and the *fascinum* was an amulet in the shape of a penis that was given to children in the Middle Ages to wear around their necks in order to ward off the powers of witchcraft.

Johann-Caspar Westphal

---

ogy behind other 17th-century philosophers such as Locke and Condillac, which put special value on the senses (Z., 1941).

[3] Descartes' "elements" are more fundamental and more useful as building blocks for the more complex emotions than the earlier schema of de la Chambre (1640), whose six elements were "love, hate, desire, aversion, pleasure, and pain." *Aversion* and *hate* are too overlapping, whereas Descartes' *admiration* is significantly different from the other five.

This practice gives further evidence of how men externalized their sexual difficulties onto women, who supposedly had "hexed" them so that they were unable to perform! The obvious amulet for this trouble would be an "extra" phallus with powers even greater than that of the *fascinatiô*. Westphal adds:

> So enormous is the power of the imagination that it can not only stir up various and extreme motions in the Soul, but, by these means, can stir up and deform the fetus growing in the womb, such that moles, discolorations, and dreadful swellings can arise, or can even cause death itself (p. 40). [Author's translation]

Arnold Wesenfeld

Meanwhile, Arnold Wesenfeld, a German professor of philosophy, took issue with Descartes' model of six primary emotions, asserting that admiration, strictly speaking, was not an emotion and, besides, everything boiled down to the two extremes anyway, namely, love and hate (1695).

ENGLISH CONTRIBUTORS

The contributions of English alienists and scholars in this century were enormous. Almost without exception, their works are characterized by rationalism, empiricism, and—especially in the case of Robert Burton—by an ability to self-reflect as a means of searching for the sources of mental distress. Even among the majority of writers who were not particularly self-reflective (who, as we would say, had no "insight into their own dynamics"), there was a recognition that emotional illness was often triggered by life circumstances, lovesickness, personal tragedy, and the like—rather than by some mysterious external force such as an "evil spirit" directed at one by a "witch."

Edward Jorden

Edward Jorden (1569–1632) was the first English physician who viewed the women who were accused of witchcraft as unfortunate persons suffering from some medical condition. Asserting that there were natural causes for their afflictions, Jorden often served as expert witness at trials of women accused of witchery. His arguments did not always persuade the judges, however. One Elizabeth Jackson, accused of causing the fits suffered by May Glover, was convicted in spite of Jorden's defense. Jorden (1603) called the disorder manifested in Jackson (and in the majority of supposed witches) by two terms: *hysterical,* and *strangulatus uteri,* or "suffocation of the mother" (*mother* here being an old-fashioned term for the uterus), since a choking in the throat was a common accompaniment. Jorden was impressed by the panoply and ever-shifting quality of symptoms associated with this condition: now shortness of breath, now palpitations, now paralysis, and so on. He was also aware that the hysterical "fits" might occur with varying regularity: yearly, monthly, or even weekly.

That the physicians of this time and place had to combat, again and again, the popular beliefs in devils, witches, and possession is attested to by another commentator, Richard Baddeley (1586–1670). Called upon to examine a boy believed to be possessed, Baddeley demonstrated instead that he was emotionally disturbed—and a malingerer to boot:

Richard Baddeley

> This boy, being about 13 yeres old . . . was thought by divers [persons] to bee possessed of the Divell and bewitched, by reason of many strange fits and much distemper. . . . In those fits hee appeared both deafe and blinde, writhing his mouth aside, continually groaning and panting . . . yet hee could not be discerned to betray the least passion or feeling. [He complained of abdominal pains and passed black urine.] But by the 3rd day following . . . by diligent watchfulness . . . he was espyed mixing Inke with his urine, and nimbly conveying the Ink-horne into a private place. When being suddenly deprehended in this his conveyance, after an earnest, but loving exhortation, this deafe began to hear, and dumb to speake: and at the sight of his ungracious and godlesse practises, he brast out into plentiful tears, confessing all. (Hunter & Macalpine, 1963, p. 100)

Fifty years passed until another physician, John Webster (1610–1682), took up the cause again of disclaiming any validity to stories of witches, devils, and apparitions, relating these phenomena instead to delusions of melancholy and fancy (Webster, 1677). Citing Baddeley's case, he then recounted a similar case of his own, in which a ten-year-old girl claimed worms came out of her ear. As Weyer had done with Barbara Krämers, Webster took the girl into his own home, watched her carefully, and caught on to the *legerdemain* by which she pretended to exhibit this strange condition, whereupon ". . . and so the wonder ceased" (p. 265).

John Webster

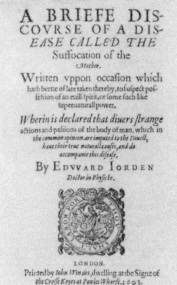

An allusion to *inner conflict* as a source of emotional distress—an early reference to what has become a customary way of thinking in our psychoanalytic era—can be found in an essay on "The Soules Conflict with Itself" by Richard Sibbs, a doctor of divinity at Cambridge. He writes (1635):

Frontispiece of Edward Jorden's book on hysteria—the first on the subject to be written in English. From Jorden, *A Briefe Discourse of a Disease Called the Suffocation of the Mother*, 1603.

> Another thing that disquiets and casts down the soule very much is, that inward conflict betwixt *grace* and *corruption*: this . . . puts us to most disquietment. It is the trouble

of troubles to have two inhabitants so neare in one soule, and there to strive one against another. (p. 386)

Richard Sibbs

Sibbs was referring to the simultaneous and contradicting desires to do what is socially acceptable and "good" versus what is socially rejected and "bad"—akin to what we speak of under the heading of superego/id conflicts.

Arguably the most important English book of the 17th century relevant to our history comes not from a physician but from the dean of divinity at Oxford, Robert Burton. His treatise, the almost 600-page-long *Anatomy of Melancholy* (1621), is remarkable not only for its encyclopedic coverage of melancholy in every aspect, but for the running commentary embedded within it—*on Burton's own case of melancholy.* The kind of self-revelation so commonplace in our post-Freudian era was exceedingly rare in Burton's time. Apart from St. Augustine, who some 1,200 years earlier castigated himself for the lustiness of his youth, one does not find many examples of self-revelation before Burton.

As Alexander and Selesnick (1966) note, Burton's childhood was apparently arid because of the aloofness of his parents. He became ". . . an Oxford scholar of great eminence and a recluse who perpetually dreamed of being able to participate in life" (p. 103). Self-deprecatory, gloomy, bitter, and angry, Burton might be called "dysthymic and avoidant" in our contemporary terminology. As a scholar of divinity, Burton seems to have accepted the existence of the Devil; he also struggled with the conflicting attitudes toward suicide that characterized this era. After giving examples of melancholic persons who had taken their own lives (by drowning or by hurling themselves out a window), Burton pondered: "It is controverted by some, whether a man so offering violence to himselfe, dying desperate, may be saved or no" (Burton, 1621, p. 543). If such a person dies suddenly, before having the chance to ask for God's mercy, he dies "impenitent" (the worst situation), whereas:

If a man put desperate hands upon himselfe, by occasion of madnesse or melancholy, if hee have given testimony before of his regeneration, . . . we must make the best construction out of it, as the Turkes doe, that thinke all fooles and madmen goe directly to Heaven. (Burton, 1621, p. 543)

Richard Burton, 1577–1640. Courtesy Stock Montage, Inc.

Burton himself manifested (and perceived in other melancholiacs) an inordinate sense of *guilt,* for which he expressed an urgent need for repentance: "I offend hourly, dayly, in word and deed" (Burton, 1621, p. 546). He did not seem to sense the exaggeration of this guilt, however: Burton, after all, led an exemplary and blameless life, as do many people with this condition. As for remedy, Burton mentioned many useful measures (besides repentance), including good diet, eight or nine hours of sleep, eating no more than a light meal before bedtime so as to minimize the possibility of having terrifying dreams,[4] exercise, "physicke" (medicines), being in the company of others as much as possible, being occupied with useful things to do, and listening to soothing music. But the most important remedy for melancholy, which Burton judged to be "more grievous than a disease of the body," was *confessing one's grief to a friend.* Before discussing this remedy, Burton elucidated the adverse effects of the negative emotions produced in the melancholiac:

> For anger stirres choler, heats the blood and vitall spirits, Sorrow on the other side refrigerates the Body . . . overthrows appetite, hinders concoction [digestion], and perverts the understanding. Feare dissolves the spirits . . . attenuates the Soule: and for these causes all passions and perturbations must to the uttermost of our power, and most seriously bee removed. (Burton, 1621, p. 239)

According to Burton, their removal could best be effected through what we would consider *psychotherapeutic means*: the interaction between the melancholiac and a sympathetic and trusted outsider:

> If then our Judgment be so depraved, our Reason so overruled . . . that we cannot seek our own good, or moderate ourselves, as in this Disease it commonly is, our best way for ease is to impart our misery to some friend, not to smother it up in our own brest, *aliter vitium crescitque tegendo* [otherwise the defect increases through concealing it]. . . . When as we shall but impart it to some discreet, trusty, loving friend, is instantly removed, by counsell happily wisdome, perswasion, advise, his good means, which we could not otherwise apply unto ourselves. (p. 242)

John Adams

At the end of the century, another minister, the Reverend John Adams, chaplain to His Majesty, spoke out against suicide. In his treatise on "self murther" (1700), Adams maintained that suicide, though it may be the end-stage of melancholy, is an "injustice toward God . . . by destroying that which is His alone [to bestow] and by the positive and willful refusal of performing that end for which Man received life" (p. 23). However, Adams also argued that suffering extreme pain might justify suicide, if death entailed the total cessation of all existence and feeling. But since the greater part of mankind—"at least ten thousand to one"—has held

[4] Three hundred years later Kraepelin cited terrifying dreams as a sign of the depressive temperament (1921).

Thomas Sydenham, 1624–1689. Courtesy National Library of Medicine

that an afterlife exists, it seems like a terrible folly to "run such a hazard against so much odds" (p. 284).

Competing theories about hysteria circulated in the latter half of the century. London physician Thomas Sydenham (1624–1689) used the term in a nonspecific sense to signify any mental disorder short of what we would call outright psychosis—"frank alienation," in the language of the day (H. & M., 1963, p. 221). This broad usage finds a counterpart in our psychoanalytic term *neurosis,* as noted in the writings of Freud and other pioneers (for Freud, hysteria was a specific *form* of neurosis). Sydenham noted a similarity between the *hypochondriacal* symptoms in men and the *hysterical* symptoms in women, although he apparently did not go so far as had LePois, who contended that men could be "hysterics" also.

Sydenham was not a theoretician so much as a clinician, whose first concern was to get his patients better. To this end he was not above benign trickery, as demonstrated by his work with a nobleman patient who suffered from melancholy. Surmising that distracting the man's attention from his misery would be a curative in itself, and noting that his efforts were thus far unavailing, Sydenham recommended that his patient consult with the "renowned" (but actually non-existent) Dr. Robinson in Scotland. Contemplating the cure that was in store for him, the nobleman felt relieved all the way to Scotland, forgetting his melancholic worries. Upon discovering there was no Dr. Robinson, he flew into a rage at Sydenham's deception—and again, forgot all about his worries. When he angrily confronted Sydenham after returning to London, the doctor explained to the patient that his faith in "Dr. Robinson" had cured his condition on the way up, and his fury at Sydenham had cured him on the way back—which was the response Sydenham had counted on in the first place (H. & M., 1963). As to Sydenham's notions of causative agents, he ascribed both hysteria and hypochondriasis to "irregular or inordinate motions of the animal spirits" (Goshen, 1967, p. 127).

Thomas Willis

A contrasting view on hysteria emerged from the work of Thomas Willis (1621–1675), discoverer of the eponymous "circle of Willis" (the anastomotic arterial circuit at the base of the brain) and originator of the term *neurology.* He also used the term *psyche-ology* to designate the study of the "corporeal soul" (H. & M., 1963). Willis was one of the founding fathers of *biological* psychiatry, placing even hysteria and hypochondriasis among the disorders of the nerves (in contradistinction to the blood vessels, as postulated by Hippocrates). Willis saw hysteria as a type of "fit" or convulsion (*Pathologia Cerebri* [*Pathology of the Brain*], 1668) specifically as a disorder less severe than *grand mal* epilepsy (in modern terms) but still convulsive in nature. As Willis described it:

These are the features—rumbling sounds, retching, distension of the abdomen,[5] uneven or impaired breathing, a suffocation in the throat, dizziness, crossing or rotation of the eyes, tearfulness, saying strange things, sometimes losing the voice or becoming motionless, a weak pulse and a cadaverous look, and meantime convulsive movements of the face and joints or, often enough, of the whole body. This can happen to women of all ages and classes—including prepubertal girls, and even to men. (p. 160) [Author's translation]

Willis rejected the notion of the "wandering womb" as a cause of hysteria, though his theories were still heavily dependent on Hippocratic humoural formulations. Willis realized that the brain was the seat of mental disturbance and that the nerves were the connections between the brain and the rest of the body, but the mechanisms involved remained elusive. Willis believed "animal spirits" (here *animal* is the adjectival form of *anima,* meaning *soul*) were somehow distilled from the blood inside the brain and conducted throughout the body via the nerves. He concurred with Burton as to the recreational treatment methods for melancholia (music, pleasurable activities like fishing, academic studies, etc.), but had no interest in, nor feeling for, the psychological (i.e., humanistic, interpersonal) interventions advocated by Burton (sharing one's malady with a friend) or practiced by Sydenham. Quite to the contrary, Willis favored extremely harsh measures when faced with "madness" (psychosis): For those who demonstrated incongruous notions, wild emotionality ("fury"), and fantasies, Willis advised restraints, beatings, "hard usage," and the all-too-typical triad of emetics, bloodletting, and purgatives.

On this subject of "madness," Willis is given credit for having sketched a clinical picture that we would equate with dementia praecox (now more commonly called *schizophrenia*). This profile is described in his important book, *De Anima Brutorum* [*On the Irrational Soul*] (1672), more than a hundred years prior to the description by his countryman John Haslam, and more than two hundred before the definitive descriptions by Emil Kraepelin and Eugen Bleuler. Willis emphasized the transition from intellectual brightness in youth to dullness (*stupiditas*) in adolescence:

There are many clear causes by which dullness may be induced in a number of formerly healthy persons. These persons, who were once upon a time clever and gifted, gradually become, without any great changes in their way of life, duller [*hebetiores*], and

---

[5] *Hypochondria* literally means region below the diaphragm.

indeed, foolish or insipid . . . rather as it is with certain wines that after fermentation is completed, lose their strength and little by little turn vapid. A good number, having been to a high degree intelligent during childhood, and extremely quick to learn, end up in adolescence enfeebled and dull. Where they were handsome in aspect before, they are now without gracefulness or pleasant demeanor. (p. 509) [Author's translation]

Passages of this sort may be as close as we can come to answering the skeptics of our own day (notably E. Fuller Torrey), who doubt that schizophrenia antedated the "Industrial Era" of the early 19th century. Although Willis did not mention delusions accompanying this adolescent hebetude, we must take into account that physicians seldom offered descriptions that were novelistic in detail and richness before 1800. Furthermore, the abnormalities to which they paid attention were those that related to the then current theories of the mind. Any behavior that could be construed as a derangement of the humours caught their eye; "bad parenting" and its effects went largely unnoticed, as did the subtleties of thought aberrations, which we now look for if we are to make a diagnosis of schizophrenia with confidence.

A curious but influential figure at mid-century was Lord Chief Justice Matthew Hale (1606?–1676). A humanist in some ways, he objected to the Cartesian view of *l'homme machine,* in which the human is viewed as an engine, one of surpassing complexity to be sure, but an engine all the same. Hale also objected to the notion that animals have the capacity for imagination and reason, as put forward by de la Chambre (H. & M., 1963). Hale argued against what, in our century, has been termed *cybernetics* (Wiener, 1948), asserting (in his 1677 treatise on "The Primitive Origination of Mankind") that human perception, memory, fantasy, and logic cannot be neatly reduced to the "modification of matter or the natural motion thereof." But Hale was also an arch-conservative in other ways that touched on mental illness. He believed firmly in the influence of the moon on human emotions, juxtaposing the term *lunacy* with acquired (moon-) madness, which was distinct from inborn madness, or *idiocy* (Mettler & Mettler, 1947). Hale's definition of idiocy was both sweeping and imprecise: All adults who did not display an intelligence equal to that of the "normal" 14-year-old were considered idiots. Hale was also responsible for the notion of *temporary insanity,* noting that some witches, for example, experienced the height of their distemper at the full moon (and also at the equinoxes) (Z., 1941).[6]

[6] This concept, based more on the convenience of the law than on the observations of medicine, has helped to create an unfortunate gray area in modern-day forensic psychiatry: Chronically psychotic persons who have occasional

Earlier, in discussing Weyer's case of the girl who feigned fasting, I alluded to the genuine cases of anorexia nervosa first identified by Richard Morton (1637–1698), physician to King James II. Ascribing this "consumptive" disorder to an abnormal state of the "animal spirits" and to an enfeebled "tone of the nerves," Morton sketched the case history of an 18-year-old girl who began to lose appetite, becoming so emaciated that she resembled a "skeleton only clad with skin" (H. & M., 1963, p. 231). Her periods ceased and she showed no fatigue, studying long hours into the night—which Morton thought added to the severity of her condition, because of the especially cold night air the year she took ill (1684). He also blamed "violent passions of the mind" for her conditions, as though these could upset the "animal spirits" by sending too much blood to the brain. There was no sign of any other known illness in any part of her body. Morton had only the most rudimentary remedies to offer: stomach plasters, ammonia salts, bitter medicines containing iron (chalybeates)—all to no avail. A few months later she died. The condition Morton described did not acquire its present name, *anorexia nervosa,* until William Gull (1868) published his treatise nearly two centuries later.

Richard Morton

As we have seen thus far, 17th century England leaned more and more in the direction of the rational and empirical in relation to mental phenomena and medicine in general. Lord Justice Hale's stubbornness aside (he condemned two witches to death), belief in witchcraft was also on the wane. But belief in the magical and miraculous by no means disappeared. There was a famous healer in England in the mid-1600s who worked cures by the "laying on of the hands": Valentine Greatraks (1628–1683). Born in Ireland to a devout Protestant family, Greatraks served as an officer in Oliver Cromwell's army, then as a justice-of-the-peace in County Cork (a post he served with exemplary honesty). In about 1660, Greatraks became aware of ". . . an Impulse, or a strange perswasion in my own mind (of which I am not able to give any rational account to another), which did very frequently suggest to me that there was bestowed on me the gift of curing the King's Evil" (1666, p. 22). This "evil" was tuberculosis scrofula; it was believed to be cured by a touch from the King, a practice begun in the 11th century by Edward the Confessor (A. & S., 1966). Cromwell made no attempt at bestowing the

The "laying on of hands" by the Irish healer, Valentine Greatraks. From Greatraks, *A Brief Account of Mr. Valentine Greatraks, and Divers of the Strange Cures by Him Lately Performed,* 1666.

---

lucid intervals may be deemed only "temporarily insane" and therefore sentenced as though sane, while others who are deemed "insane only at the time of the crime" may be excused altogether, depending on the leniency of the court.

magical touch, and after the beheading of King Charles I (1649), this power was resituated in the hands of Greatraks. Once he began working his cures, patients flocked to him by the hundreds, mostly suffering from scrofula, headaches, palsies, abdominal aches, but also from "possession," hysteria, and other nervous disorders. In fact, the distinction between the physical and the mental was often blurred, both in the conditions of the patients and in the minds of the physicians of the day. Anything as inexplicable and miraculous-seeming as Greatraks' cures was bound to inspire controversy. His book, *A Brief Account of Mr. Valentine Greatraks, and Divers of the Strange Cures by Him Lately Performed*, consists of a lengthy letter to physicist Robert Boyle, written with great humility and giving an account of his own strange powers. In the appendix of the book are dozens of testimonials by appreciative patients as well as physicians, all of whom were convinced of the efficacy of Greatraks' cures. Here is an example:

> I was by, when [Greatraks] stroked a servant of Mr. Faithornes . . . who had been lame a twelve-month by a dead Palsey on the right side. After the second stroking he was able to go about the room with the help of a stick, and in a little time grew to such strength, that he can now work at his Trade again. (signed) Simon Patrick, Rector of St. Paul's Church. (p. 61)

Greatraks' honesty was such that he gave examples of his failures alongside his successes. The importance of his method—which, of course, depended on his absolute faith in his own powers as well as on the faith of his patients—lay in his emphasis on the powers of suggestion, faith, hope, and the natural tendencies of the body to cure itself when nature, as Hippocrates so wisely quipped, is given half a chance.

Along the spectrum of what is considered curative in the healing arts, there is one extreme, the dyed-in-the-wool rationalist, who would denigrate any story of "faith healing." The other extreme, represented by the Christian Scientist, is skeptical about the efficacy of any medicines or doctors' instruments. As it turns out, both reason and imagination—sound medical tradition and faith—have their places. It is a healer like Greatraks who reminds us that medicine, in its effort to be wholly scientific, dare not altogether shun the mysterious.

The great English philosopher Francis Bacon, Lord Chancellor and Earl of Verulam (1561–1626), was instrumental in anchoring psychology on firmer scientific footing than ever before, thanks to his strong advocacy of rational inquiry and meticulous observation—an empirical approach that also informed the philosophy of John Locke (1632–1704) and the

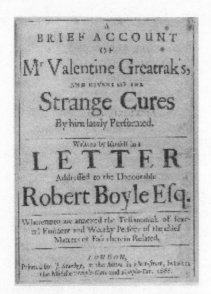

Frontispiece of the 1666 account of the cures worked by Valentine Greatraks.

clinical method of George Stahl. Bacon favored inferential reasoning (inductive logic) based on the evidence of one's senses, in contrast to Descartes, whose deductive approach relied on mathematics and on what logically "ought" to be (A. & S., 1966). Though Bacon did not reject the notion of humours, he paid them little mind, concentrating instead on what he viewed as the major compartments of the mind (elucidated in his *Advancement and Proficience of Learning,* 1640): "The Faculties of the Soule are well knowne, to be, *Reason, Imagination, Memory, Understanding, Appetite* and *Will*" (p. 209).

Sir Francis Bacon, 1561–1626.

Recognizing that little was known about many aspects of these compartments, Bacon spoke of various "deficiencies" in the formulations handed down from Aristotle and other ancient writers on these subjects. By encouraging physiological experimentation and careful description, Bacon helped demystify psychology, securing for it a future as a solid science, even though few advances were made along these lines in his own lifetime.

As to the interconnectedness between mind and body, Bacon (1640) spoke of an "alliance" or "league," commenting that:

> To describe how these two, namely the Mind & the Body, disclose one to the other . . . [i.e.,] a description of what discovery may be made of the Mind, from the habit of the body, or of the Body from the accidents of the Mind, hath begotten two Arts, both of prediction . . . The first is Physiognomy, which discovers the dispositions of the mind, by the lineaments of the Body. The second is the exposition of Naturall dreams, which discovereth the State & Disposition of the Body, from the Passions and Motions of the mind. (p. 182)

Bacon acknowledged great deficiencies in his era's understanding of dreams. He himself suspected that dreams were affected by what was going on in the body. "Thus, such as are troubled with the Hypochondriaque wind [gas in the bowels], doe often dream of Navigations, and agitations upon the waters" (Bacon, 1640, p. 183).

A tribute to Bacon's scientific spirit: He felt there was knowledge to be gained from a study of physiognomy, but he did not succumb to the fanciful speculations that had befallen Giovanni Porta (that men whose faces resembled lions acted like lions, etc.). As we shall see, men of science, including alienists, took physiognomy seriously until the dawn of the 20th century, and though we now regard their efforts as misguided, they spurred interest in mind-body relatedness and were the forerunners of modern biological psychiatry. We also see in Bacon's main divisions of mind into *reason* and *imagination* our contemporary division of dominant and nondominant hemispheres: the left brain (in all but a few true sinistrals) subserving reason; the right, mediating primary-process associations, poesy, and, in general, the imagination.

Bacon is also credited with stimulating interest in producing detailed descriptions of individual patients—which we see reflected in the work of Sydenham and Morton toward the end of this century. Likewise, Bacon's work helped justify the much needed search for correlations between brain findings at autopsy and mental illness, such as Willis undertook a generation later (H. & M., 1963). Bacon was aware of the tendency in medicine (he could as well have said, in science as a whole) to progress in circles, "with much Iteration but small Addition." Indeed, Hippocratic and Galenic notions—belief in the four humours and use of purgatives and emetics in mental disorders (to release "excesses" of these humours from the body)—were "iterated" until well after Bacon's time and into the mid–19th century.

Bacon (1640) distinguished himself in another way not immediately related to matters of the mind, but rather to the humane care of patients, in his advocacy of euthanasia:

> I estimate the office of a Physitian, not only to restore health, but to mitigate the dolors and torments of Disease . . . even when all hope of recovery being gone, it may serve to make a faire and easy passage out of life . . . But in our times Physitians . . . stay with a patient after the disease is past hope of cure; whereas . . . if they would not be wanting to their profession, and to humanity it self, they ought . . . to give the attendance for the facilitating and asswaging of the paines and agonies of Death at their departure. (p. 195)

ITALIAN CONTRIBUTORS

Tomaso Garzoni

To complete our picture of 17th century psychiatry mention should be made of several Italian contributors. Noteworthy among them was Tomaso Garzoni (1549–1589), who argued in favor of mental patients being housed in hospitals rather than penned up in prison-like "stronghouses." As to the kinds of persons to whom his recommendations might apply, Garzoni (1601) sketched some two-and-a-half dozen mental disorders and abnormal character types that one might find in such institutions. He began his catalogue with the more serious conditions: the *pazzi frenetici, malinconici, scioperati, ubbriachi, smemorati o dementi, stupidi o persi* ("madmen" who were either frenzied, melancholic, sluggish, drunk, memory-impaired or demented, or dumb or lost souls). The remaining terms are even more piquant and nontechnical. Garzoni included the "impetuous" (*sfrenati como cavallo:* literally, wild like an unbridled horse) and those who become mad only at the full moon or only episodically (*lunatici o pazzi a tempo*). But even the stubborn, the haughty, the long-winded, the "scatterbrained" (*balzani*), the vulgar-tongued (*mille forche*), and the lovesick were added to his roster, making one wonder what proportion of the population Garzoni thought fit to live outside the secure setting of the mental hospital! There is a certain judgmental quality that comes through the pages of Garzoni's treatise, as though, still very much under the influence of the Church, he equated madness with sinfulness.[7] Still, Garzoni's recognition that the mentally ill (broadly defined by his pen as they were) belonged in hospitals, there to be treated by physicians, represented an enormous advance over the much harsher fate to which they had been subjected throughout much of Europe during the Inquisition.

Shortly thereafter, Curtius Marinello published a book (1615) "on illnesses that oppress the powers of the higher soul" (*De Morbis Nobilioris Animae Facultates Obsidentibus*). The thirty conditions he described belong half to psychiatry and half to neurology (as we currently define these domains). Thus there are passages on phrenitis (defined as a delirium stemming from an inflammation of the linings of the brain), melancholia, insania, and memory impairment, but also on paralysis, tremor, tinnitus, and blindness. Marinello's work simply repeated the descriptions and advice of Galen and Arab and Latin authors. He spoke of melancholy as a "lesion of the Imagination and Reason [an idea derived independently of Bacon] not accompanied by fever" (Bk. 2, p. 5). Because Marinello still understood melancholy as representing an excess of black humour, he went along with the old recommendations for purging and bloodletting. For the *nightmare* he employed the ancient terms *ephialtes* or *incubus* (both the Greek and Latin words signify a "laying upon"), but no longer gave credence to the idea that devils prey upon the affected person during sleep. He merely stated:

Curtius Marinello

> A feeling of suffocation, stifling of the voice, a heaviness and immobility—these are the certain signs of the Incubus—all of which are brought about by the ventricles of the brain filling up with thick, cold vapours, which interferes with the transmissions of power to the nerves [*transitus facultatis ad nervos*]. (p. 12) [Author's translation]

---

[7] The tendency for rigid systems of belief to foster parallels of this sort remains with us even in the 20th century. Whereas madmen were seen as heretics by the medieval Church, heretics (those with contrary political views) were seen as madmen (schizophrenics) in Communist Russia.

Paolo Zacchia

Probably the best known of the 17th century Italian alienists was Paolo Zacchia (1584–1659), physician to Pope Innocent X. By virtue of his treatise on medico-legal questions in 1630, Zacchia is considered the father of forensic medicine (Z., 1941). His views were in line with those of Weyer's adversary, the French lawyer Bodin, to the effect that a person who had committed murder could be deemed legally sane but medically insane (we would have to say *psychotic,* since in our day "insane" is *only* a legal term). In this respect Zacchia concurred with his confreres in the Southern Europe of his day (Spain and Italy), now that the hostile spirit of the Inquisition was weakening in the northern countries (The Netherlands, Germany, and England).

Zacchia also adhered to humoural theory, at least in terminology. In his compendium on *Hypochondriasis* (1651), for example, there is a long section on melancholia. He devoted much more space, however, to clinical varieties than to the fate of one's "black bile." He used *hypochondriasis* in its root sense meaning abdominal disorders below/hypo the breastbone, or diaphragm/chondrion. All sorts of mental disorders were subsumed under *melancholy,* not just those relating to sorrowfulness. As Zacchia (1651) described it:

> There are many who imagine themselves dead, or else condemned to eternal damnation; many who believe they are persecuted by the Law or the Pope or the King—with whom they nevertheless have no relationship. We also see many who, being rich, think of themselves as impoverished, as though someone had absconded with all their possessions, for which reason they spend day and night without uttering a sound and in continual sadness. But on the other hand, there are others who, though poor, think of becoming wealthy. Then too we see those who are convinced of harboring some evil for which no cure can be found, such as harboring an abscess inside the body, or having inside them a serpent, or some other live animal, like a toad or a dog or a cat. Or those who think themselves changed into a wild beast or a bird or a fish, or who have a firm belief of being transformed into marble, or stone, or glass, or of having a head made of one of those substances, or—of being without a heart. (p. 419) [Author's translation]

This passage is interesting because of its allusions to several forms of psychotic illness, as we understand them—some of which are in line with modern conceptions of somatic delusion, melancholia, mania (delusions of poverty versus those of great wealth), or of a persecutory illness compatible with either manic-depression or even with schizophrenia. Unfortunately, Zacchia did not give us a detailed enough description of any one patient to allow us much more than a guess about the nature of these severe illnesses.

Further on Zacchia addresses the debate about the origins of "lovesickness." In line with ancient Greek theory, he concluded that this condition must also be "hypochondriacal" and not of the heart— since the latter organ subserves anger, whereas the *passioni concupiscibili* (desire and love) "belong to the Liver" (p. 493). It is obvious that we have long since established our preference for the poetic over the factual in these matters. After a romantic disappointment, no one speaks of having a "broken brain"—only a broken heart.

Chapter 5

THE EIGHTEENTH CENTURY:
THE RISE OF RATIONALITY

In the psychiatry of the 1700s, ever greater reliance was placed on direct observation and rational argument. Superstition and the dogmatism of the Church were on the wane, especially in those countries most influenced by the Reformation—Germany, The Netherlands, and England.

Though the diagnostic terms coined by the ancient Greek physicians were largely retained—*mania, melancholia, hysteria,* and the like—notions about etiology leaned away from theories about humours and "wandering wombs." Neuroanatomical theories, however primitive, now emerged, as did psychological theories regarding the "passions" (chiefly, love or anger). Cartesian dualism (the notion that the spirit was distinct from the body) still held sway with the many physicians and philosophers who also held a religious orientation. Also apparent was the emergence of materialist/monist reductionistic thought, which explained the human organism in purely mechanistic terms. For example, the English monists, impressed by Newton's physics, contended that nervous disorders arose from a "want of sufficient force and elasticity in the solids and in the nerves."

The psychiatric distinction, so significant in our era, between hospitalized and ambulatory patients was scarcely relevant until the end of the 18th century, when people with mild emotional disorders sought help from practitioners who used interventions developed by Mesmer and his followers. Before then, if one were not seriously ill, one made the best of it. If one were ill enough to warrant institutionalization, reliance on hospitals or some other form of sanctuary was necessary. These "sanctuaries" ranged in quality of care from the more humane institutions in Belgium, Switzerland, Scandinavia, Spain (and in places run by the Quakers) to the overcrowded, often makeshift places where patients were commonly brutalized, neglected, and kept in chains. The French Revolution brought about salutary changes in these hospitals and, even in the years just beforehand, the "non-restraint" movement was getting underway in Italy, France, and England.

In the beginning decades of the 1700s few figures of notable renown in the history of psychiatry appeared on the scene. In fact, there are few names from the whole of the century that contemporary psychiatrists would recognize, unless they had a special interest in the field. The exceptions would be Franz Mesmer and Philippe Pinel, and perhaps Pinel's pupil, Jean-Marc Gaspard Itard, who treated the feral child known as the "Wild Boy of Aveyron" (though the boy, who became the subject of a movie some years ago, is more famous than his doctor).

The contributions from this century, however, inspired by the rational and objective spirit of Descartes, served as a springboard from which leapt the great figures and far more numerous contributors who lived during the 19th century. From 1700 onwards most of the prominent names in psychiatric history came from countries influenced by the Protestant Reformation (the British Isles, France, and the German-speaking countries) and all that this movement fostered—the enthusiasm for methodical investigation, rational inquiry, and changing accepted beliefs.

The 18th century is considered the Age of Enlightenment; it was graced by great figures, such as Voltaire, Rousseau, Newton, Hume, Kant, Mendelssohn, Hegel, Benjamin Franklin, and toward the end, Goethe. Nevertheless, conditions for the institutionalized mentally ill remained poor, even in the most "enlightened" regions. Germany and Austria still sported *"Narrenturms"*—places where the populace could gawk at the antics of the insane. In 1730 wings for incurable patients were added to the Bethlem (Maudsley) Hospital in London (built in 1676), but conditions were still primitive: The chains had not yet come off the patients, either there or in Paris' *Salpêtrière*. Physicians were slow to give up the ancient Galenic humoural notions; bloodletting, emetics, and purges (to get rid of the "corresponding" humoural excesses) were still favorite treatments. Throughout the century there were few changes in terminology. The brief taxonomy included mania, melancholy, paranoia, dementia, idiocy, epilepsy—and little else.

GERMAN-SPEAKING CONTRIBUTORS

The most influential physician/alienist in the first third of the 18th century was Georg Stahl (1660–1734). Described as morose and sharp-tongued, and also as a man of great piety, Stahl was strongly opposed to the mechanistic theories of Willis and Descartes. For Stahl the soul was not a spirit peculiar only to humankind but rather a special "force"

George Stahl

or "drive" that infused all living beings, animals included. This idea, which presaged Henri Bergson's concept of *élan vital* in the early 1900s, represented a *synthetic* view of mind and matter as unified phenomena. By his rejection of the "man-as-machine" theories that had gained prevalence in his day, Stahl emerged as a "psychist" rather than a materialist. The concept of a vital, life-giving "force" also prefigures the Freudian concept of "libido." However, Stahl's insistence that physicians should busy themselves more with this force than with chemistry marks him as much more a psychist than Freud, who realized that the neurophysiology of the brain was as important in understanding the mind as was the mysterious force of the "libido." The idea that animals have souls was revolutionary, not to say heretical, in its day—at least in Western Europe. Such a notion was quite congenial to medieval Jewish cabalistic writers and Buddhist religious adepts (both groups believing in reincarnation). In our current times, it is clear that, though we seldom speak of *souls,* many animals (certainly the mammalian order) have *consciousness* and *subjectivity* (Searle, 1992).

Though Stahl did not specialize in mental conditions, he did express the view that mental illness stemmed from an impediment or derailment of the life-force, which might occur if a person were seized by a mood or idea that was contrary to the proper "direction" of the life-force. Stahl was also among the first to recommend specific psychological treatment for the mentally ill (Harms, 1967). Stahl's teachings impressed French alienists such as Pinel more than anyone in the immediately succeeding decades of his own country (Z., p. 280), though his psychist theory helped set the stage for the German Romanticist movement of the early 1800s, spearheaded by Reil and Heinroth.

Christian Wolff

Although Rudolph Goeckel used the word *psychology* almost two centuries earlier (1590), it is the German writer Christian Wolff who is usually given credit for coining this term, since he used it in a way more in keeping with customary usage today: Wolff's two important works were *Psychologia Empirica* [*Empirical Psychology*] (1732) and the *Psychologia Rationalis* [*Rational Psychology*] (1734). Wolff still spoke of psychology and philosophy as interrelated subjects, as did Maine de Biran and Kant. It was not until the 19th century that the two disciplines were teased apart, with psychology more allied with physiology (B., p. 69).

Hermann Boerhaave of Leyden

In the Netherlands the prominent physician of this time was Hermann Boerhaave of Leyden (1668–1738), whose medical opinions were gathered into 1,495 *Aphorisms* (1728). His basic theory was still rooted in humoural concepts: For him, melancholia was indeed a matter of black bile. He described melancholia as "that condition in which one remains persistently delirious yet without fever, the mind always fixed on one thought" (p. 257). If uncorrected, melancholia could progress to apoplexy, madness, inappropriate laughing or crying, and bizarre fantasies. Boerhaave's observation about the melancholic's "one-track" mind was quite accurate: it puts him in accord with the subsequent observers, who have employed such terms as "monomania" (Esquirol), "obsessional neurosis" (Freud, Sandler), and more recently, *obsessive-compulsive disorder*. Mania, which Boerhaave thought might be a different phase of the same condition (a conception that became standard a century later), was characterized by flushed skin (the "sanguine" temperament), intense watchfulness (*"pervigilium"*), frightful fantasies, and a remarkable tolerance for hunger and pain (p. 268). To remedy melancholia, Boerhaave recommended taking the patients by surprise and immersing them in water, just to the point short of drowning. This was the same as the "ducking" method advocated by Benjamin Rush in 1812. In retrospect, this cruel treatment (decried by Pinel) can be understood, perhaps charitably, as a kind of primitive "shock therapy."

The remainder of the 18th-century contributors from German-speaking countries manage to be, at once, obscure and important. Leopold Auenbrugger (1722–1809), for example, is hardly remembered even as the father of auscultation, let alone as the originator of shock therapy for mania. The son of an Austrian innkeeper, Auenbrugger was also a musician with a keen ear. He translated his habit of tapping beer barrels to determine their fullness into the art of listening to the chest for signs of disease. In the 1750s he turned his attention to patients with mania or alternating mania/melancholia, treating them with camphor to induce mild seizures. Eleven such patients are described in his 1776 monograph, several whose moods shifted from lethargic and morose to manic as the full moon approached.[1] Usually Auenbrugger gave six to twelve treatments, one to several days apart. Many of the patients improved dramatically and were still well a year later. Yet this remarkable innovation remained unnoticed. The discovery of a similar method 150 years later by Meduna and (using electricity) by Cerletti and Bini should be understood as a chance "rediscovery," since there are no indications the latter were aware of Auenbrugger's treatise.

Leopold Auenbrugger

A still more obscure contributor was Friedrich Scheidemantel, a German contemporary of Auenbrugger who was interested in the relationship between mind, body, and the "passions" (Z., p. 291). He spoke of the soul (*die Seele,* or the "psyche") as the part of us responsible for our capacity to think, to exhibit virtues or vices, and to show emotion (the passions). This was a more rational view, stripped of religious overtones, than that of his predecessors, and it fits in comfortably with our notions of consciousness, subjectivity, and self as manifestations of

Friedrich Scheidemantel

[1] For example, see case #2, p. 11.

brain function. In his major work, *Leidenschaften als Heilmittel* [*The Passions as Curative Agents*] (1787), Scheidemantel outlined over a dozen main passions, including fear, fright, sorrow, love, hate, joy, hope, rage, and envy. He considered the negative emotions (hate, envy, jealousy, and arrogance) to be unusable for therapy (Harms, 1967); in fact, they could induce all manner of harmful effects in the mind and body. The curative emotions were joy and its close relative, laughter, which "revitalized the vascular system" (p. 52). He enumerated many illnesses (diarrhea, colic, women's disorders, lung ailments) as susceptible to cure through the instrumentality of joy. At all events, his awareness of the profound effects of strong emotions on the body, whether for ill or for good, establishes him as a pioneer, if not the "father," of *psychosomatic medicine*.

Johann Lavater

Scheidemantel stood apart from most 18th-century physicians, the majority of whom were preoccupied with strictly "scientific" matters, such as the measurable aspects of the body and its physiology. Such a person was Johann Lavater (1741–1801), who hailed from an old Swiss family of physicians: A 16th-century Lavater had written on the topic of hallucinations and illusions; a 17th-century forebear, on renal calculi. Our Lavater, however, was not a physician but a clergyman whose interest lay in physiognomy. Carrying on the tradition in "biological psychiatry" of Giovanni Porta and Cardano, he influenced Franz Gall, the most widely known of the physiognomists. In a workshop filled with rulers and calipers, Lavater described what he thought were the personality characteristics peculiar to the subtle differences in his measurements of the head. His aim: to discern the inner man from the outer man.[2]

Christian Spiess

At the crossroads between the Age of Enlightenment—with its focus on empiricism, observation, and classification—and the period of German Romanticism is a curious and all but unknown author: Christian Spiess. His *Biographien der Wahnsinnigen* [*Biographies of the Insane*] (1796) contains 10 extensive case histories, each 30 to 70 pages long— the first detailed accounts of *individual patients* to have appeared in the literature. To give some idea of how the tenets of both Enlightenment and Romanticism—close observation of, and sympathetic interest in, the individual—were united in Spiess' accounts, I offer a synopsis of his first biography, that of "Esther."

Esther was a woman of about 20, the daughter of a wealthy Jewish merchant. An accomplished pianist, she had formed a friend-

---

[2] According to Benjamin Rush, Lavater was apparently hypomanic; he talked compulsively, darted about his laboratory with dizzying speed, and frantically measured every angle of the head with his instruments. Lavater, by the way, was a close friend of Goethe (A. & S., p. 131).

ship with a young violinist, Friedrich, from the German nobility. This blossomed into a passionate, if as yet platonic, love. Religious differences made this a hopeless match, and her father, though sympathetic to Friedrich, made him break off the engagement. Agreeing reluctantly, Friedrich went so far as to move away, giving Esther via an intermediary the false information that he had married. Despondent, she went into a depression. Not long after, her father died, leaving her (her mother having died years ago) a fortune of half a million gulden. Esther secretly converted to Catholicism and entered a convent, taking the name "Karoline." She makes over her fortune to the convent. After some years, Friedrich discovers where she is, tells her (via a letter attached to a stone he hurls into the convent garden) he is free and has come to marry her. They escape, marry (in the Protestant faith), and travel, meantime being befriended by a princess sympathetic to their cause. Friedrich also inherits a fortune—but gambles it away. Now destitute, Friedrich, during a duel over debts, is killed, dying in Karoline's arms. She returns, pregnant, to her old convent, expecting mercy and sanctuary. Instead, she is treated as a criminal for breaking her vow of chastity and is imprisoned within the convent. When her time comes, the baby is sent away and she is told that she "killed" it. Eventually a new and more lenient abbess takes over, and Karoline is allowed a few freedoms. Meantime, she had become delusional where the baby is concerned (though lucid in other areas), fashioning a "baby" out of rags, which she fondles and clings to. Later she supplants this with a cane that has a tuft of feathers on top. Later still, the princess discovers where Karoline is and rescues her—but not before the real baby had died at the age of one and a half. A servant of the princess had to wrest her from the convent physically, because she was still too engulfed in madness to answer clearly whether she wanted to escape. She lives two years under the princess' protection, still clinging to her cane-baby. She contracts tuberculosis. Two days before her death, Karoline regains her reason and thanks the princess profusely. The princess sees to it that she is buried with her tufted cane.

FRENCH CONTRIBUTORS

The spirit of the Enlightenment in 18th-century France was embellished by its two most famous philosophers, Rousseau and Voltaire. Both died in the same year (1778). Rousseau, who was born in Geneva (1712) to a Calvinist family (his mother died a week after his birth), rebelled against the conservatism, formalism, and authoritarianism of

Rousseau

his day (and probably against the coldness and strictness of his father). His was the Dionysian antiphon to the Apollonian temper of his time: Rousseau advocated emotion, humanism, democracy, and living in a "state of nature." In nature we could be free, independent, happy— unlike in society, where we are controlled and stifled, not only by authority but by our own intellects, which separate people from nature and from each other. His emphasis on our "lost unity with nature" and on the value of emotion over reason placed Rousseau at the vanguard of the Romantic movement. Voltaire, who was devout yet opposed to organized religion, stood for empiricism and liberal humanism.

Another important contemporary was Etienne Bonnot de Condillac (1714–1780), who espoused an extreme form of materialism and reductionism. He believed that if inert matter could somehow be endowed with sensation, it might eventually acquire the intelligence of the human mind (Z., p. 283). Here we see the presage of our contemporary proponents of artificial intelligence (namely, Minsky) who believe that the brain is computable and that the manifestations of the human mind could be "reduced" to some (presumably quite complex) binary strip via some algorithm: This is the "man-as-machine" argument taken to its extreme and constitutes the theory and attitude against which the Romanticists had begun to rebel.

Simon Tissot

The French counterpart of Scheidemantel was Simon Tissot (1728–1797) from Lausanne in French Switzerland. Interested in the interrelationship between physiology and the passions, this physician combined the psychosomatic ideas of Scheidemantel with the moralism found in Boerhaave. As Harms (1967, p. 75) mentions, some of Tissot's ideas can be seen as forerunners of Freudian sexual theory and even dream theory. Tissot believed that dreams carry forward the preoccupations of the day and that nocturnal emissions happen as a result of unfulfilled sexual desires, which then produce activity in the sexual organs, leading to emission. He also saw hysteria as the baleful result of sexual abstinence in persons not temperamentally suited to that mode of life. Menstrual irregularities were similarly seen as a kind of suppression of normal biological processes, which then led to mental illness and disease.

By far the two most famous figures in 18th-century French psychiatry were Franz Mesmer, who worked primarily with ambulatory patients, and Philippe Pinel, who worked as a hospital based psychiatrist. (Mesmer was not French- but Austrian-born.) Much the more colorful personage of the two, Mesmer was a maverick, a charismatic healer, and would have earned the label of charlatan were it not for the complete sincerity with which he pursued his irrational theories. Early in his career he was

Franz Mesmer, 18th century. Courtesy National Library of Medicine

not always above ethical lapses, as when, after switching from law to medicine, he lightened his burden by plagiarizing the works of Richard Mead (below) for his doctoral thesis. In the meantime, while still in Vienna, he married a wealthy, much older widow. It was on the lawn of her estate that she and Mesmer invited Mozart, a boy of 12 at the time, to stage his first opera, *Bastien and Bastienne* (1768).

Impressed by the newly discovered phenomenon of electricity (thanks to Coulomb and Franklin), of which his grasp was meager, Mesmer began to speculate that an invisible fluid existed in animal bodies, comparable to whatever it was that gave magnets their force. Assuming that various illnesses were the expression of insufficient or maldistributed "animal magnetism," Mesmer sought to cure patients by energizing them by touch or by use of a special "wand," while they stood in a huge oaken bucket. He himself donned a purple robe, dressing like a magician, as he went about inducing a "hysteric crisis."

Accused of touching a young, blind female patient inappropriately while still in Vienna (probably he did nothing indiscreet), he was chased out of Austria by the authorities, relocating in Paris in 1778, whence he began his highly productive *Wanderjahre*. His *Mémoire sur le Découverte de la Magnétisme Animal* [*On the Discovery of Animal Magnetism*] appeared the next year. Mesmer won a large coterie of enthusiastic followers—some physicians, most savants from the gentry—but he also "won" the outrage of the conventional medical community. He was forced to submit to an investigation, commissioned by Louis XVI, as to the merits of his claims. Headed by men of no less stature than Lavoisier, Guillotin (of the eponymous decapitation machine), and Benjamin Franklin (in Paris at the time), the commission offered the king their impressions in 1784. Their conclusion: There was no rational, scientific basis for "animal magnetism"; rather, the effects—for there were profound effects—could be ascribed to the *power of the imagination* (as Westphal had noted 77 years before).

Surely a forest of trees was felled to create the paper for all the broadsides, pamphlets, and books that now appeared, from both Mesmer's supporters and detractors. For example, there was Bailly's *Secret Report to the King* (1784) in which objections were raised to the use of touching. Noticing that there were always more women than men who underwent the "magnetic" treatment and who fell into the trance state, Bailly, with typical Gallic delicacy, explained:

Women's nerves are more excitable, their imagination more active than men's . . . . This greater excitability, in providing them with senses that are more delicate, render women more susceptible to the effects of being touched. In touching them in any place whatsoever, one may say that one has touched them all over. (p. 2) [Author's translation]

But at the same time there was an outpouring of favorable reports, even of seemingly miraculous cures, of hitherto intractable nervous ailments. Several such testimonials were reported by one of Mesmer's staunchest supporters, the Marquis de Puységur.

Among the main followers of Mesmer—D'Eslon, Deleuze, Bergasse, Puységur—it is the latter who deserves the most credit for showing that Mesmer's method could work even without the magical trappings— that is, without the bucket, the wand, and the purple cloak. This was a great step forward, since the medical community was more congenial to a method that appeared reasonable and conventional than one that smacked of hocus-pocus.

Risible as Mesmer's *theory* now appears to us (and to his opponents back then), there is no question that his technique often worked remarkably well—so much so that 1784 can be seen as the turning point in our history. Prior to this year there was not much psychiatry done in the world and not very many books about it. Following this year, however, the library of psychiatry expanded exponentially, there was the birth of "out-patient" psychiatry and of psychoanalysis, and psychiatry became an increasingly respected discipline worldwide.

Indeed, the influence of Mesmer and his followers was so great that I cannot give an adequate account without getting ahead of our story, jumping into the next century and across national boundaries. One can identify three main lines of this influence, only one of which is central to our topic. The other two concern *faith healing* and *spiritism*. For example, there is a direct line from certain French Mesmerians, who came to the American northeast and to Louisiana, to one of their pupils, Phineas Quimby (1802–1866), who in turn treated his patient, Mary Baker Eddy, via the "suggestion method" (as it was then called); she in turn became the founder of Christian Science (Ellenberger, 1970, p. 82). The second line of influence evolved into Swedenborgian mysticism—use of the trance state to make contact with the departed— which became popular in England in the 19th century, especially if supplemented with the ouija board.

Phineas Quimby

The main Mesmeric line, however, is the one that led eventually from trance—to *transference*. There is a direct connection from Mesmer's method, to the refinements introduced by Puységur, to James Braid (the Scottish physician in the mid-19th century who introduced the term *hypnosis*), to Charcot in Paris, Liébault and Bernheim in Nancy, and thence to their most famous pupil—Sigmund Freud. There are more similarities than might be expected between the therapeutic framework of Freud's psychoanalytic method—hour-long sessions four

Phillipe Pinel, 1745–1826. Courtesy
National Library of Medicine

or five times a week—and the Mesmerians of the early 1800s, who induced trances and routinely spent an hour with their patients—five times a week! (the journal *Hermes,* 1826).

Philippe Pinel (1745–1826), whom many consider to be the father of modern psychiatry, was accepted in his own day as a great physician. He managed to offend so few that he survived the French Revolution of the 1790s, whereas Lavoisier and Bailly, a few years after busying themselves with the report on Mesmer, were beheaded by the contraption of their colleague, Guillotin (A. & S., p. 129). Influenced by Locke and Condillac, Pinel rejected the old-fashioned humoural theory as well as the purging and bloodletting treatments the theory inspired. He became the director of two psychiatric hospitals in Paris: the *Bicêtre* (for men) and the *Salpêtrière* (for women, though, as its name reveals, it had formerly been a storehouse for gunpowder).

In Pinel's view mental illness stemmed from heredity or from intolerable "passions," such as fear, anger, hatred, elation, or sadness. The latter assumption is in harmony with the views of Scheidemantel and Tissot. As did many physicians of the Enlightenment, Pinel took literally Rousseau's shibboleth: "Man is born free yet is everywhere in chains." Pinel strongly advocated—and put into practice—the removal of chains from the hospitalized insane. He was not actually the first to do so, though he is often given credit for this reform.

As Dora Weiner mentions (1992) in her introductory remarks to her translation of Pinel's 1794 "Memoir on Madness," Pinel began removing the chains from insane persons at the Salpêtrière in about 1800, three years after his assistant, Jean Baptiste Pussin, had done so at the men's hospital, Bicêtre (replacing them with camisoles!). Weiner credits Pinel with having been the first to write "sympathetic and eloquent" case histories (p. 727), portraying the mentally ill as unfortunate men and women meriting respect and compassion. His 1794 memoir, read at the society for Natural History, helped reduce people's fear of the insane and paved the way for humane methods of treatment.

Pinel was surely among the first to pen sympathetic accounts of the insane, though no one can truly claim absolute priority in this regard.

Pinel in the courtyard of the Salpêtrèire. Courtesy National Library of Medicine

Joseph Daquin

Spiess's *Biographies of the Insane* was published in Germany in 1796, and in France other sons of the Enlightenment who wrote in a similar vein during the momentous years surrounding the French Revolution. Under the influence of Arab doctors (who did not view the insane as devil-possessed), Spanish physicians who tended the insane in Valencia early in the 15th century had removed their patients' chains and had also instituted the kinds of "moral treatment" Pinel recommended: exercise, entertainment, useful activities, agricultural work, and the like (A. & S., p. 116). One such figure of historical importance was Joseph Daquin (1733–1815), whose story is worth a moment's digression.

Born in Chambéry in what was a city in Savoy (then, a separate kingdom; now, a Department of southeast France), Daquin received his medical training in Torino. At the age of 54 he assumed directorship of a 40-bed hospital for the insane at Chambéry. A humble and apologetic man, Daquin had little previous experience with the mentally ill but hoped to bring to their treatment the same methods he had learned in internal medicine. He felt that only in hospitals could one observe enough patients with the same illness to make possible a scientific study of each malady. He strove to rid himself of all prejudices from the past about the care of mental patients and to apply "moral treatment" (*moral* meaning humane, interpersonal). He published a book in 1791 called *La Philosophie de la Folie* (the term *philosophy* in 18th-century France often signified natural science). The book, as Semelaigne (1930) mentions, went all but unnoticed. In it were examples of the same moral treatment, including removal of chains, for which Pinel has long been accorded precedence.

Besides removing the iron fetters from patients, Daquin allowed them to roam freely within the hospital courtyard and made sure (as had Chiarugi) that only the most humane and mild-mannered of attendants were entrusted with their care. Daquin himself credited William Cullen with replacing the cruel chains with the camisole. As an example of humane care, Daquin described the treatment of a woman, who

. . . in the midst of family strife, became obsessed with the idea of killing her children. Interned at Chambéry before she could implement this desire, she was at first noted to pace with extreme agitation, to talk incessantly and to claim that she was the

"Virgin Mary," although she was Protestant, or else the "Wandering Jew". . . . The directress of the hospital offered her copious
words of consolation, and countered the woman's irrational ideas
with words of common sense. After a year of such daily inter-
changes, the woman became less volatile, and requested to return home. She totally regained her reason, and even mentioned
to her friends that the conversations she had had with the
directress had done her the most good, and that her kind words
had contributed to her recovery. (Brierre de Boismont, 1854, p.
6) [Author's translation]

Daquin's biographer, Guilland, said that if Pinel knew of Daquin's
work, he did not acknowledge it. From what we see in the brief biography by Semelaigne, a distant relative of Pinel, the second edition of
Daquin's work (1804) was actually dedicated to Pinel. It is difficult to
imagine that Pinel was unaware of its existence. Pinel's silence on the
subject perhaps reflected some residual pride and rivalry in a man
whose nobility and greatness overshadow these minor flaws. Semelaigne
charitably suggests that, after all, William Tuke was introducing the
same humane reforms in England at about the same time, and that
Tuke, Pinel, and Daquin were all three of the same high rank. The
issue of precedence aside, about this there is little doubt: Pinel was the
most famous and the most widely read of the new breed of alienists
who described in great detail and with great compassion the personal
histories of mentally ill persons.

In every respect, Pinel's suggestions for therapy were based on rational consideration and direct observation. He urged physicians in charge
of the mentally ill to live on the hospital grounds and to spend time
getting to know them. Even when his recommendations strike us as
quaint—such as his advising early marriage and frequent pregnancy as
a remedy for recurrent and severe menstrual pain—they had a scientific
rationale and were a vast improvement over the leeches and purgatives
of his predecessors. Even in dealing with the most violent patients, Pinel
took a sensible and nonviolent approach: "The secret in dealing with violent patients, without receiving or causing injury, is to have the hospital
staff come toward them in number, such as would instill some fear and
make resistance useless" (1801, p. 90) [Author's translation]. Following
this tactic, rational dialogue between patient and staff could take place.

The diagnostic schema Pinel employed was simple yet still constituted an advance over the nosologies in vogue earlier. He spoke of melancholy, "mania without delusion," "mania with delusion," dementia,
and idiotism. I have put *mania* in quotations because Pinel's usage did
not correspond to our notion of manic-depression (bipolar disorder) but

Jean-Marc Gaspard Itard, 1775–1838.
Courtesy National Library of Medicine

referred to severe psychiatric disorders with or without derangement of understanding. Cases of compulsion to engage in violent acts, where there was no defect of reason, exemplified his
"*manie sans délire*" [mania without delusion]. In addition, Pinel
described hysteria, anorexia, bulimia, hypochondriasis, obsessions, and compulsions. He noted that patients with religious
obsessions were extremely difficult to cure. In Pinel's works
there are examples of cases similar to the obsessive-compulsive disorders of our own day. He also mentioned the case of a
"murderous compulsion": that of a missionary who immolated
his children in cold blood, ostensibly to guarantee for them
eternal life in heaven.

The same spirit of compassion and humanism that Pinel
brought to the treatment of the insane, his pupil, Jean-Marc
Gaspard Itard (1775–1838), brought to bear on the treatment
of the mentally retarded. In the last year of the century Itard,
by then appointed as physician to an institution for the deaf-mute, heard
about a feral child, found wandering about in the woods of Aveyron. Not
quite the "noble savage" of Rousseau, the boy was dirty, unclad, eking
out a precarious existence in the forest, inarticulate except for animal-
like grunts, and insensitive to heat or cold. Itard volunteered to rehabilitate the wild boy, whom Pinel, with uncharitable candor (and unfortunate
accuracy) declared a congenital idiot. For several centuries there had
been sporadic reports of feral children, the majority of whom were also
retarded or otherwise mentally incapacitated, such that their impoverished parents had abandoned them to the fields. Itard struggled hero-
ically, guided by the principles of Condillac and an optimism born of
naïveté, with results that were both miraculous and disappointing. The
miraculous part was that, after Itard took him into his home for two
years, little by little the boy became tractable, sensitive in the normal
ways to changes in temperature, affectionate, and able to understand
much that was said to him. He had grown quite attached to Itard, whose
efforts had by this time earned him an international reputation. The
disappointing part: The wild boy was never able to say more than two
words: *milk* and *God*. Itard's humane attitudes and techniques for working with the retarded were passed on to his pupil, Edouard Séguin, who
was to become the leading figure in the treatment of the retarded in the
19th century (see Chapter 6).

ENGLISH, SCOTTISH, AND IRISH CONTRIBUTORS

The spirit of the Enlightenment shone through all the works of the English physicians of the 18th century, as they themselves were enlight-

ened by the philosophy of the two Scottish philosophers, David Hume (1711–1776) and Thomas Reid (1710–1796). Hume sought to bring the experimental method, as had been employed in physics with such success by Sir Isaac Newton (1642–1727), into the study of the mind (Blackburn, 1994, p. 179). Hume hoped that the seemingly separate ideas, feelings, and impressions of the mind could be ordered via the discovery of patterns and fundamental principles, in the way that the random-seeming events of nature could often be woven together via common patterns. Contrary to Kant, Hume rejected the notion of *a priori* principles of reasoning. He asserted that the mind, in which our perceptions arise, is never given to us *in* perception. Hence the concept of "Self" is an abstraction: the product of our imagination.

David Hume

Objecting to Hume's empiricist reliance on *ideas* as units of knowledge, Thomas Reid (1710–1796)—the "common sense" philosopher—argued that the proper unit of knowledge is a *judgment* about *things* in the external world, whether or not there are minds to know them. These disputations are not casuistical, for they bore relevance, a century and a half later, to the burning issues in psychoanalysis: How far can we delve into ourselves with introspection, and to what extent can we escape subjectivity when we attempt to contemplate our own subjectivity?

Thomas Reid

Despite the many physicians in the British Isles who, during the 18th century, turned their attention to mental illness, none achieved the prominence of Pinel or the glamour of Mesmer. The first to win some notoriety was the Scottish physician George Cheyne (1671–1743), who was one of the first to write about his own nervous disorder. His book, *The English Malady* (1733), explored the melancholy, anxiety, and biliousness that afflicted him for many years. Cheyne asserted that these troubles affected mostly the highly intelligent (like the author, presumably!), since "fools, weak or stupid Persons . . . are seldom troubled with Vapours or Lowness of Spirits." But his book was not the confessional tome we might expect from someone in our era divulging the details of his or her own neurosis. There are no *personal* revelations here: instead, mostly complaints about his digestion, of a sort that suggests his condition was related to his gallbladder!

George Cheyne

Richard Mead (1673–1754), one of Britain's most highly respected physicians in the 18th century, developed two influential theories relevant to mental illness. Noting that, as one of his tubercular patients became delirious, her physical condition improved—only to deteriorate once again when her mind had cleared—Mead speculated that the body could not harbor a physical and mental disease at the same time. This mistaken notion led to the practice of giving the mentally ill a physical disease on purpose, as though to cure them. Theories of this kind persisted into the 20th century; for example, the belief that epilepsy and schizophrenia could not coexist led to the "rationale" for shock therapy.

Richard Mead

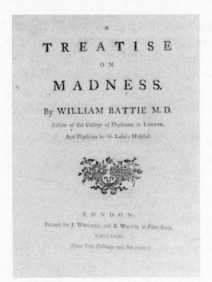

William Battie's 1758 *Treatise on Madness* was the first extensive text on purely psychiatric conditions.

Mead's other contribution concerned the influence of the sun and the moon on mental illness: *De Imperio Solis ac Lunae* [*On the Influence of the Sun and the Moon*] (1746). This treatise dealt mainly with menstrual afflictions, which often occurred in conjunction with the full moon. He also cited several examples of men whose diseases (usually in the form of hemoptysis or other bleeding) broke out just at the time of the full moon. These notions, long regarded as fanciful in our century, have been taken more seriously now that we note similar correlations in certain bipolar and violence-prone persons whose frenzy coincides with the full moon (Stone, 1976). The word *lunacy*—a common designation of Mead's era for mental illness—is itself a testimonial to the frequency with which physicians ascribed mental disorders to the lunar cycle. Mead was among the physicians of his time who suspected that mania and melancholia were different aspects of the same process.

The first extensive text on purely psychiatric conditions (*A Treatise on Madness,* 1758) was that of William Battie (1703–1776), who was probably the first to teach psychiatry in England (A. & S., p. 119). The director of Bethlem Hospital in 1742, Battie was so appalled by the conditions there that he founded a new hospital (St. Luke's) in 1751.[3] Battie argued against the then current enthusiasm for bloodletting as a general antidote for illness, including cases of "madness." As he put it: "The lancet, when applied to a feeble and convulsed Lunatic, is no less destructive than a sword" (H. & M., p. 408). Battie made an important distinction between *internal* and *external* causes of insanity (akin to our usage of *endogenous* and *exogenous*), though for him the latter had to do with damage to the brain. He did not recognize what we consider *functional* illness, stemming from emotional conflict. As for Battie's distinction between internal and external causes, he made the following comments:

First then, there is some reason to fear that Madness is Original, when it neither follows nor accompanies any accident, which may justly be deemed its external and remoter cause.

[3] The Priory of St. Mary of Bethlehem in London was seized by the Crown in 1375 and converted into a repository for "lunatics" in 1403. The "madhouse," as it was known, received so little funding that the inmates had to go begging in the streets as piteous "Tom-o'-Bedlams," as mentioned in Shakespeare's *King Lear.* Conditions remained unwholesome until its rebuilding in 1814.

Secondly, there is more reason to fear that, whenever this disorder is hereditary, it is Original. For, altho' even in such case it may now and then be excited by some external and known cause, yet the striking oddities that characterise whole families derived from Lunatic ancestors, and the frequent breaking forth of real Madness in the offspring of such illconcerted alliances, . . . strongly intimate that the nerves or instruments of Sensation in such persons are not originally formed perfect and like the nerves of other men. (p. 59 of the original text, the frontspiece of which is reproduced on p. 66)

Contributions made by Scottish neurologist Robert Whytt (1714–1766) occurred in two main spheres. He expressed philosophical ideas concerning the nature of the mind, where he took issue with those (such as Stahl) who compartmentalized the mind into *anima* (the sentient soul) and *animus* (the reasoning soul or "intelligence"). Instead Whytt postulated that there is but one unifying principle, which is equally the source of sensation, action—and also of reason. This he expressed in his 1751 treatise on the involuntary motions of animals. In his view, if the "reasoning mind" had to be actively engaged in the activation of behavior, the mind therefore ought to be conscious of this "activation" process. Whytt held that we must be "sensible of the ideas formed within us by the internal operation of our minds, because their existence depends on our being conscious of them" (H. & M., p. 390). To say that such ideas could exist without our consciousness of them seemed like a contradiction in terms to Whytt, who thus would have opposed the psychoanalytic concept of "unconscious ideas."

Robert Whytt

From the standpoint of nosology, Whytt worked with the milder mental conditions (in effect, the neuroses), categorizing them into the *hysteric,* the *hypochondriacal,* and those characterized by "nervous exhaustion" (similar to the *neurasthenia* described by Beard in the 1870s). Whytt explained these conditions, and the varying degrees that certain groups experienced them, on the basis of differing motilities and subtleties of the nerves. As with the fashioners of the Secret Report to Louis XVI, Whytt, too, assumed that women's nerves were more motile than men's—and children's were even more vulnerable. Here he carried forward the view expressed by Purcell in 1707 on women (whom the Age of Enlightenment still left mostly in the shadows): "Because from the weaker texture of their Brains and Nerves [women] are more subject to violent passions" (Whytt, 1765, p. 38).

Although the Witchcraft Acts in England were repealed in 1736, this did not stop many persons from continuing to fear and despise the mentally ill. Sometimes deluded inmates hurled accusations at themselves of being devils or witches, inadvertently sabotaging the process of changing the perception of ordinary people to see them in a more sympathetic light. To help offset this sorry situation, a minister, Hugh Farmer (1714–1787), wrote a well-researched book—*An Essay on the Demoniacs of the New Testament* (1775)—debunking the old superstitions and stating plainly that "possessed" persons were invariably "mad [i.e., psychotic], melancholy, or epileptic." He reframed the Biblical description of demons "entering" a person as being *symbolic* of the person becoming afflicted with a mental illness. When Christ and the Apostles "cast out the demons," this symbolized that they had *cured* the "demoniacs" in question.

A similarly enlightened preacher, Charles Moore (1743–1811), a vicar from Kent, took up the issue of suicide, writing what was one of the earliest and most comprehensive books on the subject: *A Full Inquiry into the Subject of Suicide* (1790). In amongst its 800 pages is an outline of the factors Moore saw as contributing to suicide in England, the main ones being melancholy, liquor, and the deplorable "want of composure and equanimity of temper" that Moore felt was endemic among his countrymen. He also blamed their "refinement of principle": If they fell into dilemmas (debts from which they could not extricate themselves, for example), their scruples left them no choice but suicide. As a cleric, Moore necessarily judged suicide to be an offense against God as well as against society and the person in question. He saved his sharpest remarks for Goethe's *The Sorrows of Young Werther,* whose publication in 1774 brought in its wake a wave of suicides throughout Western Europe. Commenting on this "pernicious publication, first broached in Germany by one Goethe," Moore departed from the compassionate tone found elsewhere in his treatise: " . . . what an outrage is committed on every sensation of our 'rational' compassion, when a love-sick tale, founded on the voluntary continuation of a very censurable and unlawful species of attachment, is all that is to be met with in the 'Sorrows'" (Moore, 1790, vol. II, p. 123). In sexual matters Moore was "Victorian" a generation before Victoria.

Toward the end of the century John Ferriar (1761–1815), a general physician in Manchester, wrote two books touching on the topic of mental maladies: *An Essay towards a Theory of Apparitions* and *Medical Histories and Reflections.* In his essay on apparitions, he argued that a "morbid disposition of the brain" could produce the impression of having seen ghosts or specters, even in the absence of delirium or insanity. In working with the mentally ill, Ferriar advocated pure *clinical observation* that was not attached to any preconceived ideas or system of belief. In his empirical approach to the treatment of mania, he listed a number of medicaments—tartar

Hugh Farmer

Charles Moore

John Ferriar

emetic, digitalis (which had recently come into use), opium, even the camphor Auenbrugger had found so effective—and declared them all useless. Bleeding he found worse than useless, and he also recommended isolation of violence-prone patients rather than the use of restraints. He originated the term "hysterical conversion" in referring to the condition in which, when one organ is affected, another and distant organ also acts abnormally, as though out of "sympathy" with the first. Freud was to revive the term a century later in referring to hysterical paralysis engendered by the "conversion" of an unbearable idea into a bodily symptom.

ITALIAN CONTRIBUTORS

The most important 18th-century contributor from elsewhere in Europe was the Florentine-born Vincenzo Chiarugi (1759–1820). Chiarugi is known chiefly for his insistence on humane treatment for the insane and for his opposition to physical restraints or harsh measures. Though the latter recommendation antedated Pinel's removal of chains in Paris hospitals by a few years, it is probably more accurate to speak not of "who was first," but of a new philosophy of humane treatment. Spurred by the Enlightenment and the spirit of social reform that led to the French Revolution, a new consciousness was emerging independently in many European countries at about the same time.

Vincenzo Chiarugi

Chiarugi's patron, the Duke of Tuscany, Pietro Leopoldo, was himself a zealot for reform, who brought about such changes as the medical treatment of the insane and the humane care of delinquent adolescents. He built the Hospital of Bonifacio in Florence and appointed Chiarugi as its director. This came on the heels of Chiarugi's publication of a three-volume work on insanity, *Delle Pazzia in Genere e in Specie* [*On Madness in General and in Specific*] (1793–1794), based on Morgagni's theory that insanity stemmed from deterioration of the brain.

Pietro Leopoldo

The *Delle Pazzia* included Chiarugi's practical, if unoriginal, taxonomy, emphasizing *melancholia, mania,* and *amensia* (imbecility). Pinel disparaged the work for simply following the old scholastic order, of "Cause, Diagnosis, Prognosis, Symptoms" (Pinel, 1801, p. xli). As to treatment, Chiarugi recommended either *calming* methods (for those who were in a manic excitement) or *exciting* methods (for those in melancholic torpor). He was one of the first to attach great importance to post-mortem examination of the brain. To his credit, Chiarugi did understand the interrelationship between mania and melancholia: "Mania signifies raving madness. The maniac is like a tyger [sic] or a lion, and in this respect mania may be considered as a state oppo-site to true melancholia" (Beddoes, 1803).

In Chiarugi's earlier book (1789), which included a meticulous de-scription of the new hospital and of the detailed duties of all the staff, his humanistic approach is apparent: "It is a superior moral duty and medical obligation to respect the mentally ill patient as a person." This respect for the individuality of each patient facilitated a natural transi-tion into the next great movement in psychiatry—Romanticism—where all attention was focused on individual patients and particularities of their life histories.

Chapter 6

NINETEENTH-CENTURY GERMANY:

FROM ROMANTICISM TO EMPIRICISM

In the 19th century, psychiatry began to take a form which we, at the end of the 20th century, can recognize. The very term *psychiatry* was used for the first time in the early 1800s; *psychosis* took the place of *lunacy* and *insanity,* the latter now serving mostly as a forensic label in the courtroom. Psychiatry gained a firmer footing as a branch of medicine; advances in neurology somewhat reduced the mystery of the brain and its anatomical subdivisions; persecution of "witches" became a rarity.

Psychiatrists concerned themselves more and more with the mildly ill, not just with institutionalized patients: The latter were now seen as suffering from "diseases"; the former, from "conditions." Juvenile delinquency, along with the more clearly psychiatric entities, such as anorexia nervosa and *folie du doute* (later to become our "obsessive-compulsive disorder"), gained attention. Psychopharmacology was still in the gestational phase, not even in its infancy yet, but the sanitaria were much improved and humane treatment for the retarded became widespread. Psychiatry would become worldwide by the end of the 19th century, and although Western Europe still dominated the scene, it was no longer the only scene. America had come into the picture: Important advances were already taking place here at mid-century (such as the inauguration of the American Psychiatric Association in 1844), and by the century's end, we had become a psychiatric "super-power" along with Germany, France, and England.

THE ROMANTICISTS

For roughly the first half of the 19th century the philosophical atmosphere in Germany was permeated by interest in the irrational, in the strivings and values of the individual, and in a longing to return to nature. This attitudinal shift was given the name *Romanticism.* If we divide mental faculties, as Bacon did, into *reason* and *imagination,* it was upon the latter, with its emphasis on empathy and emotional sensitivity, that the spotlight now focused.

One outgrowth of this trend was a preoccupation with matters pertaining to the *individual,* such as dreams, sexuality, and hidden desires (for which the term *unconscious* came into use) (B., p. 49). One can catch the scent of the romantic atmosphere in a comment from G. Schubert's book on dream symbolism (1814)—"Dreams are a freeing of the soul from the bonds of the senses"—which Freud later cited as an example of the pietistic and unscientific outlook of this period. Scientific or not, the physicians and writers of German Romanticism (including the philosopher Schopenhauer), with their concern about each person's sorrows and joys and secret longings, helped pave the path toward psychoanalysis at the end of the century. Traces of Schopenhauer's *will,* to which reason and knowledge are subservient, could be found in Freud's use of *libido* and the *unconscious.*

Johann Reil

One of the most important contributors in the first years of the new century was Johann Reil (1759–1813), if for no other reason than that he originated the term *psychiatry,* which appeared in an article he wrote in the newly launched journal he helped edit in 1808: *Beytraege zuer Befoerderung einer Kurmethode auf psychischen Wege* [*Contributions to the Advancement of Healing Methods in the Mental Sphere*]. Reil believed that *Psychiatrie,* by which he meant *treatment of the mind,* was an essential component of training for all physicians, since surgery, internal medicine, and psychiatry each affects the individual at different levels of organization (Marx, 1990). Actually, Reil was not wholly committed to the Romantic philosophy, insofar as he believed that physics and chemistry were the basic sciences from which a proper physiology would be constructed. He did not accept the concept of a "world soul," as promulgated earlier by Stahl and later by the more thoroughly committed members of the German Romantic school, such as Heinroth, Fichte, and Ideler. The Romantics, in their belief in the supernatural, the intuitive, and the unity of "personal" ego and world, have a kinship with the holistic views of Hinduism and Buddhism, although there is no evidence that the German school had any meaningful contact with the East.

Reil was also influenced by Immanuel Kant, whose empiricism was less reductionistic and hard-edged that that of his contemporaries in England and France. As Marx points out (1990), Kant contended that true science depended on laws that could be expressed mathematically—which was impossible for psychology. The notions of human freedom and mathematical "explanations" of life seemed incompatible to Kant. Whereas Locke and Hume viewed the mind as the passive recipient of sense impressions, Kant considered sensory perception and reasoning to be active processes.

Reil spoke of a basic feeling of "being and experience," which he called *Gemeingefühl*, an insufficiency of which could lead to a minor "loosening of control." A serious loss of this basic feeling was associated with psychosis. Conditions akin to our concept of schizophrenia were described as well: *Narrheit* or "oddness" was accompanied by a loosening of associations and *fixer Wahnsinn* was similar to our paranoia.

For Reil the brain was clearly the locale of thought and of the "psyche" or mind; thoughts were described as reflecting an image-forming process evoked by stimuli and experience. Temperament was seen as innate disposition, not as a manifestation of the four humours. Reil's ideas about pathogenesis were typical of the day: heredity, climate, the seasons, overwork, excessive luxury (a point made earlier by Tissot), or education could all serve as sources. But he showed no awareness of what we consider to be *psychodynamic factors:* those intra- and interpersonal conflicts stemming from past experience.

Even so, Reil was ahead of his time in recognizing the close connection between mental and somatic states and in making uncommonly practical suggestions for the relief of various conditions, including sexual ones. In an important passage of his 1803 book, *Rhapsodieen,* he stated: *"Gefühle und Vorstellungen, kurz Erregungen der Seele, die eigentümlischen Mittel [sind], durch welche die Intemperatur der Vitalität des Gehirns rectificirt werden müsse* [Feelings and representations—in short, whatever arouses the soul—are the characteristic means by which the altered temperature and the vitality of the brain must be restored]" (p. 50). Though the son of a Lutheran minister and a man of strict habits, Reil recognized that sexual frustration or failure to conceive in a woman who longed to have children could lead to "hysteria." For the former condition, he did not shrink from recommending intercourse as a remedy—an idea already sanctioned by Chiarugi. (This calls to mind Freud's quip along the same lines, when he recommended *"penis normalis, dosim repetatur"* [a normal penis, dose to be repeated] as the antidote for hysteria.)

Reil was also among the first to employ occupational therapy as well as music and drama therapy by way of reeducating patients into developing more adaptive ways of coping (A. & S., p. 136). As healing methods Reil advocated good food, adequate sleep, and sunlight, along with measures already mentioned. Some of his recommendations, however, were less benign. Dividing patients into the "competent" and "incompetent" (those who had, or who lacked, self-sufficiency), Reil would employ "shock" methods at times to arouse the torpid or to provide "rewards and punishments" for the "incompetent." To bring patients out of an unresponsive state, Reil might drip hot wax onto their palms or even place mice under a glass upon their skin. Dunking patients under water—a measure utilized in many asylums during the late 18th/early 19th centuries—appears cruel and barbaric to us now, yet seemed justified during this time period on the grounds that certain agitated patients were known to have attempted suicide by drowning, only to have regained their sanity after rescue from the water (Marx, 1990). Hence the rationale for therapy by submersion.

More exotic still was a form of shock treatment Reil sometimes used to "revive the sense of the incurable": He would create a "cat piano" consisting of live cats whose tails were nailed to the table. Punishment, which might take the form of whipping, was meted out only to patients who had committed an offense *and* were aware of what they had done and understood why they were being punished. Reil encouraged patients to take an active part in their own recovery, to which end he advocated cognitive training, gymnastics, and other exercises aimed at enhancing self-esteem. Some of Reil's ideas about occupational therapy were derived from his familiarity with England's York Retreat.

Carl Carus

In his 1829 text on psychology, Carl Carus (1789–1869) expressed the view that biological processes function according to a psychological "plan," which underlies the aims that inform our conscious behavior. The fundamental biological force was the "unconscious," which he subdivided into a "general-absolute" layer underlying bodily processes and a "relative unconscious" containing ideas and feelings that were once conscious but later became unconscious (a concept that anticipates the Freudian notion of repression) (A. & S., p. 169).

Ernst von Feuchtersleben

Two other important figures from the Romantic period (circa 1800–1850) were Ernst von Feuchtersleben and Eduard Beneke, both of whose works have a decidedly modern ring to them, especially in relation to psychosomatic concepts. Von Feuchtersleben (1806–1849) viewed psychotherapy as a reeducative process that helped patients untangle the problems resulting from their disordered personalities. He contended that mind and body were one, a viewpoint that placed him in opposition to Descartes and in line with the materialist philosophers of his day as well as other "monist" psychiatrists of the next generation (such as Wilhelm Griesinger).

Eduard Beneke

The psychosomatic perspective formed by Eduard Beneke (1798–1854) was that abnormal ideas could become symbolized and transformed into bodily reactions. Trained in philosophy, theology, and psychology, Beneke was of a decidedly maverick disposition. He opposed Hegel, objected to the materialism of Friedreich (for whom mental experience was "just the workings of the nerves"), and disagreed with Kant's idealism (A. & S., p. 144). For Beneke, ethics was not grounded in some abstract, metaphysical system but derived from natural law. Since humans were creatures of nature, our ethics, therefore, were an expression of our need to get along with one another. Mental phenomena were real (as, indeed, they are!), and could be studied, Beneke believed, by means of objective introspection (a stance quite in harmony with the compelling argument of Searle, 1992). His remarks concerning psychotherapy are compatible with both contemporary psychoanalytic and cognitive approaches: Fixed (abnormal) ideas are replaced with positive, healthier ideas. Occupational therapy was particularly useful, since it often had the power to distract patients from their maladaptive ideas. Beneke's insistence on evaluating each clinical case individually marked his perspective as an individual-centered psychology.

A predecessor to the psychoanalytic thinkers (though seldom credited as such) was Johann Christian Heinroth (1773–1843), who developed a theory of mind involving a "tripartite" structure identical with that of Freud's a century later. Couched in religious language derived from his Lutheran background, the theory he set forth in his major work—*Treatise on the Disturbances of Mental Life* (1818)—contained three layers: The lowest layer is represented by the instinctual forces, the next layer is that of consciousness (*Bewusstsein* or *das Ich*), which includes intelligence and awareness of self; finally, there is the superior layer of conscience, which Heinroth referred to as the *Über uns* [that which is "over us"]. He also introduced a concept of "internal conflict," which was the product of the two forces of sin versus conscience pulling us in opposite directions. *Sin* included thoughts that offended one's moral sense as well as actually sinful *acts*. Sins provoke moral shock and drive the offender to a lower psychic level of "instinctual forces." (Easily recognizable is the similarity of Freud's id-egosuperego tripartite vision of mind in his 1923 revision.)

Though Reil was the originator of the term *psychiatry,* Heinroth has the distinction of being the first physician to occupy a university chair in psychiatry. This was in his native Leipzig in 1811, three years after Reil's new coinage (Cauwenbergh, 1991). Because Heinroth located the root causes of mental illness in the soul rather than in the body, he was known as a *psychist* in contrast to a *somaticist*. Yet, as with others of the German Romantic School, he was a unifier who saw mind and body as interrelated: He was, more properly speaking, a *psychosomaticist*.

Heinroth indeed used the term *psychosomatic* as a way of expressing his objection to Cartesian dualism and conveying his contention that mind and body were two aspects of the same entity and that health was a function of harmony between body and soul. Furthermore, he was in agreement with Kant's assertion that the natural sciences (physics and chemistry) were fundamentally different from the psychological sciences. The mind could not be reduced to neat mathematical equations, the way Heinroth's contemporary, Herbart, insisted was possible (see below). Cauwenbergh (1991), who has made an intensive

Johann Cristian Heinroth

study of Heinroth's prolific writings, sees a parallelism between the latter and the works of Hegel, whose *Science of Logic* appeared (in the 1810s) around the same time as Heinroth's early works.

Impressed not only with the unity between mind (or soul) and body, Heinroth also believed each individual is linked inextricably with nature. Humankind is not a collective of self-contained essences but of *relational entities,* whose "animal, vegetative and human" qualities are held together in unity (Cauwenbergh, 1991, p. 378). As with other Romanticists, here we see a holistic viewpoint reminiscent of, but unconnected with, Eastern religion and philosophy. Even Heinroth's "primary diseases"—passion, delusion, and vice—are similar to the Buddhist triad of sins: greed (under which he subsumes passion and lust), anger, and foolishness. For Heinroth, these conditions were preludes to the "secondary" (deeper) diseases of *melancholy, madness,* and *rage,* respectively. Those who were in the grip of passion, especially of the greedy desire to have more and more, were no longer "free." This lack of freedom was akin to what others in this era were calling "neurosis" (and, parenthetically, what Buddhists had always referred to as the absence of *satori* or enlightenment). In his later writings, Heinroth took up the famous case of the jealous murderer Woyzeck (upon whom several modern operas are based). As Cauwenbergh (1991) mentions, Heinroth saw Woyzeck as responsible for his crime, ". . . because he deprived himself of human freedom, and so became the cause of the passion which made him a murderer" (p. 381).

In line with his predecessors among the German Romanticists, Heinroth stressed the importance of treating patients according to their individual qualities and symptoms, demonstrating kindness and warmth with some, firmness with others (A. & S., p. 142). In the tradition of Hippocrates, he also gave credit to nature's healing powers. Holding each person responsible to his own conscience—which could thus lead to conflict between the inferior and superior mental layers—was a basic tenet of Heinroth's Protestant *Weltanschauung.*

Heinrich Neumann

Karl Ideler

In a similar prefiguration of psychoanalytic theory, Heinrich Neumann (1814–1884) spoke of sexual (and other) "drives," which, if not satisfied, could generate "anxiety." The same assumptions were echoed in the writings of Karl Ideler (1795–1860), who recognized the importance of the emotional life and that unfulfilled sexual longings could serve as a source of mental disturbance. Ideler, for many years director of Berlin's Charité, published works on such topics as religious insanity, aggressive drives that could erupt and cause persecutory delusions (Z., p. 476), and the biographies of psychotic patients. In the latter book (1841) each of the eleven biographies is accompanied by an etching of the patient.

Two patients with depression. From Karl Ideler, *Biographieen Geisteskranker*, 1841.

THE BIOLOGICAL SYSTEMATIZERS

With the passing of Ideler, Carus, and Heinroth the era of Romanticism and focus on the individual came to a close. The pendulum now swung toward the biologically oriented systematizers, including the "neuropsychiatrists," whose basic orientation was neurology. Medicine in general had become more advanced—more "modern," as we would think of it—thanks to the work of such luminaries as Lister, Pasteur, Virchow, and Romberg. In this second half of the century, Germany was becoming more powerful, unified now under Bismarck; France was weakening, owing to internal mismanagement during Napoleon III's Second Empire (A. & S., p. 151). Germany's success spurred progress in science and medicine. Investigations in experimental psychology were pioneered by Gustav Fechner (1801–1887), who studied the relationship between the intensity of external stimuli and the strength of the corresponding internal sensation. Fechner also developed the concept of a "pleasure principle" and introduced the principles of "stability" and "repetition" in the psychological arena—ideas that were to become part of a Freudian metapsychology (the "repetition compulsion").

Gustav Fechner

At mid-century Otto Domrich became the first in the field of medical psychology to write about "anxiety attacks." This term replaced

Otto Domrich
"Anxiety attacks"

earlier notions of "neurocirculatory neurasthenia," "soldier's heart," and "hyperventilation syndrome" that dated back to the French Revolution (Angst, 1995) and depicted the state of combined anxiety and cardiopulmonary symptoms that might be induced by the terrors of the battlefield. Freud's description of the "anxiety neurosis" in 1895 was a wider concept that covered milder anxiety states as well as actual *panic attacks,* of which Domrich's description was the forerunner.

Wilhelm Griesinger

The most important contributor in the early phase of this new movement was Wilhelm Griesinger (1817–1868), a pupil of the great neurologist Romberg (of "Romberg's sign" in *luetic tabes dorsalis*). For Griesinger mind and body were one: Mental disease was somatic disease. Therefore, he searched for relationships between psychological phenomena and brain anatomy. In this sense, Griesinger adopted a decidedly monist position: Neuropathology and psychiatry were one and the same field. Objecting to the earlier tradition of considering every mental symptom a different "disease," Griesinger trimmed down psychiatric nosology and modernized the language. He assigned great importance to temperament and began each case description in his written works with a comment on the patient's premorbid temperament and personality. Drawing on the observations of Johann Friedrich Herbart (1776–1841), Griesinger recognized that not all behavior was consciously determined. Part of his interest in looking for organic causes for mental illness was stimulated by the work of L.-F. Calmeil in France, who had demonstrated a connection between "general paresis" and certain brain pathology.

Johann Friedrich Herbart

Indeed, for Griesinger all mental disease must stem from abnormalities of brain cells; there were no "functional" disorders. Even so, Griesinger was not blind to purely psychological constructions: He proposed, for example, that dreams might represent *wish fulfillments.* As he put it, "The dream realizes what reality refused." He also endorsed the idea, borrowed from the Romanticists, that strong affects could induce mental distress, and that such distress might be the expression of conflicts involving the stifling (*Verdrängung,* or repression) of sexual urges or other strong emotions. During the last two years of his life, Griesinger was the director of the psychiatry department of Berlin's Charité Hospital, where he introduced non-restraint as a policy. Other recommendations included work (occupational therapy), baths, medications, conversations, and games. Through all these measures he hoped to restore the former, healthier personality that had come to be buried under the psychotic process.

Herbart's role in shaping the direction of the field cannot be overlooked. According to Rosemarie Sand (1988), Johann Friedrich Herbart, the professor of philosophy who succeeded to Immanuel Kant's chair in Koenigsberg, influenced a whole generation of psychologists and contributed importantly to the intellectual atmosphere surrounding Freud during his formative years. Herbart himself was influenced not only by Kant but by Isaac Newton, and his writings on psychology (1816)—then still a subdivision of philosophy—carried a mathematical perspective, reflecting his attempt to accord this field the kind of precision and respectability given the more "exact" sciences. Herbart's position opposed Kant's, who assumed psychology "could never be scientific because it could not be quantified" (p. 467). As Brett mentions (1953), Herbart did not think that psychology could be treated experimentally, even though he did believe it could be made into an exact science.

His ideas about the "statics" and "mechanics" of the *Vorstellungen,* or representations, reflect his enthrallment with Newtonian physics, where much attention is paid to the statics and mechanics of solid objects. All "ideas" (which *Vorstellungen* can also mean) move on a semicircular path, from a point below the level of consciousness upward to its zenith, only then to dip below again, giving way to the emergence of another idea into consciousness. Herbart spoke of the "mental structures" derived from apperception, a notion that greatly influenced German psychology in general and Freud's developing theories in particular. In contrast to Freud, however, Herbart's psychology remained restricted to the realm of cognition; he did not venture into the arena of drives, sex, and aggression, though he did describe an *unconscious,* which contained those ideas that are driven down beneath consciousness by other ideas that are temporarily "stronger." He used the word *Verdrängung*—which Freud used for repression—to signify this driving-down process. Herbart's theory was one of psychic determinism, as we also see in Freud's works.

For Herbart, the intensity or strength of the cognitive representations constituted the elusive *quantity* of psychology whose existence Kant had denied. While it remains unclear whether Freud read Herbart specifically, in high school he had become acquainted with an 1858 text by Adolf Lindner, *Lehrbuch der empirischen Psychologie nach genetischer Methode* [*Textbook of Empirical Psychology by the Genetic Method*], which is strongly Herbartian in flavor. The ideas contained therein may well have provided the seeds for Freud's theories about the spatial model (conscious/unconscious) of the mind, the "quantities" of representations (as sketched in his 1895 *Project for a Scientific Psychology*), and the development of the ego (*das Ich*).

After Griesinger, the pendulum swung even more sharply to the side of biological/neurological psychiatry in Germany and Austria. Theodore Meynert (1833–1892), with whom Freud studied in Vienna, outlined different layers of the cerebral cortex according to cell type and found correlations between histology and cerebral function. An extreme somatologist, Meynert objected to the very term *psychiatry* and classi-

Theodore Meynert

fied mental disorders purely on an anatomical basis. He ascribed delusions and hallucinations to irritation of the subcortical layers; melancholia and mania resulted from abnormalities of the cortical blood vessels.

Karl Wernicke

Meynert's pupil, Karl Wernicke (1848–1905), developed a theory of associations based on cerebral histology and distinguished the different psychoses according to whether they concerned the external world (as in hallucinatory conditions) or the internal world, as in aberrations of personality. Having worked briefly as a surgeon during the Franco-Prussian war (1871), Wernicke came under the influence of Heinrich Neumann (1814–1884) of the Breslau psychiatry department (Lanczik & Keil, 1991). At the age of 26 Wernicke earned fame with his discovery of the *sensory* speech center in the brain, showing that "Broca's area" (the *motor* speech region) was not the only speech-related area in the brain. Wernicke located this sensory speech center in the temporal lobe, building on the theory of his teacher (Meynert) that this area served as the repository for "remembered images" (*Erinnerungsbilder*). Meynert had also postulated that the frontal area stored the *Bewegungsvorstellungen* or "impressions of action."

Wernicke's contributions to our understanding of cerebral localization, both in the normal and pathological states (such as aphasia), demonstrate just how far the field had advanced in the mere 50 years that separate him from the phrenologists of the 1820s. The advance was no less than revolutionary, for the long tradition of fantastical notions about physiognomy and brain regions (as represented in the works of Porta, Cardano, Lavater, Gall, and Spurzheim) was at last giving way to science.

Wernicke understood certain forms of psychopathology as symptoms of "irritability" (*Reizsymptome*), caused by a build-up of energy in the nerve cells as a result of interrupted flow along various associated pathways (Lanczik & Keil, 1991). Because hallucinations are false impressions about the environment, Wernicke referred to them as *allopsychoses,* in contrast to *autopsychoses,* which stemmed from false impressions about oneself (such as delusions of grandeur or persecution). Wernicke also recognized a third variety—*somatopsychoses*—wherein the abnormality involved distorted perceptions of one's own body. The latter is in keeping with the *dysmorphophobia* that Morselli (1866) had described a decade earlier, and which, in the current *DSM,* is called "body dysmorphic disorder."

P. E. Flechsig

Meynert's rival, P. E. Flechsig (1847–1929), from Leipzig, helped define projection and association areas in the cortex and distinguished motor from sensory aphasias. Flechsig is also famous in psychoanalytic history as the doctor who successfully treated the jurist, Daniel Schreber, during the latter's 15-month stay in a sanitorium, where he wrote the strange memoirs that became the basis for Freud's (1911)

Schreber case. Meanwhile, the physiological psychologist Wilhelm Wundt (1832–1920), Gustav Fechner's greatest follower (Ellenberger, 1993, p. 94), was studying the phenomenon of psychological associations; his major textbook, *Die Grundzüge der Physiologischen Psychologie* [*The Fundamentals of Physiologic Psychology*], was published in 1874.

Both Wundt and Flechsig were teachers of the man who became arguably the most famous, influential psychiatrist (as distinct from psychoanalyst) of the 19th century: Emil Kraepelin (1855–1926). While studying with Wundt, Kraepelin wrote on the effects of acute diseases on mental diseases and attempted to ascertain the cerebral actions of various drugs. In collaboration with Flechsig he carried out neuropathological studies. Inspired by Morel's 1860 treatise on adolescent dementia (Willis had written on this same topic in the 17th century), Kraepelin devoted much attention to the psychoses. By the late 1890s he had unified psychiatric nosology in this domain, placing many hitherto "separate" conditions under the rubric of "dementia praecox."

Emil Kraepelin, 1855–1926. Courtesy Stock Montage, Inc.

The last decades of the 19th century were characterized by what has been called the "paranoification" of psychiatric taxonomy, whereby every slight variation of a persecutory or otherwise paranoid condition was viewed as a separate disease. Kraepelin, a "lumper" rather than a "splitter," considered the "catatonia" described by Karl Kahlbaum and the "hebephrenia" sketched by both Kahlbaum and his pupil Ewald Hecker to be variants of his dementia praecox. Likewise, the "simple dementia" of Arnold Sommer and the dizzying array of paranoid disorders (such as the famous *Capgras' syndrome*, the delusion that a person was not "real" but only a "double") were all variants of dementia praecox.

Perhaps Kraepelin went a bit too far with his integrative or "lumping" approach. One of the many varieties of paranoia written about in the latter part of the 19th century, which Kraepelin viewed as subtypes of dementia praecox, was that of *folie raisonnante*, described by Sérieux and Capgras in a 1909 treatise. The "reasoning madness" was limited to severe distortions of interpretation, in which innocent events or remarks were construed as menacing or in some way suffused with hidden meanings intended for the patient. But hallucinations and other stigmata of schizophrenia, as we now understand it, were not part of this particular clinical picture. The condition is therefore more properly understood as a type of delusional disorder and a variety of psychosis apparently distinct from schizophrenia (Kendler, 1980).

In hopes of finding the cerebral-histological substrate for dementia praecox, Kraepelin enlisted the help of his neurologist colleague Alois Alzheimer (1864–1915). Alzheimer found histological abnormalities

Alois Alzheimer

in a certain form of senile dementia—the eponymous "Alzheimer's disease"—but was unable to establish a link between dementia praecox and any consistent microscopic abnormality of the brain.

Kraepelin's systematization of psychiatric nosology was hardly limited to the psychoses. He studied thousands of patients during his lifetime, searching for commonalties, and in the process brought clarity to the cluster of manic-depressive disorders as well as to what we now call (after Eugen Bleuler) "schizophrenia." Endowed with a subtler mind than he is sometimes given credit for, Kraepelin also described "borderline" variants of manic-depressive psychosis, created a whole catalogue of character types, and enumerated the traits peculiar to the temperaments associated with manic-depression: namely, the *depressive, irritable,* and *manic* temperaments, plus *cyclothymic,* a combination of the depressive and manic. Current editions of the American Psychiatric Association's *Diagnostic and Statistical Manual of Mental Disorders* have often been called "neo-Kraepelinian," because of the profound influence Kraepelin exerted on contemporary biometricians.

For all his breadth of knowledge and experience, Kraepelin had nothing but contempt for his predecessors among the German Romanticists. For example, he considered Ideler's contributions to be so much "play of thought." Nor did he have any use for Freud, who, like Ideler, also busied himself with *individual patients*. The two never met, nor was there any common ground to unite them, except perhaps for their one patient they both treated: Sergei Pankeyeff, the depressed Russian aristocrat, better known in psychoanalytic circles as the "Wolf-Man" (so named because of a memorable dream he had about wolves perched on a tree outside his bedroom window). Pankeyeff first consulted with Kraepelin, who could do nothing for him; he then spent some time in treatment with Freud, who eventually gave up on him also, viewing him as totally *existenz-unfähig* [unable to take care of himself] (Gay, 1988). (Freud entrusted the Wolf-Man to the care of Ruth Mack-Brunswick in the 1920s.)

Before turning our attention to Freud, a few other names in German psychiatry are noteworthy. Richard von Krafft-Ebing (1840–1902) is most known for his research on sexual aberrations, and is also credited for establishing the connection between general paresis and neurosyphilis (Z., p. 399).

A pioneer in the field of child psychiatry was Hermann Emminghaus (1845–1904), who also originated the term *psychopathology* (in 1887). Noting that mental disorders of children were incommensurate with those of adults, Emminghaus contended that the two domains deserved separate status (Harms, 1967, p. 173). It was his humanistic view that the delin-

The Wolf Man's dream. From Freud, "The Dream and the Primal Scene,"*The Standard Edition of the Complete Works of Sigmund Freud,* xvii: 30.

quent child was emotionally ill, not morally bad. Emminghaus understood that poor home conditions could lead to emotional disorders in children, so that conceptually, childhood psychoses due to physical abnormalities of the brain needed to be separated from disorders with a primarily psychogenic etiology.

Karl Kahlbaum (1828–1899) also attended to the disorders of childhood and established a pedagogium for the treatment of mentally ill children—the first of its kind. A systematist and strict empiricist in the manner of Kraepelin, Kahlbaum outlined three types of "partial pathology": paranoia, dysthymia, and diastrephia, which affected judgment, mood, and the will, respectively.

Karl Kahlbaum

A contemporary of Kahlbaum, Karl Westphal (1833–1890) wrote about the neuroses, including phobias, sexual disorders, and what would now be called "obsessive-compulsive disorder."

Karl Westphal

In 1885 there appeared an epoch-making monograph by Hermann Ebbinghaus (1850–1908), professor first at Halle, later at Breslau. His book, *Über das Gedächtnis: Untersuchungen zur experimentellen Psychologie* [*On Memory: Examinations in Experimental Psychology*], is considered the first in the area of *learning theory,* and placed experimental psychology on a firm footing, even in the more abstract realms of higher mental functioning. Using the techniques developed by Ebbinghaus, it became possible to study processes like memory without neurophysiological investigation of the sort that intrigued Séchenov and Pavlov in their reflex action and conditioning. For Ebbinghaus the two essential features of memory were repetition and time: Memory was enhanced by repetition, diminished by time. By using "nonsense syllables" Ebbinghaus was able to show that, if one had first learned a series A, B, C, D, E and later on just rows of A, C, and E, the recollection of A, C, and E was enhanced because of prior learning. An opponent of the "intuitionist" school, which emphasized an irrational will answering to the dictates of self-preservation and sex, Ebbinghaus declared that, once we understand sensation, ideation and feeling, we understand the "soul." The forms of the psychic life that he acknowledged were attention, association, habit or attitude, and finally, movement (akin to behavior). Ebbinghaus accepted the notion of an unconscious as an explanatory principle and recognized that the power of words depends on our associations to them (the impact of a word like *death* is infinitely greater if the death is of one's child than of a mouse in the kitchen). In this sense Ebbinghaus recognized the domain of emotion (akin to his notion of "attitude"), though his orientation toward "hard science" and biology led him away from dwelling on emotion per se. Ebbinghaus' achievements, nevertheless, helped lay the foundations for both 20th-century cognitive psychology and, in the realm of psychoanalysis, theories of a "conflict-free ego sphere" (involving processes like memory and cal-culation) as elaborated in the 1950s by Heinz Hartmann.

SIGMUND FREUD: THE EARLY YEARS

In the whole history of psychiatry the name of Freud is the only one to have become a household word. Born in Příbor (Freiberg) in what is now the Moravian part of the Czech Republic, Sigmund Freud (1856–1939) spent most of his life in Vienna, where his family moved when he was three years old. He began his studies in neurophysiology in 1876 with his first mentor, Ernest Brücke, himself a former pupil of Hermann von Helmholtz. It was Brücke's conviction that physics and chemistry would supply the answers to questions about living organ-isms, not belief in some "vital force."

Ernest Brücke

Freud's initial eagerness to find neuroanatomical substrates for psy-chological processes stemmed from the six years he spent in Brücke's laboratory. For the next four years (1882–1886) he worked with Meynert, during which time Freud published a preliminary report on the anes-thetic properties of cocaine. He had hoped to win fame for this discov-ery but was "scooped" in this research by Karl Koller, who discovered the usefulness of cocaine for numbing the eye during ophthalmic sur-gery. While in Meynert's lab, Freud became acquainted with the ideas of Herbart and Griesinger, who spoke about unconscious processes and speculated that conscious thought reflected only those ideas, among all the competing ideas in the brain, that captured the person's attention at any given moment. Freud's contributions during the neurological phase of his work included some excellent papers on aphasia. The next phase of Freud's work began in 1886 with his trip to Paris to study hypnotism and hysteria with Charcot. Impressed by the power of hypnotherapy to relieve hysterical symptoms (including paralyses), at least in some cases, Freud returned to Vienna after a year and formed a close friendship with physician Josef Breuer (1842–1925), who lent a sympathetic ear to Freud's enthusiasm for the hypnotic method.[1] To Meynert, hypnosis seemed like so much jiggery-pokery, and the two men parted ways in 1886, the same year that Freud married Martha Bernays.

Josef Breuer

Beginning in 1880, Breuer treated a young woman, "Anna O.," for hysterical limb paralyses as well as visual and other disturbances. He used hypnosis, during which she revealed hidden resentment for her father as well as feelings of love for Dr. Breuer—which prompted him to abandon the case. Freud and Breuer began to real-

---

[1] Freud met Breuer in Brücke's laboratory, where they had both trained (B., p. 126).

ize that not all patients were susceptible to hypnosis, nor did all hysteric patients improve.

Seeking to refine his techniques, Freud traveled to Nancy in 1889 to work with A.-A. Liébault (1824–1904). There he also met another famous proponent of the hypnotic method: Hippolyte Bernheim (1840–1919). Freud became aware that hypnosis was a type of sleep induced by *suggestion,* to which many patients, not just hysterics, were susceptible. Under hypnosis, *unconscious* material could become *conscious*.

Freud soon realized, however, that even experts, such as those of the Nancy School, had their failures; his own efforts did not always meet with "cures" either. In 1893 Breuer and Freud published their first paper on the psychic mechanisms of hysterical phenomena; in essence it was a "transitional" work between the focus on hypnotherapy and the emergence of psychoanalysis proper. In 1895 Freud discovered that the unconscious could be made conscious without the use of hypnosis through the method of *free association,* in which one idea or image leads to another, seemingly irrelevant, idea—until the patient unwittingly reveals a key, often embarrassing, experience, whose exposure relieves neurotic tension (in varying degrees). It is likely that Freud's notion of free association was influenced by his knowledge of the Jewish cabalistic sages (most especially, Abraham Abulafia in 13th-century Spain): Freud would have heard about them either from his paternal grandfather, who was a rabbi, or from other members of the Czech and, later, Austrian Jewish community, most of whom were steeped in cabalistic lore (Grözinger, 1994; Scholem, 1946; Weiner, 1969). Abulafia had used meditation and free association to dissolve mental images in the hope of coming closer to apperception of the Divine. Though his purpose was different from Freud's, the process was very similar.

In all events, this transition marked the beginning of *psychoanalysis,* a term that Freud introduced in 1896. In his new method, at once a therapy and a theory of mind, Freud united strands from empiricist, "neurologizing" psychiatry, as he had learned it from Brücke and Meynert. He was also influenced by the French school of the latter half of the 19th century as well as by the German Romanticist school, both of which focused attention on the *individual* patient.

In their efforts to free-associate, patients regularly mentioned their associations to dreams, which proved a particularly fertile source of emotionally relevant, unconscious material. Freud's discovery of this "royal road to the unconscious" culminated in his *Interpretation of Dreams* (actually published in 1899 but given the publication date of 1900 to extend the publisher's rights)—his one work, if there were to be only one, that would stand for all time. Whereas previous speculation about the meaning of dreams had been couched in mystical for-

A.-A. Liébault
Hippolyte Bernheim

mulations or, at best, in simplistic absolutes in which each common dream symbol had but one "translation" (losing a tooth meant concern about "losing one's property," etc.), Freud realized that it was the dreamer's unique chain of associations to the dream that unlocked its meaning. Furthermore, the meaning often reflected the hitherto unconscious conflicts with which the dreamer had been struggling in his or her waking life.

Freud also noted that sexual symbolism was all but omnipresent in dream language. Thus unresolved sexual conflicts, such as the Oedipus complex, seemed to be at the root of the dream camouflage. The realization that the dream mechanism was grafted onto the rapid eye movement (REM) phase of sleep in the higher animals, not just humans, and that REM sleep was accompanied by sexual tumescence, did not occur until the work of Aserinsky and Kleitman in 1953. In effect, Nature had "stacked the cards" with respect to the sexual meaning of dreams. Even so, Freud's discovery, which is still compatible with contemporary conceptions of the dream state as a problem-solving mechanism, was revolutionary, not to say breathtaking, in its impact. For Freudian dream interpretation created a solid foundation for a conflict-based theory of emotional disorders (especially, of the "neuroses," milder mental disturbances), and paved the way to a *psychodynamic* understanding of mental life and to *psychoanalytic treatment.* Whatever the merits and demerits of Freud's method as a theory of mind, whatever its successes and failures as a therapy, psychoanalysis offered a psychological profile of the individual, based on observation, intuition, and introspection, that was incomparably more detailed and satisfying than any of its rival methodologies.

The psychoanalytic approach yielded insights into the *whys* of a patient's choices and life-course that had been left unexplored by earlier investigators. Sexuality, in particular, but other "dark corners" of the psyche as well, touched on only timorously or passed over entirely in previous generations, were henceforth to be explored carefully. One has only to read the heart-rending though etiologically barren case histories of Spiess or Ideler or the vignettes of Freud's contemporary, Pierre Janet—detailed, dry, and all but devoid of early childhood material—to sense what was missing in the works of his predecessors.

Chapter 7

NINETEENTH-CENTURY FRANCE: EFFORTS TOWARD SYSTEMIZING ILLNESS

Whereas the emphasis in German psychiatry in the first half of the 19th century was on the individual, and in the latter half on taxonomy and organic correlates, in France the situation was nearly the reverse. Important discoveries concerning general paresis were made by the French of the first half-century. Phrenology, which was all the rage, constituted an effort (albeit fanciful) to establish a biopsychological science. In the second half-century considerable attention in France was turned toward the individual patient and away from "neurologizing."

THE "NEUROLOGIZERS"

A number of French philosophers explored the areas of sensation and memory—topics that would later be relegated to psychology. Two in particular, at the turn of the century, influenced Pinel: Pierre Maine de Biran and P. J. G. Cabanis. Maine de Biran (1766–1824), in his *Influence de l'Habitude sur la Faculté de Penser* (1803), contended that habit dulls our ability to recall from memory the perceptions and ideas that originally led to the formation of the automatic behavior. The vocal signs (i.e., the words) associated with events, objects, and experiences are learned at Mother's knee, as it were, and the adult can no longer recall precisely how or when each linguistical habit was acquired. In a classification that has a distinctly modern ring to it (cf. Mishkin et al., 1984), Maine de Biran outlined three

Pierre Maine de Biran
P. J. G. Cabanis

The head of Shakespeare, as sketched in Spurzheim's book, showing superiority in the traits of "Ideality" (xix) and "Imitation" (xxi).

The supposed hypertrophy of the "organ of acquisitiveness" in the violinist, Nicolo Paganini. From Poupin, 1837.

types of memory: *mechanical* or habit memory (involving retention and recall of words, numbers, etc.); *sensitive* memory (the recollection of sensations, emotions, desires, and the like); and *representative* memory (long-term, associational memory that underlies abstract thought, intellect, planning, etc.).

P. J. G. Cabanis (1757–1808) also explored sensation in his *Rapport du Physique et du Moral de l'Homme* (1802), as well as the various instincts, such as those subserving self-preservation, movement (including the innate behavior patterns by which cats and dogs, though born blind, find their mothers' teats), and nutrition. Cabanis cited the work of William Cullen, who wrote on the similarity between dreaming and "madness" (*délire*)—an idea that also occurred to Jung a century later, when he analogized the schizophrenic to someone dreaming yet awake. Cabanis also credited Pinel with the observation that "imbeciles often have either a skull-depression or a general diminution in their brain-size" that accounts for their mental limitation—an incorrect notion, appealing at the time, that gave a scientific cachet to the topic of idiocy.

Apropos of overly enthusiastic speculations about the body's influence on the mind, the pseudoscience of phrenology dominated Europe and America in the early 19th century, owing to the popularity of Franz Gall (1758–1828), a German scholar who contended that palpation of the skull yielded information about 37 brain "organs," the size of which determined corresponding personality traits. Gall's theory was so materialistic (in the sense of denying the soul) that it was regarded as being irreligious. As a result, like Mesmer before him, he was deported from Vienna (A. & S., p. 124). His six-volume treatise, *Sur les Fonctions du Cerveau et des Facultés Intellectuelles de l'Homme* [*On the Functions of the Brain and of the Intellectual Faculties of Man*] appeared in 1825. Soon thereafter, Gall published another tome co-authored by his pupil, Johann Spurzheim (1776–1832). Spurzheim lectured in Boston in 1832 and was enormously popular because he claimed that proper moral influences could change a person's character for the better, whereas Gall was discouragingly fatalistic.

Despite the fanciful nature of phrenology, its focus stimulated interest in cerebral localization on the part of the more truly scientific neuroanatomists, such as Meynert, whom we have already met. The French writer Theodore Poupin went so far as to subject various famous figures of the day to phrenological analysis. The skull configurations of Paganini, for example, were presumed to determine the virtuoso's "acquisitiveness."

Biological psychiatry made impressive advances in France with

1. Organ of destructiveness
2. Organ of amativeness
3. Organ of philoprogenitiveness
4. Organ of adhesiveness
5. Organ of inhabitiveness
6. Organ of combativeness
7. Organ of secretiveness
8. Organ of acquisitiveness
9. Organ of constructiveness
10. Organ of cautiousness
11. Organ of love of approbation
12. Organ of self–esteem
13. Organ of benevolence
14. Organ of reverence
15. Organ of firmness
16. Organ of conscientiousness
17. Organ of hope
18. Organ of marvellousness
19. Organ of ideality
20. Organ of mirthfulness or gayness
21. Organ of imitation
22. Organ of individuality
23. Organ of configuration
24. Organ of size
25. Organ of weight and resistance
26. Organ of coloring
27. Organ of locality
28. Organ of order
29. Organ of calculation
30. Organ of eventuality
31. Organ of time
32. Organ of tune
33. Organ of language
34. Organ of comparison
35. Organ of causality

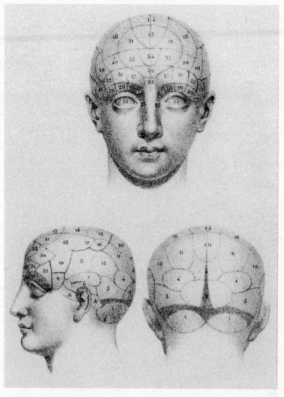

A phrenological map of the head, as depicted by Theodore Poupin, based on the works of Gall, Spurzheim, and Lavater. Each of the thirty-five regions was considered a separate "organ," controlling a different characteristic of the personality or the mind. From Poupin, *Caractéres Phrénologiques et Physiognomoniques*, 1837.

the work of Antoine Bayle (1799–1858) and L.-F. Calmeil (1798–1895). Both discovered the link between certain forms of meningitis and clinical symptoms of grandiose delusions accompanied by paralysis—the general paresis later shown to be a manifestation of syphilis. Diagnostic criteria for the disease were elaborated in the 1850s by Delasiauve and J. P. Falret. The disease itself was outlined more fully a generation later, in the 1870s, by Fournier in France and Krafft-Ebing in Germany. The spirochete responsible for syphilis was not identified for still another generation, in 1913 by Noguchi.

Bayle and Calmeil both worked at the Charenton Hospital in Paris and both of their books appeared in 1826. In 1845 Calmeil also published a general psychiatric text that covered description and taxonomy as well as forensic considerations.

Antoine Bayle
L.-F. Calmeil

THE "SYSTEMATIZERS"

Jean-Etienne Esquirol

Guillaume Ferrus

Unquestionably the most renowned psychiatrist in 19th-century France was Jean-Etienne Esquirol (1772–1840). A disciple of Pinel, Esquirol distinguished himself in many areas, including descriptive psychiatry, institutional reform, and statistics. He originated the term *hallucinations* and differentiated them from *illusions* (the latter being "false impressions based on misinterpretation of reality") (1838, pp. 159 ff.). With his colleague Guillaume Ferrus (1784–1861), Esquirol was instrumental in bringing about the law reforms of 1838 that led to improvements in the conditions of asylums. Actually, Esquirol had written an important monograph in 1819 on the disgraceful conditions in European asylums. It becomes apparent from his work that the reforms initiated by Chiarugi and Pinel did not sweep through the continent in a day. "This is what I saw almost everywhere in France, and this is how the mentally ill are treated almost everywhere in Germany and Italy as well," Esquirol wrote, adding:

> These unfortunate souls, as though they were criminals of the State, are thrown into pits, or into dungeons where the eye of humanity never penetrates. We let them waste away in their own excrement, under the weight of chains that rip at their flesh. Their faces are pale and emaciated. They await only the day that gives surcease to their misery—and to our shame . . . . Heaped up and tossed together in a jumble, they are kept in control only by terror: whips, chains and dungeons are the only means of persuasion used by caretakers who are as barbaric as they are ignorant. (p. 5) [Author's translation]

(Compare these remarks to those of Dorothea Dix in America a generation later, who still had to inveigh against the same sordid conditions.) Esquirol also rose to the defense of criminals who were mentally ill (Z., p. 391), arguing for compassionate treatment.

During this era in French psychiatry attention was directed to the systematic observation of patients, to the correspondences between the "physical" and the "moral" (the French word for *moral* signifies something more akin to our usage of "mental" or "emotional" than to ethical concerns), and to the discovery of organic etiologies for the various psychoses. There was also some interest in exploring the psychological factors underlying the less severe conditions. These early psychodynamic notions concerned mostly disappointments in love and financial worries (both

Jean-Etienne Esquirol, 1772–1840.
Courtesy National Library of Medicine

of which had been alluded to by LePois a century before). Esquirol contributed to advances in all these areas.

Esquirol's nosology was relatively simple, consisting of main headings such as *délire général* [general madness], *délire partielle* [partial madness], and *affaiblissement intellectuelle* [weakening of the intellect]. The first term was reserved for what we could consider to be an all-encompassing psychosis, as opposed to a compartmentalized condition involving, say, paranoid thinking in just one area of life (*délire partielle*). In time, *délire général* became known as *manie*, but its meaning was not confined to our usage of "mania" as it occurs in bipolar illness. *Délire partielle* became *monomanie:* There was "affective monomania" (which could be of the *triste* type—our "recurrent depression"), *pyromanie*, or *kleptomanie*—terms still in use today. Esquirol used the term *lypemanie* [grief-madness] for melancholy, though it never gained wide use. He also divided "intellectual weakness" into congenital and acquired types. The latter might take the form of what Morel was later to call "démence précoce": a loss of intellectual powers beginning in adolescence, described earlier by Willis and later by our term *schizophrenia*.

A woman suffering from *lypemanie*, or severe depression. From Esquirol, *Des maladies mentales*, 1838.

Esquirol was among the first to report on mental illness and on suicide in particular from a statistical standpoint (Moore in England preceded him). He reported that among some 200 female suicides in France, the most common means was hanging (25%), followed by drowning; the use of firearms or poison was rare. His textbook (1838) also cited cross-cultural epidemiological statistics to the effect that suicides accounted for 0.4% of the London population, 1.26% of those in Berlin, 2.5% in Paris, and 10% in Copenhagen. These figures, though scarcely credible, at least represent the beginning of statistical analysis in psychiatry; they also indicate a higher suicide risk in Scandinavia than in France or Germany, which is consistent with contemporary data.

Among the important figures in the generation after Esquirol were Jean-Pierre Falret (1794–1870) and Jules Baillarger (1809–1890). Both helped clarify that mania and melancholy were different clinical manifestations of the same illness: Baillarger spoke of *folie à double forme* [double form insanity]; Falret, of *folie circulaire* [circular insanity]. (Hippocrates had suspected as much two thousand years earlier, but following the work of Falret and Baillarger, the connection was much more convincing.)

Jean-Pierre Falret
Jules Baillarger

The "inside" story of these two prominent figures has been beautifully told by Pichot (1995). Both Falret and Baillarger had been trained by Esquirol, and both then became heads of private clinics: Falret, with his colleague Félix Voisin at a clinic in Vanves near Paris; Baillarger, with Moreau de Tours at a clinic in Ivry. Falret had given a series of lectures on mental diseases in 1850. Psychiatry was not taught as a subject in French medical schools until 1862—and then, by a pupil of Falret's: Lasègue (of the eponymous *Lasègue*'s sign in neurological examination). In his last lecture Falret mentioned a special form of insanity called "circular": alternating excitement and *affaisement/depression*. Falret's original brief note about his *folie circulaire* in 1851 was expanded in a more detailed presentation in a book he published in 1854.

About a week later, Baillarger gave a lecture about a "type of madness . . . consist[ing] of two periods, one of depression, the other of excitement, in immediate succession"—to which he gave the label *folie à double forme* (p. 4). Baillarger fought with Falret over the matter of who said what first as well as the precise nature of the illness they purported to describe. The battle became acrimonious, though the hostility was mostly on Baillarger's side, with the older Falret remaining more detached. After both had died, Falret's son Jules, who had succeeded Moreau de Tours at the Salpêtrière, and who had meantime introduced the term *folie à deux*, made, in 1894, a conciliatory speech praising both his father and Baillarger for their pioneering work on what we now call bipolar illness. As Pichot tells it, the next speaker was a pupil of Baillarger: Magnan—who referred to the old controversy as a "battle between giants" where "both won the victory" (p. 7). With that Gallic gallantry, the drama came to a happy end.

At Falret's urging, during the reforms of 1838 the older terms of "imbecility" and "furor," with their pejorative connotations, were replaced by *"alienation"*—a gentler term signifying estrangement from society because of illness. Baillarger, who served as the editor of the prominent journal *Annales Médico-Psychologiques* [*Annals of Medical Psychology*], carried forward the work of Bayle, which concerned the topographic outline of the various brain centers and was inspired by the philosophical works of John Stuart Mill and Condillac. Each cerebral hemisphere, Baillarger noted, had lobes whose architecture depended on their specific area and function. As Beauchesne (1993) notes, the brain was now seen as a "mosaic of centers capable of being excited or ablated" (p. 55).

Félix Voisin

Another intriguing figure from the generation after Esquirol was Félix Voisin. Born in Mans in 1794, he trained at the Salpêtrière, where he was befriended by Esquirol and Jean-Pierre Falret. He and Falret founded a sanitarium at Vanves in 1822. Voisin was a firm organicist and lifelong supporter of the phrenological theories of Gall. He asserted that the brain, far from being influenced by the uterus in cases of hysteria, exerted strong influences upon the sexual organs. His first major work (1826) dealt with hysteria, nymphomania, and satyriasis, for all of which he postulated an organic rather than a psychological source.

Voisin's description of nymphomania is of particular interest, not alone for its grandiloquent style but for his division of the condition into "three stages"—a nosographic approach that became popular in 19th-century France. Le Grand du Saulle, for example, was later to describe *folie du doute* (our obsessive-compulsive disorder) as a disease of three stages. This idea of inevitable progression to a more serious form is implicit in certain 20th-century theories as well: In the 1940s it was common to view schizophrenia as evolving from a "borderline" stage to a more florid one and, finally, to a chronic, deteriorated stage.

Voisin's "stages" of nymphomania, which he ascribed to abnormalities of the cerebellum, began with an internal struggle to contain lustful feelings, which nevertheless break through as a coquettishness that "betrays the inner fire with which she is consumed." In the second stage, "she delivers herself unreservedly to the full impetuousity of her sense." Concerning the third stage, however, "the pen refuses to record the attendant symptoms . . . I can only say that frenzy increases to the point of abolishing altogether the faculty of reason" (p. 291). Because pregnancy was noted to "free the patient from the worst part of the illness," Voisin recommended early marriage to a strongly sexed man as the logical remedy.

Later he published a trilogy: *The Analysis of Human Understanding*, addressing our "moral, intellectual and animal faculties." This division is reminiscent of Freud's 1923 division of mind into superego, ego, and id. The "complete man," for Voisin, shows a high degree of morality and great intelligence—both resting upon a vigorous body. He saw moral and intellectual faculties as the products of culture; our animal aspects, the product of nature.

Voisin also organized a hospital for the retarded—one of the first— at the Bicêtre hospital. He recommended "moral" (humane) treatment and wrote on the subject with the support of Guillaume Ferrus.

Toward the end of his life (he died in 1872), Voisin addressed forensic issues. He believed that criminals came from the lower classes and had a faulty organization of the brain. In this respect his views reflect the temper of his time (France at mid-century), when the political and economic ills of the country were seen as the consequences of moral "degeneration"—a topic taken up in greater detail by Benedict Morel. The presumption was that hereditary factors greatly contributed to this degeneration.

In the 1860s the areas of the brain subserving speech were identified by Jean Baptiste Buillaud (1796–1881) and Pierre Paul Broca (1824–1880). The latter noted that in right-handed persons, aphasia stemmed from a lesion in the left frontal lobe (now the eponymous "Broca's area").

In this time period there were several French savants who commented on dreams. The Marquis d'Hervey de Saint-Denis (1823–1892) published a work on *Dreams and How to Guide Them* (1867), in which

Jean-Baptiste Buillaud
Pierre Paul Broca
Le Marquis d'Hervey de Saint-Denis

he recorded several years' worth of his own dreams—apparently the first person ever to do so in the West (a Korean Buddhist monk of the 8th century had recorded his dreams, but this was unknown in the West until recently). The Marquis' book was cited by Alfred Maury (1862) in his monograph on dreams, and later cited by Freud, who regarded the Marquis as someone who recognized the importance of dreams (even though he had not unlocked their meaning).

Alfred Maury (1817–1892) merits an important position in the history of psychiatry out of proportion to his modest reputation. He was not a psychiatrist to begin with, though he had studied law and then medicine (the same sequence as in Mesmer and Wilhelm Reich), not even completing his medical studies. History was the profession he settled on, and eventually he succeeded as professor of history (at the Collège de France) Jules Michelet—who had also been an opponent of Catholicism. Yet his life story, eloquently told by Dowbiggen (1990), highlights the major battles in 19th-century French psychiatry and in French politics, and is not without reverberations in our own day as we approach the new millenium.

The son of a devout Catholic mother (who taught him that atheism was a crime and a sign of depravity) and a free-thinking engineer father, Maury identified more strongly with his father, becoming in his turn militantly anticlerical. He had a hatred and a fear of the Jacobin excesses of 1793–94, the Reign of Terror, when fanatics such as Robespierre and Marat put to death many a scientist whom they considered insufficiently "revolutionary." Though these events occurred a few years before Maury's birth, his early years were marked by revolutions of both the royalists and the republicans. The 1830 revolution reestablished a monarchy (that of Louis Philippe) and restored power to the Church. This so unnerved Maury that he suffered a nervous breakdown that included hallucinations and delirium. To Maury the Church meant superstition and belief in magic or miracles—the antithesis of rationalilty and science. Science, for Maury, was the "conscientious search for truth, and truth, inscribed in our hearts, is the path to goodness"(remarks of 1864, cited by Dowbiggen, 1990, p. 277).

Maury had friends and supporters in high places within the psychiatric community: Jules Baillarger, Jacques Moreau de Tours, and Benedict Morel. Morel's theory of hereditary degeneration was in part a symptom of the times, as one after another French intellectual became discouraged with the antiscientific atmosphere of the 1840s and the deteriorating political situation in France (economic depression and starvation, reminiscent of what was taking place in Ireland in 1845).

Maury and his medical colleagues were all vehemently opposed to the ideas of Brierre de Boismont, whose treatise asserted that the hallucinations of Joan of Arc and of Martin Luther were a product of their era and culture, not necessarily a manifestation of mental illness. To

Maury and the psychiatrists, this notion was abhorrent, since it spoke of something mysterious and supernatural, outside the realm of biology. They contended that abnormal changes in the mind, such as hallucinations or ecstatic experiences, reflected organic changes in the brain. This placed them, as Moreau de Tours asserted, squarely within the province of the physician.

Maury had a particular interest in dreams all his life, recording many of them, as had d'Hervey de Saint-Denis before him. For Maury, dreams were at the crossroads of reason and madness, a view held by his illustrious predecessors, Cabanis and Maine de Biran. Maury understood that dreams were comprised of sensory impressions from both childhood and more recent experiences, which the brain, in its "passive" state during sleep, put together higgledy piggledy, creating a content that was, in his opinion, devoid of meaning. In this respect Maury came close to the more complete understanding of dreams that Freud achieved, and indeed was one of the two or three predecessors in this domain whom Freud singled out for high esteem. Freud went the further step, as we know, of discovering that the seeming hodge-podge of dream imagery did encode psychological meaning after all.

Maury was aware of the necessity of sleep, stating that "insomnia, or the privation of sleep, irrespective of its cause, conduces to madness, because the cerebro-spinal system is then forced to provide an unending supply of nervous energy that is not replenished" (1862, p. 9) [Author's translation]. Maury believed that, as the muscles and senses become benumbed during sleep, the intellectual faculties likewise become dulled. This belief may be why he dismissed the idea that dreams had any special meaning. For Maury, mesmeric trance, clairvoyance, hypnotism, telepathy, ecstatic states, somnambulism, and hallucinations were all, like dreams, rooted in organic changes in the brain.

The notion, at once romantic and ecclesiastic, that dreams were quasi-divine messages that "spoke" to people of genius in ways they could grasp but that the common people could not, was attractive to the followers of Mesmer and to a number of prominent persons (like Balzac) who were much influenced by them. Maury fought against this irrationality in what became an uphill battle toward the end of his life, when a wave of renewed interest in spiritism, ecstatic experiences, ouija boards, and the like swept over the European continent. This is a battle that is never completely won. In our own day, a new wave of millenarians has made an appearance as we approach the year 2000; side by side with the rational psychotherapies, we confront, admittedly in small number, "past-life therapists," "astral tunneling therapists," and other sincere but misguided practitioners whose claims rest on beliefs no more defensible than those Maury and his friends were at pains to debunk in the 1850s.

Maury was impressed by what seemed to him the lightning-like rapidity with which the brain could fashion a dream, as though it were an artist that could create a painting in a matter of seconds. To prove his point, he mentioned an experience from his twenties that culminated in a fascinating dream, not unlike the famous dreams Freud later shared in his *Traumdeutung*. I translate it here in what I believe is the first time it will have appeared in English:

> I was a little indisposed, and found myself abed in my room, with my mother sitting nearby. I dreamed of the Terror and was present at scenes of massacre. I was then at the revolutionary tribunal, and I see Robespierre, Marat, Fouquier-Tinville, all the most villainous figures of that dreadful epoch. I enter into conversation with them, but after a time, I am judged, sentenced to death, carried in the tumbrel—surrounded by an immense crowd—and taken to the Place de la Révolution. I mount the scaffold; the executioner binds me atop the fatal board, tips it, the cleaver drops—and I feel my head separate from my body! I awaken in the grip of intense anxiety. I feel the pole of my bedpost, which has suddenly grown loose, fall down and strike my neck vertebrae in a like manner to the blade of the guillotine. All this transpired in an instant, as my mother confirmed—yet it was this external sensation that must have triggered the dream. At the moment I was struck, the memory of that fearful machine, which the bedpost represented to such good effect, had all at once aroused all the images of that epoch, of which the guillotine had been the symbol. (1862, pp. 133–34)[1]

Jacques Moreau de Tours

Jacques Moreau de Tours (1804–1884), who had studied under Esquirol, viewed mental disorders as signs of disturbance of the whole personality brought about by "hidden, irrational forces." Intrigued with the effects of hashish upon its users, Moreau de Tours declared in a manner more forceful than Cullen or Cabanis that madness (*délire*) was identical to the state of dreaming—except that it occurred in a person who happened to be awake. This perception was reflected in the title of his 1852 book, *L'Identité de l'État de Rêve et de la Folie* [*On the Identity of the Dream State with Insanity*].

Alexandre Brierre de Boismont

Alexandre Brierre de Boismont (1797–1881) wrote extensively on hallucinations (1845) and suicide (1856). In the former he listed a long catalogue of "causes" of hallucinations, such as fear of the devil, the full moon, masturbation, fever, the long silences in prison, and the

---

[1] Note that Maury's dream flies in the face of Freud's assertion that one cannot dream of one's own death. We know now that in certain vulnerable individuals, such dreams can occasionally occur (Stone, 1979).

effects of opium or hashish. Certain dreams also appeared to be "hallucinations" of stored up memories, recalled according to the "laws of association" (p. 411), and capable of serving as the inspiration of painters and sculptors. Here again is a hint of what Freud was to expand on in his dream research, but which Brierre de Boismont carried no further. There is an equally long catalogue of causes in his commentary on suicide, which he divided into two types: "predisposing" and "determinative." The former included heredity, seasonal changes, gender (males were at higher risk), age (40–50 was the most suicide-prone age range), and certain professions. As for determinative causes, the most important were alcoholism, poverty or wretched life conditions, unemployment, libertinage, and sloth (p. 102).

An important contributor in the chain of psychiatrists who have worked on what we now call schizophrenia was Bénédict Morel (1809–1873), in whose 1860 treatise on mental disorders we find the phrase "démence précoce." Morel coined this term to refer to adolescents whose intellectual faculties, which were unremarkable in childhood, begin to deteriorate. This is the evolution of schizophrenia sketched by Thomas Willis nearly 200 years earlier. Influenced by Darwin's work, Morel ascribed this "precocious dementia" to heredity; faithful to the moralistic climate of the times, he further assumed that drunkenness in the father might be passed on to the sons, whose degeneration would be even more severe (i.e., accompanied by dementia). Social causes (poverty, debauchment) also seemed causative but also correctable— as though *regeneration* early enough in life (via social hygiene) might counteract the *degeneration*.

This might be the moment to interject a note about the outward *form* (or "phenotype") of schizophrenia, as it has changed throughout the ages. E. Fuller Torrey (1979) contends that schizophrenia is a "new" disease, going back no further than about 1800. Most schizophrenia researchers disagree, contending that cultural factors and epochal changes over long time periods alter the clinical picture at any given time and place. For example, the con-

Bénédict Morel

Young men diagnosed with idiocy. From Morel's 1860 treatise.

viction that one's life was controlled by demons would be deemed much "crazier" in 1995 than in 1595, but other beliefs would have been regarded as equally delusory back then. Some of the clinical signs we now regard as crucial to the diagnosis (thought insertion, loosening of associations, persecutory delusions) either were not understood centuries ago or were not described in the literature that has survived. But it is much more likely that genuine schizophrenia (as opposed to tumor- or toxicity-induced phenocopies), with its hereditary predisposition, has been with us for a very long time.

P. Briquet

What we currently call "somatization disorder" was referred to earlier as "hysteria" or "Briquet's syndrome." The latter takes its name from P. Briquet (1796–1881), whose monograph, *Traité de l'Hystérie* [*Treatise on Hysteria*], appeared in 1859. The syndrome consists of multiple, vague, or exaggerated somatic complaints for which no physical cause can be found. The accompanying symptoms are often gastrointestinal or sexual; the latter might include sexual indifference or vomiting during the whole of pregnancy. Plato assumed that this *hysteria* was the result of sexual continence. Briquet disagreed with this notion, which he noted had been accepted without challenge by Hippocrates, Galen, and their successors up through Briquet's time.

Through his methodical observations, Briquet was able to correct the old prejudices, stating that married women were only slightly less prone to hysteria than unmarried women, that a fifth of cases occur even before puberty, that having a sexual life is not a guarantee against developing hysteria, and perhaps more importantly, that men could also develop the syndrome (as LePois had mentioned years before). For treatment Briquet relied on various medications, but he also realized that, in the majority of cases, the women (for most of the patients were women) suffered from difficult or embarrassing life circumstances and therefore needed a physician who was able to serve as confidante to their troubles. In other words, Briquet was attuned to the need for *psychotherapy*, over and above the somatic measures usually resorted to in his day.

Edouard Seguin

A former student of Itard, Edouard Seguin (1812–1880) brought into the care of the mentally retarded the more humane measures introduced by his mentor. Seguin's work led to improvements on a large scale: He initiated reforms whereby corporal punishment was no longer used in institutions for the retarded. Simply put, Seguin changed the method of interacting with retarded patients from one of aversive conditioning to positive conditioning (relying on coaxing, kindness, rewards, etc.). Seguin (1886) wrote: "For our pupils, science, literature, art . . . may each do something; but love alone can truly socialize them; those alone who love them are their true rescuers" (p. 245). Later in his career, Seguin spent time in the United States, effecting the same improvements in the care of the retarded here as he had brought about in France. The first American private school for the "moral treatment" of the retarded was opened under Seguin's guidance by Dr. H. Wilbur at Barre, Massachusetts in 1848. Shortly thereafter a similar residential school was opened in New York State, named after Dr. Wilbur.

Guillaume Ferrus

Guillaume Ferrus (1784–1861), mentioned above in connection with his work with Esquirol and the institutional reforms of 1838, also introduced occupational therapy into the therapeutic milieu of the psychiatric hospital. Trained by Pinel, Ferrus had become the director of the Bicêtre in 1826. Patients capable of work tended animals or participated in various workshops. Although criminals and the insane were often still housed in the same facility, Ferrus sought to improve the care of the criminal internees as well, making sure they didn't escape, but urging the authorities to give them meaningful work to do. Despite Pinel's reforms, the policy of non-restraint was often honored in the breach: Many patients were still chained to the walls, a practice that Ferrus sought to abolish. Under his direction the Bicêtre became a teaching hospital where he conducted public interviews of patients in a gentle and non-threatening manner (Z., p. 384). In his views on etiology Ferrus never went beyond the perspectives characteristic of his day: For example, he could not grasp how psychoses could become chronic without there being a distinct underlying organic base.

Henri Le Grand du Saulle

Another prominent psychiatrist at the Bicêtre was Henri Le Grand du Saulle (1830–1886), an enormously prolific investigator who wrote lengthy treatises on obsessive-compulsive disorder, delusions of persecution, hereditary mental disorders, jurisprudence, epilepsy, and agoraphobia. His description of *folie héréditaire* most closely resembles our concept of "schizotypal personality." Noting that these patients sometimes occupy high positions in society and perform their duties with exemplary lucidity, they nonetheless ". . . show eccentricity of character, peculiarities that seem inexplicable. . . . sometimes the condition persists, and the patient becomes incurably insane." The clinical vignettes in his 1866 monograph on obsessive-compulsive disorder are particularly vivid, as in the following example of an obsessional woman:

> Mademoiselle Hortense G . . ., 24 years of age, distinguished artist. She is intelligent, active, punctual, conscientious, and enjoys a fine reputation. Whenever she walks in the street, she becomes preoccupied with these thoughts: Might not someone fall from a high-up window and land at my feet? Would it be a man or woman? Will the person be dead or merely wounded? If wounded: at the head or the feet? Will there be blood on the sidewalk? If the person dies instantly—how will I know it? Should I call for help, run away from the scene, or recite *Pater Nosters* and *Ave-Marias*? Will people accuse me of having been the cause of the accident?

Then won't my pupils quit coming to me? Then again, maybe my innocence will be recognized? (p. 12) [Author's translation]

Le Grand du Saulle credited Pinel with having described similar cases earlier, though Karl Westphal, a contemporary, also gave examples of ego-dystonic, alien, intrusive thoughts of the obsessional type.

Equally detailed and compelling are the author's 1878 descriptions of *folie des espaces* or "what the Germans call 'agoraphobia.'" A young engineer, for example, was terrified to walk in the street because he felt as though the ". . . pavement ran like a torrential river under his feet, as though he were a swimmer who, suddenly coming out of a canal, found himself in a vast pool that was much too large for him to cross" (p. 16).

Georges Gilles de la Tourette

In the 1880s Georges Gilles de la Tourette (1857–1904), who had trained at the Salpêtrière under Charcot, described the syndrome that was named after him, which was characterized by motor and vocal tics. His first report appeared in the 1884 volume of the *Archives de Neurologie* in a brief article mentioning that such cases had been reported in America, Malaysia (known there as *latah*) and, quite commonly, Siberia, where the compulsive jumping and odd vocalizations were called *miryachit*. Three years later he published an extensive work on hypnotism, containing chapters on the nature of suggestion, hysteria, and the medical applications of hypnosis.

Gilles de la Tourette (1887) also discussed the exploitative use of hypnotism by unscrupulous persons. An example concerned a young man, described as a scruffy and unprepossessing vagrant with a club foot, who ingratiated himself with a farmer and his family who lived in a small village. After winning their confidence, he managed to get the daughter alone, whereupon he put her in a trance and, on several occasions, raped her. When he was caught and tried, the examining psychiatrists concluded that it was possible to overcome the will and the moral compunctions of highly suggestible women through the illicit use of "magnetic effect." As a result of this testimony, the vagrant was found guilty and sentenced to 12 years of hard labor.

Jean-Martin Charcot

As for Gilles de la Tourette's teacher, Jean-Martin Charcot (1825–1893), the preeminent French neurologist of the 19th century, he trained many of the most influential psychiatrists of the era—most notably, Freud, Bleuler, Janet, and Bechterev. Charcot's interest in hysteria, combined with his great stature as a physician, conferred acceptability on the study of related phenomena (the "unconscious," hypnosis, and the neuroses) to the conservative medical establishment of his day. As a medical student, Janet wrote his thesis on hysteria while on Charcot's service at the Salpêtrière, where Charcot had also organized a laboratory for the study of experimental psychology.

Unlike many of his predecessors, Charcot took hysteria seriously.

He was too much the psychologist to share their conviction that hysteria was "something imaginary," yet he was too much the neurologist to retreat from his belief that there must be a "weakness of the nervous system"—something organic—at the root of it. That he perceived a psychological connection of any kind aligned him with Sydenham, who, in the 17th century, had also postulated a psychological explanation (A. & S., p. 191). As mentioned above, Charcot's belief that only hysterics were susceptible to hypnosis was overturned by the hypnotists of the Nancy School: Liébault and Bernheim. Yet Charcot understood that the convulsive episodes of the hysteric were not related to epilepsy (Z., p. 362). In Freud's early papers there are hints that Charcot (and other neurologists of the time) believed that many female hysteric patients had suffered sexual traumata in their early years, including incest (Stone, 1992). But, as we would phrase it today, it was "politically incorrect" to make an issue of this correlation at the time. Freud himself found it necessary to downplay the connection, and it was not until much later (the 1980s) that childhood sexual trauma could be investigated more openly.

Nevertheless, Charcot helped greatly to "de-demonize" hysteria by showing conclusively that the "demonic possession" of the late Middle Ages and pre-Enlightenment era was a variety of hysteria (Z., p. 364). In bestowing legitimacy on the condition as something worthy of the physician's attention, Charcot also facilitated Freud's research on hysteria and thus contributed to the creation of a climate congenial to the development of psychoanalysis.

Whereas Freud plumbed the depths of the childhood experiences of his hysteric patients, Charcot ventured only a short distance into this forbidden territory. In one of his clinical vignettes concerning hysteria with contractures, Charcot (1875) wrote:

> At the moment of the attack, the patient was in the grip of a delirium that related to the events that presumably gave shape to the initial crises: she addressed imaginary persons with furious invective: "Criminals!, Thieves!, Burn them!, Burn them! Oh, the dogs! They're biting me!" So many memories, doubtless, of emotions of her youth. (p. 344)

Charcot's work exerted a strong influence on psychologist Theodule Ribot (1839–1916). With support from Janet he became the chairman of the department of experimental psychology at the Collège de France in Paris, where he specialized in abnormal psychology. Ribot envisioned a continuum spanning the normal and the pathological ranges in "personality"—a term he used in 1885. Influenced by Darwin and other British philosophers, he stressed the importance of heredity in determining individual as well as national characteristics. He regarded he-

Theodule Ribot

redity as playing a comparable role for the *species* to that memory served for the *individual* (B., p. 75). He reasoned that if we remembered "everything," our brains would become swamped with much useless information and, therefore, *forgetting* was a necessary component of the memory mechanism. He spoke of a pleasure/pain principle as well as of "drives" for sex, self-preservation, hunger, thirst, and even "killing and stealing" (presumably representing what we more commonly subsume under the heading of "aggression"). Our sociability as a species nonetheless gave rise to moral sentiments. Ribot also accepted the idea of an "unconscious" that served as a reservoir of past experiences and of emotions.

Charcot was also the mentor of another important commentator on hysteria: Paul Richer, who was to dedicate his encyclopedic 976-page work on *la grande hystérie*, published in 1885, to his teacher. By then Richer had become the director of the clinic for nervous diseases at the Salpêtrière. The terms "grand hysteria" or "hystero-epilepsy" were used to designate a severe form of hysteria in which the contortions of the body and outbursts of overwhelming emotion that characterized hysteria were accompanied by convulsions (either during the outbursts or at a separate time). The presence of convulsions pointed to what previous authors (Louyer-Villermay, Tissot, Briquet, Charcot himself) considered a grave sign prognostically.

Richer understood the condition as evolving in stages—three, usually, though sometimes four: (1) the epileptoid, (2) the period of contortions and exaggerated movements, (3) the period of attitudes and poses displaying great emotion, and (4) delirium or madness. During the third stage, striking exaggerated poses, spontaneous expressions of sexual feeling or else "lubricious hallucinations" were characteristic. One such patient described by Richer would shout out: "Camille, *je n'ai jamais aimé que toi!* [Camille, I've loved no one but you!]" or "*Donne-moi ton amour!* [Give me your love!]."

Despite all this evidence, the taboo against open acknowledgment

of the sexual underpinnings in *la grande hystérie* was so great, even in France of the 1880s, that Richer did not mention as even a possible etiological factor, the unrelieved sexual desires that affected either those who took vows of chastity or who, for other reasons, lived lives where this natural drive went unfulfilled. This omission does not mean that either Richer or Charcot was unaware of this connection. It was Charcot, after all, who said in 1886 concerning women's nervous troubles: "*C'est toujours la chose génitale* [It's always the sexual thing]" (Gay, 1988, p. 82). Richer's book is nonetheless noteworthy in another respect: There are 197 drawings and 10 etchings (all by Richer, who was also a gifted artist) illustrating *la grande hystérie* in all its forms.

Richer also included a long chapter on the history of the phenomenon, which previously was ascribed to the workings of the devil. The parts of the body where the devil was alleged to have taken up residence—the breasts, the heart, the forehead—were the very areas where hystero-epileptoids were wont (according to Richer) to experience their auras. Richer noted past outbreaks of what he saw as hystero-epilepsy in Aix la Chapelle in 1374, Strasbourg in 1418, and the celebrated case in 1632–33 at the convent of Loudun near Bordeaux. In this particular outbreak of hysteria among the Ursuline nuns at Loudun, a priest, Urbain Grandier, was accused of casting evil spells upon them or somehow causing them to be possessed by the devil. Triply unfortunate in being handsome, witty, and well-mannered, Grandier could scarcely avoid stirring up unwelcome passions in women sworn to chastity—the more so, as he was known to have an eye for the ladies and probably took advantage of the nuns on several occasions. However this may be, Grandier, due to the influence of Cardinal Richelieu, was condemned and burned at the stake. (Aldous Huxley immortalized this story in *The Devils of Loudun* [1952].)

Hysteria, as illustrated by Richer in his 1885 book on *la grande hystérie*.

Chapter 8

NINETEENTH-CENTURY BRITAIN: INTERESTS IN TAXONOMY AND HEREDITY

Similar developments in psychiatry occurred in Great Britain in the 19th century as were occurring on the continent: systemization of the diagnostic taxonomy, movement toward the use of non-restraint, more humane attitudes toward mentally ill offenders, and an interest in heredity. But the keen attention given to the individuality of the patient, which had characterized the German Romanticists and the French psychiatrists after mid-century, was not as apparent in England or Scotland, apart from a few exceptional figures who surfaced every so often.

William Tuke

Samuel Tuke

John Conolly

The first decades of the 19th century in Britain witnessed the same humane movement toward releasing institutionalized psychotic patients from restraints as had begun to form in Italy and France. The famous York Retreat was founded by a Quaker tea merchant, William Tuke (1732–1822), an admirer of Pinel. At this institution patients were treated with sympathy, allowed unrestrained access to the grounds, and housed in comfortable settings (A. & S., p. 120). William's son Henry and grandson Samuel Tuke (1784–1857) continued to direct the retreat and Samuel published a book describing the institution in 1813. The practice of non-restraint was introduced shortly afterwards at the Hanwell asylum by John Conolly (1794–1866), whose textbook on insanity appeared in 1830; his monograph on non-restraint was published in 1856.

SYSTEMATIZERS

William Cullen, 1710–1790. Courtesy National Library of Medicine

The most influential school of medicine in the British Isles in the late 1700s and early 1800s was located in Edinburgh, Scotland. The most renowned physician was William Cullen (1710–1790), whose works were translated into French by Pinel. Others who became his disciples included John Ferriar (who wrote on "apparitions"), William Hallaran (whose 1818 book discussed causes and cures of insanity), Thomas Trotter (whose *A View of the Nervous Temperament* was published first in England in 1807 and then in America in 1808, the first American psychiatric textbook), and Benjamin Rush (who was the first American psychiatrist to achieve prominence). Cullen introduced the term *neurosis* to designate various diseases of the brain and nervous system—specifically "all those preternatural affections of sense and motion, without pyrexia" (H. & M., p. 475). The neuroses were subdivided into four types; one type, *vesania,* designated disorders of judgment and intellectual function. An old Latin word (even Horace used it), it means *madness.* Eighteenth-century French alienists used *vesania* to refer to disorder in both reason and emotion. But Cullen used it more specifically, to refer to conditions involving hallucinations, melancholia, "oneirodynia" (disturbed imagination during sleep), and "amentia" (which could be either congenital or acquired). It was only much later that *neurosis* became the general term used in psychoanalysis to designate mildly disordered conditions rooted in early developmental conflicts.

The first physician in Britain to study medicine with the avowed purpose of working with the mentally ill was Joseph Cox (1763–1818), who, like Cullen, was Scottish. Cox achieved fame, albeit brief, through his use of the swing—in which he would spin his patients, effecting (sometimes) a "cure." As Cox (1804) explained it: "The various peculiarities and changes, both mental and physical, produced by the mode of swinging, must be attributed to the state of the sensibility, joined to the sympathy and reciprocity of action that subsists between the mind and body" (p. 131). In other words, fear induced by being swung in a rotating chair supposedly drove out the disturbing thoughts and emotions that had comprised the patient's mental illness. Cox's method was also employed by William Hallaran (1765–1825), the owner of a private asylum near Cork in Ireland. He wrote the first Irish textbook (Hallaran, 1818) on insanity, advocating not only "swinging" but also occupational therapy (including painting and sketching). Hallaran discharged his patients as soon as possible and was often agreeably surprised that their conduct in public remained acceptable (H. & M., p. 650).

Joseph Cox

William Hallaran

Thomas Arnold

One of the early British systematizers was Thomas Arnold (1742–1816) of Edinburgh, a pupil of Cullen. His two-volume text (1806) is primarily devoted to diagnosis. He took issue with the "splitters" of the French school, de Sauvages in particular, who enumerated a dozen species of melancholy and almost as many varieties of "demonomania." Using the word *insanity* in a very broad sense (to mean mental illness, whether severe or mild), Arnold divided the severe cases into two broad categories: *ideal* and *notional*. He defined "ideal" as indicating the presence of pervasively abnormal ideas or hallucinatory images. He divided the "notional insanities" (some of which resembled delusory conditions, others not) into so many subtypes as to establish himself, unwittingly, as a "splitter." Under "hypochondriacal/pathetic" type, he enumerated a dozen still smaller subtypes, which focus on what we would consider to be personality disorders. Indeed, there is a surprisingly close correspondence between Arnold's nosology and *DSM*'s "Axis II" categories of personality disorders:

DSM-IV *Terminology*	*Arnold's Terminology*
Schizoid personality	Misanthropic insanity
Paranoid personality	Suspicious insanity
Histrionic personality	Amorous insanity
Narcissistic personality	Arrogant insanity
Avoidant personality	Bashful insanity
Obsessive personality	Avaricious insanity
Depressive personality	Sorrowful insanity
Explosive personality	Irascible insanity

Arnold's description of "fanciful" insanity resembles our schizotypal personality. Furthermore, he noted that "all these species can be combined and interchanged with one another" (p. 245). He included a category for impulsive sexuality: "satyriasis" in a male; "nymphomania" in a female. Our concept of borderline personality can be found in Arnold's language by combining the jealous, lascivious, sorrowful, and irascible. Arnold added nothing new to his list of causative factors that had not been enumerated earlier: somatic injury, mental factors (such as overly intense application to one's business), the passions (his list is similar to Descartes'), and imbecility.

John Haslam

In the area of descriptive psychiatry John Haslam (1766–1844) provided clinical profiles of general paresis and schizophrenia that remain applicable to this day, almost two centuries later. His 1809 text, *Observations on Madness and Melancholy,* written when he was still medical director at Bethlem Hospital, is sometimes credited with containing the "first" cases of what we would identify as "schizophrenia," including what probably are the earliest described in children. But some of Arnold's vignettes (of "ideal insanity") might claim priority equally well—as might Pinel's cases, and so on, back at least to Willis' cases of adolescent "hebetude." Bethlem Hospital often received violent or even criminal patients, as is reflected in many of Haslam's clinical examples. One concerns a particularly "outrageous" boy of ten who:

> . . . contrived after two or three minutes of acquaintance to break a window and tear the frill of my shirt. . . . He never became attached to any unfamiliar animal: to these creatures his conduct was that of a brute: he oppressed the feeble, and avoided the society of those more powerful than himself. Whenever a cat approached him he plucked out his whiskers with wonderful rapidity. . . . After this operation he commonly threw the creature on the fire. . . . He felt no considerations for sex, and would as readily kick or bite a girl as a boy. (p. 204)

In 1810 Haslam published *Illustrations of Madness*, the first medical book devoted to the explication of a single case of insanity (H. & M., p. 634).[1] The patient in question, one James Tilly Matthews, was a paranoid psychotic man who believed that an "infernal machine" was controlling his life and subjecting him to all manner of excruciating tortures. These included, according in the patient's own words, "lobster-cracking, bomb-bursting, and brain lengthening." Matthews illustrated his plight with a drawing, depicting the persecutions to which he was supposedly subjected. (Matthews' machine presages the "influencing machine" of which Viktor Tausk's patient was to complain in the 1920s.)

Though many practitioners in mental health disciplines today know of the term "moral insanity" as a precursor of more recent concepts of antisociality or "psychopathy," fewer know of the term's author or of the different connotations it implied. James Cowles Prichard (1786–1848) studied in Edinburgh and then directed several hospitals in England. He was a systematizer like Arnold, though he followed Heinroth's division of mental life into thought, affect, and behavior ("understanding, feeling, and will,"

The "infernal machine" (that produced "bomb-bursting, lobster-cracking, lengthening of the brain") by which paranoid patient James Tilly Matthews imagined himself tortured. From Haslam, *Illustrations of Madness*, 1810.

[1] Haslam was familiar with the biographical accounts of the insane by Spiess (Chapter 5), mentioning that they were of great interest and "deserved to be rendered into English."

in the language of the day). Prichard spoke of aberrations of *feeling* as examples of *moral insanity,* by which he meant mental disorders involving "morale" (in the French sense) of one's spirits or general emotional state. He was not using the word in the way Benjamin Rush used it: as a label for the mental faculty that distinguishes the socially right from the socially evil (as when we today make a statement such as, "What he did was morally wrong"). Nevertheless, Prichard did lump all kinds of affectional disorders under this rubric: melancholy, personality disorders of various types, conditions characterized by lack of ordinary feelings of compassion, plus the commission of violent or improper acts against others. That manic-depression came under Prichard's (1835) umbrella of moral insanity is clear from his comment:

> A considerable proportion among the most striking instances of moral insanity are those in which a tendency to gloom or sorrow is the predominant feature. . . . A state of gloom and melancholy depression occasionally gives way . . . to an opposite condition of preternatural excitement. (p. 18–19)

Arthur Wigan

A novel theory about the origin of insanity was set forth by Arthur Wigan (1785–1847). Noting how similar the two cerebral hemispheres appear, Wigan postulated that they constitute, in effect, two separate brains, each with its own set of separate functions. He referred to this as the "duality of mind" in his 1844 monograph. To some extent he based this theory on autopsy findings in certain cases of "insanity," where disease was present in just one hemisphere or just one cerebellar hemisphere. Wigan postulated that one brain-half was superior in its powers, compared with the other (we would say *dominant*), and that this was the *rational* half. The other hemisphere was the *irrational* half. The notion of two cooperating hemispheres, each specialized for different functions (scientifically demonstrable only since the 1970s), was perhaps implicit in Bacon's *Imagination and Reason* 200 years before Wigan, now given the bare beginnings of anatomical support by Wigan's observations. The two streams of thought generated by the two brains could be present simultaneously. The rational hemisphere, as it monitored the content of the other side, could ascertain when certain ideas, images, or strange perceptions (hallucinations) were the irrational figments of our imagination. If the strength and function of the rational hemisphere were impaired in some way, then abnormalities of varying degrees would occur—all the way from *déjà vu* experiences (which Wigan called "sentiments of pre-existence") to outright insanity. Wigan gave credit to novelist Walter Scott for what we now refer to as *déjà vu,* for Scott described the experience of suddenly feeling as if one has been in precisely the same place before, seen the same things, etc. Wigan supplied illustrations of the effects of damage to the rational hemisphere from his own life as well as from clinical experience. For example, he knew of a young man who, after the death of his mother, saw visions of her in the night. These so terrified him that he traveled to France to be with his father—who, it turned out, was having similar visions of his dead wife. The man's brother, in a still different city, revealed that *he,* too, was tormented by the "ghost" of his mother. Wigan contended that this unusual experience could be understood as the result of the temporary disempowerment of the rational brain, due to the impact of the recent loss, such that the irrational brain's misperceptions were no longer recognized as unreal.

MENTAL ILLNESS AND CRIMINALITY

As time went on "moral insanity" took on the meaning of *antisociality,* much as *psychopathy* (which merely signified "mental disorder" for Kraepelin) later acquired the pejorative meanings of antisociality, moral insensitivity, and criminality. Prichard's contributions helped focus attention (but did not shed much light) on the controversial area of the relationship between mental illness and criminality: Under what circumstances is it meaningful to speak of a violent offender as being "mentally ill"?

This issue of the boundary between mental illness and criminality was taken up by a contemporary of Prichard: William A. F. Browne (1805–1885), superintendent of the Montrose Asylum in Edinburgh and former student of Esquirol at the Charenton Hospital. In 1837 Browne published a collection of lectures on the need for reform in mental institutions: *What Asylums Were, Are, and Ought to Be.* The fame earned him by the book led to his receiving a large sum from a patroness, Elizabeth Crichton, the founder of the Crichton Royal Institution. He accepted the post of medical superintendent in 1839. One of his humane reforms: drama therapy, in which mental patients performed plays within the walls of the asylum. The first play was performed in 1843, followed a year later by the publication of a magazine, written and edited by the patients (H. & M., p. 886). Dorothea Lynde Dix, the great American reformer, visited Browne in 1855. Browne's approach rested chiefly on the principles of *kindness* and *useful occupation;* his vision of the ideal—actually, *idyllic*—asylum is worth quoting at length:

> Conceive a spacious building resembling the palace of a peer, airy, elevated, and elegant, surrounded by extensive and swelling grounds and gardens. . . . The inmates all seem to be actuated by the common impulse of enjoyment, all are busy, and delighted by being so. . . . You meet the gardener, the common agriculturalist,

William A. F. Browne

the mower, the weeder. . . . Some of the inhabitants act as domestic servants, some as artisans, some rise to the rank of overseers.
The bakehouse, the laundry, the kitchen, are all well supplied
with indefatigable workers. . . . There is in this community no
compulsion, no chains, no corporal chastisement, simply because
these are proved to be less effectual means of carrying any point
than persuasion, emulation, and the desire of obtaining gratification. . . . You will [upon entering the buildings] pass those who
are fond of reading, drawing, music, scattered through handsome
suits of rooms, furnished chastely but beautifully. . . . In short, all
are so busy as to overlook, or are all so contented as to forget,
their misery. Such is a faithful picture of what may be seen in
many institutions, and of what might be seen in all, were asylums
conducted as they ought to be. (p. 229)

Very much an organicist (he was also a surgeon and had dedicated
his book to Andrew Combe, physician to the Belgian Royal Family),
Browne believed that the mind consisted of "four classes of powers:
instincts (impulses), sentiments (pride, hope . . .), intellectual powers
(reasoning), and observing powers (perception). The integrity of these
powers depends on the structure of the brain and its coverings." How
the connections are made between mind and matter was a fit subject
for study in Browne's view, although the ultimate link ". . . will perhaps
ever escape human research." Insanity was equated with impaired action of the mind, which was produced by an organic change in the
brain that caused conditions which "destroy property or the public
peace, and must be treated with isolation." Sometimes, however ". . .
the offender proves to be a delinquent: a criminal, rather than a lunatic—and the asylum becomes more of a penitentiary than a hospital."
Browne spoke of *delinquency* and *moral insanity* in the same breath—
i.e., more in the modern sense than in the neutral sense of "mental
illness involving the emotions."

Browne's diagnostic schema, borrowed from Arnold and Heinroth,
included four main categories: *idiocy* (non-development of the faculties), *fatuity* (obliteration of the faculties), *monomania* (derangement
in one or a few of the faculties), and *mania* (derangement of all the
faculties). Because *monomania* had so many subtypes (satyriasis, homicidal mania, suicidality, pride, avarice, etc.), it referred to what we
would now divide into general psychiatric conditions versus forensic
divisions.

In keeping with the times, Browne (1837) considered women to be
more susceptible to mental illness because their education was poorer,
which conduced to "sickly refinement, insipidity or absolute disease"
(p. 68). As a buffer against illness, marriage was recommended, "since
it acts as a barrier to our hidden sorrows and gives employment to our

noblest qualities" (p. 67). As an aside, Browne stated that there were more lunatics in America than in England: "The fact cannot be overlooked that the source of the tide of the population which has been flowing to America has been impure and poisoned" (p. 65).

The medicolegal consequences of insanity, adumbrated in Prichard's work, were examined again in the 1840s by Forbes Benignus Winslow (1810–1874) early in his illustrious career. His book, *The Plea of Insanity in Criminal Cases,* was published in 1843, the same year as the celebrated court case of Daniel McNaughton, a Glasgwegian woodturner, who, intending to kill Home Secretary Sir Robert Peel (whose name gave rise to the British derisive term for policemen—"peelers"), misfired and killed his private secretary Edward Drummond. Subjected to persecutory delusions that the local Tories "followed and pursued" him wherever he went, McNaughton was found "not guilty, on the ground of insanity" owing to psychiatric opinion that "the deed of murder flowed immediately from the delusions" (H. & M., p. 919). The outcome of this trial set the tone for decisions regarding criminal responsibility in the presence of legally defined insanity that has endured into the present.

Forbes Benignus Winslow

Commenting on the many subtleties with which the psychiatrist must grapple while serving as expert witness in the courtroom, Winslow noted that persons have been known to commit murder while in the state of somnambulism.[2] He argued: "If it could be satisfactorily proved that the person perpetrated the murder whilst in this state—if the fact was unequivocally established—then it ought to be considered as a good exculpatory plea." But he added, "It should never be forgotten that these cases are easily simulated."

Elsewhere in his monograph Winslow gave support to the same criteria now enshrined in the McNaughton Rules: Namely, that there must be "total" as opposed to "partial" insanity, such that at the time of commission of the crime, the accused was laboring under such defect of reason, from such disease of the mind, that he did not know the nature and quality of the act he was doing, or if he did know it, that he did not know he was doing what was wrong.

Winslow's final comments in his monograph presage the sentiments debated over the ensuing 150 years:

> I am ready to admit that if insanity be clearly established to exist, a *prima facie* case is made out in favor of the prisoner. But to believe that a person may be proved to be strange and wayward

[2] See Chapter 28 and articles on persons committing violent acts during sleep or somnambulism by Nofziger and Wettstein (1995) and Schenck and Mahowald (1995).

... ought of necessity to be exonerated ... is a doctrine as untenable as it is opposed to the safety and well being of society.

Here Winslow touches on the crux of the issue: Where do the rights of the individual cease in favor of the rights of society?

BRAID'S HYPNOSIS

The year of 1843 was important in the history of psychiatry for another reason: This was the year the Scottish physician James Braid (1795–1860) published his book, *Neurhypnology—Or the Rationale of Nervous Sleep,* in which we find the first use of the term *hypnosis* as well as a renewal of interest in the individual patient. Braid became intrigued with "mesmerism" after he attended a popular demonstration of its effects in Manchester in 1841. He became an effective hypnotizer, curing many patients who had milder nervous afflictions; in the process of which Braid incurred the wrath and skepticism of the medical establishment—much as had Mesmer before him. But Braid was conventional enough, and "magnetism" firmly enough accepted (at least on the Continent), that his methods were not altogether dismissed.

Because of the sober and rational tone of Braid's written works, he became the next important link in the chain alluded to earlier, which led from Mesmer to Freud. Braid rejected materialism, stating:

I look upon the brain simply as the *organ* of the mind ... [I hold] that the mind acts *on* matter and is acted on *by* matter. ... This, however, does not imply that mind is *a mere attribute of matter.* My thinking and willing and acting, so as to influence the mental and bodily condition of another, surely does not destroy our separate individuality. (p. 81)

In Part II of his book Braid provided details of cures he had effected through the use of hypnotism and suggestion on cases of hysterical blindness, deafness, and muteness, tics, paralyses, and spasms. He recognized the difference between cases in which there *was* organ pathology (whereby hypnosis was inefficacious) versus those in which there was no pathology (and hypnosis might be efficacious). Thus in the case of Elizabeth Atkinson, who was suffering from hysterical aphonia (there was no pathology in the vocal cords), Braid worked a cure—for which she thanked him profusely in a subsequent testimonial!

DARWIN'S INFLUENCE

Surely the most well-known man of science in 19th-century England was the biologist and naturalist Charles Darwin (1809–1882). His greatest work, *The Origin of Species by Natural Selection* (1859), had the effect of taking humankind out of the center of the animal kingdom, just as Copernicus had taken the earth out of the center of the universe. Humans are apes, albeit clever ones, not creatures tossed by God "as-is" on our planet some 6,000 years ago. As for the philosophy of creationism, Darwin's theory drove the last nail into the coffin of its respectability. In some circles, Darwin's views produced humility; in others, outrage. (At her husband's funeral, Mrs. Darwin hazarded that God would probably forgive her husband's offense.)

Into his theory of natural selection Darwin incorporated the work of his near-contemporary, Georg Mendel (1822–1884), whose experiments with peas had laid the groundwork for the laws of genetics. Now that the subject of heredity had passed from the level of hunches and prejudice (as permeated the psychiatric literature until well into the 19th century) to that of scientific endeavor, the degree of hereditary predisposition involved in the psychoses could be explored. The bulk of this work, however, was not initiated until the early 20th century. It became clear to Darwin that many behavior patterns in humans were analogous to patterns observed in animals. We are as we are because of the thousands of adaptations made, species-wide, to an ever-changing environment, over millions of years. These adaptations, which produced subtle changes in our genetic structure that afforded us advantages in the harsh game of survival, included gestures and facial expressions that reflected emotions, helped us gauge the friendly stranger from the hostile, and so forth. In 1872 Darwin published *Expression of the Emotions in Man & Animals,* demonstrating the mechanisms and the role of facial and bodily expressions in humans and higher animals (horses, cats, dogs).

Darwin also demonstrated the utility of the various emotional displays in relation to survival value. Small members of the cat family, for example, arch their backs and put their hairs *en fourrure* when approached by a dangerous enemy. They do so, according to Darwin's convincing argument, in order to make themselves appear as large and formidable as possible. Lions and tigers do not show this pattern because, presumably, they do not need to: Other animals are afraid of

Georg Mendel

A "cat terrified by a dog." From Darwin, *Expression of the Emotions in Man & Animals,* 1872.

A man expressing terror. From Darwin, 1872.

them, *as is*. Cats will spread their claws and "knead" the chests of their owners—as they did as kittens to maximize milk-flow from their mothers. In other words, *out of habit*, they show behavior that betokens a similarity of emotion (fondness for mother; fondness for master) even when the original, hereditarily maintained behavior can no longer produce the intended result (mother's milk). In situations of overwhelming distress, humans may curl up in a "fetal position," as would have brought the solace of mother's comforting to the infant, even though the distressed adult may be far way from any such source of comfort. The survival value of grief in a social species (like ours) consists in conveying a message to those nearby that the person is suffering and should be pitied or consoled, not taken advantage of or injured.

Most people possess innate mechanisms for expressing and understanding (having empathy for) such displays. Persons lacking the ability to understand the emotions of others or, worse yet, who recognize but remain unmoved by others' sorrow, are considered abnormal and given labels, such as "social-emotional learning disability" or "psychopath." Darwin understood the role of *associations* in these processes— of which Pavlov was to make so much toward the end of the century. One might say that students of theory and therapy received much of their impetus from this phase of Darwin's work as well.

The widespread interest in heredity during the third quarter of the 19th century inspired Sir Francis Galton (1822– 1911), a cousin of Darwin, to examine the influence of heredity on intelligence. His treatise, *Hereditary Genius: An Inquiry into Its Laws and Consequences,* appeared in 1869, and was endorsed by Darwin. Galton created a "bell curve" with seven levels on either side of the median. (Standardized intelligence tests had not yet been created.) His measures, necessarily crude, depended on such factors as, on the high side, unusual mathematical ability (e.g., being a "First Wrangler" in mathematics at Cambridge) or eminence in various professions; and degrees of mental retardation on the low side. Using the population

Expressions of sadness. From Darwin, 1872.

statistics that were available to him, and some elementary probability equations, Galton concluded that 84% of people fell in the two middle portions (*a/A* and *b/B*) on the low/high sides of the midline; his next two groups (*c/C* and *d/D*) took up 15.5%; a very thin margin of "outliers" comprised his remaining three groups: the geniuses (*E, F, G*) and the imbeciles (*e, f, g*). This is a much more compressed curve than the gaussian curve we are all familiar with, which places 68% as "average," 11% above average, 11% below average, and 5% each in the brilliant or retarded categories. Galton offered examples of family pedigrees that demonstrated how people clustered in one group or another: Simply put, average people tended to have average relatives; men and women of eminence had many unusually gifted relatives.

Galton, whose avowed purpose was to contribute to the eventual betterment of humankind, called his study "eugenics." The whole science fell into disrepute 70 years later, when the Nazis used eugenics to support their myth of racial superiority. Although statistical techniques applied to intelligence differences in monozygotic versus dizygotic twins, a century after Galton, have shown that a portion of intelligence is under genetic control, the determinants of intelligence have proven to be much more complex (there are many more intervening variables) than Galton envisioned.

Henry Maudsley

In this same third-quarter of the 19th century, Henry Maudsley (1835–1918) published *Pathology of the Mind* (1879). Regarded as an important textbook at the time, its assumptions are materialistic and, for the most part, anti-psychological, as was Griesinger's text of a few years earlier. Insofar as possible, Maudsley based his nosology on physical etiology, ascribing the various mental conditions to such bodily troubles as anemia, infections, and toxins. While it is true that Maudsley viewed mental disease as primarily organic in nature (Z., 1941), he was not wholly blind to the psychological, nor was he opposed to introspection. He devoted a long chapter to the "insanity of early life," which antedated Emminghaus' monograph on child psychiatry by 20 years. In this chapter he described children with hallucinations, epilepsy, fits of involuntary laughter, "cataleptoid" states of mystical abstraction (i.e., assumed by some people to be caused by supernatural forces), and melancholia of such severity as to lead to suicide. Some of the suicide cases, he admitted, were driven by fear of parental punishment for getting poor grades in school—a psychological etiology, to be sure.

In keeping with the Victorian era, there is an intensely moralistic tone to Maudsley's comments on licentiousness and promiscuity in certain adolescents. As for "the degenerate acts of the insane child," he argued that, "there is the rapid undoing of what has been slowly done through the ages; the disruption . . . of faculties which have been tediously acquired; the dissolution of what has been the gain of a long process of evolution" (p. 295). Here Maudsley's remarks anticipated those of neurologist John Hughlings-Jackson. But before we turn our attention to his contributions, a word about Maudsley's view of dreams is in order.

Considering his biological bias, it is remarkable that Maudsley's first chapter discussed the nature of sleep and dreaming. He recounted several of his own dreams as well as his associations to them, either from events of the preceding day or even from his childhood. According to Maudsley, dreams partake of "ancestral modes of thought" (which we now call "primary process" thought), whereby the imagination gains ascendancy over reason. He was also aware that dreams sometimes incorporated sensations that are impinging upon the dreamer, as though "not all the senses are equally asleep." He cited an example of how a Dr. Gregory, "having gone to sleep with a bottle of hot water at his feet, dreamt he was walking up the crater of Mt. Etna" (p. 28). In France Alfred Maury had actually conducted experiments where someone tickled or pinched him as he lay asleep so that he could determine the effects of these sensations upon his dreams. Freud was later to understand these phenomena as subserving the function of "preserving sleep" (a hypothesis that is no longer accepted).

It does appear that Maudsley, whom Freud cited (1900, p. 612) only to support his contention that "mind" is larger than consciousness, had an inchoate awareness of many aspects of dreaming elucidated by Freud a generation later, even if Maudsley remained unaware of the conflict-oriented and sexual components. Maudsley clearly demonstrated a measure of psychological awareness in recognizing that the dreams of childhood are "sometimes of a painful character, being accompanied by great terror and distress" (p. 47). Though he felt these were usually provoked by teething, indigestion, or other purely bodily causes, he understood that the suffering was interpreted during sleep according to whatever forms of terror and affliction with which the child's imagination had been indoctrinated. Thus resulting dreams contain visions of lions or tigers or wicked men who have come to carry off naughty children. As Maudsley charitably worded it, "The emotional life preponderates much over the intellectual life in children . . . [and] they are consequently very susceptible to fear, just as savages are" (p. 47).

John Hughlings-Jackson

The Darwinian concept of evolution influenced neurologists of the late 19th century, the most outstanding of whom in England was John Hughlings-Jackson (1835–1911). He devoted particular attention to the condition of epilepsy, probably because his wife suffered from partial or "localized" seizures (which we still refer to as "Jacksonian"). Evolution, as it applied to the nervous system, manifested itself in three ways: Structure and function spanned a spectrum from the most to the least *organized;* from the most to the least *complex;* from the most *automatic* to the most *voluntary.* The lowest (spinal cord, medullary, etc.) are already highly organized at birth, whereas the highest (cortical) centers continue to grow more organized throughout life.

In his *Croonian Lectures* (1884), Hughlings-Jackson stated that nervous system disease only produces "negative" symptoms that reflect the degree of *dissolution* (the opposite of evolution); the so-called positive symptoms (hallucinations, illusions, extravagant conduct) are merely the outcome of the activities of parts of the nervous system that are *untouched* by the pathological process of dissolution. These activities are the products of the lower levels of evolution that still remain intact. In other words, there is survival of the (still) "fittest" neurological layers (he borrowed the notion of survival of the fittest from the writings of philosopher Herbert Spencer).

Thus he contended that the illusions of the insane are caused *not* by disease but by the isolated activities of those centers that are still functioning. (This is a most casuistical argument! Of course, disease "causes" the symptoms, rendering the top-most layers inoperative and forcing the patient to function from the more automatic, less modulated "lower layers.") In alcoholic intoxication, for example, the most complex, least organized *cortex* gives out first; the most organized, least complex centers hold out the longest (in a drunken stupor, one still breathes).

Here there is a strong analogy to the concept that higher centers *inhibit* otherwise automatic actions of the lower centers, which was articulated by Freud in his *Project for a Scientific Psychology* (1895). For Freud, the executive, controlling parts of the brain—the ego—consists of neurons capable of inhibiting, at least transiently, the potential actions that the lower reflex centers would initiate if left to their own devices. Stripped of ego, the organism behaves in an *unmodulated* and *impulsive* fashion, not unlike the behavior described by Hughlings-Jackson's notion of *dissolution* and Freud's *disinhibition.*

Hughlings-Jackson encountered conceptual difficulty when he tried to incorporate a view of *consciousness* into his theory. He saw memory, reason, and emotion as "artificially distinguished aspects of consciousness." Furthermore, he contended that consciousness attends to only the activities of the highest (least organized, most complex) centers. To what extent consciousness permeates the lower "layers" was uncertain. The idea of *un*conscious mental states made Hughlings-Jackson uncomfortable, though he was willing to grant that "less consciousness attends the most automatic, highly organized centers." "Insanity" (he still used the term generically for all mental disorders) resulted from the dissolution of the higher centers. For example, aphasia (partial) involved the loss of voluntary (complex) language and retention of emotional (automatic) language.

In *On the Correlation of Consciousness and Organization*, Thomas Laycock (1812–1876), under whom Hughlings-Jackson worked

Thomas Laycock

for a time, took the position that consciousness was a reflection of "continuous cerebration" (i.e., of the brain's continual working), much of which never reached the "mind." Here *mind* is equated with that of which we are fully conscious. Laycock also noted the then popular view that "every mental state has a nervous [meaning *brain*] state for its immediate antecedent"—a view espoused by Hughlings-Jackson—but cautioned that "we are wholly ignorant of the characteristics of these nervous states." Laycock introduced an interesting evolutionary twist to the notion of consciousness when he stated that self-love, sexual love, and love of offspring are necessary implants in conscious life, since upon these varieties of love depend the survival of any species and its individual members.

Though the emphasis in 19th-century British psychiatry was on the broader issues and more common categories of conditions, some attention was given to exotic conditions that were rarer and did not fit well into the traditional nosology. For example, Winslow devoted a large text to *Obscure Diseases of the Brain* (1861), which included examples of elective mutism, persecutory delusions triggered by disturbing dreams, compulsive "thinking aloud," and many others. He also described cases of bulimia and severer forms of anorexia nervosa under the heading "refusal of food." In some patients the refusal was made on the grounds that the food was poisonous; in others, that they pursued a course of hunger because a "higher power" had ordered them to fast until death. (These might have been examples of anorexia complicated by a coexisting condition of schizophrenia or other psychosis.) More mundane cases of what we would include in the disorder of anorexia nervosa were described by Sir William Gull (1868), who carried forward the work of Morton. Both authors, along with Ernest Lasègue, drew attention to the diagnostic triad of fasting, amenorrhea, and hyperactivity ("wasting without lassitude").

At all events, by the latter part of the 19th century many of the conditions we encounter today and that are defined in the *Diagnostic and Statistical Manual* (*DSM-IV*, 1994) were already known and described, though often with different labels.

Chapter 9

NINETEENTH-CENTURY AMERICA:
MODERN PSYCHIATRY EMERGES
WITH TECHNOLOGY

In surveying the history of psychiatry in America and Europe, we find several points along the time continuum when the pace of change suddenly quickened or when the philosophy of treatment suddenly took a new, more humane, course. The reasons behind these abrupt changes are hard to pinpoint; they seem to lie buried underneath the welter and confusion of historical events, some of which related directly to medical science; others, to developments that had no obvious bearing on the field.

One such historical influence, which took place over a stretch of years, was the Protestant Reformation. This, coupled with the invention of the printing press in the mid-15th century, ultimately dispelled people's superstitions about witches and devils and introduced more realistic and humane ways of thinking about the mentally ill. Hitherto demonized, the mentally ill were now seen as suffering human beings, the worthy recipients of compassion, not execution. The advanced thinking of this new mentality could now be disseminated far more quickly and to a far greater audience than ever before, thanks to inexpensive books—once treasured possessions of the learned and wealthy few, now the property of an ever more literate populace.

Another steep ascent in medical/psychiatric progress occurred in the late 1830s and early 1840s. The use of non-restraint was spreading; better hospitals were being built; more rapid exchange of ideas was taking place among the savants of the field. As we review them a century and a half later, the language and methods of psychiatry were beginning to look "modern."

What was behind this turning point? My best guess is the *steam engine* and the *railroad* (the same railroad Phineas Gage was helping to expand when the tamping rod backfired through his skull). James Watt had perfected the design of the steam engine in 1775, but in 1795 the first railroad, which was constructed in England, was still horse-drawn. In 1832 the first steam-driven railroad was opened in St. Etienne in France. The first steamship to cross the Atlantic was the *Savannah* in 1818 (the trip took 26 days).

These changes brought about dramatic improvements in communication. A person with a new idea in Boston could give a talk to an audience in Washington, D.C. or the Carolinas in a day or two rather than a week or two; an American expert in the care of the mentally ill could exchange ideas with colleagues in England or France within weeks rather than months.

In 19th-century America psychiatry was just beginning to enter the medical arena as a legitimate field of inquiry. Whereas America is now the major source of new knowledge in the mental health disciplines—and is now the world's teacher (this has been so since World War II)—in the 1800s America was the student. Mainly we learned from physicians in England, France, and Germany. We modeled our psychiatric institutions after European ones, such as that of Tuke's York Retreat. We used a nosology borrowed from Pinel, Prichard, or Griesinger. Treatment methods were copied from, or inspired by, the techniques used in England, Ireland, or Western European countries. One notes a certain self-consciousness. For example, the language in our texts, especially from the first half of the century, was mellifluous, even grandiloquent—as if to demonstrate, in no uncertain terms, that we in "the colonies" could muster as fine, or fancier, a brand of English as that of our elder brethren in Great Britain.

A NUMBER OF "FIRSTS"

The first American psychiatrist of prominence, and the first to write a medical text (in 1812) devoted solely to the mentally ill, was Benjamin Rush (1745–1813), known also as the one physician to have been a signatory of the Declaration of Independence. Recognizing that the brain was the "seat of the mind," he believed that psychopathology stemmed from abnormalities of the cerebral blood vessels, as exemplified by mania, which represented an inflammation of those vessels. Rush coined new diagnostic terms, such as "manicula" for mild (hypomanic) manic-like disorders and "tristemania" for depressive states in which patients blamed or disparaged themselves—in contrast to melancholia, in which "the error

Bejamin Rush, 1745–1813. Courtesy Independence National Historical Park Collection

of mind extended to objects external to the patient" (p. 74).

Rush also parodied terminological "splitters," like his teacher Cullen, by making up a whole catalogue of different phobias: Among them were dirt phobias, insect phobias, and even "home phobias"—the dislike of the home by men who much preferred the tavern (H. & M., p. 665). Rush's recommendations for treatment were somewhat paradoxical: Although he advocated the removal of chains, at the same time he employed intimidation measures of swinging (described earlier), total immobilization in the "tranquilizing chair," and sudden ducking in water. These barbaric methods were legacies dating back to the time of Celsus, when it was assumed that the insane were being "stubborn" and could be brought to their senses via some pain-inducing treatment. Rush still paid homage to the humoural theory through his use of emetics, purgatives, and bloodletting.

Rush's "Tranquilizer," which enforced the most complete restraint of a patient ever devised. From Hunter and Macalpine, 1963, p. 671. Reprinted with permission.

The first psychiatric book printed in America was actually an 1808 New York reprint of an English work: *A View of the Nervous Temperament* by Thomas Trotter (1760–1832). Trained in Edinburgh, Trotter wrote his medical thesis on alcoholism, which he believed should be considered a disease of the mind rather than merely an example of degeneracy. He associated the condition with civilization, believing that "the savage tribes of the new continent, when compared with European manners, are observed to be chaste, temperate and abstemious" (p. 16). Also inculpated as causes of mental illness were tea, coffee, overwork, the reading of trashy novels, the clothes fashions of his day (either too little or too much), and worse still: stage-dramas, which "communicate poison in a new way: such poison as has no antidote on the shelves of the apothecary" (p. 89). Prudery aside, Trotter made a very sensible suggestion regarding the treatment of alcoholism: the immediate cessation of drinking as opposed to a gradual reduction in alcoholic intake. He also understood the properties of alcohol: that the initially stimulating effects are followed by sedative and narcotic effects.

Thomas Trotter

Trotter's work influenced Samuel Woodward (1787–1850), one of the founders of the Hartford Retreat. He was also the first president of the Association of Medical Superintendents of American Institutions of the Insane—the forerunner of the American Psychiatric Association. Woodward had also established, in 1858, the first hospital for the "cure of intemperance," The New York State Inebriate Asylum (H. & M., p. 588). The first meeting of what was to become the American Psychiatric Association took place on October 16, 1844, in Philadel-

Samuel Woodward

Amariah Brigham
American Journal of
Insanity

phia. The most well-known (in our time) of the 13 founders, besides Woodward himself, are Thomas Kirkbride, Amariah Brigham, Isaac Ray, Pliny Earle, and Luther Bell.

Amariah Brigham was the first editor of the *American Journal of Insanity,* which also began in 1844, and which later became *The American Journal of Psychiatry.* One of the articles in the first issue of the 1844 journal was devoted to "illustrations of insanity from the histories of distinguished men and by the writings of poets and novelists" (no author was listed). The article expressed a view popularly held at the time: "Insanity is a disease particularly incident to persons remarkable for their talent or genius. Dryden correctly says: 'Great wits are sure to madness near allied / And thin partitions do their bounds divide.'" Examples offered included Fielding, Pope, Dryden, Tasso, Byron, Cellini, Rousseau, and Dr. Johnson. I suspect most of these men were, at worst, a bit "melancholic" at times, but by no means psychotic, so here again the term *insanity* was being used in an excessively broad and non-specific way. It should be noted that 1844 was just a year after the McNaughton case; it would still be many years before *insane* dropped out of psychiatric parlance altogether, to become purely a legal term.

THE BEGINNINGS OF FORENSIC PSYCHIATRY

Isaac Ray

Isaac Ray (1807–1881) was the most widely known and highly respected psychiatrist in the middle of the century. He had been superintendent of the State Hospital for the Insane in Augusta, Maine; later, of Butler Hospital in Providence, Rhode Island. Praised for his humanism and enlightened eclecticism, Ray was nonetheless a staunch advocate of restraint, asserting that Europeans tended to be obedient, whether insane or not, and therefore safer to trust with a policy of non-restraint. Americans, however, because of their "love of liberty," were not apt to be so compliant (Z., p. 387). His 1838 treatise, *Medical Jurisprudence of Insanity,* was the most important American work on forensic psychiatry of its time. He bemoaned the lack of a standard nomenclature, for want of which reliable statistics—such as might have shed light on problematical forensic issues—could not be accumulated (H. & M., p. 974). Indeed, the problem of distinguishing real from feigned insanity posed tremendous difficulties in Ray's time (here nothing has changed![1]), though Ray confidently stated: "Those who have been long-

---

[1] A controversial experiment by Rosenhan (1973) reported that actors pretending to hallucinate were seen by psychiatrists in an emergency unit—and hospitalized. Though Rosenhan felt this error reflected on the acumen of the doctors, their behavior was consistent with that of responsible professionals who do not *expect* to be duped by actors in the course of their normal work (Maher, 1991).

est acquainted with the manners of the insane . . . assure us that insanity is not easily feigned, and consequently that no attempt at imposture can long escape the efforts of one properly qualified to expose it" (p. 305).

Ray was also aware of the absurdity of many claims of "recovery," whereby patients with recurrent manic excitement were hospitalized, calmed down in a few weeks, released as recovered, only to be readmitted shortly thereafter, with the same course repeating itself. Writing on "partial moral mania," Ray gave examples of pyromania, described as "a morbid propensity to incendiarism where the mind though otherwise sound, is borne on by an invisible power, to the commission of this crime" (p. 177). Certain murderers were considered to show what Esquirol had call *"manie homicide"* [homicidal mania], which, for Ray, was a "propensity to destroy; where the individual without provocation . . . imbrues his hands in the blood of others; oftener than otherwise, of the partner of his bosom, of the children of his affection . . ." (p. 179).

Ray also addressed paradoxical issues concerning capital punishment when applied to the "insane." Some "monomaniacs" commit murder, Ray explained, hoping to be caught and executed, especially when, out of religious compunctions, suicide was even more repugnant to them than murder. In such cases, Ray concluded that "nothing can be more absurd than to inflict the very punishment which the delusion of the monomaniac often impels him to seek: what is it but to convert a dreadful punishment into the dearest boon the earth can offer?" (p. 241).

Toward the end of Ray's life the legal climate had changed considerably in the direction of leniency, partly due to his humanizing influence. For example, a superior court in New Hampshire ruled that if a criminal act was the product of "mental illness" (a softer term than *insanity,* though just as vague), then "criminal intent" could not be formed. This set in motion a process that culminated a century later in the 1954 Durham decision (in a District of Columbia murder case), in which mental illness was held to "diminish criminal responsibility" (A. & S., p. 349)—an issue that has been hotly debated ever since. Ray noted other intriguing examples of this lenient tendency, such as that of the alcoholic ship's captain who developed delirium tremens upon sudden cessation from drinking, and in this delirious state, killed his Second Mate. The court saw fit to excuse him on the grounds that his insanity was secondary to the effect of *not* drinking, whereas had he been under the influence of alcohol, he would have been deemed culpable!

Probably the most celebrated psychiatric case in 19th-century America, and surely one of the most fascinating, was that of Phineas Gage. A 25-year-old railroad foreman working in Vermont, Gage had been drilling holes in rock with blasting powder in order to prepare the

Phineas Gage

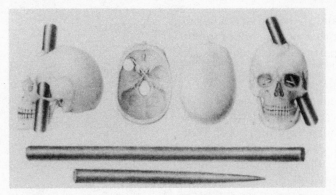

The skull of the railroad worker, Phineas Gage, through which an iron bar passed in a nonfatal, yet personality-altering, accident involving blasting powder. From Dr. Henry Bigelow, *Dr. Harlow's Case of Recovery from the Passage of an Iron Bar through the Head*, 1850.

ground for tracks. On a fall day in 1848, in a moment of distraction, Gage tamped some powder before his assistant had added sand. An explosion ensued, sending a three-and-a-half foot missile-shaped tamping rod shooting straight through Gage's skull and landing some yards away! Gage miraculously survived the accident: He was no more than momentarily stunned, in fact, but afterwards underwent a drastic change in personality. The story of his recovery was told in a brief article by the surgeon Henry Bigelow (1850). A more extensive description of his personality change was recounted in 1868 by his doctor, John Harlow, and repeated recently by Damasio (1994), who did a computer analysis of Gage's skull to ascertain the precise areas of the brain that had been ablated by the injury.

Formerly an "efficient and capable man," whom others regarded as shrewd, smart, and temperate in his habits, Gage, though still possessed of all his ordinary faculties, became:

> . . . fitful, irreverent, indulging at times in the grossest of profanities which was not previously his custom, manifesting but little deference for his fellows, impatient of restraint or advice when it conflicts with his desires, at times pertinaciously obstinate, yet capricious and vacillating, devising many plans of future operation, which are no sooner arranged than they are abandoned.

This profound personality change, which persisted until Gage's death (of *status epilepticus*) in 1861, has been shown by the Damasios to have been in response to lesions in the ventral and medial sectors of both frontal lobes. They theorized that this region of the brain apparently subserves social decisions and, to that extent, moral choices.

Though Gage's story is by far the most dramatic example of frontal lobe damage leading to personality change, other examples have been reported, including that of a 37-year-old man who, in 1888, sustained a severe penetrating frontal fracture after falling from a fourth-storey window (L. Welt, 1888; cited by Levin et al., 1991). This man, like Gage, having been honest and industrious, now became aggressive, malicious, disrespectful, and paranoid. The case of Phineas Gage, and other cases like it, have inspired research investigating centers of empathy, compassion, and moral decision-making. Still, it has taken over a century to reach the technological and scientific levels where meaningful correlations can be identified.[2]

INSTITUTIONAL REFORMS AND IMPROVEMENTS

Beginning in the 1840s, a powerful and positive influence was exerted not by a learned psychiatrist, but by a dedicated Boston schoolmistress: Dorothea Lynde Dix (1802–1887). When in 1841, at the age of 39, Miss Dix conducted the Sunday school service for the female convicts in a Boston jail, she was ". . . so appalled by the indiscriminate mixing of insane with criminals, healthy with sick, herded together in terrible conditions, that she from then on devoted herself to the cause of the insane" (H. & M., p. 911). In moving words, she described the miserable conditions of the institutionalized mentally ill, as she addressed the state legislature in Massachusetts in 1843 and the general assembly in North Carolina and Congress in Washington, D.C.—both in 1848. She traveled to England in 1854, met with Samuel Tuke at the York Retreat, and then surveyed the terrible conditions of the asylums in Scotland. By taking the night train to London, she managed to put her criticisms of these asylums before the Home Secretary in London before her Scottish adversaries could intervene. In 1855 she was commissioned to survey the "lunatic asylums" in Scotland and ultimately to initiate significant improvements in those facilities. Here is a sample of her rhetoric from a memorial to the general assembly of North Carolina in 1848:

> I come not to seek personal claims nor to seek individual benefits; I appear as an advocate of those who cannot plead their own cause; I come as a friend of those who are deserted, oppressed and desolate. In the Providence of God, I am the voice of the maniac whose piercing cries from the dreary dungeons of your jails penetrate not—your Halls of Legislation. I am the Hope of the poor crazed beings who pine in the cells, and stalls and cages, and waste-rooms of your poor-houses. I am the Revelation of hundreds of wailing, suffering creatures, hidden in your private dwellings,

Dorothea Dix, 1802–1887. Courtesy National Library of Medicine

[2] In our own time Solyom (1987) reported a most unusual case of a young man with intractable obsessive-compulsive disorder, who had attempted suicide by shooting himself through the mouth. He survived the injury and, in effect, "cured" his OCD, apparently by interrupting certain basal ganglion tracts with his self-inflicted injury—what could be called an "auto-leucotomy." His underlying personality, however, remained unchanged.

Pennsylvania's Central Hospital for the Insane. From Thomas Kirkbride, *On the Construction, Organization and General Arrangements of Hospitals for the Insane*, 1880.

and in pens and cabins—shut out, cut off from all healing influences, from all mind-restoring cares.

As a result of the reforms set in motion by Dix in her compassion and determination, by the time of her retirement in 1880, the number of institutions for the mentally ill and retarded had increased from 13 to 123, of which 32 had been founded directly by her efforts (H. & M., p. 911).[3]

One of the men who "caught the fever" from Dix's impassioned pleas was Thomas Kirkbride (1809–1883), who became the "guiding spirit of model-hospital building" in the third quarter of the 19th century (A. & S., p. 405). In his book, *On the Construction, Organization and General Arrangements of Hospitals for the Insane* (1880), Kirkbride provided minute details about every facet of the ideal psychiatric hospital (including architectural plans), much as Chiarugi had done a century ago on behalf of the hospital in Florence, of which he became director. Among Kirkbride's concluding remarks were the following:

> The contents of this volume are a contribution . . . toward securing a more elevated sentiment, and a greater harmony of thought and action in regard to the insane, as well as a more just appreciation of the objects and the work of institutions for their care and treatment. These institutions can never be dispensed with . . . without retrograding to the conditions of a past period, with all the inhumanity and barbarity connected with it. (p. 300)

In the last quarter of the century, a number of prominent hospital superintendents began to have second thoughts about the rate of "curability" of their patients. There was greater recognition that some of the earlier optimism in this regard had been unwarranted because it had been founded on discharge statistics based on "cases," without regard to how often those cases reflected *the very same person,* admitted over and over again due to "periodic insanity."

---

[3] Readers interested in further material on the life of Dorothea Dix should consult the excellent biography by Gollaher (1995).

Luther Bell (1806–1892), superintendent of McLean Hospital near Boston, distrusted statistics altogether. Toward the end of his life, he regretfully concluded that the "cure" rate was not 75% or 50%, but some lower number. Pliny Earle (1809–1892), superintendent of Northampton, Massachusetts State Hospital, agreed with Bell. In his 1887 book, *The Curability of Insanity,* he expressed the hope that *accurate* statistics would rectify the situation by distinguishing between *persons* and *cases.* Recognizing that the true cure rate of persons who never needed re-admission, while lower than once believed, was still substantial, he suggested that "the sooner the person attacked with insanity is placed under curative treatment, the greater the prospect for recovery" (p. 63).

Luther Bell

Pliny Earle

Throughout the century there was increasing awareness that "moral causes"—what we would call social or emotional factors—underlay many cases of mental illness, that there were more variables to etiology than those of heredity, climate, and bodily abnormalities, such as "inflammation of the cerebral vessels." In *Remarks on the Influence of Mental Cultivation upon Health,* Amariah Brigham (1798–1849), focused on these factors, enumerating "pecuniary embarrassment, domestic griefs, disappointments in love, erroneous education, overexertion of the mind, and religious anxiety" (1832, p. 74). In sympathy with Rousseau and Trotter that civilization contributed to these woes, Brigham believed that the "noble savage" was somehow immune to insanity. Citing Esquirol, Brigham noted that certain women who bore children during the time of the French Revolution seemed to transmit their nervousness to their offspring, who were supposedly extremely susceptible to mental illness.

Amariah Brigham

Brigham also wrote extensively on the ill effects of excessive devotion to religion, especially when heavily laden with rites and rituals. He endorsed a much more austere kind of religion, stating in his 1835 book, *Observations on the Influence of Religion upon the Health and Physical Welfare of Mankind:*

> Religious sentiment is innate in man, but often acts blindly and to the injury of man; Christ established no ceremonies at all; God has no supernatural dealings with men . . . and the religious fanaticism of the revivalists is not essential to Christian faith or conduct; that numerous meetings for religious purposes, night meetings, camp meetings, protracted meetings etc. injure the health and may cause insanity. (p. 330)

Pasted into my copy of Brigham's book are undated old newspaper clippings, perhaps of the period, attesting to an "epidemic of religious suicides and murders." One story tells of a farmer in Ohio who, while seized by religious madness, drowned two of his children, suffocated his wife, prayed "long and fervently," and then went about his work. It was probably unfair to single out religion as the culprit in these cases, given what has become so apparent to us in the 20th century: Fanaticism can lead to misery and bloodshed, whatever flag waves over it, be it religious fundamentalism, bigotry, political extremism, or ardent nationalism. Only a few of the people caught up in these movements are mentally ill in any meaningful sense of the term; instead, the majority are ordinary people—often in hard circumstances, with poor adaptive capacities—who lose their moral sense under the pressure of the group or of a charismatic leader, becoming capable of a viciousness otherwise foreign to their character. We think of underlying psychosis or "insanity" because of the egregiousness of the resulting acts—when the real trouble, where there is any psychiatric trouble at all, lies in the *personality*.

CONTRIBUTIONS FROM NEUROLOGISTS

Silas Weir Mitchell

In the latter half of the century many of the contributions to American psychiatry came from neurologists. Two of the most influential were Silas Weir Mitchell and George Miller Beard. Mitchell (1829–1914), who had also served in the Civil War as a surgeon, wrote on *Diseases of the Nervous System, Especially in Women* (1881) and also on the topic of "double consciousness" in a later book, *Mary Reynolds: A Case of Double Consciousness* (1889). His therapeutic regimen consisted of simple and sensible measures, including "rest cure" (for which he was most well known), good nutrition, comfort, and removal from the pressures of work. These measures, basic to any adequate mental hospital, would be subsumed nowadays under the headings of providing beneficial *milieu therapy* in the *sanctuary* of the institution.

The case of Mary Reynolds was not quite like the multiple personality cases that have attracted so much attention in recent years, although her behavior did present strong evidence of dissociation. Born in England in 1793, Mary moved to Pennsylvania as a child. Until 18, she was noted to be avoidant, melancholic, and devoted to reading her Bible throughout the day. But at 18 she began to have episodes of "hysterical attacks," which were preceded by a prolonged sleep. She awakened from her first deep sleep "deaf and blind for five weeks," after which time these senses were somehow restored to normal functioning. After a second attack, she awakened bereft of all memory of her past and without the ability to speak. She did not recognize any kinship to her siblings or parents and was like an infant who had to learn language from scratch. She did manage to learn to read and write within a few weeks, though with a handwriting somewhat different from that which she formerly used.

More strikingly, her personality underwent a dramatic change, and she was now cheerful, prankish, and fearless before the bears and snakes of the Pennsylvania woods. Following another two months, she awakened from an 18-hour sleep as her former melancholic, fearful self, well aware of her family ties and completely unaware of the other state through which she had just passed. These switches recurred periodically until she reached the age of 36, after which she remained in her buoyant state, though more subdued and less prankish than in her previous episodes. She gradually accepted her family as her own, taught school, lived with her nephew, and died at 61. Case histories of that era included no information about possible abuse, so we have no way of knowing whether her childhood was unusually severe compared with her age-mates, as is so regularly recorded with multiple personality patients of our time.

The other eminent neurologist, George Miller Beard (1839–1883), achieved greater fame, if less respect, than Mitchell for his somatic treatments based on the use of electricity. A fellow of the New York Academy of Science, Beard introduced the term "neurasthenia," which had a meaning similar to Whytt's "nervous exhaustion" of the previous century. Disappointed with the then available medications for nervous conditions, Beard turned to the various forms of electricity to provide a "tonic" for patients who were depressed, lethargic, lacking in energy, "burnt out" (to use our modern term) from overwork, or lacking in sexual vitality. His 1875 book, *A Practical Treatise on the Medical and Surgical Uses of Electricity,* was enormously popular, as were the machines he described for delivering electrical stimulation. Beard provided a history of the subject, mentioning the use of static electricity, which he called "franklinization," that had fallen out of favor by mid-century. He cited "voltaic-galvanic" stimulation, in use since 1791, and "faradic" stimulation, named after Michael Faraday, who had introduced magnetic induction of electricity in 1831. Discussion of the advantages and disadvantages of each form of electrical stimulation occupies several chapters.

Beard contended that galvanic current produced muscle contraction in some cases where faradic had failed; however, faradic stimulation was less apt to cause unpleasant side effects. Illustrated pages of the "motor points" of the human body accompanied the text and the pictures resemble the acupuncture points of ancient Chinese medicine. The belief underlying these treatments was that the body could be "recharged" or "reenergized," much as we now recharge our cellular phones and hand-held drills. There were hardly any conditions or areas of the body where Beard's machines could

George Miller Beard

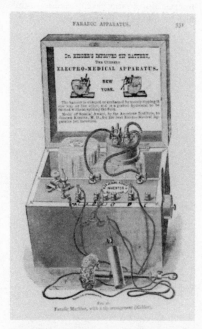

A mid-nineteenth-century American faradic machine used by George Beard to cure all manner of emotional illnesses and and nervous conditions. From Beard, *Practical Treatise on the Medical and Surgical Uses of Electricity,* 1875.

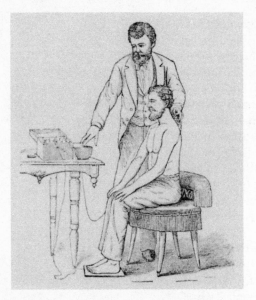

"General Faradization—application to the spine. The hand of the operator is on the metallic tube, in a position to increase or decrease the current as may be needed." From Beard, 1875.

not work their wonders. He gave examples of cures in cases of mania, menopausal insanity, dizziness, paralysis, atrophy, ataxia, hysteria, as well as somatic disorders of the joints, skin, larynx, heart, lungs, digestive organs, and the reproductive system.

Though long ago discredited as a kind of mechanical snake oil, electrical treatment was quite the rage in the 19th century and might be said to have kept alive the tradition of biological psychiatry, which has become as respectable in our day as it is impressive. In the 1870s, however, anyone with the price of Beard's book, or of C. M. Haynes' *Elementary Principles of Electro-Therapeutics* (two dollars, postpaid), could learn the rudiments of the trade and set himself up as an electrotherapist.

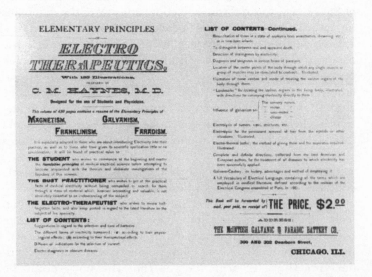

Advertisement at the end of Beard's book, illustrating that anyone with the $2 to purchase Dr. Haynes' text could present himself as an electrotherapist. From Beard, 1875.

Chapter 10

ITALY, RUSSIA, AND SPAIN IN THE

NINETEENTH CENTURY:

CONTRIBUTIONS FROM LESS

ACTIVE AREAS

Psychiatry in the 19th century was still dominated by the French-, German-, and English-speaking countries. Nevertheless, two men outside these linguistic/geographical areas made a strong impact on the psychiatry of their day. Both were representatives of other disciplines: anthropology, in the case of Cesare Lombroso; physiology, in the case of Ivan Pavlov.

ITALY

Cesare Lombroso (1836–1909), professor of anthropology in Torino, Italy, was interested in physiognomy. He may be said to have carried the baton passed from Gall, who had received it from his predecessors, Italians both: Cardano and della Porta. Whereas Gall sought correlations between certain psychological traits and the shape or size of the skull, the Italian physiognomists concentrated on the face. Gall had been inspired when, while still a schoolboy, he noticed that a certain fellow student with protruding eyes was an excellent scholar. As an adult this solitary observation motivated him to examine skull volume and shape for clues to individual differences. He thereby became interested in innate predispositions and subsequently concluded that criminals who showed this predisposition, in his view, were less responsible for their acts.

Etching in Lombroso's book, *L'Uomo Deliquente* (1878), entitled "Robber from the Basilica, held in custody in Pesaro."

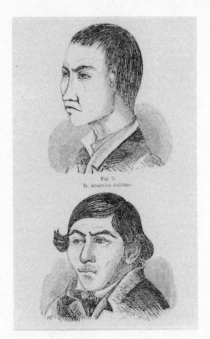

A Sicilian murderer (top) and a murderer from Lucca (bottom). From Lombroso, 1878.

Murderers and thieves. From Lombroso, 1878.

Lombroso's attitude was less charitable. He believed that there was a strong correlation between certain facial configurations and various criminal propensities; these configurations marked the bearers as "inferior men." According to Morel and others earlier in the century, the outer self partook of the same "degeneracy" that supposedly was manifested by the "inner self" of the insane. The etchings and photographs Lombroso used to illustrate his thesis do, indeed, portray some very mean-looking characters. As one can imagine, Lombroso's work became immensely popular, not so much as a forerunner of modern somatic psychiatry (although, in a way, it was), but as a consolation to the "moral majority," who took cheer at the idea that *they* (the criminal class) not only acted but even *looked* worse than the average person.[1]

Lombroso's foray into the realm of genius and physiognomy rests on even shakier ground (if this is possible) than his theories on criminality. His *Man of Genius* (1891) is a potpourri of prejudices cloaked as science. For Lombroso, lunacy was the back side of the coin of genius. To fit so many brilliant persons under the rubric of *insanity*, it was necessary to broaden the term until even eccentricity could be counted "insane." Thus poets Torquato Tasso and Edgar Allen Poe were insane geniuses, as was Galileo's predecessor, Giordano Bruno—". . . all of whom were restless, compulsively traveling" (p. 316). Genius was also accompanied by *degeneracy*—and here Lombroso included even rickets, from which Alexander Pope, Talleyrand, Moses Mendelssohn, and the painter Giotto suffered. As for Aristotle, Aesop, Virgil, and Demosthenes, well, they all stammered; others were left-handed (!), like Michelangelo and daVinci. Being *sterile* (i.e., without children) also struck Lombroso as a brand of degeneracy, allowing him to include Isaac Newton, Ben Johnson, John Milton, Spinoza, Kant, Jonathan Swift, and the "composer Mendelssohn" (was Lombroso unaware that the composer married and had five children?). As if to show that the study of genius was no great distance from his previous work on criminality, Lombroso mentioned the "criminality" of Sallust, Seneca, and Bacon (accused of peculation) and of Rousseau and Byron (as excessively passionate); also of Avicenna, an "epileptic who in old age plunged into debauchery" (p. 59).

---

[1] Anyone today who has perused the recent literature on serial killers realizes that the perpetrators span the physiognomic spectrum—from the shifty-eyed and intimidating (Jerry Brudos) to the conventional and even handsome (Ted Bundy, Jeffrey Dahmer). In fact, a *normal appearance* is helpful to serial killers in luring their unsuspecting victims into fatal trustingness.

Perhaps Lombroso was on surer ground in pointing out the "melancholy" of Schumann, the misogyny of Schopenhauer (whose mother refused to see him due to his ill humor and grandiosity), and the decadence of Baudelaire (who dyed his hair green, etc.). In actuality, the men in whom genius and "madness" truly intersected constituted a tiny fraction of the names cited in Lombroso's text: Perhaps Schumann is the one compelling example.

Elsewhere Lombroso offered evidence that men of genius often had larger brain capacity than ordinary men, reaching such enormous figures as 1,740 cubic centimeters in Kant, 1,660 in Thackeray, and 2,012 in Turgenev (as against the usual 1,300). Furthermore, he asserted that the brains of geniuses had more convolutions than those of ordinary men, as "proven" in the etching of Gauss's brain compared with that of a German workman. Here, at least, Lombroso had hit upon a testable hypothesis, but he did not carry out the controlled study that would have been necessary to challenge the null hypothesis.

Counterfeiters, thieves, and other criminals. From Lombroso, 1878.

Francesco Bonucci

Psychiatric wisdom was by no means confined to famous authors. For example, an obscure alienist named Francesco Bonucci at the St. Margherita Asylum in Perugia, Italy, wrote a brief but important account in 1858 of the patients housed there and of the causes of their mental illnesses. He accorded greatest significance to hereditary factors. Also worthy of mention were certain organic conditions such as alcoholism and pellagra. Chief among the "moral" (meaning psychological or environmental) causes were: lack of solid life goals (as when young men from good families waste their resources on gambling, fall into debt, and end up ruined), "misery" (primarily in the form of grinding poverty), and sexual repression. About the

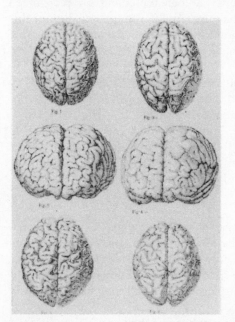

Fig. 1 Gauss's brain.
Fig. 2 Frontal lobe of same.
Fig. 3 Brain of a German workman.
Fig. 4 Frontal lobe of same.
Fig. 5 Dirichlet's brain.
Fig. 6 Hermann's brain.

This illustration from Lombroso's *Man of Genius* (1891) purportedly demonstrates the greater number of convolutions in the cortex of geniuses' brains (those of mathematicians Gauss, Dirichlet, and Hermann) than in those of ordinary men.

latter, Bonucci had these modern-sounding remarks to make, presaging those made by Freud 40 years later:

> Madness brought about by restraining of the force of the sexual instinct, often manifests itself in perversions of the other instincts—as though its power once repressed [*risospinto*] is carried over into other instincts, and not being able to adjust to their laws and nature, stirs them up in a manner both vehement and disordered. [Author's translation]

RUSSIA

Ivan Petrovitch
Pavlov

Ivan Petrovitch Pavlov (1849–1936) was a physiologist who became famous for his studies on conditioned reflexes. A lesser known fact is that for his studies on digestive glands (published in 1897 and translated into German the following year), he won the Nobel Prize in 1904.

Pavlov was influenced by Ivan Mikhailovitch Séchenov, considered the father of Russian physiology (A. & S., p. 157), who had contended that psychological acts were simply the final expression of external stimuli impinging on our sense organs. The stimuli led to changes in the brain, which then occasioned various observable behaviors. Séchenov was not blind to the psychological element: He recognized that stimuli elicited different responses in different people. But for this phenomenon, too, his explanation was totally mechanistic—so it came across as not very psychological after all in his 1873 book:

> Some people have the capacity in their imagination for sharp recall of sights and sounds; and there are those whose imagination in this regard is dull. This means, in effect, that the only real difference between an actual impression and someone's recollection of it involves *vividness* [of one's imagination]. There are all manners of gradations, from the one extreme of dull imagination—to the other, of morbid hallucinations. [Author's translation]

Pavlov carried Séchenov's ideas a step further when he demonstrated how repetitive learning could be used to create *conditioned reflexes* out of the organism's *unconditioned reflexes*. The best known example was his experiment with the dog, whose unconditioned reflex of salivating upon being given food was paired with a bell rung simultaneously with the presentation of the food, over and over again, until the dog eventually began to salivate just upon hearing the bell (the conditioned reflex). Pavlov recognized that, in humans, thought, especially in the form of logical reasoning, required the temporary inhibition of action, as the brain presumably mulled over the various options appropriate to this or that external stimulus. Even so, he believed that simple conditioned reflexes comprised the basic units of the human psyche, even the complex phenomena involved in psychological life.

The notion of temporary inhibition of action was in agreement with the ideas Freud expressed in his 1895 *Project,* where he assumed the existence of "psi-neurones" as the substrate of the ego, whose task was to inhibit or modulate action until the most adaptive response was selected.

For Pavlov, irritating external stimuli called forth different response styles in different persons that generally reflected their differing temperaments. The four temperaments of the ancient Greeks were accepted by Pavlov but renamed in mechanistic terms: non-reactive (phlegmatic), under-reactive (melancholic), over-reactive/negative (irritable), and over-reactive/positive (sanguine).

The behaviorists who drew upon the work of Pavlov, such as Bechterev and Skinner, are discussed in Chapters 11 and 12, but for now it is important to note that similar ideas were expressed long before Pavlov, in some instances by persons outside the mainstream of psychological thought. For example, Sir Kenelm Digby (1603–1665), a 17th-century non-medical savant, demonstrated how unaccustomed responses could be induced in animals artificially—a process he called "assuefaction" (derived from the Latin *assuefacio,* meaning "getting used to"). He noted how dogs bred to kill deer "will live friendly with one" if bred since puppyhood with a fawn. Digby even claimed that a tiger cub who was raised with a deer (presumably in a zoo) would not harm the deer in any way during its adult years, even if it were starved. He drew a parallel to the human condition of *folie à deux:* the induction of otherwise foreign or unaccustomed attitudes in a "weaker" person by a person of "strong imagination."

Sir Kenelm Digby

SPAIN

Lombroso and Pavlov influenced the clinical realm of psychiatry. In the realm of neuroscience the towering figure at the century's end was Spanish histologist Santiago Ramón y Cajal (1852–1934). In 1887 Ramón y Cajal learned about the method for staining nervous-tissue specimens developed by Camillo Golgi (Salvador-Carulla, 1995). Making improvements on the Golgi method, Ramón y Cajal, who did much of his research in a small laboratory in his own home, was able to show that axons from various nerve cells ended only in contiguity with the dendrites of other nerve cells. Previous neurohistologists, including

Santiago Ramón y Cajal

Golgi himself, had insisted that the nervous system was a vast rete (net), in which all the fibers were part of one continuous network: the so-called continuity doctrine. Ramón y Cajal roundly rebutted the continuity argument in 1894:

> The most general conclusion concerning the morphology of the cells of the nerve centers is the *absence* of continuity of substance between the expansions of the nerve cells. The nerve cell elements represent distinct cellular entities or "neurones," to use Waldeyer's expression.
>
> Given that continuity of substance does not exist, the currents must be transmitted from one cell to another by contiguity or contact, much as happens where two telegraph wires are tied together. This contact takes place between the terminal arborizations or the collaterals of the cylindrical axes [axons] of one side, and the cell bodies and the protoplasmic arborizations [dendrites] of the other side.
>
> The probable direction of nervous motion in the cells that are supplied with two types of expansion is: cell-seeking (in the protoplasmic elongations) and cell-exiting (in the cylindrical axes). (pp. 171–172) [Author's translation]

In 1906 Ramón y Cajal won the Nobel prize, along with his spiritual guide and rival, Camillo Golgi. Certainly Ramón y Cajal's reformulation of central nervous system histology paved the way for the next century's discovery of *neurotransmitters,* whose job was to conduct electrical impulses from one nerve-cell to another across the, indeed, *non-continuous* gap that we now call the *synapse.*

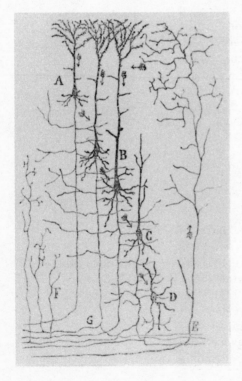

Diagram showing the probable direction of currents and the nervous/protoplasmic connections in the cells of the cerebral cortex. From Ramón y Cajal, 1894.

PART III

Modern Psychiatry: 1900–1959

Chapter 11

1900–1929: AN ERA OF EXPANSION

As the 20th century now draws to a close, we can begin to see trends in psychiatry that were less apparent a generation or so ago. The age of the person observing those trends influences how they are evaluated. As I enter my sixties, what seem very much like "historical events" to my trainees, as they wonder about psychiatry at mid-century, were merely "current events" to me; what to me constitutes the history of the pioneer years of the psychoanalytic movement feels like current events to my mentor, Dr. Henrietta Klein, who is 94 years old as of this writing, and cousin to Ruth Mack-Brunswick, who treated the Wolf Man after Freud felt he could do so no longer.

Certain aspects of our recent history can be approached conveniently through chronological review, decade by decade. There are other aspects—large-scale trends, especially—that span several decades and usually have no fixed beginning or ending. These trends are best discussed conceptually. First, to the chronology.

1 9 0 0 – 1 9 0 9

Descriptive Psychiatry and Psychology

In 1903 Alfred Binet (1857–1911) published his important study on intelligence in France. Director of the laboratory for psychological physiology at the Sorbonne (begun by Ribot), he worked with his colleague, Simon, to develop a metric scale for intelligence. Their efforts culminated in the famous Binet-Simon test, which appeared in 1905. Intelligence could now be evaluated with greater precision and meaningfulness than was possible in the days of Galton. The emerging gaussian curve was flatter than Galton's, with 68% of the population regarded as "average."

Alfred Binet

Pierre Janet

A key figure in descriptive psychiatry was Ribot's student Pierre Janet (1851–1947), who later became one of the founders of French dynamic psychiatry. Janet was a prolific writer: A book on neuroses and *idées fixes* was published in 1898; another (with the collaboration of Raymond) on obsessions and neurasthenia in 1903. Later, other works appeared on hysteria (1911), religious mania (1926), and personality (1929). Janet relied on his own clinical experience with each patient, eschewing both experimental methods and statistics (B., p. 84). He endorsed the concept of cerebral structures (the "layering" Hughlings-Jackson had outlined earlier) and spoke of a "subconscious." Janet's treatment consisted in helping patients express their "fixed ideas." Our present corollary to Janet's notion of fixed ideas would be the concept of maladaptive "underlying assumptions" (as in the Beck school of cognitive therapy), exemplified by the depressive person's conviction that "I'm no good," or the paranoid person's assumption that "You can't trust anybody." Wrestling with fixed ideas was not the same intervention that Freud was emphasizing at this time: that of making the unconscious conscious. In comparison to Freud, Janet was less interested in the content of his patients' early childhood memories and more focused on their present thought patterns. For this reason, in reading Janet, we don't feel that we are getting to the essence of the underlying conflicts or troubles. Be this as it may, Janet's works are a treasure trove of case descriptions of every sort: There are patients we would now diagnose as having borderline personality disorder or obsessive-compulsive disorder; indeed, most of the disorders we regard as typical of our day were depicted nearly a century ago by Janet.

"fixed ideas"

Psychoanalysis

Freud published his landmark *Three Theories of Sexuality* in 1905, wherein he discussed the inverse relationship, as he saw it, between neuroses and perversions. Freud identified phases of peak sexuality in early life: one in children between the ages of three and five (the time of the Oedipus complex, with its interest in the opposite-sex parent and fear of retaliation by the same-sex parent); another in adolescence. The process of detachment from parental authority was completed through the gradual suppression of incestuous fantasies. In adults with a *neurosis,* these fantasies and strivings are largely unconscious; in those with a perversion, the fantasies are acted out instead of being repressed.

Freud also published analyses of hysteria in the case of "Dora" (1905) and of phobia in the case of "Little Hans" (1909). Five-year-old Hans was terrified of horses, which

Sigmund Freud in 1909. Courtesy The Warder Collection

Freud resolved through conversations with the boy's father in which he explained how Hans' fear of the oedipal father's penis had been displaced onto that of the horse.

In Freud's theory of anxiety during this early period of psychoanalysis, he assumed the existence of neural "energy" that gave force to the drives (including sexual), such that if there were sexual frustration, this energy (as *libido*), lacking its normal outlet, would manifest as anxiety. (The revision of this theory occurred in 1920s.) Neurosis, at all events, was seen as the product of unresolved conflicts involving our basic drives versus the need to conform to the limitations imposed upon us by society.

theory of anxiety

In 1909, at the invitation of G. Stanley Hall, Freud visited the United States and gave his *Introductory Lectures* at Clark University in Worcester, Massachusetts. He was accompanied by Carl Jung and Sandor Ferenczi, and upon disembarkment met in New York by Abraham Brill, who had emigrated some years earlier. Brill, an ardent disciple of Freud, translated a number of the professor's works into English and also founded the New York Psychoanalytic Society in 1911. Freud did not like America; it is unclear whether he would have been happy or sad to realize that psychoanalysis would reach its zenith here, on these shores, some 20 years after his death.

Introductory Lectures

Viennese-born Alfred Adler (1870–1937) was among the small group who met at Freud's house in Vienna on Wednesday evenings to discuss important issues and developments in psychoanalysis. Adler believed that the crucial dynamic motivating human action was the wish for power. He articulated this notion in his 1907 book on *Organ Inferiority* (the source of his coinage: the *inferiority complex*).

Alfred Adler

The first international meeting of analysts was organized by Jung in 1908. Freud read his paper on the "Rat Man," a case of obsessional neurosis. At this time C. G. Jung was Freud's "fair-haired boy." Freud regarded him as brilliant and, of equal importance, hoped that this Christian physician, the son of a Swiss pastor, would help make psychoanalysis—thus far practiced almost entirely by Jewish professionals in Austro-Hungary—acceptable in the wider, gentile circles beyond the Viennese "inner circle."

General Psychiatry

Vladimir Bechterev (1857–1927) developed his theory of "psychoreflexology" in the 1910s. Psychoreflexology carried forward the concepts of Séchenov, particularly the view that the brain was an inhibitory reflex-center mediating between sensory impressions entering the brain and motor

C. G. Jung. Courtesy National Library of Medicine

responses emanating from the brain. Bechterev had studied with Wundt, Charcot, and Flechsig, and was influenced also by Pavlov (B., p. 71). With the use of aversive conditioning, Bechterev achieved cures in alcoholic patients. Bechterev had the misfortune to achieve such renown in his native Russia that it was he whom Stalin's entourage called upon to determine, in 1927, if their leader were "paranoid." Bechterev examined Stalin, concluding (correctly, as it turns out) that the leader was indeed paranoid, whereupon Bechterev was immediately executed.

Hospital Psychiatry; Schizophrenia and Manic-Depression

Clifford Beers

In 1908 a former mental patient, American Clifford Beers, wrote a book describing his psychosis, hospitalization, and recovery. The hospital stay had been degrading and unpleasant in the extreme. His book, *A Mind That Found Itself* (1908), was hailed as a "voice heard 'round the world" by virtue of the tremendous impression it made on lay persons and professionals alike. Beers' illness had been bipolar mania (though it was not recognized as such at the time). He went on to lecture on the need for reform of mental institutions, much as Dorothea Dix had done in the 19th century. Prominent psychiatrists and philanthropists—including Henry Phipps (of the Phipps Clinic in Baltimore) and Adolf Meyer—championed his cause and often appeared with him on the lecture circuit. Beers was instrumental in effecting positive changes and in improving the lot of other mentally ill patients.

reform of mental institutions

Biological Psychiatry

treatment of syphilis

During this first decade some progress was made in the treatment of syphilis and its neurological complications. Though "general paresis" had been described in the 19th century, the cause was as yet unknown. The spirochete was isolated in genital lesions in 1905 by Schaudinn and an accurate blood test was developed the following year by Wasserman. In the area of conduct disturbances, Still (1902) reported cases in *Lancet* that may be regarded as forerunners of what we now diagnose as "attention deficit disorder."

1910–1919

Psychoanalysis

Freud severed relations with both Adler and Jung in 1911. He had criticized Adler for his excessive focus on the power motif and on social, as opposed to childhood-developmental, factors as the key to the genesis of neuroses. Freud clearly accorded greater significance to infantile sexual development; Adler, to the social environment. As Gay (1988) mentions, Adler was both a member of the Socialist Party and a social activist—leanings that influenced his theoretical stance—whereas Freud was less involved in political issues (apart, that is, from the politics of the psychoanalytic movement).

As for Jung, he had begun to "chafe under Freud's authority" (Gay, 1988, p. 225). Jung's burgeoning preoccupation with mystical themes of a "collective unconscious" or of male ("animus") and female ("anima") minds in each of us would not have appealed to Freud's way of thinking, which was alien to poetical/religious explanations of that sort. Jung soon began to take issue with Freud's dream theories (namely those pertaining to wish-fulfillment), proposing his theory of "archetypes" instead (in 1913; published 1935). The "father-son" relationship (Jung was 19 years Freud's junior) ceased at this point.

In contrast to Adler and Jung, German Karl Abraham (1877–1925) remained loyal to, and esteemed by, Freud to the end of Abraham's short life. Among Abraham's papers were several dealing with the various character types adumbrated by Freud—oral, anal, and genital—each associated with progressive stages in early development. These three stages were supposedly correlated with dependent, obsessive, and hysteric character development, respectively.

Karl Abraham

In 1912 Otto Rank (1884–1939) published his work in German on the "incest motif" in psychoanalysis. The same year he and Hanns Sachs, both non-medical analysts, established the journal *Imago* (A. & S., p. 215); a year later Rank founded the *Internationale Zeitschrift für Psychanalyse* [*International Journal of Psychoanalysis*].

Otto Rank

Freud published a number of important papers in this time period, of which perhaps the best known are the following: the case of Schreber (1911), "On Narcissism" (1914), "Introductory Lectures" (1915–17), "Mourning and Melancholia" (1917), "The Wolf-Man (A Case of Obsessional Neurosis)" (1918), and "A Child Is Being Beaten" (1919).

In Freud's analysis (1911) of the diary Daniel Schreber[1] had written during his hospitalization, which was filled with ambivalent feelings toward his physician, Flechsig, Freud proposed that Schreber's paranoia grew out of thinly disguised homosexual longings toward his doctor—which Schreber then had to repudiate. Freud suspected that,

---

[1] Schreber was a prominent jurist who suffered a psychotic break, probably of a manic-depressive type, during his forties. The timing of his break coincided with his promotion to a higher post. Schreber's father was a pedagogue of some fame, who was extraordinarily punitive and controlling of his children. One of Schreber's brothers committed suicide.

although he believed there was a constitutional basis for homosexuality, paranoia represented the mechanisms of *denial* and *projection:* "I don't love *him; he* loves *me!*" followed by the assertion, "and that disgusts me!"

narcissism

In his 1914 paper on narcissism (a term introduced in the late 19th century by Paul Näcke), Freud introduced the concept of an "ego-ideal," the forerunner of his "super-ego" concept enunciated in 1923. Earlier Freud had expressed the belief that schizophrenic patients (whom he referred to having a "narcissistic neurosis") were so caught up in "self-love" as to be unable to make attachments to others or to experience a

transference

transference to the analyst. Without this latter ability, there could be no successful analytic working through, in Freud's view, though some members of his circle challenged this point.

Alfonse Maeder and Swedish analyst Poul Bjerre, both writing in 1910 and 1911, believed that schizophrenic patients were capable of forming a transference, and they claimed to have worked successfully with several such patients (these patients certainly were paranoid; whether we would call them *schizophrenic* by contemporary standards is another question). As for the term *narcissism,* there was, and is, much confusion in psychiatry over its meanings; it is used to denote normal self-regard as well as pathological investment in the self (with a corresponding impairment the ability to achieve intimate relations with others).

internalization

In "Mourning and Melancholia" (1917) Freud discussed the process whereby the lost person is *internalized* by the mourner (the loss may be through death or the rupture of a relationship). Melancholic patients (in today's nosology, those with severe depression), Freud noted, tend to disparage themselves in ways that seem paradoxical (what is the "point" of heaping contumely upon oneself?), which Freud explained as the sadistic, hypercritical voice of the actually lost, but now internalized, loved one.

masochism

In his paper, "A Child Is Being Beaten" (1919), Freud examined the fantasy, common to certain classes of patients, of being beaten for some misdeed. The fantasy is one of pain and pleasure commingled and seems to underlie certain sexual perversions, including masochism. Masochism had become an important topic in psychoanalytic circles, partly because, in its strict sense, it represented an interesting sexual perversion (pain as a precondition to sexual arousal and fulfillment), but more importantly, because, in its figurative sense, masochism represented the whole domain of paradoxical behavior, in which certain emotional gains were purchased at the price of displeasure or inconvenience. Masochism takes its name from the writings of Count Leopold von Sacher-Masoch (1836–1895), who described

Count Leopold von Sacher-Masoch

his own self-abasement before a haughty mistress in *Venus in Furs.* Apparently the count had been beaten mercilessly in his childhood years by his father, which established a pattern he (and persons like him) unconsciously sought to reenact in their adult lives.

At the end of the decade Melanie Klein (1882–1960), who had begun an analysis with Ferenczi in Budapest, published her first papers on the analysis of children. She later moved to Berlin and underwent further analysis with Karl Abraham. The year after his death, she moved permanently to London, where she eventually set up a psychoanalytic group in opposition to that of Anna Freud and Ernest Jones. Her ideas about the early phases of infant/child development included the concepts of *splitting,* a defense whereby good and bad aspects of self and important others are kept in separate mental compartments; *introjection,* whereby the child incorporates aspects of the mental life of his or her caretakers; and *projective identification,* whereby unacceptable aspects of the self are attributed to another.

Klein's awareness of the mutuality of the mother-child relationship led to an interpersonal theory of psychoanalysis. Unfortunately, her first "patient" happened to be her own daughter, Melitta Schmideberg, who later became a prominent analyst in her own right for her work with delinquent adolescents. (Schmideberg [1971] remained resentful of her mother all her life for having intruded into her childhood in that way.) Melanie Klein attracted loyal and highly respected followers, including Edward Glover and W. Fairbairn.

Melanie Klein, 1882–1960. Courtesy Special Collections, A. A. Brill Library, The New York Psychoanalytic Institute

In America, psychoanalysis became a popular branch of psychiatry. Isador Coriat founded the American Psychoanalytic Institute toward the end of the decade. In 1917 he published a paper relating his successful analytic treatment of five schizophrenic patients. Years later, George Vaillant (1963), in reviewing Coriat's cases, rediagnosed most of those patients as having suffered instead from manic-depressive illness (with its inherently better prognosis).

Isador Coriat

General Psychiatry

Emil Kraepelin's textbook on psychiatry went through many editions, several of which were published in this second decade. In this four-volume compendium are chapters discussing manic-depressive psychosis and the four temperaments associated with it: depressive, manic, irritable, and cyclothymic (the latter being a combination of the first two). Kraepelin used the term *psychopath* to designate mental disorders in general, although among them he described several varieties of antisocial behavior similar to our modern usage of the term. For Kraepelin, dementia praecox had a downhill course, in part because his definition depended on "hard signs" (delusions and hallucinations), which were more apt to be associated with poor-prognosis cases.

Emil Kraepelin

John Watson

American John Watson (1878–1958) founded the field of *behaviorism* in 1913, based on his experiments on animals. Challenging the assumptions of psychoanalysis, Watson's behaviorism stressed the *observable* as opposed to the *unconscious*. He also studied the reactions of infants in the hopes of discovering the human organism's basic reaction patterns, which he identified as love, anger, and fear. He instilled conditioned responses in infants (including his own son, who later committed suicide), proving (to his satisfaction) that phobias arise out of conditioning in early life and could be treated by desensitization. Watson influenced others who took up the cause of behaviorism, such as Thorndike and B. F. Skinner.

Hospital Psychiatry

August Forel

Swiss physician August Forel had been influenced by the Nancy hypnotists, Liébault and Bernheim, as had Krafft-Ebing and Freud. Forel (1905) wrote on the topic of female sexuality, including themes popular at the time, such as that of the *femme fatale* and the "flirt." He also addressed the general topics of sadism, masochism, exhibitionism, fetishism, and homosexuality in men and in women. Turning toward forensic matters, his 1905 *Die Sexuelle Frage* [*The Sexual Question*] included case histories of mothers who had strangled their babies.

Eugen Bleuler's (1857–1939) interests were quite different. Succeeding Forel as the director of the famed Burghölzli clinic in 1898, Bleuler worked intensively with psychotic patients, visiting and talking with them five or six times a week, such that his familiarity with them was comparable to that of psychoanalysts with their patients (who were also seen about five times a week in this era). His great monograph on the group of schizophrenias appeared in 1911; here he proposed a new definition of the condition Kraepelin and others had been calling *dementia praecox*. Bleuler identified the "primary signs" of this condition, which have become known as the four "A's": *a*utism, loosening of *a*ssociations, *a*mbivalence, and *a*ffect inappropriateness. The latter trait was the key element for Bleuler: The patient who smiled while talking of the death of his mother, or who cried while talking of inheriting a fortune, was showing a split (Greek: *schizo*) between thought and affect: hence his term *schizophrenia*. *Ambivalence* and *autism* were also words Bleuler coined.

In recent years we have come to regard Bleuler's definition of schizophrenia as too broad, including many "false-positives" more indicative of patients with manic-depression. For example, Bleuler regarded the composer Schumann as schizo-

Eugen Bleuler, 1857–1939. Courtesy National Library of Medicine

phrenic, whereas the evidence suggest that manic-depression would be the more accurate diagnosis. Bleuler's broader criteria nevertheless lent a more hopeful outlook to the prognosis; those who use his criteria report higher recovery rates than do those who rely on Kraepelin's criteria.

Bleuler had been favorably impressed by Freud and asked Jung to report on Freud's *Interpretation of Dreams* to the Burghölzli staff in 1906 (Gay, 1988, p. 201). For a brief time Bleuler became a member of the budding psychoanalytic organization. He attended its 1908 international congress and founded, with Freud, the *Jahrbuch für psychoanalytische und psychopathologische Forschung* [*Yearbook for Psychoanalytic and Psychopathological Research*] (with Jung as editor). Bleuler wrote a small volume in defense of Freud's psychoanalysis, which appeared in 1911, by which time Bleuler had already parted company with the movement on the basis of what he considered to be Freud's excessive emphasis on infantile sexuality.

Biological Psychiatry and Genetics

Further progress was made in the treatment of syphilis shortly before World War I. In 1910 Paul Ehrlich developed an arsenical compound (Salvarsan), which was fairly effective. Shortly thereafter, German Julius von Wagner-Jauregg (1857–1940) introduced fever therapy, purposely giving his paretic patients malaria. This measure was predicated on the observation that syphilitic patients who subsequently got (febrile) infections of one sort or another seemed to improve.[2] In 1927 von Wagner-Jauregg received the Nobel Prize for this work. He is thus one of three persons making contributions to the field of mental health to win this coveted honor, and is (still) the only psychiatrist (Pavlov was a physiologist; Moniz, a neurologist).

Julius von Wagner-Jauregg

In Munich in 1916, Ernst Rüdin published *On the Inheritance and Origin of Psychic Disorders,* in which he examined the siblings of 701 patients with dementia praecox. He found that 4.5% percent of the siblings older than 17 had the same psychosis; 4% had other psychoses. The percentage of dementia praecox rose to 6.2% when one parent exhibited the same disorder. These figures did not support the previously held notion of simple recessive inheritance, therefore inclining Rüdin to favor a theory based on two recessive genes. At all events,

Ernst Rüdin

[2] As Braslow points out (1994), there is no convincing evidence that malaria therapy actually worked, yet this form of biological therapy encouraged doctors to listen compassionately to their syphilitic patients and to treat them with greater optimism. In this way, malaria therapy contributed indirectly to improvement in the doctor-patient relationship.

Rüdin and his coworkers succeeded in establishing the genetic independence of schizophrenia and manic-depression.

1920–1929

Descriptive Psychiatry and Psychology

Ernst Kretschmer

Interest in possible interrelationships between mind and body was articulated in the work of German Ernst Kretschmer (1888–1964), who believed that the major psychoses were associated with certain body conformations. Similar theories, ultimately dating back to the ancient Greeks, had been proposed in France shortly before: Supposedly it was possible to distinguish the "cerebral," "digestive," "respiratory," and "muscular" types (B., p. 95). Kretschmer understood *constitution* to mean the combination of inherited attributes of body and mind. In his 1922 monograph, *Body Build and Character,* he described manic-depressives as having a "pychnic" physique (i.e., tending toward overweight) and schizophrenics as being "leptosomes" (i.e., thin persons); epileptics were supposedly beefy or muscular. These were extreme types, which were distributed by degrees across the normal population. Thus one encountered people who were on the "shy" side (whom he called "schizoids") and those who were more outgoing than average (whom he called "cycloides" because of their mild cyclothymic tendencies). Kretschmer influenced W. H. Sheldon, whose work on "somatypes" enjoyed popularity in America at mid-century.

Kurt Schneider

Another German, Kurt Schneider (1887–1967), wrote an important treatise on "psychopathic personalities" (1923), by which he meant abnormal, not antisocial, variants. His characterology was "atheoretic"— that is, it was not tied to any assumptions about etiology—unlike Kraepelin's "temperaments," which he saw as attenuated forms of manic-depression. Although Schneider used a different set of terms, there are close correspondences between his typology and the personality disorder labels in current use. Thus Schneider's "insecure" type, with its two subtypes of "sensitive" and "anankastic," correspond to our "dependent" and "obsessive"; his "fanatic" is like our "paranoid"; his "attention-seeking" like our "hysteric." Persons we now distinguish as "psychopathic/antisocial" were "affectionless" in Schneider's terminology.

Later (1959), Schneider would enumerate some eleven symptoms he felt were pathognomonic of schizophrenia. His first-rank symptoms included "thought aloud," "thought insertion," "thought broadcast," and "hallucinations where the patient hears voices describing his activity as it takes place." As Carpenter showed in the 1970s, none of these attributes is unique to schizophrenia: They may occur, if less frequently, in mania as well.[3]

In 1921 Hermann Rorschach's (1884–1922) significant work on the inkblot test was published. Having done his medical dissertation with Bleuler in Zurich, Rorschach, whose father was an artist who worked with ink sketches, became intrigued by patients' reactions to the random shapes of inkblots and what those reactions might reveal about their personalities. The results of his research, the *Psychodiagnostik* [*Psychodiagnostics*] (which came out less than a year before his untimely death), laid the foundation for the development of a whole subspecialty of psychology having to do with the assessment of personality and underlying psychodynamic themes.

Hermann Rorschach

Psychoanalysis

In 1920, Ernest Jones was chosen as editor of the new *International Journal of Psychoanalysis,* the first psychoanalytic journal in English. In general there was continued interest in applying psychoanalysis as a treatment for schizophrenia: Work was done on the unconscious determinants of schizophrenia by Hermann Nunberg; the concept of "ego boundary" was elaborated by Viktor Tausk in his 1919 paper on the "influencing machine"—an imaginary machine conjured up by a delusional (probably schizophrenic) patient, who believed his thoughts and actions were being controlled from outside by this "machine." A similar delusion was experienced by the patient Haslam described a century earlier.

In Austria, Otto Rank (1884–1939), at first a close adherent of Freud and one of the "inner circle" (who included Ernest Jones, Sandor Ferenczi, Karl Abraham, and Hanns Sachs) published his work on *The Trauma of Birth* in 1924. Rank postulated that the primal act of being born, with its inevitable crying and other signs of physiological distress, is the source of all later anxiety. He contended that people, in general, seek to recapture the security of intrauterine life ("womb fantasies") via returning to the mother as an "antidote" to this anxiety. Rank thus repudiated Freud's view in which the Oedipus complex (fear of the "castrating father") was the central source of anxiety. The ensuing clash of theories led to Rank's break with Freud in 1929.

---

[3] Actually, the search for the elusive sure-fire "pathognomonic" symptoms is just as fruitless in psychiatry as it is in general medicine—where, apart perhaps from Koplik's spots in measles, there are scarcely any to be detected. Diagnoses are instead dependent on *constellations* of signs and symptoms which, taken in the aggregate, lend more certainty to a particular diagnosis.

Sandor Ferenczi (1877–1933) remained Freud's closest colleague. Whereas Freud was primarily a theoretician, Ferenczi was first and foremost a clinician. As such, he felt that the emotional reliving of the infantile neurosis in the transference relationship was more curative than intellectual interpretations. In his experimentation with different techniques, at times Ferenczi went too far, as when he sought to compensate for the loveless past of one of his patients by allowing her to sit on his lap. Freud criticized this attempt to give direct gratification; ever since this episode, such practices have been regarded as inappropriate. In his 1924 book on sexuality Ferenczi noted a parallel between the sexual drive, in which the sperm enters the "sea" of the womb, and the organism's "wish" to return to the sea, the origin of life. Like Rank, he saw the mother as a parent no less important—perhaps more so—than the father.

Melanie Klein also emphasized the importance of the *dyadic* mother-child relationship, which antedated the *triadic* mother-father-child Oedipal situation emphasized by Freud. Thus the *primary* component of affective life was the maternal relationship. In the course of working with her child patients, Klein developed *play therapy* during the 1920s.

A most problematic figure in the history of psychoanalysis was Wilhelm Reich (1897–1957). The son of a wealthy Jewish-Romanian landowner, Reich was educated by tutors, one of whom had an affair with his mother when Reich was 14. Reich revealed this disturbing fact to his domineering and overbearing father, whereupon his mother committed suicide. Three years later his father exposed himself to the cold in a suicide attempt and died shortly thereafter of tubercular pneumonia. After serving (on the German side) in World War I, Reich (like Mesmer) started his career in law but switched to medicine. Fascinated by lectures on psychoanalysis, he made this his profession, achieving distinction while still in his twenties. For a time he became Freud's most promising disciple.

In 1925 Reich wrote the *The Impulse-Ridden Character,* in which he described personality aberrations similar to what we now call "borderline." In 1927 he published *The Function of the Orgasm,* in which he presented a very literal interpretation of Freud's libido theory. For Reich, neurosis is the result of imperfect, insufficient orgasm, wherein there is a failure to release all of the orgasmic "psychic energy" (as would be released in a "perfect" orgasm): Thus the pent-up energy stays within the system, causing neurosis. Freud repudiated this simplistic and mechanistic explanation.

In 1929 Reich, who had already begun to lead a seminar in analytic technique, completed the first part of his *Character Analysis,* in which he sketched the main character types he had encountered in analytic work. As Reich realized, character (we would now say *personality*) is an ego-syntonic layer of mental organization that may become injured through disadvantageous or traumatic rearing, giving rise to a disordered personality. Reich noted that this layer remains behind after the *symptoms,* which have led patients to seek analysis, have been adequately resolved in the early phases of psychoanalytic therapy. Here Reich's influence was enormous: Henceforth analyses became much more thorough and lengthy. At the outset Freud's analyses tended to be comparatively brief: several weeks or months in duration.

Reich's own personality was becoming progressively more brittle and tetchy during the late 1920s. When he sought a personal analysis with Freud, he was turned down as being too paranoid and referred to Isador Sadger; then, when Reich moved from Vienna to Berlin, he worked with Sandor Rado. Just after being rejected by Freud in 1927, Reich developed tuberculosis and spent time in a Swiss sanatorium. Increasingly paranoid thereafter, he departed more and more from standard theory and began elaborating pseudoscientific notions about "deadly nuclear energy" that caused cancer. This delusion was spurred by Freud's lip cancer, which emerged around this time and which Reich hoped to cure. All of Reich's writings after age 30 are vitiated by delusional preoccupations of this sort. He became increasingly alienated from the orthodox psychoanalytic community.

Expelled from the psychoanalytic society in 1934, Reich eventually went to Norway, then to the United States, where he developed his "orgone box"—as if to capture the "good" orgone energy and to combat the deadly, cancer-producing energy. Reich set up a laboratory in Rangely, Maine, staffed by his adherents. By now he had abandoned conventional analytic technique in favor of working from the *outside in:* That is, he tried to uncover the source of the neurotic's "character armoring" by releasing the physical rigidity through deep manipulation of the body rather than by interpreting the neurotic's unconscious need for the physical rigidity.

In the early 1950s the U.S. government pursued Reich for what appeared to be his touting of a quack cancer cure. There was a trial where Reich, acting as his own lawyer, claimed that the orgone box was a device not only for curing neurotic patients but also for undoing the ill effects of the Communists, who were actively seeking to poison the West with deadly orgone energy! (Reich became an ardent anti-Communist only after a brief dalliance with Communism in his Vienna days.) Reich was incarcerated in a minimum-security prison in Lewisburg, Pennsylvania. There, after deliberately exposing himself to the elements, just as his father had done, he died of pneumonia in 1957. Thus ended a tragic life, the first half of which was spent as a brilliant and original theoretician; the second, as a "mad scientist." Interestingly, *Character Analysis* was divided into two halves, the first, with writings before 1929; the second, with the pseudoscientific material after 1929. Nevertheless, this work lay the groundwork for the whole next phase of psychoanalytic methodology, which concentrated on the analysis of the personality rather than just on symptoms and id content.

Jung's contributions during this decade also focused on the personality: In his *Psychological Types* (1921) he described the *introvert* and the *extravert*, terms he borrowed and that we still use today, to refer to the continuum of shy-to-outgoing tendencies, respectively.[4] Schizoid persons are introverted (turned in on themselves) and represent the diluted version of the schizophrenic tendency; persons with a manic temperament are usually extraverts (turned toward the outside world).

It was in this period that Freud revised his original theory of anxiety. His monograph, *Inhibition, Symptoms and Anxiety* (1926), promulgated the theory that anxiety acts as a signal, warning us of dangers to our psychic well-being coming from other persons or from the general social environment. Internalization of the prohibitions from both parental and societal injunctions leads to the formation of the *super-ego*, the mental agency embodying conscience, values, and life goals. This agency was added to Freud's original conception of the mind, which had emphasized only the *id* (the repository of basic drives and wishes) and the *ego* (the executive agency responsible for modulating the often socially unacceptable wishes and drives, and selecting the most appropriate—often "compromise"—behaviors).

General Psychiatry; Group Psychotherapy

Adolf Meyer

Adolf Meyer (1866–1950) exerted enormous influence on psychiatry in America, not just in the 1920s, though this decade offers a convenient time frame to discuss his work. Like Jung, he was the son of a Swiss pastor. He studied under August Forel in Zürich, then worked in France with Déjerine, and later in England, where he was impressed with the work of Hughlings-Jackson, from whom he derived his ideas about the layers of brain organization and the organism's adaptation to the environment.

Meyer came to the United States in 1893, working first as a neurologist. His interest in psychopathology was stimulated by William James. He established a friendship with another prominent psychologist and educator, John Dewey. In 1907 Meyer met Clifford Beers and, joining hands with this former mental patient, now reformer of hospitals, started a mental-hygiene movement in America. Meyer also had an illustrious teaching career; he taught at New York State Psychiatric Institute, later at Johns Hopkins and the Henry Phipps Psy-

---

[4] These terms were already in the popular literature in the 19th century, as Eysenck noted; Jung brought them into psychiatric parlance (Stone, 1993a).

chiatric Clinic, both in Baltimore. In 1927 he was president of the American Psychiatric Association.

Meyer wrote very little, communicating his teachings via lectures (a four-volume set of papers and lectures was published in 1952). He opposed the biological bias of Kraepelin, proposing instead a *psychobiological* view in which all relevant data—biological and psychological—about each patient was taken into consideration. Emphasizing the patient's "longitudinal" picture as it developed over the lifetime, he urged the taking of careful and detailed case histories. Meyer spoke in terms of "reaction types" rather than discrete disease entities. Theoretically, a schizophrenic "reaction" could come about not only as a result of heredity but as a reaction to a combination of negative influences, some perhaps constitutional, others environmental. Thus Meyer offered a more hopeful attitude toward mental illness, one that was less determined by the seemingly immutable "hereditary" conditions outlined in 19th-century diagnostic taxonomy. Friendly to both psychoanalysis and behaviorism, Meyer helped Watson set up his behavioral laboratory; he also encouraged epidemiological study of mental illnesses and their prevalence. Most American psychiatrists of the mid-century generation were trained in the Meyerian philosophy combined with psychoanalytic theory—and comparatively little in the way of biological psychiatry—an approach that was little modified until the 1970s.

Advances were made in group therapy in the 1920s when it became a popular adjunct to dyadic therapy as well as being utilized as the sole treatment modality for certain patients. This occurred in response to the observation that many patients concealed relevant material from their analysts in the one-to-one setting, which could be evoked through the interaction with other patients in the group. Some group work had been done, especially with children, as early as 1905 (A. & S., p. 334); Alfred Adler and his followers had worked with children in group settings and then with adults. Jacob Levi Moreno (1889–1974) introduced *psychodrama* to the United States, where he emigrated in 1925. He had developed his technique in Vienna, where he used dramatic classes to help disturbed children act out their emotions. The idea behind psychodrama was to utilize spontaneity in evoking an outpouring of emotionally relevant material, which, in turn, would effect a catharsis—a release form the neurotic conflicts that had been troubling the patient. Shortly thereafter, Samuel Slavson used play therapy in his group work with children (A. & S., p. 335).

Jacob Levi Moreno

Throughout the 1920s Morton Prince (1854–1929) wrote extensively on various unconscious and dissociative phenomena, such as automatic writing, depersonalization, hypnosis, and dream interpretation. But he is most remembered for his detailed account of Sally Beauchamp, a case of "multiple personality" reported in the *Journal of Abnormal Psychology* in 1920. Her main self and two alters showed varying pat-

Morton Prince

terns of emotion: Sally was playful or angry, "B-1" was fearful, and "B-4" was suggestible. Prince ascribed the psychogenesis of her condition to an unhappy childhood. Sally's aloof and rejecting mother had died when she was 13. Living "under nervous strain" with her father, Sally ran away at 16, never to see him again. In 1893, at age 18, while serving as a nurse at a hospital, she had a traumatic experience during a thunder-and-lightning storm, in which she saw a vision of a man who apparently awakened forbidden sexual feelings in her: forbidden in the sense that they clashed with her exalted and "saintly" image of herself. We are not told whether she ran away from home because of sexual (or other) improprieties on the part of her widowed father (something we would routinely assume in the 1990s) or whether she had been seduced by the man, "Jones," of her 1893 vision. Prince does assure us that eventually Beauchamp reintegrated and "like the traditional princess in the fairy story, soon married and lived happily ever afterward."

Despite the lengthy description of the Beauchamp case and the self-report of another "multiple personality" in Prince's collected papers, the details of interest in the 1920s are different enough from the clinical details we look for now in assessing personality that we cannot say, for example, whether these patients were "borderline" by contemporary criteria. Many borderline patients of that era were called "preschizophrenic" on the (mostly mistaken) assumption that they were diluted or incipient cases of schizophrenia.

Hospital Psychiatry; Treatment of Psychotic Patients

Due either to serendipity or a fortuitous mistake, the benefit of shock therapy, largely forgotten since the days of Auenbrugger, was rediscovered by the Hungarian psychiatrist Ladislaus von Meduna (1896–1964).

Ladislaus von Meduna

Because of differences he noted (not confirmed by subsequent investigators) in the glial cell structure of schizophrenic, in contrast to epileptic, patients, von Meduna concluded that the two diseases were "incompatible," such that *causing* epileptic convulsions in schizophrenics would somehow *cure* them (A. & S., p. 281). At first he used camphor (unaware of its similar use 150 years before) and then the less toxic Metrazol. He published his results with the Metrazol in 1937, though his work in this area began in the 1920s.

Because of the curiously promising result with (chemical) shock therapy—curious, in the sense that the mechanism was unclear—and because the method was crude and often frightening to patients, others tried less hazardous methods. Ugo Cerletti (1877–1963) collaborated

Ugo Cerletti
L. Bini

with L. Bini in Genoa in the use of electroshock, which they applied successfully to a schizophrenic patient for the first time in 1938.

One of the major exponents of applying the psychoanalytic method to the treatment of schizophrenia during this period was Gustav Bychowski. A Polish-Jewish analyst who later emigrated to America because of the Nazis, he had participated in Wilhelm Reich's seminar on therapy for a time, along with Richard Sterba and Helene Deutsch. Bychowski advocated a more energetic approach to psychotherapeutic work with schizophrenics, owing to their tendency to remain aloof from the analyst or to make only meager responses.

Gustav Bychowski

Many analysts, including Kurt Eissler and Gregory Zilboorg, who worked with schizophrenic patients to any great extent came to similar conclusions. One must bear in mind that the label *schizophrenia* was applied very loosely in this generation; many of these patients might be diagnosed differently today. Even so, analysts were already beginning to recognize that the standard analytic technique (the use of the couch, four or five sessions per week, comparatively little verbalization on the part of the analyst) was ineffective or even disturbing and counterproductive for a certain group of patients. It was this group for whom special "parameters" were developed and permitted (talking more readily, saying the first word during a session if the patient seemed tongue-tied).

Taking a position midway between the optimism of Coriat and the pessimism of Freud as to the efficacy of the analytic method with schizophrenics, Leland Hinsie of the New York State Psychiatric Institute felt that with many hospitalized schizophrenic patients, psychoanalysis was contraindicated or, at best, not very useful. Still, there were some who could develop "enough insight to release their repressions and fixations" and thus make significant improvement (Hinsie, 1929, p. 12). For the majority, however, he felt that a mixture of therapeutic measures was necessary—that would most often include "reeducation" and "removal from a stressful environment."

Leland Hinsie

Biological Psychiatry and Genetics

In 1928 the first study of twins regarding the inheritance of schizophrenia was carried out by H. Luxenburger in Munich; he also studied manic-depressives and epileptics using this method. Out of a base of nearly 10,000 cases with any one of those three conditions, Luxenburger isolated 163 patients who were one of a twin-pair: 106 with "dementia praecox," 38 with manic-depression, and 19 with epilepsy. The concordance in monozygotic schizophrenic twins was 67%. This is a high figure by contemporary standards and probably reflects the severity of the underlying condition in his sample. His statistics led him to think of dominant inheritance rather than recessive, in contrast to Rüdin.

H. Luxenburger

Child and Adolescent Psychiatry

A number of books began to appear in the 1920s that reflected attempts by psychoanalysts to apply their methods of understanding and treatment to children. For example, in *The Diary of an Adolescent Girl,* Hermine Hug-Hellmuth gives examples of how children express themselves more readily, revealing their fantasy life and their main conflicts, in *play* than in ordinary conversation. Also noteworthy were *Ambivalence in Children* by G. H. Graber, and *Psychoanalytic Education in Soviet Russia* by Vera Schmidt.

The most well-known of these works today is that of August Aichhorn (1878–1949): *Verwahrloste Jugend* (1925), usually translated as *Wayward Youth* (*verwahrlos* means both "neglected" and "allowed to run wild"). Aichhorn began as a teacher and became known for his sensitive treatment of difficult or delinquent youngsters. Anna Freud heard of his work and persuaded him to undergo psychoanalytic training (A. & S., p. 378). As the director of two reformatories, Aichhorn was convinced that the way to rehabilitate delinquent children was through warmth and understanding of a kind that earned their respect and created a new ego-ideal they would wish to emulate. He saw punishment as futile, even with those who were openly aggressive (they constituted a small subgroup of his students). In Aichhorn's view aggression was a "reaction of hatred" against earlier caretakers who had been punitive and was not likely to be lessened by strong punishments from teachers. Aichhorn noted etiological factors in the families of delinquents:

> The family constellation was never perfect in these cases. The parents lived in an atmosphere of hatred and discord; insults and fighting were parts of their daily life; either that, or the parents were divorced, remarried, with the children raised by a step-parent, or else the parents were dead and the children wandered about in unfamiliar places.

Aichhorn apparently had success not only with aggressive adolescents but also with some of the chronically dishonest and deceitful ones. He did so by showing them the superiority of his values over their parents' values; in the meantime he cultivated their identification with him by engaging in mutually interesting activities. In the years that followed, many centers for the treatment of behavior-disordered adolescents were modeled on Aichhorn's perspective.

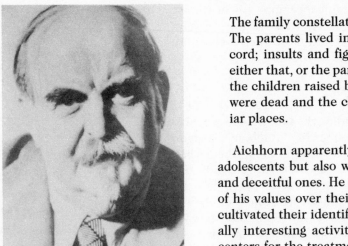

August Aichhorn, 1878–1949. Special Collections, A. A. Brill Library, The New York Psychoanalytic Institute

Chapter 12

1930–1949: PERSECUTION AND WAR CAUSE MANY PSYCHIATRISTS TO EMIGRATE FROM EUROPE

Descriptive Psychiatry and Psychology

More precise definitions of normal and abnormal personality traits were the focus of much psychological research during this period. Gordon Allport and Henry Odbert (1936) from the Harvard Psychological Laboratory combed the dictionary for personality-trait words, ending up with a list of 18,000 words! This mammoth list was later pared down to a more manageable number by Cattell (1945), and even further refined into the *Five-Factor Model* (see below).

personality traits

In Sweden throughout the early part of the century, Henrik Sjöbring (1914) also tried to systematize personality evaluation by identifying three crucial dimensions that he believed shaped personality. Influenced by Janet, his tridimensional model consisted of "validity" (the amount of energy available to the nervous system), "stability" (degree of maximum potential), and "solidity" (amount of experience needed to actualize that potential). Persons he rated as "subvalid" were akin to our obsessives; the "substable" folks were similar to cyclothymics; and the trait of "subsolidity" might be noted in our borderline or hysteric patients.

Henrik Sjöbring

Psychoanalysis

In 1936 Anna Freud's (1895–1982) *The Ego and the Mechanisms of Defense* was published; here she described the important defenses ex-

Anna Freud

Anna Freud, 1895–1982, in about 1920. Courtesy Corbis-Bettmann

hibited not only by patients in the course of analytic therapy but by people in general, as part of their personality organization. She explored the higher-level defenses seen in "neurotic" patients with hysteria (repression) or obsessions (rationalization, intellectualization, and isolation), as well as more the pathological defenses of denial and projection. Identification with the aggressor was also described.

Though Freud worked with adult patients, her main clientele was children (her treatise on child psychoanalysis appeared in 1927). The rift between Anna Freud and Melanie Klein occurred during the late 1920s and early 1930s, chiefly caused by Klein's postulating a much earlier time frame for the emergence of oedipal feelings and superego formation than was consistent with the position of orthodox analysts.

The deterioration of the situation for Jews in Europe began in earnest once Hitler assumed power in 1933. As a result, many analysts began emigrating, chiefly to England and America. Gradually the center of the psychoanalytic world shifted from Vienna and Berlin to London and New York. In England, Ernest Jones, who had been president of the British Psychoanalytic Society continuously since 1923, was totally allied with Freud. There were a few "Kleinians" working in Britain in the late 1920s and early 1930s, but they were not much noticed by the Freudians until the late 1930s, when the German-Jewish analysts were resettling in England and the United States. After that, those who had been identified with Melanie Klein strengthened her group. Ernest Glover, who had been Jones's assistant, now swung over to the Kleinians, causing a schism in the British psychoanalytic community. There were the conservative ego psychology-oriented Freudians (with Anna Freud at their head), and the more interpersonally-oriented Kleinians in the other camp. John Bowlby, long interested in the effects of mother-child separation, became a member of the Kleinian group. Also affiliated with the Kleinians was Wilfred Bion, who had become interested in group dynamics as an outgrowth of his work during World War II with groups of soldiers (Malcolm Pines, 1995, personal communication).

In the United States, Bychowski had settled in New York, as had Sandor Rado; Heinz Hartmann, who had been analyzed by Rado, also went to New York, where he did his impressive work on ego psychology. Ernst Simmel became director of the Los Angeles Psychoanalytic Association; in Germany he had been director of the analytically-oriented Sanatorium at Tegelsee. While there, Simmel had initiated changes in the way hospitalized patients were treated: The confidentiality of the analyst-patient dyad was put aside with the more seriously ill psychotic or alcoholic patients in the sanatorium, because the members of the other disciplines—the nurses, social workers, occupational

Ernst Simmel

therapists, etc.—all needed to know what was transpiring in the analytic sessions. The analyst also needed to know how the patient was interacting with the hospital staff. Simmel understood that all parties involved in a patient's treatment needed to communicate, and he facilitated and encouraged this process.

Franz Alexander

Franz Alexander emigrated from Budapest to Chicago, where he became director of the analytic institute in 1932. Alexander's work included a book on the theoretical principles and applications of psychoanalysis. Written with Thomas French (Alexander & French, 1946), it contained chapters on the treatment of phobias, sexual problems, ulcers and other psychosomatic conditions, and alcoholism. With Sheldon Selesnick, he also wrote a book (1966) on the history of psychiatry several decades later. Alexander's interest in finding possible correlations between certain somatic diseases and psychological "precursors" inspired Flanders Dunbar's (1902–1959) research into this area. She felt that certain psychological patterns were discernible in a number of "psychosomatic" conditions, such as ulcer, colitis, asthma, and coronary heart disease (1938, 1944). She ultimately described a personality that supposedly underlay each variety of illness.

Flanders Dunbar

Later work by Arthur Mirsky showed that, in the case of duodenal ulcer, gastric hypersecretion of pepsinogen on a hereditary basis was present in those who developed ulcers. In other words, psychological factors may provoke ulcer formation in predisposed individuals, though many experts now question whether there is any *specificity* to the personality variables in the future ulcer victim. It seems more likely that a variety of psychological stressors may interact with many different personality types—in the presence of the hypersecretion—to bring about ulceration. The specificity factor in a psychosomatic condition may reside only in the inherited vulnerability of certain organs rather than in particular configurations of personality.

Arthur Mirsky

Helene Deutsch and Karen Horney, both analysands of Karl Abraham, also emigrated to America: Deutsch to Boston, Horney to New York. Deutsch wrote extensively on psychoanalytic theory as it pertained to women and gave much attention to the condition of *masochism*. Karen Horney (1885–1952), influenced by Adler, believed that the biological substrate in analytic theory (relating to developmental changes over the life cycle) was overly emphasized. She (1937, 1939) turned the spotlight on *culture* as the source of conflicts fueling neurosis: Specifically, Western culture gave rise to a conflict between the drive toward economic success versus our grounding in the philosophy of brotherly love. Unfortunately, the explanatory power of Horney's theory, as with all other theories of human behavior that omit the factors of

Karen Horney, 1885–1982. Courtesy National Library of Medicine

heredity and constitution, is severely limited. The same shortcomings affected the formulations of Adler and Melanie Klein.

Freud flees Austria

In 1938 Freud and his family were forced to flee Austria following the Nazi occupation. His fame was hardly enough to protect him and his family from the clutches of the Gestapo (who detained Anna Freud for several hours before releasing her). The Freuds would not have been able to move to London without the help of many influential gentile friends, some in government, others from within the psychoanalytic circle. Princess Marie Bonaparte, herself an analyst and staunch supporter of Freud, was particularly helpful (Peter Gay, 1988, tells the story in detail). Freud was slowly dying of oral cancer at the time. He had written *Civilization and Its Discontents* (1930) shortly before leaving Austria; *Moses and Monotheism* (1939) was completed in London, where he died the following year.

Psychoanalysis was an active enterprise in America during the 1930s: There was the orthodox Freudian school as well as alternative movements, of which the school founded by Harry Stack Sullivan (1892–1949) is the most important. In the late 1920s Sullivan was working with schizophrenic patients at St. Elizabeths in Washington. His orientation was *interpersonal* in much the same way that Melanie Klein's was *object-relational,* and for analogous reasons. Sullivan proposed that just as infants form a primary bond with their mothers, and thus have "preoedipal" concerns well before the triadic difficulties of the oedipal period are manifest, psychotic patients show difficulties in relating that are much more primitive (i.e., preoedipal) in their ontogenesis than is the case with neurotic patients.

Furthermore, it was clear to Sullivan (1953) that the intense emotional storms that so often flare up in psychotic patients evoked powerful emotions in their therapists as well. There was no way a therapist could quietly serve as a "blank screen" on which the patient could project various transference feelings. The therapist of the schizophrenic patient was an equal *participant,* at times constrained to reveal his or her real feelings as these were elicited by the affect storms of the patient: Hence the *interpersonal* nature of the therapeutic transaction. Sullivan himself was marvelously intuitive and attuned to the unconscious processes of his schizophrenic patients; he was at once compassionate yet blunt in his responses—a very different scenario from the contemplative analyst at work with the generally calm and undemanding neurotic patient.

Although Sullivan recognized the importance of biological factors, in his writing (1953, 1962) he clearly emphasized the mother-child bond, and how its abnormalities could affect the child's psychological development. Schizophrenia was attrib-

Harry Stack Sullivan, 1892–1949. Courtesy Corbis-Bettmann

uted to the mother's anxiety, which she transmitted to her infant. Sullivan created a special terminology in describing mental operations that covers much the same territory as orthodox psychoanalysis but with different words. Thus "transference distortions" become "parataxic distortions," and so on.

Sullivan's influence was strongest among American psychiatrists who worked with schizophrenic patients, especially at mid-century, when psychotherapy (rather than medications and rehabilitation techniques) was still the mainstay in treatment. There was an optimistic chord in Sullivanian theory: The schizophrenic mode of thought was a reaction to severe psychological stress, whose removal through therapy would be accompanied by resumption of normal modes of thought. It was as though anyone could "become" schizophrenic temporarily, given enough stress: Normal, neurotic, and psychotic thought patterns were viewed as occurring on a continuum, along which one could slide back and forth, depending on circumstances. It was this perspective (quite incorrect in the light of subsequent research) that lent such a sense of hopefulness to the psychotherapy of schizophrenia.

General Psychiatry; Group Psychotherapy

In outright opposition to the Freudian school of psychoanalysis was the school of behaviorism championed by psychologist Burrhus Frederick Skinner (1904–1990). Objecting to the "non-scientific" nature of psychoanalytic theory and adopting Watson's position that because behavior is observable, it provides a more objective basis for understanding psychological life. Skinner proposed that neuroses could be understood more scientifically as sets of learned (as opposed to innate) behaviors that happen to be maladaptive for the individual. These behaviors, like all behaviors, are acquired through the process of conditioning; maladaptive results arise from the learning of disadvantageous conditioned-response patterns. Skinner's publications began in 1930 with a paper on eating reflexes and culminated in *The Behavior of Organisms* published in 1938. Earlier, Thorndike (1874–1949) had promulgated a "law of reward" (1911) based on the ability of certain actions to gratify a need and thus reinforce the behavior pattern in question.

Burrhus Frederick Skinner

Smith Ely Jelliffe (1866–1945), neuropsychiatrist and editor of the *Journal of Nervous and Mental Diseases,* and his colleague and co-editor, William Alanson White (1870–1937), were instrumental in gaining acceptance for the teaching of psychoanalysis in psychiatry departments at university medical schools. They had been favorably impressed by A. A. Brill, whose founding of the American Psychoanalytic Association in 1911 had received the support of Ernest Jones, who had lectured on psychoanalysis in Canada and the United States

Smith Ely Jelliffe

William Alanson White

from 1908 until his return to London in 1913. Jelliffe was among those who, along with Angel Garma in Argentina, had tried to link each psychosomatic disease with a specific abnormal psychological profile (A. & S., p. 391).

Hospital Psychiatry

Manfred Sakel

In Berlin in 1933 Manfred Sakel (1900–1957) applied induced-insulin coma to the treatment of schizophrenia. The technique seemed more effective in acute than in chronic cases. However, the difficulties in its administration and the uncertainty of its scientific rationale led to its discontinuance some twenty years later, even while electroconvulsive therapy (ECT) retained a measure of usefulness in the acute phase. During the 1930s Cerletti was also establishing the usefulness of ECT in the treatment of melancholia—a usefulness which, with refinements added in the intervening years, it retains to this day.

Few advances were introduced in the treatment of hospitalized schizophrenic and manic-depressive patients during this decade, apart from the new, analytically-oriented psychotherapeutic methods, introduced by Hermann Nunberg (among the orthodox analysts) and Harry Stack Sullivan. In 1939 Abraham Myerson advocated an aggressive approach that he called "total push," which consisted of getting patients who were languishing in the back wards re-involved in life. Recreational activities, vocational training, crafts, psychotherapy, group therapy, whirlpool baths—Myerson made use of anything and everything the ward-milieu could provide.

Abraham Myerson

Jacob Kasanin

Intermediate forms of psychoses became more recognized in the 1930s. In 1933 Jacob Kasanin, a Boston analyst who worked in a hospital setting with psychotics, coined the term "schizoaffective" to designate a psychosis whose features reflected equal measure of schizophrenic and manic-depressive symptoms. Debate has clouded this diagnosis ever since: Are these "atypical psychoses" *really* variants of one or the other classical disorder? Schizoaffective illness is usually characterized by clear-cut precipitants (such as loss of a love-relationship) and a better level of premorbid function than is characteristic of schizophrenia; the prognosis is usually better as well.

Gabriel Langfedlt

The issue of prognosis and ultimate outcome took on special importance for Norwegian investigator Gabriel Langfeldt who, in 1937, divided the diagnosis of schizophrenia into two groups: "process" and "reactive." The latter, in which the outcome was often favorable, was equivalent to what Kasanin was calling *schizoaffective;* others, *atypical.* In the process cases the course was usually deteriorating. Both types might show delusions and hallucinations (what we now call "positive symptoms"), but those with a process condition also showed anhedonia, blunted affect, loss of will ("abulia") (what we now call "negative symptoms"). Their premorbid personalities were usually schizoid and the onset was insidious rather than acute.

Biological Psychiatry and Genetics

Not all the refugees from Germany were psychoanalysts. Before emigrating to New York, psychogeneticist Franz Kallmann had worked at the German Research Institute for Psychiatry, where he studied the inheritance of schizophrenia and other conditions (epilepsy, alcoholism) via analysis of families and concordance rates in monozygotic versus dizygotic twins. His mentor was Rüdin; Luxenburger was a co-worker. Kallmann continued accumulating probands in the United States, until he had amassed 106 twin-pairs for whom the index case was schizophrenic (along with 38 pairs with at least one manic-depressive). His concordance figures were high: in monozygotic pairs 86% of the co-twins of a schizophrenic were also schizophrenic. In other family analyses, 63% of the offspring of parents, *both* of whom were schizophrenic, also became schizophrenic as adults. These rates were consistent with the assumption of single dominant-gene inheritance. But subsequent studies have not duplicated rates as high as Kallmann's, perhaps because of the severity of the schizophrenic illness in his probands. This severity factor is known to be associated with higher twin concordances than when the disease in the probands is milder (McCabe et al., 1971).

Franz Kallmann

Around the same time Eliot Slater in England was studying the families of manic-depressive probands. In a paper published in 1938 he noted an incidence of manic-depression in one form or another in 11% of the parents and 22% of the children—figures that rose to 17% and 26%, respectively, if suicides were counted as probable instances of the serious depressive form of the illness. In a later twin study of schizophrenia (1953), Slater found a concordance rate of 68%.

Eliot Slater

In America physiologist Walter Cannon (1881–1945) was demonstrating the effects of intense emotional states, such as rage and fear, upon the endocrine system. He discovered that the adrenal glands become activated during these states so that more energy (from carbohydrates) becomes available to the organism. Cannon's work established a firmer foundation for the psychosomatic research being carried out during this period by providing a solid biochemical explanation for the way in which chronic emotional stress might adversely affect bodily function and even organ integrity. This biochemical basis reduced the esoteric (as the behavioralists envisioned it) aura of those who claimed the mind could indeed influence the body.

Walter Cannon

Cannon's work was supplemented by the studies of James Papez, a neurologist, who suggested that the limbic system played a role in emotional control, not just in olfactory processes (Snyder, 1988).

James Papez

Papez's (1937) research on rabies revealed that the characteristic brain lesions that resulted were located in the Negri bodies of the limbic system. Since rabies is associated with severe emotional reactions of fearfulness, rage, and hyperexcitability (Snyder, 1988), Papez hypothesized that the components of the limbic system—chiefly, the hippocampus, hypothalamus, and cingulate gyrus—are not only interconnected but serve to mediate the emotional responses of the organism. These responses include the subjective experiences of emotion as well as the motoric activity (flight, fight, sexual arousal) appropriate to and accompanying each specific feeling state.

In this same time frame Klüver and Bucy (1938) were demonstrating the phenomenon of "sham rage" in animals rendered extremely irritable following the surgical removal of the hypothalamus. Despite these important experiments, the anatomy and functions of the limbic system were little taught or understood in medical education until the 1960s and 1970s, when the neurochemistry of emotion was further clarified. Indeed, the work of Valzelli (1981) and others on the psychobiology of aggression and violence was inspired by the pioneering work of Papez and Klüver.

Child Psychiatry

Leo Kanner

In 1935 Leo Kanner published the first textbook in English on child psychiatry. Therein he referred to schizophrenia and other thought disorders as "parergastic"; to mood disorders, as "thymergastic" (p. 484). He viewed masturbation and homosexuality as distinct abnormalities (p. 397) brought about by disruptive biological factors. Kanner was a pioneer in the area of infantile autism. He viewed the characteristic aloofness and uncommunicativeness of autistic children as the primary result of the "coldness" of the mothers, whom he described as generally being intelligent but distant. Later it was shown that autistic children come from a variety of backgrounds and that neither the mothers' high intelligence nor aloofness had anything to do with their children's autism. The explanation for Kanner's assumption is that the first cases he encountered were those brought to him by a small number of women with doctoral degrees, who happened to be working in the same hospital where Kanner worked. For some years thereafter, the mothers of autistic children were unfortunately branded as "refrigerator mothers." Now it is widely recognized that infantile autism is an organic condition unrelated to the comparative warmth or detachment of the parents.

Lauretta Bender

Working out of Bellevue Hospital in New York, Lauretta Bender viewed autistic children, especially those who were unable to talk and who treated other people like objects, as examples of "childhood schizophrenia" (1947). At least Bender recognized that the condition was rooted in constitution, even though it turns out that autism is (for the most part) etiologically distinct from schizophrenia and autistic children do not have family members with schizophrenia in numbers greater than one would expect from population averages.

1940–1949

Descriptive Psychiatry and Psychology

Kretschmer's work on finding correlations between body type and mental illness was continued in the United States by W. H. Sheldon, whose *Varieties of Human Physique* was published in 1940. Sheldon depicted three extremes of body habitus—very thin (*ectomorph*), very fat (*endomorph*), and very muscular (*mesomorph*)—which he used for assessing all "body types." As Kretschmer had found, Sheldon noted correlations between the thin type and schizophrenia; the fat type and manic-depression. Aggressive and criminal men were often mesomorphic, though Sheldon observed that many delinquent adolescents were "gyandromorphic"—that is, they had bodily features of both men and women. Sheldon gave credit to Beneke for his "precise measurements of . . . external anatomy" that had paved the way for Kretschmer; also to Lombroso, whom Sheldon praised: "His work will provide leads and hypotheses for many generations of investigators yet to be born" (p. 306). Only recently (1995) did it emerge that Sheldon, as part of his research efforts, had taken thousands of nude photographs of freshmen at various prestigious colleges around the country—some of whom had gone on to achieve prominent places in society. Mercifully, these photographs have now been shredded, and, along with Sheldon's specious (but once popular) work, have taken their place on the scrap heap of tendentious pseudoscience.

W. H. Sheldon

In 1948 Alfred Kinsey and his colleagues in Indiana published the results of their large-scale survey of sexual habits and practices of American males. Their work suggested that a third of American males have had homosexual experiences at some point in their lives and that about 6% of males were fixedly homosexual. Their study, as with other studies on sexuality in recent years, was methodologically flawed: The sample was not truly representative of the population; the responses, not all trustworthy. Even so, Kinsey's figures were more realistic than the assumptions held by the general public prior to this research, which helped to decriminalize homosexuality.

Alfred Kinsey

The process has been slow, since antihomosexual sentiments run deep wherever Judeo-Christian teaching has been dominant. As Elaine Pagels (1988) points out, in desert tribes—which is where the Western religions got their start—to be fruitful and *multiply* was to survive:

Small groups were easily taken over by large groups, so sexual practices that did not result in reproduction—masturbation, adultery, prostitution, and homosexuality—all became taboo. Western society has been reluctant to view homosexuality as a natural biological variant in our species, just as it had been reluctant to accept masturbation as biologically inevitable and prostitution as socially inevitable. The decriminalization of homosexuality was followed a generation later by its demedicalization—that is, by its removal as a mental condition from *DSM–III* in 1980.

David Wechsler

Improvements in the standardization of intelligence testing were introduced by David Wechsler in his Wechsler-Bellevue IQ test, which generates a "quotient" derived from dividing a subject's intellectual achievement (as measured by the test, calibrated according to the age at which various questions can usually be answered correctly) by the chronological age. The test is considered valid when administered to children of at least elementary-school age.

Hans Eysenck

In England Hans Eysenck created a system for evaluating personality based on three "super-factors": neuroticism, extraversion, and psychoticism (1947), each derived from analysis of a large array of personality traits. The factors are used dimensionally, in the sense that each person being assessed can be situated somewhere along these dimensional axes, according to his or her responses to standardized questionnaires.

Jean Piaget

In Switzerland throughout the 1940s and beyond, Jean Piaget (1896–1980) made important contributions to our understanding of the normal development of intellectual faculties as they steadily progress from infancy to adulthood. He was professor of psychology at the University of Geneva from 1937 to 1954 (A. & S., p. 255), where he established the norms for, and outlined four phases of, a child's cognitive development (1941). The progression Piaget described included a *sensory-motor* stage, wherein the child learns about surrounding space and how to manipulate it in order to fulfill his desires (for example, by pulling a toy towards himself); a *pre-operational* stage, (wherein verbal symbols are learned, so that words come to represent objects); a stage of *concrete operations* (wherein objects become classified according to similarities); and a stage of *formal operations* (beginning in early adolescence), wherein adult logic is utilized more and more (for example, the tall glass might *not* hold more water than the short glass—because the short one might be much wider).

Starke Hathaway
J. C. McKinley

Building on the psychometric work of the 1930s, much of which was not very successful, Starke Hathaway and J. C. McKinley developed a self-report instrument for the detailed assessment of personality: the *Minnesota Multiphasic Personality Inventory,* usually abbreviated to the MMPI. This is arguably the most widely-used test of personality, one that has spawned many hundreds of articles and books.

Over the years certain modifications have been made; the test now contains nearly 600 questions relating to ten clinical scales: (1)hypochondriasis, (2) depression, (3) hysteria, (4) psychopathic deviance, (5) masculinity/femininity, (6) paranoia, (7) psychasthenia, (8) schizophrenia, (9) hypomania, (10) social introversion. There are additional scales for evaluating dishonesty of response (the "Lie" scale), validity, and atypicality.

The authors of the MMPI strove to make their factors as conceptually distinct as possible. The scale names betoken only personality *tendencies*. For example, a high score on scale #8 does not establish a diagnosis of schizophrenia; rather it suggests the presence of alienation and bizarreness of sensory experience found in schizophrenics (and also in other diagnostic categories). The test is suitable for the assessment of both normal and abnormal personality traits. What is important is the *profile:* For example, borderline patients often show an #8-4-2-6 profile (i.e., high scores on these scales, respectively).

Psychoanalysis

Psychoanalysts in the 1940s still tended to think about causation in purely psychological terms. This trend was established by the pioneer generation, even though Freud himself, grounded in medicine through his neurological training, always acknowledged the importance of constitutional factors. Melanie Klein, who was not medically trained, was especially prone to ignore possible constitutional underpinnings, as did most of her followers. Further reinforcing the psychological bias was the connotation of incurability attached to heredity, which made the analysts of this generation reluctant even to consider the possibility of inherited predispositions.

In 1942 an important article was published by Helene Deutsch on the "as-if" personality. Her work laid the foundation for modern psychoanalytic formulations concerning borderline personality organization, as elaborated by Otto Kernberg. Deutsch described how object-relations are disturbed in characteristic ways in borderline patients, of which the as-if patient is a subtype. The as-if patient, lacking a strong sense of identity and solid values, manages to get along by adopting, in chameleon-like fashion, the attitudes, values, and beliefs of whoever is the friend or lover of the moment. Deutsch thought that these patients, with their lack of warmth and substance, might represent incipient cases of schizophrenia; this aspect of her formulation no longer seems valid.

Interest in borderline conditions was growing, partly because analysts were becoming more aware of certain patients

Helene Deutsch, 1884–1982. Courtesy Special Collections, A. A. Brill Library, The New York Psychoanalytic Institute

whose psychodynamics were easy to decipher but whose condition did not improve. In 1938 Adolph Stern described such patients and gave a workable, if loose, definition, which helped put borderline conditions on the "mental map" of the analytic community. In her 1947 paper, Melitta Schmideberg characterized these patients as "stably unstable." Others noted their weak ego structures, inability to deal with common interpersonal situations without becoming inordinately anxious, and paranoid or depressive tendencies.

W. Ronald Fairbairn

Meanwhile, in Scotland, Kleinian-oriented psychoanalyst W. Ronald Fairbairn (1954) was proposing a modification of Freud's instinct-based metapsychology along *object-relational* lines. Fairbairn viewed regression as the withdrawal from a bad external world—often enough, from the bad or negative aspects of the mothering figure—into the security of an inner world. As Guntrip mentions (1969, p. 56), this is the essence of the "schizoid problem": the deepest element in all psychopathological development. Fairbairn wrote extensively on the schizoid personality, situating it on a continuum with the schizophrenic. He described schizoid persons as fearful of intimacy to the point of preferring isolation to social intercourse, even at the risk of losing all loveobjects or even their own egos. There is considerable cogency to Fairbairn's clinical picture (here, of the withdrawn, schizoid patient), but less cogency to his theoretical formulation. As with others of the Kleinian school, he fails to address the biological factor in the major condition of schizophrenia, to which many "withdrawn" patients are allied only by *analogy,* not by *biology.*

General Psychiatry; Group Psychotherapy

World War II spurred interest in several areas of psychiatry that concerned problems encountered by soldiers facing battle. Some psychiatrists gathered experience working with soldiers experiencing "shell shock," the recurrent nightmares, flashbacks, and anxiety attacks that we now label "posttraumatic stress disorder" (PTSD). Other psychiatrists dealt with the fear and reluctance of certain inductees to face the rigors of war; Whitman et al. (1954) described such men as "passiveaggressive." This was the birth of a new personality disorder label, although the characteristics were encountered in many other situations, both before and after the war: e.g., covert hostility toward a boss, showing up as slow or sloppy work; promises on the part of uncooperative children to do various chores that they then do belatedly or conveniently forget to do altogether.

Wilfred Bion

Wilfred Bion (1897–1979), the British psychoanalyst affiliated with the Kleinians, had been a tank officer at the age of 17 during World War I (barely escaping death during a battle) and had served again in World War II. He worked with groups of soldiers on an interpersonal plane and evolved a theory of group function that had a level of sophistication equal to that of conventional psychoanalytic theory of individual function. Bion (1952) postulated that, ontogenetically speaking, the individual inevitably begins life as a member of a "group"—the family—and experiences anxiety (which Bion likened to "psychosis") in relation to the primary "objects" (usually, mother and father). In group settings later on, certain primitive affect states are reawakened. Bion referred to these affect states as "basic assumptions": dependency (that someone will take care of the group members), coupling (that one can find a mate within the group), and "fight-flight" (that there are "enemies" external to the group, whom one must either attack or flee from, depending on one's assessment of the group's strength relative to that of the dangerous outsiders).

It is difficult to grasp the full force and comprehensiveness of Bion's postulates unless one participates in a group experience, such as a workshop organized by the A. K. Rice Institute—a British organization, inspired by Bion's work, devoted to the study of group process. In these workshops a dozen or so group members, offered no clues as to how they are supposed to conduct their group, begin to select a leader, as if by some magical "chemistry," and then to form pairings, developing both a sense of group pride and a wariness of other groups that have formed during the workshop.

Experiences of this sort help us to understand the unconscious operations that can permeate many group situations, including the typical meetings on psychiatric wards as well as larger groups in everyday life—even political groups and the behavior of groups of nations. With a practical knowledge of Bion's work, it becomes less mysterious how it was possible, for example, for a dark-haired, bigoted, paranoid, vagrant hack-artist with a gift for oratory to emerge from a homeless shelter in Vienna to become the Nazi Führer of the blond "super race." Hitler became the leader when the "group"—in this case, the whole German-speaking part of central Europe—was enraged to the point of desperation by the economic collapse of the 1920s that resulted from the impossible reparations payments Germany owed the Allies. The ensuing inflation, joblessness, and dispossession of the working class made Germany ripe for blind obedience (Bion's "dependency") to a charismatic, paranoid leader, who promised to put the group's troubles to rest.

Group dynamics of this sort can also be observed in much smaller settings—for example, on a psychiatric ward composed of patients of different functional levels. During calm periods the better organized, higher functioning members tend to dominate the community meetings, but during times of great stress (loss of key staff members, for example) often a very disorganized, schizophrenic patient may set the tone for the meeting—emoting baleful expressions of rage that tap directly into the troubled emotions of the healthier members, who are too diffident to complain openly.

Bion's principles facilitate our understanding of the inner workings of therapeutic groups of all sorts, whether with hospitalized or ambulatory patients. But as a technique, the A. K. Rice model, where the non-directive leader maintains prolonged silences and gives minimal suggestions, is appropriate only for better functioning persons. As is generally true in individual psychoanalysis, the paucity of interactions on the part of the therapist usually proves too anxiety-provoking for severely disturbed patients.

Hospital Psychiatry; Treatment of Psychotic Patients

Egas Moniz

Portuguese neurologist Egas Moniz (1874–1955) was impressed by the recurrent morbid thoughts of melancholic and obsessive-compulsive patients. Believing that these reflected reverberating circuits in the brain, he hypothesized that it might be possible to interrupt them by severing the nerve tracts leading from the centers subserving the reverberating circuits to the presumed centers of consciousness in the frontal lobes. This was the thinking behind his idea of *prefrontal lobotomy.* Moniz used this operative procedure on schizophrenic patients who failed to respond to other measures, as well as on obsessives and melancholics. The success he reported won him worldwide fame plus a Nobel Prize. The original procedure proved too radical to be practicable: Many patients were rendered, albeit calmer, mere shadows of their former selves. Lobotomy has mostly fallen out of favor, except in cases of intractable obsessive disorder, where the modern operation is limited to a cingulotomy instead of a whole frontal lobotomy.

The discovery of penicillin by Alexander Fleming in Britain in the 1940s led to the possibility of truly effective treatment of syphilis; cases of general paresis are now quite rare on psychiatric wards.

Don Jackson
"double bind"

In the treatment of schizophrenia, Don Jackson and his colleagues pioneered the concept of the "double bind" in which the future schizophrenic patient was ensnared by the "double messages" from key family members (Bateson, Jackson, Haley, & Weakland, 1956). For example, a hostile mother might say, "Of course, I love you!" in such an angry tone of voice and accompanied by such a scowl that her child becomes bewildered as to what Mother really feels. The resulting confusion was believed to be the etiologic agent in the psychosis that later developed.

A whole school of theoreticians formed around this postulate: Gregory Bateson, the family therapists Theodore Lidz, Lyman Wynne, Murray Bowen, and Jay Haley. This school dominated psychiatric thought about schizophrenia in the late 1940s, throughout the 1950s, and on into the 1960s. The theory is purely psychological in its etiology, denying any role for biological factors, clearly overlooking the obvious fact that many children grow up in homes where they are exposed to "double binds" day in and day out, without ever developing schizophrenia.

The tragedy here was that a whole generation of mothers of schizophrenics was branded as "schizophrenogenic," as though they were evil, disease-producing witches, deserving the opprobrium of the psychiatric profession. Subsequent research has made it clear that some families of schizophrenics are indeed rageful, accusatory, and humiliating toward the affected family member (Vaughn & Leff, 1976a, 1976b), but it is the inborn vulnerability that interacts with these hostile displays to exacerbate the underlying condition. There are no more families with the above traits among schizophrenic patients than in the general population. In fact, many schizophrenics come from families where the parents are nurturing, patient, as well as cooperative with therapists who try to help them understand the nature of their child's illness.

"schizophrenogenic"

In the late 1940s John Rosen, an analyst in Pennsylvania, developed a vigorous approach to the treatment of schizophrenia which he called "direct analysis" (1947). Rosen would make extremely blunt, "direct" interpretations, couched in a purposely repugnant, not to say scatological, language, of a patient's supposed underlying dynamics. Thus he might say to a lethargic patient from the "back wards": "What you really want is to suck your father's dick!" This would often jolt the patient temporarily into unaccustomed perkiness and activity, which Rosen interpreted to be the "cure" he had striven to effect. He would then minister to the next such patient, using the same confrontative technique, without reexamining what had become of the first patient at a later time. When others conducted a follow-up study (Horwitz, Polatin et al., 1958), it was learned that the patients relapsed into their former lethargy within about two weeks.

John Rosen

An altogether different approach with hospitalized schizophrenic patients was taken by Frieda Fromm-Reichmann (1899–1957), who emigrated from Munich and became a staff psychoanalyst at the Chestnut Lodge Institute in Maryland. A woman of incomparable intuitive ability and unfailing humanism, she was able to reach the most regressed patients. She was also the much admired therapist of Hannah Green, who wrote *I Never Promised You a Rose Garden,* which described her healing experience under Fromm-Reichmann's care when she was a disturbed adolescent.

Among Fromm-Reichmann's many written works is *Principles of Intensive Psychotherapy* published in 1950, containing her insightful comments about how therapists of very disturbed patients might use their countertransferential feelings to advantage in the therapeutic work. In her remarks about the proper manner of conducting "in-

Frieda Fromm-Reichmann, 1899–1957. Courtesy National Library of Medicine

tensive psychotherapy" (her term for psychoanalytically-oriented therapy, with three to five sessions per week), particularly in working with hospitalized patients, Fromm-Reichmann urged the exact opposite of Rosen's confrontative approach. As she cautioned: "[The therapist] will not intentionally push or force patients into reexperiencing these [oedipal or other disturbing] feelings with him, as was frequently done in the early days of psychoanalysis" (1950, p. 100). Writing several years prior to the era of drug-specific treatments for the major psychoses, Fromm-Reichmann continued to place reliance on verbal interpretations, as did most therapists at mid-century:

> With the schizophrenic, interpretation of dynamics is the approach needed. One of the schizophrenic's responses to excess emotional pain . . . is to withdraw his interest from the outside world and to live in a private inner world of his own. . . . Hence he expresses himself in a private language or in a way that sounds like mere tenuous allusions to the nonschizophrenic listener. (p. 86)

The therapist's task was to help the patient re-enter the everyday world through careful and well-timed interpretations, which would diminish the need to withdraw to the "private inner world of his own."

Biological Psychiatry

J. F. J. Cade

In the late 1940s J. F. J. Cade, an Australian researcher interested in the effects of purines on behavior, began using lithium urate to reduce the nephrotoxicity to uric acid in his animal experiments. This substance seemed to have a calming effect. From this unanticipated finding, Cade then thought to use lithium with manic patients: he reported some positive results in a 1949 article. Cade's research marked the beginning of the era of condition-specific psychopharmacology, most of which unfolded in the 1950s (and is discussed in the section on that decade).

Interest in neural feedback mechanisms, neural networks, computer models of the brain, etc., got much of its start from the work of Shannon and Weaver on mathematical logic, information measurement, and neural networks as set forth in a *Bell Systems Technical Journal* in 1948.

This was also the beginning of the modern computer era: John von Neumann had been instrumental in constructing the first generation of computers, such as the Eniac, which was used by the U.S. Armed Forces in World War II. Not long thereafter, another extraordinary polymath, Norbert Wiener (1894–1964), published his monograph on "Cybernetics" (1948), in which he discussed feedback mechanisms,

Norbert Wiener

computing machines, and the nervous system. In his remarks on the brain Wiener stated: "The brain under normal circumstances is not the complete analogue of the computing machine, but rather the analogue of a single run on such a machine" (p. 143). In regard to memory, he mentioned the feedback analogy: ". . . a satisfactory method for constructing a short term memory is to keep a sequence of impulses traveling around in a closed circuit, until this circuit is closed from the outside. There is much reason to believe this happens in our brains during [memory]" (p. 143).

Wiener speculated that *functional* psychological disorders (those without demonstrable brain lesions) might be "diseases of memory," in which the "circulating information [is] kept by the brain in the active state." Then "the alteration of synaptic thresholds" causes "secondary disturbances of traffic," in turn causing an "overload of messages" (p. 171)—which ultimately manifests as neurosis, psychosis, or a reverberating circuit-like condition such as obsessive-compulsive disorder. Wiener's self-correcting "negative" feedback operators in the nervous system are analogous to the inhibitory *psi* neurones of Freud's 1895 *Project*.

The invention of the computer and the research on feedback mechanisms and neural networks (both mathematical and neurophysiological) transformed psychiatry in the post-World War II era. Tools were now at hand to test the hypotheses elaborated earlier in the century by the psychoanalysts and psychotherapists who had focused on the individual. In addition, a spirit of rigorous scientific method now pervaded a field whose scientific credentials had, to be quite candid, begun to tarnish for lack of such things as control groups, statistical methods, objectifiable questionnaires, and carefully collected patient-samples of a size large enough to permit meaningful comparisons. Soon it would no longer be possible to interview half a dozen schizophrenic patients, three of whose mothers seemed "overbearing," and get an article published on the "schizophrenogenic mother."

Child Psychiatry

Observing that infants who are severely neglected from birth fail to thrive, and at times even waste away (a condition then called "marasmus") and die, Margaret Ribble wrote on the way the mother's handling of her infant affected whether it would be overly active or listless (1945). She viewed insufficient nurturance to be the cause of various tics and rhythmic disturbances seen in young children, such as rocking and thumb-sucking.

Margaret Ribble

Sybylle Escalona and Mary Leitch (1949) saw parallels between the mother's tension level and that of her infant. However, even highly

Sybylle Escalona

anxious mothers who "transmitted" high anxiety levels to their infants did not necessarily produce a schizophrenic reaction; the future of such children might take any of a number of clinical courses.

David Levy

David Levy wrote about a particular form of maternal anxiety that had adverse consequences—namely, *overprotectiveness* (1941). In his view, overprotectiveness could be expressed in two forms: *overindulgence,* which might lead to excessive dependency in the child, or excessive *control,* which might cause intimidation and slavish conformity in the child.

Adelaide Johnson

In the area of juvenile delinquency, Adelaide Johnson published an important paper on the "superego lacuna," by which she referred to a postulated defect in the conscience of certain parents (from any social class), who subtly condone "cutting corners" or transgressing social norms. Learning that it is acceptable to steal, play hooky, throw rocks at someone's car, etc.—even sensing that such behavior gives secret pleasure to the parent(s)—the child (usually in adolescence) then feels permitted, even encouraged, to commit these acts.

Chapter 13

1950–1959: DEVELOPMENTS IN THE UNITED STATES BECOME PROMINENT

DESCRIPTIVE PSYCHIATRY AND PSYCHOLOGY

The current fourth edition of the *Diagnostic and Statistical Manual of Mental Disorders (DSM–IV)* (1994) is the great-grandchild of *DSM–I*, which appeared in 1952. The significance of the first edition, as Spitzer points out (1994), was that it represented the first attempt to provide operational definitions of all the various categories of mental disorders. Earlier diagnostic systems were either simplistic to the vanishing point of offering a single category[1] or else simply simple, using five or six categories (mania, melancholia, paranoia, amentia, dementia, hysteria). *DSM–I* was modeled after the theory of Adolf Meyer, who stated that the various conditions were "reaction types"; indeed, the term reaction is used throughout this manual. Diagnostic entities were divided into two overarching groups: organic and functional; functional disorders were subdivided into psychotic, psychophysiological, and personality-disordered categories.

Diagnostic and
Statistical Manual
of Mental Disorders

---

[1] In the early 19th-century United States, *idiocy* was the sole category; in Germany there was E. Zeller's 1844 term *Einheitspsychose* [unitary psychosis]; and in the 18th century, the alienists listed only *lunacy*.

PSYCHOANALYSIS

Sandor Rado

Hungarian emigré Sandor Rado came into prominence in the 1950s, partly due to the fact that he left the New York Psychoanalytic Society in order to found the Columbia Psychoanalytic Institute a few years earlier (1945), and partly due to his many articles on schizophrenia, normal psychology, and psychoanalytic theory and technique. Regarding the ideal outcome of analytic therapy to be the patient's adaptation to his or her interpersonal world, Rado stressed attention to the here-and-now, not just to early childhood memories. In Rado's view, focus on the remote past, which the psychoanalytic method fosters via use of the couch and frequent sessions that evoke dependency on the analyst and a reliving of the child-parent relationship, must be a means to an end —better adaptation as an adult—and not an end in itself. The transference (which he called "parentifying") must be analyzed, to be sure, but the patient must always be brought back to the current situation. Rado invented a terminology of his own, perhaps by way of giving a new look to old ideas. Mercifully, most of his terms have fallen into disuse ("ipsation" for masturbation, "non-reporting brain" for unconscious, and so on).

"schizotype"

One of Rado's major accomplishments was to reintroduce biology where it had been sorely neglected. Rado was convinced (and he was right) that schizophrenia had strong hereditary underpinnings; he proposed the notion of the "schizotype" (later used by psychologist Paul Meehl) to indicate the phenotype of the inherited predisposition to the full form of the illness. Rado saw the schizotypal person as representing one pole of a *spectrum* comprised of gradations of "anhedonia" and "proprioceptive diathesis" (by which he meant a tendency toward distorted awareness of the bodily self). At the mild end of the spectrum was "compensated schizoadaptation" (his term for the schizoid personality); at the other, "schizotypal deterioration" (schizophrenia).

Rado was interested in the application of psychoanalysis not just to neurotic patients ("reconstructive" cases) but also to less integrated (borderline) or psychosomatic patients, who required a less rigorous but still analytically-oriented treatment (these were "reparative" cases). Although analysis of more severely ill patients had been in vogue for some years, by mid-century it was widely recognized that alternative measures ("parameters") were necessary in the context of treatment. Such patients should remain in a sitting position, the here-and-now should be emphasized over the remote past, the therapist should intervene in life-threatening situations, the therapist should say the first word if the patient is silent for too long at the beginning of a session, and so on. Different terms were used to designate this altered style of analysis, such as "psychoanalytically-oriented psychotherapy" (as suggested by Racamier). (Later on, terms like *exploratory* or *expressive* were advocated.)

In the middle of this decade, when the new psychoactive medications came into use, heated debate took place within the analytic community as to whether these agents fostered or hindered the analytic process. Some argued that they dulled the senses, making it hard for patients to gain access to relevant psychic material; others claimed that the drugs gave surcease from anxiety, thus allowing schizophrenic or agoraphobic patients, for example, to explore the relevant areas more calmly. Purists abjured the use of the drugs altogether. (The staff at Chestnut Lodge, in particular, eschewed the use of such medications even with schizophrenic or manic-depressive patients until very recent times.)

psychoactive medications

Another critical issue of the time concerned the limits of psychoanalysis as a therapy. Which psychiatric conditions were amenable to analysis? Which illnesses or personality configurations were likely to prove utterly resistant? This was a time when symposia were organized to discuss the "borderline" conditions, which many had defined in terms of the patient's analyzability, or lack thereof. Meanwhile, others continued to use the label as an indicator of "diluted" schizophrenia. This was true even of Robert Knight, a psychoanalyst at the Austin Riggs psychiatric hospital in Massachusetts, who was the first to use *borderline* as a separate diagnostic entity (see below, Hospital Psychiatry), all the while paying lip service to the tradition that viewed borderline conditions as falling within the domain of schizophrenia.

"borderline" conditions

In the late 1950s Edith Jacobson (1953, 1973) had recognized that certain "resistant" cases of depression were probably "borderline" with respect to manic-depression, an astute observation not made in analytic circles since the days of Oberndorf (1930) some 25 years before.

Edith Jacobson

Donald Winnicott (1896–1971), an English psychoanalyst of the Kleinian school, had first trained and worked as a pediatrician—a background that greatly fostered his appreciation of the mother's role in her infant's development. In papers of the early 1950s Winnicott first conceptualized the "transitional object" as something chosen by an infant or toddler to serve as a comforting symbol and substitute for the "primary object," the mother, during her temporary absences. The object may be a teddy bear, a "Linus blanket," a special pillow . . . any object connoting warmth and comfort to the young one. Many clinicians have noted that anxious children and certain adults (those with borderline personality disorder, for example) tend to clutch on to their transitional objects longer than do others of similar age and circumstance.

Donald Winnicott

Winnicott (1965) also originated the concept of the "good-enough mother," the largely empathic, nurturing mother who, despite minor shortcomings, is about as good as one could look forward to in this world, and who serves quite adequately as a source of identification and validation. Another related concept we owe to Winnicott is that of the therapist as "container," whereby the patient's intense and often hostile emotions are temporarily "contained" by—allowed to reside in—the therapist, who is not frightened or unsettled by them, thus creating a safe space within which the affect storms can be explored and therapeutically resolved or mitigated.

countertransference

Beginning in 1951, Annie Reich wrote extensively on the topic of countertransference, which was, in fact, one of the main themes discussed by psychoanalysts during the 1950s. Earlier, Clara Thompson had observed that unconscious determinants played a role in a patient's choice of analyst (Fine, 1979), which might lead to a stalemate if the analyst had a corresponding set of unresolved countertransference problems (an interesting comment, considering that Harry Stack Sullivan was her analysand: Sullivan, who was homosexual, felt only men could treat men; only women could treat women. Was it meaningful that he chose Thompson?). In his 1949 paper on "Hate in the Countertransference," Winnicott had suggested that analysts who work with psychotic patients could hardly escape from feeling hatred, fear, and other powerful emotions at various times, and that they might need to communicate these responses in some compassionate (and dispassionate) way in order for treatment to progress. (A decade later Searles was to give many examples of this countertransference reaction in his papers on intensive therapy with schizophrenic patients.) Analysts began also to distinguish between "neurotic" versus "inevitable" countertransferences: The former were related to unresolved conflicts from the developmental years of the analyst; the latter were reactions no ordinary human being could avoid—such as the wave of disgust Searles (1964) registered when one of his schizophrenic patients moved his bowels on the analytic couch!

Heinz Hartmann

The 1950s was also the decade when analysts shifted their attention away from content analysis to analysis of ego components. At the vanguard of this movement was Heinz Hartmann, an orthodox Freudian analyst from the New York Psychoanalytic Society. Already a decade before, he had begun to criticize the then popular conceptions of the ego, which limited its functions to that of mediator between drives and conscience. He contended that there was a whole catalogue of other ego functions that were neutral with regard to the sexual drives and their vicissitudes. Mathematical reasoning, memory, perception, language—all belonged to what Hartmann called the "conflict-free" spheres of ego functioning. These autonomous ego functions served the individual's *adaptation* to the environment, a viewpoint similar to what Rado was developing in his "rebel" school on the other side of the city.

At the end of the decade Erik Homburger Erikson's most famous work, *Identity and the Life Cycle,* was published. His prominence highlights one of the vexing questions that has plagued the field of psychoanalysis: Is it a branch of medicine, whose practitioners should be medically trained? Or is it a science that cuts across several disciplines (medicine, philosophy, and anthropology), such that non-medical "lay" analysts should be recognized and welcomed? Freud (1926) took the latter position; however, many (especially in America) have felt that medical training was a necessary precursor. Like Freud's daughter Anna, Erikson had no medical training (or *any* formal training); yet both indisputably made important contributions to the field and were highly regarded for their clinical work.

Erik H. Erikson, 1902–1994

Whereas Freud's developmental stages (oral/anal/genital) cover only the formative first six years of life (with adolescence tacked on as a kind of unpleasant afterthought), Erikson envisioned a whole continuum of stages stretching into old age. Each normal stage had a pathological counterpart. Table 1 shows the eight stages Erikson outlined. Identity diffusion, the pathological counterpart to Stage 5, occupies a key position in the criterion set for borderline personality organization as formulated by Otto Kernberg in 1967. The lack of cohesive identity development, according to Erikson, may take the form of deep uncertainty about one's values, ambitions, goals, gender, and occupation, or a contemptuous attitude about the sorts of friends, mates, and jobs one's parents feel would be appropriate. In either case, the young person steers a course precisely opposite to those choices, thus forming a "negative identity."

TABLE 1   ERIKSONIAN STAGES OF THE LIFE CYCLE

Stage	Normal Development	Pathological Counterpart
0–1 years	Basic trust	Basic mistrust
2–3 years	Autonomy	Shame, doubt
4–5 years	Initiative	Guilt
Latency	Industry	Inferiority
Adolescence	Identity	Identity diffusion
Early adult life	Intimacy	Self-absorption
Adult years	Generativity	Stagnation
Mature years	Integrity	Despair, disgust

GENERAL PSYCHIATRY; FAMILY THERAPY

Nathan Ackerman

Throughout most of psychiatry's long history, the family had been glimpsed only with peripheral vision by psychiatrist and psychoanalysts alike. As noted previously, in the 1870s Lasègue and Falret had written about the folie à deux, whereby maladaptive attitudes are transmitted from one family member to another, as if by contagion (B., p. 204); Freud had treated Little Hans at a distance via the father (Freud's one foray into child psychiatry). Family therapy did not, however, achieve separate status as a mental health discipline until the work of Nathan Ackerman, whose interest in this area had begun back in the late 1930s, although his main book, *The Psychodynamics of Family Life*, did not appear until 1958. Ackerman sought to develop a taxonomy of family abnormalities analogous to those of the individual. He also tried to link certain abnormal patterns with the major disorders: Thus he saw the "schismatic" family, where no one communicates effectively with anyone else, as an etiological factor in schizophrenia; a hostile symbiosis, wherein mother and child become entangled in a malignant interdependency, contributed to either schizophrenia or depression.

Theodore Lidz (Lidz, Fleck, & Cornelison, 1965) of Yale thought that this symbiotic pattern was as much a causative factor in schizophrenia as was the schismatic pattern. Others, including Lyman Wynne, drew attention to a pattern of insincere "togetherness"—an outer show of good form and pretended love—observed in families where there was a psychotic member, who became the "designated patient" (or scapegoat) forced into the patient role, even though the rest of the family was just as ill. Often enough, the designated patient was a child or adolescent. Wynne (1958) referred to this phenomenon as "pseudomutuality."

Ackerman, who founded an institute in New York for the study and treatment of families, was a charismatic interviewer of families and a lecturer of boundless enthusiasm. He preferred to work with the *whole* family, meaning all the children, the parents, even the pets, irrespective of which one had been singled out as ill and in need of help. Like most founders of a new school or method, Ackerman believed ardently that family therapy was *the* format in which psychotherapy ought to be conducted.[2] Nowadays we recognize that there are clearly unworkable, highly destructive families, with whom "family therapy" would

---

[2] When I was in training in the 1960s, I can recall asking Ackerman if he could think of a clinical situation where family therapy might be contraindicated; he gave no answer.

erupt into a shrill shouting match of no earthly use to anyone. Those who specialize in this area have become more discerning as the field has matured.

A theoretical problem that was not adequately addressed in the heyday of optimism about family therapy involved the absence of control groups. There are many "schismatic" and "hostile symbiotic" families where the "designated patient" is *not* schizophrenic. Furthermore, epidemiological studies reveal that there are many such families where there is discord and unpleasantness, but no definable mental illness in the children. The early family therapists, like their counterparts in the domain of individual psychoanalysis, did not take sufficiently into account the significance of constitutional and inherited factors in the ontogenesis of the major psychoses. However, in the domain of borderline personality, their claim that family pathology is etiologically relevant is much more convincing (Stone, 1990; Zanarini & Gunderson, 1990).

absence of control groups

While family therapy's theoretical roots were planted mostly in psychoanalytical ground, other treatment modalities were developing in quite different soil. Pure Skinnerian behaviorism was beginning to fall out of fashion by 1959, thanks in part to adverse criticism from Noam Chomsky (Stein, 1992). In *Logical Theory of Linguistic Structure* (1955) Chomsky sparked considerable interest in psycholinguistics by showing that the grammars of all languages share similarities that therefore must reflect the brain's *innate* predisposition to learn a language.

Noam Chomsky

This discovery, by itself, did not father a new form of treatment, but in combination with the then burgeoning research on artificial intelligence and the pervasiveness of computer analogies to the brain, *cognitive science* began to take shape, and with it, *cognitive psychology*. As in behavioral psychology, cognitive psychology is concerned with input (stimuli) and output (responses); unlike behavioral psychology, it is also concerned with the processing in between the input and the output: what goes on in the "black box" of the brain. As Stein (1992) mentions, Newell and Simon were contending in the 1950s that there were strong similarities between the problem-solving mechanisms of computers and the human brain, leading them to propose the possibility of artificial intelligence. Simon (1967) was later to contend that *emotion* could also be accounted for in cognitive terms: "Emotion in humans is comparable to the prioritized interruption of different processes by one another in complex artificial intelligence systems with multiple goals and limited resources" (cited by Stein, 1992, p. 9). Focusing on people's reactions, Simon (1967) further noted:

cognitive psychology

> The most active part of the environment for man . . . consists of living organisms, particularly other men. . . . The behavior of problem-solving groups is commonly observed as taking place at

two levels: "task oriented" behavior and behavior directed toward the group's social-emotional needs. . . . A human being in the course of development and socialization acquires an increasingly sophisticated set of cues to indicate which responses of another person call for interruption of his own ongoing program. . . . As (we mature and) the behavior of others becomes more predictable, the ego's behavior can more readily be planned, and the emotionality of the situation decreases. (p. 37)

This passage, quoted at some length, gives an idea about the kinds of parallels between computer operations and mental operations cognitive psychologists were beginning to draw in the 1950s. Cognitive *therapy* evolved as a special set of interventions inspired by the emerging principles of cognitive psychology.

In the area of substance abuse, the biggest problem was, and (numerically, at least) remains, alcoholism. The most effective treatment for alcoholism is enrollment in Alcoholics Anonymous. Although "A.A." is not a psychiatric organization, to the extent that it is of inestimable value to affected persons as well as to the community at large, A.A. certainly deserves mention in any history of psychiatry.

Alcoholics Anonymous

A high proportion of alcoholic patients exhibit the traits of one or another personality disorder or suffer from serious depression. Suicide rates are much higher in alcoholics than in the general population, partly because alcohol lowers inner controls against impulsive behavior. In the United States estimates of prevalence run in the range of 10% for alcoholism. A still larger proportion of the population is directly and negatively affected by this illness, since family members, colleagues, and friends often suffer in one way or another as a consequence of behavioral abnormalities caused by alcoholism.

A.A., which is still the exemplar of support groups designed to combat alcoholism, was founded in 1935 by "Bill." Anonymity is one of the important traditions of A.A., "reminding us," as Bill put it, "to place principles before personalities." Part of this tradition involves the use of first names only at meetings and in A.A. literature. A former alcoholic, Bill Wilson from Akron, Ohio became part of a lay religious movement in Britain in the 1920s called the Oxford Group, founded by Frank Buchman. Bill's spiritual mentor was a member of that group, Reverend Samuel Shoemaker (Houck, 1995). When Bill met Bob Smith, another recovering alcoholic who had also been part of the Oxford Group, they decided to join forces and together formulated the now famous Twelve Steps. The first step is the admission that one is powerless over alcohol and that one's life had become unmanageable. The twelfth and final step is a spiritual awakening resulting in a desire to carry the message to other alcoholics and to practice the 12-step principles in daily life. A.A. urges reliance on a Higher Power—but this is not necessarily the God of any particular religion. As Bill wrote in a passage about atheists: "I have had many experiences with atheists, mostly good. . . . But I do always entreat these folks to look to a 'Higher Power'—namely, their own group. When they come in, most of their A.A. group is sober, and they are drunk. Therefore, the group is a 'Higher Power.' That's a good enough start, and most of them do progress from there" (1938, p. 276). Bill also urged A.A. members to guide themselves with this message: "God [or the Higher Power] give me the serenity to accept the things I cannot change, the courage to change the things I can, and the wisdom to know the difference."

A.A. has also become the model for the many other support groups for people with impulse-control disorders, such as O.A. (Overeaters Anonymous), N.A. (Narcotics Anonymous), and G.A. (Gamblers Anonymous). Each relies on the 12-step program devised by Bill and his colleagues. A.A. encourages daily attendance, especially for new members. The consistent group support and non-authoritarian attitude of A.A. gratify the dependency needs of the newer members and, at the same time, encourage them to conquer their disease, as the older, now abstinent members have conquered theirs. A.A. started small, but in time grew into a national, then international, organization. By the 1950s A.A. had achieved national prominence.

Even so, in psychiatric circles the atmosphere was not yet fully favorable toward A.A. Many psychiatric centers still viewed alcoholism in ways disturbingly reminiscent of the 19th century, when alcoholics were labeled "morally degenerate." Many psychoanalysts, in particular, still clung to a purely psychodynamic formulation of alcoholism, contending that it represented an "oral regression" brought about by a "wish to suck at the breast." This perspective fostered an evaluation of the alcoholic as, at best, a naughty and pathetically passive child. Alcoholic patients rarely responded to psychoanalytic therapy anyway, which further contributed to their disparagement by analysts, who, no more than is the case with other practitioners, do not like to be confronted with their failures.

By the late 1950s and the 1960s, as a result of the successful efforts of A.A., alcoholism was acknowledged as a treatable and curable disease (curable *if* patients remained in A.A.). Finally, the stigma previously attached to this group began to lessen. But these positive changes owed no debt to psychiatry. Rather, something undefinable took place "out there," beyond the purviews of orthodox medicine, in the self-help groups Bill had brought into being. Certainly an important facet of A.A.'s success relates to its focus on a non-denominational spirituality that acknowledges the existence of a higher power and on one's obligations beyond the self, to the much larger groups of community and human society. Any mention of spirituality was alien to the tenets of mid-century psychoanalysts, who stressed reliance on one's own inner resources and objected to bringing God (or anything that faintly smacked of Him) into the treatment room. Today the value of A.A. is universally recognized, and psychiatrists and analysts, whatever their orientation, are also more accepting of the important place of spirituality in the individual's welfare.

HOSPITAL PSYCHIATRY; TREATMENT OF PSYCHOTIC PATIENTS

borderline patients

In accord with the decade's psychoanalytic emphasis on countertransference, several authors drew attention to a particular variation of this phenomenon peculiar to therapeutic work with borderline patients or with "V.I.P." patients. Stanton and Schwartz in Boston and Thomas Main in England wrote about the unnerving impact on hospital personnel exerted by patients who demonstrate narcissistic entitlement by demanding special treatment and attentions. These patients elicit all manner of intense feelings in the treatment staff, ranging from misplaced affection and excessive sympathy to envy, outrage, and contempt—any of which act as a stumbling block to effective therapy. V.I.P. patients who treat staff members with arrogance and impatience routinely evoke anger; borderline patients, who truly suffered serious abuse as children and who now show a weepy, pathetic facade, tend to evoke pity—even as they "get away with murder" at other times during their stay on the unit. Sexual transgressions and other sorts of boundary violations (forming inappropriate friendships, accepting expensive gifts, doing special favors) occur much more frequently on the part of staff in dealing with borderline than with most other types of patients.

These problems became the center of discussion among treatment units all during the 1950s and beyond. Various solutions were conceived, such as the formation of groups comprised of staff members from all the different disciplines on a unit, wherein countertransference feelings could then be voiced openly. The recommendations set forth in Stanton and Schwartz's book, *The Mental Hospital* (1954), and in Main's article, "The Ailment" (1957), led to improved treatment strategies and to a more understanding and compassionate stance toward these difficult patients—especially those who spent long periods of time in residential treatment facilities, interacting over many months with the staff members.

For example, thorough discussions were devoted to the myriad ways in which such patients catalyze "staff splitting" by behaving contemptuously toward the nurses but ingratiatingly toward the therapist (or vice versa). Such splits would elicit conflicting behaviors in staff members; the therapists would evaluate the patient as being ready for a weekend pass but the nurses would disagree (or vice versa). Frank discussion of these splits often led to staff insights about how similar maneuvers had been enacted in the family of origin and may even have led to some of the troubles that had necessitated hospitalization in the first place. Once such discoveries were made, the material could be discussed with the patient in the hopes of effecting an integration of the hitherto split behavior.

In addition to focusing on troublesome borderline, narcissistic and other personality-disordered patients, hospital-based psychiatrists were directing their efforts toward achieving more effective therapy with schizophrenics. To be sure, sometimes the diagnostic distinctions between these groups of patients were blurred, especially in the United States, where the diagnosis of schizophrenia was applied much too loosely. In 1949 Hoch and Polatin of the New York State Psychiatric Institute coined the term "pseudoneurotic schizophrenia"; Hoch and Cattell addressed the topic again in 1959. Throughout the decade of the 1950s (even until the 1970s) the condition they described was considered to be a form of schizophrenia, albeit a milder, atypical variant. The *pseudoneurotic* qualifier derived from the puzzling clinical picture of these patients, who manifested seemingly *all* the known neuroses *at once:* These patients were troubled by phobias, obsessiveness, depression, anxiety, and a chaotic sexual life characterized by promiscuity and multiple perversions! Psychosis in these patients tended to be short-lived and was manifested via somatic delusions and paranoid ideation (more apt to surface as referentiality than as chronic persecutory delusions). The treatment of choice was intensive (three to five sessions per week) analytically-oriented psychotherapy. The favorable outcomes, as with Isador Coriat's "cured schizophrenics" forty years before, had as much or more to do with the fact that the patients were *not* schizophrenic (in our contemporary, *DSM–IV* sense of the term) as it did with the therapy they received. In reviewing the records of these "pseudoneurotic" patients years later, it became clear that the label had been applied indiscriminately, covering what we would now call "borderline personality disorder" (the bulk of the cases) as well as a few "true" cases of schizophrenia (in a small minority) (Stone, 1990).

Marguerite Sechèhaye at the Burghölzli in Zürich probably worked more closely with the "real" (more disabling and chronic) schizophrenia than did Hoch and Polatin. Sechèhaye developed a technique she called "symbolic realization," first described in 1947 in a book by the same name, which was translated into English in 1956. The technique was also an integral part of her detailed description of her treatment of a deeply disturbed young woman, which appeared in English in 1951. To summarize: Due to a bout of anorexia and tuberculosis at the age of 13, "Renée" spent two years in a sanatorium. After her release, she had a mental breakdown involving visual hallucinations, delusory ideas

therapy with schizophrenics

Marguerite Sechèhaye

of extreme guilt and unworthiness, and strange perceptual abnormalities in which objects viewed from one perspective seemed "different" to her when viewed from another angle.

Nineteen years old when Sechèhaye first worked with her, Renée suffered "hebephrenic-catatonic" crises and persecutory auditory hallucinations; her speech was peppered with neologisms. In the course of daily treatment Renée revealed that she feared she "would die, for they had taken her most precious belonging: her apples." In response, Sechèhaye spontaneously offered her "beautiful apples" as a replacement, but Renée replied: "I don't want the apples of grown-ups; I want Mama's apples" (Sechèhaye, 1956, p. 18). Sechèhaye's (1951) intuition informed her of the "deep symbolism" of the apples, and armed with this insight, she

> . . . at once gave [Renée] a piece of apple, saying, 'It's time to drink the good milk from Mama's apples; Mama is going to give it herself to her little Renée.' And Renée, her head resting on my shoulder, ate her piece of apple with all the concentration and contentment of a nursing baby. (p. 19)

This act of mothering, mediated through a *symbol* (here, of breast-feeding), constituted the *symbolic realization.* Sechèhaye cautioned, however, that "only those among all schizophrenic expressions may be selected for realizations which are recognized as translations of a vital, real and fundamental need" (p. 77). Evaluating her technique Sechèhaye (1951) concluded: "Above all, [symbolic realization] requires deep understanding not only in terms of the observer's point of view, but especially of the patient's point of view. It is a perpetual attempt to break the enchanted circle in which he has shut himself" (p. 190).

Sechèhaye believed that Renée's actual mother had been aloof and depriving. It is not clear whether the woman was not a "good-enough" mother in Winnicott's sense, or whether Renée was constitutionally autistic or schizophrenic to such an extent that she would have been ill in any case. My reading of the text inclines me to put more weight on the latter factor, whereas Sechèhaye (1951) clearly saw Renée's condition as a "massive schizophrenic regression to an elementary level of affective life" (p. 76).

Sechèhaye's treatment of Renée is a triumph of intuition, compassion, steadfastness, and a patience of superhuman proportions—but therein lies the difficulty. One is reminded of those rare artists who build three-masted galleons inside bottles or who weave massive silk rugs with 800 knots to the square inch. In a whole lifetime one can create scarcely half a dozen such works. But in a world with five billion people, 0.85% of whom (according to epidemiological data) are schizophrenic—an army of 43 million suffering men and women—where are the Sechèhayes to treat them? Even if we add many others to this honor roll—such as Frieda Fromm-Reichmann, Harold Searles, Elvin Semrad, Margaret Little, Herbert Rosenfeld, Silvano Arieti, Alberta Szalita, Harry Albert—and even if the method always worked (which it does not), the number of schizophrenic patients who could be helped would be pitiably small.

In the remaining decades of this century, this intensive mode of therapy fell into increasing disfavor, due in large part to the psychoactive medications that were being developed, but also due, in no small measure, to the sheer impracticality of it. Simply put, daily therapy over many years is not a *useful* treatment for schizophrenia. Sechèhaye and the handful of valiant others can be seen more helpfully as a band of intrepid explorers, whose work has illuminated some very dark corners of the human mind. But those who nowadays offer schizophrenic patients the most practical sort of help are a much more mundane lot: the developers of neuroleptic drugs, "social skills training," occupational therapy, and family education. Gone is the poetry—but at least the methods are effective for a large number of people.

BIOLOGICAL PSYCHIATRY AND GENETICS

As with other sciences, psychiatry has not progressed in a neat, linear fashion. Every so often, a sudden change of direction or a dramatic breakthrough, worthy of the words *turning point* or *revolution*, has occurred. Some speak of the removal of chains in the asylums as the first revolution; of Freud's psychoanalysis as the second. If so, surely the third was the birth of "psychopharmacology" scarcely fifty years ago. Considering that people have been ingesting plants and juices for millennia (not just for years) in an effort to alter their mental states, it is a wonder that this revolution did not precede the others. All the more amazing is the fact that this revolution was not so much worked towards as stumbled upon—and by chemists with no special interest in psychiatry and researchers who were looking for the answers to questions that had nothing to do with psychiatry.

There is no chief protagonist in this drama, though much of the impetus came from the laboratory of Jean Delay in France and his co-workers, Deniker and Pichot. A strong interest in biological psychiatry had surfaced in France after World War I, owing in part to the influenza epidemic of 1917 and 1918. Many victims developed von Economo's encephalitis and suffered residual "organic" psychoses. These conditions were studied by Gaetan de Clérambault (1872–1934), who had also written on epilepsy, alcoholism, and on the psychosis that was named after him—"de Clérambault's syndrome," a form of

Jean Delay

Gaetan de Clérambault

erotomanic delusion (usually involving an unmarried woman of modest circumstances who imagines that a man of high status is secretly in love with her). A little later Henri Claude developed an eclectic approach, combining the biological and the psychological. Claude's successor was Delay, who was also influenced by Janet and Hughlings-Jackson (B., p. 126).

chlorpromazine

Delay and Deniker published two papers in 1952 describing favorable responses in 38 psychotic patients to chlorpromazine. Earlier the same year, Laborit, Huguenard, and Alluaume, French surgeons who had been looking for a better pre-anesthetic sedative, had written about the effects of this drug, one of which was to render a patient indifferent to his surroundings. Delay and Deniker tried using the drug with psychiatric patients and noted ". . . an increase in the efficacy with which barbiturates sedated manic and other psychotic patients" *if* chlorpromazine were added to their regimen (Baldessarini, 1985, p. 15). In 1954 chlorpromazine was introduced into the United States. Thereafter, a large number of similar compounds (the phenothiazines) were developed. These were divided, according to their chemical structure, into three sub-groups (here given by chemical name followed by brand name): *aliphatic* (including chlorpromazine/Thorazine), *piperdine* (thioridazine/Mellaril), and *piperazine* (triflouperazine/Stelazine). Other antipsychotic drugs soon became available: thiothixene/Navane (from the thioxanthene group), haloperidol/Haldol (from the butyrophenone group), and pimozide/Orap (a diphenyl-butyl-piperidene compound). Collectively, these agents are known as

neuroleptics

neuroleptics; they are now generally reserved for use with schizophrenic patients, although they are also prescribed in small doses for highly anxious patients, irrespective of diagnosis.

Preceding the development of these neuroleptic drugs, a derivative of the snakeroot plant, *Rauwolfia serpentina,* was used as a remedy in India for both hypertension and "insanity" (Sen & Bose, 1931).

reserpine

The drug, marketed here as reserpine, was used as a neuroleptic in 1951 (Kline, 1959). Because the phenothiazine compounds soon proved more effective and better tolerated, reserpine enjoyed only a brief popularity.

antidepressant drugs

The antidepressant family of drugs was discovered in the same circuitous and serendipitous way as were the neuroleptics. Before the 1950s, amphetamines were sometimes used as a stimulant to overcome the lethargy of chronic depression or as an antidote for brief, acute cases of depression. But amphetamines were neither useful nor safe as a treatment in the more typical, longer-lasting melancholic depressions. During World War II isoniazid, a derivative of nicotinic acid, was found to be useful as an antibiotic in the treatment of tuberculosis. Then in the early 1950s a chemical cousin of isoniazid, iproniazid, was observed to induce euphoria. Delay was again involved with the psychiatric application of this chance observation: In 1952 Selikoff et al. reported on the usefulness of iproniazid (Marsilid) in the treatment of depression. Nathan Kline, then with the research department of the Rockland State Psychiatric Center in New York, was able to confirm the antidepressant properties of iproniazid.

At about the same time that the psychoactive properties of reserpine and iproniazid were discovered, it was also determined that both these agents exerted their effects upon the same cell components— the monoamines—which, in turn, were found to play a pivotal role as *neurotransmitters* (cited in Grenell & Gabay, 1976), compounds that catalyze the transmission of impulses from one nerve cell to another. The biogenic amines include *norepinephrine, dopamine* (both catecholamines), and *serotonin,* each of which is responsible for transmission within particular, definable nerve-tracts in the brain; the level and appropriate functioning of the neurotransmitters determine whether the corresponding nerve tracts operate efficiently, excessively, or sluggishly. Iproniazid was found to act as a monoamine oxidase inhibitor (MAOI), which means that it interferes with the enzyme that ordinarily inactivates monoamine neurotransmitters in the synaptic cleft between one nerve connection and another. By blocking this deactivation process, the MAOIs keep the active transmitter substances in circulation (within the synapse) a bit longer, thus facilitating the transmission of impulses within the nerve-tracts, where they operate.

monoamines

In 1954 A. H. Amin et al. identified the presence of serotonin in brain tissue; in 1957 Brodie and Shore hypothesized that norepinephrine acted on nerve fibers within the sympathetic (alerting, emergency-oriented) nervous system; serotonin, on the parasympathetic (autonomic) nervous system. Clinical depression was found to be associated with insufficiencies in the *noradrenergic* (norepinephrine) or the *serotonergic* (serotonin) systems. Iproniazid and the other MAOIs that were developed later relieve depression by boosting the noradrenergic system.[3]

The antidepressant properties of yet another class of compounds were identified in the mid-1950s: the tricyclics. A decade earlier *imipramine,* a tricyclic compound structurally similar to the phenothiazines, had been found to produce sedative effects; it gave promise of exerting antipsychotic effects as well, but this did not prove to be the case. Instead, as reported by Kuhn in 1958, imipramine worked as an activating and mood-elevating drug (Baldessarini, 1985, p. 133).

tricyclics

Although Cade had already begun to demonstrate the anti-manic properties of lithium, the work of Mogens Schou (1958) in Denmark

lithium

[3] In the light of recent research, this statement is too simplistic, but it nonetheless presents the broad theoretical picture that is relevant to the pharmacological effectiveness of this class of compounds.

during the mid-1950s bolstered its reputation as the drug of choice in bipolar mania. As for lithium, its mechanism of action was, and has remained, more obscure than that of the catecholamines. It may be that lithium effects changes in intra- versus extracellular ion distribution in nerve cells; it also appears to inhibit norepinephrine release in the brain. If so, lithium would have an effect opposite to that of the antidepressants. This may account for lithium's anti-manic properties (though it leaves unexplained its general mood-stabilizing property even in many depressed patients). Despite the extensive use of lithium in Europe during the 1950s, it remained an experimental drug in the United States until its approval for clinical use in 1969. Much of the experimental work to establish the therapeutic efficacy of lithium was carried out here by Ronald Fieve and his colleagues in New York.

anxiolytic agents

Another major class of psychoactive drugs was developed at the end of the decade: the anxiolytic or antianxiety agents. Although other compounds (MAOIs, tricyclics, etc.) also have antianxiety properties, *anxiolytic* is usually reserved for the *benzodiazepine* compound of drugs. *Chlordiazepoxide*/Librium was the first anxiolytic drug to be used in clinical trials (Sternbach, 1960), after having been shown to have calming and anticonvulsant effects in animal experiments during the 1950s. In 1951 a muscle-relaxant drug, *meprobamate*/Miltown, was developed (Ludwig & Piech, 1951, as cited in Baldessarini, 1985) and found to be mildly anxiolytic (N. Dixon, 1957, as cited in Baldessarini, 1985). Before these safer and more specific anxiolytics became available, there was little else for clinicians to prescribe in cases of anxiety apart from the bromide salts, which had been used first in the treatment of epilepsy by French psychiatrist Bécoulet (1869) and M. J. Falret (1871).

Amazingly, in this one decade drugs became available for the relief of symptoms associated with schizophrenia, depression (especially of the "endogenous," inherited type), mania, and anxiety disorders. (Table 2 presents a summary of the psychoactive medications discovered and investigated during the 1950s.) Even amphetamines, though no longer used as a main antidepressant, were applied therapeutically in the treatment of narcolepsy. Later in the decade, another stimulant, *methylphenidate*/Ritalin, was found to be useful in the treatment of attention-deficit hyperactivity disorder (ADHD) in children and adolescents (Wender, 1971).

psychopharmaco-
logical revolution

The psychopharmacological revolution of the 1950s brought about a corresponding revolution in our standards of diagnosis, particularly in the United States. Because of our endorsement of Bleuler's (rather than Kraepelin's) conception of schizophrenia, until the last generation this disorder was grossly overdiagnosed here, while mania was underdiagnosed. Until the advent of more effective drugs, there was little one could do for either, apart from prescribing ECT, barbiturates (for acute states of frenzy), patience, and prayer. Suddenly, the arrival of lithium made a world of difference in diagnosing whether a patient were

TABLE 2   PYSCHOACTIVE MEDICATIONS OF THE 1950S

Drug/Class	First Discovered or Used	Reference
Rauwolfia/reserpine	1931 (India)	Sen & Bose, 1931
	1952 (U.S.A.)	Pearl et al., 1956; Kline, 1959
Antidepressants		
Iproniazid/Marsilid (MAOI)	1951 (France)	Selikoff & Delay, 1952
Imipramine/Tofranil	1957 (U.S.A.)	Kuhn, 1958
Anti-manic		
Lithium	1949 (Australia)	Cade, 1949
	1954 (Denmark)	Schou, 1957
Neuroleptics		
Chlorpromazine/Thorazine	1951 (France)	Laborit, 1951; Delay & Deniker, 1952
Anxiolytics		
Meprobamate/Miltown	1951 (produced in U.S.A.)	Ludwig & Piech, 1951
	1954 (relaxant properties)	Berger, 1954
	1957 (anxiolytic properties)	Dixon, 1957
Chlordiazepoxide	Late 1950s (U.S.A.)	Sternbach, 1960
Stimulants		
Methylphenidate/Ritalin	Late 1950s	Sprague & Sleator, 1970 (review article)

schizophrenic or bipolar-manic. In the acute state, particularly in young people, the two conditions are often difficult to distinguish, even for experienced practitioners. But now there was a strong incentive to make the diagnostic distinctions. Accordingly, a flurry of activity was directed to helping clinicians learn how to do precisely that. Questionnaires were developed to aid in making more accurate diagnoses; lectures were given to educate the psychiatric community; European colleagues, who had always been careful about these distinctions due to their less psycho-analytic, more descriptive tradition, were invited to come here to expand our consciousness about manic-depression and to participate in cross-cultural studies (Kendell & Gourlay, 1970).

diagnostic distinctions

Alongside the chance discoveries of specific remedies, research was also conducted in the 1950s on the so-called "model psychoses" induced by naturally occurring drugs such as LSD, in the hopes of shedding light on brain mechanisms involved in schizophrenia and manic-depression. Since ancient times humans have willingly used extracts from certain plants to induce hallucinations and other altered states of consciousness, often as part of religious rites.[4] Mushrooms of the *Psilocybe* family, extracts of the peyote cactus, and cannabinoids from the marijuana plant are examples; all can induce euphoria, and, in sufficient concentration, hallucinations. In the United States mescaline, from the peyote cactus, has been used as a hallucinogen since the early 1920s (indeed, novelist Aldous Huxley experimented with it and wrote about it in the 1930s). By 1943 LSD was known to be 3,000–6,000 times as potent as mescaline, gram for gram (Himwich, 1971, p. 363). Nevertheless, once the psychoactive properties of LSD were glimpsed, it was studied extensively because the hallucinations it induced presented a model psychosis for schizophrenia. In the late 1950s and early 1960s a wave of enthusiasm passed over the psychiatric community as possible medicinal uses of LSD were sought. Perhaps the strange mental phenomena of "hearing visions and seeing sounds" and the deluge of memories from early life routinely reported by LSD users would "free up" tightly controlled obsessional patients, so that they could come into better contact with their long-submerged emotions (Leuner, 1962). Ultimately it was learned that little good, and at times much harm, came from such uses of LSD, and the drug was quickly dropped from the psychopharmacological armamentarium.

Meanwhile Hollister and Sjöberg(1964), noting that chlorpromazine was a useful remedy for LSD poisoning, proposed that LSD affects the dopamine neurotransmitter system in ways opposite to that of chlorpromazine. Though it turned out that this is not the only site of LSD action, Hollister's observation did lend support to theories that attributed schizophrenia to abnormalities of the dopamine system.

Unfortunately, the general public was not as quick to become disenchanted with LSD and the other hallucinogens as was the psychiatric profession. Quite to the contrary: Thanks in part to the misguided enthusiasm of the Harvard psychologist Timothy Leary, who in the early 1960s preached the "virtues" of such drugs, many young people were inspired to "drop acid and drop out." The drug epidemic spawned then is with us still and has forced psychiatrists to learn methods of combating the ill effects of illicit psychoactive drugs. (We will take up this story again when discussing the 1960s.)

---

[4] Frohman and Gottlieb mention (in Grenell & Gabay, 1976, p. 757) that ergot alkaloids from wheat rust contain psychomimetic substances, among them lysergic acid diethylamide—LSD—as a result of which, "In the 17th century whole villages in southern France went temporarily insane from eating rust-infected wheat."

CHILD AND ADOLESCENT PSYCHIATRY

Piaget's developmental scheme influenced those who took up the task of improving the lot of normal children, such as Maria Montessori (1870–1952), who sought to better the education of children in the slums of Italy. Among her many innovations was the recommendation that particular changes be made in the way perceptual stimuli were presented to pupils in the classroom: Single properties were made more observable and thus more easily learned by eliminating overly complex, distracting elements. For example, when the concept of size was being taught, all the demonstration objects were of the same color and shape. As Deutsch pointed out, this similarity maximizes attention to, and perception of, size differences. Because the Montessori method gives the child an opportunity to "select materials consistent with his own developmental capabilities," it fosters the experience of success, lends a positive reinforcement to the learning process, and thus enhances the child's motivation to learn.

Maria Montessori

The predominant view of psychopathology in children and adolescents in America in the 1950s was psychoanalytic. Formulations about causation were almost uniformly wedded to Freudian conceptions of a linear developmental path. Matters of constitution or hereditary predisposition, though not entirely ignored, were mentioned only in passing. Many of the prominent contributors of this era published in the prestigious *Psychoanalytic Study of the Child,* founded in the mid-1940s and edited by such luminaries as Anna Freud and Heinz Hartmann.

Early in the 1950s Elsa Pappenheim, who had been Freud's case of "Anna O," became an important figure in child psychiatry. In a paper on separation anxiety between mother and child (Pappenheim & Sweeney, 1953), she presented a case involving the child of a severely disturbed mother. The child, despite the "intense preoedipal relationship," remained comparatively healthy, which led Pappenheim to suggest that, although a child remains long dependent on the mother, "the latter is partly only environment and thus her influence is limited by the child's constitutional endowment" (p. 112).

Elsa Pappenheim

René Spitz developed a taxonomy of "psychosomatic diseases of infancy" (1951) classified according to the types of pathological mothering, in which he identified "deficiency diseases": anaclitic[5] depression (1946) and marasmus, reflecting "partial" or "complete" maternal deprivation, respectively. Colic at three months was ascribed to "primary anxious overpermissiveness"; excessive rocking, to the mother's

René Spitz

[5] *Anaclitic* is derived from the Greek "to lean on," signifying a state of depression wherein there is a strong element of clinging to a protective person.

"oscillating between pampering and hostility" (p. 259). These and others were the "psychotoxic diseases." Given that the mothers of schizophrenic and autistic children were castigated for being "double-binding" or "cold," we can see that mothers in the 1950s were something of an endangered species! This is not to say that the analysts of this generation were totally wrong in pointing out the negative impact of certain maternal qualities. However, they did have inordinate difficulty seeing *beyond* a putative "maternal factor," such that the causes for emotional disturbances in children were laid at mother's doorstep, as if by some cerebral reflex, irrespective of whether or not her behavior had contributed to her child's illness.

Regarding the advisability of maternal breast-feeding to ensure the infant's optimal development—a much debated issue at the time—Dorothy Burlingham (1951) provided an interesting historical context to the question. She recounted how Comenius, in the 17th century, had counseled mothers to nurse their own children and Jacques Guilleneaux, a French commentator, had advised against giving an infant to a nurse, because "the natural affection which should betwixt mother and child by this means is diminished" (p. 247).

Margaret Schoenberger Mahler

During this same time period Margaret Schoenberger Mahler was describing autistic and symbiotic infantile psychoses (1952). The autistic child, she noted, is intolerant of human contact, which becomes apparent during the nursing phase. However, the symbiotic child "often cannot be detected before awareness of separateness from the mother throws the infant into a state of panicky separation anxiety" (p. 301). Often, elements of both conditions are commingled in the same child.

David Beres

David Beres addressed the question: To what extent is aggression a *reaction to frustration* versus an *innate response*? This issue was extremely controversial in this era, owing to the belief that any problem that was inborn was incurable. To believe that aggression had roots in our very constitution was seen as sourly un-Rousseauian and pessimistic. Beres (1952) opposed this general view in his formulations: Aggression, for him, was an "innate instinctual drive emanating from the Id, which by its biological nature, seeks constant gratification. One function of the Ego and Super-Ego is to mediate its demands" (p. 153). Beres also understood childhood perversions and delinquent behavior as stemming from the intertwining of libidinous and aggressive drives.

schizophrenia

That schizophrenia was still understood mostly in psychological terms at this time within the analytic community is clear from Hartmann's formulation (1953) in which he stated that schizophrenia "has been situated in the oral-aggressive stage," citing Melanie Klein's work. He did acknowledge a constitutional component in the form of a "thin" stimulus barrier—the *Reizschutz* of which Freud spoke—which fails to protect against impingement in schizophrenics and certain "sensitive" children (as described by Bergman & Escalona, 1949). Ekstein and Wallerstein (1957) considered this hypersensitivity to be instrumental in precipitating psychotic or "borderline" reactions in children who showed this vulnerability.

Further contributions to object-relations theory were made by Edith Jacobson (1954), who wrote on the manner in which at the end of the oedipal period and the beginning of latency, "representations of the self and object world gain lasting configuration" (p. 125).

object-relations theory

Throughout the 1950s there was considerable interest in the topic of juvenile delinquency in child analytic circles. Melitta Schmideberg became the director of APTO, the Association for the Psychotherapy of Offenders, and wrote prolifically on the therapy of delinquents, especially delinquent girls (1958; Schmideberg & Orr, 1959). Her organization did outstanding work in a manner similar to August Aichhorn's institution for "wayward youth." Schmideberg was indefatigable in her efforts (1947); willing to spend prodigious amounts of time with her young patients, she often accompanied them on walks, gradually nudging them in the direction of dressing and behaving in more socially acceptable, less "tart" ways.

Melitta Schmideberg

In commenting on female delinquents, Peter Blos addressed another much-debated issue: Who has the harder task dealing with the developmental phases on the way to adulthood—boys or girls? He took the position (1957) that, because the first love-object for all children is the mother, the girl must abandon her love object—and endure the mother's disappointment—in order to seek a sense of completeness and femininity by turning toward the father. The boy's love-object, in contrast, never changes sex; therefore, his development is more direct and less complicated than the girl's (p. 234).

Peter Blos

While there may be something to this point in the case of (heterosexual) boys, Blos's position ignores other developmental tasks related to *identity formation.* One could argue equally well (and many subsequently have) that the girl need only remain identified with her primal love-object in order to gain a sense of femaleness; the boy, in forging a male identity, has to detach from his mother and reattach to his father several years later. Therefore, *boys* have the harder job. Perhaps a more reasoned view is our more modern one, which asserts that children of both sexes have an equal lot: Some developmental tasks are easier for girls; others, easier for boys.

To comprehend the degree of one-sided thinking that characterized this era in both psychoanalytic and psychiatric communities, it is important to examine the formulations concerning a condition we now understand as being 99% innate or constitutional—maybe even 100%. I refer to "strephosymbolia," a form of dyslexia in which the child reverses letters (a *b* becomes a *d*) or even writes from right to left. Writing in 1955, Victor Rosen saw as the "culprit" in this situation abnormalities in the unfolding of the Oedipus complex, resulting from primal-scene fantasies in which the father is associated with *visual*

dyslexia

activities and the mother with *auditory* activities. Registering his parents as "two unloving people," the child presumably develops a conflict that invades the area of (normally conflict-free) synthetic ego functions. The result: difficulty in the transitional stage in learning to write, between ideographic forms and a syllabic alphabet.

In retrospect it is easy to cast aspersions on ideas that seem so wrongheaded in the light of what we understand today. What I find so remarkable is that this "oedipal" explanation of a type of dyslexia was not something culled from the musty covers of some 18th-century tome; it comes from a book just 40 years old, whose pages are as white as when they were new! This example highlights how far we have come in so short a time—how, in fact, there has been more "psychiatry" (and more psychiatrists) in the last 40 years than in all recorded history up to 1955.[6]

"corrective emotional experience"

Still in this decade, Augusta Alpert (1954) applied Franz Alexander's concept of a "corrective emotional experience" to therapy with children. What has curative value for children is the experience of interacting with the therapist in more humane and adaptive ways than what is offered at home. It was hoped, and assumed, that these corrective experiences would override the old "programs" of thinking and behaving that had generated the child's maladaptive patterns.

psychotic or "borderline" children

Those working with children who were psychotic or "borderline" (the diagnostic criteria for borderline behavior in children were quite vague at this time) still emphasized abnormalities in the mother-child relationship as being central to the problem. Elisabeth Geleerd (1958), for example, spoke about the "pathological development of object relations with Mother," whose lack of gratification of elemental needs leaves the child with a concomitant lack of self-confidence. Such children, she held, "react to any frustration with Mother as though it were a total loss, a disaster" (p. 223).

FORENSIC PSYCHIATRY

As used by Kraepelin, the term *psychopath* referred to anyone who was mentally ill. Since the beginning of the century, however, psychiatric terminology had undergone changes. Psychopath began to take on connotations of moral irresponsibility; such a person was characterized as having "constitutionally psychopathic inferiority." Consti-

---

[6] It is this exponential growth of information that makes the writing of a new "history of psychiatry" so problematical; the choices of what to include and what to leave out, so difficult. Surely if we continue to climb the steep S-curve of knowledge in this fashion, future historians of our field will find it a daunting task to sketch the developments of the previous *decade,* never mind the three millennia we are attempting to cover here.

tutional here signified not so much inherited as ingrained behavior, in the sense of being chronic and unmodifiable. These persons, often referred to by the acronym CPIs, were a constant problem for both the courts and the psychiatric profession. Summoned before the courts for their outrageous, repugnant, or dangerous behavior, CPIs would be adjudged sane, competent, and thus responsible for their actions. A crafty lawyer might succeed in portraying them as the victims of madness, winning their removal to a mental hospital rather than to prison. Once in a hospital, CPIs would quickly be evaluated as "sane" and just as quickly released. Often relatives then implored the courts to reconsider the case because of the terrible troubles inflicted on them by the just-released "patient." The latter, having no wish to be confined, would then charm the judge with what appeared to be obvious sanity and reasonableness, thereby earning his right to remain at large. This was the psychopath's vicious circle, or more properly, vicious triangle: home, court, hospital.

The man most responsible for trying to create some order out of this linguistic and diagnostic chaos was Hervey Cleckley, a professor of neuropsychiatry at the University of Georgia. Cleckley was educated at Oxford and then returned to the States to complete his medical degree. Whether he developed his noteworthy style at Oxford is unclear, but he wrote with a dramatic flair and wit more typical of British than American physicians. His most well-known book, *The Mask of Sanity,* first appeared in 1941, though his later editions of the 1950s and 1960s (the last was in 1972) were less novelistic and more influential.

Hervey Cleckley

Though much of Cleckley's book is devoted to vivid and lengthy portrayals of individual psychopaths, he also provided a synthesis of the impressions he had accumulated over the years. This synthesis enumerated some 21 pathological attributes lurking behind the "mask of sanity." Though not every psychopathic person shows *all* 21 traits, many are present (see Table 3).

Among the many vignettes in Cleckley's book are several from "good" families, whose efforts to rescue and rehabilitate their alcoholic ne'er-do-well sons or brothers invariably come to naught. For example, the psychopathic patient in a mental hospital artfully cons the doctor into believing that he is ready for release by convincingly swearing that he has learned his lesson and will never touch another drop—only to be picked up by the police 24 hours after discharge, ". . . floundering among rubbish and weeds in the mire of a canal bank in a squalid neighborhood . . . his new clothes torn by brambles, tin cans and broken glass, stained with mud and urine" (1941, p. 99).

These descriptions resonate with the newspaper stories of our own day, which tell of violence-prone "ex"-cocaine addicts, who normalize while in mental hospitals, claim their "civil rights," win release, and immediately resume terrorizing their old neighborhoods.

TABLE 3 CLECKLEY'S PATHOLOGICAL ATTRIBUTES

1. Superficially charming
2. Does not display irrationality, psychosis, or nervousness
3. Lacks all sense of responsibility; remains unaffected when confronted with his disloyalty or failures
4. Shows a total disregard for the truth
5. Blames others; blames self but in an insincere and ingratiating way
6. Lacks any sense of shame
7. Undependable; cheats and lies, and is without compunction or any apparent goal
8. Lacks judgment
9. Unable to profit from experience
10. Supremely egocentric
11. Shows a poverty of affect
12. Lacks insight and ability to see self as others do
13. Callous; without regard for the feelings of others
14. Apt to overindulge in alcohol
15. Given to bizarre conduct, exploits, and pranks
16. Shows no potential for suicide
17. Shows sexual peculiarities; tendency to trivialize sex
18. Has adverse heredity
19. Able at times to demonstrate good behavior earlier in life (such that one cannot say *all* cases are "constitutional")
20. Shows an inability to follow any life plan
21. Makes every effort to fail; even if placed in a secure position by a wealthy relative, for example, such a person will fail with "spectacular and bizarre splendor"

Though Cleckley considered psychopaths to be mentally ill, suffering from what he called "semantic dementia" (despite their surface rationality, they could not grasp social meanings), he had nothing to offer by way of treatment, apart from the hope that someday some form of therapy might reeducate them.

Cleckley's psychopathic attributes, though they convey the range of behaviors from confidence trickster to callous career-criminal, cannot be reliably assessed during the course of an interview—or even several interviews. Often one has to be fooled, cheated, betrayed, or hoodwinked by the psychopath in order to make the diagnosis. The fact that psychopathic behavior only unfolds in "real time," not in the artificial atmosphere of a clinic or job interview, highlights the difficulties of creating a workable definition for diagnosis and research.

PART IV

The 1960s

Chapter 14

THE RENAISSANCE OF BIOLOGICAL PSYCHIATRY AND THE DIVERSIFICATION OF PSYCHOTHERAPY

The psychopharmacological revolution of the 1950s did more than prompt the new look at nosology that resulted in the mini-revolution in diagnosis alluded to in the previous section. This very change itself catalyzed a new interest in the biological aspects of psychiatry and led to a shift in focus between "psyche" and "soma" as profound as that which occurred when Ideler's Romanticism gave way to Griesinger's somaticism. Dramatic social changes were also erupting—some nationwide, some worldwide—many of which had a direct impact on the way psychiatric patients were treated, even on *who* became a psychiatric patient.

Early in the decade, illicit psychoactive drugs became fashionable again, mostly in America, but also in Western Europe. America had flirted with cocaine until the Harrison Act of 1909 made heroin and other illicit drugs less popular for half a century. Alcohol never left the scene, even during Prohibition; heroin made a comeback after World War II. But in the 1960s abuse of marijuana, LSD (and related drugs, such as mescaline, psilocybin, and eventually "angel dust" or "PCP"), amphetamines, barbiturates, and to a lesser extent (initially, that is), cocaine grew quickly out of bounds and became an epidemic. Many adolescents with hitherto hidden vulnerabilities to psychosis had this potential shockingly actualized after they took (or, in some cases, were given surreptitiously at parties) hallucinogens. Many an emergency-room visit, some hospitalizations, and not a few suicides were precipitated in this manner.

illicit psychoactive drugs

The divorce rate in the United States and the West rose steeply in the 1960s. Partly this was for acceptable reasons: More women worked

divorce rate

and were thus better able to leave their husbands in cases of abuse. Partly it was due to a cultural shift away from idealism and self-restraint and toward greater self-gratification. This was the "culture of narcissism" of which Christopher Lasch wrote in his 1978 book.

"sexual revolution"

Related to the growing divorce rate and the increasing number of women in the workplace was the "sexual revolution," to which the popularity of psychoanalysis contributed through its emphasis on one's entitlement to healthy sexual gratification. As prudish Victorian restraints were weakened and the demonization of masturbation overturned, better contraceptive devices (including the "Pill") led to greater sexual freedom and smaller families. With less need for mother to stay at home as brood-mare, there was greater opportunity for sexual experimentation and a concomitantly greater threat to the integrity of marriage.

stepparents

As divorce became increasingly common, more children were raised (at least partly) by stepparents with half-siblings—families with "his," "her," and "their" children. Single mothers living in reduced circumstances or on welfare assistance became more common, which left a greater number of children less supported financially and emotionally

incest

than in the preceding generations. Incest, the best-kept secret, also was more common (though not recognized until the 1970s), partly because of the rising number of stepfathers. Religious affiliation and

religious affiliation

church attendance dropped off noticeably in the 1960s, further weakening the support system upon which young people relied. The suicide rate spiked throughout America and the West among those in their thirties who now had less parental support, less church support, and, increasingly, fewer jobs to fall back on (Diekstra & Moritz, 1987).

disillusionment

Many young people felt disillusioned with government and authority in general—and there were ample sources of disillusionment. Those born after World War II were adolescents in the 1960s: the first generation of people who never knew a time when there *wasn't* the atom bomb. After the Krushchev-Kennedy showdown over the missiles in Cuba (1962), many Americans felt even more reason to adopt Horace's philosophy: *Carpe diem; quam minimam credula postero* [pluck the day; trust but little in the morrow]. The string of assassinations of the 1960s—John and Robert Kennedy, Martin Luther King—came at the same time as the war in Vietnam was escalating. The America that had saved the world and fostered its recovery via the Marshall Plan had now soiled its hands and lost its honor.

Disillusionment was hardly confined to America. German youth swung from the far right of their Nazi fathers to the far left of the Baader-Meinhof gang; similar trends appeared in Italy with the Red Brigade and in France with the young Maoists. The British Empire, whose "pink" areas on the map once encircled the globe, had shrunk back to its island boundaries, and soccer hooligans replaced Churchill in the daily news. In Russia Lenin's dream dissolved in alcohol, and psychiatric hospitals became a repository for political dissidents—who were "zombified" with the same chlorpromazine that was emptying out hospitals in the West.

As for that "emptying out of hospitals," the 1960s was the era of *deinstitutionalization:* The wonder drugs of the 1950s had indeed permitted the psychiatric hospitals to dispose of the straightjackets (though some people complained that the drugs were "chemical straightjackets"), but the assumption that chemistry had made living all *that* better (in the case of schizophrenia, in particular) proved lamentably naive. For some, leaving the hospital was a God-send. For others, however, the closing of these doors meant going from the straightjacket to the street, from a life of shabby dignity in a state hospital that at least provided food and shelter, to one of sleeping under cars, eating out of garbage cans, and voiding on the sidewalk. Confinement of the severely ill had become a "bad" thing, even in a good place. New laws were enacted granting patients the right to refuse medication, even if the drugs were helpful. In essence, the prevailing attitude contended that the freedom of the outside was a "good" thing, even if it were the freedom to stay crazy.

deinstitutionalization

DESCRIPTIVE PSYCHIATRY, PSYCHOLOGY, AND EPIDEMIOLOGY

As the result of a cooperative study between the United States and Britain, the original *Diagnostic and Statistical Manual* (DSM) was overhauled. The eighth edition of Europe's diagnostic "Bible," the *International Classification of Diseases* (ICD–8) was published in 1965. The new *DSM–II* came out three years later and reflected efforts to bring American diagnostic standards more in line with those of Britain and the Continent. The main categories in the *DSM–II* included "organic brain syndromes," the psychoses and neuroses, psychophysiological ("psychosomatic") conditions, the special syndromes, transient conditions (brief reactions to various stresses), and mental retardation. As Spitzer mentions (1994), the *DSM–II* encouraged the use of multiple diagnoses, when applicable, in contrast to the earlier diagnostic habits of giving just one diagnosis, no matter how complex the case.

K. Leonhard continued the work of Kraepelin and Kretschmer in identifying correlations between manic-depressive psychoses and certain abnormal temperaments. By interviewing nonpsychotic relatives of manic-depressives, Leonhard (1962; Leonhard, Korff, & Schulz, 1963) found that the relatives of persons who suffered only manic attacks tended to have a "hypomanic" temperament, while the relatives of

K. Leonhard

bipolar patients tended to show a cyclothymic temperament (though some bipolar patients had purely depressive relatives). Because he noted more ill relatives among the families of bipolar- than of unipolar-depressed patients, Leonhard speculated that the two conditions were genetically distinct. While few researchers still concur with that conclusion, Leonhard is credited with reintroducing the important subject of inborn temperaments, which had been neglected during the heyday of psychoanalytic theory.

"character disorders"
personality

Psychoanalysts usually spoke of *character disorders,* where psychologists were more apt to use the term *personality.* The psychoanalytic view of "character disorders" was still organized in reaction to "fixation" along the linear developmental track: Passive-dependent and depressive or depressive-masochistic character types were fixated at the oral stage; obsessional and sadistic types were fixated at the anal stage; phallic-narcissistic and hysteric types were genitally fixated. By the 1960s a person's "make-up"—habitual reaction patterns, typical mode of self-presentation—was seen as an amalgam of innate and learned (environmental) factors. *Personality* now became the inclusive term for all such attributes: the *innate* portion determined one's *temperament;* the *environmental* components comprised one's *character.* The latter also included one's ethical and moral development, as implied by the word's usage in everyday parlance.

"five-factor model"

Meanwhile, Tupes and Christal (1961, 1962) were conducting further factor-analysis work on the fractionation of personality into its irreducible ingredients. Where Cattell had refined Allport's giant trait list to 16 basic qualities, Tupes and Christal achieved a further distillation, creating a "five-factor model." Their five factors included the *neuroticism* and *extraversion* of Eysenck's three-dimensional model and added *agreeableness, conscientiousness,* and *openness.* Currently there is wide, though not universal, acceptance of the five-factor model, and, as we shall discuss later, most of the traditional personality disorders (as enumerated in the *DSM–IV*) can be subsumed under one or another of the "Big Five."

epidemiological
research

The results of Leo Srole's epidemiological research were published in 1962 as the *Midtown Manhattan Study.* After analyzing structured questionnaires given to 1,600 New York City residents, Srole and his colleagues identified significant emotional problems in 23% of those surveyed. Their study had been carried out a few years after another landmark publication, *Social Class and Mental Illness,* by Hollingshead and Redlich (1958), one of whose findings was a strong (and inverse) correlation between social class and mental illness: The lower the socioeconomic status, the higher the proportion of people with mental disorders.

PSYCHOANALYSIS

In Britain the psychoanalytic movement had been spearheaded by orthodox Freudians, such as Ernest Jones in the 1920s and Freud's daughter, Anna, after the Freuds had fled to London in 1938. A bifurcation soon took place: Melanie Klein and her followers set up a separate institute. Not long thereafter, a third group formed, unhappy with the theoretical positions of the other two. This became the "Independent Group," whose predominant interest was in object-relations. It included such names as Donald Winnicott, Michael Balint, William Gillepsie, and Charles Rycroft. They contended that psychoanalysis is a two-person event wherein the analyst is always an active participant who *interacts with* the patient; the analyst is not merely a "blank screen" that registers the patient's thoughts and emotions with machine-like neutrality.

In this sense the object-relations school resembles the Sullivanian interpersonal school: Both stress the importance of analysts becoming aware of their countertransference reactions. Klauber would later speak of how "patient and analyst need one another," as they form their private, intimate, secret relationship (Kohon, 1986, p. 53). Ella Freeman Sharpe had noted over a decade earlier: "To say that the analyst will still have complexes, blind spots, limitations is only to say that he remains a human being. When he ceases to be an ordinary human being he ceases to be a good analyst."

Perhaps because of their rejection of some tenets of both the orthodox Freudians and the Kleinians, the analysts of the Independent School wrote in a language that was free of the special, often jargonistic vocabularies of the other two groups (especially the Kleinians) and thus more accessible. Michael Balint (d. 1970), addressing the unique difficulties of establishing emotional contact with borderline patients (in Kernberg's use of the term), published an important monograph on the subject in 1968: *The Basic Fault.* This "fault" had to do with the strange way in which the analyst, with his "adult language," seemed unable to communicate with the patient, who took the words in the wrong way, understood something different by them than what the analyst intended. Such patients, who acquire labels like "deeply disturbed," "seriously schizoid," "profoundly split," or "narcissistically wounded," characteristically complain of a "defect": something *missing* from their early childhood life that ought to have been there, as though someone had failed them. The problem is not one of conflict, as in the neurotic's oedipal complex, but of *fault*. Furthermore, the problem had arisen out of a *two-person* situation (typically, mother and child), not a triangular one. The trouble was *earlier than* the oedipal phase, say in the first year or two (though Balint was unhappy with the term

Michael Balint

"preoedipal," since it lay so much stress on the oedipal period, tending to downplay the importance of the preceding phase).

Balint described two polarities among patients exhibiting the basic fault: those who deal with their distress by clinging excessively to other people (the "ocnophile type"), and those who rely excessively on their own ego resources, eschewing contact with other people (the "philobat type"). From the standpoint of therapy, Balint emphasized the importance of remaining unobtrusive. The more the analyst's technique and behavior suggest omniscience and omnipotence, "the greater is the danger of a malignant form of regression" (p. 173). Balint acknowledged that, in some cases, the "basic fault" might arise out of "congenital" factors, though he did not expand on this.

Donald Winnicott

Also appearing in the 1960s was Donald Winnicott's book *The Maturational Process and the Facilitating Environment,* containing papers written from 1958–1964. Many of the articles discussed child psychoanalysis and therapy. One of the more general, and influential, articles presented his concept of the "*false self,*" which he acknowledged had been explored in earlier psychiatric and philosophical writings. In Winnicott's contemporary application, the false self is the façade people create in order to function more smoothly in social situations. Creating this façade is a means of surviving in a family where the parents impose expectations and insist on forms of behavior that are at variance with the underlying "true self." Clearly, the more accepting one's parents, the less false self one need create. The more destructive the family, the "thicker" a false self one must erect, as a defense against "annihilation," as when the mother is quite the opposite of "good-enough."

"false self"

Though both Balint and Winnicott made no attempt to relate their formulations to strict diagnostic categories (for which reason we cannot be certain just what kinds of patients they were addressing), the concepts of the *basic fault* and the *false self* are particularly relevant to *borderline* patients, as we now understand this personality type. For it is from this group of patients, especially, that one hears of serious neglect or abuse in the early ("preoedipal") years; and it is this group who describe feeling poignantly incomplete, short-changed, or strong-armed into adopting false attitudes (smiling sweetly when feeling angry, etc.) by parents with little concern for what might be the natural bent (true self) of their children.

John Frosch

In a number of papers written during the 1960s, John Frosch in New York brought more precise definition to this shadowy concept of the borderline. Frosch (1964) preferred the term *"psychotic character"* in describing what others had labeled *borderline* (Knight, 1953; Schmideberg, 1947), *pseudoneurotic schizophrenia* (Hoch & Polatin, 1949), and *latent psychosis* (Bychowski, 1953). The chief characteristics of the psychotic character were preservation of reality-testing;

object-relations which, though faulty, were better than those seen among psychotic patients; quick recovery from a psychotic episode; and primitive defenses (denial, projection). Frosch (1964) had a more thorough view of etiology than had most of his predecessors. For example, he acknowledged (as had Oberndorf and Edith Jacobson) that manic-depressive illness might be present in a *forme fruste* and that psychotic character need not be an expression (in a mild form) of schizophrenia.

Otto Kernberg

Otto Kernberg, then director of the Menninger Clinic in Topeka, Kansas, published a paper (1967) on borderline personality organization that became a classic. Writing from a structuralist[1] object-relations point of view, Kernberg envisioned three levels of general mental functioning: *neurotic, borderline,* and *psychotic.* In the highest (neurotic) level, both reality-testing and sense of identity were well preserved. The borderline level was characterized by a preservation of reality-testing in the presence of a weakened sense of identity (the "identity diffusion" of which Erikson [1956] spoke). In the psychotic level both these functions were severely crippled. Borderline patients showed primitive defenses—particularly, splitting and projective identification—and a pattern of oscillation between devaluation and idealization (noticeable in close relationships, including that with the therapist). One usually saw impulsivity, a meager ability to withstand stresses ordinary people handle with aplomb, and a seriously compromised capacity for work and hobbies. Kernberg mentioned a variety of subtypes within the borderline domain: some patients were *hysteric* (outwardly, as described by Easser and Lesser [1965] in their paper on the "hysteroid" patient; inwardly they were much more fragile and hostile); others were paranoid or hypomanic, etc. The work of Robert Knight (1953) in decoupling the concept of schizophrenia from that of borderline was carried further by Kernberg, who, unlike Knight, saw borderline organization as quite distinct and not even a subtle manifestation of schizophrenia. As to etiology, Kernberg drew attention to both environmental and constitutional antecedents: faulty child-rearing patterns during the developmental stage of separation and individuation (as conceptualized by Mahler, 1968), and an excess of "innate aggression" of a sort that conduces to the anger, impulsivity, and stormy relations that characterize the interpersonal life of borderline patients.

All through the 1960s many important contributions were made by Joseph Sandler and his colleagues in London. A member of the more

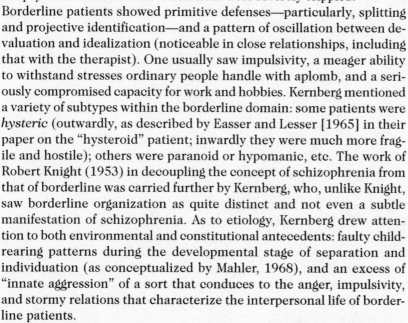

Joseph Sandler

---

[1] "Structuralist": derived from concepts about mental structures, as embodied in the work of anthropologist Claude Levi-Strauss.

orthodox Freudian school in which Anna Freud had long been spiritual guide, Sandler had been chiefly responsible for setting up the Hampstead Index at the Hampstead Child Guidance Clinic. This project was designed to give greater precision to analysts' impressions as to what kinds of interventions they were making during analytic sessions and also to lend greater precision to diagnosis. The project took advantage of the dynamic equilibrium between clinical observation and theory-formation, each enhancing the other.

Sandler has also been instrumental in computerizing the material, an exercise that has led to a number of ground-breaking papers. One example of this concerns the factor-analytic work done on the classification of obsessional character traits and symptoms (Sandler & Hazari, 1960). Data collected from 50 men and 50 women, when analyzed statistically, showed that "the term 'obsessional' has at least two distinct connotations . . . the *reactive narcissistic character* and the *true obsessional picture*." This work presages the contemporary distinction between obsessional *personality* and the (symptom-based) *disorder*.

Jacques Lacan

In France Jacques Lacan (1901–1981) had begun to achieve great popularity in this decade, although *The Four Fundamental Concepts of Psychoanalysis* was not published until 1973. The book is actually one of several volumes, each representing one year of Lacan's seminars (which began in 1953). In contrast to most of his contemporaries (in France or elsewhere), Lacan was no longer concerned with common clinical conditions and their treatments (as he was in the 1940s). Rather, he became interested only in Freudian theoretical concepts of the unconscious, repetition, transference, and drives. Focusing on the analogies between psychoanalytic theory and modern linguistic theory, Lacan discussed these concepts in a deconstructionist manner, later popularized even further by the French philosopher Jacques Derrida. As is the case with Derrida, Lacan's writing is at once glittery on the surface and hollow on the inside, rather like a mannequin in a sequin dress. Because of its airy intellectualism and solipsistic language, Lacan's work obscures what it purports to illuminate. Throughout his later writings he attempted to explain the mind and human relationships via an endless playing-with-words, using Freud's metaphors in his own idiosyncratic way, without recourse to other frames of reference, until his theory coils in on itself, becoming meaningless. An excerpt from his 1973 book exemplifies this problem:

> Through the effects of speech, the subject always realizes himself more in the Other, but he is already pursuing there more than half of himself. He will simply find his desire ever more divided, pulverized, in the circumscribable metonymy of speech. The ef-

fects of language are always mixed with fact, which is the basis of the analytic experience, that the subject is subject only from being subjected to the field of the Other, the subject proceeds from his synchronic subjection in the field of the Other. (p. 188)[2]

There were many prominent French contributors during this period whose works remain within the realm of conventional psychoanalytic thought. Among these are Andre Green, Janine Chasseguet-Smirgel, and Serge Lebovici. Dr. Lebovici had been president of the International Congress of Adolescent Psychiatry. Chasseguet-Smirgel has written (1965/1985 Engl. tr.) on the ego-ideal. She expressed the view that father-daughter incest rarely leads to psychosis (1985, p. 33), contending that only incest with the mother represents a return to the original state of fusion (and this is more akin to psychosis). Her impression is not easy to reconcile with clinical experience in America, where the correlation between father-daughter incest in childhood and subsequent psychosis is fairly pronounced. This may be an example of where prediction based on psychoanalytic theory is not always borne out by clinical experience or epidemiological study.

Janine Chasseguet-Smirgel

Another important French contributor of the 1960s was Sacha Nacht. Unlike many of his contemporaries, Nacht was vividly aware that the healing elements in the analytic process were *not* confined to the verbal interpretations. He was among the first to acknowledge the impact of the nonverbal transactions, the gestures made by both participants, and the whole analytic *mis-en-scène*—the furnishings of the office, the calm and quiet of the room, and so on (1963).

Sacha Nacht

The subject of masochism received considerable attention in the 1960s, to which Nacht made an important contribution. Earlier Freud (1924) had identified three types of masochism: erotogenic, moral, and feminine. These types are equivalent (respectively) to (1) a specific perversion in which sexual gratification is dependent on experiencing physical pain; (2) the unconscious and indirect seeking of suffering; and (3) "typical" feminine submissiveness. Nacht (1965) conceptualized moral masochism as "enveloping the whole personality"; it is not an end in itself but a *means* whereby the masochist "consents to a partial sacrifice" in order to safeguard the rest of a necessary relationship.

masochism

Rudolph Loewenstein viewed the masochist's passivity and helplessness as an appeal to the mercy of the parental figure, who might then be willing to switch from the role of tormentor to that of protector

Rudolph Loewenstein

---

[2] For those interested in a detailed explication of Lacan's work, written in clear language, the excellent review of Eugen Bar (1974) will be rewarding.

(1957). Thus a mother who was cruel, menacing, and humiliating—but capable of softening if approached humbly enough—would be likely to foster a masochistic response pattern in her child. To this extent mother becomes the "beloved bitch" to whom the child clings, using the masochistic posture as an insurance measure to secure what love the mother is willing to offer.

Victor Smirnoff

Victor Smirnoff (1969) took these ideas a step further, asserting that "the essential phenomena of masochism may well not be in the suffering but in the position of the masochist in the masochistic relationship" (Hanly, 1995, p. 63). Paradoxically, masochists may be seen as orchestrating their own victimhood by eliciting just enough "punishment" to appeal to their need to feel "in control." In essence, there is a symbiotic dance choreographed to blind the "powerful one" to the dependent, but no longer so helpless, masochist. A relationship of this sort is more likely to unfold in cases where the mother alternates between two roles in relation to her son: that of seducer and rejecter. An adult parallel to this childhood experience of the mother can be found in the madonna-prostitute fantasy many men entertain (especially masochistic men); throughout their lives they oscillate between an attraction to the woman who is pure, asexual, and rejecting or loving but unavailable (because she is already married, of a different religion, etc.), and the whorish woman with whom sex is easily available but whom one would never "stoop" to marry. In his concluding remarks Smirnoff noted:

> The symbiotic relation, as found in masochism, makes use of suffering, pain and humiliation, not in order to obtain pleasure, but as a symbolic representative of both the unattainable fusion with, and the impossible separation from the primary object. (p. 72)

"negative therapeutic reaction"

A phenomenon related to masochism, the "negative therapeutic reaction," was the subject of a paper by Stanley Olinick (1964), in which he discussed the paradoxical pattern seen in certain patients in therapy who behave as though they were intolerant of gratification. Some have referred to these patients as "help-rejecting complainers." Since many borderline and depressive patients exhibit this reaction, especially in the opening phases of treatment, the topic received much attention within the analytic community during this period.

In the ensuing years, there has been considerable clinical confirmation of the impressions expressed by Nacht, Loewenstein, Smirnoff, and Olinick. Their formulations may be said to have "stood the test of time," to have proved their usefulness to therapists who confront "moral masochism" in their patients. We shall consider "feminine masochism" when we discuss its transmogrification into "self-defeating personality" in the 1980s.

GENERAL PSYCHIATRY

Because of the enormous expansion of psychiatry after World War II, not only in the sheer number of practitioners but also in the number of subspecialties within the field, no one psychiatrist could claim any longer to know *all* of psychiatry. A number of prominent men had earned their fame partly through writing a widely read textbook, such as Kraepelin in the early part of the century and Lawrence Kolb of New York Psychiatric Institute in the 1950s (who rewrote and expanded Alfred Noyes' earlier text). However, the era of single-author textbooks was coming to a close as multi-authored textbooks began to appear (which were usually multi-volume as well). One such enterprise was edited by Silvano Arieti (1968); another by Harold Kaplan and Benjamin Sadock (1967). Several others have been added in the recent decades.

multi-authored textbooks

In the early 1960s Irving Bieber published *Homosexuality: A Psychoanalytic Study of Male Homosexuals,* based on his analysis of 106 homosexual men (30 of whom were bisexual) and 100 heterosexual men. Bieber found that the homosexual men were more apt to have avoided fights as children, less apt to have engaged in competitive sports, and more likely to be effeminate (the latter attribute was seen in only 27% of the homosexual men and 5% of the control group). Although homosexuality was finally (if gradually) becoming decriminalized in the United States, it was not yet *demedicalized.* Bieber still perceived homosexuality as an illness, which was the prevailing view at the time among psychoanalysts. The then popular analytic theory was that homosexuality resulted from being raised in families where the mother was "seductive" or "overinvolved" and the father "aloof." The belief was that, if "caught" early, homosexuality could be modified, and that most homosexual men would welcome such an outcome. Ironically, this notion reflected a powerful *normative* streak in psychoanalytic metapsychology, according to which, in fact, *no one* is truly "normal"—because, at best, we all have some unresolved conflicts and moments of irrationality. Homosexuality "couldn't" be normal because it falls short of "full genitality": in the Freudian sense, a developmental track that ends with oedipal resolution, overcoming the "castration complex," and achieving the capacity for heterosexual intimacy.

Irving Bieber

homosexuality as an illness

Only to the extent that one ignored epidemiological data and the results of genetic research (see p. 321 and Friedman & Downey, 1993) could one persist in these views. In the 1960s, alas, few in psychiatry were peering outside the narrow confines of a purely psychological construct. Some criticized Bieber (rightly so) for comparing homosexual *patients* with heterosexual *non-patients.* Only much later would it also become clear that (a) most American (probably most Western) families show a constellation of "aloof father/overinvolved mother," and (b) many fathers of homosexual-to-be boys are befuddled and ill-at-ease—in other words, *aloof*—with their sons, because their interests are so often at odds with those of the fathers. Thus these fathers would become aloof or rejecting in response to what is perceived to be irreconcilable differences, not necessarily because they were, by nature, detached and unresponsive individuals. In the next decade we will see how ideological differences on this controversial topic led to pitched battles of the most acrimonious sort.

The issue of homosexuality highlights another problem that was surfacing in the 1960s: The efficacy of psychoanalysis as a method for understanding the mind was not always matched by its efficacy as a treatment modality. Even if one accepted the premise that homosexuality was a condition for analysts to correct, the results did not inspire optimism—at least, not the results of therapists with integrity. There was always an Edmund Bergler (1957) to claim that he could convert homosexuals to heterosexuality with the greatest of ease—but this was sheer fakery, as the profession soon realized. This realization nudged some psychiatrists and analysts in the direction of searching for *constitutional,* as opposed to purely psychological, underpinnings for homosexual object-choices.

There were still other conditions where psychodynamic understanding was only occasionally rewarded with a cure, such as agoraphobia and obsessive-compulsive disorder. Disappointments of this sort stimulated the development of alternative treatment methods for these refractory conditions. Freud and later Franz Alexander had stated that, sooner or later, phobics need to be "pushed" into facing the feared situation (airplanes, elevators, leaving home, etc.), lest they languish endlessly in a state of avoidance. In the 1960s a number of clinicians from other areas of psychiatry were making impressive advances with

cognitive and behavioral approaches

cognitive and behavioral approaches to the very conditions that were either impervious to psychoanalytic therapy or, at least, could be treated far more quickly and less expensively by the newer techniques. Chief among the contributors were Isaac Marks in England, whose *Fears and Phobias* appeared in 1969; Aaron Beck in Philadelphia, who published numerous papers (1963, 1967) on cognitive/behavioral treatment of depression and anxiety disorders; and Joseph Wolpe, whose *Practice of Behavior Therapy* was published in 1969.

In the late 1950s and early 1960s Wolpe developed a technique called "systematic desensitization" for counteracting phobia. This method involved training patients in muscular relaxation and then exposing them to graded degrees of anxiety-provoking situations. Wolpe had been influenced by Pavlov, Thorndike, Watson, and Skinner, whose work he had discovered after becoming disenchanted with psychoanalysis, of which he had been a strong supporter in the 1950s.

Beck's method for treating phobias is built upon Wolpe's systematic program of exposure. Beck recommends that therapist and patient draw up a list of fear-inducing situations, then rank them from least to most anxiety-producing. The patient then is urged to confront the situations in a graded series of steps. Successful completion of each small step lessens the anticipated anxiety of the next step and helps to depotentiate the negative assumptions that had become part of the patient's inner "script" in dealing with the external world. The therapeutic approach is directed at altering these consciously-held assumptions rather than at uncovering underlying, unconscious conflicts (as would be the focus in psychoanalysis). Cognitive therapy aims at reeducation, tends to be brief, and requires "homework" on the part of the patient. The ultimate goal is to uproot the old habits of thought, via appeal to reason, and replace them with more adaptive ways of thinking, which, in time, will become new habits of making positive assumptions.

Beck's method

"Flooding," another behavioral technique developed for anxiety disorders (especially phobias), requires phobic patients to inundate themselves with frightening situations in the imagination until the anxiety begins to abate. In other situations, patients may use flooding to physically immerse themselves in some anxiety-laden aspect of the environment. For example, a patient with a germ phobia might be asked to place his hands in a sandbox or in mud, which forces him to see that one can do such a thing without suffering adverse consequences. "Participant modeling" was a related technique developed for conquering phobias: The phobic patient watches someone else confront the feared situation, which then ideally emboldens him to do likewise. Using the above example, the therapist would submerge his hands in the mud and then encourage the patient to do the same. Flooding techniques had actually been tried years before: Westphal, who first described agoraphobia in 1871, tried to get his patients to cross the feared place every day (Pichot, 1990), though his efforts were not successful.

"flooding"

"participant modeling"

Cognitive/behavioral therapies soon became widely accepted in the 1960s as treatments of choice for anxiety disorders. The uncovering techniques of psychoanalysis were successful in a fair number of such cases, but the lower cost and briefer time required for the behavioral methods soon made them more popular. Some analysts, however, were able to combine the traditional analytic methods (dream analysis, the couch) with exhortation (which may be understood as behavioral intervention), all within the context of a brief (three-month) and highly successful therapy. An illustrative case was Thorkil Vanggaard's work with a patient suffering from panic disorder, who had remained asymptomatic 20 years at follow-up (1989).

Another analyst of the 1960s noted for his liberal use of parameters in the therapy of agoraphobic patients was Lionel Ovesey (1915–

Lionel Ovesey

*severely phobic
patients*

1995). A member of the Columbia Psychoanalytic Institute, Ovesey recognized early on that many severely phobic patients did not improve if treated only by a psychoanalysis conducted according to strict guidelines. He introduced such innovative measures as giving his agoraphobic patients a handwritten "safe-conduct pass" (1966) that promised them no harm would come to them were they to venture out to visit a friend or do an errand. Often enough, when done at the right time in the course of the analysis, this gesture would catalyze a forward movement, emboldening a patient to surmount the phobia. In a similar manner, Ovesey would help a patient with overwhelming separation anxiety to cope better with the analyst's vacation by sending the patient a postcard from wherever he was at the time. Ovesey recognized that there were many patients whose anxiety was so extreme that the interpretive work of the analysis, no matter how skillfully employed, was not sufficient to contain the upsurge of anxiety during prolonged separations, at least in the first few years of therapy. Unfortunately, Ovesey's sensible recommendations struck the more "purist" among his colleagues as contrived. Now our understanding has deepened; interventions of this sort no longer seem outlandish with severely phobic patients—they seem very human and appropriate. And besides, the "bottom line" is, they are often therapeutically effective.

*"pseudo-homosexual
anxiety"*

Ovesey is also known for the distinctions he drew between true homosexuality and what he called "pseudo-homosexual anxiety" (1955, 1969). As Friedman (1988) has summarized the dynamics, pseudo-homosexual conflicts ". . . are intimately related to insecurity about one's masculinity," and may be experienced by some men who feel they have failed to live up to societal standards for masculine performance. These men arrive at the (unconscious) equation: *I am a failure = I am not a man = I am castrated = I am a woman = I am a homosexual* (p. 171). Pseudo-homosexual anxiety is a phenomenon of heterosexual men, in contrast to *homosexual anxiety,* which afflicts men who harbor genuine homosexual desires which, perhaps because of their upbringing in a culture intensely hostile toward homosexuality ("homophobic"), they suppress in a losing battle against their own nature. Homosexual anxiety concerns unacceptable sexual desires; pseudo-homosexual anxiety concerns issues of power and dependency. In both situations, as Friedman points out, actual homoerotic fantasies are usually absent.

HOSPITAL PSYCHIATRY

By the end of the decade enthusiasm for psychoanalytically-oriented psychotherapy for schizophrenia had begun to wane. Before this attitudinal shift was in full swing, however, two analysts achieved particular prominence in this area: Silvano Arieti and Harold Searles. According to a popular survey book of this period, these men ranked first and second, respectively, as the most widely known psychiatrists in America. It is a testimony to the rapid pace of change over the past 25 years that the extensive publications of these authors are very little read by psychiatric trainees today.

Fleeing Pisa, Italy, during World War II, Silvano Arieti (1906–1981) settled in New York, where he became director of an analytic institute (Flower Fifth Avenue) of Sullivanian orientation; later he was a founding member of the American Academy of Psychoanalysis and first editor of its journal. Arieti had a special interest in schizophrenic thought disorder, which utilizes a "paleologic" (primary process modalities: condensation, concrete thinking, neologisms) and betrays ego-boundary confusion (as when a patient says, "I'm growing my father's hair").

Silvano Arieti, 1906–1981. Courtesy National Library of Medicine

Arieti believed that analytic therapy had much to offer the schizophrenic patient, provided modifications appropriate to the patient's needs were utilized. It was commonly accepted by Arieti and others (Fromm-Reichmann, Sullivan) that the therapist was the schizophrenic patient's "ambassador to reality" (Bellak & Loeb, 1969, p. 349), serving as a bridge from the inner world, to which the patient has retreated, to the hitherto frightening world of everyday reality. Arieti (1955) outlined three phases of the therapeutic work: (1) establishment of relatedness (achieving rapport through awareness of transference and countertransference), (2) helping the patient gain insight, and (3) active intervention or involvement in the life of the patient.

Arieti believed that schizophrenics begin to hear hallucinations only in anxiety-provoking situations—just when they *expect to hear them*. These patients put themselves in a "listening attitude," thus taking an active stance (as though somehow "controlling" the situation), instead of experiencing themselves as the passive victims of "persecutors." Initially, Arieti conceptualized the schizophrenic reaction to be the result of abnormal family life, whereby the child, offered too little security, was consigned to live in a state of "ominous expectancy." Later in his career Arieti recognized that, while *some* schizophrenic patients come from highly disturbed backgrounds (he estimated 25%), the majority come from reasonably nurturing families, making it more likely that constitutional, rather than primarily environmental, factors were the key to etiology.

Such enlightenment was not to grace all who treated schizophrenics in the 1960s. In England, R. D. Laing, for example, remained loyal to the false philosophy of family bashing to the very end. As coarse as he was charismatic, Laing eulogized the "noble schizophrenic" much as

schizophrenic thought disorder

R. D. Laing

Rousseau had waxed eloquent over the "noble savage" in the 18th century. Laing influenced those who organized certain "communes" for schizophrenic patients, such as Soteria House, where they were to live and govern themselves. Ultimately his experiment was a dismal failure, but not before earning its originator some years of fame.[3]

The fame of Harold Searles (b. 1919), in contrast, rested on a much firmer conceptual foundation. Born in upstate New York, near the birthplace of Harry Stack Sullivan, Searles was trained in the Sullivanian tradition and went on to spend many years on the staff at Chestnut Lodge in Maryland, where Frieda Fromm-Reichmann also taught. To his intensive therapy with schizophrenic patients Searles also brought an uncanny intuition and remarkable candor—qualities that aided him in penetrating further into the darkness of the schizophrenic's mindset than anyone else had ventured.

More clinician than theoretician, Searles' forte lay in speaking directly from his unconscious, as it were, to that of the patient. In his compassionate but bantering interviewing style, Searles would tease out the patient's hidden, heavily defended dynamics, and then, with sardonic humor, make an interpretive remark designed to tug the patient gently toward reality.

For example, a homosexual paranoid schizophrenic young man who, in a fit of jealousy, had strangled his lover's German Shepherd denied having killed the dog, admitting only that he had "touched the animal's collar." "Oh, I see," Searles replied, "the dog just *chose* that moment to die!" Faced with this absurdity, but reassured by Searles' good-natured "naiveté," the young man conceded that he had, indeed, been the direct cause of the dog's demise.

The poignancy of Searles' writing made him a favorite author, not only among those dedicated to this difficult area of work, but also with schizophrenic patients themselves, who often took comfort in his *Non-Human Environment* (1960) or his *Collected Papers* (1964). Searles was particularly astute in perceiving dynamics peculiar to schizophrenic patients. One patient might look longingly at a tree; another might speak nostalgically about a puppy his family once owned. Searles would comprehend the patient's envy of the tree, which was both beautiful and free of the need to interact with hostile and unpredictable human beings; or the envy of the puppy who had been the sole recipient of any affection from the parents.

Harold Searles, b. 1919

[3] Serious illness always spawns ill-conceived treatments, of which Laing's was only one of dozens that surfaced in the 1960s. Toward the end of the decade, for example, megavitamin therapy was touted as a cure, winning many advocates among the desperate.

In supervision Searles was a master at sensing countertransference feelings in his supervisees and then helping them understand what these feelings were reflecting about the emotional lives of their patients. He influenced a generation of trainees in Washington and New York throughout the 1960s and 1970s. Like Arieti, Searles conceptualized the treatment of schizophrenic patients (some of whom he worked with for 30 years) as unfolding in stages, which he likened to the developmental phases through which the patients had passed with their mothers (though not in sequence): First comes a stage of ambivalent symbiosis; next, one of "preambivalent symbiosis"[4] (usually several months later, when the storminess of the first stage has given way to a more relaxed atmosphere); then, a stage of resolution of the symbiosis; and, finally, the long, late phase of resolution of the symbiosis.

Toward the end of the 1960s currents were already building that would eventually sweep this kind of lengthy analytic therapy of schizophrenia into a corner. The advocates of this arduous technique—Searles and Arieti in the United States, Gaetano Benedetti in Switzerland, Racamier in France, Margaret Little in England—would soon be compared to the makers of stained glass for the great cathedrals or of woodblock prints in Japan: consummate artists whose skills were no longer in vogue. One who spurred this transition was Philip May in California, whose 1968 study comparing different modes of treatment of schizophrenic patients was conducted at Camarillo State Hospital. Among the comparison groups, one received ECT; another, neuroleptics plus milieu therapy; a third, "intensive psychotherapy" alone; and still another, neuroleptics and psychotherapy. The group receiving only intensive psychotherapy fared the worst; the patients receiving medications plus milieu therapy did as well as those with psychotherapy and medication. May's study was seriously flawed in design: The "long-term" therapy was only a few months; the therapists were residents in training; the patients were not the sort who would be expected to benefit from analytically-oriented therapy; and many had only a poor grasp of English! Even so, this was a turning point. The seeds of doubt had been planted; the efficacy of psychoanalytically-based therapy for schizophrenia was now openly in question. As future, better designed studies would show, the same results occurred with better educated schizophrenic patients: Even with these patients, this form of therapy was rarely useful by itself.

Meanwhile, Roy Grinker, Sr. and his colleagues (Grinker, Werble, &

Philip May

---

[4] The preambivalent phase, akin to unperturbed mother-infant symbiosis, is developmentally *earlier* than the ambivalent phase (similar to the "terrible twos"), but usually emerges *later* in the course of psychotherapy with schizophrenics.

borderline

subtypes

Drye, 1968) conducted an important study of 52 hospitalized patients diagnosed as borderline according to criteria selected by the Chicago Psychoanalytic Clinic: Assessment of ego strengths, symptoms, and social patterns of these patients led to further division into subtypes. Those with the most impulsivity, hostility, and disturbed thought became *Type I* patients, representing the "border with psychosis." Next, came *Type II* or "core borderlines," followed by *Type III,* called "as-if" patients.[5] Finally, the *Type IV* or "anaclitic-depressed" group were the least handicapped and resembled those we now place in the dysthymic category. Follow-up of these patients over a decade later revealed that only one or two could be considered schizophrenic, and that the outcome was poorer in the Type I patients, who remained more awkward socially and were more prone to brief psychotic episodes, than was the case with Type III or IV patients (Grinker & Werble, 1977). Grinker's typology remained useful for a number of years, partly because it complemented Kernberg's use of *borderline* as a level of function, providing four distinct layers within that layer.

manic-depressive
psychosis

In the area of affective disorders controversy continued as to whether manic-depressive psychosis was one condition or two. Jules Angst in Switzerland (1966) and George Winokur and Paula Clayton (1969) in the United States took the position that it made more sense to speak of two *forms* of affective psychosis: *bipolar* and *unipolar-depressed.* It then becomes casuistical whether this implies a unitary condition with two subtypes or two distinct entities under one general diagnostic umbrella. In either case, the relatives of bipolars, if also ill, tend to be bipolar; and the relatives of unipolars were at greater risk for unipolar illness—both by a factor of about 20 in their studies.

national community
mental health
program

Beginning in the first half of the 1960s, the federal government expressed a commitment to a national community mental health program. President Kennedy expressed great enthusiasm for a long-range plan to establish 2,000 mental health centers, under the aegis of the federal government, in order to care for the mentally ill and the mentally retarded. (The president's sensitivity to the need for such a program derived in part from having a mentally retarded sister.) The centers would consist of clinics, half-way houses, day-hospitals, and other forms of partial hospitalization that would facilitate the care of chronically mentally ill adults and children, at whatever stage of recovery or illness they were in, at any given time. Comparable programs were already in place in Scandinavia and Switzerland. Luc Ciompi's center in Bern, specializing in the total care of schizophrenic patients, is an ex-

[5] These patients were similar to the patients described by Helene Deutsch (1942) as lacking a firm sense of identity, assuming instead the attitudes and values of persons they attached themselves to at any given time.

ample. (In one of Ciompi's units, patients were taught useful crafts and trades that would allow them, in time, to occupy positions of respect in similar employment in the city.)

Alongside this activity of setting up community mental health centers in America was a new policy of *deinstitutionalization,* executed primarily by the states (the public hospitals were state run, for the most part, since Dorothea Dix's time), though with the blessing of the federal government and the administrators of the National Institute of Mental Health (NIMH). Though begun with the best of intentions, Kennedy's program soon encountered serious difficulties. The goal of 2,000 clinics would have required a vast increase in the number of psychiatrists and other mental health professionals. If professional standards were to be maintained, there was no way to recruit or train the necessary personnel. The cost to the government would be overwhelming, unless only small segments of the population demanded the services these clinics were intended to provide. Already by the late 1960s it was clear that the program was neither feasible nor affordable, resulting in various halfway measures and budget cuts by the federal government. Meanwhile, the states, banking on the ability of the newer drugs to maintain chronically ill patients *outside* the hospital, continued their policy of closing or reducing the state hospitals. The tragic consequence of this policy (increased homelessness) was not yet so manifest in the 1960s.

deinstitutionalization

Chapter 15

BIOLOGICAL PSYCHIATRY,

NEUROSCIENCE, AND GENETICS

dream state

REM sleep

A major breakthrough now occurred in our understanding of the dream state and its functions, thanks to the discoveries of Aserinsky and Kleitman (1953) and Dement and Kleitman. These researchers demonstrated on an electroencephalogram (EEG) that dreaming was accompanied by a rapid-eye-movement phase of sleep ("REM sleep"). This led to an outpouring of studies by Dement and others during the 1960s (Dement, 1960, 1964; E. Hartmann, 1968, 1969; Roffwarg, Muzio, & Fisher, 1962), which proved the need for revisions in the psychoanalytic theories of dreaming as formulated by Freud and the first generation of analysts. Dreaming occurred roughly every hour and a half throughout the night, beginning about 80 minutes after the onset of sleep, and lasting about 10–15 minutes per cycle. Ernest Hartmann (the son of ego psychology's Heinz Hartmann) showed that the in-between phase—NREM ("non-REM") sleep—was an anabolic period of protein synthesis. REM sleep supported homeostatic processes of adaptation to the environment—in effect, *problem-solving*. In other words, dreams are concerned not so much with "preserving sleep" or with "fulfilling wishes" but with re-working the emotional and interpersonal problems of the day, from the perspective of primary process thought. Since animals from the lamprey on up also show REM sleep—dogs and cats and horses certainly dream—it made sense to hypothesize that problem-solving (in humans, at least) is a psychological mechanism engrafted during childhood onto an already pre-existing neurophysiological mechanism widespread throughout the animal kingdom.[1]

GENETIC RESEARCH

Research in psychogenetics during the 1960s dealt with the following issues: To what extent do the major psychoses breed true? What are the patterns of inheritance? Is "schizoaffective psychosis" a distinct diagnostic entity or is it a blend of schizophrenia and manic-depression? How strong are the hereditary factors? Which clinical disorders express the milder degrees of inherited predisposition?

Ødegaard (1963) in Norway and Mitsuda (1967) in Japan concluded (independently) in their studies of relatives of schizophrenics and manic-depressives that there was a strong tendency (just over half of Ødegaard's series; 80% in Mitsuda's series) for these conditions to "breed true": Affected relatives of the index cases usually had the same type of illness. This argued for *genetic heterogeneity,* or to use Ødegaard's term, "multifactorial" inheritance in which *several* genes interact rather than one *dominant* gene. The more severe the illness in the index cases, the more similar were the conditions in the relatives; in the relatives of diluted or borderline cases (*borderline* with respect to the major psychosis in question), the psychiatric conditions did not so closely resemble that of the index case. Actually, Mitsuda (1979), though he pictured schizophrenia, manic-depression, and epilepsy as separable categories, also posited a variety of *overlap* conditions, including *atypical* psychoses (such as schizoaffective, schizophreniform, and cycloid).

In the area of affective psychoses, George Winokur and V. Tanna (1969) provided evidence that bipolar mania is transmitted from mother to son via an X-chromosome-linked dominant gene. Their report was exciting news and engendered considerable enthusiasm that this discovery would lead to rapid progress in treatment as well. Confirmatory studies fol-

research in psychogenetics

genetic heterogeneity

affective psychoses X-chromosome-linked dominant gene

---

[1] The poets knew this long before the analysts and physiologists. Pushkin, for example, writing his most famous work, *Eugene Onegin,* in the 1830s, has his heroine, Tatyana, solve her problem—should she marry Onegin (a "gloomy and dangerous crank," in the poet's words) or should she break off the engagement—via a dream. In her dream a huge bear carries her off through the woods to a house where various horned and beaked monsters are panting for the chance to possess her. She awakens with a fright, looks up the symbols in her "dream book," to no avail—and yet has a flash of insight that marrying Onegin would be a disaster. What Freud hinted at, and Hartmann realized, Pushkin had anticipated many years earlier.

lowed shortly thereafter (Fieve, Mendlewicz, & Fleiss, 1973), but there were also reports of father-son transmission (by David Dunner, et al., 1976) which called into question the X-chromosome linkage theory (Goldin & Gershon, 1983). In response to these confusing results, Ming Tsuang (1975) proposed that genetic heterogeneity characterized the affective psychoses as well: An X-linked major gene might be the main factor in some cases; a polygenic system might underlie other cases.

studies of twin pairs

Studies of monozygotic versus dizygotic twin pairs, carried out in a more rigorous method than in previous years, were reported by Einar Kringlen (1968) in Norway and Pekka Tienari (1963) in Finland. The concordance rate in schizophrenia was reduced from the 86% of Kallmann's earlier series (1938) to more modest figures, in the range of 40% (Tienari's results were initially much lower, but later follow-up showed a similar ratio). This psychogenetic research further fueled the nature vs. nurture debates. Some interpreted the 40% heritability figure to mean that schizophrenia was 40% nature/60% nurture. Others, such as Lucille Erlenmeyer-Kimling (personal communication, 1985) in New York, believed that schizophrenia requires an *a priori* condition of hereditary predisposition—*but* whether a person actually develops the clinically recognizable illness depends on a number of factors. These could be *hereditary* (the intensity of the genetic loading), *constitutional* (low birth weight, fetal hypoxia, etc.), or *environmental* (an extremely chaotic or abusive family would be more likely to push a child with "middling" genetic loading into "frank" schizophrenia, whereas a warm and accepting family, given the same child, might be able to protect that child from becoming overtly ill).

nature versus nurture debates

PSYCHOPHARMACOLOGY

In the area of psychopharmacology, considerable progress was made in the development of compounds related to the originally small roster of neuroleptics and antidepressants: neuroleptics, such as trifluoperazine/Stelazine, that were less sedating than chlorpromazine; tricyclic antidepressants, such as desipramine/Norpramine, that have fewer anticholinergic side effects than imipramine/Tofranil (i.e., less dry mouth, constipation, blurred vision). Since not all bipolar manic patients respond to lithium (perhaps only two out of three), and since not all tolerate its side effects, there was a search for other anti-manic compounds. One such drug was discovered serendipitously in France: valproic acid. Though the drug had been synthesized in 1882 (as an organic solvent), it was discovered quite by accident to have anticonvulsant properties by Meunier in 1963 (Keck, McElroy, & Bennett, 1994). Only three years later the anti-manic property of valproic acid was discovered by another French investigator (Lambert, 1966).

The various pathways in the brain where norepinephrine, seroto-nin, and dopamine are concentrated were studied intensively in the 1960s. Hornykiewicz (1962, 1966) showed that dopamine is primarily concentrated in the extrapyramidal areas: substantia nigra, caudate, and putamen. The caudate and putamen are parts of the basal ganglia; high concentrations of dopamine in these regions may account for vul-nerability to extrapyramidal disorders (most notably, Parkinson's dis-ease) following localized lesions. Hornykiewicz established, for example, that patients with Parkinsonism show decreased brain levels of dopam-ine, detectable especially in the substantia nigra (1962). Garattini and Valzelli (1965) outlined the serotonin pathways (found especially in the limbic regions of the septum, amygdala, and hippocampus). Glowinski and Baldessarini (1966) showed that norepinephrine con-centrates in similar areas as does serotonin, though in lower amounts, and that these norepinephrine tracts involve two ascending pathways: the central tegmental tract and the dorsal tegmental bundle beginning in the locus coeruleus. In the years to follow, the identification of these pathways was to prove important not only to our understanding of the mechanisms of action in the antipsychotic drugs but also to our under-standing of the more subtle shadings of personality.

pathways in the brain

dopamine

serotonin

norepinephrine

BRAIN RESEARCH

Research on differential functioning of the two cerebral hemispheres, adumbrated in Wigan's writings in 1844, made dramatic progress in the 1960s. Much of this work was done in hospitals, by neurologists and neurosurgeons operating on patients with intractable epilepsy, whose condition, it was hoped, would be controlled by sectioning the corpus callosum. Those with the most extensive experience in this procedure and who wrote most prolifically on their findings were J. Bogen (1962, 1969), R. W. Sperry (1966), and Michael Gazzaniga (1965, 1967). Their "split-brain" studies demonstrated that each hemisphere specializes in mediating certain functions. The dominant hemisphere (the left hemisphere in right-handed, and even in some left-handed, persons) subserves lexical processes: linear, sequential speech and thought, arithmetic reasoning, tasks requiring logic. The non-domi-nant (usually the right) hemisphere subserves visuo-spatial tasks, music appreciation (registering the emotional overtones as opposed to sim-ply recognizing the melody) (Kimura, 1964), comprehending puns and jokes on the basis of similarity of sounds or associations, and (per-haps) the visual aspects of dreaming.

differential functioning of the two cerebral hemispheres

split-brain research

Split-brain research also proved relevant to the problem of dyslexia. Dyslexia in children had been identified earlier in the century, first by Hinshelwood (1900) and then by neurologist Orton (1928), who founded

dyslexia

the Orton Dyslexia Society. Orton (1937) had already noted that two-thirds of his dyslexic patients showed opposite handedness and eye dominance. Another neurologist, Martha Denckla (1981), confirmed that two-thirds of her dyslexic patients were right-handed and right-footed but *left*-eye-dominant. In psychiatric areas differences in normal people between left-brain superiority for logical/linguistic processing and right-brained superiority for primary process operations and the emotions led Pierre Flor-Henry (1969) to speculate that schizophrenia was mostly a dominant hemisphere disease; manic-depression, a mostly non-dominant condition. Subsequent investigation did not bear out these neat dichotomies; the neurological deficiencies in schizophrenia, for example, are not limited to the dominant hemisphere. Mandell (1980) later suggested an association between the left-brain attributes of linearity, non-intuition, and affective flatness and the *obsessional* personality; the right-brain attributes of visual and spatial sensibilities, excitability, intuition, emotionality, and the non-logical were associated with the *hysteric* personality. Others drew a parallel between degree of creativity and degree of interplay between the two modes of processing (the corpus callosum serving as the connecting pathway for the interhemispheric cross-talk). One of the most famous examples of this cross-talk: The chemist Kekule, unable to determine the chemical structure of benzene, had a dream in which he saw a snake biting its own tail. He awakened from this dream with a flash of insight: Benzene is *not* a linear compound—the carbons form a *circle!*

evoked potentials

Another bridge being built between neurology and psychiatry during this period was occurring as a result of research on "evoked potentials" (EP). In work with electroencephalography it was noted that the "delivery of a sensory stimulus triggers a series of voltage peaks and troughs lasting for several hundreds of milliseconds" (Kutas & Hillyard, 1990, p. 1). Some of the original work on evoked potentials was done by Walter, Cooper, and Aldridge (1964), Kornhuber and Deecke (1965), and Sutton, Braren, and Zubin (1965). Much of the pioneering work with EP applying the phenomenon to psychiatric conditions was done by Charles Shagass and his colleagues, beginning in the early 1960s (for example, Shagass, 1968; Shagass & Schwartz, 1962). There was some initial hope of finding an EP "signature" unique to each major disorder, which would make EP analysis an important diagnostic tool. A number of interesting correlations were indeed noted (and will be discussed in the section on the 1970s), though not the ideal, one-to-one mapping between EP pattern and clinical diagnosis.

CHILD AND ADOLESCENT PSYCHIATRY

During the 1960s anecdotal material was accumulating on physical abuse of children. Emergency-room cases of children with fractures or in states of unconsciousness, coma, or "sudden death" were now being recognized as evidence of beatings and other kinds of injurious treatment by parents or other caretakers. For many centuries, the home and what went on within its confines had been regarded as a terra sancta that lay above suspicion and inquiry. As a result of this attitude, assertions on the part of the parents that these injuries resulted from "falling down the stairs" or "bumping into furniture" were taken at face value. It is true that in the newspapers of Freud's Vienna in the 1890s cases of child murder and other grotesque examples of child molestation were occasionally reported (Wolff, 1988). But the topic did not become a *cause célèbre* until the 1960s and did not receive much national attention until the 1975 publication of the National Family Violence Survey in the United States. Meanwhile, Arthur Green and other psychiatrists in the 1960s were observing and reporting on such cases, thus bringing the whole sordid topic to the attention of both mental health and child welfare professions.

The displacements and losses imposed by World War II upon untold numbers of children stimulated interest in the topic of separation, especially in regard to its impact on small children who have lost their mothers or been separated from them for protracted periods. The most prolific commentator on this subject was British psychoanalyst John Bowlby (1954, 1980). His articles, which had begun to appear in the 1950s, emphasized that a close and warm relationship with the mother was essential to a young child's mental health. Bowlby disagreed with Melanie Klein's (1952/1975) assertion that infants routinely go through a "depressive position" at about six months of age. Klein had postulated that the young child is fearful when mother disappears (even briefly) because the child believes he has "devoured and thus destroyed his [mother]" (p. 63). In addition to guilt, the child feels a sense of "permanent" loss.[2] In contrast, Bowlby contended that grief reactions in the face of loss were similar in both adults and children and could be compartmentalized into three stages of *protest, despair,* and *detachment.* The last stage, when completed, paved the way for attachment to a new object. Bowlby's papers during the 1960s included "Separation Anxiety" (1960a) and "Ethology and the Development of Object Relations" (1960b). *Attachment,* the first volume of his important trilogy on child psychology, appeared in 1969 and was followed by *Separation* (1973) and *Loss* (1980).

John Bowlby. Courtesy Richard Bowlby

[2] Most analysts now regard such claims as incorrect—perhaps the result of projecting dynamics gleaned from analytic work with grieving adults onto the mind-set of preverbal infants.

High-Risk Children

studies of "high
risk" children

The decade of the 1960s marked the beginning of an impressive series of studies, in which evaluations were made periodically of "high-risk" children born to a psychotic parent(s). Most of the studies concentrated on parents suffering from schizophrenia or manic-depression. Sarnoff Mednick (1960) from California, in cooperation with the Danish government, set up the first such study of 207 children whose mothers were schizophrenic (as determined by strict criteria). Mednick and his colleagues also examined a control group consisting of similarly aged children from similar socioeconomic backgrounds. Among the significant findings reported when the children were assessed at intervals up to ten years later: The children who eventually became psychiatrically ill were much more likely to have lost contact with their mothers at an early age due to the mothers' psychiatric hospitalizations. The sick children were more likely to have been described by their teachers as disruptive, aggressive, and apt to create discipline problems in school. Difficult pregnancies for the mothers and more birth complications were also noted in the sick group. In addition, several psychophysiological abnormalities were noted with significant frequency in the sick group, such as abnormal electrodermal responses.

Similar projects were launched at the University of California at Los Angeles (UCLA) in 1964 and Washington University in St. Louis in 1966. Eliot Rodnick, Michael Goldstein, and others of the UCLA group (1984) focused on patterns of "communication deviance" in the families of schizophrenics. They noted a correlation between (a) families high in communication deviance and (b) offspring who develop disorders of the schizophrenia-spectrum (i.e., schizophrenic psychosis, borderline schizophrenia as defined by Kety et al., 1968, and possibly schizoid and paranoid personality disorders).

Bonding

Harry Harlow

critical period

Using an animal model to investigate the nature of the mother-infant bond, Harry Harlow (1963) observed baby monkeys who had been separated from their mothers and divided into two groups: One group was fed by a bottle attached to a soft "cloth monkey" (a "surrogate" mother), while the other group took its feeding from a toy monkey made only of wire. Those "reared" by the wire-mother showed more emotional disturbances as they matured than those who had contact with the cloth-mother; some were even unable to mount potential sexual mates. Harlow's research suggested that there was a "critical period" during infancy when mother-child bonding optimally took place, without which severe and not easily rectified emotional and relational problems were the likely sequelae.

This notion of a *critical period,* though it belongs mostly to the conceptual framework of the ethologists (such as Konrad Lorenz, who reported on the time when "imprinting" of the mother takes place in various animals), is also applicable in relation to human development. The concept is implicit in the theoretical formulations of Margaret Mahler, when she outlined the successive developmental stages through which infants and children typically pass. In her 1968 book, *On Human Symbiosis and the Vicissitudes of Individuation,* she described five developmental stages. The *autistic* phase (approximately the first two months of life) is followed by a *symbiotic* phase (from the second through the seventh month); then comes the *separation-individuation* phase (up to a year and a half), when the toddler makes its first efforts to develop autonomy and assert its own personhood. The *rapprochement* phase, through age two and a quarter, marks the time when *self* and *other* ("object" in psychoanalytic parlance) are differentiated, but the good and bad aspects of each are not yet integrated. This in turn is followed by *object-constancy,* during which time an integrated view of self and other begins to form.

In the 1960s child psychiatrists frequently spoke of the "stranger anxiety" that infants so characteristically demonstrate at the onset of the symbiotic phase. At about eight months of age, infants often dislike being held by persons other than the parents. This phase was seen as a "critical period" for bonding to the mother, especially, but also to other main caretakers, usually including the father. (Of course, some infants show this reaction to strangers earlier; others, later—and some, not at all.)

Mahler's work may be seen as a refinement of the linear developmental track suggested by Freud's oral, anal, and genital stages. Like Freud, Mahler was open to the idea that heredity and constitution are important factors in shaping personality; that there is more to the psychopathology seen in certain adults than can be explained solely in terms of the ill effects of parental mishandling at this or that early stage. Even so, throughout the 1960s (and 1970s) the assumption was often made, especially by those who worked with adult borderline patients, that patients' separation problems must perforce reflect "bad mothering" during the separation-individuation phase. James Masterson (1981) was an ardent proponent of this view. Later it became clear that, while adverse mothering is indeed a factor in some borderline patients, others develop their separation anxiety in response to different sources (and even with adequate mothering), such as sexual molestation or genetic predisposition for affective illness.

Margaret Mahler 1897–1985. Courtesy Special Collections, A. A. Brill Library, The New York Psychoanalytic Institute

ETHOLOGY

human gestures

Paralleling the post-World-War II research on animal behavior, with its focus on innate "fixed action patterns," was considerable research on hereditarily-determined and culturally-driven behavior patterns in our own species. This latter area is the domain of "human ethology." In the middle part of the present century, ethologic studies by Konrad Lorenz and Nikolaas Tinbergen (who shared the Nobel Prize in 1972), were confined almost exclusively to nonanimals. Tinbergen (1948, 1951) was among those who later contributed to our understanding of human gestures. Research on gestures was enhanced by careful slow-motion photography of people in typical social gatherings. For example, it was noted how men, when being introduced to an attractive woman, tend to straighten their ties and pull in their stomachs—an unconscious behavior pattern designed, apparently, to create a more "masculine," powerful image.

As a science, ethology may be seen as an offspring of Pavlov's research on conditioned reflexes. (Perhaps we should consider it one of Pavlov's *grandchildren,* since the behaviorism of Watson and Skinner was the direct descendant, antedating ethology.) Ironically, behaviorism was diametrically opposed, philosophically, to psychoanalysis, yet both championed the notion that the human brain at birth is a *tabula rasa*—Locke's "clean slate"—free of predetermined, inherited behavior patterns and, therefore, free to be shaped, either by interpersonal relationships or by the narrowly delimited system of rewards and punishments. For both warring camps, to believe otherwise was to submit to the "hopelessness" of unalterable patterns to which genetic influences would have consigned us.

Irenäus Eibl-Eibesfeldt

Through the work of Lorenz and Tinbergen, ethology emerged as a respectable field of scientific inquiry. The great pioneer in human ethology is Irenäus Eibl-Eibesfeldt, who has worked for almost 50 years at the Max Planck Institute in Germany. In 1967 he wrote a chapter on "Concepts of Ethology and Their Significance for the Study of Human Behavior," based on field research in many countries and cultures. As he wrote in the introduction to his *magnum opus, Human Ethology* (1989), "The discovery that even the behavior of higher vertebrates is preprogrammed in well-definable ways through phylogenetic adaptation has initiated a process of reconsideration in the human sciences . . . " (p. x).

Drawing upon observations with both human and nonhuman species, Eibl-Eibesfeldt noted similarities between the *agonistic* sexuality in reptiles, which is characterized by male dominance and female submissiveness, and certain patterns in human behavior, which are influenced by the "reptilian," phylogenetically primitive portion of the brain.

For example, male swaggering and posturing, by way of asserting dominance, may be seen as carry-overs of this agonistic brand of sexuality. In birds, mammals, and humans, *affiliative* sexuality predominates and is characterized by love or limerance or bonding, wherein mothers form intimate ties to their offspring (and where, in certain species, there is long-term mating and distinct roles for the father). Female fearfulness and submissiveness, though apparently not as "essential" to the mating game as was once true in our species (and still is in many animals), are still manifested in certain women under a variety of circumstances.

In discussing advances in ethology in the 1980s, we will examine new ways of thinking about the long-problematic human practices of adultery and homosexuality. Already in the 1960s, however, the findings from ethological science were beginning to force modifications in the theoretical constructs of psychoanalysis and the other psychologies. Still, it would be unfair to state that psychoanalysis remained blind to the existence of biological influences until the work of the ethologists became more widely known in other circles. As far back as 1939 psychoanalysts Theresa Benedek and B. Rubenstein had reported on the fluctuations in the content of women's dreams during the menstrual cycle. These authors noted that in the estrogenic phase normal women experienced more active libido and desire for sexual gratification. The few days prior to ovulation, when estrogen levels suddenly diminish, Benedek noted increased narcissistic concerns in the women she was studying, along with heterosexual hostility and fears relating to the mother. Heightened relaxation and dependency accompanied the post-ovulation phase, followed by heightened wishes for impregnation and nursing during the mid-luteal phase. Finally, in the premenstrual phase aggressive tendencies were noted, especially in women whose relationships with their mothers were predominantly hostile. These observations of mood shifts that correlated with points in the menstrual cycle, while admittedly more pronounced in "neurotic" than in normal women, meant, in effect, that there was more to the understanding of psychodynamics than could be explained solely on the basis of oedipal conflicts or problems in the first two or three years of life. While human psychology is not *determined* by biology, it is *shaped* by biological influences, as ethology was to show more clearly than any other discipline.

SYSTEMS THEORY

Another new science to arise in this era was called "systems theory." Its most famous expositor was Hungarian Ludwig von Bertalanffy (b. 1901), whose articles and books began to appear in the 1940s, but

Ludwig von Bertalanffy

whose work did not come to more general attention till the 1960s. His book, *General Systems Theory* (GST), appeared in 1968. Concerned with homeostatic mechanisms and hierarchical arrangements of the different levels of organization within a complex system, this theory expanded the narrow deterministic assumptions of the time. Von Bertalanffy derived some of his inspiration from the work of Walter Cannon and Claude Bernard. He cites Cannon's "Organization from Physiological Homeostasis" (1929). Other influences included Wiener's (1948) treatise on cybernetics, Shannon and Weaver's (1948) essay on information theory, and von Neumann and Morgenstern's (1944) book on game theory.

Until mid-century, both the hard sciences and psychology had shown a *deterministic* and *reductionistic* cast, in which human behavior was viewed as operating within a "closed system." This simplistic perspective was implicit in the early psychoanalytic libido theory, in which humans were believed to have a fixed quantity of psychic "energy." Thus if *x* amount of energy (total energy = *e*) was invested in one activity, then only *e* minus *x* energy would be "left over" for other activities. This strange calculus was alleged to hold sway even in the amatory sphere: If Tom loved Sue with a grand passion, he would have rather less left over to bestow upon other relatives or persons in his closest orbit.

Reductionistic explanations were part and parcel of psychoanalytic metapsychology even in the 1960s; President Kennedy's ambition was "merely" the unfolding of sibling rivalry within the context of oedipal conflict. And so on. Deterministic explanations were characteristic of both behaviorism and psychoanalysis. The belief was that if *enough* information about a person could be accumulated (his psychological antecedents, interpersonal world, work situation, medical history, etc.), then his future could be mapped out in detail. However, this was an *unfalsifiable hypothesis,* since no matter how much information is made available about someone, it can always be claimed that, if the predictions are incorrect, it is because still more information is needed.

It was against this elegant nonsense that von Bertalanffy rebelled. Admittedly, the appeal of determinism is easy to understand; it promises orderliness and comprehensibility in the face of a bewilderingly complex world. Furthermore, there is an accompanying belief that absolute understanding would foster perfection in the ordering of society—utopia. Not long after von Bertalanffy's book had appeared, several independent areas of research would all blend together to expose the fallacy of determinism: Heisenberg's "uncertainty principle"; Gödel's unprovable mathematical axioms; and the later work of Mandelbrot on non-linear equations, fractals, and chaos theory. Together—though independently—these disparate revelations would breathe humility into psychological theory and restore individuality to humans. As von Bertalanffy (1968) wisely cautioned:

Human society is not a community of ants or termites, governed by inherited instinct and controlled by the laws of the superordinate whole; it is based on the achievement of the individual and is doomed if the individual is made a cog in the social machine. (p. 52)

Von Bertalanffy is particularly known for his presentation of schemata in which interrelated systems are organized within a *hierarchy.* One might diagram such a hierarchy, as it pertains to our species, as shown in Table 4.

Attention to level of discourse within a hierarchical system, as in Table 4, helps to clarify questions that, if viewed within the narrow framework of just one level, may resist solution. An example: Many find it difficult to understand how the existence of homosexual men and women, or of maiden aunts, could be other than some kind of aberration. Viewed solely within the level of the *individual,* all such persons face genetic death by becoming the end of their particular lineages. If *everyone* were a non-breeder, the race would "die out"; therefore, persons in these categories are *ipso facto* abnormal. *But*—if viewed from the next level up (the family), or even three levels up (society), the perspective acquires additional dimensions. For example, homosexual men and women (as well as maiden aunts) may contribute to the economic welfare of their nieces and nephews—who share a fourth of their genes—permitting these younger family members to survive and flourish in ways that the biological parents could not as easily guarantee if bereft of the resources of their siblings.

TABLE 4 *HIERARCHY OF SYSTEMS,* EACH LARGER AND MORE COMPLEX THAN THE ONE BELOW IT, RELEVANT TO OUR SPECIES

Level	*Related Discipline or Science*
Humankind	Philosophy, political theory
Society/nation/culture	Anthropology, political theory, sociology
Group	Ethology, anthropology, sociology
Family	Family psychiatry
The Individual	Individual psychology, psychoanalysis, cognitive/behavioral psychology
Organ	Medicine, physiology
Cell	Cellular physiology, chemistry
Organelles	Molecular biology
Molecules	Atomic physics, chemistry

As to the *societal* level, there would appear to be a superiority among homosexual people, as a group, in the realm of creativity, such that they confer benefits to society as a whole that compensate for the lack of progeny. One need only reflect on the contributions of Michelangelo, da Vinci, Walt Whitman, Schubert, Oscar Wilde, Tchaikovsky, Gertrude Stein, Yukio Mishima, and a host of others, including many famous actors and actresses.

Taking the perspective to the top level of humankind, one recognizes that there have *always* been homosexual people in each and every culture; to believe that each generation produces homosexual members, and has done so throughout all recorded history—*to no purpose whatever*—is now seen as untenable. The purpose is not something one could discern by pondering solely the individual level. The sacrifice to the non-breeding relative is genetically "worth it" if several "quarter-gene" nieces and nephews can be helped to survive. Dawkins (1976) and other neo-Darwinian ethologists have even worked out a mathematics that answers under what conditions the sacrifice "pays."

Particularly because our capacity for language is unique in the animal world (nonhuman animals communicate by meaningful sounds, to be sure, but they do not have our ability to symbolize or our extensive vocabulary), von Bertalanffy (1968) contended that mental illness is a specifically human phenomenon. For this reason, he expressed objections to the notion that human behavior could be explained by (reduced down to) homeostatic theory, biological drive theory, abnormal mothering, etc. Rather, he called for a medley of theories addressing all the relevant hierarchical levels. For example, juvenile delinquency requires an understanding of the *cultural* context that supplies the value system no longer honored by the offender. Von Bertalanffy insisted that mental soundness was determined by whether a person has an "integrated universe consistent within the given cultural framework" (p. 219). What is normal for the members of one culture may be pathological in another. For example, "magical thinking" is a normal attribute for people in certain cultures, whereas in Western culture it is one of the defining features of schizotypal personality disorder. From a systems theory standpoint, contemporary therapy with schizophrenic patients would be seen as incorporating the concerns of several hierarchical levels: Exploration of the past (the *individual* level) is emphasized less than reeducation of the close relatives (the *family* level) and developing social skills and occupational skills (the *societal* level).

Von Bertalanffy also stressed that some of the age-old problems in philosophy and psychiatry melt away when reexamined in the light of systems theory. Among these are the Cartesian dualism between matter and mind and the question of free will. According to von Bertalanffy, the question of free will is resolved by the realization that individuals experience themselves as acting freely only because "the category of causality is not applied in direct or immediate experience." People are not in touch with the degree to which certain behaviors are driven by biological forces or of how their language is organized partly by the neural architecture of the brain itself. Assigning causality is the means by which we try to make sense of mental and behavioral phenomena by "taking into account ever more factors of motivation" (p. 221). For reasons having to do with inherent unpredictabilities in the nervous system and the world in general, we can only *refine,* never *perfect,* our understanding. Will is thus not "determined" but "determinable"—progressively more, and only up to a point. In this regard von Bertalanffy's ideas have broad implications concerning both the *limits* beyond which biological psychiatry cannot take us and the *degree* to which individual behavior remains unprogrammable and unpredictable.

REVOLUTIONS IN THOUGHT

In America the late 1960s marked the beginning of the student revolution, the sexual revolution, and the feminist movement. Obviously the sexual revolution did not erupt in one moment in time: social changes were already well underway (smaller families, easy access to birth control, higher divorce rate, more women working), and discoveries in biology that challenged many long-cherished assumptions about sexuality in men and women were reported steadily. Better communication between the disciplines of gynecology, psychiatry, and psychoanalysis makes it impossible to credit any one source or person for the intellectual breakthroughs that were achieved.

This aside, one of the most important—and in its way, revolutionary—contributions to our understanding of human female sexuality came from the pen of psychoanalyst Mary Jane Sherfey. In her landmark article of 1966, Sherfey reviewed and integrated data from embryology, ethology, gynecology, and psychoanalysis. The older psychoanalytic view about the "bisexuality" of the embryo had given way to the discovery that "all mammalian embryos, male and female, are anatomically female during the early stages of fetal life" (p. 122). Older Freudian postulates about the "vaginal orgasm" also had to be modified to reflect the fact that "the nature of [women's] orgasm is the same regardless of the erotogenic zone stimulated to produce it" (p. 123). She reported that women show considerable variation as to which zones require stimulation before orgasm is achieved and as to the length of time such stimulation must be maintained. Some cases of coital frigidity stem from anatomical variations in the genital region; others from insufficient stimulation by the partner—and neither reflects psychological inhibitions. Prior to Sherfey's work, the prevailing tendency

Mary Jane Sherfey

was to assume that frigidity was the end result of a sexual neurosis that could be resolved by psychoanalysis.

Turning her attention to ethology, Sherfey (1966) noted that, unlike men, women are capable of having multiple orgasms without definite limit as to number—meaning that *satisfaction* (feeling pleasure and relief) may occur without *satiation* (being physiologically incapable of having another orgasm). "It could well be," Sherfey stated, "that the 'oversexed' woman is actually exhibiting a normal sexuality—though because of it, her integration into her society may leave much to be desired" (p. 116). From the standpoint of human evolution, she concluded that "women's inordinate orgasmic capacity did not evolve for monogamous, sedentary cultures" (p. 118). Sherfey pointed out that what we think of as the human mating system, emphasizing monogamy, kinship ties, inheritance laws, etc., grew out of the survival needs of our species as we ceased to be nomadic hunter-gatherers and developed agriculture and geographically stable communities. The more men's work and steadfastness to family were necessary to the survival of children, the more it was necessary to suppress women's potential for multiple sexual partners: A woman's mate/husband would not remain with her unless he were certain that the children he was working to support were his own. This need resulted in long engagements (more than nine months to ensure that the first child his wife bore was indeed his own) and the demand for absolute marital fidelity on the wife's part.

Neither sex, as it turns out, is programmed biologically for monogamous marital life. Subsequent ethological studies in the 1980s suggest that humans occupy a position intermediate between prairie voles and geese (who are faithful for life) and chimpanzees (who are highly promiscuous). As Sherfey noted, with the development of agrarian societies (somewhere between 10,000–14,000 years ago), a compromise had to be struck between an earlier survival strategy, which had depended on females mating indiscriminately and often (in order to produce a quantity of offspring, at least some of whom would survive), and the "modern" custom, whereby offspring survival is optimized by monogamous mating. Sherfey speculated that ". . . the forceful suppression of women's inordinate sexual demands was a prerequisite to the dawn of every modern civilization and almost every living culture" (1966, p. 119). Her views have been supplemented in recent years by other ethologists (viz., Rushton et al., 1986), who have pointed out the greater need for monogamous family structure in cold-climate regions (where survival of children is optimized by small families with two parents) as compared with hot-climate regions (where larger numbers of children, requiring less parental involvement, is a more successful strategy).

Sherfey's work inspired a psychoanalytic reexamination of the psychology of women in regard to the themes of feminine submissiveness and masochism (as noted in the writings of Freud and Helene Deutsch). As a character trait, submissiveness may not have been typical of ancestral, pre-agricultural women; it may have emerged because it was more in harmony with the patriarchal family structure that is optimal for modern civilization. In both sexes, but particularly in women, society's survival is best served by people animated more by love (implying devotion to one mate and to one's children over the whole life span) than by lust (which, in the case of women, conduces to pregnancy but not to maternal devotion).

Because human *culture* changes demonstrably over the ages, while the human *brain* (and thus the human *nature* of which it is an expression) does not, in contemporary society a discrepancy has arisen between what our culture demands and what our genome inclines us to. Freud addressed this issue in *Civilization and Its Discontents* (1930). Sherfey, with insight derived from biological/ethological data not available in Freud's day, helped us view the particularities of the nature-culture conflicts with a sharper focus.

PART V

The 1970s

Chapter 16

THE FLOURISHING OF

OBJECTIFIABLE SCIENCE

Those branches of psychiatry that represented hard science (or at least objectifiable science)—biological psychiatry, biometrics, epidemiology, psychogenetics—continued to flourish in the 1970s. Psychoanalysis came under further fire because of its reliance on speculative assertions not substantiated by solid data, adequate control groups, and respectable sample sizes. Psychotherapy in general faced increasing challenges from the biological sector, which demanded that proof of efficacy replace faith in efficacy. Whereas the chairmen of psychiatry departments throughout the 1950s and 1960s had mostly come from psychoanalytic backgrounds, new chairmen began to be recruited from the ranks of the biological psychiatry. And the chairmen were no longer always chair*men*: Paula Clayton become the first woman department head (in Minnesota). The roster of the American Psychiatric Association grew to about 30,000 members, or about one psychiatrist per 8,000 U.S. citizens—the greatest concentration in any of the developed nations.

first woman department head

By this decade, however, almost every country had at least a small contingent of psychiatrists. In Thailand, for example, there were 150 psychiatrists among a population of 50 million: about one per 300,000 people. Psychiatric journals were published in almost ever country as well; it was far beyond the powers even of specialists to keep up with all the literature pertinent to their areas. The increasing popularity of psychiatry, the public's heightened awareness of emotional disorders both mild and severe, coupled with the high cost of the long-term intensive (several sessions per week) psychotherapies led to the fashioning of short-term solutions to treatment for both the milder neurotic conditions and schizophrenia.

popularity of psychiatry

Air travel facilitated the convening of *international* conferences, which in turn led to heightened respect within the Western nations for

international conferences

the healing arts in China, Japan, and India. Transcendental meditation, Zen meditation, acupuncture, Buddhist teachings, and other Oriental approaches to the understanding and treatment of mental conditions gained increasing popularity. Asia was no longer a *terra incognita* on the map of psychiatry. But because of the prominence of American psychiatry, English was emerging as the *lingua franca* of the psychiatric world: Increasingly, conferences around the world were held in English, and papers, if they were to have a wide readership, were written in English.

TAXONOMY, PSYCHOLOGY, AND BIOMETRICS

Objectifiable Criteria

There was feverish activity throughout the 1970s in the area of diagnosis. Especially throughout the United States attempts were made to create and field-test new sets of objectifiable criteria for diagnosing all the major psychiatric conditions. The first such set to win wide recognition was that of John Feighner and his colleagues in St. Louis (1972). The "Feighner criteria," as they soon became known, applied to some 14 conditions in which high levels of reliability among raters could be achieved. The criteria developed for schizophrenia, in contrast to those of Bleuler, emphasized chronicity and the primary signs of delusions and hallucinations; as such, the criteria were considered "neo-Kraepelinian." Inevitably, the new criteria affected future views about prognosis. For the most part, only the more severe forms of "Bleulerian" schizophrenia met the criteria of Feighner or of other biometricians in the 1970s who addressed this issue.

John Feighner
"Feighner criteria"

Considering the pace of change in post-World-War-II psychiatry, the concept of schizophrenia has remained remarkably stable: For the past quarter century the Feighner criteria have comprised our standard nomenclature, with only minor revisions. Table 5 compares Feighner's criteria for schizophrenia with those of the *DSM–IV.*

rival criteria

Shortly after the Feighner criteria appeared, rival criteria sets were published. Some focused on schizophrenia (the International Pilot Study of Schizophrenia by Carpenter, Strauss, and Bartko, 1973; the New Haven Schizophrenia Index of Astrachan et al., 1972; the Modified Research Criteria of Taylor and Abrams, 1975); others were part of a broader taxonomy embracing other diagnoses (such as the Research Diagnostic Criteria of Spitzer et al., 1975, 1978). Robert Spitzer and his colleagues at the New York Psychiatric Institute were soon to become the major players in the setting of new diagnostic standards: Spitzer became the director of the large team who created the next revision of the *Diagnostic and Statistical Manual: DSM–III,* published in 1980.

Robert Spitzer

TABLE 5   CRITERIA FOR THE DIAGNOSIS OF SCHIZOPHRENIA

Feighner (1972)	*DSM–IV (1994)*
• Chronicity of illness, with at least six months of illness or more. • Absence of sufficient depressive or manic symptoms to qualify for affective disorder. • Presence of delusions or hallucinations or verbal production that makes communication difficult. • Three of the following five: single status, poor premorbid adjustment, family history of schizophrenia, absence of drug abuse, onset before age 40.	*Two or more of the following:* • No schizoaffective or mood disorder. • Delusions, hallucinations, disorganized speech, disorganized/catatonic behavior, negative symptoms (flat affect, etc.). • Social/occupational dysfunction. • Duration of six months or more. • Not due to drug or alcohol abuse.

Not all these criteria sets were in competition, strictly speaking; some (such as the Feighner criteria) were designed for ordinary clinical use, while others were designed primarily for research purposes. The latter relied upon narrower criteria in the hopes of minimizing the number of "false positives" in any research sample. There was the further hope that such a purification process would facilitate the discovery of biological markers and even the essential "risk genes" (if any were to be found), whose presence could be ascertained in future patients by the specific tests. Such markers would validate the original diagnostic criteria and hopefully lead to even further refinements—whose use would then isolate an ever higher percentage of cases that bore the marker or genes in question.

This dynamic equilibrium between diagnosis and biological markers would exist, presumably, only in those patients for whom diagnosis answered to a particular biological predisposition and *only rarely* resulted from causative factors *other than* the biological factor. Schizophrenia and the bipolar form of manic-depression seemed excellent candidates for this research process. Estimates in the domain of schizophrenia suggested that only 10% of cases diagnosed by the new criteria arose from "extraneous" causes, such as frontal-lobe tumors, hormonal

diagnosis and biological markers

abnormalities, etc.; the bulk of cases were thus patients with "genuine" (i.e., genetically-based) schizophrenia, in whom relevant markers might be found most of the time.

questionnaires/more reliable diagnoses

Questionnaires of every description began appearing in the 1970s not only in the hopes of establishing stricter and more reliable diagnoses but also of determining general levels of social adaptation. Jean Endicott, Robert Spitzer, and their colleagues published the "Global Assessment Scale" (G.A.S.) in 1976, which used a rating scale from "0" (dead by suicide) to "100" (superior function in every area of life) to evaluate the general daily functioning. The G.A.S. was itself the outgrowth of Lester Luborsky's "MHSRS" (Mental Health/Sickness Rating Scale), which had appeared in 1962. The current *DSM–IV* employs a still further revised scale: the Global Assessment of Functioning Scale (G.A.F.). Because groups of clinicians simultaneously rating a given person rarely disagree by more than five scale-points, the instrument is highly reliable.

Schizophrenia and Manic-Depression

diagnostic distinctions

Making diagnostic distinctions between schizophrenia and manic-depressive illness (especially the bipolar form) was becoming increasingly important in the United States now that lithium was available as a remedy for bipolar conditions. Psychiatrists in Europe were part of a tradition where such diagnostic differences had mattered greatly, even before the advent of lithium, which was accessible to them a decade earlier. Kendell in Scotland wrote extensively on the different diagnostic customs in Great Britain and the United States. He was also keenly aware that some patients showed intermediate forms of illness (Kendell & Gourlay, 1970), which suggested a *continuum* of disorders, with schizophrenia at one extreme and manic-depression at the other. The so-called schizoaffective disorders might represent "heterogeneous inheritance" (i.e., having risk genes for both conditions) rather than inheritance from one common source, or they might be peculiar outward manifestation (phenotype) of genes for *either* of the two psychoses.

This issue would be debated throughout the 1970s, and beyond. In any event, as a result of the cooperation between such groups as Spitzer's in the United States and Kendell's in Great Britain, diagnostic criteria in the two countries were more closely standardized, leading to improvements in cross-cultural research.

Eating Disorders

changes in the distribution

Meanwhile epidemiologists were paying attention to changes in the distribution of the various psychiatric disorders over time. During the

1970s there was an absolute increase in the incidence of anorexia nervosa in Switzerland (Willi & Grossman, 1983), which confirmed what clinicians thought was occurring in America and Western Europe since the 1960s: Eating disorders (bulimia as well as anorexia) were becoming more widespread—and the increase was real, not simply a function of heightened awareness on the part of diagnosticians. The reasons for this increase were not immediately clear: A cultural equation of thinness with beauty might be part of the answer, it was thought; later, some clinicians suggested that there was a correlation between having a history of sexual abuse and experiencing anorexia in adolescence or young adulthood. (The incidences of sexual abuse and anorexia are more common in females.)[1] Epidemiologists took up the latter issue more extensively in the 1980s; as we shall see, there remains much controversy over the etiology of eating disorders and "the jury is still out."

Suicide

The findings of epidemiologists in the 1970s concerning suicide were of particular importance. In the United States and Canada an increasing rise in suicide rates in young people was becoming apparent. Since the pioneering work of Emil Durkheim, first published in 1897, the suicide risk for persons in Western Europe had increased with each succeeding decade of life, until reaching a peak in the sixth decade. After World War II, in the United States the suicide rate for white males (the most suicide prone group) in the third decade of life increased dramatically from about 10 per 100,000 per year in the 1950s to almost 30 per 100,000 per year in the late 1970s (Solomon & Murphy, 1984). The rate in white females also increased, though somewhat less dramatically, doubling from 3.5 to about 7 per 100,000 per year.

rise in suicide rates

Other epidemiologists reported similar noteworthy increases in deaths via automobile accidents and homicides in adolescents and young adults during the generation ending in 1976 (Holinger & Offer, 1981). Causative factors cited for this increase in violent deaths among the young (noted also in Western Europe during this period) included decreased opportunity for employment, weakening religious influence, and widespread family breakdown (Diekstra, 1987)—all of which combined to enfeeble the emotional-support system upon which adolescents rely as they make the transition to independent life.

accidental and violent deaths

Other epidemiological studies investigated such issues as the relationship between sociopathy and hysteria (Cloninger, Reich, & Guze,

---

[1] Many contend the correlation between *bulimia* and sexual abuse is stronger than for anorexia without bulimic episodes (see chapter 23).

1970), the likelihood of affective disorders in adoptees whose birth parents were manic-depressive (Cadoret, 1978a), the risk of sociopathy in adoptees whose birth parents were antisocial (Cadoret, 1978b), and the risk of fetal alcohol syndrome in babies born to alcoholic mothers (Clarren & Smith, 1978).

Overview of the Field

importance of epidemiology

The importance of epidemiology was well expressed by Morris (1975), who identified such uses as establishing historical trends in mental illness, assessing the degree of individual risk, providing a more complete picture of the extent and nature of any given condition, and pointing to probable causative factors. In the realm of personality disorders, for example, many persons with borderline or antisocial disorders never present themselves to clinics or hospitals. Reliance on data from treatment centers would give too low an estimate of the true incidence of both conditions. The difficulties that beset epidemiological research are numerous. Random samples of a population are not easily acquired, especially in a country like the United States where the society is heterogeneous as to country of origin and as to social class (compared with Japan, where there is greater homogeneity on both counts).

difficulties that beset epidemiological research

In evaluating subtle conditions such as personality disorders, the sample size must be very large—and is therefore costly to study. And even if the money and manpower were available to interview *every* inhabitant in, say, a New Hampshire town of 25,000 (a daunting task!), what would that tell us about Los Angeles, with its strikingly different demography, or about America as a whole? This caveat aside, epidemiology has enormously broadened our knowledge about the major psychoses as well as etiological factors that reflect the darker side of our society: the frequency of incest and the rates of violence, including parental violence toward children.

Statistics

Reliance on statistical methods had been the norm in psychology for a number of years, partly necessitated by the large population samples that research psychologists routinely dealt with (for example, in assessing personality variants in a normal population). Psychoanalysts and clinical psychiatrists usually had only dozens of persons to diagnose and treat, whereas research psychologists worked with samples in the hundreds and even thousands. Controlled studies of treatment efficacy were still rarities in clinical psychiatry and all but unknown in psychoanalysis, so it is no surprise that practitioners in these latter groups did not feel the need to enlist the aid of statisticians. Psychopharmacologists, however, were able to carry out controlled studies more easily (they had fewer variables to contend with than would be the case with verbal therapies) and they relied heavily on statistical methods.

By the 1970s the sheer amount of information that was accruing in all branches of medicine was voluminous and overwhelming. The question arose of how to sift and sort through it all, so that reliable data and "real facts" could be separated out from unprovable assertions, mistaken assumptions, and plain nonsense. Once psychiatrists began to pay statistical analysis its proper due, the inferential assumptions of psychoanalysis could even be put to the test. Is it really the case that fantasies of a "corrosive mother" play a causative role in the development of ulcers? An outside observer could now test 25 ulcer patients, 25 asthma patients, and 25 normal control subjects and compare their reported fantasies. Does having an "aloof father" and "overinvolved" mother really "cause" homosexuality in men? Or was that parental pattern so widespread in our culture that it would be noted with equal frequency in a heterosexual comparison group?

inferential assumptions of psychoanalysis put to the test

There were many mathematicians and mental health professionals who contributed to the explosion of statistical applications in psychiatry and whose aim was to "contain" the even greater explosion of information. Among them: Guilford and Fruchter (1973), Colton (1974), Daniel (1974), and Cohen (1977), all of whom wrote textbooks on statistics in the health sciences. Spitzer and Fleiss (1974), who also worked with Cohen, described methods for statistically assessing the reliability of psychiatric diagnoses. Clinical researchers were much more prone in this era to include a statistician as an integral part of the research team. Examples were Lolafaye Coyne, who collaborated with Otto Kernberg and others on the Menninger Project, and J. Bartko, who worked with William Carpenter and John Strauss on the International Pilot Study of Schizophrenia.

statistical applications in psychiatry

The statistical approach was not embraced by everyone: Some psychoanalysts and other psychiatrists of a more humanistic stance worried that people were being "reduced to numbers." Another criticism was that, while statistical analysis was well suited for controlled drug studies or, for example, studies of how many juvenile delinquents had a history of head injury, it had little relevance to the day-to-day workings of dynamic psychotherapy. Actually, certain cherished assumptions in psychoanalytic theory (about family patterns, human sexual response, and the like) were severely challenged by careful statistical analyses, and the overturning of those assumptions most assuredly *did* influence the diversified field of psychotherapy. Clinicians no longer tried to "convert" homosexual men to heterosexuality, as though to rescue them from a supposed pathological "fixation point"; dynamic therapy was no longer pursued as the treatment of choice for schizophrenic patients.

certain cherished assumptions in psychoanalytic theory were severely challenged

statistics and the
individual

"Monte Carlo
Paradox"

forensic issues in
psychiatry

Statistical methods do indeed have their shortcomings—though not the ones the humanists were most concerned about. Statistics has considerably less reliability in relation to the *individual* and his long-term fate than it does when predicting the percentages of certain outcomes within a large collection of people. I call this the "Monte Carlo Paradox." The roulette croupier knows, for example, that if the house pays 36:1 for a correct number, the house retains about a 5.4% advantage, because the roulette wheel also has a "0" and a "00." Given hundreds of players over hundreds of evenings, the house will profit to that extent. But this fact does not make the croupier any smarter at guessing *which* player on *which* evening will lose his entire stake or else make a killing. There are simply too many variables and idiosyncrasies in the individual to permit accurate prediction of behavior.

In psychiatry, statistics can validly demonstrate that the lifetime risk of death by suicide in a large group of patients who have recurrent depressive illness is greater than that in the general population by a factor of 20 or more, perhaps even a factor of 50. This information about a large group can be further distilled, again with the help of statistical analysis, so that a smaller group is identified: Depressives with certain high-risk factors (Caucasian, single, unemployed, alcohol-abusing, with a history of previous serious attempts) are the most likely persons within the larger group to commit suicide, compared with other depressives who do not exhibit those qualities. Even so, faced with the *individual* depressive patient, we do poorly at prediction, whether in the short- or long-term.

The impossibility of translating even the most compelling statistical data from large-group studies into information that is predictive of the individual is highlighted by certain forensic issues in psychiatry, where the knowable, the scarcely knowable, and the unknowable become difficult to distinguish. Here is an example, if we may skip ahead a decade. By the late 1980s fluoxetine/Prozac, having already been widely and successfully used as an antidepressant in Europe, became popular in the United States. (It is also useful in the treatment of obsessive-compulsive disorder.) Several patients committed suicide while on this medication and some families have sued the pharmaceutical company arguing that their relative was driven to suicide by a rare side effect of the drug in which irritability, impulsivity, and suicidality are experienced in a few patients, even though its effects are the opposite in most patients.

Armed with a knowledge of statistics, how could this problem be evaluated? Obtaining baseline data on a number of variables would be the first requirement: What is the yearly risk for suicide in a population of unipolar depressives? What percentage of these patients have been taking Prozac exclusively in the recent past? What percentage is on other medications? What is the suicide rate in these two groups?

The problem is one ordinarily approached by Bayesian algebra, provided the necessary baseline figures are available.

As it turns out, we know something about the suicide rate in unipolar depression: about 200–500/100,000 annually in the United States, as against 11/100,000 in the general population. But there are no such comparable data on suicide in untreated depressives (because most seek help and, nowadays, medication), let alone inpatients treated with just Prozac or just with tricyclics or MAOIs. If Prozac were associated with a substantial increase in the suicide rate (greater than in patients treated with other classes of medication), taking it off the market would be legitimate possibility. We would not, however, be able to tell *which* suicides were attributable to Prozac, unless the patients treated with other drugs *never* committed suicide. Not only is that *not* the case, but there is also no evidence that Prozac is associated with a heightened suicide rate.

Consider the position of the plaintiffs in the suit against the U.S. government relating to excess cancer deaths downwind from the Almogordo atom-bomb experiments in the 1940s. Here there *was* an excess of cancer-related deaths, but the excess did not manifest in the form of rare tumors never before seen in that population—such tumors would have indicated which persons were killed by the bomb experiment. Instead, there were simply *more* of the customary tumors. The radiation released in the atmosphere probably was responsible— the statistics suggest this—but as to *which individuals* would otherwise have remained cancer-free?. . . To this there is no answer.

Since Prozac is not even associated with high suicide rates, there is still less reason to inculpate the drug. One would have to argue that a small percentage of patients *do* have paradoxical reactions and that, although they already belonged to a very high-risk group (for which reason they were taking the drug in the first place), they would not have committed suicide if they were not taking the drug. To assert this, however, is to abandon the realm of science and statistics for the realm of faith.

The example does serve to illustrate a limitation of statistics that continues to bedevil the mental health field. Many questions pertaining to the individual patients and their long-term fate cannot be answered with certainty, no matter how much information is provided at the outset. This aside, there has been tremendous progress since the 1970s in our understanding of many issues relating to *classes* of patients. But when it comes to the fate of one patient—for example, to thorny issues about the potential for violence, suicide, recovery from schizophrenia—we often find ourselves in situations of the scarcely knowable (the cost of the study that could yield the answer would be too great and the time to harvest the results too long) or the unknowable.

NORMALIZING HOMOSEXUALITY

human sexuality

Beginning in the 1960s and extending into the 1970s, enormous attention was devoted to the topic of human sexuality: The characteristics and variations of normal sexuality were redefined and greater clarity about issues regarding sexual pathology and sexual-disorder therapy was achieved. At the vanguard of these efforts were William Masters and Virginia Johnson, whose *magnum opus* on normal sexuality, *Human Sexual Response*, appeared in 1966. This was later followed by their *Textbook of Sexual Medicine* (of which Robert Kolodny was first author) in 1979, which addresses the whole panoply of normal and abnormal conditions: geriatric sex, sex in patients with heart disease or cancer, rape, transsexualism, homosexuality, the paraphilias (exhibitionism, voyeurism, sexual sadomasochism, etc.), and sexual dysfunction in men and women.

focus of research

Homosexuality was perhaps the most important sexual issue of the day: More people, lay and professional alike, were beginning to question the age-old view (in the Western world, particularly) that homosexuality, even between consenting adults, was immoral and abnormal. In small numbers at first, homosexual men and women were openly declaring their sexual orientation. The focus of research on the etiology of homosexuality was on the biological basis of sexual object-choice, since the more scientific the evidence, the more understandable and acceptable homosexuality would seem to those in the heterosexual majority, who had hitherto condemned it, primarily on religious grounds. The data in the 1970s about genetic factors, possible hormonal differences, and family backgrounds yielded mostly conflicting results.

genetic basis

As Kolodny, Masters, and Johnson (1979) noted, in the 1950s Kallmann had argued for a genetic basis, because of the high concordance rate for homosexuality in monozygotic twins. But isolated instances of discordance in monozygotic twins were also reported, which called into question the genetic theory. Articles on both sides of the issue were likewise reported concerning male and female hormonal levels in homosexual men and women. Most of the newer studies refuted the notion that homosexual men are more attached to their mothers than are heterosexual men. There seemed to be no real evidence that disturbed parental relations are either a necessary or sufficient causative factor (Hooker, 1969). All these conflicting data led many of the leading investigators (viz. Masters and Johnson, 1966; Marmor, 1965), to conclude that homosexuality was "multifactorial" in origin.

psychiatric profession acknowledges homosexuality as a normal variant

The new findings, however confusing, were enough to incline the psychiatric profession to acknowledge homosexuality as a normal variant, reserving the notion of abnormality for the "true" perversions, such as pedophilia, zoophilia, and sexual sadism. Behavior modification therapies were developing for the perversions, with the goal of lessening the desire to engage in the undesirable behaviors through use of aversive conditioning (Bancroft, 1974) or positive conditioning (Stoudemire, 1973).

The psychoanalytic community, by virtue of its "normative" psychology (according to which homosexuality was merely a way station on the road to heterosexuality), was slow to embrace the new attitudes. Many strenuous debates—or pitched battles, as they often became—erupted on this issue. The younger generation of analytically trained psychiatrists (such as Spitzer) took the position that homosexuality was a normal variant; the older generation (represented by Irving Bieber) maintained the traditional view of homosexuality as pathological. Spitzer did succeed in having homosexuality removed from the official nomenclature as a pathological mental condition. This significant change mirrored the spirit of the times and helped diminish the burden of unnecessary shame that many homosexual people endured as a result of parental and societal contempt.

PSYCHOANALYSIS

Heinz Kohut

The work of Heinz Kohut (1913–1981), an Austrian emigré who settled in Chicago, became widely known and appreciated during the 1970s following the publication of *The Analysis of the Self* (1971) and *The Restoration of the Self* (1977). The only child of an upper middle-class Jewish family, Kohut was born in Vienna in 1913—in the same month that Hitler left Vienna as a vagabond, only to return 25 years later as a dictator, causing the expulsion first of Freud (June 4, 1938), then of Kohut and his family (Cocks, 1994). Kohut actually witnessed the departure of Freud, having been informed about the situation by August Aichhorn, with whom Kohut had earlier been in analysis. Barely able to complete his medical-school final exams in October of 1938, Kohut and his parents went into hiding until they were able to obtain visas for England, where they arrived in March of 1939. A year later, Kohut was able to enter the United States, settling in Chicago, where he remained the rest of his life.

In his brief biographical introduction to Kohut's collected correspondence, Cocks has suggested that Kohut's interest in narcissistic disorders and his belief that lack of parental warmth underlay them may have stemmed from his early experiences with his own distant and unempathic parents.

Heinz Kohut, 1913–1981. Bachrach photo courtesy Institute for Psychoanalysis

*spotlight on parent-
child interactions*

However this may be, Kohut eventually created a psychological system related to, but in a way separate from, mainstream psychoanalysis—a system that put the spotlight on parent-child interactions in the first few years of life.

Kohut created a psychological system related to, but in a way separate from, mainstream psychoanalysis. According to Kohut's system, the organizing principle in psychic development is the self, as it evolves throughout the successive life stages.

self psychology

As Cooper et al. (1990) notes, the focus of Kohut's self psychology is on the "maturation of the sense of self from its infantile state of fragility . . . into the cohesive and stable structure of adulthood" (p. 11). Young children gradually achieve this state, in Kohut's view, via a combined process of "exhibitionism" (wishing to be admired by the parents) and "idealization" of the parents. In infancy there is an overpowering need for the significant other person (the mother, especially), who is perceived as part of oneself, and without whom the young child feels incomplete. Kohut called this significant person the "selfobject" (i.e., the object through whom one begins to acquire a sense of self).

"selfobject"

*importance of the
therapist's empathy*

From the standpoint of treatment, Kohut (1959) emphasized the importance of the therapist's *empathy* for the patient, which is similar to the empathic understanding ideally shown by Winnicott's "good-enough mother." Many patients, having lacked such mothering, develop neurotic illnesses—which Kohutian therapy hoped to cure by supplying this empathic understanding and becoming, in effect, a latter-day "selfobject" for the patient. In this regard, Kohut's position was in accord with Sullivanian interpersonal analysis and placed less emphasis on interpretation or analysis of negative transference (such as Kernberg emphasized in the initial phases of work with borderline patients).

*Kohutian view of
diagnosis*

Though his influence has been far-reaching, especially on the topic of narcissism (Kohut, 1966), his writing style is opaque and difficult—in contrast to the charm and lucidity of his letters, the bulk of which have only recently been published (Cocks, 1994). The clearest expositor of his message is Ernest Wolf (1980). Kohut's use of the term *borderline* referred to psychoanalytic failure in one's work with a narcissistic patient and thus bears no relation to proper diagnostic definitions (made at the time of initial consultation), such as those of Kernberg, Gunderson, or the *DSM*. In a 1981 letter he wrote to the prominent Los Angeles psychologist Marion Solomon, Kohut went so far as to contend that diagnosis does not entirely inhere in the patient, but hovers unstably in the air, as it were, between patient and therapist, depending on the skill and empathy of the latter.

The therapist with special responsiveness to a particular analysand will be able to . . . tolerate the [often enormous] demands [the transference] makes on him—the patient is then a "serious narcissistic personality disorder"—while another therapist who does not possess the same empathic capacity will not. . . be able to tolerate the archaic selfobject transference. . . . With the latter analyst, the patient is now "borderline" or "psychotic." (Cocks, 1994, p. 432)

Kohut is making an interesting point here insofar as diagnosis does depend, to a certain extent, on the personalities of the *observers* and their impact upon patients. Certainly a rude or hostile diagnostician may anger a patient into appearing "sicker" than would a calm and sympathetic diagnostician. Even a group of sympathetic interviewers will not always agree because of differences in their orientation and experience. The logic of diagnosticians is not one of mathematical precision but of "fuzzy-set" approximations, as outlined by Lofti Zadeh (1965) and explicated in relation to medical diagnosis by Rocha et al. (1992). Even so, by placing diagnostic decisions so far *after* initial contact with a patient, and by ignoring the importance of diagnostic instruments for enhancing objectifiability and reliability, Kohut placed himself outside the domain of scientific approaches to diagnosis.

outside the domain of science

Throughout the 1970s and beyond the time of his death in 1981, Kohut sparked debate concerning the ideal therapeutic approach to take with narcissistic and borderline patients: Kohut emphasized sympathetic understanding whereas Kernberg dealt with the patient's hostility and negative transference at the outset via candid confrontation and discussion. Furthermore, Kernberg disputes Kohut's contention that narcissistic personality represents fixation at an early stage of development. Kernberg views this abnormal personality development to be the outgrowth of pathological ego/superego structures in response to faulty pathological object-relations (Kernberg, 1975). Given the magnitude of the difficulties that beset any attempt at a controlled study of the two techniques, there is no clear answer to this controversy. Probably much of the answer depends on differences in symptom picture (Kohut treated ambulatory patients; Kernberg works with both ambulatory and hospitalized borderline patients) and on differences in personal styles among therapists.

Kohut versus Kernberg

Shifting Parameters

Controversy among psychoanalysts regarding Kohutian theory and practice also reflected more general changes in psychoanalysis during the 1970s. Ralph Greenson, whose book, *The Technique and Practice of Psychoanalysis* (1967), embodied all that was best in conventional analytic work and became a *vade mecum* for trainees, recognized that the orthodox, oedipal, conflict-based theory and treatment did not reach out to many of persons who were entering analytic therapy in the 1960s and 1970s. Greenson continued to emphasize the importance of dream analysis (1970) but recognized that more and more patients were exhibiting serious psychopathology. There were more patients with borderline and narcissistic disorders, more with "preoedipal" problems similar to those the British Independent School had been writing about under the heading of the "basic fault" (Balint, 1968).

serious psychopathology

The patients needed something beyond standard interpretive work; they required "parameters" (deviations from orthodox technique): reassurance, sympathy, guidance, exhortation, containment of stormy affect—in essence, more of the kinds of interventions Kohut had been recommending. Certainly the days when analysts (at least in the United States) could fill their practice with "high-level neurotic" patients were over (Dewald, 1992). These were the patients for whom the resolution of oedipal conflicts (and the often inappropriate choices of intimate partners such conflicts engendered) was all that was necessary for a successful outcome.

"parameters" (deviations from orthodox technique)

Several factors underlay these changes occurring in the clientele of psychoanalysts. The popularity of psychoanalysis after World War II had led to the training of large numbers of non-medically trained "lay" analysts and psychotherapists who by their very numbers, and often lower fees, made inroads into the practices of the medically trained analysts. Discrete phobias and sexual difficulties, for example, could usually be treated less expensively and more quickly by behavioral (or other) methods, with which the non-medical therapists (including the lay analysts) were often more familiar.

"lay" analysts

Cost factors became crucial: Classical analysis, with four or five sessions per week, usually worked better with young persons—students in their twenties, professional people in their thirties—for whom $60-visits (a typical fee in the late 1970s) and a bill of $1,000–1,200 per month were beyond their budgets. Analysts began seeing many of their patients three, or two, or even one time a week, which necessarily altered the atmosphere by interfering with the development of a "transference neurosis" and redirecting the focus onto the "here and now" rather than on early childhood memories.

cost factors

"here and now"

Furthermore, psychoanalytic vocabulary came under criticism in the 1970s from a number of quarters. Roy Schafer (1976) voiced his objections to the tendency—present, to an extent, in Freud's writing and much magnified in the works of his followers—to confuse (as Wittgenstein had put it) *substantive* with *substance;* metaphors, that is, hardened into "things" (a process psychiatry calls "reification"). The term *libido,* for example, originally used as an abstract concept for the *energy* (another abstraction referring to the intensity and direction of drives and wishes), became a kind of nebulous "something"

psychoanalytic vocabulary

"reification"

that was located in the brain—somewhere! Wilhelm Reich certainly used *libido* in this non-metaphorical way, even at a time when Freud had said of it, " *es ist nur ein Spiel mit Worter* [it is only a playing with words]"(Eissler, 1967).

Schafer also took exception to the freewheeling use of *ego* as a tangible force in the brain that motivates or compels behavior (i.e., "His Ego compelled him to choose a career in . . . , though his id would have preferred . . ."). The misuse of the entire psychoanalytic vocabulary of words (self, superego, internalization, incorporation) came under fire in Schafer's book. In its place Schafer recommended an "action language" wherein emotional states are expressed in simple, declarative sentences ("I wanted to call Mary, but I feared she would not accept a date") that employ the active voice. Inveighing against the notions of *the* unconscious and *the* conscious, Schafer stated that to think consciously is not the only mode of thought: "a person may also think *unconsciously* or *preconsciously*" (p. 365) [italics added]. Where psychoanalysis had used nouns (the unconscious), Schafer called for adverbs (think unconsciously).

"action language"

Schafer also took issue with the convention among analysts to talk about various abstract concepts as if they were located *inside* the brain. The brain, Schafer explained, is the organ that mediates mental activity, sure enough, but to state that desire, hatred, love, etc., are "in" the brain is to confuse different levels of discourse (two different *systems,* as Bertalanffy would say): that of neurophysiology with that of *mind.* As an abstraction, *mind* includes the physiological activity of the brain—and all that is *subjective* as well. Because of this personal or subjective aspect of mind, Schafer contended that *actions* do not have *causes* in any neat and simple fashion: There is always the added element of a person's understanding and interpretation that preceded and shaped the action—and so on back, in an infinite regress through one's personal history. Earlier psychoanalytic thinking on the subject of causality tended to be reductionistic and deterministic; sweeping causal statements were often founded on meager or questionable evidence ("because his mother thwarted his drive toward individuation he became overly dependent"). In this context, Schafer's work may be seen as heralding the intense interest in the phenomenon of subjectivity and mind/brain issues to which philosophers and neurophysiologists were to devote their attention in the 1980s and 1990s (Penrose, 1994; Searle, 1992).[2]

confusing neurophysiology with the mind

[2] Schafer's admonitions may be having a salutary effect on the writing style of analysts, who seem less uncomfortable replacing passive constructions ("The patient was then offered the interpretation by the analyst that . . .") with active phrases ("I then told the patient . . .").

Object-Relations in Theory and Practice

Object-relations theory and its applications to the understanding and treatment of severe personality disorders gained greater influence in both the psychoanalytic and general psychiatric communities following the publication of key works by Otto Kernberg in the United States and Jean Bergeret in France. Kernberg's first book, *Borderline Conditions and Pathological Narcissism,* was published the same year as Bergeret's *La Depression et les États-Limites* [Depression and Borderline States]—1975. The latter was an expansion of *Abrégé de Psychologie Pathologique* [Synopsis of Pathological Psychology], edited by Bergeret in 1974.

structuralist concepts of Claude Levi-Strauss

These works reflected the structuralist concepts found in the anthropological treatises of Claude Levi-Strauss (1974) from the 1940s and 1950s. In object-relations theory, *structure* refers primarily to the inner mental representations of important other persons (of one's parents, to begin with) and of oneself, as these take shape in earliest childhood and evolve over the life-course. As Levi-Strauss noted, there are always positive and negative aspects to these structures.

Otto Kernberg

normal progression of these representations

Kernberg drew attention to the normal progression of these representations from a state of *fusion* (in which both good and bad images of self and other are jumbled together) in early infancy, to a state in which *good* images of self and object (other) are held, as it were, in a compartment separate from the *bad* images. From one-and-a-half to about two years of age, self and object are normally distinguished, but the good and bad images of each are not yet integrated. In about the third year, this integration begins to take place.

"splitting"

What one sees in borderline patients, as both Kernberg and Bergeret noted, is a persistence of the "splitting mechanism," wherein self ("I") and object ("other people") are recognized as distinct but where the good and bad aspects of each are still not integrated. In object-relations language, the term *borderline* was used to designate an intermediate level of mental organization, between the *neurotic* level (where integrated self- and object-representations are present) and the *psychotic* (where distinctions between self and object are confused). The persistence of splitting is a core problem in borderline patients; therefore, therapeutic interventions are designed to lead the patient toward more unified pictures of self and other (e.g., mother was not, alternatingly, a saint or a witch, but a troubled woman with a mixture of good and bad qualities).

By the end of the 1970s Kernberg's formulations had gained ascendancy within the psychoanalytic community and, thanks in part to the Menninger Foundation Psychotherapy Research Project (Kernberg et al., 1972), also influenced clinicians in traditional hospital psychiatry. Some aspects of Kernberg's diagnostic schema (those that were less inferential and thus easier to measure) were later incorporated into the criteria set in *DSM-III* for borderline personality disorder.

In Kernberg's view (1975) the narcissistic personality differs from the borderline in structural terms, insofar as those with a narcissistic personality have an "integrated though highly pathological grandiose self" (p. 265). His etiological perspective differed from Kohut's: for Kohut, narcissistic personality is a fixation (lasting into adult life) of an archaic "normal" primitive self; for Kernberg, it is a pathological structure that is phenomenologically distinct from normal infantile narcissism.

narcissistic personality differs from the borderline

Chapter 17

GENERAL AND HOSPITAL PSYCHIATRY

The same cost factors that impinged upon psychoanalysis in the 1970s also affected many people seeking other forms of treatment. At least this was so in the United States. Many patients of all diagnostic types clamored for help: some who could not afford a lengthy psychotherapy, others who had the money but not the time. This need spurred the development of briefer modes of therapy, some of which were based on psychoanalytic principles, others on cognitive/behavioral models, still others on the traditional supportive techniques upon which all treatment relies. Since it is not possible to revamp the human personality in a matter of weeks, short-term therapy of whatever kind cannot hope to "change" a person, only to alleviate some symptom or resolve a relational crisis.

SHORT-TERM APPROACHES

Habib Davanloo

blunt confrontation

In Montreal Habib Davanloo (1980) wrote extensively on the use of short-term "dynamic" (i.e., analytically-oriented) psychotherapy when treating ambulatory patients suffering from psychoneuroses of various types.[1] Davanloo's method of breaking down resistances in difficult patients (as he described in a 1986 paper) was to utilize blunt confrontation that sometimes sacrificed tact and caution. To compel patients to admit embarrassing feelings before they are ready can rarely be accomplished without becoming intrusive or even intimidating. Ideal short-term treatment does not dispense with tact. In the 1970s a profusion of short-term solutions appeared—some highly respectful of the

[1] The term *neurosis* had fallen out of use by the late 1980s, but it is still used by many practitioners to refer to the milder personality and anxiety disorders.

patient's comfort; others (like Davanloo's) well-intended but often uncomfortable; and still others that veered toward verbal abuse.

The gentler short-term approaches may have derived their inspiration from the analytically-oriented interview techniques developed earlier by Felix Deutsch and William Murphy (1955) in dealing with psychosomatic conditions. These authors showed how clinicians could quickly ascertain a patient's core problems by listening carefully to "key" words which, like dream images, slipped out unnoticed by the patient, only thinly disguising the patient's deepest fears.

Felix Deutsch and
William Murphy

An example from an interview with a veteran who was suffering a "hysteric" arm weakness following a minor wound to the thigh (near the penis) illustrates their techniques. Asked to describe his condition, the man began: "Well, it started right here, in the muscle of the forearm . . . I do a lot of shooting, you know, and I could hold the gun up . . . but I couldn't pull the trigger . . . and I used to have to yank it, you know, to get it off . . . " (p. 90). The many veiled allusions to male sexual function (*hold it up, yank it, get it off*) were the key words that alerted the interviewer to what was troubling this man "underneath" the surface: his worries about his masculinity and his relationship with his wife. These worries were elicited later in the interview by gentle questioning that utilized these emotionally-loaded words.

Deutsch and Murphy called their approach "sector analysis," since it zeroes in on only the most troublesome area of the patient's overall problems. This specialized focus allows a therapist to bring help where it is most needed (perhaps in 10 or 20 sessions), meantime purposely ignoring remarks that point to less pressing problems. This approach has been carried forward more recently by Arnold Winston (1994). Other forms of short-term crisis-intervention therapies were described by Mann (1973) and Sifneos (1981).

"sector analysis"

Quick Fixes and Cults

All manner of superficial "quick fixes" were touted in this era: Arthur Janov's "Primal Scream Therapy," Werner Erhard's "EST," "Rolfing," to mention but a few. As in every generation (one thinks of Emil Coué's *My Method* in 1923), a few charlatans flourished briefly, outshining momentarily their more responsible counterparts in conventional psychiatry.

Charlatanry is at times transformed into dangerous cults, as in the case of Scientology, which achieved a certain popularity in the 1970s. Though discredited, Scientology still attracts adherents. One among a number of competing cults, partly religious, partly pseudo-psychological in nature, Scientology utilizes brainwashing methods developed by the charismatic leader, L. Ron Hubbard. Because cults often succeed in achieving total control over their initiates through isola-

cults

tion and alienation from their families, a whole branch of psychiatry developed in response to the need to deprogram those who had been ensnared. Two psychiatrists who have won prominence in this field, and who have aided families in rescuing young persons from coercive cults, are David Halperin (1978, 1983) and Marc Galanter (1982, 1989).

Because there was such a rapid growth of alternative therapies in the 1970s, and because their claims of efficacy rested more on faith than on scientific proof (there are so many variables in the study of psychotherapy, proof is elusive), some clinicians claimed there were cult-like elements even in the highly respectable therapies. Zvi Lothane (1983), for example, contended that there was such a quality to Kohut's self psychology, whose followers, like its charismatic promulgator, emphasized the attribute of empathy—which everyone agrees is a key ingredient of all good therapies—but used the term so often, that it struck Lothane as a mantra.

MENTOR AFFILIATION

signature concepts

All psychotherapeutic movements, however, contain the elements of *leader*, *followers*, and *signature concepts* (such as Adler's "quest for power" and Rado's "adaptation," to mention only two). There was nothing new about this phenomenon in the 1970s. Rather, psychiatrists were becoming more self-conscious about the much heavier reliance on faith—theirs, in a revered teacher; their patients, in the psychiatrists themselves—than characterized the "hard sciences." Facts, once established, "forget" their authors; belief never forgets its prophet. Thus a modern-day physicist who grasps quantum mechanics does not call himself a Heisenbergian. But in the mental sciences, where proofs comparable to physical proofs are not obtainable, expert opinion takes the place of mathematical demonstration.

Perhaps the closest we come to the ideal of physical proof is in the field of psychopharmacology, where controlled studies sometimes show correlations as convincing as in the physical sciences. In the vastly more complex area of psychotherapy we rarely have *facts*; we have *impressions*. And, ever since psychotherapy became respectable, professionals have acknowledged their allegiance to a mentor by appending "-ian" to the mentor's name: Thus one is a Freudian, Adlerian, Kleinian, Reichian, Sullivanian, Rogerian, Lacanian, Kohutian, *ad infinitum*. Psychotherapists are often twitted about this tendency by their colleagues in the (only somewhat "harder") neurosciences. But because any effective therapy depends upon a foundation of expert opinion and coherent (if unprovable) theory, in recent years it has become more widely accepted for novices in the art of therapy to begin their careers by identifying themselves as "____-ian," even if they become more eclectic as they gain experience.

Much of the stiltedness of psychoanalytic writing, especially during the early years, was a reflection of the efforts to give analysis a higher scientific "mortgage." This was achieved by spicing the writing with physicochemical analogies and (as Schafer rightly criticized) by replacing the personal pronoun "I" (which announces our inescapable *subjectivity*) with passive constructions carrying the aroma of *objectivity*. In recent years psychiatry has grown less ill-at-ease over not being physics; psychotherapists have grown more accepting about the necessity of belief, faith, and hope as essential elements in the human equation—and in their work with patients. Therapists, if they are to do good work, must believe in a coherent theoretical system, must have faith in their own abilities and in the worthwhileness of what they offer, and must be able to instill hope in their patients. As research on the "basics" of psychotherapy was soon to suggest (Smith, Glass, & Miller, 1980), these elements, along with empathy and emotional warmth, are the fundamental building blocks of *all* effective therapies, irrespective of their conceptual and methodological differences. Follow-up studies of the 1980s, as we shall see, tended to confirm that academic orientation is less important as a curative factor than are these "human" qualities (coupled with life experience!).

stilted psychoanalytic writing

"basics" of psychotherapy

GENERAL TRENDS

Belief in the efficacy of psychotherapy received support in the 1970s from the work of Myrna Weissman and her colleagues. As an epidemiologist, she had already shown that affective disorders are the most prevalent mental disorders in the United States (Weissman et al., 1978). In a comparison study shortly thereafter, she demonstrated that *psychotherapy* by itself could be as efficacious in the treatment of depression as *pharmacotherapy* (whether alone or in combination with psychotherapy) (Weissman, 1979).

efficacy of psychotherapy

Twelve-Step Programs

The societal tendency toward *impulsive* as opposed to *inhibited* forms of psychopathology continued during the 1970s in both the United States and Western Europe. To cope with the many disorders of *craving* (for drugs, alcohol, sex, gambling, bingeing), twelve-step programs modeled after Alcoholics Anonymous sprung up, each oriented toward the curbing of a specific craving. These groups included Narcotics Anonymous, Overeaters Anonymous, Gamblers Anonymous, even Sexaholics Anonymous.

impulsive forms of psychopathology

Borderline Personality Disorder; Incest

In the domain of borderline personality disorder, articles during this decade ascribed causative significance to risk genes for manic-depressive illness (Akiskal, 1981; Andrulonis et al., 1981; Stone, 1977b) in patients whose close relatives have bipolar mania or recurrent depression. Toward the end of the decade a connection was made between childhood experiences of incest and the subsequent development of borderline personality disorder (Stone, 1981), later confirmed by others (Ogata et al., 1988; Zanarini, 1989). David Finkelhor, director of the Family Violence Research Program at the University of New Hampshire, increased psychiatrists' awareness of the magnitude of the incest problem with his book, *Sexually Victimized Children,* which appeared in 1979. Around this same time, other studies and anecdotal reports were published (Armstrong, 1978; Forward, 1978).

incest and border-line personality disorder

Like a smoldering volcano that suddenly exploded, books, articles, and stories about incest appeared everywhere and all at once in the United States and Western Europe. The stage was set for the intensive research on incest that would occur in the 1980s: How true were the stories? How widespread was the problem? How did incest affect symptom-formation and personality?

Hypnosis

During the decade of the 1970s the use of hypnosis was gaining respect as a therapeutic modality in psychiatry as well as in medicine, perhaps resulting from the extensive use of hypnosis for treating war neuroses in World War II and in Korea (Lucas, 1990). In addition, the split-brain research of Gazzaniga and Sperry during the 1960s had provided a way of understanding hypnotic phenomena in scientific (neurophysiological) terms. The relationship between hypnosis and certain processes mediated by the non-dominant hemisphere (such as meditation) was now recognized, and hypnosis was no longer viewed as hocuspocus. Important works on clinical applications of hypnosis in various psychiatric disorders were published by Crasilneck (1975), Spiegel and Spiegel (1978), and Frankel (1974, 1975). In work with phobic patients, for example, it was found that treatment resistance (to behavioral or other techniques) could be lessened via hypnotic suggestion.

hypnosis and non-dominant hemisphere

HOSPITAL PSYCHIATRY

Eating Disorders

anorexia nervosa

The treatment of anorexia nervosa underwent significant changes during the 1970s. For many years psychodynamic psychotherapy was used extensively, especially with patients whose weight loss had not yet necessitated hospitalization. Hilda Bruch (1973) was a prominent advocate of this approach. In the more serious cases, drastic measures (such as tube feeding) were widely employed, usually as an adjunct to dynamic therapy. The condition was, and remains, predominantly one that afflicts young females, and its etiology is typically characterized by power struggles between daughter and mother, morbid fears of becoming fat, fear of assuming adult female roles of wife and mother (*fat* ultimately means *pregnant*).

Cultural factors are also recognized as influencing anorexia as a "symptom choice": There is a long tradition in Christian countries of young girls overdoing fasting rituals to drastic extremes, as we saw in the cases of Princess Margaret of Hungary and the Venerable Lukardis (see Chapter 2). In countries where there are chronic shortages of food, anorexia would be an absurd "choice" as a means of expressing psychological conflict. As Professor Lambo of Nigeria said (at a World Psychiatric Congress in Denmark in 1986), anorexia nervosa does not appear in his country.

At some point in the 1970s it became increasingly (and embarrassingly) clear that the success rate of curing anorexia with psychoanalytic methods was poor. Other methods were developed and soon proved more effective, especially with hospitalized patients. Positive reinforcement techniques were especially useful (Agras et al., 1974), such as rewarding the patient with some privilege (having a TV, seeing a boyfriend) if she gained a certain amount of weight within a specified time.

Cases of bulimia nervosa, encountered with some regularity since the 1950s, were now becoming much more frequent. A particularly serious variant was also on the increase: bulimia (bingeing) followed by purging (self-induced vomiting) and often a period of anorexia— only to be followed by a repetition of this cycle (Russell, 1979). Depression was a common accompaniment, more so than with pure anorexia cases. As a result, antidepressant medications were prescribed alongside behavioral methods such as involvement in Overeaters Anonymous groups or in other cognitive/behavioral programs. In college populations bulimia began to reach prevalence rates of 6% or even 10–15% (among the female students) (Halmi et al., 1981).

bulimia nervosa

Research on Schizophrenia

Research on every aspect of schizophrenia was summarized in a series of encyclopedic works edited by Leopold Bellak, which appeared every 10 years. Throughout the 1970s psychiatrists used the 1969 volume as a resource book, with its thousands of references. Bellak presented an "Ego-Function Scale" for establishing a "profile" in the

*establishing a
profile in the
evaluation of
schizophrenic
patients*

evaluation of schizophrenic patients. The scale utilized a dozen factors, including reality testing, judgment, stimulus barrier, and object-relations.

In 1979 the fourth such volume appeared: *Disorders of the Schizophrenic Syndrome.* Each chapter was written by an outstanding investigator in the field of schizophrenia: Herbert Meltzer on biochemical studies, Robert Cancro on genetics, Monte Buchsbaum on neurophysiological aspects, William Carpenter and John Strauss on diagnostic issues, John Gunderson on individual psychotherapy, and Morris Lipton on pharmacotherapy. Manfred Bleuler, who continued the work of his father, Eugen Bleuler, at Zürich's Burghölzli Clinic, wrote the foreword, in which he surveyed his 60 years of research on schizophrenia. In 1972 Bleuler's own masterwork was published, *Die schizophrenen Geistesstorungen im Lichte langjähriger Kranken- und Familiengeschichten* [Schizophrenic Disorders in the Light of Long-term Illness and Family History]. In this volume M. Bleuler reported the results of follow-up on 208 schizophrenic patients with whom he had maintained contact for over 20 years. Using the diagnostic criteria outlined by his father, Manfred showed that the life trajectory and final outcome in schizophrenia is quite variable: Some patients remain ill from the onset of their first psychotic episodes; others show an intermittent course; still others, one prolonged episode in midlife with lasting recovery.

Similar results, perhaps even more encouraging, were reported by Luc Ciompi and C. Müller, also using Bleulerian criteria, in 1976. Most of their 289 patients spent the greater portion of their lives outside of hospital confinement, a finding that argued against the more pessimistic reports of some investigators. For example, Gerd Huber and his colleagues in Bonn reported on a still larger sample (449 patients), in which there was a correlation between prominent "basic symptoms" of schizophrenia (Huber's term for the negative symptom of flat affect, lack of willfulness, etc.) and a less favorable life course (Gross & Huber, 1973; Huber, 1981).

In an effort to assess more definitively the value of analytically-oriented therapy in treating schizophrenia, Alfred Stanton at the McLean Hospital in Boston organized a group of clinicians and researchers to form the "Psychotherapy of Schizophrenia Project." John Gunderson was co-director and took over the lead role upon Stanton's death. The research design was superior to that of the May (1969) study, in that the patients had higher educational levels, the therapists were more experienced, and the treatment was truly long-term. Patients were randomized into two groups: those who received analytically-oriented therapy and those who received supportive therapy. When outcomes of the two groups were examined some ten years after the project had been initiated, the schizophrenic patients given the intensive therapy

lives outside hospital confinement

assess analytically-oriented therapy in schizophrenia

had fared no better on average than those who had received "treatment as usual" (Gunderson et al., 1984).

As analytic therapy for schizophrenia was losing favor throughout the 1970s, other forms of treatment were demonstrating greater effectiveness. For example, Marvin Herz, then at New York State Psychiatric Institute, found that combining *brief* inpatient hospitalization with day-hospital visits yielded better results than long-term inpatient stays. Furthermore, group therapy was often more helpful than individual therapy—and when individual therapy *was* useful, it was the *supportive* rather than the *analytic* interventions that made the difference (Herz, 1979; Herz, Endicott, Spitzer, & Mesnikoff, 1971). Herz also showed that training the treatment staff to become more aware of prodromal symptoms (as early warning signals of impending psychosis) helped them to intervene quickly and obviate relapse (Herz, 1984). The community-oriented programs Herz and others were now championing in the United States (and which were already flourishing in Europe) also helped deal with the consequences of the "downsizing" of psychiatric facilities (especially the government-run ones), which continued throughout the 1970s. In the United States, and to a lesser extent in Europe, deinstitutionalization often proceeded faster than alternate facilities could be arranged. In the process, some schizophrenic patients became homeless or dependent on families not well-equipped to shelter an ill relative over an extended period.

other forms of treatment for schizophrenia

Research on Manic-Depression

Research on manic-depressive disorders was extensive during the 1970s. Lithium, whose clinical applications had been pioneered by Mogens Schou in Denmark (1968), was further analyzed in regard to its prophylactic properties (Angst et al., 1970) and to its general effectiveness in treating mania (Goodwin & Ebert, 1973). Van Praag and Kort (1971) attempted to identify a biochemical classification of affective disorders according to chemical factors, such as the presence of disturbance in the metabolism of 5-hydroxytryptamine in "endogenous" depressions. Bunney and his colleagues (1972) studied the "switch process" that takes place in the brain at the neurophysiological level in manic-depression. In Denmark Strömgren (1973) found that unilateral electroconvulsive treatment could be effective, and more easily tolerated, in patients with recurrent depression.

lithium

electroconvulsive treatment

Parallels were noted in the responses of bipolar and unipolar depressives to evoked potential (EP) experiments and their clinical response tendencies: Manic patients usually augment the stimuli during EP testing, just as they react too intensely to stressful interpersonal situations; patients with unipolar depression tend to show diminished EP responses, just as they often show sluggishness or "psy-

evoked potential experiments

chomotor retardation" in stressful situations (Buchsbaum et al., 1973).

Milder clinical forms of affective illness resembling manic-depression were analyzed by Donald Klein (1974), who used the term "endogenomorphic" in describing subacute biological depression, and by Hagop Akiskal et al. (1978), who spoke of "subaffective" forms of bipolar illness.

"subaffective" forms of bipolar illness

George Winokur (1975) argued in favor of genetic heterogeneity in manic-depressive illness. Elliot Gershon of the National Institute of Mental Health reexamined the X-linked postulate of manic inheritance elaborated in the 1960s and failed to find any close linkage with the known X-linked gene for colorblindness (Gershon et al., 1979), suggesting that, at the very least, it could no longer be claimed that an X-linked gene was *the* responsible factor in bipolar illness. That inherited factors of some sort were important was underlined in Gershon's review (1975) of twin studies: The pooled monozygotic concordance was five times greater than that of dizygotic twins (69% versus 13%)

Borderline Conditions

John Gunderson

definition of border-line personality disorder

John Gunderson of Boston's McLean Hospital rose to prominence in the domain of borderline conditions with his 1975 paper (written in collaboration with Margaret Singer) on the definition of borderline personality disorder. Striving for a less inferential diagnostic system than that of Kernberg, Gunderson relied on criteria that were easier for raters to assess and agree upon, such as the presence of manipulative suicidal acts, along with impulsivity, inordinate anger, mild or brief psychotic episodes, disturbances in close relationships, and good socialization but poor work history. When the *DSM* committee accepted *borderline* as a separate personality disorder in the 1980s, the official definition was an amalgam of Kernberg and Gunderson descriptors.

impulsivity

limit-setting

Despite the many controversies surrounding the diagnosis and treatment of borderline patients in this era, the one diagnostic feature all authors agreed upon was that of *impulsivity*. From a therapeutic standpoint, this meant that some form of *limit-setting* would be appropriate, whether the main lines of treatment were analytically-oriented or supportive. The role of medication was also hotly debated: Some felt that medications should be avoided, as though to prescribe them were to give in to the patient's demands for immediate relief; others contended that medication was indicated in cases where the anxiety was so strong that it interfered with attempts to address the crucial interpersonal problems.

If drugs were to be used and limits were to be set (concerning a hospitalized patient's wish for a weekend pass, etc.), the question arose, should such decisions be made by the therapist or by an "administrator" (a psychiatrist who was *not* the primary therapist)? Both Kernberg and Gunderson accepted the "therapist/administrator split" approach, though for neither was it an inflexible recommendation.

Indeed, the idea of *multimodal* treatment of inpatient borderline patients was becoming the most widely accepted approach (Gunderson, 1984; Kernberg, 1975). This approach included individual therapy, group therapy, work with family members, rehabilitative measures (such as recreation and occupational therapies), and a ward milieu tailored to the treatment of borderline patients.

multimodal treatment of inpatient borderline

Optimally, these patients were housed in units that specialized in their care and the staff had the opportunity to discuss the strong emotions such work engendered. For example, staff morale and "savvy" were enhanced by "T-groups," where the staff themselves met to discuss their own emotions and reactions, and by educational sessions, where the problems peculiar to borderline patients (suicidal acts, particularly) were elucidated in order to facilitate a more unified approach to these problems.

The changes in diagnostic criteria for *borderline* during the 1970s placed the condition more toward the *affective* pole of psychiatric disorders than the schizophrenic. Borderline patients often manifested significant levels of depression and anxiety, such that treatment with antidepressants, sometimes in combination with anxiolytics, was indicated. Some borderline patients showed a clinical picture closer to "bipolar type-II" disorder (mild euphoric episodes but serious depressions), for which lithium was a useful addition to the medical regimen.

antidepressants anxiolytics

Chapter 18

BIOLOGICAL PSYCHIATRY AND

GENETICS

One of the puzzling aspects of schizophrenia, especially for clinicians, was the tendency for the illness to "disappear" for a time, only to reappear after lapses that might be many years' duration. Some patients seemed to suffer only one episode where the diagnosis could be convincingly made. Those who interviewed such patients in the in-between periods were often hesitant to diagnose schizophrenia, especially because of the pessimism surrounding this condition. Some spoke of "latent schizophrenia," as though the illness were probably there, somewhere beneath the surface, even when the patient had apparently recovered.

"latent schizophre-nia"

Among those who brought clarity to this confusing situation were Joseph Zubin and Bonnie Spring, who advocated the concept of "vulnerability" in 1977. Instead of viewing these patients as being sometimes schizophrenic and sometimes not, Zubin and Spring proposed that patients had a *vulnerability* to the condition *all the time*, but this vulnerability (or *diathesis* or *predisposition*) only became clinically manifest and recognizable under certain stressful circumstances. Persons with low vulnerability presumably succumbed only under severe stress; those with the highest vulnerability might remain recognizably schizophrenic most of the time.

"vulnerability"

In referring to the hereditary component of the disease, Matthysse and Kidd (1976b) spoke of a "schizophrenia quotient,"[1] analogous to

"schizophrenia quotient"

---

[1] SQ represents the amalgam of liability from all prenatal sources—genetic and constitutional—to develop schizophrenia. While it is similar to Zubin and Spring's "vulnerability," it is not the same, since "vulnerability" includes environmental factors as well.

the intelligence quotient: Those with the highest "SQ" might never appear well once they had their first breakdown; those with the lowest SQ would only show the condition under heavy stress, and perhaps only in an attenuated form (such as bohemianism, unconventionality, or schizotypal personality). Vulnerability was an amalgam of many factors: risk genes, hypercritical family members who undermined the confidence of the vulnerable relative—as well as mollifying influences, such as artistic talent or high intelligence, that might buffer the impact of the negative factors. Vaughn and Leff (1976b) used the phrase "high expressed emotion" (high E.E.) in referring to the overly critical families, whose schizophrenic offspring were hospitalized more often than comparably ill children of less abusive families.

"high expressed emotion"

vulnerability model

Zubin and Spring's vulnerability model helped reorient our thinking about other psychiatric disorders—actually, the greater bulk of psychiatric disorders—where nature *and* nurture both play a role. The model is equally relevant to the affective disorders, for example. Many patients with recurrent unipolar depression, though likely to have periodic episodes even in the absence of stressful life events, have more such episodes in the presence of stressors. Also, certain stressful situations to which a predisposed patient is vulnerable can trigger a depressive episode, making it appear "merely reactive," when, in fact, it is both a reaction to stress *and* a manifestation of constitutional vulnerability. Even manic episodes—which are not usually stress-related and are not as understandable or common a human reaction to, say, job loss, death of a loved one, or romantic disappointment—sometimes occur immediately following stressful experiences in persons carrying risk genes for bipolar illness.

BIOLOGICAL MARKERS

Much of the research on the major psychoses in the 1970s concentrated on the search for *biological markers*. These might come in the form of abnormal body chemistries or physiological reactions peculiar to psychotic patients and their close relatives. An "ideal" marker would be one not only specific for a clinically diagnosed psychosis but also detectable during normal interludes in the patients as well as in a proportion of their siblings, parents, or children (first-degree relatives). Philip Holzman and his co-workers hit upon one such marker for schizophrenia: "abnormal smooth pursuit eye movements" (1973). Whereas a normal person tracks a moving pendulum in a smooth sinusoidal fashion, many schizophrenic persons show a disrupted pattern. This jagged pattern was found in 69% of schizophrenic subjects, 22% of manic-depressives, and only 8% of normals. Furthermore, 44% of the first-degree relatives of schizophrenic subjects (as against 10% of non-schizophrenic patients) showed the abnormal pattern (Holzman, 1975). Others who figured prominently in this area of research were Shagass

"abnormal smooth pursuit eye movements"

(1974) and Siever et al. (1984), who showed that this biological marker could help identify persons with schizotypal personality within a "normal volunteer" population.

Smooth pursuit eye movement abnormalities are but one example of many such markers investigated during the 1970s, which was a decade characterized by such an outpouring of biopsychiatric research findings that the books published in this area were almost invariably multi-authored. Some examples (with their respective editors): *Biochemistry, Schizophrenia, and Affective Illness* (Harold Himwich, 1970), *The Biology of the Major Psychoses* (Daniel X. Freedman, 1975), *Biological Foundations of Psychiatry* (Robert Grenell and Sabit Gabay, 1976), and *The Impact of Biology on Modern Psychology* (Elliot Gershon, Robert Belmaker, Seymour Kety, and Milton Rosenbaum, 1977). Typical topics explored in these works included hemispheric specialization, memory mechanisms, evoked potentials, neurochemical and neurophysiological bases of emotion, the psychophysiology of sleep, genetic factors in the major psychoses, and psychotropic drugs and their effects on brain neurotransmitter mechanisms in the synaptic cleft.

multi-authored books

Another marker relevant to schizophrenia was a response of "abnormal event-related potential" following random presentation of tones to the two ears. Shagass (Shagass, Straumanis, & Roemer, 1977; Shagass, Roemer, & Straumanis, 1978) described the reduction in amplitude of the P-300 (a wave occurring 300 milliseconds after the stimulus) component that he and his colleagues noted in schizophrenic patients. This P-300 reduction was also noted in some children at risk for schizophrenia. In respect to everyday function, this abnormality is correlated with *indifference* to the importance, or surprise value, of the stimulus, compared with the reaction of normal persons. This finding is consistent with the misinterpretation or under-reaction of many schizophrenics to stimuli whose surprise value is greater when experienced by normal persons.

"abnormal event-related potential"

Noting that schizophrenic patients treated with chlorpromazine sometimes showed lactation as a side effect, Göran Sedvall and his colleagues at Stockholm's Karolinska Institute demonstrated that this phenomenon was related to the secretion of prolactin triggered by the postsynaptic dopamine receptor blockade in the central nervous system (1975). Prolactin assay analysis became a useful marker for the evaluation of neuroleptic drugs for schizophrenia and for other research involving the dopaminergic system.

prolactin assay analysis

GENETIC MARKERS

The genetic aspects of the major psychoses remained a subject of great importance throughout the 1970s, as it had been in the decades since 1910. Seymour Kety, whose book, *Transmission of Schizophrenia,* was a leading resource on this topic in the 1960s (Kety, Rosenthal, & Wender, 1968), reviewed the literature in 1975 and noted the convergence of monozygotic-twin concordance rates for schizophrenia toward a figure of 40%. Kety's work continued to support the "spectrum" notion, since certain milder disorders (schizoid personality or "borderline schizophrenia") were still found to occur more often among relatives of schizophrenics than among the relatives of control-group patients. But the findings did not point to a "unitary" basis for schizophrenia, since the data were "equally compatible with a syndrome of multiple etiologies and different modes of genetic transmission" (p. 205).

monozygotic-twin concordance rates

"spectrum" notion

In the domain of affective disorders, Gershon (1975) discussed various theoretical models of transmission for the different forms of manic-depression and proposed a "single major locus model" (adapted from the work of Kidd, 1975), in which there are different thresholds for recurrent depressive and bipolar illnesses. Each threshold represents a combined total of genetic and environmental influences; the thresholds form, in essence, a continuous scale of liability to illness. Persons with liability beyond the first threshold are likely to manifest the illness (most likely, depression) associated with that level. As liability increases, one may show other forms of illness, such as bipolar-type II (more depressed than manic) or at still greater levels, full-blown manic illness.

models of transmission of affective disorders

The hitherto vexing question of whether manic-depressive psychosis and schizophrenia are truly distinct genetically was answered in the affirmative, to the satisfaction of most investigators. Gershon and Rieder (1980), drawing on research in the 1970s, contended that the data supported this conclusion. As a corollary, it was noted that patients with schizoaffective and atypical psychoses tended to have relatives with bipolar, unipolar, or schizophrenic conditions, suggesting that in some families risk genes for *both* classical psychoses may be present. That is, cases of schizoaffective illness may result from genetic "admixture." (The problem was taken up again in the 1980s.) From epidemiological studies of the affective disorders, it emerged that males are more prone to develop bipolar and schizoaffective psychoses; females, more likely to develop depression (Angst, 1980).

distinct psychoses

The issue of creativity, an interesting sidelight to the topic of manic-depression, was introduced by Nancy Andreasen, currently the editor of the *American Journal of Psychiatry,* who obtained a Ph.D. in English before earning her medical degree. Highly qualified to examine this issue (especially in relation to writers), she noted (1980; Andreasen & Canter, 1974; Andreasen & Powers, 1975) that writers, when compared with a control population, were more apt to have affective disorders or cyclothymic personality. In separate studies of eminent and creative persons (not just in the realm of literature),

creativity

manic-depression

personality and affective disorders were again more common (as was alcoholism) than in the control groups. Andreasen (1980) concluded that there was a "relationship between affective disorder and some forms of creativity" (p. 384). Examples among writers and poets include Sylvia Plath, Anne Sexton (both of whom committed suicide), and William Styron (who went through severe depressions). Vincent van Gogh went through periods of mania and depression, committing suicide at age 37. The composer Handel was manic-depressive, as was Robert Schumann (whom Eugen Bleuler thought was schizophrenic). Schumann's chronology of compositions has been carefully worked out, and we now know that he composed almost nothing during the years when he was depressed, whereas he was enormously productive when manic.

PSYCHOPHARMACOLOGY

anti-manic properties of carbamazepine

In the area of psychopharmacology another serendipitous discovery was made, this time about the anti-manic properties of a drug ordinarily used for the control of epilepsy (mainly temporal lobe). The ability of carbamazepine (Tegretol) to ameliorate mania was noted by a Japanese team headed by Okuma in 1973, and Ballenger and Post (1978) later confirmed this work. The mechanism of action was not altogether understood but appeared to involve changes in the metabolism of norepinephrine (decreased levels of which were noted in the cerebrospinal fluid of manic patients [Post et al., 1978]) and of dopamine. Post (1980) also speculated that carbamazepine might lower limbic-system excitability, as lithium appears to do (Delgado & DeFendis, 1967). As a result of these studies, the roster of anti-manic medications grew to three (lithium, valproate, carbamazepine), offering further hope of controlling bipolar illness in persons who happened to be refractory to lithium.

By the 1970s the number of researchers exploring brain pathways concerned with emotion (and implicated in emotional disorders) was enormous. One cannot do justice to all these men and women in a book of ordinary dimensions; even a mere catalogue of their names, which would reflect the four corners of the globe, would create an unwieldy tome. There is no one "father of psychopharmacology" comparable to Pinel or Freud in their respective fields. Still, there is one investigator whose discovery of hitherto unknown neurotransmitters and prolific publications lend him a prominence that overshadows even such important contributors as O. Hornykiewicz (1966), Joseph Schildkraut (1965) (who elaborated the catecholamine hypothesis), Maria Åsberg (Åsberg, Träksman, & Thoren, 1976) (who pioneered the identification of serotonin mechanisms in suicide and violence), Monte

Buchsbaum (who worked on platelet monamine oxidase in various psychiatric conditions), Donald Klein (Klein, Gittleman et al., 1980) (who worked on all disorders for which drugs were relevant), and Herbert Meltzer (Meltzer, Sachar, & Frantz, 1974) (who conducted important research on prolactin in schizophrenia).

I refer to Solomon Snyder of Johns Hopkins Department of Psychiatry, whose articles and other publications (which number nearly a thousand), opened whole vistas on the landscape of brain mechanisms. Whether or not he becomes psychiatry's second Nobel laureate (Wagner-Jauregg won his in 1927 for much more limited accomplishments), Snyder's place in the history of psychiatry is assured. He and his co-workers were among the first to detect endogenous opiate receptors and opiate-like compounds in certain brain pathways (Snyder, 1978). Snyder helped outline the pathways related to the most widely studied neurotransmitters: dopamine, norepinephrine, and serotonin (Snyder & Banerjee et al., 1974; Snyder, 1976), and also detected and mapped the pathways of many other transmitters, which now number about two hundred. Among the more obscure compounds: *substance* (which may function as a transmitter of pain) and *cholecystokinin* (a co-transmitter with dopamine in the mesolimbic tract) (Snyder, 1985).

Solomon Snyder. Courtesy National Library of Medicine

Aggression and Violence

While Snyder's attention has been directed at the "micro" level (in systems terms) of molecular neurobiology, the neuropsychopharmacologist Luigi Valzelli, chief of the Mario Negri Institute of Pharmacological research in Milan, was extending the work of Papez and Klüver at the "macro" level. Valzelli's primary focus had been on identifying the psychobiology of aggression and violence, as these tendencies manifest themselves behaviorally in animals and humans. His extensive research—much of it carried out in the 1970s (Valzelli, 1970, 1977, 1978)—is summarized in his monograph of 1981. Citing MacLean's (1970) concept of the "triune brain," Valzelli showed how the most primitive of these compartments—the "reptilian" brain (of which Eibl-Eibesfeldt had spoken)—subserves such functions as territorial defense, hunting, mating, competition, dominance, aggression, and imitative patterns. The major components of the reptilian brain are the caudate, putamen, globus pallidus, and amygdala, along with the olfactory bulb and optic chiasm.

Surrounding the reptilian brain is the "paleomammalian" brain, consisting of the hypothalamus, thalamus, hippocampus, corpus callosum, cingulate gyrus, and portions of the amygdala. This is the limbic sys-

Luigi Valzelli

psychobiology of aggression and violence

"triune brain"

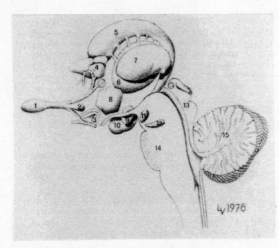

1. Olfactory bulb
2. Olfactory tubercle
3. Optic chiasma
4. Septal nuclei
5. Caudate
6. Putamen and globus pallidus
7. Talamus
8. Hypothalamus
9. Mammilary body
10. Amygdala
11. Interpeduncular nucleus
12. Substantia nigra
13. Quadrigeminal bodies
    (Tectrum mesencephali)
14. Pons
15. Cerebellum

Schematic diagram of the so-called reptilian brain, i.e., the portion most primitive and ancient in evolutionary terms. From Valzelli, 1981.

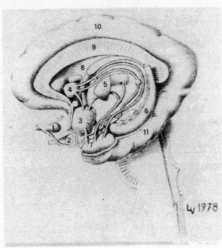

1. Olfactory tubercle
2. Optic chiasma
3. Hypothalamus
4. Septal nuclei
5. Thalamic nuclei
6. Hippocampus
7. Amygdala
8. Septum
9. Corpus callosum
10. Cingulate gyrus
11. Hippocampal gyrus
    (temporal lobe)

Schematic diagram of the paleomammalian brain showing structures that became more prominent in the ancient mammals, as they began to appear around 100 million years ago. From Valzelli, 1981.

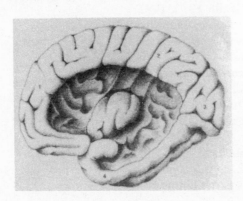

1. Frontal lobe
2. Parietal lobe
3. Occipital lobe
4. Temporal lobe

Schematic diagram of the neomammalian brain, with the newest and most advanced structures, especially the large cortex. From Valzelli, 1981. Printed with permission of Lippencott-Raven Publishers.

tem (named by MacLean in 1952), which subserves emotion and affect regulation as well as certain feeling states important to survival (recognition of hunger, thirst, pain, familiarity versus unfamiliarity).

Finally, enveloping these structures is the "neomammalian" brain, consisting of the cortex with its four main sections: the frontal, temporal, parietal, and occipital lobes.

Valzelli outlined the many varieties of aggression encountered in the animal kingdom, most of which also pertain to our own species: *predatory, competitive, defensive, irritative, territorial, maternal-protective, sex-related,* and *instrumental*. In social species such as our own, there is a trade-off between the behavioral pattern of competitive aggression (each person wants all the goods and glory for himself: a "narcissistic" ambition) and that of dominance/submission. Because unifying as a group helps ensure success in fending off enemies, those lower in the hierarchy come to accept (without too much protest) the leadership of the dominant member(s), whose abilities simultaneously earn respect for the leaders as guarantors of the group's survival and minimize competitive antagonism (out of gratitude for one's safety).

In discussing the ethological aspects of depression, Price (1972) made a related point on this imbalance between competition and cooperation: Persons prone to depression are more willing to blame themselves for shortcomings than to blame others. This "intropunitiveness" results in a readiness to accept criticism, such as that of a boss to an employee. Rather than resort to *irritative* aggression, which might culminate in harming the boss or destroying company property in "revenge," depression-prone employee looks into herself, strives to do better, and harms no one. This attitude causes misery to the depressive person but is clearly more socially adaptive and survival-oriented in relation to the group than is wantonly destructive behavior. Price speculated that people living in densely populated countries, such as Italy, would be more prone to depression than those living in sparsely populated regions, such as Sweden, for whom it might be more adaptive to have schizoid (instead of depressive) traits and stronger territorial attitudes. These qualities would help the population adapt to living in isolated units in regions where neighbors were relatively far apart and where each person needed to demonstrate self-sufficiency and a high tolerance for being alone.

Testosterone plays a role in several forms of aggression. In *irritative* aggression, for example, males are far overrepresented among antisocial/aggressive persons; it has been noted that U.S. Army veterans in the top 10% of testosterone levels have significantly higher likelihood of having engaged in antisocial activities (Dabbs & Morris, 1990), even more so if the men were from a lower socioeconomic group. Environmental influences affect testosterone, in the sense that competing men who show increased hormone levels, while those who lose show levels

varieties of aggression

ethological aspects of depression

geography and mental illness

testosterone

lowered from their previous baseline (Archer, 1994). As for *instrumental* aggression, which has to do with threatening behavior (intended to keep subordinates in line), this type is shown, for example, by "boss" monkeys (the "alpha-monkeys" whose testosterone levels are incidentally higher than that of the subordinates) in their efforts to reaffirm dominance. As Valzelli mentions, instrumental aggression "may be considered as being conceptually similar to authoritative command behavior" (1981, p. 84).

compounds affecting the expression of aggression

Valzelli studied other compounds affecting the expression of aggression, including serotonin (Valzelli et al., 1977), noting that there are rhythmic variations (maximal levels in winter, minimal in summer) as well as daily variations (greater emotional stability occurs in the morning hours). The peak rates for suicide, which occur during the spring (and to a lesser extent, autumn) months, may also be related, in part, to seasonal fluctuations in brain levels of serotonin (Eastwood & Peacocke, 1976); serotonin may also play a role (though not necessarily a direct one) in homicide rates, which show seasonal changes (Lieber, 1978; Lieber & Sherin, 1972), and in women who commit suicide or murder (they usually do so around the time of their menstrual periods) (MacKinnon et al., 1956).

serotonin

In the mid-1970s Åsberg, Träksman, & Thoren (1976) showed the connection between low CNS serotonin levels and heightened impulsivity/irritability. Later she (Åsberg, 1994) demonstrated a link between low serotonin levels and violent behavior, whether as suicide (hanging, jumping, shooting) or as murder. Thanks to the research of Valzelli, Åsberg, and others, the old psychoanalytic shibboleth about "suicide as aggression turned inward" received biological validation.

Chapter 19

CHILD PSYCHIATRY

The decade of the 1970s witnessed a significant increase in awareness—on the part of physicians, psychiatrists, and lay people alike—of the magnitude of child abuse. Many investigators and clinicians contributed to this awareness, such as Richard Gelles (1975) and Murray Straus (1973), whose collaboration produced an important compendium on the subject. Their book, *Physical Violence in American Families* (1990), was based on the National Family Violence Survey of 1975 and a follow-up survey 10 years later. In this large-scale study (over 8,000 families), the authors found that 24 children out of 1,000 suffered severe abuse (being kicked, bitten, punched, beaten up, burned, scalded, attacked with a weapon); if "merely" hitting a child was included as a possibility, the rate went up to 110 per 1,000—or about 7,000,000 children per year in the United States. About two-thirds of children hit siblings, sometimes doing severe damage; this factor further increases the level of child abuse, and the worst examples wreak the same kinds of psychological damage as does parental/caretaker abuse.

magnitude of child abuse

Comparable epidemiological data about sexual abuse and incest were not to become available until the next decade, though reports about incest were beginning to accumulate in populations of college students and in patients with borderline personality disorder. Certain factors were shown to heighten the risk of incest to young girls (and to a lesser extent, young boys): having a stepfather, coming from a family of low socioeconomic status, and living without the mother (Finkelhor, 1984).

sexual abuse and incest

What was not so clear was whether the abuse problem—now of epidemic proportions in the United States but of considerable dimensions in Western Europe as well—had been this great for decades but gone unrecognized or had increased dramatically only recently. The most reasonable assumption was that child abuse had always been present but currently afflicted a larger percentage of households, due to the

abuse

social breakdown

same post-World-War-II factors of social breakdown mentioned earlier: more broken families (hence more stepparents, whose protective feelings toward their stepchildren seldom equal those of the biological parents) and less respect for religion and other institutions of authority. It also seemed that Western cultural values were becoming increasingly narcissistic, which subtly influenced adults to become more self-involved at the expense of their children's welfare. The pervading ethos of narcissism also weakened the barriers to abusive and exploitative behavior of children.

Advanced medical technology in the preceding generation provided one means of more clearly assessing levels of abuse. Certain cases of "sudden infant death syndrome" (SIDS), for example, could now be shown to have resulted not from natural causes but from deliberate smothering by the mother. Sometimes a mother would stage repeated instances of smothering, followed by "heroic" rescue efforts, such as mouth-to-mouth resuscitation and summoning an ambulance to whisk the infant to a hospital emergency room. Until the real reason for the child's distress was suspected and proven, all manner of unnecessary tests and inaccurate diagnoses were given. Because the child's factitious illness was induced not by himself but by another person, this condition was named "Munchausen syndrome by proxy" (MSBP) by its discoverer, British pediatrician Roy Meadow, who first described it in 1977 (Olsen, 1995).[1]

"sudden infant death syndrome" (SIDS)

"Munchausen syndrome by proxy" (MSBP)

Although this syndrome is admittedly rare, it may be seen as a symptom of *something* gone very wrong in the body social. MSBP and related crimes almost always involve women whose natural capacity for empathy has been aborted by incest or other forms of abuse during their own childhoods. These women—such as the mothers who smothered to death one infant after another (Mary Tinning, described by

---

[1] Since this is a text on the *history* of psychiatry, perhaps this is the place to put to rest the common misunderstanding about the origin of the term *Munchausen syndrome* as a synonym for factitious illness. There *was* a Baron von Münchausen in the 18th century, but the literary frivolity that bears his name—*The Surprising Adventures of Baron Münchausen*—was not written by the baron himself. The author was an impoverished German student living in England, Rudolph Eric Raspe, who wrote the book in 1785. Raspe had met Baron Hieronymus Karl Friedrich von Münchausen earlier in Goettingen and simply ascribed the tales to Münchausen (copyright laws did not exist at the time) in hopes of winning a wider readership and earning a few guineas (Seccombe, 1927). To the end of his days the baron had to endure ridicule as having "authored" the far-fetched accounts of his "travels" depicted in the *Adventures*. Thus the tall tales told to physicians by patients with factitious illnesses harken back not to the baron but to the fantastical tales falsely attributed to him by Raspe.

Eggington, 1989; Waneta Hoyt, described by Hickey et al., 1996), the delivery-room nurse who killed infants (Genene Jones, described by Moore and Reed, 1988), and mothers who attempted to kill their babies for insurance money (Ellen Boehm, described by Coston, 1995) or to unencumber themselves when about to remarry (Diane Downs, described by Rule, 1987)—represent the extremes of narcissistic behavior and serve as examples of how victims can turn into victimizers, seeking revenge for past wrongs by exploiting even their own children for selfish purposes (van der Kolk, 1989).

Fortunately only a small percentage of child-abuse victims become murderers as adults. More often they become emotionally handicapped, unable to form lasting relationships and/or prone to severe depression (as in the case of Ellen Boehm's daughter, who survived her mother's attempt to kill her when she was eight [Coston, 1995]). Nevertheless, the child-abuse cycle is on its way to spiraling out of control: Family breakdown leads to increased abuse of children, which creates a higher proportion of children with depression or revenge fantasies who, when they become adults, are less capable of harmonious and sustained marriages and more prone to abuse their own children, leading to more family breakdown . . . as the vicious circle begins again.

child-abuse cycle

Psychiatry works with individual victims of child abuse in the hopes of repairing the damage inflicted. Incest survivor groups, which began to form in the late 1970s, offered a group-based source of reparation. But psychiatry is relatively powerless (except in an advocacy function) to effect the social changes necessary to ameliorate the abuse problem.

MORAL/COGNITIVE DEVELOPMENT

In the area of moral development, the work of Lawrence Kohlberg has been especially important. His chapter on "Moral Stages and Moralization" appeared in 1976 and became the basis of a later book (Kohlberg et al., 1983) on the development of moral awareness from its beginnings in childhood through its further evolution in late adolescence. Kohlberg and his colleagues reexamined the earlier, and much simpler, model (viz. Freud, 1896), which traced the child's progress from a shame-oriented position (requiring the presence of a disapproving "other") to a guilt-oriented position (where the child finally internalizes parental/societal negatives and refrains from certain actions, even in the absence of others, to avoid feeling badly for transgressing the accepted values).

Lawrence Kohlberg

Kohlberg and his colleagues (1983) identified seven stages (Table 6), beginning with the "egocentric perspective" (stage 1), moving through a "core justice structure" similar to the Golden Rule (stage 3),

seven stages of
moral development

TABLE 6   KOHLBERG'S STAGES OF MORAL DEVELOPMENT

Basis of Judgment	Stage of Development	Characteristics of Stage
Preconventional moral values reside in external, quasi-physical happenings, in bad acts, or in quasi-physical needs rather than in persons and standards.	Stage 1	Obedience and punishment orientation; egocentric deference to superior power or prestige, or a trouble-avoiding set: objective responsibility.
	Stage 2	Naively egoistic orientation; right action is that instrumentally satisfying one's own and occasionally others' needs; awareness that value is relative to each person's needs and perspectives; naive egalitarianism and orientation to exchange and reciprocity.
Conventional moral values reside in performing good or right roles, in maintaining the conventional order, and in meeting others' expectations.	Stage 3	Orientation to approval and to pleasing and helping others; conformity to stereotypical images of majority or natural role behavior and judgment by intentions.
	Stage 4	Orientation to doing one's duty and to showing respect for authority and maintaining the given social order for its own sake; regard for the earned expectations of others.
Postconventional moral values are derived from principles that can be applied universally.	Stage 5	Contractual-legalistic orientation; recognition of an arbitrary element in rules or expectations for the sake of agreement; duty defined in terms of contract, general avoidance of violation of the will or rights of others, or of the majority will and welfare.
	Stage 6	Orientation to conscience or principles, not only to ordained social rules but also to principles of choice appealing to logical universality and consistency; conscience is a directing agent, together with mutual respect and trust.

From Kohlberg, 1971. Reprinted with permission from Lippencott-Raven Publishers.

wherein equality, reciprocity, and equity are integrated, to a level where moral judgment is organized ". . . around a clearly formulated moral principle of justice and respect for persons that provides a rationale for the primacy of this principle" (stage 6) (p. 61). Beyond these stages is a stage seldom attained, wherein there is a sense of participation in, and identity with, a cosmic order. At this level of development, moral values are no longer viewed as arbitrary human inventions but as "principles of justice which are in harmony with broader laws regulating the evolution of human nature and the cosmic order" (p. 42). There is an accompanying sense of spirituality which may, or may not, be expressed through the medium of religious concepts and beliefs.

Kohlberg's model, inspired in part by the contributions of Piaget (1932) and Rawls (1971), helped establish more secure guideposts for assessing the moral level attained by children and adolescents under evaluation for psychological problems, including conduct disorders and delinquency.

Awareness of attention-deficit disorders (with or without hyperactivity) was increasing during the 1970s, spurred by the research of Paul Wender (1971) on the clinical aspects and Dennis Cantwell (1975a, 1975b) on the genetic aspects. Morrison and Minkoff (1975) also studied inheritance patterns and reported that one form of hyperactivity in children occurred predominantly in the male line and that "explosive personality" was often the adult sequel to the syndrome.

attention-deficit disorders

Rachel Gittelman-Klein and Donald Klein (1976) concentrated on the pharmacological approach to hyperactivity, comparing the effectiveness of methylphenidate (Ritalin) with thioridazine (Mellaril). (Methylphenidate and dextroamphetamine, both stimulants, have the paradoxical effect of calming hyperactivity in children.) Mendelson and her colleagues reported a follow-up study of hyperactive children (1971) that indicated poor functioning five years after diagnosis (impulsivity, immature behavior, and use of illicit drugs were still common symptoms) but improved functioning ten years later (by which time the probands were young adults), to the degree that there was scarcely any difference from the control subjects.

TEMPERAMENT

Considerable attention was devoted during this decade to the study of temperament in children. The stimulus for much of this work had come from the research carried out by Alexander Thomas and Stella Chess in New York during the 1960s, who had observed infant behavior and identified nine categories that could be understood as the phenotypes of various hereditary influences. These consisted of *activity level, rhythmicity, approach/withdrawal, reaction intensity, response threshold, mood quality, distractibility,* and *attention span/persistence* (Thomas & Chess 1963, 1977).

Alexander Thomas and Stella Chess

hereditary influences

Arnold Buss and Robert Plomin (1975) focused on the attributes of *emotionality, activity level, sociability,* and *impulsivity,* later defining temperament as "inherited personality traits present in early childhood" (Buss & Plomin, 1984, p. 84). These authors showed that the heritability[2] was impressively high for emotionality (0.58), activity (0.75), and sociability (0.45) (Buss, Plomin, & Willerman 1973). Other researchers studied parental ratings of temperament factors in monozygotic versus dizygotic twins, which showed similar, though less robust, levels of heritability (Willerman, 1973; Wilson, Brown, & Matheny, 1971).

PSYCHOPATHOLOGY SCALES

Progress in the development of diagnostic instruments for adult disorders was mirrored in child psychiatry by the development of scales for child psychopathology, often adjusted for discrete age levels. Achenbach and Edelbrock (1978) wrote on general issues in the classification of childhood disorders, and also developed a scale pertinent to boys ages 6–11 (Achenbach, 1978). Kestenbaum and Bird (1978) devised a "Mental Health Assessment Form" for school-age children; Michael Rutter and David Schaffer developed a "Multiaxial Classification of Child Psychiatric Disorders" (1975).

Depression and Mania

Kovacs and Beck (1977) adapted the well-known Beck Depression Inventory for use in evaluating what was emerging as a new phenomenon: depression in children. Another such scale was elaborated by Ella Poznanski and her colleagues (1979). Theodore Shapiro, director of the child psychiatry department at New York Hospital, observed that child psychiatrists were becoming much more aware during the 1970s that serious depressive disorders could occur in the prepubertal years (personal communication, 1995). This awareness came about, in part, through research on children at risk for affective disorders (by virtue of having one or both parents who were manic-depressive). Certain symptoms and traits seen in young children, which did not appear to be depressive in nature (not like depressive symptoms in adults, that is) were now understood as manifestations of depression *in statu nascendi*.

depressive disorders in prepubertal years

A number of investigators sketched the clinical profile that would justify a diagnosis of childhood depression: Brumback et al. (1977), Carlson and Cantwell (1979), Cytryn et al. (1980), Malmquist (1971), and Poznanski and Zrull (1970). Poznanski highlighted the clinical difficulties of evaluating a potentially depressed child, especially a child

clinical profile of childhood depression

[2] Heritability is expressed as the degree to which correlations in monozygotic twins (mz) exceed that for dizygotic twins (dz): $(mz)–(dz)/1–(dz)$.

younger than 10. In the very early years, children are less verbal, less able to put feelings into words, less aware of the finality of death, and less solidified in identity and conscience-formation to be able to experience the markers of low self-esteem or guilt as might an adolescent or adult. So instead of the "classical" signs of depression, one might see loss of enthusiasm for play (rather than anhedonia), a deterioration in school performance (rather than a complaint of poor concentration), or a sullenness or irritability (rather than the customary sadness or bitterness of the depressed adult).

Child psychiatrists in the 1970s also learned to recognize the early counterparts of mania (Feinstein & Wolpert, 1973), though the clinical picture is more questionable in children under 10 than in adolescents. Some manic adolescents (the more readily recognizable if they have parents or other close relatives with bipolar illness) show extremes of irritability, along with intrusive behavior (including persistent teasing) or rebelliousness, well before they show pushed speech, grandiosity, or other clear-cut adult manic symptoms.

counterparts of mania

Schizophrenia

The "soft signs"—premonitory symptoms and attenuated features—of schizophrenia were elucidated further in the high-risk studies of the 1970s, where children were examined periodically (usually over a minimum span of 10 years) for possible abnormalities that might be related to genetic liability for schizophrenia. Such studies were carried out in New York City (Erlenmeyer-Kimling, 1975), Stony Brook, New York (Weintraub, 1978), Minnesota (Garmezy & Neale, 1974), and Rochester, New York (Wynne et al., 1977), among others.

premonitory symptoms and attenuated features of schizophrenia

The New York study enumerated several factors in high-risk children (aged 7–12) that presaged later development of a schizophrenic psychosis necessitating hospital care: lower IQ, poor performance on the Bender-Gestalt test,[3] and abnormalities in attention (Erlenmeyer-Kimling, Kestenbaum, Bird, & Hilldoff, 1984). The attentional deficits that were identified on the Continuous Performance Test[4] were thought

Bender-Gestalt test

[3] A test of one's ability to reproduce with pencil and paper several abstract forms of increasing complexity. Poor performance on the test is suggestive of impairment in space perception and a possible malfunction in related areas of the brain.

[4] The Continuous Performance Test (CPT) is a test of sustained visual attention in which the person taking the test is required to respond to the second of two identical stimuli. Children at high risk for schizophrenia tend to do poorly on the CPT. This deficiency is considered attributable to decreased capacity for stimulus-discrimination.

abnormalities in brain chemistries

social behavior

different type of attention deficit

nonorganic psychoses

genetic basis of schizophrenia and manic-depression

to correlate with certain abnormalities in brain chemistries (reduced monoamine and dopamine-B-hydroxylase activity) noted in adult schizophrenics (who routinely also show disturbances in attention) (Erlenmeyer-Kimling et al., 1984).

Weintraub and his colleagues focused on social behavior, reporting that the children of schizophrenic parents tended to show impatience, disturbing classroom behavior, disrespect, withdrawal, and irrelevant responses to a greater extent than was true of a control group. Lowered competence and heightened vulnerability to stress were seen in children of both depressed and schizophrenic parents, though the former, if they showed abnormal signs at all, were the more deviant (Weintraub & Neale, 1984). The children of severely depressed parents were shown to be at risk for adult depression (Perris, 1973) but rarely for schizophrenia. Children at risk for schizophrenia showed a different type of attention deficit than was seen in hyperactive children: Those at risk for schizophrenia had difficulty distinguishing relevant from irrelevant stimuli, whereas hyperactive children were impulsive and more easily distracted (Garmezy & Devine, 1984).

Still another research team examined the children of women with a variety of nonorganic psychoses—schizophrenia and "cycloid psychosis," in particular—and found that neonatal neurological abnormalities were common in infants born to mothers in both diagnostic categories. Children in both sub-groups tended to be characterized by their teachers and relatives as "slow to warm up" or "difficult"; they also showed less attachment and less "stranger anxiety" as infants (McNeil & Kaij, 1984).

The aim of all these studies was to ascertain (1) the likelihood of high-risk children succumbing to the corresponding parental psychosis (what percentage would fall ill?), (2) the biological markers best suited to foretell children's fate, and (3) the best strategies for early intervention and prevention, if possible. The results of this body of research established a firmer foundation for the genetic basis of schizophrenia and manic-depression. Phenocopies[5] apart, the genetic factors were henceforth understood as the necessary, though not sufficient, elements of the classical psychoses. If one carried the risk genes for schizophrenia, for example, one might still not develop the full-blown condition (mollifying influences might prevail; the genetic loading might

[5] Phenocopies are characteristics (whether normal or abnormal) usually brought about by specific hereditary factors, but caused instead by other influences. Certain frontal lobe tumors, for example, cause a clinical picture *resembling* schizophrenia (this was the case with George Gershwin), but in this case the "schizophrenia" is a pheno*copy* not a genuine *phenotypic* expression of the schizophrenic genotype.

be too weak, etc.). But without at least some of the relevant risk genes, a "true" schizophrenic disorder would not develop.

One outgrowth of these studies was to sharpen the diagnostic distinctions between *infantile autism* and *childhood schizophrenia*. The research on high-risk factors showed that some children of schizophrenic parents developed problems in cognition and in relating to others early in life, but usually *not* within the first year or two. Gross speech and relational abnormalities occurring between birth and age three were now thought to be more likely signs of autism (Kolvin, 1971; Rutter, 1972); however, Barbara Fish (1975) described the two disorders as bands on an age continuum, such that childhood schizophrenia, with its hallucinations and formal thought disorder, represented the "after-age-five" band. Because both of these childhood conditions are rare (2 or 3 in 10,000), it was difficult to create samples large enough to conduct convincing family studies. Still, it appeared that children of a schizophrenic parent, were they to become ill in the early years, were more likely to do so after the age of five. Children with marked autistic signs below age three were more likely to have infantile autism and not to have schizophrenic relatives.

diagnostic distinctions between infantile autism and childhood schizophrenia

SHIFTING TIDES

General trends in child psychiatry during the 1970s were dominated by a diagnostic shift away from the organismic "biopsychological" model (espoused by many of the prominent child psychiatrists in the preceding decades, such as Lauretta Bender) and toward what was soon to become the *DSM* categorical approach, whereby the total psychopathology of a given patient is compartmentalized into symptomatic versus personality conditions. Theodore Shapiro has expressed serious concern to me about this contemporary trend, since it leads away from the more integrated way of thinking about psychopathology in children that characterized the earlier, pre-*DSM* generation.

DSM *categorical approach*

On a more positive note, there was greater enthusiasm for empirical studies based on large-enough samples of children to permit statistical analysis. René Spitz (1951) had inaugurated this trend in the 1950s at a time when many child psychiatrists, especially those with psychoanalytic training, were basing their impressions on small numbers of children. In England Michael Rutter was a leader in the domain of empirical studies (Rutter et al., 1975). Increasingly, child psychiatrists were specializing in making diagnoses and organizing treatment programs, many elements of which might then be carried out by nonmedically trained personnel: psychological testing by a psychologist; play therapy by therapists from any one of several disciplines, and so

enthusiasm for empirical studies

on. Treatment of children was becoming less psychoanalytically-oriented in the United States and correspondingly more focused on specific presenting problems. There was an increased willingness to use behavioral techniques, especially since conduct problems are common in any child psychiatry practice. Many in the field still avoided giving psychoactive medications to young patients, apart from those with attention-deficit disorder/hyperactivity or who had been hospitalized with early forms of schizophrenia.

tensions between the "Old Turks" and the "Young Turks"

Sometimes the tensions between the "Old Turks" and the "Young Turks" in this period of transition took on a comical aspect. I recall a young woman who was in supervision during the early 1970s as part of her training in child psychoanalysis. Her patient was a boy of 14 who was in treatment for his moodiness and disrespectfulness. Three of his close relatives were taking lithium for bipolar illness. Some months into the four-times weekly therapy, he struck a classmate with a bat after a trivial provocation, for which he was nearly expelled from school.

The supervisor, an elderly analyst from the "Old School," would address only the patient's dreams; she criticized the trainee's "preoccupation" with the boy's behavior as a "parameter" that detracted from the analysis. The trainee, recognizing the boy's impulsive aggression as an early sign of mania, finally prescribed lithium on the sly, never telling the supervisor (lest the latter consider her unready for graduation). Many trainees in child psychiatry (and in adult psychiatry, too) felt caught between tradition and change—between analytic therapy and behavioral/cognitive/pharmacological therapy. To adopt the new ways meant not only "breaking ranks" but also being seen as abandoning one's religion.

Preventive Psychiatry

high-risk studies

There was a positive synergism between the high-risk studies of the 1970s and efforts to develop a preventive psychiatry. Since it was now easier to identify which children were likely to develop serious emotional disturbance in the future, there was hope that early intervention could abort many such troubles or at least lessen the severity of illnesses that could not be prevented altogether. For this same high-risk research also demonstrated how strong the genetic and constitutional factors could be in certain children, some of whom were sadly destined to show a vulnerability beyond the powers of psychotherapy, skill training, or medications to extinguish. The interest in prevention and early intervention nonetheless led to better integration of psychological services in schools and communities and to more effective liaison between hospital staff and child psychiatrists. One example: It now became routine to permit mothers to spend the night in the hospital with children who were undergoing surgery or intensive medical pro-

integration of psychological services

cedures, by way of minimizing the children's fears of separation and of the trauma of treatments they were about to undergo.

The number of practitioners in the field of child psychiatry (here I also include those who work with adolescents) had grown substantially during the 1970s. In the United States, the largest organization of such specialists, The American Academy of Child and Adolescent Psychiatrists, now had some 5,000 members (as of this writing, it is about 6,000). Many of the specialists in adolescent psychiatry worked at residential treatment centers where long-term (one-to-two-year) stays were common, especially for adolescents who were chronically ill (schizophrenic), who had made repeated suicidal acts (many of these young people came from highly disturbed families, from which the young patients needed literally to be rescued), or who were beginning to show signs of delinquency. The Devereux Schools in Pennsylvania are examples. Despite the great need for such institutions, adverse economic factors put treatment centers of this type out of reach for most families in America. Residential care for disturbed adolescents was more readily available in the Netherlands, France, Switzerland, Australia, Germany, and the Scandinavian countries, though fiscal belt-tightening later affected these countries as well, rendering long-term care less affordable and less popular as an intervention.

*residential treat-
ment centers*

Chapter 20

NEO-DARWINIAN ETHOLOGY: A NEW

LOOK AT THE HUMAN "GAME PLAN"

human soul

Throughout most of recorded history we have viewed ourselves as being endowed with souls that were God-given and marked us as distinct from the "lower" animals—even as the many similarities between us and the animals were also recognized and acknowledged. Buddhist and Jewish cabalistic philosophers attributed souls to animals as well, but hierarchically, the human soul was something loftier: a culminating point in psychical development from which one's soul might slip back in the next life into one or another non-human species, depending on how poorly one had led the previous life. Human life had a purpose—and this purpose was understood primarily in religious terms.

social creatures

Made in God's image, our main objective was to reach His state of perfection, or rather to *aspire* to this perfection, for it was commonly accepted that we could approach this state only asymtotically. Even saints could not attain God's level. Implicit in this view was the understanding that we were, inescapably, social creatures; hence, the imperative to "Do Unto Others As You Would Have Them Do Unto You" is expressed in different ways by all religious systems. To this extent the key ingredient of life's purposefulness had a strong moral coloration: During our brief sojourn we were to live in harmony with our neighbors, thence to return to God's place—or the Other Place—in accordance with our personal history or *karma*.

"be fruitful and multiply"
religious belief

Adherents of the Judeo-Christian religions were further enjoined to "be fruitful and multiply"—not so much to fulfill our *biological* imperative to procreate as to increase our number and extol God's glory all the more. Hidden underneath this religious philosophy was, perhaps, a bit of practical wisdom. As the theologian Elaine Pagels reminds us (1988), as members of small desert tribes (where Judeo-Christian and Islamic religions got their start), being part of a populous group conferred powerful survival advantages over membership in a group that was weak in warrior sons. But this is getting ahead of our story. It was not of great importance whether people believed they were tainted with Original Sin (Christians), needed to perform good works in order to achieve redemption (Orthodox Jews), or could find the path to salvation solely through faith (certain Christian, Hasidic, and Buddhist groups). Whatever the particular content, it was religious belief that gave shape and purpose to human existence.

During the Enlightenment, the explanatory power of religion concerning the forces directing human life grew weaker and alternative theories gained ground. Some, like that of English philosopher Thomas Hobbes, were pessimistic. Hobbes (1651) saw life as "nasty, poor, brutish and short"—in short, humankind as self-centered and predatory. We might liken this to a "scorpions-in-a-bottle game plan." Other theories were more optimistic, like Rousseau's idealized picture of the noble savage, who would live in harmony with nature were it not for the "corrupting" influence of society. This view was echoed later by Russian anarchist Prince Kropotkin, who believed that humankind would pursue a purely *cooperative* Game Plan if left unassailed by government.[1]

Enlightenment theories

Shortly before the Enlightenment period Jean Senault (1649), neither pessimist nor optimist, was content to enumerate the "passions" (similar to the notion of basic drives). He took exception to Plato's concept of hierarchy, where (as we saw in Chapter 1) pride of place was given to lust (with anger as the second strongest). Senault saw anger as "more ardent, but it is not of durance" (p. 33). For Senault, *all* human passions are derivatives of love: "All the rest are but effects of her producing" (p. 38). His concept of love as the *primum mobile* [prime mover] is analogous to Freud's concept of *libido*. But neither Senault nor the philosophers of the Enlightenment carried us deeper toward our biological roots.

PSYCHOLOGICAL ETHOLOGY

It remained for Freud to bring us one step further down the epistemological staircase toward an understanding of the human game plan. With Freud we move from the plane of religion to that of psychology— and he *almost* took us to the still deeper plane of biology, for especially during his early years, his was a *biologically-informed* psychology. Recognizing the limitations of neurology in his time, after the turn of the century, Freud relied less on biological explanations, though he never did turn his back on biology.

Freud's biologically-informed psychology

The principal components of Freud's psychological model of human behavior are incorporated into his postulate of an Oedipus complex. Derived from his reading of anthropological treatises by Malinowski

Oedipus complex

---

[1] For further explication of the *cooperative* as opposed to the *defector* strategies within the "game" of Prisoner's Dilemma, see Nowak et al., 1995.

and others, this model depicts a basic human Game Plan for males: the ambition to supplant the father (killing him, for example, with the help of the "primal horde" of one's brothers) and thence to enjoy the sexual favors of the mother, as in the famous Sophoclean play. For females it is necessary to reverse the genders: In the "negative Oedipus," the girl unconsciously yearns for the sexual attentions of the father. Usually, though, she merely replaces the wife: There is no "sisterhood" poised to eradicate her rival.

incest

For the first three quarters of this century, wherever Freudian theory predominated, notions about human nature were patterned after the Oedipus complex. Corollaries were added: Incest became taboo since the father (focusing once again on the male) would punish a son's efforts to encroach upon his territory with (what else?) castration. To avoid this ghastly fate, the son eventually learns to suppress his incestuous desires, sublimating them into various socially acceptable activities and accepting as a substitute for mother—a gal (as in the old song) "just like the gal that married dear old Dad." Even Freud's pithy response to a reporter asking him, in his old age, what life was all about— Freud said, *"Liebe und Arbeit"* [love and work]—does not so much explain our essences as it does mark out the main compartments into which our activities can be assigned. Whatever our essence is, these are the agencies through which it is expressed.

EVOLUTIONARY ETHOLOGY

evolutionary biologists

In the 1970s a new stream of thought flowed into the discussion, its origin from a different source than psychiatry. The new assessment of what makes us as we are, and what we strive for at the most fundamental level, came from the neo-Darwinian (or "evolutionary") biologists and ethologists. In systems-analytic terms, evolutionary biologists work at the level of the genes—above which lie the levels of *brain biology* (e.g. Valzelli's theories on drives for sex and the various forms of aggression), *individual psychology* (Freud), *society* (our relationship to our fellow creatures), and the *cosmos* (our relationship to God and our place in the cosmos).

level of our DNA

Richard Dawkins

The neo-Darwinian biologists directed our attention down to the level of our DNA. If Freud showed us what Shakespeare had always known— "We are such stuff as dreams are made of"—Richard Dawkins showed us we are such stuff as genes are made of. Former student of Niko Tinbergen at Oxford, ethologist-zoologist Dawkins is the author of the *The Selfish Gene* (1976), in which he explained how animals, including humans, are at once "the most complicated and perfectly designed pieces of machinery in the known universe" *and* "survival machines—robot-vehicles blindly programmed to preserve the selfish molecules known as genes" (pp. ix–x). These ideas were not originated entirely by Dawkins.

Evolutionists had been saying something similar ever since Mendel laid down the fundamental laws of genetics late in the 19th century. But in recent years there had been a rebirth of interest in the field, to which the outcropping of books and articles in the 1970s gave testimony: Edmund Wilson's *The Insect Societies* (1971) and *Sociobiology* (1975); W.D. Hamilton's "Altruism and Related Phenomena" (1972); Robert Trivers' "Parent-Offspring Conflict" (1974); and J. Maynard-Smith's "The Theory of Games and the Evolution of Animal Conflict" (1974), *Theory of Evolution* (1975), and "The Logic of Animal Conflicts" (co-authored with J.R. Price) (1973).

As evolutionists are fond of quipping, looking at the world from the gene's point of view, a hen is an egg's way of making another egg. The germ-plasm is potentially immortal: The hen lives a brief moment and dies, but if she succeeds in breeding, the DNA of the egg she produces contains a replica of the strand that once produced her (and so on, back to the time chickens first appeared on earth, and so on into the future, to the extent that her particular progeny manage to attract mates and to make eggs). Natural selection concerns the myriad forces that impinge upon this process, causing some DNA strands to flourish in the game of replication and others to fail, with their corresponding family lines, or even the species, dying out.

natural selection

Males and females have different strategies for optimizing the chance of passing their genes into the next generation—genes that will be encased within their viable offspring. In *The Selfish Gene* (1976) Dawkins illustrated how this process could best be served, using examples from many different animals. These illustrations at the gene level shed light on what we observe at the level of human psychology, and by extension, of psychopathology. More importantly, this evolutionary approach elucidates much that has remained obscure concerning the forces that prompt us to behave as we do.

strategies for optimizing the chance of passing genes

A COMMENT ON COURTSHIP

The "mating game" as observed in many human cultures provides an excellent example of the biological and evolutionary aspects of behavior we generally view as psychological in nature. Typically there is a courtship period in which the man woos the woman, who often plays "hard to get." Each tends to worry about the fidelity of the other, but this is particularly true for women, since men more often stray from the marital bed than do women. The annals of literature, opera, drama, and ballet are replete with testimonies to this pattern; therefore, they must be reflections of some eternal verities about our species. In general, there do seem to be more Don Juans and Albrechts than Carmens and Mme. Bovarys. Are there clues from the gene level why this is so?

the "mating game"

To begin with, we are land mammals. As Dawkins reminds us, fertilization in land animals must take place inside the female's body,

land animals

where moisture can be maintained, lest the mobile element—the sperm—dry up. There is no such problem for fish. The male fish simply spews his sperm into the water in proximity to where the female is casting her eggs, fertilization taking place externally. In mammals, the need for internal fertilization creates a special problem for the female: She is literally "stuck" with the developing embryo, whereas the male is free to decamp, investing little time or energy, if he so chooses, in the rearing of his offspring. What makes the playing field even less "level" is the fact that females have a limited number of eggs during their reproductive lives, in comparison to the billions of sperm males produce during their reproductive careers (in our species the figure would approximate three trillion). In short, females are the more precious commodity, reproductively; males are more expendable.

internal fertilization

males are more expendable

In a social species like our own, males have evolved to take on the function of defending the tribe—often dying in the process. Considering how easily sons are replenished as long as there are adequate females for the few remaining males to impregnate, this is a small loss. A tribe with a hundred fertile females and one male can produce a hundred children in a year; in the reverse situation, only one child can be added to the tribe.

Extended maternal care is the norm among land animals; paternal care is more typically "catch as catch can" or negligible. But in humans, not only as social creatures but as a species for whom prolonged parental care is a necessity for the survival of the offspring, paternal investment is *not* negligible, especially where food is not easily available (as in temperate and cold regions). So the forces of natural selection have favored a situation where males experience *limerance* (i.e., falling in love and wishing to stay with the same mate throughout life) and also love their children. But if men are willing to invest fairly heavily in the process of child-rearing, they need to have some assurance that the children they are working to support do indeed carry their own, and not some other man's, genes. Hence the advantage of a long courtship—longer than nine months if possible—for if the future wife has not had sex with any other man during that long an interval, her children will also be his children. The genes he will be toiling to perpetuate will be (half) his genes. From the man's point of view, this is a fair bargain.

limerance

Dawkins' Typology of Mating

The history of human societies makes it abundantly clear, however, that not all men or all women pursue the same strategies for ensuring genetic survival into the next generation. Dawkins referred to the pattern that we see instead as an "evolutionarily stable state" (ESS). This state consists of a mixture that is "just right" for the maximal genetic

"evolutionarily stable state"

success of individuals within a communal group. Dawkins divided these strategic patterns into four types: for females, *coy* versus *fast*; for males, *faithful* versus *philanderer*. Next he submitted these variables to the logic of the "Gedank experiment": If, by way of ensuring their mates' fidelity, all women pursued the coy strategy and made their suitors wait a long time before granting them sexual favors, inevitably some men would be too impatient. Therefore, the first fast woman, who was not so fussy or slow to grant her favors, to enter the scene would whisk away the impatient men from the majority group of her coy sisters.

Unchecked, this scenario could in time dominate the picture: Fast women and philandering men would become the majoritarians. There would be a price to pay, though. Many hitherto fast women would begin to experience hardship at having to raise their children without the help of their still philandering men, who long ago left the scene in pursuit of other fast women. Faithful men, now at a premium, would begin to look very desirable; they would of course favor coy/patient/faithful women (in order to maximize the survival of *their* children, whose health and welfare would naturally be better served by a devoted, monogamous mother). *fast women and philandering men*

Over many generations, an ESS would establish itself: There would emerge, and persist with only modest changes, a certain proportion of men and women embodying each of the four strategies. We would expect to see relatively more coy women than faithful men—perhaps something on the order of five women out of six being coy; four out of six men being faithful. In real life the situation is more complex, since some men and women change from one predominant strategy to another as they pass through early and late stages of adult life. *an ESS would establish itself*

Evolution and Menopause

Because good mothering is more vital to the survival of a child than is good fathering, and because human children spend almost the first two decades of their life span more or less incapable of independent survival, natural selection would have also favored the survival of women whose menopause occurred at a particular age. This age limits the possibility of a child being born whose mother would be at risk of dying before the child were psychologically and occupationally independent, since such an outcome would be calamitous for the child's welfare (and for the continuance of its mother's genes). One must remember that we have inherited our genes from ancestors whose life span was far shorter than our own. It is only in the last 200 years (since medical knowledge could forestall disease such as smallpox and puerperal sepsis) of our million-year history that some women over 40 have had a reasonable chance of surviving long enough to rear a child to independence.

Attraction Through the Gene's Eye

*evolution and
female beauty*

Granted women ought to be choosy (with their 350–400 eggs/lifetime), in our species both sexes have reasons to be so. Though the deciding factors differ somewhat from culture to culture, the basic "game plan" is very similar. For example, evolutionary forces have inclined men to be attracted to, and to choose as sexual partners, females who show promise of fertility and good health (the latter being passed on, presumably, to their offspring). Facial and bodily symmetry, as it happens, are reliable indices of physical health. This is so throughout the animal kingdom and has been much studied in recent years (Etcoff, 1994; Howlett, 1993; Kirkpatrick & Ryan, 1991; Perrett et al., 1994).

There is evidence that the philosophical conundrum, What is beauty?, can be resolved in evolutionary terms, at least in relation to feminine beauty, by recognizing that men have been programmed to select as "beautiful" women with attributes that foster survival: Their fertility is made apparent by their youthfulness (i.e., they are somewhere between the ages of 15 and 45 and therefore fertile), by the dimpling of their cheeks (as happens after puberty), by their curvaceousness as manifested by a waist-to-hip-circumference ration of 0.7 or less (this "gynoid" fat distribution signals a pelvis ample enough to rear children [Ridley, 1993]), and by an ample bosom (suggesting a capability for nursing offspring adequately), along with the aforementioned symmetrical appearance.

*evolution and male
attractiveness*

Females' choice of males is also dictated by their prospects of being able to sire healthy offspring, but not necessarily of staying alive. Dawkins (1976) portrayed the male's dilemma in this way: Be drab and survive, though without offspring, or be attractive and replicate but get eaten up due to visibility. The flamboyant plumage of the male peacock is an example. Since the plumage renders the peacock more visible (and hence more vulnerable) to predators, it would seem to confer only disadvantages (apart from its esthetic appeal to humans, who of course play no role in the bird's life cycle). But because the male's *parental* function is minimal among peacocks, its early demise would not hamper the species' survival. The female peacock selects for male attractiveness because it signals association with healthy daughters and healthy, flamboyantly-plumaged sons—the latter helping to ensure the continuance of her line as they mature and attract females.

In our species the situation is different. Given the importance of the paternal role as protector and provider, males are potentially as valuable in their way as women are in theirs—or may even slightly overshadow their partners as to their accorded "value" in the breeding process. A powerful male (by virtue of wealth or high status), though drab in appearance, may be so much in demand as to make it worth-while for females to compete fiercely for his attention. It has not al-ways been the case in every culture that women dress more colorfully and attractively than men, but this is *usually* the case. Feminine beauty tends to promote upward social mobility, just as masculine wealth or power conduces to the affiliation with beautiful women—whose beauty, again, is unconsciously registered as an index of robust health that will be inherited by his children. From the standpoint of appearance, it is enough for a man to be symmetrical (thus healthy); he can be "drab" (i.e., not remarkably attired) and need not be strikingly handsome. If, in addition, he is the "faithful" type, his desirability will be very high—the counterpart of the attractive female whose personality is also one of fidelity and affiliativeness.[2]

the drab but desired male

Since in our species the "dating game" generally precedes the "mat-ing game," another set of personality characteristics have come into play: compassion, empathy, and assertiveness.

Empathy (the ability to recognize the other person's feeling state) is perhaps the key quality. Men who are deficient in empathic ability (and there are more men than women in this category) are severely disadvantaged in courtship: Such a man does not "read" the woman's signals as to whether she is eager for him to move a step closer in intimacy or whether the message is "go no further!" Both schizoid and sociopathic men are commonly poor in empathic ability: Some give up in defeat (and thus do not breed); others become aggressive, taking by force (via rape, for example) what they cannot win by normal court-ship. If they sire children in the process, the children will usually grow up fatherless and may be more at risk for antisociality, substance abuse, criminality, and incarceration, and a host of other "negatives" that lower their evolutionary "fitness" and their ability to pass their genes on to the next generation.

ETHOLOGY AND PSYCHOLOGY

Though the preceding comments give only a cursory glimpse of etho-logical research in the 1970s, hopefully they establish the importance of the evolutionist's way of thinking, if we are to develop an under-standing of human behavior that is more encompassing than (espe-cially) the non-biologically-based psychologies can provide. Suffice it

[2] Ethology helps us understand the failure of the Marxist experiment. Among the more egregious impositions by the State upon its populace was the refusal to reward persons who worked hard (flying in the face of natural human ac-quisitiveness) and the insistence, as in Maoist China, that women dress drably (flying in the face of women's natural desire to appear attractive).

to say that each reader of this book is the descendant of some 40,000 generations of humans, following our divergence from the higher apes (human DNA differs from that of chimpanzees in only 0.5% of its gene structure). What is more, each reader is the latest in long line of humans who, because of fortunate genetic combinations, were successful enough at courting, copulating, parenting, working, socializing, making alliances, and dodging enemies to have reproduced and, ultimately, to have created—each one of us living and breathing.

The Ethology of Incest

For a more specific example of how ethological research should stimulate us to rethink psychological theory, we might turn once again to the problem of incest. In *Totem and Taboo* (1913) Freud assumed that the desire for incestuous mating was driven by instinct—as though incest were a natural tendency against which persons in civilized communities had to struggle. This assumption was the essence of the Oedipus complex, which was seen as involving incestuous striving, castration anxiety, and eventual renunciation. As Marc Erickson (1994) points out, Freud's position was later contradicted by Edward Westermarck, whose observations had led him to conclude that family members living in close proximity (dwelling in the same household, for example) experienced *incest avoidance.* For Westermarck, such a stretch of early-life-together constituted a "sensitive period" (akin to the ethologist's concept of *critical periods* in development) that determined future behavior—in this instance: *dampening,* rather than fostering, any impulse toward incest. Ethological studies of animals from the 1960s and 1970s indicated that incest is rare. For example, among macaque monkeys, mother and son almost never mate but do remain involved in various altruistic behaviors, such as grooming and protection. Sibling and father-daughter incest is likewise rare in nature: These combinations were noted in only 4.5% of lions, 3.5% of gorillas, 1.5% of chimpanzees, and not at all in macaques. In line with Dawkins' speculations, females are more incest avoidant than males, probably because females expend more energy in the rearing process than males do and thus have more at stake. The survival advantages of genetic diversity constitute another evolutionary force that works against incest by minimizing the likelihood of adverse recessive genes uniting to produce offspring that could not survive or thrive. Natural selection would thus favor genes that promoted repugnance of such matings, thereby eventually eliminating from a species' gene pool those genes that would have promoted or even allowed incest.

Interestingly, prairie voles separated at birth and brought together later *did* mate incestuously, whereas those reared together did *not.* The tendency *not* to mate with close relatives is supported in nonhuman animals by "histocompatibility genes" that code for odors: Animals with the same, or nearly the same, odor *help* each other but do not *mate* with each other (Eibl-Eibesfeldt, 1989). A human parallel: In studies carried out in Israel in the 1970s, exogamy—the practice of marrying *outside* of one's tribe or clan—emerged as the norm in kibbutz-raised children, who came to regard each other as siblings, the more so if they had spent all of the first six years of life together.

In general, we can speak of two varieties of attraction: *familial,* which is directed *toward* kin and is characterized by attachment, incest-avoidance, and altruistic behavior; and *sexual,* which is directed *away* from kin and is a component of mating and parenting behaviors. These two types of attraction are, as Erickson (1994) emphasizes, evolutionarily *distinct.* In humans actual instances of incest occur in *inverse* proportion to the degree of secure bonding in the first six years. Since kin-recognition enhances, and incest reduces, reproductive viability, species-specific genetic programs have developed over the millennia to foster both kin-recognition and incest avoidance. In kin-recognition the pituitary hormones, vasopressin and oxytocin, play important roles.

two kinds of attraction

Reexamined in the light of modern ethology, Freudian theory of psychosexual development is in need of overhaul. The notions embedded within the Oedipus complex should be modified so as to reflect neo-Darwinian principles. If Little Hans was attracted to his mother, for example, the attraction was not prompted by sexual desire, only then to be deflected by castration threats from his turf-conscious father. Rather, the little boy was experiencing *kin-attraction* and bonding to his mother (no doubt reinforced by her desire to bond with her son). Little Hans might indeed wish for exclusive possession of, and endless attention from, his mother. These desires would inevitably conflict with his father's insistence upon attention, and sexual favors, from his wife. We can even hazard a guess that, at some point early in childhood, Little Hans made the association between his father's big "widdler" and his special entitlements, such as getting to sleep the whole night with mother, while Hans had to content himself with being read a bedtime story by her. This is not to deny that a boy naturally comes to place a high value on his penis and would not only fear losing it, but would quake at any threat that acquired the meaning of castration.

The point to be made here is that what Freud believed was a "universal" element in the construction of the human psyche is actually the product of the particularities of *culture.* There is indeed a universal incest taboo, and many cultures go to great length to reinforce it. But the prohibition is directed against an impulse that, according to ethological research, is seldom mobilized in siblings who were reared together during their formative years or in children raised during their first six years by their biological parents.

PART VI

Recent Trends: 1980-1996

INTRODUCTION

With respect to the past 15 years, one might argue that we are no longer in the realm of history, properly speaking: We have entered "current events." Just where the one concept shades into the other cannot be defined precisely: the two areas describe a "fuzzy set" with interconnected and blurred borders. I have chosen to say something about developments of these recent years because they are, after all, the culmination of our history, even as they set the stage for what will follow. Our recent progress, remarkable as it has been, will meantime recede into the past, becoming the material for future historians of psychiatry to ponder, pick over, and incorporate (or omit) in their essays.

Psychiatry and, along with it, psychiatric literature have grown exponentially in the past decade and a half. It would be no exaggeration to say that the weight of the books and articles of the past 15 years would easily tip the scale, even if all the books and articles of the preceding 1500 years were placed on the other pan. This trend toward massive productivity was well underway, as mentioned, after World War II. During Hitler's regime (1933–1945) Germany did not strive for creditable work in psychiatry, as evidenced partly by the expulsion of Jewish psychiatrists and psychoanalysts, partly via the crass politicization of the "ethnic" German psychiatrists who remained behind.

A similar kind of politicization corrupted psychiatry in Soviet Russia until well after World War II: Political disagreement was equated with having a "thought disorder" and was "treated" as a borderline type of "schizophrenia." Dissidents were sequestered in mental hospitals and zombified with chlorpromazine over months or years. German psychiatry regained respectability quickly after the war, under the leadership of such men as Huber in schizophrenia and Mitscherlich and Thomä in psychoanalysis. Russia has been slower to regain prestige, since her full participation in modern psychiatry awaited the fall of communism in the late 1980s.

Travel by jet plane has facilitated the cross-fertilization of ideas and has helped resolve (though not eradicate) terminological differences among colleagues from different countries and cultures. Perhaps more importantly, psychiatry is no longer a "plant" that grows only in Western Europe and North America; psychiatry is *everywhere*.

In the summer of 1995, the annual meeting of the American Psychiatric Association was attended by 10,000 psychiatrists from around the world. My own travels that year took me to Italy, Ireland, England, France, Greece, and China. In Athens there were simultaneous meetings of 5,000 psychologists and 600 adolescent psychiatrists and psychologists, where one could trade ideas with colleagues from Uruguay, Mozambique, Japan, Nigeria, Norway, South Africa, Australia, Russia, Romania, Egypt, Portugal. . . . This kind of interchange was scarcely possible even in the 1960s and 1970s, when the jets were not quite as fast or inexpensive. It is both inspiring and humbling for a psychiatrist from a "rich" country to learn what the field is like in a "poor" country—and to learn how colleagues in the poor countries often do better by their patients, though with much fewer resources at their disposal, than we do in the "developed" countries.

Comprehensive centers for the treatment of schizophrenic patients are to be found in Switzerland (Dr. Luc Ciompi's unit in Bern; Dr. Jules Angst's at the Burghölzli in Zürich), in Sweden (Stockholm's Beckomberga Sjukhuset), and in many other countries in Europe. In the United States, similarly comprehensive care and rehabilitation can be found at the Menninger Clinic in Topeka, Kansas, and at the Laureate Hospital in Tulsa, Oklahoma. But equally impressive is the Fountain House center, directed by Dr. M. Rashid Chaudery, in Lahore, Pakistan, where schizophrenic patients live with dignity—learning crafts, caring for their own needs, preparing their own meals, praying in their own mosque, and enjoying the entertainers who come from the city to dance and play music for them in their own small theater.

In the last few years, communication between colleagues has begun to move from the speed of the jet plane to the speed of light, as more and more practitioners and researchers have become interconnected via "fax," E-mail, and Internet. My task of describing how certain diagnostic terms are used around the world ("borderline personality," for example) was made easier, and accomplished almost instantaneously, by exchanges of fax mail from colleagues in Italy, Germany, France, Japan, and Sweden—a task that would have taken months, now resolved in a matter of days.

Chapter 21

BIOMETRICS, TAXONOMY, EPIDEMIOLOGY: PROGRESS IN MEASUREMENT

A new version of the American Psychiatric Association's *Diagnostic and Statistical Manual* (*DSM-III*) was published in 1980 (followed by a revised edition, *DSM-III–R*, in 1987). The authors of *DSM-III* aimed at achieving a greater inclusiveness of all possible psychiatric conditions and compatibility with the European-based *International Classification of Diseases* (*ICD*). Robert Spitzer, who was the editor in charge, and the other authors felt that not enough was known about the etiology of most psychiatric disorders to warrant an etiology-based taxonomy. Instead, their stance—and the descriptors utilized in the manual—was *atheoretical*. Another new feature of this edition of the manual was a *multiaxial* organization: Axis I delineated symptom-based disorders; Axis II, personality disorders; the remaining three axes identified medical conditions, severity of stressors, and the (best) level of psychological function during the preceding year.

DSM-III offered a mixture of both advantages and disadvantages. The conditions described (about 180 in all) allowed for fairly high inter-rater reliability because they were based on *categories* defined as distinctly as possible, with descriptors as objective as possible (they did not rely on inferential impressions, that is). This, in turn, facilitated both research and crosscultural comparisons. *DSM-III* was soon translated into many languages, as it became clear that the more serious symptom-based disorders, such as schizophrenia and mania, do not differ in their clinical presentation from one country to the next. Here *DSM-III* proved its utility, even though it was basically an American product.

The same could not be said of the personality disorders described in Axis II, however, for here the manual's *Americocentrism* showed

objective descriptors

crosscultural limitations and advantages

302 HEALING THE MIND

through undeniably. For example, the *magical thinking* ascribed to schizotypal personality is so common among the populations of countries like Haiti or Thailand as to artificially inflate the prevalence of this disorder, were one to rely only on *DSM-III* criteria.

Each personality disorder was defined by seven to nine descriptors, of which only four or five need be present to clinch the diagnosis. This system had advantages and drawbacks. An advantage: Persons who are exceptionally *vain* or exceptionally *power-hungry* may be equally *narcissistic;* they need not be vain *and* power-hungry. Here an either-or approach works well. A drawback: A patient could be diagnosed as *borderline* according to *DSM-III* but lack the three items *anger, self-damaging acts,* and *impulsivity;* yet this would be contrary to the diagnostic inclinations of most practitioners, who would not see this patient as borderline. Many patients who fulfill *DSM-III* criteria for borderline personality also meet criteria for several other personality disorders (Oldham, Skodol et al., 1992). This crossover effect can become a source of confusion; how best to resolve the confusion has itself been a controversial topic (which we take up again in Chapter 25 on personality disorders).

Despite their imperfections, *DSM-III* and *III-R* represent a laudable attempt to bring global unity to the field of psychiatric diagnosis. Among the relatively minor changes in *DSM-III–R* were the omission of a few older diagnoses and the addition of a few others. "Body dysmorphic disorder" was one of the additions: It was placed in the section on somatic disorders, even though it has much in common with obsessive-compulsive disorder. As Spitzer (1994) has acknowledged, political considerations affected the final form of the manual: Pressure from feminists led to the exclusion of "paraphilic coercive disorder" (basically, *rape)* from *DSM-III–R* on the grounds that its classification as a mental disorder might be used by defense lawyers to argue for "diminished capacity" (see Chapter 28 on forensic psychiatry for further discussion). Similarly, "premenstrual syndrome" was recast as "late luteal phase dysphoria" and relegated to an appendix; "masochistic personality" was transformed into "self-defeating personality" so as not to stigmatize women.[1]

political consider-
ations

In the most recent edition, *DSM-IV* (1994), the personality disorders in the *DSM-III* appendix (sadistic and self-defeating) are omitted altogether, as is passive-aggressive personality. These changes constitute a

DSM-IV: *deletions,*
additions, diagnos-
tic changes

---

[1] Freud and the pioneer generation of analysts tended to view masochism and submissiveness as women's lot, though Helene Deutsch gave examples of male as well as female masochists in her papers of 1930 (reprinted in her 1965 book). More recently, Baumeister (1988) conducted a study (based on respondents to advertisements in sex-oriented magazines) showing that male masochists (in the sexual sense of seeking humiliation or pain in sex) out-

sweeping under the rug of politically uncomfortable entities; obviously the many people who have these disorders did not suddenly disappear. As for the positive aspects of *DSM-IV,* it achieved compatibility with the *ICD-10* and added a number of useful diagnoses, including Asperger's syndrome (autism without language disturbance), the paraphilia of telephone scatologia, and bipolar-II disorder (mild euphorias with pronounced depressions). Actually, *DSM-IV* has over 330 diagnostic entities, compared to 210 in *DSM-III.* The term *organic mental disorder* was dropped from the *DSM-IV,* partly because it has become increasingly meaningless as the neurophysiological roots of more and more conditions have been discovered, and partly because it conduced to stigmatizing mentally ill patients. The diagnosis of *neurosis,* still utilized by psychoanalysts, was omitted in the recent *DSM* editions, replaced largely by various anxiety disorders and some of the personality disorders (such as avoidant, obsessive-compulsive, and histrionic—the latter a change of term from the older *hysteric).*

THE IMPACT OF LIFE EVENTS

Though a connection between certain stressful life events and psychiatric disorders had been discerned for a long time—recall Briquet's observations about hysteria in the 1850s—methodical research in this area is relatively new. A number of studies in the 1980s focused on the correlation between certain antecedent stressors (job loss, death of a spouse) and suicide (Cross & Hirschfeld, 1986), depression (Benjaminsen, 1985), and personality disorders (Seivewright, 1987). Swedish psychiatrists Gyllenhammer and Börstedt (1987) noted an inverse relationship between adverse life events and endogenous depression (i.e., the more "endogenous," the less likely there had been antecedent life events). In these studies the spotlight was on traumatic experiences at any point in the life cycle that stemmed from sources *other than* one's original caretakers. Divorce, job loss, and death of a spouse were among the most pathogenic stressors.

As the frequency of incest and parental physical and psychological abuse became more widely appreciated (at least for the American population) in the early 1980s, a large literature grew up around these topics: the traumata inflicted on children by their parents or other close relatives, and the psychiatric conditions that seemed related as the sequelae. Judith Herman's book on father-daughter incest appeared in

incest and physical abuse

numbered their female counterparts. As for the more subtle type of psychological masochism (repetitive choice of mates who subject one to distress and humiliation, aside from the sexual sphere), there is reason to believe that men and women are about equally apt to show these characteristics, though no surveys have specifically examined the subject.

1981; Bessel van der Kolk's outstanding article on the compulsion to repeat earlier traumata was published in 1989. Diana Russell, who emigrated to the United States from South Africa, completed her epochal epidemiological study of incest (broadly defined: any relative, any form of inappropriate contact) in the San Francisco area in 1986.

abuse and border-line personality disorder

Shortly thereafter, Zanarini, Gunderson, Marino, Schwartz, and Frankenberg (1989) showed how a history of incest was revealed in the background of patients with borderline personality disorder more frequently than those with any other personality disorder. Though this finding does not prove a causative relationship, it has been confirmed in many other studies and strongly suggests one. The trauma of incest probably accounts for the marked excess of females (in American populations) with borderline personality disorder (especially those requiring hospital care). How this association between incest and borderline pathology differs from the European experience is discussed in the upcoming section on psychoanalysis.

The complete list of traumata relevant to psychiatry is very long and its literature correspondingly vast, including, as it does, such diverse events as surviving the Holocaust, witnessing the traumatic deaths of loved ones, surviving accidents, war, terrorist attacks, and natural disasters (an example of the latter: Beverly Raphael's book [1986] on the fire near Adelaide, Australia).

SUICIDE

In Western Europe and in the United States throughout the first half of this century, those at greatest risk for suicide were white males in their fifties and sixties, especially if living alone. The situation changed during the late 1960s, such that by 1975 the risk in older males, though still high, was decreasing, while for males in their late teens and twenties the risk was tripling or quadrupling (Solomon & Murphy, 1984). These trends have persisted through the 1980s and into the 1990s.

crosscultural causes

There has also been some shift in risk groups within various countries. Suicide had always been common in Hungary, Denmark, Sweden, and Japan, of intermediate frequency in the United States (11/100,000/year, on average), and low in Italy. By the 1990s, suicide in adolescents and young adults was highest in New Zealand. This puzzled many observers, whose best guess as to why New Zealand had earned this dubious distinction was that intense pressure was placed on young men to be "macho" and successful in the sanctioned mayhem of rugby (their national sport) as well as in the ability to guzzle huge quantities of beer. Those who failed to excel in these manly arts, particularly if they were, in addition, homosexual, often succumbed to serious depression and suicide.

QUESTIONNAIRES HERE AND ABROAD

Though questionnaires designed to make more reliable assessments were in use well before the 1980s, at first they were comparatively few in number and usually addressed only major diagnostic issues. Examples were the Beck Depression Inventory (Beck, Ward, & Mendelson, 1961) and the Hamilton Rating Scales (1960), also for depression. Luborsky's Mental Health/Sickness Rating Scale (1962) became the precursor for the widely used Global Assessment Scale (Endicott, Spitzer, Fleiss, & Cohen, 1976), now incorporated into the recent editions of the *DSM*. These global scales, "anchored" to cover the whole range from death by suicide to ideal mental health, have proven immensely useful in clinical work; since disagreement between raters is usually very small (less than 5%), they clearly describe behavioral variables that are readily identifiable by most practitioners.

global scales

Several scales had been developed for the more precise evaluation of personality: Eysenck's Maudsley Inventory (1959), Millon's Multi-axial Personality Inventory (1977), and Gough and Heilbrun's Adjective Checklist Manual (1983 revision of an earlier manual), which contains 300 words that capture much of the variation in personality type. Zung had developed a scale for anxiety disorders (1971) and Horowitz, Schaefer, and Hiroto (1977), a questionnaire for eliciting important life events as potential psychological stressors.

In the past 15 years there has been a virtual mushrooming of instruments, interviews, questionnaires, and self-rating scales of every variety, covering the most focused and minute clinical areas. With the greatest possible precision these measurement devices elicit information pertaining to diagnosis, personality subtype, substance abuse record, history of parent/caretaker abuse (including incest), family history of mental illness, defense mechanisms, work and sexual histories, suicide risk (Linehan, 1981), tendency to schizophrenic thought patterns (Johnston & Holzman, 1979), and so forth. In part this proliferation is a reflection of the shift in psychiatry over the past 20 years away from the inferential approach of psychoanalysis and toward more objective means of evaluation in which agreement between several observers, rather than the impressions of one very private observer, has become the standard. In part, the change also reflects a heightened interest among clinicians for answers to specific problems ("Does the patient have a dissociative disorder?"), whereas the aim of psychological testing in earlier years was to ascertain a broader picture—a complete characterological evaluation, for example (Clarkin & Sweeney, 1990). Needless to add, the now more widespread availability and use of the computers has made it

specialty scales

attitudinal shift

feasible—and, hence, attractive—to develop instruments that facilitate both accuracy in evaluation and communication among researchers all around the world.

American measurement irony

Although questionnaires are hardly the exclusive province of American psychiatrists and psychologists, the United States has achieved a preeminence in this field. There is a certain irony in this: America has the most abysmal record of violence—child murder (upwards of 2,000 a year), murder in general (10/100,000/year), serial sexual homicide, physical abuse of children, incest, and rape—of any industrialized country—*and* the most sophisticated, energetic teams of epidemiologists to track all this down and record it. It is only fair to add that America has also developed many of the best teams of mental health professionals to treat and restore the survivors and victims of all this violence.

non-American epidemiology and childhood sexual abuse

Among the epidemiological teams outside the United States that study the issue of childhood sexual abuse (CSA), the Swiss group at the Burghölzli Clinic in Zürich has done outstanding work. Cecile Ernst, Jules Angst, and Monica Földenyi (1992) from this group have tested and followed up some 591 subjects, beginning in 1978. Using a narrow definition of CSA (in contrast to Diana Russell's [1986] broad definition, whereby cousin-cousin, sib-sib cases were also included), a history of CSA was noted in 11.5% of the females; 3.5% in the males. Their figures are more in line with other data from England, Germany, and New Zealand. Incest was about as common a form of CSA in Swiss females as was molestation by a stranger. The instances of males who reported CSA consisted of homosexual contacts outside the family. High-risk factors for CSA included coming from a broken home, low parental support, punitive early environment, and chronic illness in the mother. The only problems the Swiss investigators could identify that seemed definitely related to the CSA history were described as "persisting sexual problems" as the affected subjects reached their thirties. There was a trend toward heightened incidence of suicidal acts, but no increase in the incidence of anorexia or bulimia (as is reported in a number of other studies). Ernst et al. concluded:

> [The] relative inoffensiveness of CSA for later mental health may be a consequence of the rarity of severe abuse among our subjects. . . . Women who have experienced severe abuse [father-daughter incest with intercourse at early age and over prolonged periods] . . . will cluster in clinical samples [such as hospitalized borderline patients] but seem to constitute a small minority of the population. (p. 299)

It may be that the Zürich study is more representative of the CSA situation in Europe than in America—where, I suspect, the problem really is greater, at least in the current generation.

As for epidemiology in general, the U.S. position in the vanguard of this specialty is hardly limited to the study of traumatic life events. As the outstanding book by Harvard epidemiologist Ming Tsuang and his collaborators testifies, excellent studies have been conducted in every area of psychiatry (Tsuang, Tohen, & Zahner, 1995). The epidemiology of a broad spectrum of conditions described in *DSM-IV* has been investigated by Allen Frances and his coworkers (1995) at Duke University and at New York State Psychiatric Institute. Mental disorders in the United States have been tracked by Dohrenwend and his colleagues (1980), who have also examined the impact of socioeconomic class (Dohrenwend et al., 1992). Another panoramic view of mental illness can be found in the work of Darrel Regier and Lee Robins (1991).

comprehensive range of U.S. epidemiology

The epidemiological work by Darrel Regier and his colleagues has been especially impressive and important in determining the general *prevalence* of mental disorders in the United States. His team interviewed over 18,000 persons in five major cities, using a diagnostic questionnaire based on *DSM-III*. Among their main conclusions (Regier et al., 1988): 15.4% of interviewees over age 18 fulfilled criteria for at least one episode of alcohol or drug abuse or other mental disorder during the month preceding the interview. As expected, men had higher rates of substance abuse and antisocial personality; women, higher rates of affective, anxiety, and somatization disorders.

prevalence of mental disorders

In response to these findings, some investigators commented that it seemed unrealistic to assume that one-sixth of the population had a significant emotional disorder. Yet Regier's figures are not surprising in the context of previous epidemiological findings: 1% of the population suffers from a schizophrenic disorder, 0.5% are bipolar-manic, 2.5% have recurrent depressions, 1% are mentally retarded, and several percent are alcoholic, severely phobic, anorectic or bulimic, antisocial, schizotypal, borderline, etc. With these sobering statistics in mind it becomes clear that a one-in-six estimate is quite reasonable. Focusing on posttraumatic stress disorder (PTSD), Breslau and her coworkers (Breslau, Davis, Andreski, & Peterson, 1991) found that four of ten young adults in Detroit had been exposed to traumatic events and about one-fourth of them had developed symptoms of PTSD (yielding a lifetime prevalence of 9%). People who had a family history of anxiety or who scored high on "neuroticism" were more likely to develop PTSD in the aftermath of trauma than those lacking these factors.

posttraumatic stress disorder

In general the biometric and epidemiological research of the past 15 years, greatly enhanced in its power through the now widespread use of computers, has built a more solid foundation for psychiatry as a scientific endeavor. Psychiatry has always been, and because of the "human factor" always will be, partly science, partly art. But thanks to the precision afforded by this research, psychiatry has become a more scientific art than ever before.

Chapter 22

PSYCHOANALYSIS: A WORK
IN PROGRESS

Psychoanalysis celebrated its centennial as a *metapsychology* and as a treatment method sometime during the 1990s (for there was no exact moment when, in Freud's mind, it was born). As many have remarked, psychoanalysis is a "work in progress," ever changing, ever being remolded by new material from within the field as well as by data emerging from the biological sciences. As always, practitioners vary in their willingness to incorporate new ideas and new facts. The followers of Jung and Melanie Klein tend to be slow in integrating newer findings in the fields of biology and genetics. Others, such as Joseph Sandler and Peter Fonagy in London and Otto Kernberg and John Gunderson in the United States, are more involved in, and open to, new research.

As the efficacy of cognitive-behavioral and psychopharmacological technique continues to be demonstrated in the treatment of various conditions (phobia, obsessive-compulsive disorder, borderline personality disorder, panic disorder), the territory on the psychopathologic map occupied by psychoanalysis as the treatment of choice has inevitably shrunk. To treat schizophrenia in the 1990s solely with analysis, eschewing medications and social-skills training, would be regarded by most as malpractice. Psychoanalysis has also come under much criticism—sometimes from those who are gratuitously hostile to it (Hans Eysenck, Jeffrey Masson, the journalist Janet Malcolm), sometimes from those who point out, quite correctly, that other, less expensive methods work better for certain conditions.

shrinking of the psychopathologic map

The sheer logistics of analysis create a problem. In the United States, for example, there are some 4,000 medical analysts and again as many non-medical analysts. This is a small army when pitted against 250 million people: one analyst for every 32,000 people. If each analyst treated patients in the "classical" five-times-a-week mode and could

logistical impossibilities

thus handle eight patients a week, one person in 4,000 could become an analytic patient! But the number of persons seeking psychiatric help is far greater than that, and the number who could afford so intensive a program ($24,000–$36,000/year), vanishingly small.

psychoanalytic parameters

Instead, as noted in connection with the 1970s, many analysts see those patients desiring classical analysis on a less frequent schedule and work with still others (otherwise analyzable patients as well as patients who are too fragile for unmodified analysis, such as those with borderline personality disorder) in an "analytically informed" manner, utilizing some of the classical analytical techniques, adding supportive or other measures along the way. At this point in time, few analysts maintain a practice given over solely to strict psychoanalysis for these reasons. This change has led to expressions of concern about the fate of psychoanalysis as a therapy as we approach the 21st century.

PSYCHOANALYSIS ABROAD

Eastern European popularity

Ironically, as psychoanalysis in a rich country like the United States has lost clientele and prestige, its popularity has grown enormously in a number of comparatively poor countries, such as the former Russian satellite states of Hungary and the Czech Republic. For decades, until the fall of communism in 1989, psychoanalysis was suppressed, since freedom of thought was inimical to the smooth running of a communist regime. Analytic treatment was carried out in secret and with great trepidation, lest a patient turn out to be an informer. As Prague analyst Michael Šebek has recounted (1994), analysts had to see their patients on the sly in their own homes, and were loath to address a patient's transference anger, less this stir up hostility that might incite the patient to complain to the authorities.

With the communist millstone off their necks, Czech analysts have been enjoying a renaissance: Today there are more psychoanalysts in training in Prague than in the seven-times more populous New York City. And at 100 Koruna (about $3) a session, the financial hurdle is not insurmountable. Before World War II, Poland, Czechoslovakia, and Hungary had strong psychoanalytic movements; the soil was already prepared for regrowth. It remains to be seen whether the freedom of thought that psychoanalysis represents will give it a foothold even in post-communist Russia, given that throughout the Soviet phase of Russian history psychoanalysis was basically outlawed.

European orthodoxy

In France, apart from the Lacanians and other splinter groups, Freudian psychoanalysts are typically more orthodox in their practice than are many American analysts, and more open to ideas stemming from philosophy than from the neurosciences. There are exceptions: Daniel Widlöcher, who directs an inpatient unit at the Salpêtrière Hospital, is concerned with serious forms of depression. He and his colleagues, Yves Lecrubier and Robert Jouvent, developed a scale for the precise measurement of psychomotor retardation. Philippe Jeammet, past president of the International Society for Adolescent Psychiatry, runs a residential treatment center for adolescents in Paris and has written extensively on anorexia nervosa (Jeammet, Jayle, & Terrasse-Brechon, 1984). Serge Lebovici, past president of the International Psychoanalytic Association, has made important contributions to the understanding of the mother-infant relationship, furthering the application of psychoanalysis to children and adolescents.

Cultural differences between the European continent and the United States may help account for some of the differences in what analysts in the two regions mean by such terms as *aggression* and *trauma*. In 1897 Freud had spoken of the "instinctive cruelty" of the infant, and in his *Three Essays* of 1905 he described an infantile (pregenital) aggression that was bound eventually with the libido but initially existed independent of sexual activity. Here Freud used the term *Bemaechtigungstrieb:* the drive toward possession (which the French call *la pulsion d'emprise,* the urge toward possessive control over the other). As Bergeret (1984, 1994) makes clear in his monographs on "Fundamental Violence," the libido was seen as the primary motivating force; the Oedipus complex, as the "nuclear complex" of psychic organization. These notions could be applied to the aggression exhibited by adults engaged in war, or to the fantasies Freud described in his 1919 essay, "A Child Is Being Beaten." In this work, Freud drew attention to the fantasies of certain patients, in which some other child was being beaten, for what turned out to be the guilt over sexual desires toward the parent: "This being beaten is now a convergence of the sense of guilty and sexual love" (p. 184). Further on Freud expressed the view that infantile sexuality, "which is held under repression, acts as the chief motive force in the formation of symptoms; the essential part of its content, the Oedipus complex, is the nuclear complex of neuroses" (p. 204).

Despite the horrors of two European world wars and of Stalin's depopulation of his own countrymen, there seems to be less naked aggression in European everyday life (during peacetime) compared with what Americans witness, if not in their everyday lives, at least in the newspapers and media reports. At all events, the term *trauma*, when used by European analysts (Jeammet, in Paris; Ladame, in Geneva; Scarso, in Torino), refers generally to the inevitable disruptions and difficulties children encounter during the developmental years—including the years during which they grapple with the shifting loves, disappointments, and aggressive feelings of the oedipal stage. The death

the "trauma" of developmental milestones

*trauma as physical
brutality*

of a parent early in life also constitutes a *trauma,* as does being reared (or more likely, neglected) by a seriously depressed parent.

These are really metaphorical traumata, however, very different in quality from the all too physical traumata of being beaten with an electrical cord by one's mother, having one's ribs broken by a caretaker enraged at one's crying, or having to submit to incest. Few European analysts encounter patients who have been subjected to such experiences of parental malice. Most American and Australian analysts, however, encounter seriously traumatized patients in their own practices and, hence, tend to reserve the term *trauma* for those truly shattering experiences. My own bias inclines toward the latter usage, partly because of my American background; partly because I am aware that, etymologically, trauma (from the Greek word *titrosko:* to wound) has much more violent connotations than are suggested by witnessing parental sex or having a depressed mother.

*differing definitions
of aggression and
trauma*

Considerations of this kind probably also account for the preference of analysts in France and Italy to use the term *borderline,* as do Bergeret and Kernberg, to refer to a level of mental organization intermediate between neurotic and psychotic. Although patients whose outbursts of rage and self- or other-directed violence would qualify them as *DSM* "borderlines" exist in these countries, they are far fewer in number. Hence the Bergeret definition reflects their clinical experience. The "borderline" patients of Professors Rovera and Scarso in Torino and Dr. Bertolli in Milan are, for the most part, young males with avoidant or obsessional personalities, or with severe social phobia/agoraphobia. They have been less traumatized (in the literal sense) than typical American borderline patients and are more routinely amenable to modified psychoanalytic interventions.

*European version of
"borderline"*

German psychoanalysts from the generation after the Third Reich have been particularly attentive to the subject of violence and aggression. There are now two main psychoanalytic groups in Germany: the *Deutsche Psychoanalytische Vereinigung* [German Psychoanalytic Association] and the *Deutsche Psychoanalytische Gesellschaft* [German Psychoanalytic Society]. Helmut Thomä and the late Alexander Mitscherlich represent the *Vereinigung.* Mitscherlich is especially known for his monograph (1982) on aggression, a book that is more philosophical than clinical, in which he makes the point that, in general, "cruelty is the gaining of pleasure through the suffering of the tortured persons," and that "torture victims are not *others,* not a foreign race. To a greater or lesser extent, all of us can be seduced into tormenting our fellow man. . . . The wellspring of aggression is a stream that flows *in* us, that belongs to our very nature" (pp. 99–101) [Author's translation].

*post-Third Reich
views of aggres-
sion*

Mitscherlich expresses this perspective not to exculpate German actions during the Nazi period, but rather to quell any tendency to smugness on the part of those who feel they could never behave similarly under any circumstances. He sees the passion for destructiveness (*Zerstoerungsleidenschaft*) as a human drive—one that seems to be more powerful than the forces of our *culture,* since it erupts so often despite the efforts of culture to suppress its outbreaks (a view similar to that espoused by Freud in *Civilization and Its Discontents.* Mitscherlich's comments pertain to what Valzelli (1981) spoke of under the heading of "irritable aggression": not so much a basic drive like hunger, but a mechanism, latent in our neurophysiology, capable of being awakened in most (but probably not in all) people under conditions of menace, real or imaginary, that threaten the survival of oneself or one's group.

aggression as a human drive

Another important contribution of the *Vereinigung* comes from the work of Helmut Thomä and his colleague Horst Kächele in Ulm on the psychoanalytic process (Kächele, 1988; Kächele & Thomä, 1995). These authors feel the time has come to "move beyond a subjective perspective in which all theoretical positions are equal in therapeutic potency" (p. 112). Expanding on the suggestion by Merton Gil et al. (1968) to use tapes in psychoanalytic research, Kächele and Thomä have amassed thousands of tape-recorded hours (from initial interviews, short- and long-term therapy, psychoanalytic sessions), which make it possible for non-participants to register their impressions as to what was taking place between analyst and patient, what "phase" of the work was in force, and the major themes. Kächele and Thomä emphasize that the inclusion of uninvolved third parties is essential and decisive in the testing of theories.

recording and observing psychoanalysis

The work of the Ulm school (which now has collaborators in Sweden, Austria, Switzerland, and the United States) should be able to help resolve such issues as are embedded in the Kernberg debate about the relative merits of Kernberg versus Kohut. According to a group of clinicians at Menninger's, for example, who work with borderline patients, Kohut's approach to their treatment may be better understood as a type of supportive, rather than strictly analytic, therapy. Leonard Horwitz, Glen Gabbard and their colleagues (1996) draw attention to Kohut's view that borderline patients "suffer from a failure to develop soothing-holding introjects," for which reason the "primary curative factor is the patient's experience of being symbolically held and soothed by the therapist, compensating for the deficient parenting experiences of early development" (p. 12).

Kernberg versus Kohut

soothing versus analyzing

In contrast, Kernberg's approach with borderline patients, though not devoid of supportive elements, is clearly a predominantly analytic one. For example, Kernberg would focus on the borderline patient's hostility and negative transference at the very outset—via candid confrontation and discussion—all within the framework of technical neutrality (1975). Kernberg also disputes Kohut's contention that the narcissistic personality represents fixation at an early stage of development. Kernberg views this abnormal personality as the outgrowth of pathological ego-superego structures, in turn arising out of pathological object relations.

The resolution of this debate is necessarily complex, since both theoretical and practical questions are involved. From a purely theoretical standpoint, Kernberg's is the more comprehensive formulation, embracing constitutional and traumatic as well as (pathological) parent-child factors. From a purely clinical standpoint, the question becomes: Does one or the other approach succeed with a greater percentage of the borderline patients one is likely to encounter in one's clinical work? Given the cost and complexity of controlled studies, a definitive answer will not soon be forthcoming.

At present, it appears that at least a partial answer lies in finding the balance between *soothing/holding* and *expressive/interpretive* (psychoanalytical) interventions. The phase of the therapeutic work is also important. Thus, with certain borderline patients the optimal balance may tilt toward the soothing approach; with others, the more strictly analytical. The optimal therapeutic stance itself may shift between one and the other polarity during the usually quite lengthy course of treatment. Wallerstein (1995) has commented on the way in which non-interpretive, supportive interventions—even in a classical three- or four-times-a-week psychoanalysis—appear to lead to solid structural change. This finding contravened the earlier belief that structural change could come about *only* from insight-oriented analytic therapy. But the methods utilized by Kächele and Thomä, and currently by Kernberg and his collaborators in New York (both groups utilize audio- and videotaped sessions and ratings by neutral observers) may ultimately provide a clearer understanding of (1) what "is" psychoanalytic process, (2) how many supportive elements (wittingly or unwittingly supplied) occur in typical analytic therapy, and (3) which approaches work best with which diagnostic subgroups of patients.

structural change via supportive techniques

Representing the *Gesellschaft* (currently headed by Michael Ehrmann), Christa Rohde-Dachser has written extensively on ego psychology and borderline patients. Her book on the borderline syndrome (1983), which is an excellent synthesis of contributions from many experts in this area (Kernberg, Wolberg, Zetzel, Mahler, Kohut, Winnicott, Giovacchini), focuses primarily on higher functioning borderline patients, such as those described by Bergeret and Kernberg, for whom psychoanalytically-oriented therapy is relevant and well-suited. Her remarks would be less applicable to the often severely traumatized borderlines meeting *DSM* criteria, whom clinicians, especially in the United States and Australia, regularly encounter in the present generation. Her recommendations weave together the impressions of the main analytic investigators:

German views of borderline pathology

One must avoid weakening any further the relatively healthy part of the patients' defenses, avoid increasing the permeability of their Ego-boundaries or steering their attention overly much toward primary process material. . . . The goal in treating borderline patients lay in the removal of the Ego-disturbance and in the amelioration of their Ego-function, not in the stimulations of regressive unconscious material. (pp. 194–5) [Author's translation]

treatment recommendations

Rohde-Dachser also recommends adhering to certain guidelines in the structuring of the sessions toward helping the patient develop a better relationship with reality; providing the patient with substantial information about the nature of the illness; interrupting any prolonged silences fairly quickly; giving reassurance that the therapist respects the patient's integrity and that the therapist's adherence to the rule of abstinence (i.e., not giving direct gratification to the patient's wishes) does not signify a rejection (*Ablehnung*); careful tracking of the split-off aspects of the patient's emotional life with special attention to the meanings behind acting out the negative transference, and so on. These guidelines constitute a step in the direction taken by Kernberg and his associates (Clarkin et al., 1992; Kernberg, Selzer, Koenigsberg, Carr, & Applebaum, 1989), who have developed a manual for structuring the analytically-oriented psychotherapy of patients with borderline personality organization.

PSYCHOANALYTIC FLEXIBILITY AND EXPANSION

Though controversy still exists concerning the degree to which deviations from classical analytic technique can be justified, psychoanalysts in the 1980s and 1990s have become less rigid and more open to "parameters," especially on behalf of their more fragile patients. There is greater willingness to prescribe (or to have colleagues in psychopharmacology prescribe) medications when the customary target symptoms are present. When conflicts arise over the advisability of medication, they usually concern patients with depression. In contrast to schizophrenia and mania, where there is no longer much debate about the necessity of pharmacological intervention, depression can often be remediated with psychotherapy just as well as with antidepressants.

deviations from classical analytic technique

In the 1980s a number of analytically-oriented residential centers were reluctant to use even antidepressants, which led to litigation on the part of several patients who had been hospitalized for depression. Their claim, which had much merit, was that they could have achieved symptom relief more expeditiously if antidepressants had been used. By the mid-1990s there is nearly universal agreement about the indi-

concessions to the use of medication

cations for medication in these situations. And there is the added fact that, in the United States especially, the emphasis on short-term hospitalization has become so widespread that the notion of months-long residential treatment of a seriously depressed patient—that did *not* include medication—has truly been rendered of historical, if not antiquarian, interest.

In the 1990s several clinicians trained in Kohutian self psychology have made impressive applications of this approach to the treatment of depression and of (*DSM*-type) borderline patients. For example, Joan Lang (1995) uses a modified version of the principles of self psychology to work with suicidal patients. The goal is to help patients achieve a kind of *self-restoration,* via the therapist's empathic stance, enabling them to escape the confining bounds of their pessimistic world view and preoccupation with the two or three figures from early life who may have exerted traumatizing influences. Her technique aims not only at increasing patients' adaptive capacities, but also at engendering a measure of *spirituality* to help them rise above the troublesome nature of their past. Through this larger perspective, they learn to differentiate between what they experienced as the trust-*shattering* aspects of the original family and the trust-*promoting* qualities of many benign persons in the present (including the therapist). Therapy directed toward enlarging patients' psychological worlds, helping them to trust— to live *with* and *for* others—embodies some of the same goals of religion, placing Lang's technique at the crossroads between psychotherapy and religion (of which I will have more to say at the end of this book).

The topic of narcissism continued to occupy the attention of psychoanalysts throughout the 1980s and 1990s. Belgian psychologist Nicolas Duruz (1981) discussed the differences between Kernberg's usage of the term in its *pathological* sense—a grandiose self, defending against aggressively invested and primitive self- and object-images— and Kohut's more *normative* usage of narcissism as central to the experience of self-cohesion:

> With his concept of the *selfobject,* [Kohut accounted for the] identity of the individual who experiences himself as alive, in harmony with himself, and who possesses in himself the source of his self-esteem by means of *transmuting internalizations.* (p. 62)[1]

The central issues concerning narcissism, in all its varied and overlapping uses, are discussed with still greater clarity in several articles by Arnold Cooper, a past president of the American Psychoanalytic Association (1984, 1985, 1989).

Kohutian treatment: Joan Lang

Kernberg's vs. Kohut's concept of narcissism

---

[1] We have commented earlier on Kohut's tendency to obscure his own message via unnecessary neologisms: for *selfobject* one can usually read *mother*.

The phenomenon of masochism continues to engender much attention within the psychoanalytic community (despite having come under fire for political reasons). Usually applied to patients who paradoxically (and unconsciously) seek *humiliation* and the *subjugation of self,* masochism of this sort can be found with equal frequency among men as among women. The underlying dynamics depend, to a large extent, upon one's general level of integration. Better integrated ("neurotic") masochistic patients are usually dealing with a continuing *need to submit*—a pattern often learned in response to a tyrannical, physically abusive parent. Here, submission is the price paid for sheer survival or for a few scraps of affection from a cruel parent. The pattern is then reinforced in adulthood through the unwitting selection of cruel sexual partners.

neurotic masochism

Another common dynamic among neurotic masochists: the *need to expiate sexual guilt* in advance, as it were, by choosing a partner who is abusive. This pattern typically develops in persons raised in sexually repressive families, where sex is regarded as dirty or shameful. The masochist later strikes an internal deal: "I'll get to enjoy sexual pleasure, and I've paid for it in advance by getting involved with someone who mistreats me."

Like all deeply entrenched patterns, these dynamics are easier to detect than to correct psychoanalytically, but they are less formidable from a therapeutic standpoint than the masochism noted in certain psychotic or severely depressed patients. What normal persons would experience as very painful brings great relief to these patients, for it frees them temporarily from an otherwise unendurable sense of numbness or deadness. Stolorow, Atwood, and Brandchaft (1988) addressed this variety of masochism in their paper concerning a young psychotic woman who begged her therapist to "Hit me!" This patient, who also had delusions of non-existence and severe identity confusion of the "as-if" type ("Doctor, I turn into anyone I meet—you won't let that happen, will you?"), represents a masochistic structure beyond what classical analysis could correct; many supportive measures were also necessary to diminish the intensity of her craving for pain.

psychotic masochism

Psychoanalysis can be understood as a theory of mind, as a treatment, and as a training method for those interested in pursuing professional work in intensive psychotherapy (of whatever orientation). As we approach the end of the 20th century, psychoanalysis has become more sophisticated as an explanatory theory to the extent that new material from the ever-expanding fields of cognitive and neurosciences is integrated into its core. Rigorous quantitative studies *within* psychoanalysis, such as those carried out by San Francisco psychoanalyst Joseph Weiss (1990), have shed light on the workings of the unconscious. Weiss has postulated a "control hypothesis" that has explanatory value in certain clinical situations that is superior to the dynamic

the "control hypothesis" of self-revelation

hypotheses. According to the control hypothesis, patients in analysis bring forth repressed material, not because an impulse suddenly overwhelms the force of repression (the dynamic model) but because they have unconsciously overcome their worry about the consequences of what they are about to reveal (i.e., that they might offend the analyst, for example). The analyst facilitates this process by giving responses that put the patient at ease about revealing angry, embarrassing, critical, or frightening material that otherwise would tend to remain unconscious. Presumably, effective therapists of any orientation help to create an atmosphere where forbidden material can surface.

PSYCHOANALYTIC STRENGTHS

shifts in psychoanalytic utility

As a treatment method, the utility of psychoanalysis in its unmodified form has become limited to (primarily) inhibited types of high-level character pathology (hysteric, obsessive, depressive-masochistic). Psychoanalytically-informed psychotherapy, however, has applications to the more severe conditions, though here parameters as well as medications may also be necessary. As a training method (or, more realistically, combined training and treatment) for mental health professionals, psychoanalysis retains great usefulness, though, as noted, it is falling out of favor in some places and gaining favor in others, for reasons related to cost and cultural changes. Surely psychoanalysis will have a place in the coming century, as Michels eloquently discusses (1994), though its form and domain of use in 2095 no doubt will be quite different from what we see in 1995—just as Mesmer's hypnotic method in the 1780s had evolved into something rather different in the Nancy School of Liébault and Bernheim in the 1880s.

therapeutic alliance

One element of psychoanalytic treatment that will not—because it need not—change is its focus on the formation of a *therapeutic alliance,* which is the keystone in the edifice of every school of psychotherapy. As Horvath and Luborsky (1993) note, Freud (1912) had emphasized the importance of the analyst maintaining a serious interest in, and sympathetic understanding of, the patient by way of fostering a positive attachment to the analyst. Citing Bordin's (1976) observations, they posit that the patient enters therapy with a "dysfunctional interpersonal schema" that is reactivated in the course of therapy. If the therapist responds in a manner that confirms the maladaptive assumptions, the schema becomes etched in even more deeply. But if the therapist neutrally examines the patient's negative feelings, via a *good therapeutic alliance,* in time the schema may be dissolved and replaced by more adaptive patterns of thought and behavior.

This type of therapist-patient interaction is fundamental to all types of therapy. Patrick Leung (1995), at the Chinese University of Hong Kong, makes a similar point in a more abstract way that helps link both Western and Eastern therapeutic approaches. He states that the key components of psychotherapy include:

key components of psychotherapy

(a) A healing agent who is designated in the respective culture as an expert in healing; (b) a help-seeker who has difficulty in coping with problems of living; (c) a healing relationship structured covertly or overtly by the healer in such a way as to provide the social context in which the healer induces positive changes in the moods, attitudes and behaviors of the help-seeker, primarily through words, acts and rituals; and (d) an ultimate objective of removing distress and enhancing adaptive competence of the help-seeker.

I find this to be a wonderful summarization of what psychotherapy—*healing the mind*—is all about: a summarization that not only unifies the diverse contemporary therapies of the West and East, but also the therapeutic approaches of the many religious, medical, and lay healers of former times—from the very beginning of our history; really, from long before we even had a written history. The therapeutic alliance thus does not *distinguish* psychoanalysis from other therapies (free association, dream interpretation, and analysis of the transference are a few of the distinguishing features), but it does form the foundation, the sine qua non, without which psychoanalysis—or any other form of psychotherapy—could not flourish.

Chapter 23

GENERAL PSYCHIATRY: PSYCHIATRY
BECOMES A WORLDWIDE ENTERPRISE

In the waning years of the 20th century, general psychiatry has experienced an expansion of knowledge in many traditional areas and the creation of quite new areas—some hinted at prior to the 1980s, others scarcely imaginable before the past decade.

The topic of sexual behavior, both normal and pathological, has received great attention since 1980, prompted in part by psychiatry's position reversal on homosexuality as abnormal. In their comprehensive review of the subject Friedman and Downey (1994) make a number of important points, including the historical note that the term *homosexual* did not enter common usage until 1869. They mention the difficulties in carrying out truly representative population sampling in this area, such that the reported percentages of male and female homosexuals vary from 2% and 1%, respectively, to 5–8% in males and 2% in females.

*dethroning psycho-
analytic postulates*

Recent studies have *not* shown an increased frequency of any psychiatric disorder within homosexual (versus heterosexual) groups, nor are there any data to support the older psychoanalytic postulate about the domineering mother and passive/hostile father as the "causative agents" in the development of homosexual orientation. Similarly, there are no data indicating that exclusively homosexual men (as opposed to those who have experienced attraction to women) can change through psychotherapy (or any other treatment) into men who have heterosexual fantasies and feel attraction to women. In contemporary perspectives, the factors predisposing toward homosexual object-choice are believed to be primarily constitutional, rather than psychodynamic, in nature.

twin research

The evidence for this position comes from several sources. Twin research has revealed an increased concordance for homosexuality in monozygotic as compared with dizygotic twins (Bailey & Pillard, 1991; Bailey, Pillard, Neale, & Agyei, 1993) and an increased concordance for homosexuality in (male) monozygotic twins reared apart (Eckert, Bouchart, Bohlen, & Heston, 1986; Whitam, Diamond, & Martin, 1993). Physiological research, which has established the crucial role of pre-natal androgens in organizing sexual orientation in mammals (Phoenix, Goy, Gerall, & Young, 1959), has revealed that prenatal androgen *deficit* predisposes to male homosexuality; prenatal androgen *excess*, to female homosexuality. This relation suggests that the vicissitudes of prenatal androgen may help determine sexual orientation in humans, including related phenomena, such as rough-and-tumble play, whose presence in boys is associated with eventual heterosexual choice and whose absence is associated with eventual homosexuality (Friedman & Downey, 1993). Over the past five years there have been reports about differences in the volume of certain hypothalmic regions in homosexual versus heterosexual men (e.g., LeVay, 1991), but these await confirmation.

the crucial role of androgens

In their most recent contribution to the understanding of homo-sexuality, Friedman and Downey (1995) reexamine the psychoana-lytic concept of the Oedipus complex. Based on some of the evidence just cited (the biological basis of rough-and-tumble play, for example), the authors take issue with Freud's hypothesis regarding this central complex. Freud's stand, from which he did not waver throughout his professional life, was that the young boy harbors incestuous motiva-tions toward his mother, which then have to be renounced in favor of the father—whom the boy at first wishes to murder, but then, as time passes, grows to love and emulate. Freud assumed that the child's re-nunciation of incestuous desires and eventual acceptance and adop-tion of his father's moral values laid the groundwork for the emergence of the superego; i.e., for the formation of conscience. Freud saw failure to resolve the Oedipus complex as the wellspring from which the psy-choneuroses derived.

Oedipus reexamined

These ideas have come under scrutiny in the past few years: We are aware—now, more than ever before—of the whole panoply of etiologi-cal factors that singly or (more typically) in combination lead to the various psychiatric disorders. Many of these factors are genetic, con-stitutional, traumatic (parental physical cruelty), and quite unrelated to the unfolding of an oedipal triangle. Furthermore, a child's core gen-der identity is established before the oedipal phase is thought to begin, shaped primarily by biological forces, including the organizing effects of prenatal androgen, as alluded to above (Money & Ehrhardt, 1972). In addition, we also now know that young boys' identities have little to do with castration anxiety, they are not apt to entertain strong parri-cidal wishes (unless the father is really hostile or cruel), and still less do they typically harbor incestuous urges toward their mothers. As we

panoply of etiologi-cal factors

have noted, ethologists have shown that children reared from birth in harmonious families experience a suppression of sexual feelings toward the parents and siblings with whom they live. When incestuous desires are felt strongly or acted out, they are ordinarily in response to disruptions or abnormalities in the attachment process.

Oedipus revisited

The Oedipus myth, as related by Sophocles, is itself a bit suspect. Sent away at birth so he would not commit incest, Oedipus returns by chance to his natal place, on the way killing Laius, whom he has no way of knowing is his father. Later he mates with Jocasta, who, as far as he could tell, was just an attractive, slightly older lady in Thebes. This was not incest, because there was no consciousness of incest. Only the playwright and the audience are "in on it." But somewhere in Greece there must have been instances of the real thing, or why would Sophocles bother to deplore incest in the first place? And the Athenians must have had trouble accepting that (conscious) incest did occur, or why would Sophocles have to remind them in the artfully sanitized play that has come down to us?

biological determinants of male behavior

The modification Friedman and Downey (1995) introduce into our understanding of early psychosexual development is this: Thanks to the organizing effects of prenatal androgens, there is an innate, biologically determined tendency for (most sons) to feel rivalrous, competitive, and frequently, although not invariably, "aggressive toward their fathers, and vice versa." These influences, related to rough-and-tumble play, are "not invariably associated with or reactive to erotic desire for the mother" (p. 241). It appears, in fact, that rough-and-tumble play and male-male competitiveness subserve adaptive functions as rehearsals of the dominance/submission relationships that are an inextricable (because they are useful!) part of human society.

biochemical pathways of sexual behavior

Friedman and Downey (1995) postulate that sexuality and rough-and-tumble play are expressions of two different developmental lines that are mediated by two different biochemical pathways. Along one pathway, androgens organize the structure of the central nervous system via intraneuronal conversion to estrogens (where cells respond then to the estrogens). Along the other pathway, cells respond directly to androgens. "Sex-stereotypical mating behavior . . . appears to be influenced by both pathways. In contrast, rough-and-tumble play is influenced only by androgen that is *not* metabolized to estrogen" (p. 256). These androgen-induced variations between and within the sexes help account for the much greater aggressiveness (and murderousness) of many males as compared with females in our species. Aggression, as Edmund Wilson (1978) asserted, is part of our nature: It is not caused by upbringing in a cruel environment, though it may be aggravated by such factors.

The recent neurobiological findings bearing on the distinctions between the sexes and on variations in rough-and-tumble play have helped to illuminate this dark corner of the human condition and allowed us to weave a more coherent theory about our early psychosexual development than was possible in Freud's time. Friedman and Downey (1995) speculate (I believe, correctly) that because Freud was *au fond* more biologically oriented than many of his followers, he would have endorsed the modifications in his original oedipal theory they introduce.

modern theory of psychosexual development

In this sense Freud was more modern than those contemporary analysts in America and Europe who still cleave to the view that homosexuality is a manifestation of a developmental arrest at a "narcissistic" stage, intermediate between anal and genital stages. Therefore, the strictly linear reasoning goes, homosexual persons are somehow incapable of mature love—because their love partner is merely a walking symbol of themselves: their narcissistic self-love wrapped around the shoulders of a mirror-image in the external world. This outmoded view, besides ignoring modern biological research, is prejudicial to homosexual persons seeking help, because it assumes that their relationships are somehow inauthentic. Perhaps it will take another generation for these old-fashioned ideas to dissolve entirely. And perhaps their tenacity is best explained by Elaine Pagels (1988) in her theological essay, when she reminds us that, in our evolutionary history, behaviors that did not support the command to "be fruitful and multiply"—namely, adultery, prostitution, masturbation, and homosexuality—came under scorn, and in many circles, have remained so.

revisioning homosexual love relationships

Another change occurring in the recent past concerns the wider appreciation of the many life stages that reach beyond the so-called *formative* (first six) years of life. Erik Erikson (1956) had already contributed greatly to this understanding in identifying such stages as "intimacy vs. isolation" (in young adulthood) and "generativity vs. self-absorption" (in middle age). But this range still did not capture the troublesome period Gail Sheehy (1976) described as the "midlife crisis," experienced by so many people as they approach 40. This is a time when men, in particular, are wont to look back on the course of their lives and to rethink what can still be accomplished in the years that remain, recognizing their mortality in a way young men seldom do. Divorce and job changes are common during this period.

Sheehy's exposition of midlife crisis

Nowadays therapists and the public are more accepting of the disruptions that often take place in this stage of life and are more compassionate about the changes both men and women may make at this time. Earlier attitudes were typically scornful about midlife changes, as though they were merely a sign of immaturity, hopefully affecting "other" people. As women in most countries around the world have begun to have few children and greater work opportunities, the traditional roles of older women—caring for their many grandchildren, for example—have become less important. Women too often face the existential question of how to make the remainder of their lives mean-

current attitudes toward midlife crisis

ingful and satisfying, as they find themselves also buffeted by midlife crises no less real or wrenching than those men experience. In recent years helping men and women deal with these issues has occupied the attention of many therapists and sociologists—whose books and articles on the subject now constitute an ample library.

NEW DISORDERS

seasonal affective disorders

Seasonal affective disorders, particularly depressions occurring with regularity in the winter months, were seldom recognized before the 1980s. Pittendrigh of the Rockefeller Institute had been studying circadian and other rhythms in animals for many years; more recently it has become clear that the levels of many chemical components in the human body also varied with the light cycle. The pineal gland, which Descartes thought was the seat of the soul, turned out to have an important, if not quite so lofty, role as the body's *Zeitgeber*—its internal clock—via secretion of melatonin, a compound structurally related to serotonin.

Many people, especially those with manic-depressive tendencies, become prone to depression as the amount of light per day shrinks during the winter in the temperate zones (and a fewer number have a paradoxical depression every summer). The Termans in New York found that brief exposure to intense light (via a machine generating 10,000 lumens) could relieve the depression (Terman, Terman, & Schlager, 1989). Others who have contributed to this research include Faedda, Teicher, Baldessarini, Gelbard, and Floris (1993) and Wehr (1989), who has also written a historical account of seasonal affective disorder and light therapy. Robert Sack and his group in Oregon (1990) noted that administering light therapy in the morning was more effective than evening treatment. Patients with "winter depression" tended to show abnormally delayed circadian rhythms (including those involved with melatonin secretion), which morning phototherapy was better at resetting.

light therapy

attention deficit disorder

Attention deficit disorder (with or without hyperactivity) has been studied extensively in recent years. Several books for the lay public have even become available, which has led to a salutary lessening of the stigma once attached to fidgety children who could not concentrate. Paul Wender, chairman of the University of Utah Medical School/Department of Psychiatry, has made important contributions to the understanding of this disorder in relation to both diagnosis and treatment. Persistence of the syndrome into adult life is common ("adult attention disorder" or adult ADD), where it is characterized by distractibility, restlessness, excessive talking, poor concentration, and displays of temper and impulsivity (Wender, Reimherr, & Wood, 1981). More recently, Biederman and his coworkers have studied the relationship between attention deficit disorder and the major affective disorders (Biederman, Faraone, & Kennan, 1991). Advances in the treatment of ADD-related syndromes chiefly include the tailoring of pharmacotherapy to the particular admixture of conditions each patient manifests. Whereas psychostimulants, such as methylphenidate (Ritalin), may suffice for uncomplicated ADD, when accompanied by major depression, ADD may require the addition of an antidepressant (most commonly, a serotonin reuptake inhibitor [SSRI]).

NEW VIEWS ON OLD DISORDERS

recurrent depression

In the treatment of recurrent depression, increasing evidence over the past decade has indicated that long-term maintenance medication (for many years, perhaps for life) confers real benefits in the reduction of relapses. This is particularly true for patients who have suffered three or more episodes (Frank, Kupfer, & Perel, 1990). Parallel to the emerging clinical evidence is the work of Jules Angst and his coworkers (Angst, Huber, & Stone, 1990), showing that the life-curve for patients with recurrent depression is as marked by suicides in one decade as in any other: They do not "outgrow" their risk for suicide as they age. This would suggest the wisdom of maintaining such patients on a prophylactic regimen indefinitely.

suicide and low serotonin

As demonstrated by Maria Åsberg of Stockholm's Karolinska Institute, in depressed persons who do not complete a suicide attempt, there is a strong correlation between the violence of the final act (hanging, shooting, jumping to death) and a low CSF level of the serotonin metabolite 5-hydroxyindole-acetic acid (5-HIAA) (Träksman-Bendz, Åsberg, & Schalling, 1986). Many investigators have subsequently shown correlations between suicide and violence: Inamdar, Siomopoulis, Shanok, and Lamela (1982) noted that psychotic, hospitalized adolescents (27.5%) often exhibited *both* suicidal and violent behavior; Plutshik, van Praag, and Conte (1985) found that about two-fifths of psychiatric inpatients had been either violent or suicidal before admission, and many had been both. These data support the old psychoanalytic shibboleth that "depression is aggression turned inwards," though there would be more truth in an emendation to the effect that "suicide is aggression turned inwards." Depression is not *always* accompanied by aggressive feelings; suicide (except in the elderly with fatal illnesses) regularly is.

Hoyer and Lund (1993) in Norway provided an interesting sidelight on suicide in mothers in relation to the number of children: Examining records on nearly a million women, they found a strong decrease

more children—less suicide

in suicide risk with increasing numbers of children (independent of social class and education). Their data, which supports the belief enunciated by Emil Durkheim in the 1890s that parenthood significantly lowers the risk of suicide, goes a step further in suggesting that, in effect, the more the merrier! Women with six or more children had only one-fifth the risk for suicide as did nulliparous women.

impulsivity and low serotonin

The presence of a connection between low serotonin levels and impulsivity (as opposed just to depression) was supported by the studies of Mark Linnoila at the National Institute of Mental Health. Linnoila (1995; Linnoila et al., 1983) showed that impulsive, alcoholic, violent offenders had lower 5-HIAA levels than did paranoid, alcohol abusing, violent, but non-impulsive offenders—and all the more so if the former had a history of attempting suicide.

aggression and cocaine

Another substance associated with violence and drastic lowering of serotonin (and elevation of norepinephrine) is cocaine. As Yudofsky, Silver, and Hales (1993) point out, cocaine can induce "seizure kindling"; chronic use "may lead to kindling that is neurophysiologically related to the irritability and aggression that occur so commonly during the use of and withdrawal from cocaine" (p. 220). Suspiciousness and delusional disorder may also occur in cocaine abusers, who are at greater risk for outbreaks of violent behavior if they have a preexisting CNS condition (such as epilepsy or stroke). Cocaine abuse may mimic the symptoms of intermittent explosive disorder, inducing a chimerical effect: a "personality disorder" brought into being by a drug. In earlier work, Yudofsky and coworkers (Yudofsky, Silver, & Schneider, 1987) had contributed extensively to the pharmacological treatment of aggression (such as with propanolol) and developed a scale for the evaluation of aggressive behavior (Yudofsky, Silver, Jackson, Endicott, & Williams, 1986).

OBSESSIVE-COMPULSIVE DISORDER

Enormous progress in understanding and treating obsessive-compulsive disorder (OCD) has occurred in the past 15 years. Allusions to this disorder are sprinkled throughout these pages: Under different names, OCD was recognized by medieval Arabic scholars, by Pinel, Esquirol, and Le Grand du Saulle (in his monograph of 1875) (the French usually used the term *folie du doute*). Berrios (1989) has written in detail on the history of 19th-century French descriptions of OCD. In the beginning of this century Freud and other psychoanalytic pioneers (Abraham and Ferenczi, especially) identified what they felt to be the main psychodynamics: conflicts over taboo sexual activities. Handwashing compulsion, for example, was ascribed to masturbatory guilt, which the patient tried to expiate via repetitive cleansing.

This was the perspective on OCD, for the most part, until recently, when it became apparent that the psychodynamic aspects of OCD were *not* always related to sexual guilt; guilt over revenge fantasies toward cruel parents was sometimes the main issue. Paul Salkovskis and his coworkers (Salkovskis, Richards, & Forrester, 1995) have suggested that persons vulnerable to OCD often blame themselves severely for failing to prevent harm (usually to others), which they then equate with "causing" the harm. Whereas most people feel more responsible for acts of *commission* than omission, OCD patients feel as responsible for what they have not done. This may be an underlying dynamic that is equally important, or more so, than the sexual guilt emphasized earlier.

psychodynamic aspects of OCD

Furthermore, psychoanalysis as a therapy for OCD was seldom effective, no matter how accurate the dynamic understanding. Finally, over the past decade it has become clear that the SSRI class of antidepressants brings substantial symptomatic relief in about two-thirds of cases. Meantime, a huge literature has grown up around the subject; many of these advances are summarized by Judith Rapoport (1989). Abnormalities of the basal ganglia have been implicated, partly because a substantial proportion of OCD patients (25–40%) also show tics and mannerisms suggestive of physiological dysfunction in this area of the brain. Considerable clinical overlap between OCD and Gilles de la Tourette's syndrome (characterized by tics and scatology) has been described by Green and Pitman (1990) and Nellist (1994).

physiological concomitants of OCD

Tourette's syndrome

The use of modern neuroimaging techniques has led to data suggesting that some patients with OCD show atrophy of the head of the caudate nucleus, though Insel warns that not all cases of OCD stem from abnormalities of just one brain region. An interesting "two-step" theory emerging from the data thus far posits that an increase in inhibition in the caudate nucleus (step one) renders the globus pallidus less inhibitory of the thalamus (step two), creating a reverberating (obsessive) circuit (Insel, 1992).

etiological factors

Using positron emission tomographic (PET) studies, Baxter, Schwartz, and Bergman (1992) elaborated a similar model, also describing a "worry" output from the orbital region of the brain that may be driving the OCD-related circuits. Regarding treatment for OCD, several studies now point to the superiority of SSRI drugs in combination with behavior therapy (directed toward exposure desensitization or response prevention) to medication alone (Jancin, 1994; Jenike & Rauch, 1994). In rare, intractable cases, neurosurgical intervention may be indicated and has been used with success (Jenike, Baer, & Ballantine, 1991).

A number of anxiety disorders have recently been reevaluated as possible variants of OCD because of similarities in symptomatology and response to the SSRIs. Daniel Stein and Eric Hollander (1993)

anxiety disorders and OCD

discuss how some cases of trichotillomania and hypochondriasis may belong under this heading. Hollander and Katherine Phillips (1993) have focused on another possible variant: body dysmorphic disorder (or, as it was called earlier, dysmorphophobia, described by Morselli in 1866). Fallon, Klein, and Liebowitz (1993) go a step further than Hollander and Phillips in asserting that hypochondriasis, except when set in motion by the loss of a loved one, is best regarded as a variant of OCD and treated as such with SSRIs, cognitive therapy, or both.

The motor and verbal tics (including coprolalia and echolalia) that characterize Gilles de la Tourette's syndrome—thought for a time to be psychological in origin—in recent years have been found to respond fairly well to medications, such as haloperidol or pimozide (Shapiro et al., 1989).

RESEARCH ON EATING DISORDERS

sexual abuse and eating disorders

Eating disorders, which have risen during the past generation in America and Western Europe, have become the subject of a burgeoning literature, especially the ever more "popular" symptom of bulimia. Many have suspected that childhood sexual abuse figures significantly as a causative factor in bulimia. The controversy in the literature remains intense. Waller (1991, 1992), studying a group of young women with eating disorders in England, reported that the group as a whole showed no more history of unwanted sexual experiences than were reported by women in the general population (already a high figure, around 50%). But he found a marked difference between the subgroups: anorexia without bulimia, anorexia with some bulimia, primary bulimia with some anorexia, and bulimia without anorectic episodes. Whereas the "pure" anorectics had a low rate of childhood sexual abuse (6%), the pure bulimics had a strikingly high rate of 75%. The symptomatology was worse (more persistent, more self-induced vomiting) when the sexual abuse had been intrafamilial (i.e., incestuous), had involved force, and had occurred before age 14.

Steiger and Zanko (1990) in Montreal reported similar findings: The pure anorectic women had the lowest incidence of unwanted sexual experiences (incestuous or extrafamilial) and tended to be introverted, with overprotective parents. The bulimic women were more extraverted and often came from chaotic families. The researchers concluded that, since their subjects were not more prone to have sexual abuse histories than did other groups of female patients, incest served more as a marker of a constellation of untoward family features (such as impulsivity, poor interpersonal boundary preservation) that predisposed to psychiatric disorders, but which were not specific for eating disorders. In the follow-up study by Timothy Walsh and his colleagues in New

York, about 40% of bulimics eventually recovered and 20% experienced partial recoveries (their follow-up interval was two to nine years) (Fallon, Walsh, Sadik, & Lukasik, 1990). In their study, physical abuse by parents was common; sexual abuse was not—and, furthermore, was no more common in the non-recovered bulimic women than in those who recovered.

Some investigators have turned their attention recently to the *why* of symptom-choice. Jimerson and his colleagues at the National Institute of Mental Health (Jimerson, Lesem, Kaye, & Brewerton, 1992) found that bulimic patients had abnormally low 5-HIAA and homovanillic acid in their cerebrospinal fluid (indicating low serotonin and dopamine levels). They speculated that low central serotonin might contribute to blunted satiety responses in bulimics; low dopamine, to abnormal hedonic responses to food. But it is not yet possible to unscramble cause from effect. If these neurotransmitter alterations *antedate* the bulimia, an inherited vulnerability to this specific symptom would be indicated. To determine whether this is so will require further study, however.

symptom-choice and low serotonin

MULTIPLE PERSONALITY DISORDER

Because of its dramatic—not to say freakish—nature, multiple personality disorder (MPD) has captured the attention of the mental health profession and the public alike—all out of proportion to its incidence. Greaves (1980) combed the world's literature and could come up with no more than 165 cases. But since 1980 the definition itself has been stretched so as to include severe forms of dissociation even without the presence of clear-cut "alters." As a result, there now appear to be hundreds—thousands—of new cases, at least in America and Canada. James Chu (1991) from Boston's McLean Hospital, August Piper, Jr. (1994) from Seattle, and Erkwoh and Sass (1993) from Germany all warn against overexuberance in making the diagnosis of MPD. They particularly caution clinicians about influencing the highly suggestible patients who comprise the highly dissociative population by asking them to "reveal" alters that may not exist.

changing diagnostic trends

Because of the legal system in certain countries, there is an added need for caution in dispensing this diagnosis; some criminals awaiting trial malinger, displaying symptoms of what later turns out to be factitious MPD, by way of getting a reduced sentence on the grounds of "diminished capacity." Such was the case with Ross Carlson (Weissberg, 1992), who had killed his parents for insurance money, and Kenneth Bianchi (O'Brien, 1985), one of the cousin-pair who became the Los Angeles serial killers known as the "Hillside Stranglers" (also cited by Erkwoh & Sass). The reality is, only a minority

MPD and the legal system

of patients with severe dissociation disorders present the full-blown clinical picture of MPD.

The role of childhood abuse (especially sexual), remains a controversial issue, though many authors consider it the prime etiological factor (Kluft, 1985; Loewenstein et al., 1987; Putnam, 1989; Ross, 1989). In most of the convincing modern cases of MPD there is a compelling history of severe abuse, more often sexual than physical. But, as Piper (1994) points out, such histories are as common, or more so, in (hospitalized female) patients with borderline personality disorder (meeting *DSM* criteria). In most of the earlier cases (19th century to the 1930s) there is no direct mention of sexual abuse; at most, there is Goddard's brief allusion in Latin in 1926: "The *vita sexualis* was manifested through a *hallucinatio incestus patris*" (Bowman, Blix, & Coods, 1985). Goddard seemed to believe that his 19-year-old patient had been molested by her father, yet he was so in the grip of the standard psychoanalytic theory of his time (that such memories were really fantasies and not veridical), that he wrote as though her memory were merely an hallucination.

Clearly we have no way of discovering the truth about these historical cases and thus cannot determine whether sexual or physical abuse was indeed a necessary (though not sufficient) causal factor, or whether these cases resulted from different etiological sources (epilepsy, severe neglect, or other traumatic causes not related to parental treatment). Given that severe childhood abuse appears to be a precursor not only of MPD and borderline personality disorder (BPD), but also of posttraumatic stress disorder and of other forms of dissociation, we

can conclude that childhood traumatization is an important pathogenic influence but that the symptoms emerging in adult life depend on various "host" factors, such as constitutional predisposition to dissociation and gender influences on symptom-choice.

Comparing MPD and BPD, Marmer (1991) and Fink (1991) note that in BPD there is *ideational* splitting (polarization of attitudes about self and other), whereas in MPD there is *literal* splitting of identity into various parts and pieces (the *alters*), each displaying a distinct subpersonality usually representing one main affect state (anger, lust, timidity, subservience). All authors agree that the tendency toward

dissociation is aggravated by early onset of abuse (before age 13), severity of the sexual molestation, if it occurred (incest by a father/stepfather, with penetration), and by high frequency/duration of abuse (Kirby, Chu, & Dill, 1993). There is a similar level of agreement—both by the "true believers" as well as by the "doubters" of MPD—that before clinicians can claim they are dealing with a valid case of MPD, extremely careful histories must be taken, using techniques as free from leading questions as humanly possible.

In the United States the newspapers and journals of the 1990s are replete with stories of "false memory syndrome": A patient (usually female), having accused the father or other male relative of sexual violation, is discovered to have outrightly contrived the memories or to have unknowingly created false ones. Elizabeth Loftus (Loftus & Ketchum, 1991) has been at the forefront of the movement to correct the false accusations, which sometimes destroy families. It is no easy task, however, to be 100% certain that an accusation is truly false (as a defendant in a legal case might like to contend), just as it is often very difficult to be certain an incest or molestation memory is accurate.

There is a measure of hysteria in both public and professional circles about these matters (especially in the United States), making it all the more important to preserve a sense of proportion: Many such memories are, indeed, accurate; false-memory situations do exist but are probably rare (less than 7–8%) compared with the true memories. Still, Piper (1994) wisely reminds us that memory is not a videotape but rather (citing Loftus) "involves a continual process during which bits of information are altered, reworked, interpreted and reconstructed; therapists do not uncover historical truth so much as narrative truth, which is a reevaluation of the past in the light of present day experience" (p. 609).

gaining perspective on the nature of memory

Erkwoh and Sass's (1993) paper is highly recommended for historical review of the early MPD-like cases: There are citations dating back to Gmelin's case in 1791 and up through the famous *Three Faces of Eve* case of Thigpen and Cleckley in 1950. The very early cases described states of "double consciousness" or "double personality"; not until 1893 were patients with three or more alters described (Morton Prince's "Miss Beauchamp," for example, had four). Contemporary views about optimal therapy, along with recommendations for diagnostic instruments that aid in establishing the diagnosis of dissociative disorders, can be found in the issue of *Psychiatric Clinics of North America* devoted to an exploration of MPD, of which Richard Loewenstein was guest editor (1991). Piper (1994) has also noted that, besides psychodynamic therapy with copious attention to the alters, psychic reintegration may be achieved by cognitive methods, even when attention to the alters is minimal.

reference sources on MPD

POSTTRAUMATIC STRESS DISORDER

Much more common a reaction to extreme stress than MPD, posttraumatic stress disorder (PTSD) has also experienced an upsurge in frequency over the past 15 years. Originally the label was reserved for what was called "shell shock" in World War I. Until recently PTSD continued to refer, almost exclusively, to the impact of wartime experiences on certain soldiers, who complain of panic attacks, nightmares, flashbacks, and sometimes even delusions and hallucinations, in the aftermath of surviving explosions, seeing their buddies blown apart, or other terrifying traumata that make up the quotidian life of men in combat.

In countries where civilian life is fraught with invasive traumata to large numbers of children, many adults show the same symptom profile as shell-shocked soldiers. Putnam and Trickett (1993) cite an annual incidence of sexual traumata, the more common antecedent of PTSD in the United States at a level of 160,000 cases (for 1988), indicating that the country has become a rich breeding ground of this disorder. Since the typical patient with borderline personality disorder in the United States (especially in hospital settings) is a female incest victim, she will often show the signs of PTSD as well. For example, one such woman, whose father had attempted anal intercourse with her when she was five and six, had repressed all awareness of those episodes—until such moments when, sleeping next to her husband, she would feel his penis against her backside. She would react with panic, and on several occasions, had raced outside the house naked, screaming for help, only to suddenly remember with great vividness what had transpired during her childhood (an example of "state-dependent memory").

co-occurrence of PTSD and BPD

This co-occurrence of BPD and PTSD is nowadays so common in the United States and Australia that several investigators claim that BPD should be renamed as PTSD or treated as just a variant of PTSD (Kroll, 1988; Lonie, 1993). This is a parochial view that ignores the long tradition and evolution of the term *borderline* (many instances of which do *not* have a traumatic origin) but an understandable view nevertheless, given the typical patients these clinicians are currently encountering. Roger Pitman (1993) describes a Vietnam veteran with unquestionable PTSD related to high combat exposure, who went on to develop not BPD but obsessive-compulsive disorder (OCD). Nonetheless it is true that most of what is currently called PTSD is related to childhood trauma: chiefly, sexual abuse at an early age, irrespective of whether the PTSD symptoms in adult life are accompanied by BPD, MPD, OCD, or some other disorder.

physiological correlates of PTSD

Several researchers are beginning to unravel the neurophysiological correlates of PTSD. How adrenaline serves as a kind of amplifier in the brain, sharpening the recording of traumatic stimuli, has been studied by Gary Aston-Jones (1993) of Philadelphia's Hahnemann Medical School. Schiffer, Teicher, and Papanicolau (1995) at Harvard have shown that persons who experienced childhood trauma exhibit asymmetry of left-brain dominance when thinking of a neutral topic and a marked shift to right-brain dominance when asked to think of an emotionally painful memory. The non-dominant hemisphere does mediate emotion more than does the dominant. In traumatized persons there appears to be right-sided storage of the painful memories, which helps

failure in semantic translation

expanding definitions of PTSD

to explain how they are "remembered" in a nonverbal way and why such persons are often amnestic for the traumatic memories.

Bessel van der Kolk, also at Harvard, has done some unusually elegant research in this area (1995): He reports that during flashbacks of traumatic memories, there is increased skin conductance, the amygdala shows heightened activity, the visual cortex "lights up" (as though images of the painful experiences are being recalled), but Broca's area (the motor center for speech) goes blank—indicating that translation into semantic schemata does *not* take place. This physiological research points the way to an important goal of therapy in traumatized patients: at a pace compatible with their tolerance and comfort, to help them gradually put into words—to develop a semantic schema for—what they hitherto could not recall in words but nevertheless experienced via flashbacks, inchoate feelings, and (all too often) impulsive actions. These actions are customarily destructive and inappropriate reenactments of the original trauma, occurring without the persons' being aware that they *were* redramatizing something that happened long ago.

At a conference Arthur Green showed a videotape of an interview with a young African-American man who had gotten into trouble with the law because of rage outbursts and death threats toward his teacher—which were very similar to the beatings and rage outbursts his mother had directed at him when he was two and three years old, and for which he had no conscious memory. His mother was also interviewed and revealed to Dr. Green the abusiveness with which she had treated her young son 20 years earlier.

BORDERLINE PERSONALITY DISORDER

During the 1980s several long-term follow-up studies on hospitalized borderline patients were completed. Tracing patients 10 to 30 years after they left their respective hospitals gave a much more accurate picture of the life course of borderline patients than had been possible to construct (*Austin Riggs:* Plakun, Burkhardt, & Muller, 1985; *Chestnut Lodge:* McGlashan, 1986a, 1986b; *Jewish General Hospital/ Montreal:* Paris, Brown, & Nowlis, 1987; *University of Minnesota Medical Center:* Kroll, Carey, & Sines, 1985; *New York State Psychiatric Institute:* Stone, 1990). Earlier studies had covered only two-to-five-year time spans. From the long-term outcome results it became clear that the majority of borderline patients eventually do fairly well (achieving Global Assessment Scores above 60, indicating few residual symptoms and some success in work, friendships, or intimacy). Nevertheless, the suicide rate was as high as with schizophrenic or manic-depressive patients—8–10% in most of the studies, though lower when the subjects were older patients (who had already gotten beyond their twen-

favorable treatment outcomes

ties, when the suicide risk is particularly high). These encouraging results were independent of social class and type of therapy.

prognostic variables

Certain factors could be teased out that augured well for long-range outcome: high intelligence, artistic talent, self-discipline, physical attractiveness, and (in cases of concomitant alcoholism) the ability to persevere with Alcoholics Anonymous. Other factors predicted a poor prognosis: antisocial traits (since these were more frequent in males than in females, the males tended to recover less often), schizotypal traits (these were associated with marginal, isolated life adjustment), and a history of parental cruelty or incest with penetration.

clinical profiles

In addition, clinical profiles could be pieced together from all the data on the incest victims: Women were at risk more than men by a factor of about six; as adolescents, the women had often run away from home, abused drugs, mutilated themselves with wrist-cutting or burns, become sexually promiscuous, or been seriously depressed or suicidal. Many had made suicide gestures (of a non-lethal sort); others had made real attempts that they had barely survived. Psychosomatic troubles were also common in the incest victims: van der Kolk (1989) pointed out how often these women showed certain "soft signs" of PTSD, such as getting into relationships where they were victimized again by men who treated them abusively, turning "victimizer" and dealing vengefully (or with extreme jealousy) with their sexual partners, becoming demoralized and losing all faith in humankind.

Not every woman with these clinical signs has been an incest victim and not every incest victim develops these abnormalities. But these signs can alert clinicians to the possibility that sexual molestation *may* be a part of the historical background. If careful questioning corroborates this reality, appropriate therapeutic measures (including group therapy with other molested women) can be mobilized.

EVALUATING PSYCHOTHERAPY

efficacy variables

Controversy about the efficacy of psychotherapy has continued throughout the past 15 years. Psychoanalysts and psychopharmacologists sometimes divide up into "armed camps," each denigrating the efficacy of the other's methods. Discussion occasionally descends to the acrimonious and ad hominem, as when the otherwise gifted psychologist Hans Eysenck casts almost unprintable aspersions at the "Freudian empire" of psychoanalysis (1994).

The exhaustive review of various psychotherapies by Smith, Glass, and Miller (1980) provides a strong rebuttal to the nay-sayers: Therapy often is effective. Much depends on the nature of the underlying condition and on whether the therapist has the basic ingredients of empathy, emotional warmth, and solid grounding in some explanatory theory. A similar impression emerged from a study by Pilkonis, Imber, Lewis, and Rubinsky (1984), in which ambulatory patients were assigned randomly to individual, group, or conjoint therapy for about 30 sessions: Significant improvement was noted in all three therapy modalities, and the minor differences were related to the attributes of the therapists and the "fit" between patient and therapist.

In a field that deals with something as complex as the human condition (patient variables, therapist variables, family variables, intervening events such as inheriting a fortune or developing a chronic physical illness), the kind of proof that physicists can (sometimes) boast of is rare, indeed. Still, tangible benefits from psychotherapy can be claimed: With milder cases of OCD, cognitive/behavioral therapy can hold its own with Prozac; psychotherapy (dynamic or cognitive) is helpful for depressive personalities, and in more serious forms of depression adds something to the antidepressant regimen that the pills alone cannot accomplish. Much of the relevant (and enormous) literature evaluating the efficacy of psychotherapeutic techniques is summarized in the voluminous *Treatments of Psychiatric Disorders,* published by the American Psychiatric Association.

verified areas of benefit

When reviewing the claims of the more "specific" types of psychotherapy, it is easy to lose sight of the fact that *supportive psychotherapy* is an integral part of all psychotherapy, whatever the orientation (Holmes, 1995). Supportive therapy also deserves recognition as a special form of therapy in working with patients suffering from psychotic illnesses. Holmes notes that supportive therapy is *eclectic,* drawing on many theoretical approaches. It would be unusual in any case of extended therapy—except, perhaps, that of a highly integrated and well-functioning person undergoing psychoanalysis—*not* to make use of supportive measures.

supportive psycho-therapy

With borderline patients supportive interventions are often of critical importance in the opening phases of the work, even when the therapist is committed to fashioning a mainly analytically-oriented treatment. This pragmatic stance is embedded in the title of Larry Rockland's book (1989), *Supportive Psychotherapy—A Psychodynamic Approach.* Supportive therapy now stands on a firmer theoretical foundation: Holmes (1995) speaks of an integration of both Freudian *ego psychology* (as adumbrated by Hartmann), where the focus is on adapting better to reality, and *attachment theory* (as elaborated by Bowlby), which posits that there is a lifelong psychobiological need for proximity to attachment figures, and which thus conduces to an *interpersonal* mode of therapy.

ego psychology and attachment theory

As for the balance between the biological and the psychological (especially, psychoanalytical) approaches in psychiatry in general, there has been a marked shift in the United States during the past genera-

shift toward the biological

tion—for which the backgrounds of department heads can serve as the bellwether. After World War II and until the 1980s, most heads were psychoanalytically trained (for example, Lawrence Kolb at Columbia, Milton Rosenbaum at Einstein, Morton Reiser at Yale). Recently they are primarily neuroscientists or psychogeneticists (Jack Barchas at Cornell, Robert Cloninger at Washington University in St. Louis, Nancy Andreasen at the University of Iowa) or analysts whose interests have concentrated on topics outside the immediate sphere of analysis (Allen Frances at Duke).

Chapter 24

HOSPITAL PSYCHIATRY: THE MOVE-MENT TOWARD BRIEFER HOSPITAL STAYS AND GREATER USE OF ALTERNATIVE PROGRAMS

By the late 1970s most psychiatrists in the United States had recognized that analytically-oriented psychotherapy had little to offer schizophrenic patients, especially those whose conditions showed signs of chronicity. Though some diehards within the analytic community continued to advocate psychoanalytic treatment, their number was dwindling and the evidence was against them. Some of this evidence was supplied by Gunderson et al. (1984), whose study of schizophrenic patients treated with *either* analytically-oriented therapy or supportive techniques found that the former group did not outperform the latter. Supportive therapy became the treatment of choice and included such measures as reassurance and reeducation. Certain analysts—Otto Kernberg, in particular—had been recommending the more eclectic approach for many years.

NEW TREATMENT PHILOSOPHY

By the late 1980s several long-term (25-year) follow-up studies of hospitalized schizophrenic patients had been reported (McGlashan, 1986b; Stone, 1990). Most patients, in their forties and fifties by the end of the studies, showed flat life-trajectories: Their adjustment was still "marginal"; most lived in sheltered situations, had few social contacts, and remained dependent for financial support on relatives or government subsidies. Psychiatrists in most other parts of the world, not burdened with overenthusiasm for analytically-oriented therapy to begin with, had already been providing other forms of treatment for their schizophrenic patients.

When the wave of realism finally passed over the American psychiatric community, several psychiatrists established themselves at the forefront of the new treatment philosophy. For example, William McFarlane recognized that more could be accomplished in bettering the lives of schizophrenic patients if, instead of trying to "cure" the underlying condition, family members were educated about the nature of their relative's illness: its chronicity, the patient's vulnerability to rebukes and criticisms (as though the unemployed schizophrenic relative was just "spoiled" or "lazy"), the premonitory signs of impending breakdown (so that relapse could be prevented), and the necessity of long-term pharmacotherapy. McFarlane's book (1983) on family therapy was a model of this new approach, in which emphasis was placed on educating the family, often without the patient present, rather than on traditional family therapy, in which the patient is present and family conflicts and dynamics are addressed.

educating family members

The emphasis was now on providing *rehabilitation* for those schizophrenic patients who could be rehabilitated, and *sanctuary* in dignified settings for those who could not (for reasons of age or severity of illness). These changes in the American methods of treating severe mental illness represented, in effect, a reinventing of the wheel, for rehabilitation and sanctuary had always been the mainstays of treatment in most of the rest of the world. For example, Luc Ciompi in Bern, Switzerland, for years had offered a program for schizophrenic patients that included such measures as occupational training with expert craftsmen in the city. Patients were taught sophisticated and marketable skills in special workshops, and many were able eventually to support themselves with well-paying jobs, which helped them to blend in with the general community. For patients beyond the reach of such rehabilitative measures, government-run hospitals, such as Glenside Hospital in Adelaide, Australia, provide lifelong care in pleasant living quarters on their spacious grounds.

reinventing the "wheel" of rehabilitation

The rehabilitative interventions used with schizophrenic patients in America, meantime, became more refined and responsive to these patients' social deficits, thanks to the efforts of expert clinicians, such as R. P. Liberman in California (1994). The social skills training program devised by Liberman concentrates on helping schizophrenic patients learn social amenities, how to deal with typical problem situations in everyday life in polite and effective ways, how best to dress for job interviews, etc.—all by way of helping them overcome their debilitating sense of "otherness" that so often results in alienation in social settings and in the workplace.

social skills training

Paralleling these developments has been an emphasis on shorter stays in the hospital, with correspondingly greater reliance on alternative, sheltered living arrangements: quarter-way houses, halfway houses, apartments for a small number of recuperating patients, overseen by mental health professionals, and so on. There is also a greater use of day-hospitals: sites where staff provide group therapy, social skills training, vocational rehabilitation, and recreational activities, usually within a 9 A.M. to 5 P.M. schedule. Marvin Herz (1986) has been a staunch advocate of this approach—briefer hospitalizations combined with enriched extramural programs—as the best way of reintegrating the largest number of schizophrenic patients into the community. A similar program has been in operation since the 1980s at the Bispebjerg Hospital in Copenhagen, where Tove Aarkrog (1981, 1994) has directed a unit specializing in acute care and rehabilitation of schizophrenic adolescents. As the patients in her program reach the convalescent stage, they resume their schooling in the nearby town of Tølløse, where they live in a supervised apartment complex and attend the local high school.

The contemporary emphasis on social skills training for schizophrenic patients deserves further comment, since the subject well illustrates the never-ending interplay in medicine (as in all science) between *conventional* wisdom and that of the *maverick*; between what "should be" (according to the established experts) and what "should be changed" (according to the intuitions of the innovator who stands apart from the crowd). We saw this same phenomenon in action centuries ago when Paracelsus wanted to burn the books of the ancient Greek physicians, by whose works the doctors of his day remained hide-bound. We saw it again with Johann Weyer, who, discounting the religion-bound attitudes of his day that would have deemed Barbara Krämer's "starving" as a miracle, actually *observed* her closely and discovered that she was sneaking food when she thought no one was looking. Yet again there was Mesmer, whose methods shocked the established physicians of Paris, and Freud, whose methods shocked the Viennese.

Social skills training fits into the scheme of treatment for schizophrenic patients in a way no one questions any longer. Liberman and his group have written comprehensive guidelines in the last ten years for carrying out this aspect of therapy and have trained mental health workers in the many details pertinent to the whole approach. Though Liberman is certainly a pioneer in this field, his work was built on, or inspired by, the work of "mavericks" who came before him—those intuitive and compassionate professionals who were doing social skills training before the phrase had yet been coined—because they felt instinctively that such training was needed, irrespective of what they had been taught during their psychiatric residencies.

alternative living arrangements

psychiatric mavericks

the work of Harry Albert

Already in the mid-1960s, psychoanalytically-trained Harry Albert had begun to abandon the dynamic/interpretive approach he had been taught in favor of a highly practical, behavioral therapy with his many schizophrenic patients—referred to him by colleagues who regarded work with this group to be baffling, ungratifying, even repugnant. For example, Albert would videotape a patient who incessantly picked at himself and would appear for job interviews in the rumpled jacket of one suit and pants of another. Showing the patient how his social gestures were offensive to others, Albert would "model" how best to keep his hands in his lap. Then, taking a whole morning off to accompany the patient to a clothing store, Albert would teach him how to select an outfit more appropriate to his job ambitions.

Albert wrote very little about his innovative and unconventional technique (as it then seemed) and was unknown outside a small circle of colleagues. Here is another example he provided, taken from his book (Albert, 1983), which was published two years before his untimely death.

> A 35-year-old linguist remained dilapidated, and to speak frankly, smelly, during our initial meetings. He presented this as the simple outcome of his sadness, not as behavior motivated by any feeling toward those colleagues or students whose eyes or noses might be offended. Actually he betrayed a certain pride in his being able to use his academic brilliance to force others to bear up with his "shit." I refused to go along with this arrangement. We discussed various means for dealing with his odor, including repeated cleaning of the chair, having a window open, or having the patient provide a plastic sheet to separate him from the upholstery. As one might suppose, he complained that the open window let traffic noise in, cleaning was too expensive, and a sheet, for which I had no storage space, was too cumbersome. After this experimentation, he begrudgingly consented to a shower, once a week, "for me." This led quickly to a sheepish discussion of being shunned and of how his decrepitude might be contributing to his loneliness. In time his hygiene improved without the grandiose and belligerent aspects of his behavior receiving much attention in our sessions. (p. 258)

Albert's work is an example of social skills training at its best, well before the term was popularized in the United States and at a time when behavioral techniques were being developed in England (by Isaac Marks, for example) but were often shunned as "simplistic" by American psychiatrists who still advocated analytic interventions for schizophrenic patients.

PROGNOSTIC REFINEMENTS FOR SCHIZOPHRENIA

Further refinements in our prognostic understanding of schizophrenic patients have been made in the 1980s and 1990s. The more favorable life course of the patients in Courtney Harding's long-term Vermont study (Harding, Brooks, Ashikaga, Strauss, & Breier, 1987), compared with the outcomes of several urban-based follow-up studies—suggested that life in the less pressured atmosphere of a rural environment had a protective effect for schizophrenic patients. An Australian study by Parker, Johnston, and Hayward (1988) called into question Vaughn and Leff's (1976b) equation of "high expressed emotion" (EE) with poor outcome: The Australian researchers noted that high EE was a negative predictor only in one-parent households, and that the best predictor of poor post-hospital course was a poor pre-hospital course. This finding suggests that, in some cases, severely and chronically ill schizophrenic patients may elicit "high EE" *from* their relatives, especially in the less protected setting of a one-parent home—an interactive (rather than straightforward causal) effect.

urban versus rural influences

Meanwhile, Nancy Andreasen and her colleagues (Andreasen, Flaum, et al., 1990) found that schizophrenic patients who showed poor premorbid adjustment were apt to be those with prominent *negative* signs (similar to Huber's "basic symptoms"): flattened affect, loss of will, apathy, etc. These patients were likely to be male, unemployed, and to have had an early onset of illness and poor response on cognitive testing. These clinical attributes had more predictive power in their study than did the abnormally large ventricular/brain ratio that was often noted on brain imaging scans. Though schizophrenics with predominantly negative signs tend to be treatment-resistant, a new generation of medications showed promise in a fair proportion of patients. For example, Kane, Honigfeld, Singer, and Meltzer (1988) reported that 30% of schizophrenics who had failed to improve with three trials of different standard neuroleptics did improve on clozapine, even with respect to negative signs.

predictive value of negative signs

Because the life quality of many schizophrenic patients is improving at century's end, and because alternative facilities are also improving, fewer patients have remained in chronic-care institutions, many of which have been closed for good. Tragically, some patients have been caught in the middle: Neither able to exist comfortably on the outside, nor so ill as to justify permanent sanctuary in the old "custodial" institutions, they have ended up homeless.

homelessness

The notion of parity in the gender ratio for schizophrenia has been

gender ratio for schizophrenia

taught for many years. In the last generation, however, it has become widely established that males are more susceptible to whatever influences contribute to the condition, and that there are more male than female schizophrenics. As Larry Rifkin and his group at London's Institute of Psychiatry suggest (Rifkin, Lewis, Toone, & Murray, 1994), low birth weight may be a factor in this disproportionality. In their study a birth weight of less than 2,500 grams was more common in schizophrenic than in manic-depressive patients, and low birth weight in schizophrenic men correlated with poor premorbid adjustment and cognitive ability. This, in turn, was consistent with the greater male vulnerability to fetal neurodevelopmental abnormalities and obstetrical complications.

drug-induced psychotic syndromes

Beginning in the 1960s and continuing into the 1980s and 1990s, abuse of illicit drugs, such as marijuana, cocaine, LSD, amphetamines, and the like, became widespread. Sometimes the drugs induced psychotic syndromes resembling schizophrenia (LSD and high-dose marijuana can cause hallucinations; amphetamines, a paranoid reaction). In persons burdened with vulnerability to schizophrenia, abuse would sometimes exacerbate an already manifest schizophrenic disorder or provoke a dormant one into full manifestation. Linzen and his colleagues in the Netherlands (Linzen, Dingemans, & Lenior, 1994) recently noted that, in patients with recent-onset schizophrenia, those who abused marijuana heavily had more frequent relapses as well as relapses earlier in their post-hospital course than did those who had not used marijuana to any great extent.

MOOD DISORDERS

One of the most notable recent advances in the treatment of recurrent depression is the use of *early intervention* with antidepressant medication during a subsequent episode, which can shorten the length of the episode by four or five months (Kupfer, Frank, & Perel, 1989). In a like vein, there is now consensus that *continuous maintenance* on antidepressants is likely either to abort some episodes or at least to diminish the duration and intensity of those future outbreaks that the medication could not altogether prevent. In the past the temptation was strong to discontinue antidepressants shortly after an episode had subsided.

continuous pharmacological maintenance

impact of side effects

Here again, some patients were "caught in the middle": If the side effects of the drugs were too uncomfortable, there was little choice but to go off medication as soon as practicable, and simply hope there would not be too many recurrences. Curiously, sexual function has often been the bellwether: The libido, often lowered during depression, might normalize on antidepressants—only to be lowered once again by the side effect of reduced sexual responsiveness, which is experienced by 20% of patients on most of the common antidepressants. Fortunately, some of the newer compounds (e.g., bupropion/Wellbutrin) are less apt to produce this side effect.

Continuing efforts are made to determine the optimal type of therapy for depressed patients. To this end Irene Elkin and her colleagues at the National Institute of Mental Health (Elkin et al., 1989) launched a study of four treatment strategies with ambulatory depressed patients. In general, imipramine/Tofranil plus supportive therapy worked best, followed closely by interpersonal and cognitive psychotherapy. But in the more severely depressed patients, medication plus supportive therapy did best; there was some (though less) evidence for the effectiveness of interpersonal therapy in this group. Among the less impaired patients, all four methods fared equally well, including "placebo plus support." This study confirmed the impressions of many clinicians that, at least in less severe cases, psychotherapy could often hold its own alongside pharmacotherapy as well as interact synergistically with medication to produce a superior result.

evaluating therapies for depression

A coding system for monitoring the specific interventions used by therapists doing cognitive therapy with depressive patients has recently been elaborated by Castonguay, Hayes, Goldried, and DeRubeis (1995). This system helped document the differences between this and other forms of psychotherapy: The cognitive approach places more emphasis on *intra*personal than on *inter*personal issues, more focus on how other people affect the patient than on how the patient may have contributed to his or her own problems; and more attention to the here-and-now (and on mates and friends) than on parents and childhood experiences.

coding system for interventions

Improvements were also made in the treatment of refractory rapid-cycling bipolar patients, who are often unresponsive to lithium. Mark Bauer and Peter Whybrow (1990), noting that a Norwegian study of the 1930s (noted by Gjessing & Jenner, 1976) had suggested the usefulness of thyroid therapy in "periodic catatonia," treated a number of refractory rapid-cyclers with levothyroxine (added to their usual regimen). Thyroid extract proved useful in minimizing almost all depressive and manic episodes, and did so irrespective of the patient's previous thyroid status.

thyroid therapy for rapid-cyclers

The high suicide risk in manic-depressive illness has been of concern for a long time. Long-term follow-up studies indicate a lifetime risk of completed suicide in the range of 10%. Until recently it was not understood that the lifetime risk for suicide *attempts* was high in patients with panic disorder. Johnson, Weissman, and Klerman (1990) found that even in uncomplicated (no other symptom disorders) panic disorder, the likelihood of suicide attempts was as elevated as found in

suicide risk in panic disorder patients

patients with major depression: about 20%. Deaths from suicide in panic-disorder patients are probably also elevated above population norms, though to what extent is not clear. Johnson's data suggest, at all events, that clinicians should take panic disorder more seriously than they may have done heretofore. Others report that, while long-term social adjustment in uncomplicated panic disorder is fairly good, when a *personality disorder* is also present, the likelihood for continuing maladjustment is much greater (Noyes et al., 1990)

depression and the immune system

The knotty problem as to whether depression adversely affects the immune system to a degree that could foster cancer development or hasten the transition of HIV infection into active AIDs remains unsolved. Marvin Stein and his colleagues at Mt. Sinai Hospital in New York note that, despite conflicting data, the bulk of evidence thus far does not suggest that depression (or other psychosocial stress factors) has substantial effects on the immune system in relation to AIDS or other diseases (Stein, Miller, & Trestman, 1991). They also note in passing that, although viral infections and autoimmune disorders of the brain have been implicated for a long time in both depression and schizophrenia, the neuroimmunological findings that have been touted as supporting such a theory have seldom been replicated.

schizoaffective disorders

Schizoaffective disorders occupy a middle position between the two "classic" psychoses of schizophrenia and manic-depression. Long-term outcomes are less bleak than for schizophrenia and tend to parallel those of manic-depressive patients. The balance between cognitive and purely affective symptoms influences the prognosis: The more serious and persistent the thought disturbance (the more schizophrenia-like), the more guarded the prognosis. The risk of suicide is high in all three conditions: about 10% over the lifetime. In a study of briefer follow-ups in depressed schizoaffectives, psychotic depressives, and nonpsychotic depressives, William Coryell and his colleagues found that outcomes in the depressed schizoaffective patients were worse than those in the nonpsychotic depressed group (Coryell, Lavori, Endicott, Keller, & van Eardewegh, 1984). Psychotic depressive patients tracked in an intermediate way. In general, the bell curve of life-trajectories in schizoaffective patients tends to be flatter than that of schizophrenics, indicating that outcomes are more varied and more evenly distributed over a range from very impaired to minimally impaired.

THE QUESTION OF A "UNITARY PSYCHOSIS"

Any discussion of schizoaffective disorder leads to reexamination of the question: What is the relationship, if any, between the "major psychoses," schizophrenia and manic-depression? Are the conditions distinct, or was there some rationale, after all, for Einheit's 19th-century notion of a "unitary psychosis" (*Einheitspsychose*)? Christoph Mundt and Henning Sass (1992) have recently edited a volume that addresses the similarities and dissimilarities of what we now assume are two different categories: *thought* and *mood* psychoses. Michel Maziade and his co-workers in Quebec (1995) argue that factor analysis of psychotic symptoms now suggests a *three-factor model: negative symptoms* (anhedonia), *psychoticism* (hallucinations and delusions), and *disorganization* (bizarre behavior and thought disorder). But a clinical picture containing all three elements is not specific for schizophrenia, as currently diagnosed, for patients with bipolar affective disorder can also show this triad. Maziade believes that their data support one of the models proposed by Ming Tsuang (Tsuang, Lyons, & Faraone, 1990), in which two distinct causes theoretically could produce two different illnesses (such as schizophrenia and MPD), but there could be some overlap in the pathophysiologies that might not be specific to either condition.

three-factor model

Advances in psychopharmacology in the last 15 years have broadened the treatment palette available to psychiatry for most of the serious mental disorders. For example, there is now a neuroleptic (clozapine/Clozaril) that alleviates the negative symptoms in some schizophrenic patients, including those who have been refractory to most of the conventional medications. Risperidone/Risperdal has also been used with efficacious results in some schizophrenic patients who had not responded to the standard drugs. Several drugs have been used recently in Europe but are not as yet available in the United States, such as sulpiride and moclobemide (which is a monoamine oxidase inhibitor [MAOI] that does not require abstinence from foods containing high levels of tyrosine, such as cheddar cheese). Among the MAOIs, phenelzine is currently the drug of choice for social phobia.

advances in psychopharmacology

We are now at the point where many of the major symptom disorders can be relieved with one or another medication, though anorexia and bulimia are (thus far) seldom responsive to even the newer drugs. Despite this progress, few patients with the more severe disorders—let alone the chronic psychoses—become totally asymptomatic and socially "normal" under the influence of psychopharmacological agents. Interpersonal problems, issues of self-esteem, control of negative moods and traits, and the like often persist.

The rationale for psychotherapeutic treatment of one sort or another remains legitimate with most patients. Cost factors make this important aspect of treatment unavailable to some, and less than optimally available to many, especially in countries like the United States, where both the awareness about, and desire for, psychotherapy are high. Demand and supply are more in harmony in countries like China, where there are not many psychotherapists but where the typical patient is more eager to receive medication than to talk about his or her personal life.

Chapter 25

PERSONALITY DISORDERS: THE STUDY OF PERSONALITY AS A RAPID-GROWTH INDUSTRY

There is a long chain linking Theophrastus' characterology—the temperaments of the ancient Greeks—and the personality nosology of our time. Yet the topic was viewed mostly with peripheral vision until personality disorders were set apart as a separate "axis" of diagnosis in the *DSM-III* of 1980. Interest in this area of psychiatry has grown exponentially over the past 15 years. Indeed, *psychologists*—who have long been concerned with the norms as well as the aberrations of personality—and *psychiatrists*—who were formerly wont to focus on the psychoses and other severe conditions—are now communicating to an unprecedented degree.

The *Journal of Personality Disorders* was founded in 1987, and the First International Congress on Disorders of Personality took place in Copenhagen in 1988. Within this brief time frame researchers have begun in earnest to examine possible biological/genetic underpinnings of personality.

NOSOLOGICAL CHANGES

conceptual limitations

Several speakers at the 1988 meeting argued for the need to shift from a category-based nosology to a more dimensional approach to diagnosis. Juan Mezzich, for instance, suggested that personality types used by the *International Classification of Diseases (ICD)* be thought of as the vertical axis, permitting the diagnostician to mark the *height* along each bar, corresponding to the degree this or that personality type seemed to be present. Such an exercise would yield a *profile* (much as the Minnesota Multiphasic Personality Inventory [MMPI] accomplishes) that more accurately reflected the person's total personality than would the mention of only one or two pertinent categories.

Psychiatry as a whole has been slow to adopt such a shift in methodology, partly because the dimensional approach, while more accurate, is more complex, partly because it is not easy to develop universal agreement as to the most useful array of dimensions. Also, it is next to impossible to create dimensions that do not overlap. All psychopathic persons, for example, are narcissistic to one degree or another (though by no means are all narcissistic persons antisocial or psychopathic). So long as the field considers *narcissism* and *antisociality/psychopathy* to be useful descriptors of behavior, a measure of conceptual overlap will have to be tolerated.

In its three editions since 1980 the *DSM* has aimed at achieving the widest possible utility, if not universality, throughout the world. As a part of this ambition, each edition has been translated into many languages. John Gunderson, at the MacLean Institute in Boston, has served as chairman of the Personality Disorder (Axis II) section of the evolving *DSM*s. Communication among mental health professionals has unquestionably been enhanced as a result of these efforts. Still, conceptual universality in diagnosing personality disorders has remained an unrealized dream, owing to cultural differences among various nations. These differences are more profound between Asian and Western societies than within the so-called Western countries (which include Australia as well as the United States and Europe).

cultural differences in diagnosis

Some typical examples: Certain orderly, authoritarian, thrifty persons in a German community might be labeled "compulsive personalities" by foreigners, though not by their own countrymen. Kobayashi (1989) has commented on how Japanese persons, with their emphasis on group harmony, appear abnormally "dependent" in the eyes of Americans—who in turn seem unreasonably blunt, if not downright rude, to the Japanese. In general, personality *disorders*—especially those that are questionable or subtle—are best judged by members of the same culture. Personality diagnosis is much more culture-dependent than is the case with many of the symptom disorders of Axis I.

One might even say that diagnosis per se is epoch-dependent: During the Hitler years in Germany (1933–45) it was "normal" for men to be cold, cruel, and dominant and for women to function as submissive "breeders" (Sereny, 1995). Loyalty and obedience were valued over adherence to moral principles. In this topsy-turvy world, psychopathy was normal and normal humanness was "weak." Once the 12 years of the "Thousand Year Reich" had mercifully ended, the norms of personality reverted to those of conventional morality and gender roles were no longer so flagrantly stereotyped.

EPIDEMIOLOGY OF PERSONALITY DISORDERS

differences in definitions

As to the prevalence and incidence of personality disorders in various countries, a number of authors have reported on their epidemiological research using the *DSM-III* (Merikangas & Weissman, 1986; Widiger & Rogers, 1989) and the Personality Assessment Schedule of Tyrer and Alexander (1988) (Casey, 1988). In the United States and England, schizoid personality is quite rare (less than 1% of the population); in Sweden and Denmark it is less rare. Borderline personality is more common in the United States (2.5%) than in Japan.[1]

Definitions enter into the reckoning, however, as does the type of the survey conducted. Schizoid persons, strictly defined, seldom seek psychiatric help (they are content, more or less, with their aloofness), so their number would appear smaller in a clinically-based study than in a door-to-door survey of an entire city. The *DSM* definition of *borderline* is much more behavior-oriented than the older psychoanalytic definitions (which are preferred by many practitioners in Western Europe) and more accurately portrays certain patients in the United States. In contrast, there are few patients in Japan or Saudia Arabia whose behavior is as impulsive as that of the *DSM-III* "borderlines" of the United States or Australia. The distribution of the *DSM*-based personality disorders differs from country to country, in some cases so markedly (China is an example) as to cry out for a "homegrown" classification system, no matter how scientifically studied or widely used the "foreign" system.

DIAGNOSTIC INSTRUMENTS FOR ASSESSING PERSONALITY

Over the past 15 years there has been a tremendous proliferation in the production of diagnostic instruments for the assessment of personality in both its normal and abnormal aspects. Cloninger, Przybeck,

---

[1] That a number of patients exist in Japan whose personality disorders meet *DSM* criteria for BPD is attested by Ono and Okonogi (1988). Theirs was not an epidemiological study but rather a comparison study of three systems for diagnosing "borderline": *DSM*, Kernberg, and Gunderson. These and other Japanese psychiatrists are of the belief, however, that BPD is rarer in Japan than in the United States. Cultural, temperamental, and family-environmental differences between the two countries are such as to create fewer persons in Japan who become highly impulsive, openly angry, and self-destructive.

and Svrakic (1991) developed the Tridimensional Personality Questionnaire (TPQ) in such a way as to include the three neurotransmitters considered to affect personality: dopamine (novelty-seeking), serotonin (harm-avoidance), and norepinephrine (reward-dependence). The instrument was recently translated into Japanese and found to be reliable in that population (as tested on 450 Japanese university students) (Takeuchi, Yoshino, Katoh, Ono, & Kitamura, 1993).

Tridimensional Personality Questionnaire (TPQ)

Armand Loranger and his colleagues, meantime, have worked on their Personality Disorder Examination (PDE) to make it applicable internationally. A recent study (Loranger et al., 1994) showed the usefulness of the instrument across 11 countries in North America, Europe, Africa, and Asia. Designed to correlate with both the *DSM* and *ICD* personality descriptors, the PDE generates agreement on most traditional personality diagnoses in the two systems, except where antisociality is concerned: Here the *DSM* emphasizes antisocial *behaviors,* whereas the *ICD* stresses *traits* such as remorselessness and low empathy.

Personality Disorder Examination (PDE)

The difficulties inherent in creating a universal diagnostic instrument for personality disorders are compounded by cultural differences. It is probably true that diagnosticians from *any* cultural background could diagnose correctly the more *extreme* deviations encountered in other societies: The *most* compulsive, psychopathic, schizoid, paranoid (etc.) persons are easy to spot, irrespective of their countries of origin. It is in the subtler cases, where abnormality is slighter and fades into the characteristics of the general population that cultural variations play a greater role.[2]

universal diagnostic instrument unlikely

Others have sought to develop taxonomies derived not from clinical systems like the *DSM* but from trait lists or the factors that such lists may generate. These taxonomies usually address normal personality, with abnormal aspects included only secondarily. Buss and Finn (1987), for example, have proposed a schema with three sets of variables: (a) instrumental-affective-cognitive (*instrumental* here refers to traits that have an impact on the environment, such as dominance or aggressiveness); (b) social vs. nonsocial (a trait is *social* if it occurs in the context of the interpersonal field, such as submissiveness or tactfulness; *nonsocial* if the trait can be entirely private, such as guilt); (c) self vs. nonself. As the authors mention, no single classification will suffice in organizing personality traits totally; their system is thus complemen-

trait-based instruments

---

[2] This is to be expected: Personality, as Otto Kernberg (1995) has pointed out, is a *normal* attribute of self, comprised of (1) a mental organization, built up over many years, relating to social interaction (object relations or "mutuality"); (2) instinctual gratification; (3) autonomy and assertiveness; and (4) stability in work and creative pursuits.

tary to other systems already in use. In the Buss-Finn schema important gender differences have been noted: For example, men tend to score higher on such traits as dominance, rebelliousness, aggressiveness, excitement-seeking; women, on prosocial traits like altruism and nurturance.

prototypical charac-
teristics

Livesley and Schroeder (1990) have focused on defining *prototypical* personality-disorder characteristics. Actual patients may demonstrate these prototypes to varying degrees—a fact that underscores the utility of a *dimensional,* as opposed to a purely categorical, approach to personality diagnosis. *DSM-IV* divides its 10 personality disorders into three "clusters." But patients with a "cluster A" diagnosis, for example, are rarely *just* paranoid or *just* schizoid or *just* schizotypal. Instead they are likely to show some degree of all three dimensions: paranoid behaviors, social avoidance, and perceptual-cognitive distortion. Use of the dimensional systems—either solely or as an adjunct to the category-based systems—facilitates the assessment of *all* relevant information concerning personality.

lexical vs. factorial
approaches

The traditional *DSM* categories can be generated by two different approaches: the *lexical,* where a thorough listing is made of all adjectives in a language that pertain to personality; and the *factorial* where the mammoth lists of adjectives/traits are compartmentalized into relevant factors much fewer in number. The work of Goldberg (1982), which includes some 600 trait-words, is an example of the lexical approach, as is the work by Yang and Lee (1989), which uses 557 Chinese trait-words. The factorial work of Tupes and Christal (1961–6) represents the reduction of trait-lists to an irreducible minimum—the *five-factor model*—which includes extraversion, agreeableness, conscientiousness, neuroticism, and openness. But as Widiger and Trull (1992) have shown, the five "superfactors" can be viewed as large branches of the personality tree, which then divide into the smaller branches of the *DSM* categories. The lexical lists can be broken down into groupings that also correspond with the *DSM* categories.

FAMILY AND TWIN STUDIES

Family and twin studies of personality development have shed light on the nature/nurture controversy in this area. For almost any personality trait or disorder, the similarity between monozygotic (MZ) twins compared with dizygotic (DZ) twins is high enough to suggest a heritability of 40–50%. In general, genetic factors account for approximately 50% of personality differences, the remainder stemming mostly from non-shared environment (47%), with shared family environment accounting for a mere 3%. Plomin and Daniels (1987) are among the many researchers who have looked into the distribution of these factors in relation to personality.

These findings are disturbing for many people who are more comfortable believing that personality variation comes solely from environmental influences—one's parents, mostly—and are "therefore" more correctable and modifiable through treatment. Worse, the idea that many of our differences are in our genes implies (rightly) that certain people are born with strong disadvantages, sometimes predisposing them to end up "bad" from a social standpoint. Contemporary evidence, for better or for worse, supports such a view: fortunately, the proportion of people who are "bad seeds" (ending up antisocial even though coming from nurturing and stable families) is quite small. (The biography of the serial killer John Cannan [Berry-Dee & Odell, 1992] is illustrative.) As David Lykken (1995) has shown, the more benign and nurturing the early home, the more any psychopathy noted in the children from such homes must stem from constitution. The hereditary factors that precede the emergence of such traits as incorrigibility and psychopathy (Cadoret, Troughton, Bagford, & Woodworth, 1990) are as yet unclear but probably have to do with impairment in the development of empathy (Hare & McPherson, 1984), a heightened tendency toward sensation-seeking behavior (Raine & Venables, 1988), and frontal lobe damage (Damascio, 1994). The latter work carries forward the impressions gleaned from the famous accident of Phineas Gage (noted earlier), whose frontal lobe lesion led to a drastic change in his moral sense.

"bad seeds"

BIOLOGICAL CORRELATES OF PERSONALITY

Research on the biological correlates of personality has progressed at a remarkable pace over the past 15 years. Morton Zuckerman (1991) has summarized this work in his excellent monograph. Cloninger's studies (Cloninger et al., 1991), as mentioned, provided much of the impetus to these research efforts. Alec Roy and his colleagues (Roy, DeJong, & Linnoila, 1989), for example, observed the extraversion so often apparent in pathological gamblers. Not only were the gamblers indeed often extraverted, but there were also strong correlations between the degree of extraversion and the blood levels of a norepinephrine metabolite (3-methoxy-4-hydroxyphenylgly-col [MHPG]). Roy et al. concluded that a disturbance in the central noradrenergic system underlay the personality abnormality in at least a subgroup of pathological gamblers (many of whom showed signs of, or had family members with, bipolar disorder).

CONDUCT DISORDER AND ANTISOCIALITY

As Tremblay and his colleagues (Tremblay, Pihl, Vitaro, & Dobkin, 1994) note, the idea that childhood behavior can predict adult social behavior dates back to Plato, if not before. Efforts in recent times to refine our understanding about this connection include those of Loeber and Stouthamer-Loeber (1987), who noted a correlation between early conduct disturbances (aggression, lying, drug abuse) and future delinquency. Utilizing Cloninger et al.'s (1991) tridimensional measures related to the effect of neurotransmitters on personality, Tremblay et al. found that kindergarten boys who scored high on impulsivity (especially those who also scored low in reward-dependence and harm-avoidance) were at considerable risk for the development of early-onset delinquency. Conversely, five-year-olds who scored low in impulsivity were only one-third to one-tenth as likely to develop delinquent patterns.

prevention attempts

The hope, of course, is that early identification of high-risk kindergartners may lead to prevention of future antisociality via early therapeutic interventions. The issue of prevention remains problematical, however: There are few effective treatment methods for antisociality, unless the person is relatively free of psychopathic traits (as defined by the Hare and McPherson [1984] checklist). Even for antisocial persons with few psychopathic traits, response to cognitive/behavioral therapy, including programs for controlling the substance-abuse tendencies common in this group, is often unrewarding. Personality features encountered in this group, such as lack of motivation and irresponsibility about appointments, seem to undermine attempts to modify behavior. Antisocial persons with few psychopathic traits and nonviolent habits may, as they enter their forties, cease their antisocial acts, but others tend to remain antisocial as they age.

cognitive/behavioral therapy

In an Iowa-based long-term follow-up study of antisocial men, conducted by Black, Baumgard, and Bell (1985), about a fourth showed improvement over time and 42% remained unimproved. This finding suggested that antisocial personality disorder is often chronic. Their study did not address the degree of psychopathy, so it is not clear whether these traits were more marked in the unimproved group.

In the 1980s and 1990s the general feeling has been that antisocial personality disorder, though often treatment-resistant, in some instances is amenable to the type of cognitive/behavioral therapy advocated by Beck and Freeman (1990). Their method aims more at reorienting the patient in a prosocial direction than at producing a fundamental change in fantasy life and moral values. For example, they engage the patient in a dialogue about the cost-benefit ratio of different behaviors. Yelling at a boss because he assigns last minute work—

and then getting fired for the insubordinate behavior—yields a benefit of "feeling macho" but a cost of losing a job. Knuckling under and accepting the work politely yields a cost of feeling a bit humbled but a benefit of retaining both job and reputation. The therapist's hope is to get the patient to grasp the superiority (higher benefit) of the latter scenario. But as Robert Hare makes clear in his most recent book (1993), the situation with full-blown psychopaths is much bleaker: They do not accept the notion that there is anything wrong with their behaviors and they mock the mental health profession, calling them fools who treat "patsies." Psychopaths make us aware that not all problems that can be diagnosed can be treated.

THE IMPACT OF NOSOLOGY ON PSYCHOANA-LYTIC TREATMENT ISSUES

The publication of the *DSM-III* in 1980 largely redefined what does and does not belong within the domain of personality aberration. Earlier, the psychoanalytic characterology played a more important directional role among therapists, at least in the West. This change in emphasis has had a significant impact on ideas concerning treatment. The hysteric, obsessional, masochistic, and phobic patients with whom the psychoanalysts worked usually functioned reasonably well, except within the sphere of intimate relationships. Though psychoanalysis was not the only means of helping these patients with their interpersonal problems, this method (and its derivatives) often produced impressive results. (Admittedly, owing to the lack of rigorous long-term follow-up studies, the documentation of these results is meager [Stone, 1993b]).

prognostic varia-tions

The *DSM*-defined personality disorders encompass a more psychiatrically ill population. Patients meeting criteria for an Axis II disorder are less likely to benefit from classical analysis; those who do are apt to be patients with a cluster C disorder such as dependent personality. As for those in cluster A, schizoid persons seldom seek, or remain for long, in therapy (unless they have an admixture of more treatment-amenable traits). Paranoid and schizotypal patients are difficult to treat by psychoanalysis and usually require a mixed approach that combines supportive, cognitive, and educational interventions; medications may have a role as well, especially with schizotypal patients (Goldberg, Schulz, & Schulz, 1986; Serban & Siegel, 1984).

In cluster B patients the situation varies: Histrionic patients are often more dysfunctional than the hysteric patients analysts were treating at mid-century. (In contrast, however, some of Freud's "hysteric" patients seemed to be as ill as contemporary histrionic patients!) We have already noted the difficulties that beset the treatment of antisocial persons.

The diagnosis of *borderline* personality disorder (BPD) in the *DSM* is based on more severe symptoms than on personality traits and is a narrower definition than Kernberg's psychoanalytic, object-relational description (1967) or "borderline personality organization" (BPO). Many BPO patients are amenable to a psychoanalytically-oriented therapy involving limit-setting and confrontation about the negative transferences, in addition to the analytic clarifications and interpretations that are more specific to this modality. This approach does not always suffice for the often sicker, more impulsive, self-damaging, and hostile patients who meet *DSM* criteria for borderline personality *disorder* (BPD).

BPD versus BPO

As for the travails that beset the therapists who struggle to work with borderline patients within the analytically-oriented mode (which Kernberg has called "expressive" and Gunderson, "exploratory"), these are poignantly described by the prominent London analysts (a husband and wife team) Anna Higgitt and Peter Fonagy (1992). They address the need to understand the defense of projective identification so often utilized by borderline patients, as well as the mechanisms of grandiosity, contempt (Kernberg's "omnipotence" and "devaluation"), and profound dependency. Therapy may well last two to seven years—probably a generously low estimate, since many others mention ten or more years of therapeutic contact (not always as intense as the beginning) as being necessary before genuine therapeutic progress is achieved. Higgitt and Fonagy also emphasize the therapist's need to "withstand the patient's angry and hostile transference" (p. 30) and deal with the behavioral patterns imposed and provoked. One such pattern: In response to the patient's unreasonable criticisms and outburst, the therapist feels provoked, hostile, and persecuted, and unwittingly behaves toward the patient in a way that recreates the patient's early home atmosphere.

borderline defenses and treatment travails

A number of general recommendations for working with borderline patients are provided by Higgitt and Fonagy (1992): Those who are treatable with expressive therapy are apt to be among the less ill subgroup; limit-setting is especially necessary to control impulsivity; the focus in expressive therapy should remain on current relationships, especially the one between therapist and patient. They note that patients with depression, a high degree of psychological awareness, high motivation, and a relatively secure living arrangement are the best candidates for an expressive approach. This having been said, the authors warn that "suitability (or otherwise) for treatment will most commonly become self-evident only after several months of heartache, of struggling with negative therapeutic reaction, of massive distress during breaks [separations], of insistent demands for

borderline treatment approaches

special treatment. . . . of suicidal gestures and sometimes physical violence" (pp. 38–39).

In a study based in Geneva, Switzerland, Antonia Andreoli and his colleagues (Andreoli, Gressot, Aapro, Tricot, & Gognalons, 1989) showed that the presence of *any* Axis II personality disorder in patients being treated for depression tended to retard the process of recovery and to predict poor treatment compliance and long-term social risk. Although their follow-up period covered only two years, their results were in line with other data derived from longer periods of observation. Among the borderline patients followed 20 years or more in the long-term studies of the 1980s, for example, McGlashan (1986a), Plakun et al. (1985), and Stone (1990), those who committed suicide or who deteriorated in their functioning after age 40 were usually the ones with "difficult" (rageful, chronically hostile) personalities, who alienated family members and other supportive figures on whom they were dependent. Whatever the symptom picture, the presence of markedly abrasive, irritable, and demanding traits, which render a person difficult to live with (at home or in the workplace), augur for a prognosis poorer than would have been predicted by the symptoms themselves.

comingling of Axis I and Axis II disorders

ADDITIONAL TREATMENT APPROACHES

To compensate for the limitations of psychoanalysis and allied therapies in treating the more serious personality disorders, other modes of treatment have recently been developed or—if they existed before 1980—improved and popularized. Partly this advance in treatment strategies has occurred as a result of the increasing dialogue between psychiatrists and psychologists. Psychologists had always been more involved in devising and perfecting cognitive-behavioral techniques than had psychiatrists. These techniques now seemed better adapted to the needs of patients with narcissistic, histrionic, borderline, and milder instances of antisocial disorders, with whom limit-setting and other behavioral methods are of crucial importance. Still, there are no shortcuts. Though various "quick cures" are sometimes touted, they are seldom effective in the domain of personality disturbance.

As William James asserted a century ago, and Costa and McCrae (1986) recently reconfirmed, personality tends to crystallize around age 30. It is cavalier to expect profound, let alone speedy, change, whatever the method. The best that can be achieved with short-term therapy is probably an alleviation of concomitant depressive symptoms in patients with "depressive personality disorder" or with other personality constellations.

short-term cognitive approaches

An example of this type of short-term work is provided by Chris Padesky (1995). Her method is to elucidate, then gradually to alter, the *core beliefs* or "schemata" of the characterologically depressive patient. Such a patient may have a "vicious circle" schema that runs something like this: I'm no good—Others are better than I am—I must therefore cater to the needs of others—I'm always tired as a result—There's no one to help *me*—This makes me angry and resentful—[Person overreacts to trivial annoyances]—[Others express their outrage at the unwarranted anger]—"See, I'm no good!"

The cognitive therapist asks such a patient, "What could you have done differently from what you customarily do to interrupt the vicious circle?" and helps the patient to see that she could have insisted on resting when she felt tired, she could have declined diplomatically to do some favor that would require more energy or time than she could afford, and so on. Such steps lead to the discovery of an interpersonal world that is less hostile or exploitative than the patient perceived it, which in turn fosters more agreeable interactions with others. *Positive* responses from others then help to undo the self-condemning belief, "I'm no good."

growth of behavioral psychotherapy

The topic of cognitive/behavioral therapies was extensively reviewed by Ann Hackmann (1993), who mentions the growth of membership in the British Association for Behavioral Psychotherapy over the 20 years from 1972 to 1992: from 200 to over 1,700 members. The range of clinical applications is now wide, covering not only the personality disorders but also phobias, obsessive-compulsive disorder, anxiety states, depression, sexual problems, substance abuse, eating disorders, and conduct disorder—the bulk of conditions that are not complicated by psychosis.

Hollon (1993) also reviewed the range of clinical applications of cognitive therapies, mentioning panic disorder, borderline personality disorder, and even schizophrenia, in addition to those cited by Hackmann. The evidence suggests that cognitive/behavioral therapy (CBT) yields as good or better results with social phobia (and its personality counterpart, "avoidant personality") than does pharmacotherapy.

CBT with schizophrenics

Similarly, Marsha Linehan's method of Dialectic Behavioral Therapy (DBT) (1993), a variant of CBT, has been shown to be effective in reducing the frequency of self-damaging acts committed by borderline patients. Even schizophrenic patients, hitherto believed to be unresponsive to CBT, have experienced favorable results (reduction in delusory ideas in those with paranoid traits). Linehan's application of CBT avoids direct confrontation of the delusions or distortions, instead encouraging the patient to explore other possible explanations for events and experiences that had previously been misconstrued.

turn-of-the-century cognitive therapy

Actually Linehan's approach is similar to that of Poul Bjerre (1912), who used what he felt were psychoanalytic techniques in dealing with ideas of reference in a "dementia praecox" patient (probably today we

would say she suffered from delusional disorder, not schizophrenia).
Bjerre's method also had a cognitive component: He too got his patient
to explore other possibilities as to why she thought men on the street
were sticking their tongues out at her (a conviction she developed following a romantic disappointment).

THE BEST OF ALL WORLDS

As the 1990s draw to a close, there is greater agreement about the
essential elements in verbal psychotherapy. Although psychotherapy
has a role in the overall treatment of the active psychoses (where *supportive* interventions are indicated, alongside the biological), for the
most part, the "talking cure" is relevant to patients with milder conditions. Psychotherapy is also highly appropriate for persons who have
relationship difficulties or problems in coping with stressful life situations. Most such patients exhibit disadvantageous in *personality,* though
not always to the degree that would constitute a "personality disorder"
according to criteria of the latest version of *DSM*. These are the same
conditions that earlier generations of psychoanalysts treated under the
heading of "character disorders" or "psychoneuroses." (*Character* here
was understood as a synonym for *personality* and did not include the
connotation of moral/ethical integrity.)

Currently there is a host of competing therapies—perhaps more in
the United States than elsewhere—including the psychoanalytic, cognitive, behavioral, interpersonal, and rational-emotive orientations, to
name but a few. The analytic domain alone contains many schools and
orientations: orthodox, Adlerian, Sullivanian, Jungian, Horneyan,
Reichian, Kohutian, and others. All deal with personality disturbances
of whatever severity. Supportive therapy may be viewed as either a
separate form or the form that underlies *all* therapeutic approaches.
These different methodologies could be regrouped into two broad divisions: those oriented primarily toward modifying a patient's patterns
of thought and mental imagery (especially the inner representations of
the self and important others), and those oriented primarily toward
modifying behavior. Supportive therapy, because of its eclectic components (exhortation, reassurance, problem-solving, ventilation, education, etc.), cannot be conveniently placed in either subdivision. Much
of the literature comparing two or more treatment approaches can be
seen as an attempt to pit a "mind-changing" therapy against a "behav-
ior-changing" therapy. In other examples, one of these two types is
compared with supportive treatment. Recent papers reporting on the
results of such comparisons include Linehan, Armstrong et al. (1991)
on borderline patients; Gelernter et al. (1991) on avoidant patients;
Fairburn, Jones et al. (1991) on patients with bulimia; Beck, Sokol et

competing therapies

al. (1992) on panic-prone patients; and Hollon et al. (1992) on depressives.

By the mid-1980s there was a growing awareness among open-minded clinicians that the *efficacy* of these different approaches was really about the same. With regard to borderline (and other severely ill but nonpsychotic patients, for example, the Menninger Study (Wallerstein, 1986), involving long-term follow-up of 42 patients, showed that those treated by largely *supportive* measures had outcomes essentially the same as did those in *psychoanalytically-oriented* therapy—which, at the outset, had been considered the superior method. Similar results emerged from the 10- to 25-year follow-up of some 300 hospitalized patients who were borderline by Kernberg's criteria (1967) (two-thirds of whom also met *DSM-III* criteria for BPD) (Stone, 1990).

common features

The current opinion among many seasoned clinicians is that features common to *all* effective psychotherapies—empathy, caring, the therapist's integrity and "being there" for the patient—contribute as much or even more to good outcome (the *usefulness* of the treatment) than do the features that set them apart—such as dream analysis, the "homework" of Beck's cognitive therapy, etc.) (Frank & Frank, 1991). Daniel Stern (1995) emphasizes this point in regard to the competing therapies that are used in dealing with mother-infant problems. These likewise divide into two basic types: namely, psychodynamic (focusing on inner representations) and cognitive/behavioral. Here, again, the end results differ hardly at all.

mind-body equation

The most important reason for this similarity of outcome rests on the often overlooked equilibirium between our psychological inner life and our behavior. Ultimately, our thoughts and assumptions influence behavior. But improvement resulting from therapeutic attention directed mostly at behavior can ameliorate a patient's self-image and correct false assumptions—which means bringing about changes in the patient's thinking. Wherever treatment enters the system, as Stern makes us aware, it changes all the elements of that system.

false differences?

Differences in efficacy among the different orientations tend to be measured over rather short time spans—usually a year or two. Yet the promulgators of each particular approach seize upon the often modest differences in outcome as proofs of the superiority of their method. These differences are probably less powerful than they are made to seem, and what differences *do* exist may well relate to cultural differences among patients, different orientations (during their training days) among the therapists, differences in patient's cognitive styles (some rely more on emotions, some more on logic). The differences that are truly intrinsic to the therapy per se (ones that would be analogous, say, to penicillin's superiority over aspirin in treating pneumococcal pneumonia) may be rather unimpressive—and by no means easy to tease apart from the welter of patient and therapist variables.

Stern (1995) even mentions aesthetic and political considerations that enter the therapeutic equation. One need only think of contemporary China and Russia during the Soviet regime, where the emphasis in psychotherapy was on cure through work: Patients got better through encouragement, task assignments, reentry into the work world. Patients' inner life—let alone their dreams and their associations—held little interest to their therapists, who equated such concerns with "bourgeois decadence." This behavioral work-centered therapy was in harmony with the Communist/collectivist political ethos. In the West, focus on the perfection of the individual permeates the political systems—and, not surprisingly, the therapeutic systems as well.

We are beginning to recognize that there are a number of potentially effective types of psychotherapy, each founded on a coherent and comprehensive model of the mind, each requiring years to master, and each built around the teachings of one gifted, influential, and often charismatic originator. Perhaps the ideal or "compleat" therapist would be well-versed in all the important methods. But a lifetime would scarcely suffice for such breadth of training.

Certainly the ideal model for understanding and treating disturbances of personality should integrate the most valid and useful aspects of all the "competing" schools. This is a most daunting task. Yet some scholars in our field are directing their efforts toward achieving the necessary synthesis. Prominent among these are Daniel Stein (1992) and Jeffrey Young, whose recent book (Stein & Young, 1992) addresses the advantages and limitations of the cognitive approach and its relationship to the psychoanalytic model. In the decades ahead, these efforts will carry us further toward the goals of minimizing competitive "either/or" attitudes concerning the various techniques, while maximizing the development of a flexible, integrated psychotherapy woven out of the best threads of *all* the old fabrics.

Chapter 26

BIOLOGICAL PSYCHIATRY

Biological psychiatry and the related field of psychogenetics occupy a vast space on the map of contemporary psychiatry. As the century draws to a close, the transition from focus on the individual psychology to the chemistry and physics of the soul is in full swing, just as occurred in German psychiatry in the latter half of the 19th century. From the standpoint of history (as psychohistorians in the 21st century will assess us) some of the investigators mentioned in this chapter will enjoy what I believe to be secure places: Eric Kandel, Kenneth Kendler, Solomon Snyder, Nancy Andreasen, Bessel van der Kolk, Irving Gottesman, Einar Kringlen, Maria Åsberg. Others may assume an importance in ways we cannot firmly predict in the mid-1990s.

Reports that caught everyone's attention in the early 1980s, such as the dexamethasone suppression test as an index of vulnerability to depression, did not live up to their claims. Other topics—such as the study of basal ganglia abnormalities in obsessive-compulsive disorder, and the clinical responsiveness to serotonin reuptake inhibitors—captured the headlines in the mid-1980s and have retained their place at the forefront of psychobiological research.

topics at the forefront of research

In the last decade the study of "hypofrontality" in schizophrenia has yielded impressive results. Focus on the negative as well as on the more flamboyant positive symptoms of this disorder has led to the development of new medications, such as clozepine and risperidol, that show some promise of alleviating the hitherto more stubborn negative symptoms.

"hypofrontality" in schizophrenia

Seasonal affective disorder (SAD) was scarcely recognized until the mid-1980s. At this point a decade later, research on melatonin, which is implicated in SAD, has received coverage even in the popular magazines, having earned an (undeserved) reputation as the key to eternal youth and freedom from jet-lag.

seasonal affective disorder

The mechanisms behind memory and consciousness are becoming better understood. Newer techniques, such as positron emission tomography (PET) and magnetic resonance imaging (MRI), have enhanced our understanding of schizophrenia, Alzheimer's disease, bipolar illness, and posttraumatic stress disorder. Freud's hypotheses on dreaming, reevaluated at mid-century after the discovery of REM sleep by Aserinsky and Kleitman, has been reevaluated once again in the light of recent research on memory and the hippocampus.

memory and consciousness

It is no exaggeration to say that over the past 15 years there has been an intense exploration of possible biological underpinnings of just about every diagnostic entity in the standard nomenclature. Research has gone far beyond the territory of the major psychoses, where it has been obvious for several centuries that biological factors were at work. For example, biological influences were assumed by William Battie in his 1758 textbook, in which he spoke of "original" versus "consequential" madness—original madness being caused by constitutional predisposition.

intense exploration of biological underpinnings

Recent advances have been made in many areas where the biological component is more subtle. Among these areas, as we shall see, are sexual orientation (including homosexuality), eating disorders, and personality disorders. What follows are brief accounts of developments in a number of the key areas. I have been necessarily selective, since to write a comprehensive survey of recent accomplishments in biological psychiatry would be to create still another multivolume textbook.

advances in the subtle biological component

AGGRESSION

Arguing against poverty and oppression as the primary causative factors in aggression, James Merikangas (1981) offered a three-factor model of predisposition to violence and murder that identified differences in brain neurophysiology in relation to *drive level*, *stimulus threshold*, and *response inhibition*. Murder was least likely where response inhibition was greatest. In a large population of men who had committed murder, a disproportionate number had either a psychosis or an EEG abnormality. In a similar fashion, the most important predictors of violent incidents in chronic neuropsychiatric patients were found to be focal frontal lobe lesions and history of a seizure disorder (Heinrichs, 1989)—factors associated with reduced capacity for new learning and self-correction. In depressed patients low serotonin levels in the brain were found to correlate with impulsive aggression and a tendency to violent acts, including suicide carried out in a particularly violent way (Åsberg, 1994; Coccaro et al., 1989).

predisposition to violence and murder

ALZHEIMER'S DISEASE

genetic and non-genetic sources

The dementia associated with Alzheimer's disease is currently understood as stemming from either hereditary influences (predominantly affecting persons in their forties and fifties) or from non-genetic sources (usually in the elderly) (Wurtman, 1985). These sources include protein accumulation, infection, toxins, neurochemical disturbance, or vascular insufficiency. In both circumstances, abundant amyloid deposits are found in the central nervous system. The earlier quest for the "one true cause" of Alzheimer's disease now seems unattainable. As for the genetic factor, first-degree relatives appear to be at twice the risk (about 41%) as those in a control group (23%) (Martin, Gerteis, & Gabrielli, 1988). Using the PET scan and single photon emission tomography (SPECT), Kotrla, Chacko, Haper, Jhingran, and Doody (1995) were able to distinguish between Alzheimer patients with delusions (where low profusion was noted in the left frontal lobe) versus those with hallucinations (who showed low blood flow in the parietal lobe). A correlation was also found between brain serotonin levels and platelet serotonin levels: In Alzheimer patients both were reduced (Kumar, Sevush, Kumar, Ruiz, & Eisdorfer, 1995), suggesting the possibility of using the much more easily assayed platelet levels as a diagnostic tool.

gene sites

Recently a gene was identified in certain cases of early-onset Alzheimer's disease (Tanzi, 1995). This gene, which elaborates a beta-amyloid glue-like substance that is toxic to brain cells, is on chromosome 14—in contrast to another Alzheimer's-related gene Tanzi and colleagues discovered eight years earlier on chromosome 21.

literary immunity

In an intriguing study by University of Kentucky epidemiologist David Snowdon, nuns now in their seventies and eighties were found to be particularly at risk for Alzheimer's if their writing samples at *age 20* showed low "idea density." Those whose biographical essays in the 1930s consisted of sparse declarative sentences later developed senile dementia; those whose essays were chockablock with linguistic embellishments and divagations seemed somehow immune (Rogers, 1996).

ANXIETY DISORDERS

obsessive-compulsive disorder

During the 1980s and 1990s earlier psychodynamic explanations of obsessive-compulsive disorder (OCD) were giving way to psychobiological ones. In the mid-1980s a theoretical model (Wise & Rapoport, 1989) proposed that the globus pallidus region of the basal ganglia was involved. This area ordinarily contains neurons that inhibit cells in the thalamus that mobilize certain behaviors. When OCD is present, the striatum may be malfunctioning by *inhibiting* rather than reinforcing the pallidus. This would leave the thalamus *uninhibited*, leading to repetitive behaviors no longer appropriate to optimal functioning. OCD patients were also found to show a blunted response (in measures of either coritsol or prolactin) to serotonergic challenge, suggesting a diminished serotonergic responsivity (Bastani, Nash, & Meltzer, 1990).

More recent neuroimaging studies have shown increased regional cerebral blood flow in the right caudate nucleus, the left anterior cingulate cortex, and the orbitofrontal cortex on both sides (Rauch et al., 1994)—all corroboratory of previous imaging studies in OCD. Some forms of OCD were found to be related to Gilles de la Tourette's syndrome. In patients from families *with* the tic disorder, there were high rates of compulsive behaviors such as touching rituals. In those *without* the tic disorder, the prominent symptoms were cleaning compulsions and worries about contamination (Leckman et al., 1994). The latter group also showed elevated levels of oxytocin, which has been associated with various grooming, sexual, and affiliative behaviors.

neuroimaging studies

In the area of anxiety and panic disorders, possible underlying neurophysiological mechanisms have been sought. For example, anticipatory anxiety, akin to the signal anxiety of Freud's 1926 paper "Inhibitions, Symptoms, and Anxiety," correlates with activation of the hypothalamic-pituitary-adrenal axis (Hollander et al., 1989), whereas this connection is not present in (lactate-induced) panic states. It has been known since the work of Pitts and McClure in 1967 that lactate infusion can induce panic states (the mechanism remains unclear); from recent work we know that patients with panic disorder are more sensitive to the effects of lactate than are other types of patients (Cowley & Arana, 1990). Panic may be triggered by changes in the biogenic amine nuclei of the central nervous system, whereas anticipatory anxiety may be mediated by benzodiazepine-gamma-aminobutyric receptor complexes—entirely different mechanisms.

anxiety and panic disorders

The biological correlates of posttraumatic stress disorder (PTSD) have come under scrutiny only in the last few years, and Bessel van der Kolk (1989, 1995) has been at the forefront of this research. Recently it has been suggested that some of the peculiarities of memory function in traumatized persons may be engendered by reduction in one of the memory centers (for example, the inability to recall traumatic events that may nevertheless be thrust into consciousness by chance encounter with the smells, sounds, and sights associated with the events: van der Kolk, 1995). In an MRI study of PTSD patients, Bremner et al. (1995) found a smaller volume in the right hippocampus than that of controls—a finding consistent with deficits in verbal memory. This anatomical difference may be due to high cortisol levels (as part of the sustained reaction to the traumata), which are thought

posttraumatic stress disorder

to have a neurotoxic effect on the hippocampus. In a study of CNS event-related potentials, PTSD patients also showed a lower amplitude of the P-300 wave, which is related to cognitive processing. The impairments in both memory and attention characteristic of PTSD may have their origin partly in this neurophysiological abnormality (Charles et al., 1995).

CONSCIOUSNESS

neural correlates in the visual cortex

Francis Crick, co-discoverer with James Watson of the double-helix structure of DNA, speaks of the relation between mind and brain as the major question in contemporary neurobiology. A valuable approach to this question lies in the study of the visual system (Crick & Koch, 1992). In the act of mediating vision, the brain makes myriad computations of which we are unaware; what we become aware of (or *conscious* of) is the result of these computations. In the visual cortex some neurons are involved in doing the computations; others convey the results—i.e., what we actually see. There are neurons whose firing is a sign of awareness, which is distributed widely over the neocortex. For Crick the key question is: How does the brain form its global representations from visual signals? The neural correlates of consciousness seem to depend on the rhythmic and synchronized firing of neurons in the visual cortex. These oscillations may bind together activity in different cortical areas concerning the same object, or they may help distinguish figure from ground. It may be that neurons from the lower layers in the cortex are concerned with consciousness, while those from the upper layers are busy with "unconscious" processes.

the enigma of subjective experience

Mathematician, philosopher, and cognitive scientist David Chalmers (1995) has reviewed the problems associated with explanations of consciousness. Chalmers speaks of the "easy" problems (how does the brain integrate information from many different sources? How can we verbalize our inner states?) and the "hard" problem (how is it that physical processes in the brain give rise to subjective experience). A color-blind scientist, as Chalmers mentions, could know all about the structure of the optic tracts and the wavelengths of the various colors, yet would not know what it is to experience *red*. Those currently at the cutting edge of science, well-versed in matters of quantum phenomena and nonlinear dynamics, have thus far been involved only with the easy problems.

related topics

Related topics concern artificial intelligence (the degree to which the computer can or cannot simulate the qualities of the human mind), memory mechanisms, complexity, chaos theory, and neural networks. Some important books in these areas include those of Patricia Churchland and Terrence Sejnowski (1992), Paul Churchland (1992), and Marvin

Minsky (1985) on artificial intelligence, Daniel Dennett (1991) and Roger Penrose (1994) on consciousness, Gerald Edelman (1992) and David Rumelhart and James McClelland (1986) on neural networks, Murray Gell-Mann (1994) and Klaus Mainzer (1994) on complexity, Steven Rose (1992) on memory, and John Searle (1992) on consciousness and artificial intelligence from a philosopher's perspective.

DREAMING

Scientists once abhorred teleologic questions (*why* are things as they are) as much as Nature is said to abhor a vacuum. But such questions are no longer inappropriate, and at the end of this century we are free to ask about the why of dreaming, just as Freud did at the close of the last century. Sleep seems to have developed in vertebrates by way of promoting metabolic restoration of CNS tissue (especially in animals that expend a lot of energy, as in hunting). Rapid eye-movement (REM) sleep, which appears to be concerned with the consolidation of memory, developed in mammals even as primitive as the platypus (Hawkins, 1990). REM sleep may have evolved in order to subserve "off-line" processing of information (Winson, 1985), permitting much more data processing, learning, and problem-solving than brains lacking this mechanism could manage. In fact, Jonathan Winson (1990) notes that alternating slow-wave and REM sleep appear in all placental and marsupial mammals, with the exception of the Australian montreme, the echidna. This places the emergence of REM sleep at 140 million years ago.

evolutionary role of REM sleep

Neural control of sleep is located in the brainstem, whence neural signals proceed to the visual cortex (creating the visual dream). Brainstem neurons also stimulate a sinusoidal wave in the hippocampus—the so-called theta rhythm. This rhythm is involved with the nightly recording of basic memories, the processing of which allows mammals to evaluate current experience and to evolve more adaptive coping strategies. In humans this mechanism appears to underlie the dream's function of problem-solving. What we now know about the biology of dreaming makes quite credible the psychological function that Freud assigned to it, though the emphasis belongs on problem-solving, not on the "preservation of sleep" or the "fulfillment of wishes."

the dream's function of problem-solving

For a brief time some neurophysiologists claimed that dreaming was inherently meaningless (Hobson & McCarley, 1977), a mere epiphenomenon of random neural firing from its origin in the brainstem pons. This view is no longer tenable.

It has been shown recently that "long-term potentiation" (LTP) of neural cells, discovered in 1973, underlies learning and memory and, as Winson (1990) mentions, allows the "off-line" processing of memory

"long-term potentiation"

during sleep. This ability had the evolutionary advantage of consuming less space in the prefrontal cortex for information processing—space that could then be relegated to advanced perceptual and cognitive abilities crucial to survival in higher species. A derivative of a mechanism in animals that lack language, dreaming in humans relies, as it does in the other animals, on sensory (mostly visual) information processing that is unconscious. Consciousness arose later in evolution. Winson argues that there is an "unconscious" and that dreams are indeed the royal road, as Freud postulated, to our understanding it.

EATING DISORDERS

biological correlates

The search for biological correlates in the all-too-common eating disorders of anorexia and bulimia has been intensive, but the results not as impressive as in some of the other symptom disorders. In one study, patients with anorexia nervosa were tested for abnormalities in CNS monoamines, given that disturbances of mood, appetite, and neuroendocrine function are common accompaniments (Kaye et al., 1984). Decreases in serotonin and dopamine were noted, but these seemed to be state-dependent. Abnormalities were also found in levels of norepinephrine even after weight restoration, suggesting a trait-like consistency that might implicate norepinephrine in the mood changes typical of this condition.

concomitant depression

Kennedy, Garfinkel, Parienti, Costa, and Brown (1989) studied eating disorders (both anorexic and bulimic) in female patients, and noted that the group with concomitant depression showed lower levels of nocturnal melatonin than were found in the nondepressed group. Ordinarily, melatonin secretion follows a circadian pattern, with most output occurring during darkness. These and similar studies do not as yet point to a specific CNS abnormality underlying either the fasting or bingeing types of eating disorder. Perhaps related to this lack of knowledge is the lack of psychopharmacological progress in treating the eating disorders: As yet there are no specific medical remedies.

GENETICS

Recent advances in molecular genetics, as Whatley and Owen (1989) point out, are making it possible to locate the responsible gene(s) in various hereditary disorders, even when the related biochemical abnormality is unknown (as is still usually the case in the heritable psychiatric disorders). In a number of conditions—schizophrenia, manic-depression, and Alzheimer's disease—some families show a

Mendelian transmission pattern, even though these instances are atypical and probably examples of genetic heterogeneity (i.e., not all cases stem from the same genetic defect). Especially in these cases, molecular genetics can first detect the offending gene(s) on whatever chromosome(s) it is located; then, the molecular aberration involved and the immediate biochemical consequences; and, finally, the bodily changes that result in the phenotype we identify as schizophrenia (or whatever). Research that maps these steps in detail should lead to a better understanding of the pathogenesis of these disorders and to improvements in their chemotherapy well beyond what is currently available.

mapping the transmission of mental disorders

Schizophrenia and related conditions have proved a fertile ground for genetic research. Simple delusional disorder (SDD), once thought to be a variant of schizophrenia, was shown to evolve into the latter condition only rarely (Kendler, 1980) and to have weak clustering in families. Kendler considers SDD as probably distinct from schizophrenia. In their study of "spectrum" disorders related to schizophrenia, Kendler, Gruenberg, and Tsuang noted that the risk for schizophrenia was considerably greater in close relatives of schizophrenic patients than in relatives of controls. The relatives of schizophrenics were also more at risk for a schizoaffective or paranoid disorder or for an atypical psychosis (these then constituting the "spectrum" conditions) but not for unipolar depression.

schizophrenia spectrum of disorders

In a further study concerning the boundaries of the schizophrenia spectrum, Kendler and Hays (1981) found that paranoid psychosis (delusional disorder) was rare in families with either schizophrenic or manic-depressive probands, suggesting that paranoid psychosis was on a separate genetic track. This hypothesis was further supported in a study by Kendler, Masterson, and Davis (1985) wherein relatives of schizophrenics were more likely to develop schizotypal personality, whereas those of delusional disorder probands were more likely to develop a paranoid personality.

paranoid psychosis

In further refinements of the Norwegian studies of schizophrenia, Kringlen and Cramer (1989) found that the *non-schizophrenic* twins in discordant monozygotic pairs had almost as many offspring who were in the schizophrenia spectrum as did the schizophrenic twins. In another study of monozygotic twins discordant for schizophrenia, Goldberg et al. (1990) detected differences in performance on many psychological tests, especially those of vigilance, memory, and concept-formation. This lent weight to the theory that neurological dysfunction in schizophrenia was greatest in the frontotemporal cortex. The unaffected twins did as well on the tests as did normal monozygotic twins, suggesting that the neuropsychological dysfunctions noted in the schizophrenic twins was primarily related to the disease process.

twin studies of schizophrenia

Further support from the spectrum concept of schizophrenia came from the long-term follow-up study of Erlenmeyer-Kimling and her colleagues (1995). The high-risk children of her original study, now in their late twenties and early thirties, showed a heightened liability for schizophrenia, schizoaffective disorder, and the personality disorders of cluster "A": schizoid, paranoid, and schizotypal. Some children of parents with psychotic affective disorders also became schizoaffective but were not more likely to develop schizophrenia.

heightened liability

In a study that also bears on the spectrum question, Gottesman and Bertelsen (1989) analyzed offspring of "dual matings" (one schizophrenic and one manic-depressive parent) and of parents with reactive psychosis, which appears to stem primarily from life events and has no genetic relationship with schizophrenia of manic-depression. In an earlier study of matings between schizophrenic and manic-depressive people, Elsässer (1952) found that most of the children who became ill developed an affective disorder, though a few developed either a schizoaffective or a schizophrenic psychosis.

Until recently, little attention was focused on investigating the psychogenetics of milder conditions such as the personality disorders and anxiety states. Many studies from the mid-1980s forward have sought to correct this deficiency. For example, Siever and colleagues (1990) looked at the spectrum question in relation to personality disorders. In the Danish adoption study of the 1960s Kety, Rosenthal, and Wender had already shown that schizotypal personality (then called "borderline schizophrenia") occurred among the relatives of schizophrenic probands. Siever et al. showed that the reverse was also true: There is a heightened incidence of schizophrenia among the close relatives of persons with schizotypal personality. This connection was not found in relation to paranoid personality disorder, unless persons with the latter also showed schizotypal traits. These findings indicate that schizotypal personality has a firmer place along the schizophrenia spectrum than does paranoid personality.

mood disorders

In the area of mood disorders, Weissman, Kidd, and Prusoff (1982) analyzed the lifetime prevalences of non-bipolar disorders, noting a 3–12% risk in men; 5–25% in women. A family history of depression doubles or triples the risk for bout(s) of depression within one's lifetime.

Moran and Andrews (1985) found that if one began with agoraphobic probands, one in eight of their parents and siblings were also agoraphobic. The fact that this ratio exceeds that in the general population indicates a genetic component in many cases of agoraphobia. Isaac Marks in England (1986) showed that a genetic factor was relevant not only to agoraphobia but also to panic disorder and obsessive-compulsive disorder. Marks's observation that exposure therapy can be helpful in all these anxiety disorders indicates that genetically driven mental states can nevertheless be ameliorated by psychotherapeutic means.

anxiety disorders

The destabilization of mood that is often seen in severe anxiety disorders and even more routinely in persons with bipolar conditions may manifest itself as irritability. Many manic-depressives go through periods of impulsivity as well as irritability. Yet it was not recognized until recently that some persons show marked degrees of "irritable impulsiveness" that seems distinct from manic-depressive illness. Emil Coccaro and his colleagues (Coccaro, Bergeman, & McClearn, 1993) have shown that irritability and a tendency to violent rage outbursts can stem from a heritable factor. The likely existence of such a factor emerged from their study of monozygotic versus dizygotic twins. At present, *irritable impulsiveness* is recognized as an independent diagnostic entity with a significant genetic underpinning.

"irritable impulsiveness"

The same evolution of interest is observable in psychogenetic research as in descriptive and clinical psychiatry: from psychosis to milder symptom disorders to the subtleties of personality. Hereditary factors in personality (apart from traits and temperaments associated with schizophrenia and manic-depression) were not seriously investigated until the past 15 years. Robert Cloninger and Michael Bohman (Bohman et al., 1982), exploring possible connections between antisocial and hysteric (now called *histrionic*) personality disorders, focused on Briquet's syndrome (a somatization disorder related to hysteria), antisociality, and alcoholism. The latter two conditions were common in males from families who included women with Briquet's syndrome. From this and related observations, these researches hypothesized that antisocial and hysteric personality were different sides of the same genetic coin, with social and gender factors influencing the manner in which a particular personality crystallized. Next, Bohman, Cloninger, von Knorring, and Sigvardsson (1984) gathered further data from the Swedish Adoption Study, revealing that biological fathers of women with Briquet's syndrome often had a history of convictions for violent crimes dating back to adolescence.

hereditary factors in personality

Antisocial and hysteric personality are both characterized by high degrees of novelty-seeking behavior (or "sensation seeking," Zuckerman, 1991). Recently, two research groups—one in Jerusalem, headed by Richard Ebstein; the other in Bethesda, Maryland, headed by Jonathan Benjamin—identified a gene associated with this personality trait (Angier, 1996). The gene encodes instructions for the D-4 dopamine receptor, one of five receptors known to play a role in the brain's response to dopamine. This finding lends support to the theory, elaborated by Cloninger in 1986, that dopamine transmitters mediate novelty-seeking behavior and thus affect this aspect of each person's temperament. The earlier work of Goldsmith (1983) and subsequent work of Cloninger point to a genetic basis for the stability of many different dimensions of personality (for example, aggressiveness, extraversion, impulsivity, ego resiliency). Hereditary factors appear to

novelty-seeking and a dopamine receptor

account for about half the variance for the majority of personality traits.

antisocial personality

In a study of gene-environment interaction in the development of antisocial personality (ASP), Cadoret et al. (1990) noted two markers in the background of the biological parent that predisposed offspring to ASP: alcoholism and delinquency/criminality. Two environmental factors also predisposed to ASP: alcoholism when present in an adoptive parent and low socioeconomic status in the adoptive family. The latter factor was operative *only if* a biological parent had a criminal background; low socioeconomic status did not conduce to ASP when the biological background was free of criminality.

depressive illness and suicidal tendencies

Alec Roy, a psychogeneticist from England, has long been interested in the genetic contribution to depressive illnesses and suicidal tendencies. He and his colleagues (Roy, Segal, Centerwall, & Roninette, 1991) examined a large number of monozygotic and dizygotic twins where one had committed suicide. There was a greater likelihood (by a factor of six) for concordance (both twins eventually committing suicide) in the monozygotic group than in the dizygotic group. What appears to be inherited is a vulnerability to conditions, such as severe depression, that predispose to suicide.

twin studies and personality differences

In her monograph on identical twins reared apart, Susan Farber's (1981) findings serve as a general comment on inherited factors in personality. She reports that twins reared apart were *more* similar in personality than those reared together. Perhaps this paradox can be accounted for by the pressure parents often put on identical twins to differentiate enough so as to feel more separate and independent. Minor differences are seized upon in order to heighten this sense of unique individuality. For example, one twin does a bit better in languages, the other, in math. Parents then encourage the one twin to concentrate on language studies, the other on mathematics. In this way the twins develop skills that are quite distinct by the time they reach adulthood, even though any real differences in ability at the outset were marginal or even nonexistent.

IQ and genetics

Focusing on intelligence, Bouchard, Lykken, McGue, and Tellegen (1990) also investigated twins reared apart. In the 100 pairs to which they had access, they showed that about 70% of the variance in IQ was associated with genetic variation. Optimal environment could probably enhance IQ, despite the strong heritability factor. Their results suggest that in contemporary middle-class industrialized societies, two-thirds of the variance in IQ can be ascribed to genetic factors.

homosexuality: genetic underpinnings

The possibility that genetic factors might play a role in homosexuality has created a delicate sociopolitical issue, at least in those countries (mainly the largely Christian countries of the industrialized West) where prejudice against homosexuals runs high. Highly prejudiced people like to insist that homosexuality is a matter of choice: that homosexual men and women have made a repellent "choice," flaunting

God's will, out of their "perversity," etc. The idea that there is a natural *range* of possible sexual orientations—spanning from exclusive heterosexuality at one end to exclusive homosexuality at the other—determined largely by hereditary and constitutional factors would reduce prejudice. After all, establishing as scientific fact that a certain percentage of persons are born with a predisposition to homosexuality would render the notion of *fault* meaningless.

Contemporary evidence does indeed point to genetic and constitutional factors as prominent, if not crucial, determinants in the development of homosexual orientation. Sociobiologists now tend to view homosexuality in our species as a "relatively altruistic" trait (Weinrich, 1987), involving (in part) an altruistic sacrifice of one's own breeding opportunities in favor of benefits accruing to the homosexual person's relatives (via inheritance, donations, gifts, etc.). Weinrich's model takes into account that some homosexuals are bisexual and do breed (Oscar Wilde being an example), such that the trait is *relatively*, not absolutely, altruistic. At all events, theories based on evolutionary psychology and sociobiology have greater explanatory power regarding homosexuality than do theories based solely on psychodynamic formulations.

"relatively altruistic" trait

MEMORY

As Kupferman (1985) mentions, Endel Tulving in Toronto was among the first to realize that memory for various types of learning could be meaningfully divided into two categories: *reflexive* and *declarative*. Furthermore, different neuronal systems subserve these two memory mechanisms. Reflexive memory has an automatic quality and is not dependent on conscious processes (examples: motor skills, grammar). Declarative memory depends on conscious reflection and involves evaluation, comparison, and inference.

Memory storage is modulated by a variety of hormones that are normally released during painful or otherwise aversive experiences. Noradrenergic receptors within the amygdala, for example, are activated during such aversive experiences. Epinephrine serves as an *underliner* for the memory systems, its presence a signal that experiences which threaten survival are recorded in the brain in a more deeply etched manner than is the case with less threatening stimuli (McGaugh, Introini-Collison, Nagahara, & Cahill, 1989). Of course, children are taught survival-oriented messages over and over again ("Cross on the green light, not in-between!"), which become part of reflexive memory to obviate the possible occurrence of life-threatening experiences.

memory storage: the role of epinephrine

The work of Eric Kandel has been of great importance in highlighting the mechanisms of memory and, in the process, unifying the two

neurobiology and cognitive psychology

separate fields of neurobiology and cognitive psychology. Learning, as Kandel has shown, enhances the strength of synaptic connections between neurons (Kandel & Hawkins, 1992), which in turn contribute to the uniqueness of each individual—since each of us has a different storehouse of memories and would write a different autobiography.

neural mechanisms of memory

The neural mechanisms are being studied on both macro- and micro-levels. The *macroscopic* level has revealed that the hippocampus stores memory for a period of weeks, gradually transferring information to specific regions of the cortex for long-term storage. The *microscopic* level has revealed the cellular growth that occurs during the learning process. For example, in experiments with monkeys instructed to touch an object with the middle three fingers only, microscopic measurements have shown that if the animal repeats the procedure several thousand times, the region of the cortex devoted to the three middle fingers expands at the expense of areas that regulate the other two fingers. This practice can lead to changes in the cortical representation of the "over-used" musculature. Presumably, similar hypertrophic changes occur in musicians, particularly those who began learning and practicing during childhood.

effects of ECT on memory

On another topic altogether, efforts have been made to clarify the controversial issue about the effects of electroconvulsive treatment (ECT) on memory. Sobin and colleagues (1995) looked at the pre-ECT global cognitive status and duration of post-ictal disorientation as possible indices of persistent retrograde amnesia following ECT. It appeared that patients with the greatest pre-ECT cognitive impairment and postictal disorientation were indeed the most vulnerable to persistent retrograde amnesia.

MOOD DISORDERS

seasonal affective disorder

Seasonal fluctuations in mood are common in people who live in the temperate zones. There is typically a mild "dip" in mood in July and a moderate one in February. However, depressed mood is much more marked in patients with seasonal affective disorder. The changes are apparently related to the circadian rhythm regulating melatonin secretion by the pineal gland (increasing when it is dark, diminishing when it is light). Patients with seasonal affective disorder, premenstrual syndrome (PMS), and carbohydrate-craving obesity are all prone to have a disturbed serotonin-carbohydrate feedback mechanism. Ordinarily as Wurtman and Wurtman (1989) point out, carbohydrate consumption increases blood levels of tryptophan and thus serotonin levels. The latter, when heightened, "turn off" the desire for carbohydrates. In a like vein, drugs like fluoxetine/Prozac that enhance brain serotonin usually diminish carbohydrate snacking, whereas drugs that block postsynaptic serotonin receptors may cause increased appetite for carbohydrates and bring about weight gain.

Enthusiasm for the dexamethasone suppression test as a "litmus paper" for detecting depressive vulnerability was at its height in the late 1970s and early 1980s (Carroll et al., 1981). It was believed that failure to suppress normal cortisol concentrations after a dexamethasone challenge was characteristic of melancholic states, including the depressed states seen in many patients with borderline personality. However, Sherman, Pfohl, and Winokur (1984) found that the results of the suppression test depended on the timing of the dexamethasone test dose, owing to the rhythmic changes in secretory activity throughout the day. This and other studies called into question the utility of the test as a specific biological marker for depression. At all events, dexamethasone *non*suppression was associated primarily with the vegetative signs of depression (agitation, initial insomnia, weight loss) rather than with the psychological signs (guilt, hopelessness) (Miller & Nelson, 1987).

dexamethasone suppression test

Even if the test proved disappointing, research related to it increased our knowledge of other facets of depressive illness. Earlier studies had shown that depressed patients have elevated glucocorticoid levels in plasma and the CSF as well as dissynchrony of circadian cortisol secretion. Amsterdam and coworkers (Amsterdam, Maislin, Winokur, Kling, & Gold, 1987) noted a particularly marked blunting of ACTH response to corticotropin-releasing hormone. This lent further support to the hypothesis of heightened hypothalamic-pituitary-adrenal activity in depression.

neurophysiology of depression

Subsequent studies of state-versus-trait abnormalities in patients with unipolar depression pointed to premature timing of the nocturnal secretory phase of prolactin secretion (Linkowski et al., 1989). The amplitude of the prolactin changes was also lowered, with a consequent damping of the expected nighttime elevation. These changes in prolactin levels were present even during clinical remission, suggesting a trait-like stability.

state-versus-trait abnormalities

In a study of regional cerebral blood flow (rCBF), Sackheim and colleagues (1990) found a global reduction in cortical blood flow in patients with major depression as compared with the control patients. Topographic analysis revealed lowered rCBF in several brain regions, which was more marked in older and in more severely depressed patients.

regional cerebral blood flow

Recently, Dupont et al. (1995) examined bipolar patients, using magnetic resonance imaging (MRI) and found that some patients showed an increased volume of abnormal white matter. This abnormality may be associated with cognitive impairment and suggests that at least a subset of bipolar conditions are the result of anomalous development.

MRIs of bipolar patients

self-mutilators

Though not all patients who mutilate themselves have a mood disorder, a high proportion do. Simeon et al. (1992) noted not only an excess of depressive conditions among a group of self-mutilators but also a considerable degree of character pathology, impulsivity, and aggression. Similarly, Russ and colleagues (1993) found all these correlations as well as an excess of anxiety, dissociation, and trauma symptoms in their self-mutilating patients, especially in patients who reported no pain during the self-mutilative acts (compared with those who did feel pain). Their study was inspired in part by the work of van der Kolk (1985) on trauma-induced analgesia in animals, which is known to be mediated by endogenous opioids. Opioid release also appears to occur in traumatized humans and may be a factor in the "addiction to trauma" exhibited by certain patients (especially those with borderline personality disorder and a history of incest) who have been severely traumatized in childhood. These data provide a possible biological underpinning of the Freudian concept of "repetition compulsion."

PERSONALITY DISORDERS

traits and DSM clusters

In one of the earliest and most important attempts to find correlates between the major personality disorders and neurophysiological alterations, Cloninger (1986) outlined three independent, heritable dimensions of personality, each associated with altered neurotransmitter activity. *Novelty-seeking* behavior (NS) was associated with low basal dopaminergic activity; *harm avoidance* behavior (HA) with high serotonergic activity, and *reward dependence* behavior (RD) with low basal noradrenergic activity. These tendencies can be used to discriminate many (though not all) of the *DSM* personality disorders. Histrionic personalities, for example, are characterized by high NS and RD but low HA; antisocial personalities show high NS but low HA and low RD; obsessive-compulsives show high HA but low NS and low RD. The *DSM* clusters can also be understood within this framework: *dramatic cluster* personalities all show high NS; *anxious cluster* personalities, high HA; and *eccentric cluster* types, low RD (though this trait is not the most salient feature of this group).

biological markers of BPD

Because both depressed and borderline personality patients show shortened REM sleep latencies, Akiskal and his coworkers (Akiskal, Yerevanian, Davis, King, & Lemmi, 1985) theorized that the *DSM-III* criteria for borderline personality identified a group of patients with abnormal temperament that also had a strong affective component. In one of the first reports of a biological measure confirming the syndromal diagnosis of borderline personality disorder (BPD), Blackwood, St. Clair, and Kutcher (1986) found that BPD patients showed both prolonged P-

300 latency and reduced amplitude during a study of auditory evoked potentials. This configuration is not specific for BPD, however, since it is also seen in schizophrenic patients. Grosser study of the brain, via computerized tomographic (CT) scanning, did not show differences between BPD patients and normal controls (Lucas, Gardner, Cowdry, & Pickar, 1989). In other words, subtle neurologic dysfunction may be present in BPD, but no structural brain pathology.

Raine, Lencz, and Scerbo (1995) recently applied neuroimaging techniques to the study of people with antisocial personality disorder, including murderers, and found decreased glucose metabolism in the prefrontal cortical areas of murderers. This brain region has been associated with behavioral inhibition and lesions in the area with disinhibition. The researchers also reported psychophysiological abnormalities of heart rate, skin conductance, and evoked potentials that bespeak physiological underarousal, probably underlying the exaggerated need for sensation-seeking experiences in antisocial persons.

psychophysiology of antisocial personality disorder

PREMENSTRUAL SYNDROME

In an unusual example of cross-fertilization of ideas, a psychoanalytic paper on hysteria discussed the possible neuroendocrine correlates of abnormally high prolactin levels in a female patient (Meyer, 1987). These levels tend to rise in response to serotonergic and estrogenic stimulation and to fall under dopaminergic stimulation (such as that induced by the dopamine agonist bromocryptine). Stress can cause a condition of hyperprolactinemia that is correlated with hostility, anxiety, and depression: the symptoms of premenstrual syndrome (PMS). Cognitive, fantasy, and motivational processes may be integrated with physiological functions mediated by the frontal-limbic-hypothalamic network (Reiser, 1984). Psychological and biological factors are thus interconnected and influence each other. In susceptible women taking birth control pills containing estrogen, aggravation of "hysteric" personality traits, along with PMS-like depression, may occur and be accompanied by abnormally high prolactin levels.

high prolactin levels

A contribution to the understanding of PMS-depression was made recently through the study of nocturnal melatonin secretion (Parry et al., 1990). Women with PMS showed patterns of melatonin *onset* and peak concentration similar to those of normal women but had an earlier (phase-advanced) *offset* of melatonin secretion. In other words, women with PMS may manifest a chronobiological abnormality of melatonin secretion. Furthermore, these women often respond favorably measures that affect circadian physiology (in effect, resetting one's biological clock), such as sleep deprivation or phototherapy.

nocturnal melatonin secretion

PSYCHOTROPIC MEDICATIONS

lithium and the dopamine hypothesis

The fact that lithium shows both anti-manic and anti-depressant properties is not easily explained by the biogenic amine theory of depression. Bunney and Garland (1984) suggest that dopamine may be involved in lithium's anti-manic properties. Dopamine receptor hypersensitivity causes manic-like overactivity in animals, for example. Perhaps lithium exerts its mood-stabilizing effect via preventing the development of receptor supersensitivity (cf. Snyder, 1988).

clozapine, risperidone, and dopamine

Further refining the dopamine hypothesis of schizophrenia and antipsychotic drug action, clozapine/Clozaril was shown to occupy the D-2 dopamine receptor to a lesser degree than did conventional neuroleptic drugs (Nordström et al., 1995). This difference may explain the lower risk of extrapyramidal side effects associated with clozapine treatment. The same was claimed of risperidone/Risperdal, which was introduced in the United States in 1994.[1] These drugs also appear to have beneficial effects in ameliorating the negative symptoms of schizophrenia, which, as Pies (1996) points out, account for much of the chronic social and vocational disability in these patients.

SCHIZOPHRENIA

In the last 15 years research on the neurobiology of schizophrenia has taken a sharp turn from the direction it was headed during the 1960s and 1970s. In that "pre-imaging" era, the focus was on identifying various biochemical markers—abnormal compounds detectable in the

---

[1] There is some doubt concerning the risk of tardive dyskinesia (TD) with risperidone. This drug has an affinity for the D-2 receptors in the CNS, as do the conventional antipsychotic medications (such as chlorpromazine) already in use. It is this affinity that appears to be associated with the risk of TD. Clozapine, in use in Europe over 20 years, had not been approved for use in the United States because of the risk of fatal agranulocytosis. But TD has almost never been reported with clozapine (whose affinity is mostly with D-4 and D-1 receptors). Meantime the safety of this unique drug has been improved through the use of a National Registry monitoring patients who receive clozapine, and through frequent blood counts, to ensure that agranulocytosis is not developing. The fatal form of the latter can be circumvented by the immediate cessation of the drug if the white count falls below normal levels. In this way, clozapine can be offered to schizophrenic and schizoaffective patients with minimal risk (Breier, 1996).

brain—whose presence was implicated in the pathogenesis of the disease. Currently the emphasis has shifted from these possible "brain poisons" to the search for subtle structural abnormalities, whose net effect on brain function is to reduce and distort cognitive capacities in such a way as to produce the clinical picture we call schizophrenia.

subtle structural abnormalities

Noting that schizophrenic patients tend to show sub-normal frontal lobe metabolism, and that the synapses in the cortex are progressively reduced through normal childhood, Hoffman and Dobscha (1989) hypothesized a model that might help explain certain characteristic symptoms of the illness. It may be that in schizophrenia the otherwise normal synaptic "pruning" has gone too far, creating a situation where, at the "macro" level of the patient's thoughts, assumptions are then made based on too little evidence.[2] This is certainly typical of paranoid thought whereby persons oversimplify, and of the primary process thought of schizophrenia patients, whereby minor cues from the environment are hurriedly misinterpreted.

synaptic "pruning"

A study of regional cerebral blood flow in schizophrenics showed lower blood flow in the dorsal prefrontal cortex during performance of the Wisconsin Card-Sort Test (Berman, Illkowsky, & Weinberger, 1988). This test apparently calls for a prefrontally-specific cognitive response, whereas the Raven's Progressive Matrices test activates posterior cortical areas to about the same degree in both schizophrenics and normals. Demonstration of hypofrontality in schizophrenia thus depends on the type of cognitive challenge presented.

hypofrontality in schizophrenia?

Returning to the Wisconsin Card-Sort Test, Goldman-Rackič (1992) points out that schizophrenic patients are able to do routine or habitual tasks normally but show fragmented, disorganized behavior when the use of symbols or verbal information is required—as in the card-sort task. As her own elegant work has borne out, the use of autoradiographic techniques are helping to outline which areas of the brain are utilized during the performance of various types of mental tasks. Work has been done with animals as well: In delayed-response performance in monkeys, for example, there is high metabolic activity in the prefrontal cortex, hippocampus, bottom portion of the parietal cortex, and the thalamus. These areas are less active during associative memory tasks that do not depend on short-term, rapid updating of information. Goldman-Rakič believes it would be useful to think of schizophrenia as a breakdown in the process by which representational knowledge governs behavior.

breakdown in representational knowledge

[2] This pruning process probably helps account for the difficulty in pronouncing accent-free sounds of a foreign language after the age of 12. By that time the cortex, via pruning, has streamlined itself for perceiving and recreating just the sounds of one's native language.

neuronal atrophy

In a related study, researchers noted increased neuronal density in both prefrontal and occipital areas in the brains of schizophrenic patients (Selemon, Rajkowska, & Goldman-Rakič, 1995). This finding supports the view that neuronal atrophy in key areas may be the underlying substrate for the deficient processing of information in schizophrenia.

enlarged ventricles

Comparison of ventricular space in schizophrenic patients versus normals showed enlargement of the third and lateral ventricles in the patient group (Kelsoe, Cadet, Pickar, & Weinberger, 1988). This increase in ventricle space implies a diminution in the volume of cortex near these ventricular regions. Around the same time, Reveley, Reveley, and Baldy (1987) found that discordant schizophrenic twin pairs showed a less dense left-brain hemisphere, even in the unaffected twins. This finding supports the hypothesis of hemisphere dysfunction in schizophrenia.

In a neuroimaging study of the offspring of schizophrenic parents, anomalies such as ventricular enlargement were noted across the range of schizophrenia spectrum conditions (such as schizotypal personality) but were more pronounced in patients with the most severe syndromes (such as full-blown schizophrenia) (Cannon et al., 1994).

More recently, Elkis and his colleagues (Elkis, Friedman, Wise, & Meltzer, 1995) have demonstrated that even though ventricular enlargement and sulcal prominence have been documented in many studies of schizophrenia, similar abnormalities can also be detected in patients with mood disorders, though these patients showed less enlargement than did schizophrenics. Apparently some structural brain changes in the different psychoses are common and nonspecific.

hippocampal pathology

Neuroimaging scans of the hippocampus region in schizophrenic versus normal brains (from a collection of postmortem specimens) showed lower hippocampal volume and lower pyramidal cell density in the schizophrenic brain (Jeste & Lohr, 1989), suggesting the presence of hippocampal pathology in the pathogenesis of the disease, perhaps by adversely affecting key memory and information-relay circuits.

eye-tracking dysfuntion; auditory dysfunction

In a study bearing on both neurophysiology and genetics, Holzman et al. (1988) investigated eye-tracking dysfunction in schizophrenics and their close relatives, noting abnormalities in 45% of the first-degree relatives. When they evaluated this marker in identical versus fraternal twins, they found a pattern compatible with a single underlying trait that might be transmitted by an autosomal dominant gene. In another study Kutscher and his colleagues (Kutscher, Blackwood, St. Clair, Gaskell, & Muir, 1987) measured auditory P-300 event-related EEG potentials. Both schizophrenic patients and patients with borderline personality disorder showed longer P-300 latencies and lower amplitudes, suggesting a dysfunction in auditory neurointegration in schizophrenic as well as BPD patients.

There has been an attitudinal shift in psychiatry over the past two decades regarding the "essence" schizophrenia. Clinicians and investigators alike are now more inclined to view the negative symptoms as the essence, though the neural mechanisms underlying these symptoms are still not well understood. Some researchers have implicated cerebral atrophy in certain brain regions; others, abnormalities in dopamine metabolism. However, studies of cholinergic/dopaminergic interactions in schizophrenia suggest that cholinergic overdrive can create a clinical picture closely resembling the negative symptoms of flattened affect, loss of will, and so on. Furthermore, in the wake of a psychotic episode (with positive symptoms such as delusions), a contemporary increase in the activity of the cholinergic system may take place by way of counteracting the dopaminergic hyperactivity (and the attendant positive signs of psychosis) of the psychotic phase. Tandon and Greden (1989) note that this increased cholinergic activity may be accompanied by heightened negative symptoms, experienced as "depressive" (slowed down, lethargic) by patient and therapist alike. This may be the basis for the "postpsychotic depression" often observed in recuperating schizophrenic patients.

the "essence" of schizophrenia: the negative symptoms

Contemporary research has not neglected the positive symptoms, however, as we see in the efforts of Hoffman and colleagues to advance our understanding of the phenomenon of hallucinations. As a result of their efforts to create models of schizophrenic function via computer-assisted simulations of neural networks, they have suggested that the primary cause of hallucinated voices in schizophrenia may be reduced to neuroanatomic connectivity in the area of verbal memory (Hoffman, Rapaport, Ameli, McGlashan, & Harcherik, 1995). This research is an extension of Hoffman and Dobscha's (1989) theory that excessive pruning of dendritic connections during the early years of life (referred to above) is important in the pathogenesis of schizophrenia. The mechanism seems to be one in which false word "percepts" emerge spontaneously where there has been reduced neuronal activation due to an excessively pruned dendritic "tree." In other situations, reduced interconnections appear to predispose schizophrenic persons to reach hasty assumptions ("dangerous" or "harmless") in response to stimuli from the external world that have not been adequately assessed and discriminated.

the positive symptoms

SEXUALITY

Dopamine is involved in more areas than schizophrenic and novelty-seeking behaviors: it also appears that dopaminergic receptor activation is associated with penile erection, along with the inhibition of alpha-adrenergic influences. Ejaculation is apparently mediated by alpha-adrenergic fibers and may be inhibited by serotonergic transmission in the brain. This serotonergic mechanism may underlie the distressing side effect experienced by about 20% of patients taking one of the SSRI antidepressants (fluoxetine, paroxetine, sertraline, fluoxamine): blunted ejaculatory response and/or libido (Seagraves, 1989).

gender-role changes

Contrary to earlier impressions, a more recent study by Lish and colleagues (Lish, Meyer-Bahlburg, Ehrhardt, Travis, & Veridiano, 1992), using refined questionnaires concerning the relationship between exposure during fetal life to diethylstilbestrol ("DES": a non-steroidal estrogen formerly used to sustain endangered pregnancies) and subsequent masculinization in later life, failed to confirm the supposed connection. The vast majority of DES-exposed girls and women have not shown either increased masculine or decreased feminine gender-role behavior. However, this is not the case with exposure to prenatal androgen excess. In the latter instance, gender-role changes in women do often occur. In general, early sexual differentiation depends on the presence or absence of certain testosterone concentrations during key periods in fetal life. Estrogens are important in the normal development of the central nervous system (Toran-Allerand, 1984) and specifically in its structural and functional differentiation (Gur et al., 1995; McEwen, 1983).

sex differences in cognitive and emotional processing

Through the use of positron-emission tomography (PET) scans of healthy men and women, Gur et al. (1995) were able to discern sex differences. Men had relatively higher metabolism than women in temporal-limbic regions and in the cerebellum, and relatively lower metabolism in the cingulate regions. Their data suggest that sex differences exist in cognitive and emotional processing, and that these differences have a biological underpinning. It is not surprising that such differences might exist in humans, given that sex differences in brain organization have been verified for some time in other species. (The brain nuclei subserving song-production in songbirds, for example, are larger in males, who produce the song as part of the courtship ritual and teach the song pattern to their young.)

sex differences in language

Publishing in the same year, Shaywitz et al. (1995) demonstrated sex differences in the areas of the brain that mediate language. Using MRI techniques to track phonological tasks involving rhyme, they were able to show that brain activation in males lateralized to the left inferior frontal gyrus. In females the activation was more diffuse and involved by right and left inferior frontal gyri.

nitric oxide

Also in 1994, Solomon Snyder and his colleagues (O'Dell et al., 1994) made the surprising discovery that the gas nitric oxide serves as a neurotransmitter, especially in areas of the brain that help regulate emotions. Male mice lacking the enzyme for synthesizing nitric oxide behave aggressively and hypersexually. It remains to be seen whether there is a parallel mechanism in humans that may account for a proportion of pathological aggressive and sexual behaviors.

SUICIDE

Because suicide is a comparatively rare event, large-scale studies are needed if one is to make more accurate assessments of suicide risk. This point was made by Allgulander (1994), who reviewed the death statistics for some 47,000 former inpatients with either anxiety neurosis (9,912) (what we would call panic disorder) or depressive neurosis (38,529). Of the 9,910 deaths, 18% were by suicide (usually within three months of leaving the hospital). The suicide risk for depressives was greater by twice or more than that of the anxiety patients (and both rates were considerably higher than the risk in the general population).

In their search for neurophysiologic correlates of suicide, Hansenne and colleagues studied both P-300 waves in evoked potential tests and contingent negative variation (CNV), both of which are modulated by catecholamine neurotransmitters (Hansenne, Pitchot, Moreno, Mirel, & Ansseau, 1994). Reduced P-300 amplitude and abnormalities of CNV amplitude and duration have been reported in depressed patients. Hansenne et al. found significant reductions in both P-300 and CNV amplitudes in depressed patients who had attempted suicide in comparison with those who had not. The P-300 and CNV abnormalities may be reflections of dopaminergic dysfunctions, and may relate to the feelings of hopelessness and helplessness in depression, especially when accompanied by strong suicidal behavior.

neurophysiologic correlates of suicide

In relation to the suicide risk in patients with recurrent depression, Angst and colleagues (1990) worked out life-curves for risk in various patient groups, showing that those with recurrent depressive illness are prone to suicide throughout their adult lives. In other words, the tendency to suicide is not something that is eventually "outgrown." Angst's studies lend support to the endorsement of lifelong antidepressant therapy in patients with recurrent depression, as a way of minimizing the frequency and intensity of episodes—and the number of completed suicides. In an earlier study, Angst and Clayton (1986) analyzed the pre-morbid personalities of patients in various diagnostic groups, including those who committed suicide. They were able to ascertain that unipolar depressives scored high on scales of aggression and emotional lability, with those who died by suicide or accident scoring the highest of any group. The findings of their study support the more biologically-oriented research of Åsberg, which identifies the connection between suicide and aggression as stronger than the connection between suicide and lowered mood in depressive patients.

life-curves for risk

Chapter 27

CHILD PSYCHIATRY

The literature on the history of child psychiatry is scanty, whether the focus is on the early history (before 1900) or on the 20th century. Anna Freud (1966) wrote a brief history of child psychoanalysis; articles by Walk (1969) and Stone (1973) are among the few others that deal with the pre-1900 period. To address this general deficiency, Noshpitz has written a book on the history of childhood and child psychiatry (1995) from 1890 through 1980. Noshpitz covers a wide range of topics: epidemiological issues, drug abuse, government programs, child-mother interactions, and the transformation in family size and integrity. A century ago, for example, 25% of the families in the United States consisted of seven or more persons; today, only 3%. Single-parent households are becoming more and more numerous; fewer children get to spend all their dependent years in a home containing both biological parents. These changes have important consequences for child psychiatry, given the often adverse impact of divorce and paternal absence exerted upon children. Progress in child psychiatry has been impressive during the years 1980–1995. What follows is a brief survey of recent developments in a number of broad sectors.

AUTISM, CHILDHOOD SCHIZOPHRENIA, AND AFFECTIVE PSYCHOSES

The controversy concerning a possible relationship between infantile autism and childhood schizophrenia has continued into the recent years. Lauretta Bender had earlier regarded infantile autism as a subtype of childhood schizophrenia; Michael Rutter had contended that the two conditions were unrelated. As Leonora Petty and her colleagues note, infantile autism usually has an earlier age of onset (birth to age three) than childhood schizophrenia (age five and later) and much less of a family history of schizophrenia (Petty, Ornitz, Michelman, & Zimmerman, 1984). Adult schizophrenia patients usually show reasonably good function as young children, whereas infantile autism patients show serious impairments early on. But in a few instances, children with infantile autism go on to develop well substantiated schizophrenia in adult life. Petty et al. offered three detailed case histories in support of this contention in their 1984 paper.

earlier differentiations

The correlation between age of manifestation and the nature of the psychosis had been emphasized earlier by Daniel Duché, director of the child psychiatry service at Paris's Salpêtrière Hospital (1971). Duché reserved the term *schizophrenia* for those cases of childhood-onset psychosis (with thought disorder) wherein the children had reached the age when personality has begun to solidify and become "structured." This occurred, in his view, at about age ten. As described early in the century by Heller (cited by Duché, 1971), "infantile dementia" in the first few years of life was more apt to stem from organic causes such as encephalitis or a lipoidosis. The symptoms of this nonspecific condition involved progressive loss of language, stereotyped movements, rage outbursts, blunting of affect, and indifference toward family members; terrifying hallucinations and encopresis might also occur. In general, Duché felt that the earlier the onset, the more likely some serious organic condition was the primary etiological factor (and the more the clinical picture would resemble what we now subsume under the heading of infantile autism); the later the onset, the greater the likelihood of a "true" schizophrenia.

thought disorder as current index

Current views of childhood schizophrenia identify thought disorder involving loose associations and illogical thinking as the most reliable diagnostic index (Caplan & Tanguay, 1991). According to Erlenmeyer-Kimling and Cornblatt (1987), the best predictor of vulnerability to schizophrenia in "high-risk" children is performance on attentional tasks. According to their research, the children of schizophrenic parents most likely to manifest clinical schizophrenia in adolescence or adulthood were those with low verbal IQ test scores and poor ability on the Continuous Performance Test and the Bender Gestalt Test (Kestenbaum, 1994).

treatments for childhood schizophrenia

In the treatment of early-onset schizophrenia, a bewildering variety of measures and psychotherapy approaches has been recommended, as outlined by Cantor and Kestenbaum (1986): child psychoanalysis, family therapy, movement therapy (which is used widely in Hungary with adult schizophrenics as well), pharmacotherapy, and the like. As these authors point out, schizophrenic children are particularly deficient at distinguishing reality from fantasy. This being the case, "expressive" therapies that emphasize the uncovering of previously unconscious material are usually best avoided in children already engulfed in fantasy life. Cantor and Kestenbaum propose instead a real-

bipolar disorder

ity-oriented therapy, where the therapist serves as a bridge to the real world.

Manic-depressive illness may also show itself in early life, either as depression or mania. Children with one or both parents who are manic-depressive are apt to present with clinical signs of affect lability, impulsivity, rage outbursts, and rebelliousness, and personality changes in the direction of extraversion or dysthymia (Kestenbaum & Kron, 1987). Decina et al. (1983) report a marked verbal/performance split on IQ tests (with the verbal score being the higher). Carlson (1983) notes a tendency of children at risk for bipolar illness to be irritable and emotionally labile. Some cases of borderline personality disorder, especially where there has been no history of child abuse, appear to stem from genetic predisposition to manic-depression (Akiskal, Yerevanian, Davis, King, & Lemmi, 1985).

SUICIDE BY THE YOUNG

signs, symptoms, and conditions

Because of the upsurge in the suicide rate in younger persons over the past generation, the study of suicide in children and adolescents has become a subspecialty in itself. Cynthia Pfeffer of the New York Hospital/Westchester Division has contributed importantly to this field (1986). Studying the characteristics of adolescents who died by suicide, David Brent et al. (1988) identify several factors that were more prevalent among these adolescents compared with those who harbored suicidal feelings or made suicidal acts that were not lethal. Those who died were more apt to have shown clinical signs of bipolar disorder, to be "comorbid" for other symptom disorders (such as substance abuse), to have received no prior therapy, and to have had access to guns or rifles at home.[1] Along similar lines Reinherz et al. (1995) note in their longitudinal study that childhood behaviors that were counter to typical gender norms could serve as predictors of suicidal ideation by age 15 or suicidal acts by age 18: aggressive behavior in girls, for example, or marked dependency in boys.

OBSESSIVE-COMPULSIVE DISORDER

Obsessive-compulsive disorder (OCD) occurs in children and adolescents, often with a clinical picture quite similar to that of older pa-

---

[1] This finding is pertinent only to the United States (Brent's study was carried out in Pittsburgh), since firearms are much less available in most other countries.

tients. Swedo and colleagues (Swedo, Rapoport, Leonard, Lenane, & Cheslow, 1989) note the same washing, grooming, and checking rituals in their young patients as are characteristic of adults with OCD. Preoccupation with disease and danger was similarly present in both age groups. A familial factor was also apparent: A quarter of the young OCD patients had a close relative with the same disorder. Because OCD involves ego-dystonic thoughts and actions, patients sometimes conceal the nature of this condition from their therapists, preferring to speak of depression or anxiety instead. The field has been aware of childhood cases of OCD for many years, nonetheless: Swedo relates that Janet described a five-year-old with typical OCD symptoms as far back as 1905.

GILLES DE LA TOURETTE'S SYNDROME

Occasionally, cases of OCD (especially where the manifestation is a touching compulsion) and Gilles de la Tourette's syndrome are found in the same family (Pauls et al., 1991), suggesting the possibility that the two syndromes are different phenotypic expressions of the same genetic factor. The tics associated with Tourette's syndrome tend to diminish in severity after puberty (King & Cohen, 1994). Whether or not accompanied by OCD, Tourette's syndrome is believed to represent a genetic vulnerability, which may present itself in childhood as simple tics (grimaces, limb jerks, blinks) or complex tics (clapping, elaborate movement patterns, scatological verbalizations). The mainstay of therapy is pharmacological; the medications most widely used are either haloperidol/Haldol or pimozide/Orap (Shapiro et al., 1989).

TEMPERAMENT

After evaluating over 800 children, a group of Canadian researchers (Maziade, Caron, Coté, Boutin, & Thivierge, 1990) noted two main types of temperament. Extreme examples of either type are often encountered in a population of psychiatrically troubled children. They also noted a connection between the type of extreme temperament and the nature of the psychiatric condition later exhibited: Factor #1 (withdrawal from new stimuli, high intensity, negative mood) was associated with conduct disorders and attention deficit disorders; factor #2 (low persistence, high sensory threshold) was associated with developmental delay disorders.

ATTENTION-DEFICIT-HYPERACTIVITY DISORDER

The relationship between attention-deficit-hyperactivity disorder (ADHD) and future difficulties with the law was explored in a prospective follow-up design by Mannuzza, Gittelman-Klein, Konig, and Giampino (1989). When two groups of about 100 males each—one with ADHD, the other, normal controls—were compared (after passing from grade-school age to their early twenties), the ADHD males had a doubly high arrest record (39% versus 20%), more convictions (28% versus 11%) and incarcerations (9% versus 1%). ADHD was thus seen as a risk factor for future criminality, though there was almost always an intermediate stage (in the arrest cases) of having developed antisocial personality in early adulthood.

For children with ADHD, pharmacotherapy with dextroamphetamine continues to prove its efficacy, whereas fenfluramine, though related structurally to the former, has shown no therapeutic effects (Donnelly et al., 1989).

DEPRESSION

Until recently, the correlation between major depression and shortened REM latency (as measured by polysomnographic recording over one or more nights of sleep) had been established only for adults with depression. Emslie and colleagues (Emslie, Rush, Weinberg, Rintelmann, & Roffwarg, 1990) were able to obtain polysomnograms on children hospitalized for depression. Compared with healthy controls, these children also showed reduced REM latency, suggesting that their depressive illness was probably related etiologically to the adult disorder.

EATING DISORDERS

Not all childhood eating disorders are confined to post-puberty cases of anorexia nervosa or bulimia nervosa. Fosson et al. (1987) describe cases of prepubertal anorexia; Singer et al. (1992) note cases of food phobia in young children; and Chatoor et al. (1988) cite instances of food refusal following traumatic experiences such as choking on food particles. (Lewis and Chatoor, 1994, review the topic extensively.)

Anorexia and bulimia continue to peak in incidence at, or after, puberty and to occur preponderantly in young women. Mood disorders (chiefly depression) and borderline personality disorder are common (half or more of cases) accompaniments of anorexia (Bemporad et al., 1992). In recent years the forms of psychotherapy most recommended for anorexia are cognitive (Garner & Bemis, 1985) and behavioral (Halmi, 1985), with increasingly less reliance on psychoanalytically-oriented therapy—at least in the initial stages, when serious weight loss must be counteracted quickly and efficiently.

psychotherapy

There is no pharmacotherapy specific to either anorexia or bulimia, though the mood and anxiety disorders common to both may respond to antidepressants and anxiolytics. In the United States anorexia is associated with a disconcertingly high rate of suicide and death from the complications of inanition—though the mortality rates are higher in Sweden (Theander, 1983) and Denmark, where suicide rates are higher among adolescents in general. Unfavorable prognostic signs include frequent hospitalizations, extremely low weight, and quasi-delusional distortions of body image.

suicide and death

Bulimic patients are at much less risk for fatal outcomes, though they do face the same burden of chronicity as do their anorectic counterparts. The duration of either condition tends to be prolonged (into the fourth or fifth decade of life) when there is a history of trauma in childhood. The treatment methods developed in the past 15 years, while often more effective than older methods in restoring anorectic patients to better weight and curbing bulimic tendencies, still leave a residue of unresolved personality problems. Among female patients, conflicts about wifehood, pregnancy, and motherhood are common, arising typically either from troubled mother-daughter relationships or from fathers who depreciate women. To deal adequately with these conflicts, a long period of psychotherapy (whether analytic, supportive, or cognitive) is usually necessary.

chronicity

CHILD ABUSE AND ITS EFFECTS

The statistics that Arthur Green (1994) reports on the physical and sexual abuses of children in the United States indicate epidemic proportions: half a million children who, in any one year, experience one or both forms of abuse. Although child abuse occurs in all social strata, it is more prevalent in situations of divorce, poverty, or unmarried mothers. Jean Goodwin (1982, 1985) describes some of the common sequelae of such abuse in young children: nightmares, hypervigilance, psychosomatic complaints, insomnia—all of which may later be accompanied by the flashbacks and startle reactions characteristic of the adult form of posttraumatic stress disorder. Judith Herman (1981; Herman, Perry, & van der Kolk, 1989) describes the general mistrustfulness that so often develops in abused children, some of whom (especially after experiencing incest) go on to develop borderline personality disorder.

gender differences

Boys are more apt to be the victims of physical than of sexual abuse and are more prone to resort to aggression than are abused girls. Physically abused boys are at considerable risk for conduct disorder, and later on, delinquency and antisocial personality.

treatment approaches

As the occurrence of child abuse has become more widely recognized, various forms of "survivor" groups have been established. Group therapy for incest survivors has been described by Blick and Porter (1982). Intervention with the offending or non-participating parents, either in dyadic or group therapy, has been tried as well, though fathers/stepfathers who commit incest are often sociopathic and not amenable to therapy.

SIDS

In the past few years it has become apparent that a small proportion of SIDS cases ("Sudden Infant Death Syndrome") are factitious, inflicted by immature and narcissistic mothers. The cases of Mary Beth Tinning (Eggington, 1989), Diane Lumbrera (Cavenaugh, 1995), and Waneta Hoyt (Hickey et al., 1996) are illustrative. These cases receive the diagnosis of "Munchausen syndrome by proxy": The feigned illness is induced not by the patient but by another person (in this case, the mother).

CONDUCT DISORDER AND DELINQUENCY

Efrain Bleiberg (1994), director of child and adolescent psychiatry at Menninger Clinic, notes that conduct disorder is the most commonly utilized diagnosis in his field. Partly this is because the term is a broad, nonspecific "umbrella" one, covering a host of clinical entities relating to aggressive, anti-social, rebellious, and otherwise offensive behavior. An earlier generation of psychoanalytic writers (August Aichhorn, Fritz Redl, Adelaide Johnson) sought to understand conduct disorder in dynamic terms, emphasizing such factors as superego lacunae, failure of ego controls, excessive efforts to "test" relationships, and the like.

dynamic etiology

constitutional etiology

But these explanations did not sufficiently take into account constitutional factors often present alongside the unfavorable home environments. As Lykken (1995) has pointed out, in a few instances conduct disorder emerges even in adequately nurturing homes, when constitutional predisposition (to low empathy, high sensation-seeking, and impulsivity) is so marked as to overwhelm the positive family factors. Here one is in the presence of "primary psychopathy," in which the conduct disorder is often the prelude to juvenile delinquency and adult criminality.

More commonly cases of delinquency involve youngsters at risk from both constitutional and environmental factors. Lisabeth Dilalla and

Irving Gottesman (1990) use a three-part taxonomy to distinguish types of delinquencies: *continuous antisocials, transitory delinquents,* and *late bloomers.* The continuous antisocials have the highest loading for both genetic and environmental predispositions to conduct disorder and later criminality, in contrast to the transitory group (who are delinquent but not criminal), and the late bloomers (adult criminals who are not delinquent as adolescents). Heavily represented among the continuous group are children who are the class bullies by age eight, who then go on to become delinquents after puberty and felons by age 28. In rare instances, children progress from conduct disorder to extreme violence before reaching puberty, as in the highly publicized case of the three-year-old English boy, James Bulger, who in 1993 was abducted, tortured, and killed by two 10-year-old truant boys from chaotic, fatherless homes (D. Smith, 1994).

three-part taxonomy

Many children with conduct disorder show behaviors limited to classroom disruptiveness, clowning, and tantrums, and never get into trouble with the law. Rutter and Giller (1983) place these children in their "socialized" category because of their capacity for attachment and enduring friendships. Their prognosis is correspondingly better than in the "unsocialized" group. Adolescents who commit violent acts, including murder, and who become the subject of newspaper accounts (that draw attention to their callousness or lack of remorse), are more likely to fall into the latter category.

prognostic indicators

It is not clear where such adolescents would fit in the diagnostic schema elaborated by Marohn et al. (1979), who identify four types of delinquents: impulsive, narcissistic, empty borderlines, and depressed borderlines. *Impulsive* and *narcissistic,* though applicable, do not capture the severity of psychopathology in the most dangerous cases.

beyond impulsivity and narcissism

While therapy for the most callous and violent youths may be elusive, and all too often, ineffective, for those whose conduct disorder still includes a capacity for social bonding (including a potential for feeling at least some guilt), therapy of the type recommended by Paulina Kernberg (Kernberg & Chazan, 1991) may both ameliorate conduct and lead to prosocial adaptations. These authors describe an approach built on supportive/expressive play therapy in the one-to-one setting, group therapy, and intensive work with the families.

treatment

PSYCHOTHERAPY FOR CHILDREN AND ADOLESCENTS WITH "NEUROTIC" AND "BORDERLINE" CONDITIONS

Though the term *neurotic* has been dropped from the *DSM,* it remains a useful designation for milder conditions characterized by internalization and conscious suffering (usually in the forms of anxiety or depression), in contrast to externalization and acting-out behaviors. As yet, there is no firm consensus concerning the criteria for the diagnosis of borderline in persons under the age of 16 or 15.

the Hampstead Index

The concept of neurosis still enjoys wide currency among psychoanalysts, and its relevance to younger patients has been greatly enhanced by the work of Joseph Sandler (1962) in London, who was the chief organizer of the Hampstead Index. This index is the outgrowth of research carried out at the Hampstead Child Guidance Clinic (headed by Anna Freud in the 1950s), which strove to achieve a dynamic equilibrium between clinical practice and theory. The premise was that precise categorization of clinical material would lead to more reliable diagnostic standards, which in turn conduces to sounder theory and taxonomy. An example already noted was Sandler's study of obsessional disorders that led to their differentiation into obsessional personality versus obsessional "neurosis" (akin to OCD).

intermediate levels of psychopathology

In the early 1980s efforts to establish meaningful criteria for borderline conditions in children and adolescents led to the development of checklists and questionnaires designed to identify intermediate levels of psychopathology in this age group: young persons who were not clearly psychotic, yet more disturbed than children with characteristics that more nearly accorded with those of their age-mates. Many of the articles devoted to this task were collected in a book edited by Kenneth Robson (1983), and guidelines for diagnosis were offered in separate chapters by Theodore Shapiro, Paulina Kernberg, and Ricardo Vela and his colleagues.

descriptive, object relations, and developmental approaches

Vela et al. (1983) divide symptomatology into six areas, including "disturbed interpersonal relations" (extreme outbursts of love and hate toward the same person), "reality disturbances" (withdrawal into fantasy more than would be appropriate for a child of the same age), and "impulsivity" (repetitive, unmitigated fits of rage). Paulina Kernberg's (1983) approach rests more on pathological object-relations, as exemplified by extreme devaluation of the mother. But she also mentions the vulnerability to hallucinations and brevity of reality span (the child requires the presence of the other person in order to maintain a sense of reality) as common to children who merit a borderline diagnosis. Shapiro (1983) underlines the need to rely on criteria specific to the developmental stage of the child, since the analogy to adult diagnoses is apt to be meager and misleading. He also cautions that, no matter what criteria one used to determine a diagnosis of borderline in a child, one cannot assume that years later, the child would necessarily fulfill the criteria for borderline personality disorder as described for adults.

environmental and constitutional factors

Paulina Kernberg returns to this issue in a subsequent paper (1988) that addresses both diagnosis and therapy, where she also contends that environmental and constitutional factors may be more important than genetic factors in the etiology. For her, the borderline diagnosis is most justified in the presence of such signs as demandingness, micropsychotic states, marked fantasy activity, and shifting levels of ego function. In regard to treatment, Kernberg advocates the importance of supportive-expressive psychotherapy, intensive work with the parents and the family system, group therapy as a helpful measure in compensating for deficiencies in socialization, and medication where target symptoms are present (for example, imipramine for depression; methylphenidate for attention-deficit-hyperactivity disorder).

Paulina Kernberg was also one of the first to describe narcissistic personality disorder in children (Egan & Kernberg, 1984; P. Kernberg, 1989). Though in this area the same criteria can be used for both child and adult populations, children are apt to display certain unique features, such as separation anxiety, aversion of gaze, and pathological play. She also outlines a number of "risk factors," including child abuse, adoption, parental narcissism, overindulgence, and divorce.

narcissistic personality disorder in children

There are many borderline adolescents who have backgrounds of severe sexual or physical abuse, for whom long-term residential care might be the optimal first step in treatment. Sadly, centers providing such care are becoming prohibitively expensive in the United States—and therefore fewer—but remain more available in a number of European countries. In Paris, for examples, there are excellent units directed by Philippe Jeammet (University of Paris International Hospital) and Alain Braconnier (Paumelle Psychiatric Center); in Geneva, by Francois Ladame (Adolescent Psychiatric Unit); and in Milan, by Roberto Bertolli (Center for the Study and Therapy of Personality Disorders). In Brisbane, Australia, the Belmont Hospital has a special unit for borderline adolescent and young adult patients, headed by Alan Unwin and Bronwin Beacham. The five-to-ten-year follow-up of borderline patients from the Belmont unit, many of whom have histories of incest and/or physical abuse, has shown remarkably good results: Three-fourths of their patients now function in the "good to recovered" range.

long-term residential care

In relation to children with neurotic conflicts, therapy is conducted on an ambulatory basis—in clinics or private offices. Guidelines for therapy have not changed appreciably in the past 15 years, though the important role of cultural factors is becoming more widely recognized. As Daniel Stern (1995) mentions, if a patient is acculturated to one therapeutic approach, that approach will probably work best for that particular person, regardless of the method's merits, as adjudged by controlled studies reported in the literature. As Stern also notes, because effective dynamic therapy ultimately improves behavior, while effective cognitive/behavioral therapy ultimately improves self-esteem and basic assumptions, outwardly differing therapies tend, over time, to converge in regard to their beneficial effects.

In his work with neurotic children Bleiberg (1994) leans toward a

psychodynamic play
therapy approach

psychodynamic approach. Neurotic children come to the therapist, in his words, "filled with dread, haunted by shame, or tormented by guilt, yet are generally endowed with 'basic trust'" (p. 498). Conflicts typically center around sibling rivalry and ambivalence toward a parent figure. Some form of play therapy is his usual medium of interaction, and the therapist's comments are phrased in the metaphor of the play ("the baby lion wanted to smash that mean daddy lion") rather than translated into their "real" meaning. The therapist strives to develop the same kind of therapeutic alliance that is essential to work with adult patients. The transference is used to explore conflicts and negative feelings toward family members as well as toward the therapist and hopefully "fosters the alliance and improves the outcome" (p. 500).

variety of regimens

Dynamic therapy of the type Bleiberg describes can be carried out in a variety of regimens: once-weekly sessions or a schedule involving two, three, or even more visits per week, as in child psychoanalysis. Cost factors, the nature of the child's problems, and the availability of therapists with this background become factors in determining the indications for intensive treatment of this kind. The role of interpretation takes on special importance in child analytic work, as discussed by the French psychoanalysts René Diatkine and Janine Simon (1980).

ADVANCES IN PSYCHOPHARMACOLOGY

Whereas methylphenidate (for ADHD), neuroleptics (for schizophrenic reactions), and tricyclic compounds (for depression) have been used for many years in children with the relevant target symptoms, the serotonin reuptake blockers (SSRIs) have been in use only about 10 years in the United States (though somewhat longer in Europe). Reviewing the literature, DeVane and Sallee (1996) report positive results with the SSRIs in children and adolescents who have depression or OCD. To a more modest degree, results were often favorable in a variety of other conditions, such as eating disorders, social phobia, trichotillomania. The field of psychopharmacology in relation to child and adolescent populations has been reviewed comprehensively by two investigators from New Zealand, Werry and Aman (1993), whose *Practitioner's Guide* covers all conditions, the common and the obscure, where medications may be of benefit.

STRESS AND ADJUSTMENT DISORDERS

There is more to child psychiatry than the major conditions outlined in the *DSM*. Probably more common than the psychoses and other severe symptom disorders are the "adjustment disorders" related to a whole host of environmental and interpersonal stressors. Noshpitz and Coddington compiled a book (1990) dealing with over two dozen common stressors. Among them: death of a parent, divorce, illness, accidents, natural disasters, crime, prejudice, geographical change, and bodily trauma from rape or abuse.

stressors

The magnitude of these adjustment problems can be glimpsed from the fact that in the United States half a million children are in foster care in any one year—all of whom, by definition, have experienced object loss. In a concluding chapter Noshpitz outlines the various relevant treatment measures, which include self-help groups for adolescents (for those with alcohol/drug addicted parents), other forms of group therapy, behavioral techniques, crisis intervention, family therapy, and short-term psychotherapy.

treatments

LANGUAGE DISORDERS

In her research on language disorders in children, Paula Tallal (Tallal, 1992; Tallal & Stark, 1982) discovered that dyslexic and other language-impaired children require more time (on the order of 300 msec) to distinguish high and low tones and to discriminate between rhyming phonemes that begin with different consonants. It turns out that the acoustic changes within words are more important than those between words or between sentences. In dealing with a pair like *bah* and *dah*, for example, the *b* and *d* occupy only a few brief milliseconds of time, whereas the vowel can be uttered over a long burst. Because of the low-millisecond presentation, the consonants are hard to tell apart.

auditory discrimination

Even *visual* presentations in language-impaired children are often processed with errors if the presentation time is very brief, clearly suggesting crossmodal difficulties. In some dyslexic children there is damage in the magnocellular regions of the lateral geniculate bodies: The large cells there ordinarily carry the most rapid type of signals; impairment can lead to poor processing of rapid stimuli. Magnetic resonance imaging of language-impaired children sometimes shows a reduction in the volume of Broca's speech area. Ordinarily, there is a left-hemispheric advantage in the processing of rapid speech and visual stimuli, but relevant areas in the left hemisphere may also be impaired in these children.

visual discrimination

Chapter 28

FORENSIC PSYCHIATRY

INSANITY

legal vs. psychiatric definitions

In the past 15 years many commentators have expressed dissatisfaction with current regulations regarding the definition of *insanity*—a descriptor still pertaining to mental illness, but which has been, for many years, purely a legal term. Abraham Halpern (1991) argues, for example, that the insanity defense often fails to identify those mentally disabled persons who deserve to be spared moral condemnation as criminals. On other occasions, certain persons are adjudged insane but are not mentally ill—or at least not clearly psychotic—and thus drain the resources of the maximum security hospitals. On still other occasions, psychopathic criminals have been declared insane, thanks to the clever argumentation of their defense attorneys, following which they have been permitted to remain in comparatively comfortable hospitals rather than in the less comfortable and less sympathetic environment of prison. Such was most likely the case with John Hinckley, who attempted to assassinate President Reagan in 1981. Clarke (1990) in Arizona has offered compelling evidence that Hinckley would best be understood as a psychopath rather than as a schizophrenic who was also "insane."

mental illness, disease, and the question of responsibility

Parallel to the knotty problem of determining who is insane and who is not is the equally entangled problem of determining levels of responsibility in cases where someone with "mental illness" (short of legal insanity) commits a crime. This includes determination of responsibility in cases where the illness is primarily one of substance abuse—itself a controversial issue, since, in the case of alcoholism, there is much debate as to whether, and under what circumstances, it should be considered a mental condition or disease as opposed to a bad habit. There appears to be a strong hereditary factor in about half the population of alcoholics. But even if one considers just these instances as the "disease" cases, are the acts committed under the influence of the alcohol to be viewed as within, or outside of, the person's control?

Further complicating this complex area is the confusing way in which the term *insane* is bandied about and misused to serve the desires of defense or prosecution, depending on the circumstances. Peele (1990) gives the example of the mother who, in a phase of "postpartum depression," kills her child: The defense argues, "What *sane* person would kill her own child?" But here *sane* is bent to mean the opposite of psychotic or "crazy"—not the opposite of the legal term *insane*, which means not knowing right from wrong. A person can be simultaneously psychotic and sane (and therefore responsible for his or her acts). Peele also cites a case in 1994 in which a judge in North Carolina excused a man (from a murder-1 conviction) who had shot at a woman in a passing car while he was in his own car, killing her. The grounds: He was drunk and "therefore" not capable of forming the intention to kill, as demanded by a murder-1 conviction. This was an argument for "diminished responsibility." Others (including Peele) argue that such a man is all the more responsible, precisely because he knowingly put himself into a state of dyscontrol by drinking to excess, following which *anything* could happen (and did).

insanity: a legal pawn

Examples of this sort highlight the tension between psychiatry (with its medical tradition) and the law; between the rights of the individual and the rights of society. This is the crossroads where forensic psychiatry, sociology, and government intersect—perhaps not so much a crossroads as a convergence of shifting sands, since the definitions and criteria change from one generation to the next. "Diminished responsibility," invoked in California after the Durham case in the mid-1950s, was repealed in that state during the 1990s. But the defense of diminished responsibility is still on the books in other states. This means that in the United States, where one lives—and in what decade—defines whether certain antisocial acts are viewed as the products of mental illness or of sheer uncomplicated malice.

insanity as relative

A related and earlier version of the diminished capacity concept was that of "irresistible impulse." First invoked in 1844 in Massachusetts, judge in a murder case instructed the jury about the recently elaborated McNaughten Rules but added that "the accused could be acquitted if it had been proved that in committin the homicide, he acted from an irresistible and uncontrollable impulse." (Wilson & Herrnstein, 1985, p. 504). When it has remained in force, the concept of irresistible impulse has extended the range of mental conditions that can excuse or mitigate criminal offenses. Still, like all such defenses, it is highly controversial and difficult to prove, thus rendering

"irresistible impulse"

the task of the forensic psychiatrist more complex and less clear-cut than before such notions were introduced.

The issues of insanity and diminished responsibility are being continually debated by politicians who favor the rights of the individual versus those favoring the rights of the community (in cases of released sex offenders, for example), and by psychiatrists who believe in the treatability of even psychopathic repeat-offenders versus those who believe there is a line beyond which the concept of treatability is no longer valid. Thus far, debates among these participants have produced more heat than light. As a response to the attempted assassination of President Reagan, however, it now appears that conservative influences have become stronger, with the result that, in most courts, the criteria for proving insanity have become more stringent, and the criteria for releasing dangerous offenders with a history of mental illness have also become more narrow.

political and psychiatric debates

Looking to the future, we should take note of the caveat by prominent criminologist Adrian Raine, who asks whether, in a more advanced society than ours, 200 years hence, people "will look back aghast at our current conceptualization of criminal behavior, with its concomitant incarceration and execution of prisoners, with the same incredulity with which today we look back at the earlier treatment of mental patients" (1993, p. 319). Crime—and not just crime committed by those we now diagnose as mentally ill—may be viewed more generally as a disorder, more treatable (in this utopian future) than is currently the case. But, for now, Raine's optimism is unwarranted, however much his humanism is laudable—and there is still a place for forensic psychiatry.

utopian views

SERIAL SEXUAL HOMICIDE

trends in serial killing

Among the more specific issues addressed by forensic psychiatry is that of serial sexual homicide. Although the phenomenon is rare, each example, because of the devastating effects upon victims and their families, captures the attention of the media and the general population. There is a considerable overrepresentation of such cases in the United States, where about nine-tenths of the known serial killers have operated (Lane & Gregg, 1992). Whereas only sporadic cases were reported during the century from 1860 (when the phenomenon was first recognized) to 1960, several hundred have been identified in the last 30 years.

The history of serial killers has been traced by Colin Wilson and Donald Seaman (1992), who show how the primary motives for crime have shifted over the past few centuries in response to changing societal circumstances. In the 18th century crimes usually had an economic motive; in the late 19th century increasing prosperity led to crimes with a sexual motif; and in our time we see an abundance of crimes prompted by a pathological will to power and domination.

Serial killers of the current generation are most often working-class men who feel threatened by the growing assertiveness of women since the "feminist revolution" of the late 1960s. These men behave as though driven by a need to "win back the territory" through violence that women have wrested unnaturally from their Lords and Masters. This has led some students of the subject to characterize serial killers as Roman Emperors-manqué (the exemplars being Caligula and Nero), intent upon the total domination and subjugation of their victims.

winning back territory

By the 1980s the problem of serial sexual homicide had become urgent enough (perhaps 100 to 500 serial killers operating at any one time) to stimulate intense efforts by the F.B.I. to determine the main psychological *profiles* of these men by way of aiding in their earlier capture. Much of the profiling work was carried out by Richard Ressler and his colleagues at the F.B.I. In their 1988 book (Ressler, Burgess, & Douglas) they note that the typical serial killer is a Caucasian male in his late twenties or thirties, undistinguished in appearance (and thus able to blend in with ordinary people without arousing suspicion), living alone and working at a blue-collar job. A history of previous trouble with the law is common (and often includes sex offenses, such as exhibitionism or rape), as is alcoholism. There is a typical life history as well: These men come from broken homes where there was parental cruelty, sexual molestation, and the repeated witnessing of aggressively tinged sexual scenes. Firesetting during adolescence and the torturing of animals and fetishistic behavior were noted in about half the 36 offenders Ressler studied.

F.B.I. profile of serial killers

Ressler also distinguishes between "organized" versus "disorganized" killers: The former are more integrated and self-possessed, killing their victims without unnecessary gestures and carrying out their acts at some distance from where they live, with considerable care to avoid detection. Disorganized killers are often younger and live nearer their victims, whom they may stab repeatedly in a frenzy and with less caution about leaving evidence. But even in disorganized killing, there is planning, stalking, intentionality, and attempts at concealment—all of which speak against "insanity" (the offenders clearly know that what they are doing is wrong). Hence the insanity defense has routinely failed when these cases have come to trial.

organized vs. disorganized killing

In a later study based on extensive biographical material, the typical personality profile of serial killers was pieced together: Sadistic, psychopathic, narcissistic, and schizoid traits are the most common (Stone, 1994). Schizoid personality, present in 40% of serial killers, is associated with low empathy and compassion. When combined with psychopathy, schizoid personality conveys a sense of total detachment

psychiatric profile

from human society, such that the most depraved acts of mutilation and torture can be carried out with impunity.

Rorschach tests

Rorschach exams of serial killers, studied by Reid Meloy and his colleagues (Meloy, Gacono, & Kenney, 1994), reveal characteristics similar to those of psychopaths, suggesting attachment abnormality, chronic smouldering anger, pathological narcissism, and borderline reality testing. Obsessional thoughts are also common. Indeed, the early years of those who go on to commit sexual homicide are often spent in the elaboration of sadistic sexual fantasies that serve as "rehearsals" for the eventual murderous acts. In rarer instances, psychopathy is less in evidence and obsessive-compulsive traits predominate—as in the cases of Dennis Nilsen (Masters, 1985) or Jeffrey Dahmer (Schwartz, 1992)—enough so to incline some observers to conclude that serial sexual homicide might be a paraphilic variant of obsessive-compulsive disorder (Money, 1990).

predictors of future crimes

One of the most distinguished investigators of the phenomenon, Park Elliott Dietz, professor of both law and psychiatry, has drawn attention to the revenge motif underlying most examples of sexual homicide: revenge against being "humiliated" by women, or in the less common cases of homosexual men who kill homosexuals, revenge against the denied or despised homosexual element in the perpetrator himself. Dietz (1985) has identified a list of predictors that are associated with the likelihood of committing future serious crimes. Among his "first-rank" predictors, carrying a risk-rate of greater than 50%, are acts of murder with mutilation of the corpse, cannibalism, three previous rapes of strangers, forcible rape with torture. Among Dietz's "second-rank" predictors, considered a risk-rate of 10–50%, are traits of morbid jealousy with a history of any violent offense, sadistic sexual fantasies plus a history of any violent offense, and brutality toward an unresisting victim during the commission of another offense.

female serial killers

Over the past decade a few instances of female serial killers have come to light. Here the motivation is not aggression via rape and murder, as in their male counterparts, but rather revenge for sexual wrongs: incest usually, or having been made the involuntary witness of a parent's promiscuity.

Because of the untreatability of serial killers and their dangerousness, permanent removal from society is necessary. Hence they are of interest solely to the descriptive/diagnostic aspects of forensic psychiatry, not its therapeutic applications.

AGGRESSION AND VIOLENCE: BIOLOGIC/GENETIC FACTORS

Maria Åsberg (1994) introduces an important caveat into our thinking about the neurophysiologic factors in human violence: Despite the appallingly high murder rates in certain countries (in the United States, 9/100,000/year, which is the highest in the "developed" nations), rates were apparently higher by several orders of magnitude in bygone times. In Warwick, England the rate during the 13th century was 47/100,000/year—as compared with 1/100,000 in most European countries in the 1990s. Sociocultural factors (such as drug abuse, gun ownership, societal attitudes about violent display) play the most important role in determining the actual incidence of murder and other violent crimes.

neurophysiological factors

sociocultural factors

This having been said, Åsberg's pioneering work on brain serotonin has helped define the boundaries within which neurophysiology influences the tendency to violence. Even so, our efforts are hampered, as she mentions, by the lack of a satisfactory nosology of aggressive/violent behavior. Further research over the last decade on serotonin has led to the observation that children who are cruel to animals tend to have lowered CSF 5-HIAA (Kruesi, 1989), as do children who manifest impulsive aggression and disruptive behavior disorder. There is a similar correlation between low CSF 5-HIAA and violent offenders in forensic psychiatric settings: 30–40% of such offenders have made suicide attempts. The prolactin increase caused by fenfluramine challenge (correlated with CSF 5-HIAA) is blunted in patients exhibiting irritable aggression and assaultiveness. There are some as yet unpublished reports from Åsberg's group to the effect that low CSF 5-HIAA in normal young men is related to assertiveness and lack of fearfulness—i.e., the opposite of "harm-avoidance."

These data support the idea of a continuum demarcated by high CSF serotonin levels and timidity at one end, and low serotonin/violence at the other. As serotonin levels descend, normal assertiveness turns into unusual fearlessness or "courage," then abnormal impulsivity and aggressivity with marked violent tendencies. At this end of the continuum there are forensic implications, since persons exhibiting these low levels are at greater risk for getting into trouble with the law.

serotonin continuum

Since CSF serotonin levels are partly under genetic control (Sedvall et al., 1980), the gene(s) involved have an indirect relationship to criminality; while there is no known single "crime gene," there are genetic influences affecting impulsivity and empathy, which, in combination with adverse environment and sociocultural factors, may heighten the likelihood that certain persons (including certain types of psychiatric patients), will lose self-control and commit antisocial acts. Virkkunen, DeJong, Bartko, Goodwin, and Linnoila (1989) have noted that violent offenders and pyromaniacs, when followed for three years after release from prison, had recidivism rates that correlated with serotonin levels: Those with the lowest levels were the most likely to commit new violent offenses or acts of arson. Along similar lines, Donatella Marraziti and her colleagues in Rome (Marazziti, Rotondo, Palego, & Conti, 1992) have reported lowered serotonin levels in men discharged

genetic influences

from the Navy for aggressive behavior, in arsonists, and in violent borderline-personality patients.

monamine oxidase and testosterone

Even the more accessible platelet measure of monoamine oxidase, which is associated with impulsivity, sensation-seeking behaviors, and monotony avoidance, showed abnormally low activity in persons with heightened aggressivity, such as adolescents with conduct disorder. The role of testosterone has also been studied, given that antisocial/violent acts are committed preponderantly by men. In their study of alcoholic criminal offenders Virkkunen and Linnoila (1992) noted that low serotonin levels were correlated with poor impulse control, and high testosterone levels were correlated with outward-directed aggressiveness.

CNS and ANS underarousal

Further understanding of the links between constitution and criminality has come from the research of Adrian Raine and his colleagues (Raine, Venables, & Williams, 1990). Genetic factors account for some measure of the tendency to criminality, and these may relate to *underarousal* in the central and autonomic nervous systems. Fifteen-year-old boys were tested as to heart rate, skin conductance, and EEG activity, and then followed up at age 24. The results showed a strong tendency for those with low heart rate and skin conductance and more slow-frequency EEG activity to have a criminal record by age 24. Underarousal apparently predisposed the boys/young men to heightened sensation-seeking behaviors, which, in conjunction with various social and constitutional factors, may lead to indulgence in antisocial activities. Raine is careful to underline that psychophysiological differences cannot, by themselves, account for criminality and do not negate the role of social variables in predicting criminal behavior.

evolutionary influences

At the 1992 Stockholm symposium on aggression (where most of the material in this section was presented), Lidberg offered some intriguing ideas with an evolutionary slant. He noted that parents in a social species appear to punish male children physically more harshly than females. This child-rearing behavior appears to foster more aggressive behavior, and more success in mating in the males, thus contributing to enhanced reproductive "fitness." In humans specifically, lower-middle-class parents tend to be more punitive toward their sons, with the similar effect of enhancing their aggressiveness and sexual assertiveness (or "machismo," as some call it). The extreme instances of this tendency manifest as traumatized children who later become patients with such conditions as borderline personality, antisociality, impulsive aggression, or posttraumatic stress disorder. Irrespective of social class, parental brutality, especially when meted out on children with low brain-serotonin or on sons with high testosterone levels, may combine to heighten the probability of eventual psychiatric morbidity and aggressivity, including violent criminality.

Trailing along in the wake of all this fascinating neurophysiological research on violence is a touchy forensic issue: If a violent offender can be shown to have low brain serotonin or low platelet monamine oxidase, does this imply that he "couldn't help himself" and therefore should receive a lighter sentence on the grounds of diminished capacity? Obviously, defense attorneys seize upon such new data in the hopes of exculpating their clients, while prosecutors and political conservatives argue that people are responsible for their actions—whatever their neurotransmitter and hormone levels. These are difficult issues each society must settle in an optimal way. In response to the serious problem of violence that besets the United States, the defenders of the two polar positions have become strident to the point of combativeness. Indeed, one must worry about aggressivity even in those charged with the task of legislating the most effective, but still humane, laws regarding—aggression.

evidence for diminished capacity

PSYCHOSIS AND VIOLENCE

An important question addressed by forensic psychiatry concerns evaluating the magnitude of risk that psychotic persons pose to the community by way of committing violent crimes. For many years, conventional psychiatric wisdom held that schizophrenics (to take one example), though occasionally involved in crimes of violence, were not more likely to offend in this fashion than persons not burdened by psychosis. This impression lent support to the argument that schizophrenic patients should not be stigmatized as unpredictably dangerous persons who should never have been released into communities as a result of the policy of "deinstitutionalization" in the 1960s.

schizophrenic but safe

This question has been looked at anew by a number of epidemiologically-oriented psychologists and psychiatrists, including Sheilagh Hodgins in Canada and Pamela Taylor in England. In their articles (Hodgins, 1992, 1993; Taylor & Hodgins, 1994) they marshal evidence demonstrating that the risk of violence among people with schizophrenia (and probably also those with affective psychoses) is higher than among persons without such illnesses. In Swanson's epidemiological New York study (Swanson, Holzer, Ganju, & Jonjo, 1990), coexisting alcohol abuse was found to triple the violence rate in schizophrenics from about 8% to 30% (spanning a 1-year period). However, only 3% of the total violence in this large-scale study was committed by schizophrenic patients. If 1% of the population is identifiable as schizophrenic, then the "excess" of violence, though demonstrable, is very modest in this group.

schizophrenic and not so safe

Furthermore, when violent acts were committed by schizophrenics, they almost always *followed* the onset of the illness. This was true in Hakola's Finnish study (Hakola et al., 1992), Bina Coid's London study

(Coid, Lewis, & Reveley, 1993), as well as Taylor's report (Taylor, Mullen, & Wessely, 1993) and suggests that psychosis was the main factor in precipitating the violent behavior. As a corollary: Optimal control of the psychosis ought to be rewarded with great reduction in violent incidents.

intellectual defi-ciency

Hodgins (1992) demonstrated that, in a Swedish sample, *intellectual deficiency* was also associated with elevated risk for violent offenses in both men and women: The levels were comparable to what was noted for severe mental disorders. The researcher speculated that this effect would be present but less marked in an American sample, where the base rate of violent behavior is already much greater than in Sweden. Other forensic studies in the United States are in line with her observation: Serious crimes tend to be committed by men with IQs in the high 80s or low 90s.

effects of deinstitutionalization

The best explanation for the reevaluation of violence-risk following the 1960s is that, prior to that time period, psychotic patients tended to spend protracted periods within the four walls of an institution, rendering the commission of violent crimes against others less likely than was noted in the general population. But with deinstitutionalization and increased placement within group homes and halfway houses after the 1960s, many more psychotic patients (by a factor of 9 or 10) were living extramurally—often with less attention and control by mental-health personnel. Without adequate supervision noncompliance with medication greatly increased. The increased freedom of psychotic individuals to live a more varied and agreeable life in the community was purchased at the price of a measurable (though not extraordinary) increase in violent acts (that now somewhat exceeded the rate for the general population). Because violent acts by schizophrenics may take on bizarre and dramatic trappings, they inspire great fear in a community. The paranoid man who stabbed several people to death with a sword on the Staten Island ferryboat in the 1980s is a case in point.

holding the larger picture

But it should be obvious that the murders committed by impulsively rageful persons and nonpsychotic psychopaths and serial killers vastly outnumber those carried out by schizophrenics.

INVOLUNTARY COMMITMENT

Attitudes toward the involuntary commitment of mental patients underwent a sea change in the early 1970s, primarily due to improvements in therapy of the chronic psychoses afforded by the pharmacological advances of the 1950s and 1960s. Earlier, psychotic persons who were paranoid, negativistic, or otherwise disinclined to accept the advice of their families or mental-health professionals about the need for hospitalization could be admitted involuntarily with relative ease and held for 30 days. Prior to the discovery of neuroleptics, many such persons became the chronic-care patients of public or private psychiatric hospitals; those who did not respond to available treatment might spend years or their entire lives in these institutions.

Such prolonged hospitalizations became necessary less often in the neuroleptic era, and public attitudes toward the mentally ill became more compassionate. In the early 1970s patients and their families began to form organizations, such as the National Alliance for the Mentally Ill (NAMI), among whose functions were the establishment of community centers for the continuing care of those recently released from hospitals, and the political tasks of pressuring for more enlightened and liberal laws concerning the mentally ill. The laws regarding the circumstances under which a person could be involuntarily committed became stricter and narrower, and the number of days one could be so held were abbreviated (often to 72 hours). Attorneys acting as advocates for the rights of hospitalized patients became more readily available; one of their main goals was to ensure that patients were not being held without justification.

National Alliance for the Mentally Ill

Comparable changes were occurring throughout the "developed" nations around the world. As always occurs in complex matters like the optimal care of the mentally ill, these otherwise humanistic changes came at a price. The downside to deinstitutionalization, for example, was an increase in homelessness. The very term *homelessness* was itself a new coinage replacing others, like *vagrancy*, with its pejorative connotation. In the large cities of the United States perhaps a quarter to a third of the homeless were now mental patients discharged into communities that had no adequate facilities for their after-care or no ability to monitor their whereabouts.

homelessness

A small but dramatically newsworthy proportion of these patients became violent or, in other cases, created a public nuisance by such acts as depositing their wastes on the city sidewalks. These behaviors, which formerly would have led to immediate reinstitutionalization, were now rationalized vociferously by public defenders as consonant with the "rights" of the mentally ill. Their "right" to refuse the medications that would have ameliorated their mental equilibrium (and with it, their behavior in public settings) was also staunchly defended.

"rights" of the mentally ill

This sea change also showed itself in the perspectives of psychiatrists who had undergone training after 1980, in contrast to those trained before this time: The younger generation were loath to commit even the most desperately ill on an involuntary basis; they were reluctant to administer neuroleptics to paranoid schizophrenic patients, whose paranoia might well have subsided after such medication; and they were reluctant to voice their objection to unruly or offensive acts that the ambulatory but inadequately cared-for patients sometimes committed.

The involuntary hospitalization of highly suicidal patients has also become more problematical in the past 15 years. The police, when summoned by a psychiatrist responsible for such a patient, were reluctant to "violate" the patient's right to remain free—even if the exercise of this right grossly heightened the risk of a lethal attempt. By the mid-1990s, the pendulum has begun to swing back to a middle position: Legislatures have authorized longer-term commitments of mentally ill persons whose behavior in public is offensive or who are manifestably unable to care for themselves.

the middle position

VIOLENCE AND LESSER DEGREES OF MENTAL ILLNESS

Acrimonious dispute has characterized attempts in recent years to draw some sensible dividing line between what conditions do and do not constitute mental illnesses. At the extremes of behavior, there is no problem: No one quarrels with considering schizophrenia to be a mental illness. But there is a wide "gray zone" where milder symptom disorders and the personality disorders are situated, and these pose legal challenges galore. Alcoholism, which manifests in all gradations from mild to disabling, is considered a mental illness by some, especially those who see the condition as based on genetic predispositions. But perhaps only half of alcoholics qualify for the genetic category, and it is not always feasible to distinguish between etiological subtypes. Courts that accept the concept of diminished capacity have to decide whether offenses committed under the influence of alcohol deserve special consideration as stemming from "mental illness" or do not merit leniency because they stem from a bad but controllable habit.

alcoholism

In parallel fashion, Kleinman (1990) has drawn attention to the dilemma certain courts have faced when deciding the fate of offenders who were under the influence of anabolic steroids. She cited the case of a young bodybuilder in Florida who had murdered a hitchhiker. The defendant had abused steroids, become paranoid and aggressive, and was diagnosed as "insane" by an expert witness for the defense. Nevertheless he was convicted on the grounds that he knew right from wrong at the time. Florida follows the McNaughten Rule for defining insanity, which is stricter than the American Law Institute (ALI) test, which recognizes mental disorders that "substantially impair the ability to appreciate the criminality of one's conduct or to conform conduct to the requirements of the law" (p. 221)—i.e., diminished capacity—as grounds for an insanity plea.

the anabolic steroid defense

A similar case occurred in Brisbane, Australia. An adolescent took anabolic steroids—to prove he was not the "wimp" his father accused him of being—and turned into a 6'8" giant, who became progressively aggressive and paranoid. The boy, Nathan Jones (Robson, 1989) went on a rampage of armed robberies. When finally caught, it took 14 policemen to subdue him. He was imprisoned, steroid abuse notwithstanding, and soon reverted to his mild, pre-steroid personality.

Cases of this sort have become more numerous ever since the epidemic of illicit drug abuse began in the mid-1960s throughout the Western world. The epidemic continues into the 1990s, with some shift of "favorite" drugs, from heroin to cocaine (in the 1980s) and back again to heroin; from LSD to amphetamines and PCP. Marijuana remains popular but is less often implicated in criminal offenses. Many of these drugs (amphetamines, cocaine, PCP) can induce a paranoid aggressive state, causing a simulated or chimerical "mental illness." Murders committed under the influence of these drugs have sometimes been excused on the grounds of "temporary insanity," though this is happening less often in the 1990s, primarily because of changes toward conservatism in societal attitudes.

drug-induced temporary insanity

PERSONALITY DISORDERS

The situation becomes even more blurred when the mental condition is primarily a personality disorder. When, and under what circumstances, can a personality disorder be viewed as a mental illness? Perhaps the answer is, when defining criteria are symptoms more than traits. Borderline personality, for example, as defined in the *DSM-IV*, is predominantly a mixture of mood disorder and anger/aggressivity; it adheres more closely to the admittedly blurred concept of a mental *illness*. But, as noted elsewhere, sadistic personality is now not considered to be an illness so much as an offensive "way of being," and was dropped from the *DSM-IV* lest it be misused by defense attorneys as demonstrating diminished capacity. As for psychopathy, Cleckley himself viewed the condition as a kind of (moral) insanity. Yet no one seriously considers acts committed by psychopaths as excusable on the grounds of mental illness.

More subtle are cases in which criminal acts are carried out by antisocial persons who abuse cocaine or other aggression-promoting drugs, during which time they appear mentally "ill"—paranoid, uncontrollably violent—but who become mild and tractable when either incarcerated or placed involuntarily in a mental hospital.

antisociality plus drug abuse

A well-known case in New York City concerns a man who, out of jail or hospital, abuses "crack" (crystalline cocaine), becomes violent, and commits such acts as pushing people in front of oncoming buses. "Mentally ill" when on this drug, he is sent to a hospital, where he becomes calm within a week, no longer appearing mentally ill. His antisocial personality is not viewed as a mental illness either, nor does it have much opportunity to assert itself in a hospital setting. He is "therefore" soon released, whereupon he predictably reverts to his cocaine habit and violent actions. The cycle has led to over 50 brief hospitalizations and demonstrates how the rights of the individual patient and the right of community safety can be pitted against one another. Cases of this type exemplify the problems besetting mental-health professionals and law-enforcement personnel in their efforts to set guidelines that are both humane for the offender and reasonable for the community in the current sociopolitical climate—not only in the United States, but in many countries around the world.

Multiple Personality Disorder

Within the last 15 years multiple personality disorder (MPD) has become a "trendy" diagnosis in the United States and Canada, whereas many European clinicians remain skeptical of its very existence. There are important forensic implications to MPD, at least in the United States, where a number of murderers have sought to use MPD as exculpatory of their crimes. In some cases the *diagnosis* rests on fairly solid grounds, but the *legal* question remains: Is it valid to claim, as an indicator of diminished capacity or insanity, that "It wasn't I who committed the crime, it was my alter!"? In still other cases, the MPD is faked in hopes of winning an insanity defense. This was the situation with one member of the notorious Hillside Stranglers, the two cousins in Los Angeles who teamed up to commit serial sexual homicides. Kenneth Bianchi claimed to have MPD but was determined to be an imposture (Wilson, 1984) and was sentenced as a sane offender. A similar ending marked the trial of the MPD impersonator Ross Carlson (Weissberg, 1992), who killed his parents to gain his inheritance.

immunity via alter's guilt?

Multiple personality figures importantly in forensic psychiatry in another way: in the recent controversy concerning repressed memories of sexual abuse. Patients with MPD often have a history of incest or other forms of severe sexual molestation, as do many patients with posttraumatic stress disorder (PTSD) or borderline personality. But not all do. And in some instances, therapists have been accused of suggesting to patients that they had suffered such abuse, when none may have actually occurred. Family members become maligned in the process, and some have sued for damages to their reputation and have won large awards, as in the recent case of Hammanne vs. Dr. Humenansky (Grinfeld, 1995). In all likelihood, some therapists have indeed been rash in inserting such ideas into the minds of suggestible patients. But it is also likely that some of the family members protesting their innocence had really committed the acts of which they were accused. Because memory is not always reliable and family members in these cases are not always honest, the whole topic of repressed

repressed memory controversy

memory has become a forensic minefield, where the innocent are sometimes injured, and the guilty sometimes escape unharmed.

THE ABUSE DEFENSE

Multiple personality disorder is just one example of several conditions and circumstances that crop up frequently in forensic circles as arguments for the exculpation of crime, and which have the virtue (from the standpoint of the defense) of being extraordinarily difficult to prove or disprove. In Los Angeles in the early 1990s, two sons (the Menendez brothers) accused of murdering their parents (of this there was no question) raised a self-defense argument of sexual abuse by their father when they were younger. Sexual abuse has been associated with exculpation from murder charges on the grounds of justifiable homicide. Examples are the cases of Richard Jahnke (Prendergast, 1986) and Cheryl Pierson (Kleiman, 1988), wherein the evidence for the abuse was compelling. In the Los Angeles case the evidence for the psychopathy of the defendants was stronger than their allegation of prior abuse—but not so strong as to stifle the sympathies of some jurors, since the first trial ended in a "hung jury."[1]

In the United States there have been many such forensic cases in recent years, wherein the murdered victim has been accused (*in absentia*, of course) of sexual abuse, "rough sex" (the Chambers case: Taubman, 1988), or other provocative acts that, if historically true, would turn the murder into justifiable homicide. As Wilson and Herrnstein point out (1985), however, there are also powerful cultural factors that influence the innocent-guilty equation. In Japan, for example, where the crime rate is lower than in the United States by many orders of magnitude (1/30th the murder rate; 1/200th the robbery rate), the populace is more concerned with obligations to society than with individual rights. In comparison with American norms, the Japanese are more introverted, more anxious, and less impulsive. Japanese defendants are more apt to confess, whereas their American counterparts are more apt to refrain from testifying (as in the recent case of O.J. Simpson, accused of killing his former wife).

cultural factors

OBSESSIONAL STALKING

In recent years the phenomenon of "stalking" (obsessional following of persons known or unknown) has been forced upon the public's at-

---

[1] At this second trial, however, they were convicted (1996).

tention. Though hardly a new condition of humankind, as the worship of celebrity becomes more ardent in our culture, the stalking of celebrities has become routine: Few movie or TV stars or famous authors have remained immune to the curse of being followed or spied and intruded upon in innumerable ways. In the more mundane spheres of life, rejected lovers or would-be lovers have also taken to pursuing their inamorata in far greater numbers than was the case a generation ago. Meloy (in press) has characterized stalking as a "maladaptive response to incompetence, social isolation and loneliness—combined with aggression and pathological narcissism."

forensic involvement

The condition enters the domain of forensic psychiatry when the nuisance factor becomes intolerable to the "quarry" or when the stalker kills his victim. Meloy notes a threefold increase in the number of stalkers referred to a New York forensic psychiatry clinic between 1987 and 1993. Examples in the public sector are legion: the paranoid schizophrenic Scotsman, Arthur Jackson, who entered the United States illegally to pursue the actress Teresa Saldana (whom he nearly killed); Robert Bardo, who did succeed in killing the actress Rebecca Schaeffer; David Chapman, who killed John Lennon; John Hinckley, who tried to impress the actress Jodie Foster by assassinating President Reagan.

profiles of stalkers

Some psychiatrists have risen too swiftly to the defense of these persons, as when one invoked the notion that loud disco music had unhinged the mind of Robert Bardo (Ritchie, 1994) as the "cause" of his killing the actress he had been stalking. Most stalkers have a previous criminal or psychiatric history, and about 10% have erotomanic delusions of being loved by another person (usually an important person who has no knowledge of the deluded person's existence), and about half are schizophrenic; at least a fourth are antisocial. By this time, many states in the United States have followed California's 1990 decision to enact tougher anti-stalking laws. This means that men and women who obsessively pursue others can expect to be punished by the law, and that neither mental illness nor personality disorder will serve as an excuse.

CULTS, BRAINWASHING, AND DE-PROGRAMMING

As Margaret Singer and Richard Ofshe note (1990), the terms "thought reform" and "coercive persuasion" were coined in 1961 to refer to techniques used by the Chinese Communists after their 1949 takeover. There is nothing new about these concepts: Hitler used powerful coercive techniques in the 1920s and 1930s, and similar techniques have been used for good (occasionally) and for ill (often) by charismatic religious leaders, demagogues, and tyrants since time immemorial.

The topic has relevance for forensic psychiatry insofar as the victims of these various coercive cults are young persons—a significant proportion of whom suffer from mental illness, personality disorders, or simply a lack of identity. Vulnerable to the blandishments and indoctrination of the cults, these young people become alienated from parents and friends, their whole lives diverted onto a new and often destructive path. The degree of mind control may reach extreme levels, as described by Singer and Ofshe, whose 27-year-old patient was told by her cult's leader that he had life-and-death power over her and her family, and that he would have her family executed, should she try to leave the group.

The charismatic groups frequently masquerade as new religions (as in the case of Scientology, Jim Jones's and David Koresh's ill-fated sects, and Japan's Aum Shinri-Kyoh), invariable elements of which are total control of the adherents and the exercise of sexual "privileges" by the leader with any female members who catch his fancy. Because of the quasi-religious nature of these organizations, prosecution of the leaders is difficult; the rescuing of adherents, even more difficult. At first, they do not wish to be removed from the group and returned to their families, often resisting efforts by family members or mental-health professionals to pry them loose from the cult.

"privileges" and prosecution

A whole subspecialty in psychiatry has emerged in response to the coercive cults. Experts like Galanter (1983) and Halperin (1990) have become adept at "deprogramming" cult members once they have been extricated from the group, and at dealing with the acrimonious court battles that may occur in the process, whereby the cult member sues family members for the attempt to force them back, or cult representatives sue former adherents, their families, or their therapists.

de-programming and suing

MALPRACTICE CASES

Beginning with Melvin Belli, the strident Los Angeles attorney of the 1960s, the legal profession in America has subjected the medical and psychiatric communities to ever greater scrutiny; the number of malpractice cases has soared stratospherically; and settlements often reached sweepstakes proportions. The situation crescendoed until the late 1980s, when some states (for example, Massachusetts) began placing "caps" on malpractice awards in order to curb frivolously high settlement amounts by juries and offer some protection to the insurance industry and the medical community.

Genuine malpractice cases still exist of course. In psychiatry, these usually result from sexual involvement with patients, inadequate care (especially at time of hospital discharge) contributing to a patient's suicide, or harm done through the prescription of inappropriate or improper medications. The strong stand by the American Psychiatric

sexual involvement with patients

Association in the 1980s against therapist sexual involvement, during or after treatment, has underlined what constitutes proper ethical guidelines. Since nine-tenths or more of these inappropriate involvements concern male therapists, the APA's stand represents a reinforcement of the rights of women and was doubtless spurred by the "feminist revolution" of the late 1960s.

The issues of ethical guidelines, obsessional stalking, and malpractice all came together in the late 1970s with the Tarasoff case (Blum, 1986). A foreign student from India, Prosenjit Poddar, became obsessively infatuated with a young woman he met in a chance encounter. Though she barely knew him, he came to believe she was his fiancee after she picked up a gift he had left at her doorstep ("acceptance" of such a gift had this meaning in his culture). When she did not show any signs of behaving like a fiancee, he grew despondent at first and was urged to see a psychiatrist—to whom he voiced murderous feelings toward the Tarasoff girl. Eventually he murdered her, whereupon her parents sued his psychiatrist, claiming that he should have broken the confidentiality that normally exists between doctor and patient to warn their daughter. The court found in favor of the Tarasoffs.

murder and confidentiality

Ever since this case (at least in the United States), the rights of a potential victim to be warned have taken precedence over the privacy rights of a potentially violent psychiatric patient. As Tancredi (1990) has pointed out, the scope of the Tarasoff decision was extended in the 1980s to include potential victims against whom no explicit threat has been made, but who were intimately associated with a person with a history of violence, as that history became known to the treating psychiatrist.

CUSTODY CASES

The high divorce rate since the 1960s, which is just beginning to level off in the1990s, has brought with it a multitude of custody battles—many of them exceedingly ugly—in which mental-health professionals are often summoned to give opinions as to the parental qualifications of the litigants. Some professionals have created a kind of cottage industry around the need for evaluating who should be the rightful custodial parent—despite the fact that a convincing decision can rarely be made except in the most extreme cases.

unfortunate biases

An unfortunate trend has emerged in which control-hungry fathers may castigate competent ex-spouses as "mentally ill," just to deprive the mothers of their young children. Women who have any kind of psychiatric hospitalization in their history are particularly at risk for losing custody. Of course, there *are* unfit mothers—and fathers—but all too often, the court will listen more to the pleas of a sociopathic, sadistic, and vengeful father, who has no *DSM*-definable "mental illness," than to those of a formerly hospitalized mother who has been stable for years and is much more warmly disposed toward her children. In reality equating mental illness with unfit parenting is valid only in the exceptional case. Serious personality disorders are far more relevant to childrearing abilities but more difficult to assess in the adversarial atmosphere of the courtroom. Sometimes neither party submits to psychiatric examination, instead taking matters into his or her own hands. The forensic literature is filled with horror stories such as that of Betty Broderick, who could find no other anodyne to the pain of losing custody than killing her ex-husband and his new wife (Taubman, 1992).

As of this writing both the legal and psychiatric professions still have a long way to go before developing adequate guidelines for resolving custody disputes and adequate techniques for the psychiatric assessment of the disputants. Adding to the complexity of the custody problem is ever-increasing numbers of couples with alternate life styles who are raising their own or adopted children. Such questions now arise as: Is a young child better off with a homosexual father who is stable, loving, and a good provider, or with an emotionally unstable, equally loving, but financially insecure mother?

alternate life styles

CULTURAL DIFFERENCES

Psychiatry and the law can sometimes be viewed as two neighboring tectonic plates that now and then slam into one another in almost literally earthshaking ways. Consider the cultural variations in attitudes toward rape. In most countries rape is regarded as a crime, first and foremost, and only secondarily as the end-product of adverse childhood experiences and mental maladjustment. But in contemporary Sweden, even when dealing with recidivist rapists, the tendency is to focus on their "unhappy childhoods." As a consequence, rapists are placed in forensic psychiatry institutions, where the emphasis is on treatment via psychotherapy. After they are adjudged "well" enough to return to the community, these men are released.

What most nations categorize as antisocial and criminological is, in Sweden, viewed primarily as obsessional and psychological in nature. While it is true that many (though not all) rapists have adverse family and environmental factors in their backgrounds, there is no compelling evidence that therapy or psychopharmacological methods permanently remove the tendency to repeat sexual crimes in all but an exceptional minority of cases. There is reason to fear that Sweden's policy will be shown as unwarrantedly liberal and naive. For as we have learned all too often in the United States, the usual course for incarcerated repeat-sexual offenders is, upon release, to return to their former ways.

"BAD" VERSUS "MAD": DOES THE CONCEPT OF EVIL HAVE A PLACE IN PSYCHIATRY?

As a branch of medicine, psychiatry has been concerned with understanding and treating the mentally ill—even those who commit antisocial acts. The latter are apt to be seen as "mad" first and "bad" only secondarily (if at all). The law, through its concern with preserving the peace and safeguarding citizens, sees such persons as "bad" primarily, and whether they are also "mad" is but a fine point, used in determining the proper mode of sequestration: the prison or the (forensic) hospital.

The apparent rise in the number of serial killers and other "cold-blooded" violent criminals in the last generation has led a number of authors to reintroduce the concept of evil as relevant not just within the sphere of religion but within the domain of psychiatry as well. For example, Andrew Delblanco (1995) argues that however alien to our times such notions as evil and sin appear, we "cannot do without some conceptual means for thinking about the universal human experience of cruelty and pain" (back cover). Similarly, in a chapter entitled, "Whatever Happened to Sin?," Ralph Slovenko (1995) asks whether the Reverend Jim Jones, who led 909 of his flock to their deaths via cyanide-laced fruit juice, was merely "demented, crazy and paranoid," as he was so regularly characterized; "why not depraved, cruel, vicious"? (p. 275).

Psychiatrists and philosophers alike are currently more willing to consider that the term *evil* may have a place, after all, in their professional vocabularies—even in relation to persons with obvious psychiatric disorders or long-entrenched personality disorders, who subject others, especially strangers, to torture and death. Herschel Prins (1994), for example, takes the position that evil is a useful designation for "persistent, gratuitous personal violence" (p. 298), that not all persons who habitually commit such acts are treatable by psychiatry, and that some people should be held responsible for their "evil" actions, even though a mental disorder may also be present.

Gary Maier (1990) and Ronald Blackburn (1988) represent the opposing view. Maier argues that our ability to treat psychopaths has been hampered by denied, countertransference feelings of dislike; Blackburn argues against the very concept of *psychopath* and against the practice of psychiatrists making moral judgments. Nigel Walker, a

British criminologist, adopts a pragmatic approach to the issue (1991), recognizing that repeat-offenders are highly prone to commit further offenses if released, as indicated by the data of Marnie Rice et al. (1990), who noted a 40–50% rate of violent offense among released rapists. Walker advocates a policy of "humane containment" for repeat-offenders (those whom others might characterize as *evil*), given that a small proportion of them might *not* become recidivists if released. We thus have a moral obligation to create an agreeable environment for those whom we incarcerate for long periods—partly as a compensation to the few who would have been "incorrectly" imprisoned.

evil vs. "humane containment"

Complementing the controversy about evil is the controversy about responsibility. Currently in the United States there is a shift toward holding violent offenders responsible for their acts, despite the presence of possible extenuating circumstances from a neuropsychiatric standpoint. Stanton Peele (1990), writing from the legal point of view, argues persuasively against the justifiability of excusing either thieves or killers from criminal responsibility on the basis of their having been addicted to various substances. Taking a softer view, philosopher Ferdinand Schoeman (1994) has written on the complexities of the issue (his focus was on alcoholism), mentioning that between the poles of responsibility and compassion lies a region of optimally just standards. He suggests that we can be ". . . sympathetic, understanding, supportive and forgiving for a wide variety of behaviors without precluding legitimate expressions of resentment" (p. 201).

responsibility and criminal acts

Every new discovery about the nuances of brain function that neurophysiology now provides tends to be reworked into an argument for diminished responsibility, even in our contemporary "hard line" atmosphere. Thus Gaffney and Berlin (1984) report hypothalamic-pituitary-gonadal dysfunction in pedophiles, whose criminal actions can be seen as expressions of biological abnormalities. Nofziger and Wettstein (1995) report homicidal behavior that occurs in certain persons with sleep apnea, who may be scarcely conscious of their violent acts (though the defense of sleep apnea was rejected by the jury in the murder case the authors discussed).

brain research and diminished capacity

Particularly intriguing was the case of a man with childhood-onset somnambulism, who repeatedly injured his wife while he was in the somnambulistic state (Schenck & Mahowald, 1995). He responded to clonazepam/Klonopin, and at the time of the report, had gone five years without further violent acts. In the absence of conscious awareness of wrongdoing, there was no "evil" behavior on his part, even though his actions were offensive and life-threatening.

Had these acts occurred a generation ago, when effective treatment did not as yet exist, the man committing them might have been viewed differently (as more dangerous). Unlike the situation of the alcoholic man who kills a pedestrian in his fifth "driving-while-intoxicated" offense (most would regard the man as totally responsible), the somnambulistic batterer would not be regarded as totally responsible, especially now that a simple remedy is at hand. This example illustrates how new discoveries and new therapies do move the boundaries between what is excusable and not excusable within a given culture during a given epoch in its history. Meantime, the most gruesome acts committed by fully conscious—and irremediably callous—psychopaths will continue to inhabit the realm of evil . . . and are likely to do so as long as we remain a viable species.

cultural and epoch relativity

Chapter 29

OTHER RECENT DEVELOPMENTS

THE VIEW FROM ETHOLOGY

The explanatory model of human behavior derived from the work of neo-Darwinian biologists such as Richard Dawkins has been amplified considerably in recent years. The rapidly growing ranks of *evolutionary psychologists* who apply Darwinian principles to the human condition have now formed a Human Behavior and Evolution Society, whose annual meeting is attended by hundreds of experts in related fields. John Horgan (1995), reviewing material from the most recent meeting, cites the impressions of Leda Cosmides and John Tooby from the University of California at Santa Barbara, who view the brain as a "motley" collection (akin to the Swiss Army knife) of specialized mechanisms designed by natural selection to solve the daily problems of our hunter-gatherer ancestors. In contrast to behavioral geneticists, who regard genes as the source of our differences and culture the source of our commonalties, evolutionary psychologists see our *genes* as underlying our commonalities and *culture* (environment) as shaping our differences.

Neither extreme position, however, should be wholeheartedly supported. There is impressive evidence, for example, that genetic influences account for about half the variance for such "differences" as depression, extraversion/introversion (and many other personality traits), sexual orientation, and intelligence level. Open discussion, and even research, in some of these areas has been adversely affected (in the United States, especially) in recent years by touchy issues of "political correctness." Significant levels of *heritability* have been demonstrated in twin studies for such traits as aggressiveness, sensation-seeking, impulsivity, fearlessness, and empathy—a topic about which psychologist

a balanced perspective: nature and nurture

David Lykken (1995) has written extensively and compellingly. These traits, which all have a bearing on one's predisposition to antisociality, are also influenced in turn by one's parenting. A person with traits of fearlessness, impulsivity, and sensation-seeking, if exposed to abusive, neglectful parenting, might become an adult who engages in criminal activity—or might, under the influence of optimal, nurturing parenting, become an undercover detective or some other professional on the right side of the law, where daring and pluck are required.

Morality Reconsidered from an Ethological Viewpoint

the adaptive value of moral sense

Related to these themes of ethology and antisociality are comments by James Q. Wilson, Professor of Management and Public Policy at UCLA. In his book *The Moral Sense* (1993), Wilson views the topic of morality from an ethological perspective. "There is something in us," he asserts, "that leads us to hold back from a life of crime" (p. 11). We have a natural tendency to judge ourselves and others and to live by those judgments—unless, as he adds, we are distracted by passion, greed, or leadership by "rascals," a triad that harkens back to Buddha's injunctions against anger, greed, and foolishness. Moral sense must have an adaptive value, Wilson argues, or natural selection would have worked against people who had such "useless" traits as *sympathy, self-control, fairness,* and *sense of duty* in favor of ruthless predation, unwillingness to share, and an insistence upon immediate gratification. Yet this quartet of traits—sympathy, self-control, fairness, and duty—creates the *moral sense* that is the oil without which the machine of human society breaks down and grinds to a halt.

sympathy

Sympathy, as Wilson uses the term, also involves empathy: the ability to put ourselves in the position of the other via our power of imagination. Through empathy we treat the other as we wish to be

fairness

treated—the essence of the Golden Rule. Concerning the trait of fairness, Wilson mentions Aristotle's *Politics,* wherein the philosopher noted that the very wealthy tend toward arrogance and the indigent, toward malice—the former out of contemptuousness, the latter out of envy. Therefore, optimal social conditions would allow each person to have a "middling possession of wealth" that would foster fairness and eschew the dangers inherent in either extreme.

self-control

As for self-control, temperate persons (for whom self-control is an easily won virtue) are more likely to keep promises and to get along harmoniously with others. The opposite trait of impulsivity, especially when combined with aggressiveness and lack of empathy, conduces to criminality. Wilson stresses that society has the right to be "moralistic" and "judgmental" in relation not only to the violent offender but also to the seriously addicted, insofar as judging such persons morally is an important step in correcting and preventing the adverse consequences of their behavior for the society as a whole.

Wilson's remarks in relation to duty make us rethink traditional psychoanalytic commentary on so-called civilizing influences. In *Civilization and Its Discontents* Freud (1930) pictured humankind as "instinctively aggressive." Wilson argues that Freud overlooked the likely idea that it is attachment, rather than fear of the Oedipal father, that is the strong promoter of moral development. The four moral traits of which Wilson speaks combine to foster mutually helpful alliances upon which the survival of our species depends. Most of us are programmed to acquire these qualities fairly easily through the teaching and examples of our parents: The corresponding pro-social behavior patterns are to a significant extent innate and presumably of evolutionary value. We are biologically disposed to imitate and assimilate the rules of proper social behavior. Optimal social behavior, both in group and intimate relationships, promotes the survival and flourishing of our genes in the next generation.

duty

Wilson reminds us that bonding, the process underlying attachment, often occurs even in children who are not rewarded and persists despite punishment. But children who experience bonding that is a combination of love (that provides positive reinforcement of social behavior) and discipline or punishment that is fair (and therefore not an excessively negative reinforcement) in time become strong and independent, not more dependent. At the extreme opposite end of the continuum, where bonding and the four ingredients of morality are sorely lacking, we confront the psychopath: the person who can lie without compunction, injure without remorse, and cheat without fear of detection. These individuals come under the purview of psychiatry—not so much in its therapeutic as in its forensic aspect.

bonding, for better or worse

The points made by Wilson are seconded in another excellent book, *The Moral Animal* (1994), by Robert Wright, an editor of the magazine *New Republic.* Echoing Wilson's comments about our tendency to judge ourselves and others, Wright quotes Darwin's convictions about this tendency, who noted the "deep sensitivity of all human beings to public opinion." "The love of approbation and the dread of infamy," Darwin believed, "as well as the bestowal of praise or blame" are grounded in instinct. Adherence to any moral rule has an innate basis; it is, in Wright's words, "only the specific contents of moral codes that are not inborn" (p. 184).

innate basis of morality

CROSS-CULTURAL CONSIDERATIONS

To do justice to contemporary cross-cultural psychiatry would require a book lengthier than this one. Currently there are established psychiatric communities in nearly all the world's 150-plus nations, each representing a unique culture, and each culture in turn affecting local norms of diagnosis and treatment. Although there are large regions within which psychiatric experience is comparatively similar, there are other regions where both diagnostic and therapeutic practices are vastly different from those in one's own locale. For example, psychiatry as a distinct medical branch has had only a relatively brief history in Japan of about a hundred years, following the Westernization of the Meiji Restoration. In China the history is briefer still; psychiatric epidemiology, for instance, was initiated in Taiwan only at the end of World War II (Yeh, Hwu, & Lin, 1995).

Psychiatry in China

Though mental conditions were recognized by the ancient Chinese and sometimes treated by herbal remedies, sometimes by exhortations and the practical wisdom of Confucianism, there were no asylums constructed for the mentally ill until the latter part of the 19th century when the Canton Asylum for the Insane was built in 1889 by John Kerr, an American missionary. Others were founded in the first years of this century, such as the Peking Refuge for the Insane (1906) and similar institutions in Shanghai and Fuzhou (Cheng, 1995). In the 1930s and 1940s several medical schools started courses on mental health, and in 1944 Ding Zan set up the first institute of mental health. These activities were curtailed during the Cultural Revolution of 1949 due to opposition by the Chinese Communist government to psychiatry, especially to Western psychotherapy.

Only a few medical schools in the 1950s taught psychiatry, and there were scarcely a thousand psychiatric inpatient beds in all of China. Conditions improved in the 1960s with the establishment of hospitals in many of the larger cities. By 1989 there were 100,000 beds and 10,000 psychiatrists: one psychiatrist for 100,000 persons, or about one-twelfth the ratio for the United States. Psychiatry remains an unpopular specialty in China not just because of governmental opposition (which is not as strong as in the past) but also because of cultural values, which denounce the acknowledgment of mental problems as shameful. For this reason, as Bond (1991) and Leung (1995) point out,

cultural shame and somatization

there is a tendency to "somatize"—to ascribe one's emotional ills to bodily complaints rather than talk about psychological problems directly. Many Chinese practice spiritual exercises (*qi-gong*) as a way of coping with their psychosomatic conditions.

Since the mid-1960s the Chinese Society of Neurology and Psychiatry has worked on the development of an indigenous classificatory system, analogous to the *DSM* but reflecting the particularities of the Chinese population. A second edition was published in 1989.

Yeh et al. (1995) have carried out extensive epidemiological research in Taiwan. Less information is available for the much more populous mainland, though there is probably a fair correspondence between the prevalences of major disorders in both areas. Schizophrenia ranged from 2–3% in Taiwan cities and villages; paranoid disorders, 3–6%; mania, about 1%; major depression, 9% in the large cities, 17% in the towns. Anxiety and phobic disorders were very common, as were psychophysiological disorders. Antisocial personality was noted in about 1% of the population; pathological gambling in 5%.

epidemiological overview

Also common was psychosexual dysfunction, which in men sometimes takes the form of *suoyang:* shrinkage of the penis. In the folk culture this condition is believed to represent the loss of *yang* (male) force as a result of either "excessive" sexual activities or possession by an evil spirit (Wen, 1995). Similarly, some men believe that "excessive" masturbation may deplete one's *yang,* leading to a morbid condition known as *shenkui,* which is similar to our old concept of neurasthenia (a psychologically-induced lassitude and weakness). The root meaning of *shenkui* is kidney deficiency, reflecting the popular belief that the kidney stores semen. Related to this "sexual neurasthenia" is *nao-shenjing shuai-ruo*—brain neurasthenia—which is brought on usually by students' excessive studying and leads to dizziness, poor concentration and memory, and insomnia.

psychosexual dysfunction

One point that becomes clear in reviewing Chinese nosology is that the American-based *DSM* is highly culture-bound. While the *DSM* may have wide utility in the West, it has only limited applications in relation to the psychiatric conditions, especially the nonpsychotic ones, that are commonly encountered in Asia. This is true not only for China but also for Thailand, where "magical thinking," illusions, and other cognitive peculiarities regarded as symptoms of schizotypal personality disorder in the West, may be rather normal expressions of thought in many Thai people (except, perhaps, for those educated in the West).

culture-bound limitations

As explicated eloquently in a recent book by Hong Kong psychologist Michael Bond (originally from Canada), the Chinese remain predominantly a "collectivist" rather than an individualist society. Harmony within the family counts for more than the pursuit of one's individual goals, which is why disclosure of personal problems may cast shame on the family (Bond, 1991). In contrast to Westerners, who tend to see their problems as intrapsychic, the Chinese are apt to understand theirs as relational or social in nature (Leung, 1995). Trust of persons outside the family is meager, and there is little faith that secrets will be held in confidence by authorities, even psychotherapists. As a consequence, psychodynamic/psychoanalytic therapy enjoys almost no popularity. Instead therapy more typically consists of advice-giving by the therapist as authority figure; cognitive/behavioral techniques are more readily accepted because of their practicality and

collectivist perspective

greater reliance on the suggestions of the therapist. The emphasis is on action rather than insight.

meditation and the Tao Way

Some Chinese prefer the pursuits of meditation and self-help efforts by way of achieving an altered state of consciousness that is more in touch with the *Tao* (or correct) Way. Influenced by Buddhism, traditional Chinese medicine adopts a holistic orientation (Leung, 1995). The mental and physical domains are not sharply distinguished, as they are in the West. One important goal is to achieve the right balance between *yin* and *yang* (feminine and masculine). Imbalance between these two polar forces may manifest itself as one of the seven "excessive" emotions: happiness, anger, sadness, fear, love, hatred, and desire. The Chinese regard any strong emotion as a disruptive state that should not be encouraged. Sexual passion tends to be downplayed, and sexual attitudes are generally "Victorian" (though for reasons having nothing to do with Queen Victoria). Hostility is shunned as the harbinger of the dreaded state of *luan:* chaos (Bond, 1991).

Though murder rates for the Chinese mainland are not usually published by the government, there is some indication that in the mid-1980s the rate was about 1 per 100,000: a tenth that of the United States, though similar to that of most European countries. As for the suicide rate, that too is information guarded by the government. During my recent trip to Shanghai (1995), the psychiatrists with whom I spoke could say only that suicide "seemed rare," but they had no statistical data one way or the other. This may reflect a carry-over of attitudes prevalent during the height of the Cultural Revolution: Mental illness was regarded as "wrong political thinking" (as it had been in the U.S.S.R.); psychosis represented a form of supernatural punishment and was thus a source of shame for the family (Bond, 1991).

suicide in Taiwan

In Taiwan, data are available for the suicide rate: Andrew Cheng (1995) reports an incidence rate among the Han Chinese in Taiwan of 18/100,000/year (double the United States rate). He also mentioned that pre-existing mental illness (usually depression or alcoholism) was a feature in the majority of cases of completed suicides, just as in the West. To what extent Cheng's data serves as an index of the probable suicide rate among Chinese on the mainland is unclear.

Prozac goes to China

Most of the psychoactive medications currently used in the West are available in mainland China. Given patients' preferences for practical advice and impersonal solutions, medication is relied on as a therapeutic intervention. Prozac became available in 1995, but because of its cost, it is used sparingly. To put the cost factor in perspective relative to conditions in a low-income country, a secretary earns about 12,000 Yuan a year, or $1,400. A patient with obsessive-compulsive disorder, who would require three Prozac pills (60 mg) per day at $1.50 per pill, would cost the health-care system roughly $1,600 a year.

Psychiatry in Japan

As in China, psychiatry has had a relatively brief history in Japan. Mental hospitals were constructed and psychiatry practiced as a specialty only for a little over a century. Unlike in China, however, psychiatry has become modernized and advanced in Japan since World War II, in line with all the other rapid advances the country has made in the past 50 years. The ratio of psychiatrists to the general population is currently about 1 per 12,000 (similar to Australia), in contrast to 1 per 7,000 in the United States. The majority of psychiatrists rely on psychopharmacological and supportive interventions, though in recent years, cognitive/behavioral therapy has become popular and more widely taught. This has come about partly through the efforts of Yutaka Ono, who has written extensively on the applications of cognitive/behavioral therapy to the treatment of personality disorders (including borderline personality).

The proportion of psychoanalysts is small in comparison with the United States and Western Europe. Among the more prominent psychoanalysts, Keiko Okonogi has also written on the treatment of personality disorders and has translated various works of Freud into Japanese. The solidity of family life in Japan is such that incest and abuse of children are rare; therefore their "borderline" patients are less likely to have had traumatic histories than is the case in the United States or Australia.

absence of child abuse

But the work load imposed on middle executives in corporate Japan is legendary, in some instances leading to the syndrome of *ka-roh-shi,* whose literal meaning is "over-work death." Such pressures have earlier origins. High parental expectations for academic performance has led to a system of "cram schools" where students continue to pour over their books after the already long school-day has finished; those who cannot make the grade sometimes fall into depression or delinquency. The suicide rate is high in Japan, though in recent years it has been overtaken by New Zealand's. The reasons are different: in Japanese adolescents the precipitant is apt to be failure at school; in New Zealand, failure to live up to a "macho" image and to excel at rugby.

In comparison with the United States and the countries of Western Europe, Japan, like China and Thailand, is a collectivist culture, emphasizing group solidarity, interpersonal harmony, and the suppression of "ego." These values reflect Buddhist tradition, which remains a potent influence on Japanese life. Understandably, this influence is felt in the realm of psychotherapy, as noted in the following section.

collectivist culture

Zen, Brain-Wave Changes, and Psychotherapy

Tomio Hirai (1989) has made a comprehensive study of a form of

zazen and satori

Zen meditation (Zazen) in relation to psychiatric treatment. Based on the teachings of Dohgen (1200–1253), the originator of Japanese Zen, Zazen (literally, sitting meditation) is closely related to Buddhist teachings. The state of tranquility Zazen can bring about is called *satori* (enlightenment), which means a mind free of delusion. One achieves this state through a practiced foresaking of the world, the self, and the mind itself (in the sense of consciousness of what one is doing). Dohgen implied that the truly enlightened state of mind includes both the rational and the irrational, which become two sides of one consciousness.

Zen and psycho-therapy

The themeless meditation of Zazen constitutes the connection between Zen and psychotherapy. Both share a common goal of stimulating the transition from a life of emptiness to a life of fulfillment, through efforts directed at liberating the life force within the mind. Meditation and the use of *koans*—the famous Zen conundrums ("What is the sound of one hand clapping?")—compel the Zen novice (*unsui*) to break the barrier between subjectivity and objectivity, leading eventually to self-awakening.

meditation, free association, and dream analysis

Japanese people use Zen to get closer to the essence of the inner self and to help resolve troubles and conflicts. This is analogous to the use of free association and dream analysis in Western psychoanalysis, which also has the aim of helping a troubled person to abandon the straightforward, logical path of conscious thought—which thus far had *not* led to solutions—in favor of a "detour" consisting of "illogical" thoughts or images that might lead to unexpected solutions and insights. Ideally meditation leads to insight (the goal of psychoanalysis) and then enlightenment (the goal of Zen).

On the hunch that Zazen adepts undergo an apparent alteration of consciousness, Hirai began to study the brain waves of Zen priests back in the 1950s. Hirai emphasizes that the state induced by meditation—even the enlightenment achieved by mystics and sages over many centuries—is a *psychological* state, not a matter of faith or religious belief, even though the two are often conflated in religious literature and teaching. Hirai calls the state achieved through Zen meditation "basic consciousness." In essence, enlightenment is the attainment of insight via the meditation-induced shift into this basic consciousness. What Hirai demonstrated through electroencephalographic study of Zazen priests is that, as meditation proceeds, alpha-wave frequency gradually decreases and rhythmical theta waves appear. These changes parallel those that take place during sleep and hypnotic trance states. Recall Winson's (1990) findings on the sinusoidal or theta waves that emanate from the hippocampus during sleep and that appear to underlie the dream's problem-solving function.

While both Zazen and Western psychotherapy (especially psychoanalysis) aim at creating a mental state optimally suited to solving conflicts and emotional problems by a route *other than* logic, their goals do differ. The goal of psychoanalysis is better adaptation of one's needs toward greater self-gratification. The goal of Zen is to live in greater harmony with others by overcoming egoism and greed— *not* by learning better ways of satisfying one's egoistic and acquisitive impulses. Ultimately, the Zen adept seeks liberation from the "Four Sufferings" identified by Buddha (birth, aging, illness, and death) by means of meditation. A by-product of this ideal state is compassion, which includes the desire to impart this liberated state to others (as in the case of Buddha and Princess Kisagohtami, mentioned in the Preface). Put another way, the Zen adept strives to rise above the Four Sufferings through the achievement of a greater spirituality, a greater ability to accept the "neurotic misery" (of which Freud spoke) with grace and resignation. This goal is not entirely alien to Western psychotherapy, but whereas such spirituality is a primary goal of Buddhism and of the Zen practitioner, it is only a secondary goal for most persons in Western culture.

the "basic consciousness" of enlightenment

Psychiatry in Korea

The people of the Korean peninsula have a four-thousand-year history and culture. Poised between China and Japan, Korea was influenced by Confucianism and Buddhism from China and served as the bridge over which these religions, especially Buddhism, were carried to Japan during the 6th century A.D.

Luke Kim, a psychiatrist at the University of California at Davis, has written (1993) about the Korean ethos and certain symptom patterns of particular relevance to Korean people. Face-saving (or the avoidance of humiliation) is important in Korean culture, as it is in Asian cultures in general. The Korean term, *che-myun,* refers to a quality vital to the preservation of harmonious relationships. Anger or resentment that may stem from unjust treatment is called *haan* (and was once written with the Chinese character signifying reproach or grudge). An excessive build-up of *haan* may lead to the syndrome called *hwa-byung* (whose Chinese characters mean "fire-disease"), consisting of depression, anxiety, and an oppressive feeling in the chest or abdomen, as though something hot is pushing up in the chest. *Hwa-byung,* which occurs most often in middle-aged Korean women, is said to stem from the suppression of angry feelings related to marital unhappiness, domestic violence, and the like.

This condition has been studied recently by Professor Shi-Hyung Lee, director of the Korea Hospital in Seoul and chairman of the psychiatry department. Lee likens *hwa-byung* to a neurotic illness brought about by inhibition (open expression of anger being contrary to Korean culture) and advocates a combination of antianxiety medication and psychotherapy. Because Korean people are often reluctant to seek help from psychiatrists, they tend to consult an internist first, who might prescribe an antacid (or some other digestive-system drug) for his *hwa-byung* patient.

A rich variety of treatment methods exist in Korea, including those based on religious and shamanistic beliefs. Kim mentions that rural people treated by shamanistic ceremonies (directed by a *mudang* or shaman) experience a cure in about 40% of cases. As mentioned to me by Dr. Young Sik Yoo, the *mudang* may merely give advice, or he may dress in a ceremonial costume, engage in a special dance in front of the patient, and offer special foods. "Laying on of hands" is also used (in the manner of Valentin Greatraks in the 17th century), the *mudang* placing his hand on the patient's shoulder, and perhaps intoning appropriate words.[1]

Traditional Chinese medicine teaches that optimal health depends upon the right balance between emotions and bodily organs. The liver, for example, is seen as the seat of anger and courage; the heart, of pleasure and spirit; the kidneys, of fear. Depression is attributed to an imbalance of the liver and kidney, which can be restored through such measures as acupuncture or various herbal remedies. Adherents of Buddhism understand ill health and suffering as the results of inordinate desires (lust, greed, vengeful anger), to be cured by following the "Eight Noble Paths" (among them: right knowledge, right action, right mind). Important steps in eventually attaining the curative enlightenment are taken through the regular practice of meditation.

small market for Western approaches

At present about 30% of Koreans are Christian. Within this large group, persons with psychiatric problems are more apt to rely on Western approaches than are non-Christian Koreans. Still even these do so with some hesitation, given the shame that often attaches to the open admission of personal problems or failings. This diffidence has been noted among Korean-Americans as well. In an earlier study (Sue & McKinney, 1975) many such patients attending mental health clinics came only for a session or two and then dropped out, though in recent years, more meaningful treatment alliances have been achieved (Kim, 1993), especially where bilingual or bicultural therapists are available. In Korea itself, few clinicians offer Western approaches to psychotherapy, and only a handful have obtained psychoanalytic training,

---

[1] There are many cultures besides Korea where shamans or "faith healers" are used extensively by large segments of the population, usually the less educated people of the given country or region. Thus the *murshad* of Urdu-speaking India uses practices similar to those of the *mudang*, including the laying on of hands. In Russia many people seek out the *znahar*, who may, in addition to the measures already mentioned, use herbal medicines to effect cures.

usually in America or England. Few of these psychiatrists have as yet returned to their country, since there are few patients who would wish to participate in long-term psychoanalytic treatment.

Psychiatry in Thailand

Compared with the population in Thailand, the number of psychiatrists is quite small: about one per 300,000 people. Many of the psychiatrists have been trained in England or the United States and now staff the psychiatric wards of hospitals such as the Ramathibodi Hospital in Bangkok. Buddhism is the main (almost the only) religion in Thailand, and many conditions and emotional problems that in the West would be handled through psychiatry are routinely dealt with through the application of Buddhist teachings provided by religious adepts. As a result, hospital-based psychiatrists are apt to see only schizophrenic and other psychotic patients in varying states of agitation, where the possibility of amelioration through religious measures is no longer within reach.

Buddhist influence

Even rebellious adolescents can usually be contained within a religious framework: Their families simply order them to become Buddhist novitiate monks for two or three years, where they live in monasteries, donning saffron robes, begging for rice, and doing good works in the community. The results are often gratifying.

rebellious adolescents

Another feature of Buddhist life, as it affects psychiatric administration, is the lack of emphasis on competition. In place of the "publish or perish" atmosphere that academicians in the West or Japan take for granted, advancement is based purely on seniority. Thus at the time of my visit to Bangkok, the head of the psychiatry department at Ramathibodi was Dr. Sritham Thanaphum, a lovely and gracious woman who happened to be the eldest member of her department.

noncompetetive perspective

Psychiatry in India

Generalizations about a nation as populous and diverse in its cultures, religions, and social structures as India are necessarily hazardous. This having been said, a number of authors have pointed out certain characteristics of child-rearing patterns common to many groups in the Indian subcontinent that differ notably from patterns in Western countries. Alan Roland (1980) has drawn attention to several of these differences. For example, there is an extraordinarily close tie between Indian mothers and their children (of either sex) during the first three or four years of life. Correlated with this pattern, young children from Indian cultures tend to be more sensitive to relationships within their immediate family and group and less autonomous or independent than Western children of similar age. (This pattern, incidentally, is also noted

child-rearing patterns

in Japanese families where, in a child's preschool years, mothers emphasize a "symbiotic" mode of relating more than an "individuation-fostering" mode.) According to Roland, Indian adults exhibit a "heightened sensitivity as to how others view oneself" as well as to what might hurt another person's feelings, particularly the other person's pride (p. 79).

pursuing transcendence

Alongside this collectivist orientation, where ties to one's family and cultural/religious group are paramount, there is a contrasting encouragement toward the development of a spiritual or "transcendent" self (p. 84), the pursuit of which allows for considerable individuality. Though it is expected that one follows the family's main religious and caste traditions, it is acceptable to choose one's own special deity and guru. Another feature of transcendent consciousness is the "profound orientation to the psychic and the cosmic" (p. 84). As a result, there is a tendency for Indians to experience dreams as clairvoyant and to seek contact with the world of spirits.

psychoanalytic foothold

Although Indian society is clearly more collectivist than Western society, its very heterogeneity—it is composed of many different religious groups (Hindu, Buddhist, Jain, Sikh, Moslem), not to mention ethnic and linguistic groups—is a modifying influence. This heterogeneity may explain the foothold gained by psychoanalysis since its introduction to Indian society by Girindrashekar Bose, founder of the first psychoanalytic society, 1922, even to the point where analytic theory has been integrated with psychology coursework at Indian universities (Sinha, 1966). In the much more homogeneous society of Japan, where Buddhist principles are more widely accepted, psychiatry has developed along lines more in keeping with Buddhist ideals of societal harmony and suppression of the individual quest. Accordingly, the psychoanalytic movement has gained only scant ground in Japan in comparison to India and the West.

shaman as first choice

One cannot claim that psychoanalysis is widely used in India. Cost factors alone would place analytic therapy outside the range of all but a few well-to-do persons in the larger cities. For the majority of people in the subcontinent, emotional troubles are more often handled by shamans who often have ties to a particular religious group. Hospital psychiatry has grown in importance only in the past 20 years, before which few courses in psychiatry were given at the medical schools. Patients brought to hospitals are usually those whose conditions could not be handled by the shamans—severe and prolonged psychotic illnesses. Until recently, electroshock was used for most of these conditions. Currently, psychoactive medications are coming into more widespread use.

POSTSCRIPT: TWENTY-FIRST CENTURY TRENDS

Having reviewed the march of psychiatry over the past three millennia, what can we forecast about the millennium that—in the Christian calendar, at least—is just around the corner? What will psychiatry be like in the 21st century? Or, if that is too daunting a task for prophecy, where will the field be in the year 2025, a generation from now? Given the breadth of psychiatry in our era, with its ever-growing number of branches and subspecialties, it is hard to imagine that all its many components will advance in lockstep. The thrill of progress in the neurosciences may well be mitigated by the gloom accompanying the reductions in availability of psychotherapy for many persons who will find themselves priced out of the market. The epigraph to their chapter may be the words of baseball immortal Yogi Berra (immortal more for his quips than for his playing), who said, "The future ain't what it used to be."

reductions in availability of psychotherapy

In the United States, apart from the fortunate few who can afford private psychotherapy without a time limit, people with emotional disorders of whatever severity, and those with problems in intimate relationships or in the workplace, will have to make do with the much-reduced number of visits allowed by the third-party programs of HMOs and the like. As psychiatrists, psychologists, therapists, and social workers are forced to bow to the pressure of market factors, the nobility of membership in a helping profession is increasingly replaced by a much humbler status as "providers" or, humbler still, "vendors."

mental-health practitioners as "providers" or "vendors"

Yet even this gloom is not universal but, like rain clouds, hovers over certain regions, while the sun shines brightly elsewhere. Psychoanalysis is popular now in the once Communist-dominated countries of Eastern Europe. The same is true in Austria where, in its Vienna birthplace, psychoanalysis is enjoying a renaissance fueled, in part, by

psychoanalytic resurgence

Americans such as the Viennese-born Otto Kernberg, who periodically lectures there, and George Brownstone, who now resides there, charming his Viennese analysands with his American accent—just as 50 years ago, Viennese refugee-analysts charmed their American patients with *their* accents. This focus on the individual patient, now more apparent in Europe than in the States, is reminiscent of the shifting focus toward the individual in Europe witnessed during the 18th century, again in the early 19th century (the period of German Romanticism), and yet again in the early 20th century (when enthusiasm for psychoanalysis was at its height).

I suspect there will come a time, early in the 21st century, when research in the psychobiological subspecialties and the new drugs they help synthesize will reach a point of diminishing returns (albeit temporarily) in their ability to improve the lives of psychiatric patients. The most impressive advances over the next few decades will most likely occur in the area of symptom relief. The negative and positive symptoms of schizophrenic patients will come under better control, as will the mood gyrations of bipolar patients. With the newer drugs to be taken throughout the life course, severely depressed patients will have fewer and less catastrophic episodes. Patients with phobic or obsessive-compulsive disorders may be able to overcome their anxieties more effectively and lastingly than is the case with the current palette of anxiolytic medications. All this is likely.

What is *not* so likely is a discovery of quick and effective "cures" for the personality disorders or for the many persons whose personalities have been damaged (whether or not they meet "standard" criteria for one of the personality disorders listed in an official book) by prolonged physical, verbal, or sexual abuse during their formative years. These people, along with the even greater number of those whose lives have been adversely affected by the early loss of a parent, by ineffective though not cruel parenting, by entrapment in ungratifying marital or other relationships, by the loss of trust and faith in humankind (however this may have come about)—all these people will continue to need individual or group psychotherapy, just as do their counterparts in our own generation. Personality is slow to change, and it is hard to imagine that the new psychotherapeutic techniques of the coming century will successfully hasten the process of readjustment and cure.

To be sure, these methods will be better adapted to the characteristics and values of people as they and their cultures change with time. The "typical" patients Mesmer treated at the end of the 18th century were not quite like the ones Freud treated at the end of the 19th century, and these, in turn, differ in significant ways from the patients Kohut worked with or that Kernberg or Linehan now encounter at the end of our century. Still, I cannot envision "quick fixes" for personal-

pharmacological symptom relief

"cures" for personality disorders unlikely

ity disorders and for the ordinary problems in living that the majority of persons seeking help from our profession bring to us.

One theme that the next generation of therapies will need to address more vigorously than has been done in our generation is that of *spirituality*. This is a hard concept to define. Many aspects of spirituality can be viewed as the *opposite of narcissism*. Spirituality does not necessarily require belief in a particular god or higher power; it does require the conviction that each of us is inescapably a small part of the collective of *humankind*. Along with this conviction and the humility it engenders comes the belief that offering help in whatever way one can to alleviate the suffering or privation of others can give meaning to one's life, can give a sense of purpose to those who have lost all sense of purpose, and constitutes a powerful antidote to the narcissistic quests that ensnare so many of those who now seek our help.

spirituality: the opposite of narcissism

Depressive patients in particular are often strikingly lacking in a sense of spirituality, at times feeling suicidal over a rejection within the narrow sphere of close relationships (a romantic breakup, a child refusing to visit during a holiday)—as though, for want of that one gratification, life becomes bereft of meaning and one is plunged into "eternal" despair. Occasionally one encounters a patient with a severe "biological" depression who has nevertheless retained a sense of spirituality, a quality of *living for others* (more than just for oneself and one's immediate family): Here the symptom picture may be one of lethargy, enervation, and restriction in social life, minus the self-vilification, hopelessness, and suicidal feelings typical of the usual clinical profile.

living for others

The next wave of psychotherapeutic approaches, we must hope, will pay more attention to this issue. To do so requires a returning focus on the individual and on the humanistic, rather than just on the "scientific," aspects of psychiatry. One potentially helpful measure in achieving a better balance between the humanistic and the scientific perspectives would be for practitioners in the Western countries to incorporate the accumulated wisdom of Asian countries into their therapy.

integrating Eastern spiritual principles

All that I am recommending and (hopefully) forecasting here is implicit in the Buddha's treatment of Princess Kisagohtami. The Buddha succeeded in replacing the princess' "narcissistic" overinvolvement with her dead infant and (as we might call it) the psychotic depression this engendered with *enlightenment about the human condition*, specifically about the losses that everyone suffers. Kisagohtami was inspired to devote herself to others as a more important source of meaning and gratification than the narrower goals she had previously pursued. It is to this existential point that even the best psychotropic drugs cannot, by themselves, take us. Lithium and valproic acid, for example, can sometimes curb anger, but they do not foster the ideal state for which the adherents of Buddhism strive: the dissolving of anger as an opera-

Buddha's antidote to narcissism

tive dynamic in their psyche, along with other negative emotions such as greed, jealousy, and envy—for which our pharmacopoeia will probably *never* develop biological agents.

forensic psychiatry

Looking to the still darker side of human nature, we must acknowledge that psychopathy and sadism will not disappear from our midst in the 21st century, nor in any subsequent century. The branch of forensic psychiatry, which is devoted (in part) to diagnosis and decision-making in relation to psychopathic and sadistic persons, will remain busy. Better limits need to be drawn between the remediable and irremediable cases within this diagnostic realm. Currently very few people with these disorders are amenable to treatment; many incarcerated psychopaths are adept at manipulating and deceiving therapists who take up their cause, and if released back into society quickly revert to their destructive ways. The fact that a high proportion of recidivist rapists and pedophiles were severely traumatized and neglected as children warrants our sympathy, but not to the extent that we become blinded as to the treatability of such persons, especially those who have also committed murder. Psychiatry needs to take a more conservative approach when destructive personality disorders are involved—an approach that is more in sympathy with the needs of the community and is appropriately pessimistic about the treatability of psychopathic and sadistic persons.

treatability of psychopaths and sadists?

integration of the biological and psychodynamic approaches

Finally, we must hope that the integration of the biological and psychodynamic approaches in psychiatry advances more rapidly than has been the case, not only in our century but for all the recorded past of our long history. There is still far too little "cross-talk" between psychoanalysts/psychotherapists and psychopharmacologists and other biologically-oriented psychiatrists. Whatever becomes of our species in the centuries that follow, our conflicts and our chemistries will still be inextricably intertwined. Educators of mental health professionals will need to ensure that the therapists they train are equally aware and respectful of their patients' unique individuality and culture as well as of their complex constitutional and biological underpinnings.

psychohistorians of the year 2090: what will they see?

I have written this history in the hope not only of telling the story of where our field has come from and where it seems headed, but also that it may contribute to the integration of the disparate branches of psychiatry. In the last chapters of this book I have dwelt at great lengths on the "current events" of 1980–1995—which, after all, have not yet receded into "history"—by way of providing a better baseline for psychohistorians of the future. We in the 1990s have no sure way of knowing which men and women of our era, whom we consider famous for their ground-breaking discoveries, will continue to be so regarded in the 2090s. Some will remain key figures in the histories by, and the memories of, all psychiatrists in the future. Some will fall into obscurity. Still others, overlooked now, will earn their fame among later psychiatrists, who will look back in astonishment at how little attention we paid these great figures in the 20th century.

Though I will not be privileged to know the answers to these questions, I hope I have made it easier for the younger of my readers, or for their children and grandchildren, to make these comparisons and, if they find this topic of interest, to write a better and more complete history of psychiatry at some future time.

TIMELINE AND CHRONOLOGY

THE HISTORY OF PSYCHIATRY TIMELINE CHART: 1500 TO THE PRESENT

Although a timeline chart could be constructed for the history of psychiatry that began with earliest times, the chart provided here begins with the year 1500 A.D. because this year marks a convenient point of departure. Changes in psychodiagnosis, medicophilosophical ideas about the soul, and methods of treatment proceed at a much more rapid pace than heretofore. One could justifiably speak of a "revolution." Furthermore, these changes clearly resonated with the equally rapid transformations occurring in other scientific fields and with the tumultuous events of world history, especially in the Western world, that took place from just prior to the 16th century.

To make the dynamic correspondences between psychiatric history and world history more readily graspable, I have also provided a "Chronology of Historical Events and Persons," listing events, scientific discoveries, and philosophical movements from 1500 (or a little before) onward. The entries I have included (culled from Grun's *Timetables of History* (1991), the Penguin *Atlas of History*, and other sources) were selected either for their direct relevance to the main theme, or for their dramatic impact on history in general and on the *zeitgeist* of the particular era in question. Thus the Thirty Years War from 1618–1648 in Europe is included because its conclusion led to greater religious tolerance and, therefore, to greater freedom of self-expression and scientific inquiry. Similarly, the assassination of President John F. Kennedy is a useful anchoring point demarcating the 1960s from the previous era.

I have given brief sketches (rather than one-line summaries) to a number of philosophers, because their works often exerted a profound influence on the ways in which "alienists" (as psychiatrists before the modern era were called) thought about the soul or the mind, and hence about the nature of their patients' illnesses. Philosophers and religious leaders (like Martin Luther), who took issue with the Church concerning the existence of devils and witches, likewise had profound effects both on the body social and on the physicians/alienists, who were finally free to treat suffering *patients*, rather than forced to stand aside and watch while misguided churchmen burnt them at the stake as creatures possessed of "evil."

Until 1500 (or a little before, depending upon which country) the Catholic Church reigned unchallenged as a conservative force, promulgating a dogma from which citizenry deviated only at their own peril. So long as this was the case, from the standpoint of science in general and the treatment of mental illness in particular, *not much happened*. Although it is not possible to pinpoint a specific moment when the rapid changes got underway, it *is* possible to identify the signal events that helped topple the old order. Once Islam became a powerful force in the 9th and 10th centuries, for example, dominating all of Northern Africa and much of Southern Europe and the Middle East, the Church responded to the shift in power. Now threatened, forces were mobilized to "reconquer" Moorish Spain and Southern France. Equally importantly, the Church became obsessed with the desire to reclaim Jerusalem: To bring this about, the Crusades were inaugurated (eight in all, occurring from 1095 to 1291, when the Mamelukes captured the city of Acre, ending Christian rule). As an aid in the formidable task of raising money for the Crusades, the Church took to selling "indulgences": in effect, suspended sentences from purgatory for so-and-so many ducats or gulden. Catholics of genuine piety and high moral character (such as Dante) naturally decried this hypocritical practice.

It was injustices of this sort, along with the Church's intolerance of "deviations" (prompting such horrendous acts as the massacre of heretical sects like the Albigensians in the 12th century), that led to the widespread cynicism and disaffection that culminated in the Protestant Reformation. The Reformation was already underway by 1500 and took even firmer hold on the northwest of Europe under the influence of Luther in the early 16th century. The sexual repression fostered by the Church led to outbreaks of "hysteria" and, among the male clergy especially, to reaction formations (as we would understand them) like the Spanish Inquisition. The long struggle against this repression—the dying embers of which still glowed in Freud's time—led to the gradual improvements in sexual freedom and in the lot of women that characterize the present era. The challenge to authority occurring in so many arenas created an atmosphere more conducive to science—a field which further challenged authority by toppling the earth from its supposed position of centrality in the universe (thanks to the efforts of Copernicus and Galileo) and humankind from our supposed position of centrality as God's look-alike on this planet (thanks to the efforts of Darwin).

The mind-body question seemed to be satisfactorily "settled" in the 17th century by Descartes' theory of duality: The ineffable, mysterious stuff of "mind" (*res cogitans*) was quintessentially different from "matter" (*res extensa*). As Searle points out (1992), this belief in mind-body duality was a useful mind-set in the 17th century (and for a long time after), since it allowed scientists to ". . . concentrate on phenomena that were measurable, objective and meaningless, that is, free of intentionality" (p. 93). Only recently have we recognized *consciousness* (including intentionality) as a natural biological phenomenon, arising out of the complexity of the brain's myriad cells, each with its army of tiny organelles and particles. Only now, in the current era of molecular neurobiology, can we begin to approach the question of consciousness free of the limitations of Cartesian dualism.

Timeline: 1500–1995

1500	1550	1599
	GERMANY, AUSTRIA, SWITZERLAND	
	Paracelsus	
	Melanchthon	
		Goeckel
	FRANCE	
Gerson		
	ENGLAND AND IRELAND	
Sibb		
		T. Bright
		R. Scot
	OTHER COUNTRIES	
	Vives (Spain)	
	Cardano (Italy)	
	Weyer (Netherlands)	
	Huarte y Navarro (Spain)	
	della Porta (Italy)	

1600	1650	1699

GERMANY, AUSTRIA, SWITZERLAND

Plater

FRANCE

LePois

Ferrand

Sennault

Descartes

de la Chambre

ENGLAND AND IRELAND

Jorden
Wright

Burton

Bacon

Greatraks

Willis

Sydenham

Morton

OTHER COUNTRIES

Garzoni (Italy)

Marinello (Italy)

Zacchia (Italy)

1700	1750	1799

GERMANY, AUSTRIA, SWITZERLAND

Stahl
Westphal
Wolff
Boerhaave
Scheidemantel
Auenbrugger
Lavater
Spiess

FRANCE

Condillac
Tissot
Mesmer
Deleuze
Bergasse
Puysegur
Pinel
Itard

ENGLAND AND IRELAND

Cheyne
Battie
Whytt
Mead
Farme
Moore
Ferriar

OTHER COUNTRIES

Chiarugi (Italy)

1800	1850	1899

GERMANY, AUSTRIA, SWITZERLAND

Reil

Spurzheim

Beneke

Heinroth

Carus

Wernicke

Ideler

Feuchtersleben

Griesinger

Krafft-Ebing

Wundt

Emminghaus

Kahlbaum

Hecker

Meynert

Kraepelin

Freud

FRANCE

Calmeil

Briquet

Gilles de la Tourette

Esquirol

Moreau de Tours

Seguin

Ribot

Janet

A. Bayle

J. Falret

Baillarger

Charcot

Voisin

Maury

Morel

Liébault

ENGLAND AND IRELAND

Hughlings-Jackson

Cox

Wigan

F. B. Winslow

Hallaran

Haslam

Prichard

Braid

Darwin

Galton

AMERICA

Rush

Ray

Dix

Earle

A. Brigham

Kirkbride

Mitchell

OTHER COUNTRIES

Pavlov (Russia)

Séchenov (Russia)

Lombroso (Italy)

Ramón y Cajal
(Spain)

CHRONOLOGY OF HISTORICAL EVENTS AND PERSONS: 15TH–20TH CENTURIES

15th–16th Centuries

1445   Gutenberg invents the printing press.

1453   Constantinople falls to Mehmet II.

1492   Columbus discovers America.
     The beginning of the Spanish Inquisition; dominated by persecution, burnings, or expulsion of Jews and Moors.

1517   Luther (1483–1546) posts his 95 theses at Wittenberg, demanding discussion about the abuses of indulgences.

1520   Luther's efforts at reformation begin to succeed; Philip Melanchthon offers formulation of Luther's doctrines.

1523   Lutherans in the Netherlands are persecuted by Charles V; heretics are burned in Brussels.

1531   In England, King Henry VIII (1509–1547) is recognized as head of the Anglican Church.

1534   Ignatius Loyola (1491–1556) founds the Jesuit order.

1535   English clergy deny authority of the Pope, but Sir Thomas More refuses to acknowledge the supremacy of the king and is executed for treason.

1536   Calvin (1509–1564) promulgates his Protestant doctrine of predestination to either salvation or damnation.

1542   Andreas Vesalius, Flemish anatomist, presents drawings of the anatomy of the human body.

1543   Copernicus, promulgator of heliocentrism, dies.

1553   Geneva becomes center of Protestant world; Calvinism spreads to countries outside Switzerland.

1556   Holy Roman Emperor Charles V fails to win back Metz and Verdun from France and abdicates; this contributes to a gain in power for the nation state and to forfeiture of the dream of a universal Catholic empire.

1558   Birth of Queen Elizabeth (d. 1603), who retains concept of royal supremacy over the Church.

1562   Hugenot wars erupt in France; many Hugenots leave France following their defeat in 1598 by Cardinal Richelieu.

1564   Birth of Galileo.

1566   Calvinism becomes official church in the Netherlands.

1572   Twenty thousand Hugenots are massacred in France.

1588   The English destroy the Spanish armada.
     Birth of Thomas Hobbes (d. 1679), English philosopher who

asserts that "life is but motion," a reductionist theory that places no value on subjective experience.

1596 Birth of Descartes (d. 1650), who advocated rationalism and the deductive method, and asserted that nature and spirit are distinct ("dualism") and that the body, which is made up of particles that move like tiny machines, must be understood also in machine terms (thus uniting physics and biology).

17th Century

1600 Giordano Bruno is burnt at the stake for advocating heliocentrism and the concept of an infinite universe.

1601 Danish scientist Tycho Brahe, teacher of Kepler and architect of first astronomy observatory, dies.

1609 Emperor Rudolph II permits freedom of religion in Bohemia. Galileo studies the motion of falling bodies.

1618 The beginning of the Thirty Years War of religious conflict, culminating in the Peace of Westphalia, ushering in an era of greater religious tolerance and the secular state.

1619 William Harvey discovers the circulation system of the blood.

1620 Puritan separatists cross the Atlantic on the *Mayflower*.

1632 Birth of English philosopher John Locke (d. 1704), a senior figure in British empiricism who postulates that experience (ideas of sensation and reflection) form the basis of understanding. *Some* ideas (the "primary qualities"), however, come from an "all-knowing God." Locke believes that religion and morality are open to demonstration and proof, as is mathematics.
Birth of Spinoza, whose concept of oneness of thought and existence helps pave the way for the Enlightenment.

1633 The Catholic Church forces Galileo to recant his Copernican theory about the earth moving around the sun (which provokes Galileo to mutter under his breath, "*Eppure, si muove* [even so, it moves]").

1637 Descartes: analytic geometry.

1642 Death of Galileo; birth of Newton.

1644 John Milton writes "Areopagitica," arguing for freedom of the press.

1646 Birth of Leibniz, co-inventor (with Newton) of the calculus.
The "Stubborn Child Law" is enacted by Puritans in the Massachusetts Bay Colony: Parents claiming a child was stubborn or rebellious could seek state reprimands, including execution.

1647 Birth of Pierre Bayle, philosopher of the French Enlightenment, who champions freedom of thought and religion.

1648   English civil war erupts as Oliver Cromwell demands end of allegiance to the king (Charles I), who wishes to reintroduce Catholicism in England.

1649   Charles I of England is beheaded; Cromwell assumes power; Charles II goes into exile.

1661   The monarchy in England is restored and Charles II is crowned as king.

1665   Newton invents the Calculus (as does Leibniz independently in 1672).

       Robert Hooke's book on microscopy is published.

1690   John Locke's "An Essay Concerning Human Understanding" is published.

1694   Birth of Voltaire (d. 1778), French philosopher/essayist, who argued against the Church and the notion of faith.

18th Century

1704   Isaac Newton's "Opticks" demonstrates wave aspect of light.

1710   George Berkeley's essay, "A Treatise Concerning the Principles of Human Knowledge," is published.

1711   Birth of David Hume, English skeptical philosopher, whose tendency to doubt all "certain" knowledge challenges and limits the assertions of the Enlightenment: Man is a *tabula rasa* at birth, upon whom experience impresses its symbols.

1712   Birth of Rousseau, Swiss/French philosopher, whose views that man was good by nature—corrupted because he does not allow himself to be guided by his feelings—places him in the next movement following the Enlightenment.

1714   German physicist Gabriel Fahrenheit's invention of the thermometer.

1724   Birth of Immanuel Kant in Prussia.

1728   Death of Cotton Mather, Massachusetts witch hunter.

1729   Death of German/Jewish philosopher, Moses Mendelssohn, grandfather of the composer; around this time there is greater tolerance in Germany toward the Jews.

1733   Birth of German physician and hypnotist, Anton Mesmer.

1735   Linnaeus, Swedish botanist, publishes his taxonomy of organic life.

1739   Hume's "A Treatise of Human Nature" is published.

1745   Birth of Benjamin Rush, Philadelphia physician/alienist.

1751   Assembling of the French *Encyclopedie* by Diderot and D'Alembert; contributors include La Mettrie, who asserts that man is a machine, and atheist materialist philosopher, Etienne Condillac; work is completed in 1777.

1752   Benjamin Franklin invents lightning conductor.

1761 Morgagni's work marks the beginning of pathological anatomy.

1770 Birth of German philosopher Friedrich Hegel.

In Kant's inaugural dissertation he asserts that we have *a priori* knowledge of space and time only because they are forms imposed by our own subjective experience, which also determines the schema of space and time, and gives rise to the distinction between things *as they are in themselves* and things *as they are perceived by us*, and to the distinction between experience and thought.

1770s Steam power, civil liberty, and free trade give rise to the Industrial Revolution, first in England, thence throughout the world.

1771 Galvani discovers electrical nature of nerve impulses.

1774 Goethe's publication of *The Sorrows of Young Werther* marks the beginning of German Romanticism and emphasis on the individual and the emotions (the novel also sets off a wave of suicides in Europe).

1775 Digitalis used by Withering for "dropsy."

James Watt's invention of the steam engine.

1776 The American Revolution erupts.

1781 Kant's *Critique of Pure Reason* is published, whose ethic is based on the search for a supreme principle of morality, a "categorical imperative" (in practice, similar to the Golden Rule). Kant's *idealism* represents a break with empiricism, whereby knowledge is tied to experience.

1784 Louis XVI commissions Lavoisier, Guillotin, Benjamin Franklin, and others to examine the merits of Mesmer's claims.

1789 The storming of the Bastille and beginning of the French Revolution.

1790 Jews in France are granted civil liberties.

1796 English physician William Jenner synthesizes a vaccine against smallpox.

1798 English economist Thomas Malthus' "An Essay on the Principle of Population" is published.

19th Century

1800 Napoleon becomes First Consul and commissions a civil code to be drawn up: the "Napoleonic code."

1804 Napoleon is proclaimed emperor of France.

1807 Robert Fulton's paddle steamer navigates the Hudson River.

Publication of Hegel's *Phenomenology of the Mind*. Arguably the most prominent philosopher in 19th-century Germany, influencing Marx and Engels, Hegel views history as progress toward *freedom*, conceived not as mere license, but as living self-consciously in a rationally organized community via the consent of the rational conscience of its members. Hegel writes in the spirit of German Romanticism, admiring skepticism, with its respect for freedom and reason (leading to the point where the "mind knows itself"). Hegel's prescription for reaching the ultimate goal is the *dialectic*: using reason to overcome the contradiction between thesis and antithesis, via finding the proper synthesis, again and again, until perfection is reached.

1808   Napoleon abolishes the Inquisition in Spain.

1809   Birth of English naturalist Charles Darwin.

1810   Height of Napoleon's powers; after divorcing Josephine, he marries Archduchess Maria Louise of Austria.

1811   Insanity due to porphyria of King George III of England.
Charles Bell's *New Idea of the Anatomy of the Brain* is published.

1813   Birth of Søren Kierkegaard, Danish philosopher, the first existentialist.

1814   Abdication of Napoleon after a series of defeats; he is banished to the island of Elba.

1818   Birth of Karl Marx.

1819   Schopenhauer's *The World as Will and Representation* is published.

1821   Mary Baker Eddy, influenced by followers of Mesmer, founds the Church of Christ, Scientist, commonly known as Christian Science.

1822   Birth of Austrian botanist Gregor Mendel, founder of genetic science.

1823   English mathematician Charles Babbage invents the calculating machine, precursor of computer.

1827   Joseph Niepce, French chemist, develops photographs on a metal plate and two years later forms partnership with Louis Daguerre, French inventor; beginning of era of photography.

1829   Birth of F. A. Kekule, German chemist, who discovered (1865) ring shape of the benzene molecule.

1830   Poland revolts against Russia; defeated by the Russians in 1831.
Birth of future Emperor Franz Joseph of Austria.

1831   Invention of chloroform as anesthetic; Faraday's and Maxwell's work on electromagnetism; Charles Darwin sails as naturalist on H.M.S. *Beagle*.
Death of Hegel.

1833   Karl Gauss, German mathematician and astronomer, devises electromagnetic telegraph with a two mile range.

1834   Birth of Dimitri Mendeleyev in Russia, discoverer of the periodic table in chemistry.

1837	Victoria becomes Queen of England for the next 64 years. During her reign England becomes the dominant world power, with territories in every continent, amounting to a fourth of the world's land mass; London becomes the world's greatest city. Samuel Morse invents the electric telegraph.
1838	Birth of the science of sociology, developed by French philosopher Auguste Comte.
	Birth of Franz Brentano (d. 1917), German philosopher and founder of the phenomenological movement, emphasizes "directedness of intentionality" as a fundamental aspect of thought and consciousness that distinguishes the mental from the physical.
1840	Establishment of postage in Great Britain.
1842	American surgeon Crawford Long develops ether as anesthetic.
	Birth of William James, American physician, psychologist, philosopher.
1843	John Stuart Mill's *System of Logic* is published.
1844	Birth of German philosopher Friedrich Nietzsche.
1847	English mathematician G. Boole develops a mathematical analysis of logic.
	Births of Thomas Edison and Alexander Graham Bell, American inventors.
1848	Marx and Engels issue *The Communist Manifesto*.
1850	Helmholtz establishes speed of nervous impulse.
1852	First use of the term "evolution" (by Herbert Spencer).
1854	Boole's mathematical theories of probability.
	Pope Pius IX declares doctrine of the Immaculate Conception of the Virgin Mary.
1857	General Guiseppi Garibaldi begins unification of Italy.
	French chemist Louis Pasteur shows that fermentation contains living organisms (bacteria).
1859	Darwin's *The Origin of Species by Means of Natural Selection* is published.
	Birth of Edmund Husserl, German philosopher and founder of phenomenology. Attempts to reconcile the subjective/psychological nature of mental life with its objective/logical content.
	Birth of John Dewey, American philosopher/psychologist (d. 1952), who carries forward the work of William James and Charles Peirce.
1860	Abraham Lincoln is elected U.S. president.
	Fechner's *Psychophysics* is published.
1862	Bismarck becomes prime minister in Prussia.
1865	Mendel announces his laws of heredity.
1866	Alfred Nobel invents dynamite.
1867	Austro-Hungarian dual monarchy is created.

1868   Shogunate abolished in Japan; Meiji, the reign of the emperor, is restored.

1869   Parliamentarian system is reintroduced in France.

John Stuart Mill's *The Subjection of Women* and Francis Galton's *Hereditary Genius* are published.

1870   Franco-Prussian war erupts, ending the next year with France ceding Alsace-Lorraine to Germany.

Kulturkampf against the Catholic Church in Prussia; doctrine of papal infallibility is enunciated at First Vatican Council.

1871   Darwin's *The Descent of Man* is published.

1873   A republic is proclaimed in Spain.

Development of color photography.

Wundt's *Physiological Psychology* is published.

1874   Society for the Prevention of Cruelty to Children is founded in New York.

1876   Alexander Graham Bell invents the telephone.

1877   Thomas Edison invents the phonograph.

1878   Victor Emmanuel, king of united Italy, dies, succeeded by Humberto I.

In Germany, historian Treitschke begins radical anti-Semitic movement.

1879   Birth of Albert Einstein.

1880   Electric lights invented by Thomas Edison and Joseph Swan.

1881   Pogroms unleashed in Russia; many Jews emigrate to Western Europe and United States.

1882   Joseph Breuer, Viennese physician, uses hypnosis to treat hysteria.

1883   Nietzsche's *Thus Spake Zarathustra* is published. Nietzsche describes a "will to power" as the prime moving force in human nature; failure to win power breeds resentment. The so-called *Übermensch* (the "Over-Man") escapes this resentment not by bullying (as the Nazis supposed, later on) but by mastering his passions and embellishing his character with creativity. Also skeptical about objective notions of truth or fact and the supremacy of reason, Nietzsche's views were a forerunner of "post-modern" deconstruction preference for a large variety of interpretations of a text, etc.

1885   Karl Benz, German inventor, invents the motor car.

1886   Krafft-Ebing's *Psychopathia Sexualis* is published.

1888   "Jack the Ripper" murders six prostitutes in London; he is never identified or captured.

1890   Bismarck is dismissed by Wilhelm II of unified Germany.

1893   Henry Ford builds his first car.

Breuer and Freud's first paper on hysteria treated by psychoanalysis is published.

1894   Auguste Marie Louis Lumière, French inventor, builds first cin-
        ematograph, precursor of movies.
        John Dewey becomes chairman of University of Chicago de-
        partment of philosophy and psychology. A pragmatist, he op-
        poses the formal, rigid educational practices of his time, arguing
        that the child is an active, inquisitive creature, whose educa-
        tion must be fostered by experience, supplemented by knowl-
        edge and acquisition of skills. Enquiry is seen as a
        self-corrective process by Dewey.

1895   First wave of Turkish massacres of Armenians, culminating in
        mass murder of Armenians in 1915.
        Discovery of X-rays by German physicist Wilhelm Roentgen.
        Persecution of Oscar Wilde for his homosexuality.

1896   French physicist Alexandre Becquerel discovers radioactivity,
        followed by the Curies' discovery of radium and polonium
        (1898).

1897   English psychologist Havelock Ellis' *Studies in the Psychology
        of Sex* is published.

1899   Freud's *Interpretation of Dreams* is published (though with
        publication date of 1900).

20th Century

1900   Death of Nietzsche.
        Max Planck formulates quantum theory of physics in Ger-
        many.

1901   The "Edwardian Era" begins as Edward VII succeeds Victoria.
        Italian physicist Guglielmo Marconi transmits messages via
        radio.

1903   The Wright brothers invent and fly an airplane.

1904   Marie Curie's "Research on Radioactive Substances" is pub-
        lished.
        The Russo-Japanese war erupts.

1905   First workers' soviet formed in St. Petersburg, partly in reac-
        tion to Russia's loss in the war with Japan; sailors mutiny on
        the battleship *Potemkin*.
        Albert Einstein formulates his "Special Theory of Relativity"
        and the photon theory of light.
        Birth of Jean Paul Sartre, existential novelist and philosopher.
        Opposing psychoanalysis, Sartre argues against determinism
        and the notion of unconscious motivation, and in favor of "free
        will." Only humankind, with its capacity for subjectivity, has
        the possibility of stepping outside the chain of causality and of
        exercising freedom of choice.

1907   William James' *Pragmatism* is published, built upon the work of Charles Pierce (1839–1914). James' treatise denies the possibility of absolute truth in an ever-changing universe; absolute moral standards must be replaced by a system of values, taking into consideration the vicissitudes of human experience.

Women are given suffrage in Austria.

1909   Freud and Jung lecture in the United States at Clark University.

Women are admitted to German universities.

1911   Fall of the Manchu dynasty in China; a republic is proclaimed.

1912   The *Titanic* sinks on her maiden voyage.

Lenin takes over editorship of *Pravda*.

Scottish physicist Charles Wilson detects electrons and protons in cloud chamber.

1913   Birth of Albert Camus, existential novelist, who emphasizes the individual, the experience of choice, the inability to comprehend the universe, with a consequent sense of the "absurdity of life."

Publication of Edmund Husserl's *Phenomenology* and Karl Jaspers' *General Psychopathology*.

1914   Outbreak of World War I.

English philosopher/mathematician Bertrand Russell's *Our Knowledge of the External World* is published.

1915   Einstein postulates his "General Theory of Relativity."

Margaret Sanger is jailed for writing *Family Limitation*, the first book on birth control (the following year she opens the first birth control clinic).

1917   The Russian Revolution erupts; Lenin becomes chief commissar.

1918   Influenza pandemic.

1920   World population is recorded at 1.8 billion; U.S.A., 105 million.

Rorschach develops inkblot test in psychology.

1921   Bertrand Russell's *Analysis of Mind* and Wittgenstein's *Tractatus Logico-Philosophicus* are published.

Death of Prince Peter Kropotkin, Russian philosopher, who asserted that humans are social creatures who flourish best in small communities; he disapproved of the centralized state with its use of coercion.

American biologist Thomas Hunt Morgan presents his chromosome theory of heredity.

1923   Martin Buber's *I and Thou* is published.

1924   Death of Lenin; Stalin assumes power in U.S.S.R.

Publication of German Protestant theologian Karl Barth's *The World of God and the World of Man*, asserts that we cannot attain knowledge of God via use of reason; unlike traditional

Calvinists, he did not believe in the possibility of redemption for everyone.

1925   Scottish inventor John L. Baird transmits images via television.

Physicists Werner Heisenberg and Neils Bohr develop quantum mechanics at atomic level.

Tennessee forbids sex education in schools; also in Tennessee, John Scopes is narrowly acquitted for teaching evolution in a public school.

1926   *Hitlerjugend* founded in Germany.

Joseph Goebbels appointed by Hitler as *Gauleiter* in Berlin.

Leon Trotsky expelled from Moscow.

Hirohito becomes emperor in Japan.

1927   Russian physiologist Ivan Pavlov's *Conditional Reflexes* is published.

Publication of *Being and Time* by German existentialist philosopher Martin Heidegger, who urges return to "authentic communion with independent nature"; he equates "being" with people's consciousness of their place in the world (their *Dasein*). His image was ultimately sullied by his championing of Nazi Germany.

1928   Scottish bacteriologist Alexander Fleming discovers penicillin.

1929   World economic crisis ushered in by Wall Street stock market "crash" on October 28th.

1932   Hitler gaining power in Germany; Nazis achieve plurality in the *Reichstag*.

Publication of French philosopher Henri Bergson's *The Two Sources of Morality and Religion*. An evolutionist who was hostile to materialism, Bergson views evolution not in Darwinian terms as driven by natural selection, but as propelled by a "creative life force" (the *élan vital*). Modern development in evolution and neuroscience have discredited his views.

Nobel prizes awarded to Edgar Adrian and Sir Charles Scott Sherrington for their work on neurons.

1933   Hitler becomes chancellor and soon consolidates supreme power in Germany; the first concentration camps are erected. The era of the Great Depression in the United States (lasting throughout the 1930s).

1934   Publication of U. S. anthropologist Ruth Benedict's *Patterns of Culture* and Rudolf Carnap's *Logical Syntax of Language*.

1939   Outbreak of World War II; flight of many Jews, including a large number of psychoanalysts, to England and the United States.

1942   First automatic computer is constructed in the United States. Publication of German philosopher Hans Reichenbach's *Philosophic Foundations of Quantum Mechanics*, emphasizing considerations of probability rather than reductionism.

1943   Publication of French philosopher and novelist Jean Paul Sartre's *Being and Nothingness*, focusing on the structure of consciousness and emphasizing the capacity for choice as the essential feature of human nature. By virtue of our consciousness and intentionality, we are responsible for our choices.

1945   World War II ends with the defeat of Germany in May and Japan in August—the latter following the atomic bombing of Hiroshima and Nagasaki, ushering in the Atomic Age; discovery of the death camps in Poland and the full extent of the Holocaust: 8–10 million killed, including 6 million Jews from all over Europe.
Approximate beginning of steep rise in world population.

1947   Culmination of "nonviolent" movement in independence of India.

1949   Communist takeover in China under Mao Zedong.

1950   Publication of American anthropologist Margaret Mead's *Social Anthropology*.

1951   Death of Wittgenstein, whose logical-positivist position opposes scientific (especially Freudian) reductionism and the then more accepted theory of consciousness as a manifestation of atomic and evolutionary processes peculiar to organisms with highly developed nervous systems.

1953   Death of Stalin and his succession by Krushchev in U.S.S.R.; coronation of Queen Elizabeth II in England.
E. Aserinsky and N. Kleitman discover rapid-eye-movement sleep and its connection to the dream state.

1956   Publication of British philosopher Alfred Ayer's *The Problem of Knowledge*, whose *Language, Truth and Logic* appeared in 1936, combining empiricism and the focus on logic as espoused by Bertrand Russell.

1957   Death of John von Neumann, U.S. mathematician (noted for his theory of games and decision-making), whose work led to construction of newer, more powerful computers.

1960   American scientists develop the laser.

1960s   Beginning of dramatic increase in abuse of illicit drugs in the U.S. and Western Europe.

1961   First U.S. space flight.

1962   Nobel Prizes awarded to James Watson and Francis Crick for discovery of the molecular structure of DNA.

1963   Assassination of President John F. Kennedy.

1964   United States enters the Vietnam war (lasts until 1975).
Social theorist Herbert Marcuse's book *One Dimensional Man* becomes the Bible of radical students.
Death of U.S. mathematician Norbert Wiener, creator of the field of "cybernetics."

1968   Period of student rebellions in the United States and Western Europe; rise of the feminist movement; violent crime increases more than 50% since 1960.

1969   First manned landing on the moon.

1973   Women's rights advanced by Supreme Court's Roe vs. Wade decision to permit abortions.

1974   Church attendance down to 40% weekly in the United States from about 65% a decade earlier.
Nixon resigns presidency in wake of Watergate scandal.

1978   Death of Austrian mathematician Kurt Gödel, who proves that pure mathematical reductionism does not work; he also opposes the view espoused by Alan Turing that all thinking is "computational."

1980   Death of Swiss developmental psychologist Jean Piaget.

1980s   Rise of Japan and the other Pacific Rim countries as economic powers and important contributors to science.

1981   Identification of the AIDS virus (the epidemic may have begun circa 1977).

mid-1980s   Significant progress in neuroscience in the areas of memory (Kandell, Miskin, Squires-Wheeler), computer modeling of neuronal activities (Edelman, Rumelhart, McClelland), mathematical/philosophical approaches to the question of "computability" of the mind (Penrose, Searle, Minsky, the Churchlands), neuroimaging (Andreasen, the Gurs, the Shaywitzs), the circuitry underlying obsessive-compulsive disorder (Insel, Baxter, Kellner, Rubin), the nature of consciousness (Dennett).

1986   The Chernobyl nuclear-plant disaster erupts near Kiev.

1987   Gorbachev introduces *glasnost* (openness) and *perestroika* (restructuring) into the Russian political scene; becomes president of the U.S.S.R. the following year.

1989   Collapse of the Communist regime in the U.S.S.R.; beginning of fractionation into independent states, with democratically elected chiefs.

BIBLIOGRAPHY

Aarkrog, T. (1981). The borderline concept in childhood, adolescence, and adulthood. *Acta Psychiat. Scand., 64* (293), 1–300.

Aarkrog, T. (1994). *Borderline adolescents twenty years later*. Copenhagen: P. Schmidt.

Achenbach, T. M. (1978). The child behavior profile, I: Boys aged 6–11. *J. Consult. Clin. Psychol., 46*, 478–488.

Achenbach, T. M. & Edelbrock, C. S. (1978). The classification of child psychopathology. *Psychol. Bull., 85*, 1275–1301.

Ackerman, N. W. (1958). *The psychodynamics of family life*. New York: Basic.

Agras, W. S., Barlow, D. H., & Chapin, H. N. (1974). Behavior modification of anorexia nervosa. *Arch. Gen. Psychiat., 30*, 279–286.

Akiskal, H. S. (1981). Subaffective disorders: Dysthymic, cyclothymic, and bipolar II disorders in the "borderline" realm. *Psychiat. Clin. N. Am., 4*, 25–46.

Akiskal, H. S., Djenderedjian, A. H., Blinger, J. M., Bitar, A. H., Khani, M. K., & Haykal, R. F. (1978). The joint use of clinical and biological criteria for psychotic diagnoses, II: Their application in identifying subaffective forms of bipolar illness. In H. S. Akiskal & W. L. Webb (Eds.), *Psychiatric diagnosis* (pp. 133–146). New York: SP Medicine & Science.

Akiskal, H. S., Hirschfield, N. A., & Yerevanian, B. J. (1983). The relation of personality to affective disorders: An initial review. *Arch. Gen. Psychiat., 40*, 801–810.

Akiskal, H. S., Yerevanian, B. I., Davis, G. C., King, D., & Lemmi, H. (1985). The nosologic status of borderline personality: Clinical and polysomnographic study. *Am. J. Psychiat., 142*, 192–198.

Albert, H. D. (1983). Special aids to therapy with schizophrenics. In M. H. Stone, H. D. Albert, D. V. Forrest, & S. Arieti, *Treating schizophrenic patients* (pp. 245–273). New York: McGraw Hill.

Alexander, F. G. & French, T. M. (1946). *Psychoanalytic therapy: Principles and application*. Lincoln, NE: Univ. of Nebraska Press.

Alexander, F. G. & Selesnick, S. (1966). *The history of psychiatry: An evaluation of psychiatric thought and practice from prehistoric times to the present*. New York: Harper & Row.

Allebeck, P., Allgulander, G., & Fisher, L. D. (1988). Predictors of completed suicide in a cohort of 50,465 young men: Role of personality and deviant behavior. *Brit. Med. J., 297*, 176–178.

Allgulander, C. (1994). Suicide and mortality patterns in anxiety neurosis and depressive neurosis. *Arch. Gen. Psychiat., 51*, 708–712.

Allport, G. W. & Odbert, H. S. (1936). *Trait-names: A psycholexical study* (Psychol. Monograph No. 47). Princeton, NJ: Psychological Review Company.

Alpert, A. (1954). Observations on the treatment of emotionally disturbed children in a therapeutic center. *Psychoan. Study of the Child, 9*, 334–343.

American Psychiatric Association (1952). *The diagnostic & statistical manual of mental disorders*. Washington, DC: Author. *DSM-II* (1968) second edition; *DSM-III* (1980) third edition; *DSM III-R*; (1987) third edition, revised; *DSM-IV* (1994) fourth edition.

Amin, A. H., Crawford, T. B., & Gaddum, J. H. (1954). The distribution of substance P and 5-hydroxytryptamine in the central nervous system of the dog. *J. Physiol., 126*, 596.

Amsterdam, J. D., Maislin, G., Winokur, A., Kling, M., & Gold, P. (1987). Pituitary and adrenocortical responses to the ovine corticotropin releasing hormone in depressed patients and healthy volunteers. *Arch. Gen. Psychiat., 44*, 775–781.

Andreasen, N. C. (1980). Mania and creativity. In R. H. Belmaker & H. M. van Praag (Eds.), *Mania: An evolving concept* (pp. 377–386). New York: Spectrum.

Andreasen, N. C. & Canter, A. (1974). The creative writer: Psychiatric symptoms and family history. *Compr. Psychiat., 15*, 123–131.

Andreasen, N. C., Ehrhardt, J. C., Swayze, V. W., II, Alliger, R. J., Yuh, W. T. C., Cohen, G., & Ziebel, S. (1990). Magnetic resonance imaging of the brain in schizophrenia. *Arch. Gen. Psychiat., 47*, 35–44.

Andreasen, N. C., Flaum, M., Swayze, V. W., II, Tyrrell, G., & Arndt, S. (1990). Positive and negative symptoms in schizophrenia. *Arch. Gen. Psychiat., 47*, 615–621.

Andreasen, N. C. & Powers, P. S. (1975). Creativity and psychosis. *Arch. Gen. Psychiat., 32*, 70–73.

Andreoli, A., Gressot, G., Aapro, N., Tricot, L., & Gognalons, M. Y. (1989). Personality disorders as a predictor of outcome. *J. Pers. Dis., 3*, 307–320.

Andrulonis, P. A., Glueck, B. C., Stroebel, C. F., Vogel, N. G., Shapiro, A. L., & Aldridge, D. M. (1981). Organic brain dysfunction and the borderline syndrome. *Psychiat. Clin. N. Am., 4*, 47–66.

Angier, N. (1996, January 2). Variant gene tied to a love of new thrills. *New York Times*, p. A1.

Angst, J. (1966). *Zur Aetiologie und Nosolgie endogener depressiver Psychosen*. Berlin: Springer Verlag.

Angst, J. (1980). Clinical typology of bipolar illness. In R. H. Belmaker & H. M. van Praag (Eds.), *Mania: An evolving concept* (pp. 61–76). New York: Spectrum.

Angst, J. (1995). History and epidemiology of panic. *Euro. Psychiat., 10*(2), 57–59.

Angst, J. & Clayton, P. (1986). Premorbid personality of depressive, bipolar, and schizophrenic patients with special reference to suicidal issues. *Compr. Psychiat., 27*, 511–532.

Angst, J., Huber, G., & Stone, M. H. (1990). Suicide in affective and schizoaffective disorders. In A. Marneros & M. Tsuang (Eds.), *Affective and schizoaffective disorders* (pp. 168–185). Berlin: Springer.

Angst, J., Weis, P., Grof, P., Baastrup, P.C . & Schou, M. (1970). Lithium prophylaxis in recurrent affective disorders. *Brit. J. Psychiat., 116*, 604–514.

Archer, J. (1994). Testosterone and aggression. In M. Hillbrand & N. J. Pallone (Eds.), *The psychobiology of aggression* (pp. 3–25). New York: Haworth.

Arieti, S. (1955). *Interpretation of schizophrenia*. New York: Brunner.

Arieti, S. (Ed.) (1968). *American handbook of psychiatry*. New York: Basic.

Aristotle (1992). *De Anima* [On the soul]. R. McKeon. (Ed.). New York: Modern Library.

Armstrong, I. (1978). *Kiss daddy goodnight*. New York: Hawthorn.

Arnold, T. & Guillaume, A. (1931). *The legacy of Islam*. London: Oxford Univ. Press.

Åsberg, M. (1994). Monoamines and violence. *Crim. Behav. & Ment. Health, 4*, 303–327.

Åsberg, M., Träksman, L. & Thoren, P. (1976). 5-HIAA in the cerebrospinal fluid: A biochemical suicide predictor? *Arch. Gen. Psychiat., 33*, 1193–1197.

Aserinsky, E. & Kleitman, N. (1953). Regularly occurring periods of eye motility and concomitant phenomena during sleep. *Science, 118*, 273–274.

Aston-Jones, G. (1993, Feb. 19). *Locus coeruleus and the vigilance system*. Paper presented at the New York State Psychiatric Institute, Grand Rounds, NY.

Astrachan, B. M., Harrow, M., Adler, D., Bauer, L., Schwartz, C., & Tucker, G. (1972). A checklist for the diagnosis of schizophrenia. *Brit. J. Psychiat., 121*, 529–539.

Bailey, J. M. & Pillard, R. C. (1991). A genetic study of male sexual orientation. *Arch. Gen. Psychiat., 48*, 1089–1096.

Bailey, J. M., Pillard, R. C., Neale, M. C., & Agyei, Y. (1993). Heritable factors influence sexual orientation in women. *Arch. Gen. Psychiat., 50*, 217–223.

Baldessarini, R. J. (1985). *Chemotherapy in psychiatry: Principles and practice*. Cambridge, MA: Harvard Univ. Press.

Balint, M. (1968). *The basic fault: Therapeutic aspects of regression*. New York: Brunner/Mazel.

Ballenger, J. C. & Post, R. M. (1978). Therapeutic effects of carbamazepine in affective illness. *Commun. Psychopharm., 2*, 159–175.

Bancroft, J. (1974). *Deviant sexual behavior*. Oxford: Clarendon.

Bar, E. (1974). Understanding Lacan. *Psychoanalysis & Contemp. Sci., 3*, 473–543.

Bastani, B., Nash, F., & Meltzer, H. Y. (1990). Prolactin and cortisol responses to MK-212, a serotonin agonist, in obsessive-compulsive disorder. *Arch. Gen. Psychiat., 47*, 833–839.

Bataille, G. (1991). *Gilles de Rais* R. Robinson (Trans.). Los Angeles: Amok.

Bateson, G., Jackson, D., Haley, J., & Weakland, J. H. (1956). Toward a theory of schizophrenia. *Behav. Science, 1*, 251–264.

Bauer, M. S. & Whybrow, P. C. (1990). Rapid cycling bipolar affective disorder, II: Treatment of refractory rapid cycling with high-dose levothyroxine. A preliminary study. *Arch. Gen. Psychiat., 47*, 435–440.

Baumeister, R. F. (1988). Gender differences in masochistic scripts. *J. Sex. Research, 25*, 478–499.

Baxter, L. R., Schwartz, J. M. & Bergman, K. S. (1992). Caudate glucose metabolic rate changes with both drug and behavioral treatments for obsessive-compulsive disorder. *Arch. Gen. Psychiat., 49*, 681–689.

Beauchesne, H. (1993). *Histoire de la psychopathologie, 2nd ed*. Paris: Presses Universitaires.

Beck, A. T. (1963). Thinking and depression, 1: Idiosyncratic content and cognitive distortion. *Arch. Gen. Psychiat., 9*, 324–344.

Beck, A. T. (1967). *Depression: Clinical, experimental, and theoretical aspects*. New York: Harper & Row.

Beck, A. T. & Freeman, A. (1990). *Cognitive therapy of personality disorders*. New York: Guilford.

Beck, A. T., Sokol, L., Clark, D. A., Berchick, R., & Wright, F. (1992). A crossover study of focused cognitive therapy for panic disorder. *Am. J. Psychiat., 149*, 778–783.

Beck, A. T., Ward, C. H., & Mendelson, M. (1961). An inventory for measuring depression. *Arch. Gen. Psychiat., 4*, 561–571.

Beers, C. (1908). *A mind that found itself*. New York: Longman, Green.

Belfrage, H., Lidberg, L., & Oreland, L. (1992, Sept. 10). *Platelet monoamine oxidase activity in mentally disordered violent offenders*. Paper presented at the First European Symposium on Aggression in Clinical Psychiatric Practice, Stockholm, Sweden.

Bellak, L. (Ed.). (1979). *Disorders of the schizophrenic syndrome*. New York: Basic.

Bellak, L. & Loeb, L. (Eds.). (1969). *The schizophrenic syndrome*. New York: Grune & Stratton.

Bemporad, J. L., Beregin, E., & Ratey, J. (1992). A psychoanalytic study of eating disorders, I: A developmental profile of 67 cases. *J. Am. Acad. Psychoan., 20*, 509–531.

Bender, L. (1947). Childhood schizophrenia. *Am. J. Orthopsychiat., 17*, 40–56.

Benedek, T. & Rubenstein, B. B. (1939). The correlations between ovarian activity and psychodynamic processes, I: The ovulative phase. *Psychosom. Med., 1*, 245–270.

Benjaminsen, S. (1985). Coping with precipitating life stress of primarily depressed in-patients. *Compr. Psychiat., 21*, 71–79.

Beres, D. (1952). Clinical notes on aggression in children. *Psychoan. Study of the Child, 7*, 241–263.

Berger, F. M. (1954). The pharmacological properties of 2–methyl-2–n-propyl, 1–3 propanediol dicarbamate (Miltown), a new interneuronal blocking agent. *J. Pharmacol. Exp. Ther., 112*, 413–423.

Bergeret, J. (1974). *Abrégé de psychologie pathologique*. Paris: Masson.

Bergeret, J. (1975). *La depression et les états limites*. Paris: Payot.

Bergeret, J. (1984). *La violence fondamentale*. Paris: Dunod.

Bergeret, J. (1994). *La violence et la vie: La face cachée de l'Oedipe*. Paris: Payot & Rivages.

Bergler, E. (1957). *Homosexuality: Disease or way of life?* New York: Hill & Wang.

Bergman, P. & Escalona, S. (1949). Unusual sensitivities in very young children. *Psychoan. Study of the Child, 3/4*, 333–352.

Berman, K. F., Illkowsky, B. P., & Weinberger, D. R. (1988). Physiological dysfunction of dorsolateral prefrontal cortex in schizohrenia. *Arch. Gen. Psychiat., 45*, 616–622.

Berrios, G. E. (1989). Obsessive-compulsive disorder: Its conceptual history in France during the 19th century. *Comprehen. Psychiat., 30*, 283–295.

Berry-Dee, C. & Odell, R. (1992). *Ladykiller*. London: Virgin.

Bevan, E. R. & Singer, C. (1927). *The legacy of Israel*. Oxford: Oxford/Clarendon.

Bieber, I. (1962). *Homosexuality: A psychoanalytic study of male homosexuals*. New York: Basic.

Biederman, J., Faraone, S. V., & Kennan, K. (1991). Evidence of familial association between attention deficit disorder and major affective disorders. *Arch. Gen. Psychiat., 48*, 633–642.

Bigelow, L. B. & Weinberger, D. R. (1990). Neuropsychological assessment of monozygotic twins discordant for schizophrenia. *Arch. Gen. Psychiat., 47*, 1066–1072.

Binet, A. (1903). *L'Etude experimentale de l'intelligence*. Paris: Schleicher, Freres, & Cie.

Bion, W. (1952). Group dynamics: A review. *Internat. J. Psychoan., 33*, 235–247.

Bjerre, P. (1912). Zur Radikalbehandlung der chronischen Paranoia. *Jahrbuch für psychoan. und psychopatholog. Forschungen, 3*, 759–847.

Black, D. W., Baumgard, C. H., & Bell, S. E. (1995). A 16– to 45–year follow-up of 71 men with antisocial personality disorder. *Compr. Psychiat., 36*, 130–140.

Blackburn, R. (1988).On moral judgments and personality disorders: The myth of psychopathic personality revisited. *Brit. J. Psychiat., 153*, 505–512.

Blackburn, S. (1994). *The Oxford dictionary of philosophy*. Oxford: Oxford Univ. Press.

Blackwood, D. H. R., St. Clair, D. M., & Kutcher, S. P. (1986). P-300 event-related potential abnormalities in borderline personlity disorder. *Biol. Psychiat., 21*, 557–560.

Blakeslee, S. (1995, March 21). A new theory of consciousness. *New York Times*, pp. C1, C10.

Bleiberg, E. (1994). Neurosis and conduct disorders. In J. M. Oldham & M. B. Riba (Eds.), *Annual review* (vol. 13, pp. 493–518). Washington, DC: American Psychiatric Association.

Bleuler, M. (1972). *Die schizophrenen Geistesstorungen im Lichte langjahrigen Kranken- und Familiengeschichten*. Stuttgart: G. Thieme.

Blick, L. C. & Porter, F. S. (1982). Group therapy with female adolescent victims. In S. M. Sgroi (Ed.), *Handbook of clinical intervention in child sexual abuse* (pp. 147–175). Lexington, MA: Lexington.

Blos, P. (1957). Preoedipal factors in the etiology of female delinquents. *Psychoan. Study of the Child, 12*, 229–249.

Blum, D. (1986). *Bad karma: A true story of obsession and murder*. New York: Atheneum.

Bogen, J. E. (1969). The other side of the brain, II: An oppositional mind. *Bull. Los Angeles Neurol. Sci., 34*, 135–161.

Bogen, J. E. & Vogel, P. J. (1962). Cerebral commissurotomy in man. *Bull. Los Angeles Neurol. Sci., 27*, 169.

Bohman, M., Cloninger, R., Sigvardsson, S., & von Knorring, A. L. (1982). Predisposition to petty criminality in Swedish adoptees. *Arch. Gen. Psychiat., 39*, 1233–1241.

Bohman, M., Cloninger, R., von Knorring, A. L., & Sigvardsson, S. (1984). An adoption study of somatoform disorders, III: Cross-fostering analysis & genetic relationship to alcoholism & crimi-

nality. *Arch. Gen. Psychiat., 41*, 872–878.

Bond, M. H. (1991). *Beyond the Chinese face: Insights from psychology*. New York: Oxford.

Bordin, E. S. (1976). The generalizability of the psychoanalytic concept of the working alliance. *Psychother. Res. & Pract., 16*, 252–260.

Bouchard, T. J., Lykken, D. T., McGue, M., & Tellegen, A. (1990). Sources of human psychological differences: The Minnesota study of twins reared apart. *Science, 250*, 223–228.

Bowlby, J. (1954). Psychopathological processes set in train by early mother-child separation. In *Proceedings of the 7th conference on infancy & childhood* (March 1953). New York: Jos. Macy Jr. Foundation.

Bowlby, J. (1960a). Separation anxiety. *Internat. J. Psychoan., 41*, 89–113.

Bowlby, J. (1960b). Ethology and the development of object relations. *Internat. J. Psychoan., 41*, 313–317.

Bowlby, J. (1969). *Attachment & loss: Attachment* (vol. 1). New York: Basic.

Bowlby, J. (1973). *Attachment & loss: Separation, anxiety, & anger* (vol. 2). New York: Basic.

Bowlby, J. (1980). *Attachment & loss: Loss, sadness, & depression* (vol. 3). New York: Basic.

Bowlby, J. (1988). *A secure base*. London: Routledge.

Bowman, E. S. (1990). Adolescent multiple personality disorder in the 19th & early 20th centuries. *Dissociation, 3*, 179–187.

Bowman, E. S., Blix, S., & Coods, P. M. (1985). Multiple personality in adolescence: Relationship to incestual experiences. *J. Am. Acad. Child Psychiat., 24*, 109–114.

Braslow, J. T. (1994). Punishment or therapy: Patients, doctors and somatic remedies in the early twentieth century. *Psychiat. Clin. N. Am., 17*, 493–513.

Braslow, J. T. (1995). Effects of therapeutic innovation on perception of disease and of the doctor-patient relationship: A history of general paresis of the insane and malaria fever therapy. *Amer J. Psychiat., 152*, 660–665.

Breier, A. (1996). Mechanism of action of clozapine. *J. Clin. Psychiat., 14* (2), 6–7.

Bremner, J. D., Randall, P., Scott, T. M., Bronen, R. A., Seibyl, J. P., Southwick, S. M., Delaney, R. C., McCarthy, G., Charney, D. S., & Innis, R. B. (1995). MRI-based measurement of hippocampal volume in patients with combat-related posttraumatic stress disorder. *Am. J. Psychiat., 152*, 973–986.

Brent, D. A., Perper, J. A., Goldstein, C. E., Kolko, D. J., Allan, M. J., Allman, C. J., & Zelenal, J. P.

(1988). Risk factors for adolescent suicide. *Arch. Gen. Psychiat., 45*, 581–588.

Breslau, N., Davis, G. C., Andreski, P., & Peterson, E. (1991). Traumatic events and postraumatic stress disorder in an urban population of young adults. *Arch. Gen. Psychiat., 48*, 216–222.

Brett, G. S. (1953). *History of psychology* R. S. Peters (Ed.). London: George Allen & Unwin.

Brodie, B. B. & Shore, P. A. (1957). A concept for a role of serotonin and norepinephrine as chemical mediators in the brain. *Ann. New York Acad. Sci., 66*, 631–642.

Bruch, H. (1973). *Eating disorders.* New York: Basic.

Brumback, R., Dietz-Schmidt, S. G., & Weinberg, W. (1977). Depression in children referred to an educational diagnostic center. *Dis. Nerv. System, 38*, 529–535.

Buchsbaum, M. S., Coursey, R. D., & Murphy, D. L. (1976). The biochemical high risk paradigm: Behavioral and familial correlates of low platelet MAO activity. *Science, 194*, 339–341.

Buchsbaum, M. S., Landau, S., Murphy, D. L., & Goodwin, F. (1973). Average evoked response in bipolar and unipolar affective disorders. *Biol. Psychiat., 7*, 199–212.

Bukkyoh Seiten (1966). Bukkyoh Dendoh Kyohkai [Society for the Promotion of Buddhism]. Tokyo: Kosaido.

Bunney, W. E., Jr. & Garland, B. L. (1984). Lithium and its possible modes of action. In P. M. Post & J. C. Ballenger (Eds.), *Neurobiology of mood disorders* (pp. 731–743). Baltimore: Williams & Wilkins.

Bunney, W. E., Jr., Murphy, D. L., Goodwin, F. K., & Borge, G. F. (1972). The "switch process" in manic-depressive illness, I: A systematic study of sequential behavior change. *Arch. Gen. Psychiat., 27*, 295–302.

Burlingham, D. T. (1951). Present trends in handling the mother-child relationship during the therapeutic process. *Psychoan. Study of the Child, 6*, 31–37.

Buss, A. H. & Finn, S. E. (1987). Classification of personality traits. *J. Personal. & Soc. Psychol., 52*, 432–444.

Buss, A. H. & Plomin, R. (1975). *A temperament theory of personality development.* New York: Wiley Interscience.

Buss, A. H. & Plomin, R. (1984*). Temperament: Early developing personality traits.* Hillsdale, NJ: Erlbaum.

Buss, A. H., Plomin, R., & Willerman, L. (1973). The inheritance of temperament. *J. Personality, 41*, 513–524.

Bychowski, G. (1953). The problem of latent psychosis. *J. Am. Psychoan. Assoc., 4*, 484–503.

Bynum, C. W. (1987). *Holy feast & holy fast: The religious significance of food to medieval women.* Berkeley: Univ. of Calif. Press.

Cade, J. F. J. (1949). Lithium salts in the treatment of psychotic excitement. *Med. J. Australia, 2*, 349–452.

Cadoret, R. J. (1978a). Evidence for genetic inheritance of primary affective disorder. *Am. J. Psychiat., 135*, 463–466.

Cadoret, R. J. (1978b). Psychopathology in adopted-away offspring of biologic parents with antisocial behavior. *Arch. Gen. Psychiat., 35*, 176–184.

Cadoret, R. J., Troughton, E., Bagford, J., & Woodworth, G. (1990). Genetic and environmental factors in adopted antisocial persons. *Euro. Arch. Psychiat, & Neurol. Sci., 239*, 231–240.

Cannon, T. D., Mednick, S. A., Parnas, J., Schulsinger, F., Praestholm, J., & Vestergaard, A. (1994). Developmental brain abnormalities in the offspring of schizophrenic mothers, II: Structural brain characteristics of schizophrenia and schizotypal personality disorder. *Arch. Gen. Psychiat., 51*, 955–962.

Cannon, W. B. (1929). Organization for physiological homeostasis. *Physiol. Rev., 9*, 397.

Cantor, S. & Kestenbaum, C. J. (1986). Psychotherapy with schizophrenic children. *J. Am. Acad. Child Pscyhiat., 25*, 623–630.

Cantwell, D. P. (1975a). Genetics of hyperactivity. *J. Child Psychol. Psychiat., 16*, 261–264.

Cantwell, D. P. (1975b). *The hyperactive child.* New York: Spectrum.

Caplan, R. & Tanguay, P. E. (1991). Development of psychotic thinking in children. In M. Lewis (Ed.), *Child & adolescent psychiatry: A comprehensive textbook* (pp. 310–317). Baltimore: Williams & Wilkins.

Carlson, E. A. (1983). Bipolar affective disorders in childhood and adolescence. In D. Cantwell & G. T. Carlson (Eds.), *i* (pp. 61–84). New York: Spectrum.

Carlson, G. A. & Cantwell, D. P. (1979). A survey of depressive symptoms in a child & adolescent psychiatric population. *J. Am. Acad. Child Psychiat., 18*, 587–599.

Carpenter, W., Strauss, J. S., & Bartko, J. J. (1973). Flexible system for the diagnosis of schizophrenia. *Science, 182*: 1275–1277.

Carroll, B. J., Greden, J. F., Feinberg, M., Lohr, N., James, N. M., Steiner, M., Haskett, R. F., Albala, A. A., DeVigne, J. P., & Tarika, J. (1981). Neuroendocrine evaluation of depression in borderline patients. *Psychiat. Clin. N. Am., 4*, 89–99.

Casey, P. (1988). The epidemiology of personality disorder. In P. Tyrer (Ed.), *Personality disorders: Diagnosis, management and course* (pp. 74–81). London: Wright.

Castonguay, L. G., Hayes, A. M., Goldfried, M. R., & DeRubeis, R. J. (1995). The focus of therapist interventions in cognitive therapy for depression. *Cogn. Ther. & Res., 19*, 485–503.

Cattell, R. B. (1945). The description of personality: Principles and findings in a factor analysis. *Amer. J. Psychology, 58*, 68–90.

Cauwenbergh, L. S. (1991). J. Chr. A. Heinroth (1773–1843): A psychiatrist of the German Romantic era. *History of Psychiatry, 2*, 365–383.

Cavenaugh, M. L. (1995). *Mommy's little angels.* New York: Onyx.

Celsus (1935). *De medicina* [On Medicine] W. G. Spencer (Trans.). Cambridge, MA: Harvard Univ. Press/Loeb Classical Library.

Chalmers, D. J. (1995). The puzzle of conscious experience. *Scient. Am., 273*, 80–86.

Charles, G., Hansenne, M., Ansseau, M., Pitchot, W., Machowski, R., Schittecatte, M., & Wilmotte, J. (1995). P300 in posttraumatic stress disorder. *Neuropsychobio., 32*, 72–74.

Chasseguet-Smirgel, J. (1965/1985). *The ego-ideal: A psychoanalytic essay on the malady of the ideal* P. Barrows (Trans.). New York: Norton.

Chatoor, I., Conley, C., & Dickson, L. (1988). Food refusal after an incident of choking: A posttraumatic eating disorder. *J. Am. Acad. Child & Adol. Psychiat., 27*, 105–110.

Cheng, A. T. A. (1995). Mental illness and suicide: A case-control study in East Taiwan. *Arch. Gen. Psychiat., 52*, 594–603.

Chomsky, N. (1955). *The logical structure of linguistic theory.* Cambridge, MA: M.I.T. Press.

Chomsky, N. (1959). A review of B. F. Skinner's *Verbal Behavior. Language, 35*, 26–58.

Christian, W. A. (1981). *Apparitions in late medieval and renaissance Spain.* Princeton, NJ: Princeton Univ. Press.

Chu, J. A. (1991). On the misdiagnosis of multiple personalty disorder. *Dissociation, 4*, 200–204.

Churchland, P. M. (1992). *A neurocomputational perspective: The nature of mind and the structure of science.* Cambridge, MA: M.I.T. Press.

Churchland, P. S. & Sejnowski, T. J. (1992). *The computational brain.* Cambridge, MA: M.I.T. Press.

Ciompi, L. & Muller, C. (1976). *Lebensweg und Alter der Schizophrenen.* Berlin: Springer.

Clarke, J. W. (1990). *On being mad or merely angry: John W. Hinckley, Jr. and other dangerous people.* Princeton, NJ: Princeton Univ. Press.

Clarkin, J. F., Koenigsberg, H., Yeomans, F., Selzer, M., Kernberg, P., & Kernberg, O. F. (1992). Psychodynamic psychotherapy of the borderline patient. In J. F. Clarkin, E. Marziali, & H. Munroe-Blum (Eds.), *Borderline personality disorder* (pp. 268–287). New York: Guilford.

Clarkin, J. F. & Sweeney, J. A. (1990). Psychological testing. In R. Michels (Ed.), *Psychiatry* (vol. 1, ch. 7). Philadelphia: Lippincott.

Clarren, S. K. & Smith, D. W. (1978). The fetal alcohol syndrome. *N. Eng. J. Med., 298*, 1063–1067.

Cleckley, H. (1941). *The mask of sanity.* St. Louis: Mosby.

Cloninger, C. R. (1986). A unified biosocial theory of personality and its role in the development of anxiety states. *Psychiat. Developments, 3*, 167–226.

Cloninger, C. R., Przybeck, T. R., & Svrakic, D. M. (1991). The tridimensional personality questionnaire: U.S. normative data. *Psychol. Rep., 69*, 1047–1057.

Cloninger, C. R., Reich, T., & Guze, S. B. (1975). Multifactorial model of disease transmission, III: Familial relationship between sociopathy and hysteria. *Brit. J. Psychiat., 127*, 23–32.

Coccaro, E. F., Bergeman, C. S., & McClearn, G. E. (1993). Heritability of irritable aggressiveness: A study of twins reared together and apart. *Psychiat. Research., 48*, 229–242.

Coccaro, E. F., Siever, L. J., Klar, H. M., Maurer, G., Cochrane, K., Cooper, T. B., Mohs, R. C., & Davis, K. L. (1989). Serotonergic studies in patients with affective & personality disorders. *Arch. Gen. Psychiat., 46*, 587–599.

Cocks, G. (Ed.) (1994). *The curve of life: Correspondence of Heinz Kohut.* Chicago: Univ. of Chicago Press.

Cohen, J. (1977). *Statistical power analysis for the behavioral sciences, 2nd ed.* New York: Academic.

Coid, B., Lewis, S. W., & Reveley, A. M. (1993). A twin study of psychosis and criminality. *Brit. J. Psychiat., 162*, 87–92.

Colton, T. (1974). *Statistics in medicine.* Boston: Little, Brown.

Cooper, A. M. (1984). Narcissism in normal development. In M. R. Zales (Ed.), *Character pathology: Theory & treatment* (pp. 39–56). New York: Brunner/Mazel.

Cooper, A. M. (1985). The masochistic-narcissistic character. In R. A. Glick & D. I. Myers (Eds.), *Masochism: Current psychoanalytic and psy-*

chotherapeutic perspectives. Hillsdale, NJ: Analytic.

Cooper, A. M. (1989). The narcissistic-masochistic character. In R. F. Lax (Ed.), *Essential papers on character neuroses and treatment* (pp. 288–309). New York: N.Y.U. Press.

Cooper, A. M., Frances, A., & Sacks, M. (1990). The psychoanalytic model. In R. Michels (Ed.), *Psychiatry* (vol. 1, ch. 1). Philadelphia: Lippincott.

Coriat, I. H. (1917). The treatment of dementia praecox by psychoanalysis. *J. Abnorm. Psychol., 12*, 326–330.

Coryell, W., Lavori, P., Endicott, J., Keller, M., & van Eerdewegh, M. (1984). Outcome in schizoaffective, psychotic, and nonpsychotic depression. *Arch. Gen. Psychiat., 41*, 787–791.

Costa, P. T., Jr. & McRae, R. R. (1986). Personality stability and its implication for clinical psychology. *Clin. Psychol. Rev., 6*, 407–423.

Coston, J. (1995). *Sleep my child, forever.* New York: Onyx.

Cowley, D. S. & Arana, G. W. (1990). The diagnostic utility of lactate sensitivity in panic disorder. *Arch. Gen. Psychiat., 47*, 277–284.

Crasilneck, H. B. & Hale, J. A. (1975). *Clinical hypnosis: Principles and applications.* New York: Grune & Stratton.

Crick, F. & Koch, C. (1992). The problem of consciousness. *Scient. Am., 267*: 153–159.

Cross, C. K. & Hirschfeld, R. M. A. (1986). Psychosocial factors and suicidal behavior: Life events, early loss and personality. *Ann. NY Acad. Sci., 487*, 77–89.

Cytryn, L., McKnew, D., & Bunney, W. (1980). Diagnosis of depression in children: A reassessment. *Am. J. Psychiat., 137*, 22–25.

Dabbs, J. M., Jr. & Morris, R. (1990). Testosterone, social class, & antisocial behavior in a sample of 8,462 men. *Psychol. Sci., 1*, 209–211.

Dahl, H. (1978). A new psychoanalytic model of motivation: Emotions as appetites and messages. *Psychoan. & Contemp. Thought, 1*, 373–408.

Damasio, A. R. (1994). *Descartes' error: Emotion, reason & the human brain.* New York: Grosset/Putnam.

Damasio, H. (1990, May 24). Old accident points to brain's moral center. *New York Times*, p. C1.

Daniel, W. W. (1974). *Biostatistics: A foundation for analysis in the health sciences.* New York: Wiley.

Davanloo, H. (1978). *Basic principles and techniques in short term dynamic psychotherapy.* New York: Basic.

Davanloo, H. (1980). *Short-term dynamic psycho-therapy.* New York: J. Aronson.

Davanloo, H. (1986). Intensive short-term psychotherapy with highly resistant patients, I: Handling resistance. *Internat. J. Short Term Psychother., 1*, 107–133.

Dawkins, R. (1976). *The selfish gene.* New York: Oxford Univ. Press.

de Clérambault, G. (1942). *Oeuvres psychiatriques.* Paris: Presse Universitaire Français.

Decina, P., Kestenbaum, C.J., & Farber, S. (1983). Clinical and psychological assessment of children of bipolar parents. *Am. J. Psychiat., 140*, 548–553.

Delay, J. & Deniker, P. (1952). Trent-huit cas de psychoses traitées par la cure prolongée et continue de 4560 RP. In *Le Congrés des Al. et Neurol. de Langue Français: Contes Rendu du Congrès* (pp. 497–502). Paris: Masson.

Delay, J., Deniker, P. & Harl. J. (1952). Utilization thérapeutique psychiatrique d'une phenothiazine d'action centrale elective. (4560 RP). *Ann. Méd. Psychol., 110*, 112–117.

Delbanco, A. (1995). *The death of Satan: How Americans have lost the sense of evil.* New York: Farrar, Straus & Giroux.

Delgado, J. M. R. & DeFendis, F.V. (1967). Effects of lithium injections into the amygdala and hippocampus of awake monkeys. *Exp. Neurol., 25*, 255–267.

Dement, W. C. (1960). The effect of dream deprivation. *Science, 131*, 1705–1707.

Dement, W. C. (1964). Research studies: Dreams and communication. In J. H. Masserman (Ed.) *Science and psychoanalysis* (pp. 129–184). New York: Grune & Stratton.

Denckla, M. (1981). Tests that discriminate between dyslexic and other learning-disabled boys. *Brain & Lang., 13*, 118–129.

Dennett, D. C. (1991). *Consciousness explained.* Boston: Little, Brown.

de Rivera, J. (1977). A structural theory of emotions. *Psychological Issues: Monograph #40.* New York: International Univ. Press.

Deutsch, F. & Murphy, W. F. (1955). *The clinical interview.* New York: International Univ. Press.

Deutsch, H. (1942). Some forms of emotional disturbance and their relationships to schizophrenia. *Psychoan. Q., 11*, 301–321.

Deutsch, H. (1965). *Neuroses & character types.* New York: International Univ. Press.

DeVane, C. L. & Sallee, F. R. (1996).Serotonin selective reuptake inhibitors in child and adolescent psychopharmacology: A review of published experience. *J. Clin. Psychiat., 57*, 55–66.

Dewald, P. A. (1992). The "rule" and role of abstinence in psychoanalysis. In A. Sugarman, R. A. Nemiroff & D. P. Greenson (Eds.), *The Technique & Practice of Psychoanalysis* (vol. 2, pp. 135–157). Madison, CT: International Univ. Press.

Diatkine, R. & Simon, J. (1980). Some reflections on interpretation in psychoanalysis of children. In S. Lebovici & D. Widlocher (Eds.), *Psychoanalysis in France* (pp.373–389). New York: International Univ. Press.

Diekstra, R. F. W. & Moritz, B. J. M. (1987). Suicidal behavior among adolescents. In R. F. W. Diekstra & K. Hawton (Eds.), *Suicide in Adolescents* (pp. 7–24). Dordrecht, the Netherlands: M. Nijhoff.

Dietz, P. E. (1985). Hypothetical criteria for the prediction of individual criminality. In C. D. Webster, M. H. Ben-Aron, & S. J. Hucker (Eds.), *Dangerousness* (pp. 87–102). Cambridge: Cambridge Univ. Press.

Dilalla, L. F. & Gottesman, I. I. (1990). Heterogeneity of causes for delinquency and criminality: Lifespan perspectives. *Development & Psychopathol., 1*, 339–349.

Dohrenwend, B. P., Dohrenwend, B. S., Gould, M.S., Link, B., Neugebauer, R., & Wunsch-Hitzig, R. (1980). *Mental Illness in the U.S.: Epidemiological Estimates.* New York: Praeger.

Dohrenwend, B. P., Levav, I., Schwartz, S., Guedalia, N., Link, B. G., & Skodol, A. (1992). Socioeconomic status & psychiatric disorders. *Science, 255*, 946–952.

Donnelly, M., Rapoport, J. L., Potter, W. Z., Oliver, J., Keysor, C. S., & Murphy, D. L. (1989). Fenfluramine and dextro-amphetamine treatment of childhood hyperactivity. *Arch. Gen. Psychiat., 46*, 205–212.

Dowbiggin, I. (1990). Alfred Maury and the politics of the unconscious in nineteenth century France. *Hist. of Psychiat., 1*, 255–287.

Duché, D. J. (1971). La concéption organogénétique des psychoses infantiles. In P. Doucet & C. Laurin (Eds.), *Problems of psychosis: International colloquium on psychosis* (pp.169–178). Montreal: Excerpta Medica.

Dudai, Y. (1989). *The neurobiology of memory: Concepts, findings, trends.* Oxford: Oxford Univ. Press.

Dunbar, F. (1938). *Emotions and bodily changes.* New York: Columbia Univ. Press.

Dunbar, F. (1944). *Psychosomatic diagnosis.* New York: Hoeber.

Dunner, D. L., Gershon, E. S., & Goodwin, F. K. (1976). Heritable factors in the severity of affective illness. *Biol. Psychiat., 11*, 31–42.

Dupont, R. M., Jernigan, T. L., Heindel, W., Butters, N., Shafer, K., Wilson, T., Hesselink, J., & Gillin, C. (1995). Magnetic resonance imaging and mood disorders. *Arch. Gen. Psychiat., 52*, 747–755.

Duruz, N. (1981). The psychoanalytic concept of narcissism. *Psychoan. & Contemp. Thought, 4*, 3–67.

Easser, R. R. & Lesser, S. (1965). Hysterical personality: A reevaluation. *Psychoanal. Q., 34*, 390–402.

Eastwood, M. R. & Peacocke, J. (1976). Seasonal patterns of suicide, depression, & electroconvulsive therapy. *Brit. J. Psychiat., 129*, 472–475.

Eckert, E. D., Bouchart, T. J., Bohlen, J., & Heston, L. L. (1986). Homosexuality in MZ twins reared apart. *Brit. J. Psychiat., 148*, 421–425.

Edelman, G. M. (1992). *Bright air, brilliant fire: On the matter of mind.* New York: Basic.

Egan, J. & Kernberg, P. (1984). Pathological narcissism in childhood. *J. Am. Psychoan. Assoc., 32*, 39–62.

Eggington, J. (1989). *From cradle to grave: The short lives and strange deaths of Mary Beth Tinning's nine children.* New York: Wm. Morrow.

Eibl-Eibesfeldt, I. (1967). Concepts of ethology and their significance for the study of human behavior. In H. W. Stevenson (Ed.), *Early behavior: comparative and developmental approaches* (pp. 127–146). New York: Wiley.

Eibl-Eibesfeldt, I. (1989). *Human ethology.* New York: Aldine de Gruyter.

Eissler, K. (1967). *Reich speaks of Freud: Interview* M. Higgins & C. M. Raphael (Eds.). New York: Farrar, Straus & Giroux.

Ekstein, R. & Wallerstein, J. (1957). Choice of interpretation in the treatment of borderline psychotic children. *Bull. Menn. Clin., 21*, 199–207.

Elkin, I., Shea, T., Watkins, J. T., Imber, S. D., Sotsky, S. M., Collins, J. F., Glass, D. R., Pilkonis, P. A., Leber, W. R., Docherty, J. P., Fiester, S. J., & Parloff, M. B. (1989). National Institute of Mental Health treatment of depression collaborative research project. *Arch. Gen. Psychiat., 46*, 971–982.

Elkis, H., Friedman, L., Wise, A., & Meltzer, H. Y. (1995). Meta-analysis of studies of ventricular enlargement and cortical sulcal prominence in mood disorders. *Arch. Gen. Psychiat., 52*, 735–746.

Ellenberger, H. F. (1970). *The discovery of the unconscious: The history and evolution of dynamic psychiatry.* New York: Basic.

Ellenberger, H. F. (1993). Freud & Fechner. In *Beyond the unconscious: Essays of Henri F. Ellenberger in the history of psychiatry* (pp. 89–103). Princeton: Princeton Univ. Press.

Elsässer, G. (1952). *Die nachkommen geisteskranken Elternpaare*. Stuttgart: G. Thieme.

Emslie, G. J., Rush, J., Weinberg, W. A., Rintelmann, J. W., & Roffwarg, H. P. (1990). Children with major depression show reduced rapid eye movement latencies. *Arch. Gen. Psychiat., 47*, 119–124.

Endicott, J., Spitzer, R. L., Fleiss, J. L., & Cohen, J. (1976). The Global Assessment Scale. *Arch. Gen. Psychiat., 33*, 766–771.

Erikson, E. H. (1956). The problem of ego identity. *J. Am. Psychoan. Assoc., 4*, 66–81.

Erikson, E. H. (1959). Identity and the life cycle. *Psychol. Issues, 1*, 1–171.

Erickson, M. (1994, February 18*). Rethinking the Odipus complex in evolutionary perspective.* Lecture (Grand Rounds) at the New York State Psychiatric Institute.

Erkwoh, R. & Sass, H. (1993). Storung mit multipler Personlichkeit: Alte Konzeptionen in neuem Gewande. *Nervenarzt, 64*, 169–174.

Erlenmeyer-Kimling, L. (1975). A prospective study of children at risk for schizophrenia. In R. D. Wirt, G. Winokur, & M. Roff (Eds.), *Life history research in psychopathology* (vol. 4). Minneapolis: Univ. of Minnesota Press.

Erlenmeyer-Kimling, L. & Cornblatt, B. (1987). The New York high risk project: A follow-up report. *Schizophren. Bull., 13*, 451–461.

Erlenmeyer-Kimling, L., Kestenbaum, C. J., Bird, H., & Hilldoff, U. (1984). Assessment of the New York high risk project subjects in sample "A" who are now clinically deviant. In N. F. Watts, E. J. Anthony, L.C. Wynne, & J. E. Rolf (Eds.), *Children at risk for schizophrenia: A longitudinal perspective* (pp. 227–239). Cambridge: Cambridge Univ. Press.

Erlenmeyer-Kimling, L., Marcuse, Y., Cornblatt, B., Friedman, D, Rainer, J. D., & Rutschmann, J. (1984). The New York high risk project. In N. F. Watts, E. J. Anthony, L. C. Wynne, & J. E. Rolf (Eds.), *Children at risk for schizophrenia: A longitudinal perspective* (pp. 169–189). Cambridge: Cambridge Univ. Press.

Erlenmeyer-Kimling, L., Squires-Wheeler, E., Adamo, U. H., Bassett, A. S., Cornblatt, B. A., Kestenbaum, C.J., Rock., D., Roberts, S. A., & Gottesman, I. I. (1995). The New York high risk project: Psychoses and cluster A personality disorders in offspring of schizophrenic parents at 23 years of follow-up. *Arch. Gen. Psychiat., 52*, 857–865.

Ernst, C., Angst, J., & Földenyi, M. (1993). Sexual abuse in childhood: Frequency and relevance for adult morbidity. *Euro. Arch. Psychiat. Clin. Neurosci., 242*, 293–300.

Escalona, S. & Leitch, M. (1949). The reaction of infants to stress. *Psychoan. Study of the Child, 3/4*, 121–140.

Etcoff, N. L. (1994). Beauty and the beholder. *Nature, 368*, 186–187.

Eysenck, H. J. (1947). *The dimensions of personality*. London: Kegan Paul, Trench, & Trubner.

Eysenck, H. J. (1959). *Manual of the Maudsley Personality Inventory*. London: London Univ. Press.

Eysenck, H. J. (1994). *The decline & fall of the Freudian empire*. Washington, DC: Townsend.

Faedda, G. L., Teicher, M. H., Baldessarini, R. J., Gelbard, M. A., & Floris, G. F. (1993). Seasonal mood disorders. *Arch. Gen. Psychiat., 50*, 17–23.

Fairbairn, W. R. (1954). *An object-relations theory of the personality*. New York: Basic.

Fairburn, C. G., Jones, R., Peveler, R. C., Carr, S. J., Solomon, R. A., O'Connor, M. E., Burton, J., & Hope, R. A. (1991). Three psychological treatments for bulimia nervosa. *Arch. Gen. Psychiat., 48*, 463–469.

Fallon, B. A., Klein, B. W., & Liebowitz, M. R. (1993). Hypochondriasis: Treatment strategies. *Psychiat. Annals, 23*, 374–381.

Fallon, B. A., Walsh, T., Sadik, V., & Lukasik, V. (1990). *A 2 to 9 year follow-up study of inpatient bulimic women*. Unpublished manuscript.

Farber, S. L. (1981). *Identical twins reared apart*. New York: Basic.

Feighner, J. P., Robins, E., Guze, S. B., Woodruff, R. A., Jr., Winokur, G., & Munoz, R. (1972). Diagnostic criteria for use in psychiatric research. *Arch. Gen. Psychiat., 26*, 57–63.

Feinstein, S. C. & Wolpert, E. (1973). Juvenile manic depressive illness. *J. Am. Acad. Child Psychiat., 12*, 123–136.

Ferenczi, S. (1924). *Sex in psychoanalysis*. Boston: Badger.

Fieve, R. R., Kumbaraci, T., & Dunner, D. L. (1976). Lithium prophylaxis in bipolar I, bipolar II and unipolar patients. *Am. J. Psychiat., 133*, 925–930.

Fieve, R. R., Mendlewicz, J., & Fleiss, J. L. (1973). Manic-depressive illness: Linkage with the X-g blood group. *Am. J. Psychiat., 130*, 1355–1359.

Fine, R. (1979). *A history of psychoanalysis*. New York: Columbia Univ. Press.

Fink, D. (1991). The comorbidity of multiple personality disorder and *DSM-III-R* Axis II disorders. *Psychiat. Clin. N. Am., 14*, 547–566.

Finkelhor, D. (1979). *Sexually victimized children*. New York: Free Press.

Finkelhor, D. (1984). *Child sexual abuse: New theory and research*. New York: Free Press.

Fish, B. (1975). Biologic antecedents of psychosis in children. In D. X. Freedman (Ed.), *The biology of the major psychoses* (pp. 49–80). New York: Raven.

Flor-Henry, P. (1969). Schizophrenia as a dominant hemisphere disease. *Am. J. Psychiat., 126*, 400–404.

Forel, A. (1905). *Die sexuelle Frage*. Munich: E. Reinhardt.

Forward, C. (1978). *The trauma of incest*. New York: T. Archer.

Fosson, A., Knibbs, J., & Bryant-Waugh, R. (1987). Early onset anorexia nervosa. *Arch. Dis. Child., 62*, 114–118.

Frances, A., Mack, A. H., First, M. B., Widiger, T., Ford, S., Vetterello, N., & Ross, R. (1995). *DSM-IV and psychiatric epidemiology*. In M. Tsuang, M. Tohen, & G. Zahner (Eds.), *Textbook in epidemiology* (pp. 273–279). New York: Wiley.

Frank, E., Kupfer, D. J., & Perel, J. M. (1990). Three-year outcomes for maintenance therapies in recurrent depression. *Arch. Gen, Psychiat., 47*, 1093–1099.

Frank, J. D. & Frank, J. B. (1991). *Persuasion and healing: A comparative study of psychotherapy*. Baltimore: Johns Hopkins Press.

Frankel, F. H. (1974). Trance capacity and the genesis of phobic behavior. *Arch. Gen. Psychiat., 31*, 261–263.

Frankel, F. H. (1975). Hypnosis as a treatment method in psychosomatic medicine. *Internat. J. Psychiat. Med., 6*, 366–376.

Freedman, D. X. (Ed.) (1975). *Biology of the major psychoses*. New York: Raven.

Freud, A. (1936). *Das Ich and das Abwehrmechanismus*. Vienna: Internat. Psychoanalyt. Verlag.

Freud, A. (1966). A short history of child analysis. *Psychoan. Study of the Child, 21*, 7–14.

Freud, S. (1912). The dynamics of transference. *The standard edition of the complete psychological works of Sigmund Freud* (vol. 12, pp. 97–108). New York: Norton.

Freud, S. (1913). Totem & taboo. In J. Strachey (Ed. and Trans.), *The standard edition of the complete psychological works of Sigmund Freud* (vol. 13, 1–162). New York: Norton.

Freud, S. (1919/1959). Turnings in the ways of psychoanalytic therapy. In J. Riviere (Ed. and Trans.), *Fifth International Psychoanalytical Congress: Vol. 2. Collected papers* (pp. 392–402). New York: Basic.

Friedman, R. C. (1988). *Male homosexuality: A contemporary psychoanalytic perspective*. New Haven: Yale Univ. Press.

Friedman, R. C. & Downey, J. (1993). Neurobiology and sexual orientation: Current relationships. *J. Neuropsychiat. Clin. Neurosci., 5*, 131–153.

Friedman, R. C. & Downey, J. (1994). Homosexuality. *New Engl. J. Med., 331*, 923–930.

Friedman, R. C. & Downey, J. (1995). Biology and the Oedipus complex. *Psychoan. Q., 64*, 234–264.

Frohman, C. E. & Gottlieb, S. S. (1976). Model psychoses. In R. G. Grenell & S. Gabay (Eds.), *Biological foundations of psychiatry* (pp. 755–792). New York: Raven.

Fromm-Reichmann, F. (1950). *Principles of intensive psychotherapy*. Chicago: Univ. of Chicago Press.

Frosch, J. (1964). The psychotic character. *Psychiat. Q., 38*, 81–96.

Fuller, Torrey, E. (1980). *Schizophrenia and civilization*. New York: Aronson.

Gabbard, G. (Ed.) (1995). *Treatment of psychiatric disorders*. Washington, DC: American Psychiatric Association.

Gaffney, G. R. & Berlin, F. S. (1984). Is there hypothalamic-pituitary-gonadal dysfunction in paedophilia? *Brit. J. Psychiat., 145*, 657–660.

Galanter, M. (1982). Charismatic religious sects and psychiatry. *Am. J. Psychiat., 139*, 1539–1548.

Galanter, M. (1983). Unification church dropouts: Psychological readjustment after leaving a charismatic religious group. *Am. J. Psychiat., 140*, 984–985.

Galanter, M. (1989). *Cults, faith-healing, and coercion*. Oxford: Oxford Univ. Press.

Garattini, S. & Valzelli, L. (1965). *Serotonin*. Amsterdam: Elsevier.

Garmezy, N. (1974). Children at risk: The search for the antecedents of schizophrenia. *Schiz. Bulletin, 9*, 55–125.

Garmezy, N. & Devine, V. (1984). Project competence: The Minnesota studies of children vulnerable to psychopathology. In N. F. Watts, E. J. Anthony, L. C. Wynne, & J. E. Rolf (Eds.), *Children at risk for schizophrenia: A longitudinal study* (pp. 289–303). Cambridge: Cambridge Univ. Press.

Garner, D. M. & Bemis, K. M. (1985). Cognitive therapy for anorexia nervosa. In D. M. Garner & P. E. Garfinkel (Eds.), *Handbook of psychotherapy for anorexia nervosa and bulimia* (pp.107–146). New York: Guilford.

Gay, P. (1988). *Freud: A life for our time*. New York: Norton.

Gazzaniga, M. S. (1965). Psychological properties of the disconnected hemispheres in man. *Science, 150*, 372.

Gazzaniga, M. S. & Sperry, R. W. (1967). Language after section of the cerebral commissures. *Brain, 90*, 131–148.

Geleerd, E. (1958). Borderline states in childhood and adolescence. *Psychoan. Study of the Child, 13*, 279–295.

Gelernter, C. S., Uhde, T. W., Cimbolic, P., Arnloff, D. B., Vittone, B. J., Tancer, M. E., & Bartko, J. J. (1991). Cognitive-behavioral and pharmacological treatments of social phobia. *Arch. Gen. Psychiat., 48*, 938–945.

Gelles, R. J. (1975). The social construction of child abuse. *Am. J. Orthopsychiat., 45*, 363–371.

Gell-Mann, M. (1994). *The quark and the jaguar: Adventures in the simple and the complex*. New York: Freeman.

Gershon, E. S. (1977). Genetic and biologic studies of affective illness. In E. S. Gershon, R. H. Belmaker, S. S. Kety, & M. Rosenbaum (Eds.), *The impact of biology on modern psychiatry* (pp. 207–228). New York: Plenum.

Gershon, E. S., Belmaker, R. H., Kety, S. S., & Rosenbaum, M. (Eds.). (1977). The impact of biology on modern psychiatry. New York: Plenum.

Gershon, E. S. & Rieder, R. O. (1980). Are mania and schizophrenia genetically distinct? In R. H. Belmaker & H. van Praag (Eds.), *Mania: An evolving concept* (pp. 97–109). New York: Spectrum.

Gershon, E. S., Targum, S., Matthysse, S., & Bunney, W. E., Jr. (1979). Color blindness not closely linked to bipolar illness. *Arch. Gen. Psychiat., 36*, 1423–1430.

Gill, M. M., Simon, J., Fink, G., Endicott, N. A., & Paul, I. H. (1968). Studies in audio-recorded psychoanalysis, I: General considerations. *J. Am. Psychoanal. Assoc., 16*, 230–244.

Gittelman-Klein, R. & Klein, D. (1976). Comparative effects of methylphenidate and thioridazine in hyperkinetic children. *Arch. Gen. Psychiat., 33*, 1217–1231.

Gjessing, L. & Jenner, A. (1976). *Contributions to the somatology of periodic catatonia*. Oxford: Pergamon.

Glowinski, J. & Baldessarini, R. J. (1966). Metabolism of norepinephrine in the central nervous system. *Pharmacol. Rev., 18*, 775.

Goddard, H. H. (1926). A case of dual personality. *J. Abnorm. & Soc. Psychol., 21*, 179–191.

Goetzl, U., Green, R., & Whybrow, P. (1974). X-linkage revisited: A further family study of manic-depressive illness. *Arch. Gen. Psychiat., 31*, 665–672.

Goldberg, L. R. (1982). From ace to zombie: Some explorations in the language of personality. In C. Spielberger & J. Butcher (Eds.), *Advances in personality assessment* (pp. 203–234). Hillside, NJ: Erlbaum.

Goldberg, S. C., Schulz, S. C., & Schulz, P. M. (1986). Borderline and schizotypal personality disorders treated with low dose thiothixene vs. placebo. *Arch. Gen. Psychiat., 43*, 680–686.

Goldberg, T. E., Ragland, J. D., Torrey, E. F., Gold, J. M., Bigelow, J. B., & Weinberger, D. R. (1990). Neuropsychological assessment of monozygotic twins discordant for schizophrenia. *Arch. Gen. Psychiat., 47*, 1066–1072.

Goldman-Rakič, P. S. (1992). Working memory and the mind. *Scient. Am., 267*, 111–117.

Goldin, L. R. & Gershon, E. S. (1983). Association and linkage studies of genetic marker loci in major psychiatric disorders. *Psychiat. Dev., 4* 387–408.

Goldsmith, H. H. (1983). Genetic influences on personality from infancy to adulthood. *Child Develop., 54*, 331–355.

Gollaher, D. (1995). *A voice for the mad: The life of Dorothea Dix*. New York: Free.

Goodwin, F. K. & Ebert, M. (1973). Lithium in mania. In S. Gershon & B. Shopsin (Eds.), *Lithium & its role in psychiatric research* (pp. 237–252). New York: Plenum.

Goodwin, J. (1982). *Sexual abuse: Incest victims and their families*. Littleton, MA: PSG.

Goodwin, J. (1985). Posttraumatic symptoms in incest victims. In S. Eth & R. S. Pynoos (Eds.), *Posttraumatic stress disorder in children* (pp. 157–168). Washington, DC: American Psychiatric Association.

Goshen, C. E. (1967). *Documentary history of psychiatry*. New York: Philosophical Library.

Gottesman, I. I. & Bertelsen, A. (1989). Dual mating studies in psychiatry: Offspring of inpatients with examples from reactive (psychogenic) psychoses. *Internat. Rev. Psychiat., 1*, 287–296.

Gottesman, I. I. & Shields, J. (1972). *Schizophrenia & genetics: A twin-study vantage point.* New York: Academic.

Gottfried, R. S. (1983). *The Black Death.* New York: Free.

Gough, H. G. & Heilbrun, A. B. Jr. (1983). *Adjective checklist manual.* Palo Alto, CA: Consulting Psychologists Press.

Greaves, G. B. (1980). Multiple personality disorder 165 years after Mary Reynolds. *J. Nerv. & Ment. Dis., 168,* 577–596.

Green, A. (1978). Psychiatric treatment of abused children. *J. Am. Acad. Child Psychiat., 17,* 356–371.

Green, A. (1994).Victims of child abuse. In J. M. Oldham & M. B. Riba (Eds.), *Annual review* (vol. 13, pp. 589–609). Washington, DC: American Psychiatric Association.

Green, H. (1964). *I never promised you a rose garden.* New York: Holt, Rinehart, & Winston.

Green, R. C. & Pitman, R. K. (1990). Tourette syndrome and obsessive compulsive disorder: Clinical relationships. In M. A. Jenike, L. Baer, & W. E. Minichiello (Eds.), *Obsessive-compulsive disorder: Therapy & management* (pp. 61–75). Chicago: Yearbook.

Greenson, R. R. (1967). *The technique and practice of psychoanalysis* (vol. 1). New York: International Univ. Press.

Greenson, R. R. (1970). The exceptional position of the dream in psychoanalytic practice. In R. R. Greenson (Ed.), *Explorations in psychoanalysis* (pp. 387–414). New York: International Univ. Press.

Greenson, R. R. (1972). Beyond transference and interpretation. *Internat. J. Psychoan., 53,* 213–217.

Grenell, R. G. & Gabay, S. (1976). *Biological foundations of psychiatry* (vols. 1 & 2). New York: Raven.

Grinfeld, M. J. (1995). Psychiatrist stung by huge damage award in repressed memory case. *Psychiat. Times, 12*(10), 1.

Grinker, R. R., Sr. & Werble, B. (1977). *The borderline patient.* New York: J. Aronson.

Grinker, R. R., Sr., Werble, B., & Drye, R. C. (1968). *The borderline syndrome.* New York: Basic.

Gross, G. & Huber, G. (1973). Zur Prognose der Schizophrenien. *Psychiat. Clin., 6,* 1–16.

Grözinger, K. E. (1994). *Kafka and Kabbalah.* New York: Continuum.

Guilford, J. P. & Fruchter, B. (1973). *Fundamental statistics in psychology & education, 5th ed.* New York: McGraw Hill.

Gunderson, J. G. (1984). *Borderline personality disorder.* Washington, DC: American Psychiatric Association.

Gunderson, J. G., Frank, A. F., Katz, H. M., Vannicelli, M. L., Frosch, J. P., & Knapp, P. (1984). Effects of psychotherapy in schizophrenia, II: Comparative outcome of two forms of treatment. *Schiz. Bulletin, 10,* 564–598.

Gunderson, J. G. & Singer, M. T . (1975). Defining borderline patients: An overview. *Am. J. Psychiat., 132,* 1–10.

Guntrip, H. J. S. (1969). *Schizoid phenomena, object-relations, and the self.* New York: International Univ. Press.

Gur, R. C., Mozley, L. H., Mozley, D., Resnick, S. M., Karp, J. S., Alavi, A., Arnold, S. E., & Gur, R. E. (1995). Sex differences in regional cerebral glucose metabolism during a resting state. *Science, 267,* 528–531.

Gyllenhammer, G. & Börstedt, W. (1987). Life events and psychiatric disorders. *Stress Med., 3,* 239–245.

Hackmann, A. (1993). Behavioural and cognitive psychotherapies: Past history, current applications and registration issues. *J. Brit. Assoc. Behav. & Cog. Psychotherapies, 1,* 2–72.

Hajal, F. (1994). Diagnosis and treatment of lovesickness: An Islamic medieval case study. *Hosp. & Commun. Psychiat., 45,* 647–650.

Hakola, P., Vartiainen, H., Hakola, M. L. & Jokela, V. (1990). Mielisairaalapotilaiden tekemät henkirikokset 1954–1988. *Suomen Lääkärilehti, 9,* 846–850.

Halmi, K. (1994). Princess Margeret of Hungary. *Am. J. Psychiat., 151,* 1242.

Halmi, K. A. (1985). Behavioral management for anorexia nervosa. In D. M. Garner & P. E. Garfinkel (Eds.), *Handbook of psychotherapy for anorexia nervosa and bulimia* (pp.147–159). New York: Guilford.

Halmi, K. A., Falk, J. R., & Schwartz, E. (1981). Binge eating and vomiting: A survey of a college population. *Psychol. Med., 11,* 697–705.

Halperin, D. A. (1978). The psychiatrist and the paraprofessional. In K. Nash, N. Lifton, & S. Smith (Eds.), *The paraprofessional* (pp.163–174). New Haven: Advocate.

Halperin, D. A. (Ed.) (1983). *Psychodynamic perspectives on religion, sect, and cult.* Boston: J. Wright.

Halperin, D. A. (1990). Psychiatric perspectives on cult affiliation. *Psychiat. Annals, 20,* 206–213.

Halpern, A. L. (1991). The insanity defense in the 21st century. *Internat. J. Offender Ther. &*

Comparat. Criminol., 35, 187–189.

Hamilton, M. (1960). A rating scale for depression. *J. Neurol. Neurosurg. Psychiat., 23,* 56–61.

Hamilton, W. D. (1972). Altruism and related phenomena, mainly in social insects. *Am. Rev. Ecol. Syst., 3,* 193–232.

Hanly, M. A. F. (1995). *Essential papers on masochism.* New York: N.Y.U. Press.

Hansenne, M., Pitchot, W., Moreno, A. M., Mirel, J., & Ansseau, M. (1994). Psychophysiological correlates of suicidal behavior in depression. *Neuropsychobiol., 30,* 1–3.

Harding, C. M., Brooks, G. W., Ashikaga, T., Strauss, J. S., & Breier, A. (1987). The Vermont longitudinal study of persons with severe mental illness, II: Long term outcome of subjects who retrospectively met *DSM-III* criteria for schizophrenia. *Am. J. Psychiat., 144,* 727–735.

Hare, R. D. (1993). *Without conscience: The disturbing world of the psychopaths among us.* New York: Pocket.

Hare, R. D. & McPherson, L. M. (1984). Violent and aggressive behavior by criminal psychopaths. *Internat. J. Law & Psychiat., 7,* 35–50.

Harlow, H. & Harlow, M. K. (1963). A study of animal affection. In C. H. Southwick (Ed.), *Primate social behavior* (pp. 174–184). Princeton, NJ: Van Nostrand Reinholt.

Harms, E. (1967). *Origins of modern psychiatry.* Springfield, IL: Thomas.

Hartmann, E. (1968). The 90–minute sleep-dream cycle. *Arch. Gen. Psychiat., 18,* 280–286.

Hartmann, E. (1969). Pharmacological studies of sleep and dreaming. *Biol. Psychiat., 1,* 243–258.

Hartmann, H. (1950). *Ego psychology and the problem of adaptation.* New York: International Univ. Press.

Hartmann, H. (1953). Contributions to the metapsychology of schizophrenia. *Psychoan. Study of the Child, 8,* 177–198.

Hathaway, S. R. & McKinley, J. C. (1940). A multiphasic personality inventory schedule. *J. Psychol., 10,* 249–254.

Hawkins, D. R. (1990). Dreaming, neurobiology and psychoanalysis. *Psychiat. Annals, 20,* 238–244.

Heinrichs, R. W. (1989). Frontal cerebral lesions and violent incidents in chronic neuropsychiatric patients. *Biol. Psychiat., 25,* 174–178.

Herman, J. L. (1981). *Father-daughter incest.* Cambridge, MA: Harvard Univ. Press.

Herman, J. L., Perry, J. C., & van der Kolk, B. (1989). Childhood trauma in borderline personality disorder. *Am. J. Psychiat., 146,* 490–495.

Herz, M. I. (1979). Short-term hospitalization and the medical model. *Hosp. & Commun. Psychiat., 39,* 117–121.

Herz, M. I. (1984). Recognizing and preventing relapse in patients with schizophrenia. *Hosp. & Commun. Psychiat., 45,* 344–349.

Herz, M. I. (1986). Toward an integrated approach to the treatment of schizophrenia. *Psychother. & Psychosom., 46,* 45–57.

Herz, M. I., Endicott, J, Spitzer, R. L., & Mesnikoff, A. (1971). Day vs. inpatient hospitalization: A controlled study. *Am. J. Psychiat., 127,* 107–118.

Hickey, C., Lighty, T., & O'Brien, J. (1996). *Goodbye, my little ones.* New York: Onyx.

Higgitt, A. & Fonagy, P. (1992). Psychotherapy in borderline and narcissistic personality disorder. *Brit. J. Psychiat., 161,* 23–43.

Himwich, H. E. (Ed.) (1971). *Biochemistry, schizophrenia, and affective illnesses.* Baltimore: Williams & Wilkins.

Hinshelwood, J. (1900). Congenital word blindness. *Lancet, 1,* 1506.

Hinsie, L. E. (1929). The treatment of schizophrenia. *Psychiat. Q., 3,* 5–39.

Hippocrates (1923). *Complete works* (vol. 1–4). W. H. S. Jones (Trans.). Cambridge, MA: Harvard Univ. Press/Loeb Classical Library.

Hirai, T. (1989). *Zen meditation and psychotherapy.* Tokyo: Japan Publications.

Hobson, J. A. & McCarley, R. W. (1977). The brain as a dream-state generator: An activation-synthesis of the dream process. *Am. J. Psychiat., 134,* 1335–1348.

Hoch, P. H. & Cattell, J. P. (1959). The diagnosis of pseudoneurotic schizophrenia. *Psychiat. Q., 33,* 17–43.

Hoch, P. H. & Polatin, P. (1949). Pseudoneurotic forms of schizophrenia. *Psychiat. Q., 23,* 248–276.

Hodgins, S. (1992). Mental disorder, intellectual deficiency and crime. *Arch. Gen. Psychiat., 49,* 476–489.

Hodgins, S. (Ed.) (1993). *Mental disorder & crime.* London: Sage.

Hoffman, R. E. & Dobscha, S. K. (1989). Cortica pruning and the development of schizophrenia: A computer model. *Schiz. Bull., 15,* 477–490.

Hoffman, R. E., Rapaport, J., Ameli, R., McGlashan, T. H., & Harcherik, D. (1995). A neural network simulation of hallucinated "voices" and associated speech perception impairments in schizophrenic patients. *J. Cogn. Sci., 7,* 479–496.

Holinger, P. C. & Offer, D. (1981). Perspectives on suicide in adolescence. In R. Simmons (Ed.), *Social and community mental health* (pp.139–157). Greenwich, CT: Jai.

Hollander, E., Liebowitz, M. R., Gorman, J. M., Cohen, B., Fyer, A., & Klein, D. F. (1989). Cortisol and sodium lactate-induced panic. *Arch. Gen. Psychiat.*, 46, 135–139.

Hollander, E. & Phillips, K. (1993). Body image and experience disorders. In E. Hollander (Ed.), *Obsessive-compulsive related disorders* (pp. 17–48). Washington, DC: American Psychiatric Association.

Hollingshead, A. B. & Redlich, F. C. (1958). *Social class and mental illness*. New York: Wiley.

Hollister, C. E. & Sjoberg, B. M. (1964). Clinical syndromes and biochemical alterations following mescaline, lysergic ethyl diethylamide, psilocybin, and a combination of three psychotomimetic drugs. *Comprehen. Psychiat.*, 5, 170.

Hollon, S. D. (1993). Cognitive-behavioral therapy. *Current Opinion in Psychiatry*, 6, 348–352.

Hollon, S. D., DeRubeis, R. J., Evans, M. D., Wiemer, M. J., Garvey, M. J., Grove, W. M., & Tuason, V. B. (1992). Cognitive therapy and pharmacotherapy for depression. *Arch. Gen. Psychiat.*, 49, 774–781.

Holmes, J. (1995). Supportive psychotherapy: The search for positive meanings. *Brit. J. Psychiat.*, 167, 439–445.

Holzman, P. S. (1975). Smooth pursuit eye movements in schizophrenia: Recent findings. In D. X. Freedman (Ed.), *Biology of the major psychoses* (pp. 217–228). New York: Raven.

Holzman, P. S., Kringlen, E., Matthysse, S., Flanagan, S. D., Lipton, R. B., Cramer, G., Levin, S. Lange, K., & Levy, D. L. (1988). A single dominant gene can account for eye tracking dysfunctions and schizophrenia in offspring of discordant twins. *Arch. Gen. Psychiat.*, 45, 641–647.

Holzman, P. S., Proctor, L. R., & Hughes, D. W. (1973). Eye tracking patterns in schizophrenia. *Science*, 181, 179–181.

Hooker, E. (1969). Parental relations and male homosxuality in patient and non-patient samples. *J. Consult. & Clin. Psychol.*, 33, 140–142.

Horgan, J. (1995). The new social Darwinists. *Scientific Am.*, 273, 174–181.

Horney, K. (1937). *The neurotic personality of our time*. New York: Norton.

Horney, K. (1939). *New ways in psychoanalysis*. New York: Norton.

Hornykiewicz, O. (1962). Dopamin im Zentralnervensystem und seine Beziehung zum Parkinson-Syndrom des Menschen. *Deutsche Med. Wochenschr.*, 87, 1807.

Hornykiewicz, O. (1966). Dopamine (3-hydroxytyramine) and brain function. *Pharmacol. Rev.* 18, 925–935.

Horowitz, M., Schaefer, C., & Hiroto, D. (1977). Life events questionnaire for measuring presumptive stress. *Psychosom. Med.*, 39, 413–431.

Horvath, A. O. & Luborsky, L. (1993). The role of the therapeutic alliance in psychotherapy. *J. Consult. & Clin. Psychol.*, 61, 561–573.

Horwitz, L., Gabbard, G. O., Allen, J. G., Frieswyk, S. H., Colson, D. B., Newson, G. E., & Coyne, L. (1996). *Borderline personality disorder: Tailoring the psychotherapy to the patient*. Washington, DC: American Psychiatric Association.

Horwitz, W. A., Polatin, P., Kolb, L. C., & Hoch, P. H. (1958). A study of cases of schizophrenia treated by "direct analysis." *Am. J. Psychiat.*, 114, 780–783.

Houck, J. W. (1995, May 1). Speaking up for A. A. [Letter to the editor]. *New Yorker*.

Howlett, R. (1993). Sexual selection: Beauty on the brain. *Nature*, 361, 398–399.

Hoyer, G. & Lund, E. (1993). Suicide among women related to number of children in marriage. *Arch. Gen. Psychiat.*, 50, 134–137.

Huber, G. (1981). *Psychiatrie*. Stuttgart: Schattauer.

Hunter, R. & Macalpine, I. (1963). *Three hundred years of psychiatry: 1535–1860*. London: Oxford Univ. Press.

Huxley, A. (1952). *The devils of Loudun*. New York: Harper.

Inamdar, S. C., Siomopoulis, G, Shanok, S. S., & Lamela, M. (1982). Violent and suicidal behavior in psychotic adolescents. *Am. J. Psychiat.*, 139, 932–935.

Insel, T. R. (1992). Toward a neuroanatomy of obsessive-compulsive disorder. *Arch. Gen. Psychiat.*, 49, 739–744.

Jackson, D. (1960). *The etiology of schizophrenia*. New York: Basic.

Jacobson, E. (1953). Contribution to the metapsychology of cyclothymic depression. In P. Greenacre (Ed.), *Affective disorders* (pp. 49–83). New York: International Univ. Press.

Jacobson, E. (1954). *The self and the object world*. New York: International Univ. Press.

Jacobson, E. (1973). The depressive personality. *Int. J. Psychiat.*, 11, 218–221.

Jancin, B. (1994). Behavior therapy bests drug in obsessive-compulsive disorder care. *Clin. Psychiat. News*, 22(5), 1.

Janet, P. (1911). *L état mental des hystériques*. Paris: F. Alcan.

Janet, P. (1926). *De l'angoisse à l'extase: Un délire réligieux*. Paris: F. Alcan.

Janet. P. (1929). *L'évolution psychologique de la personnalité*. Paris: Chanine.

Janet, P. & Raymond, F. (1903). *Obsessions et la psychasthenia*. Paris: Alcan.

Javit, D. C., Doneshka, P., Grochowski, S., & Ritter, W. (1995). Impaired mismatch negativity generation reflects widespread dysfunction of working memory in schizophrenia. *Arch. Gen. Psychiat., 52*, 550–558.

Jeammet, P., Jayle, D. Terrasse-Brechon, G., & Gorge, A. (1984). Le devinir de l'anorexie mentale. *Neuropsychiatrie de l'Enfance, 32*, 250–263.

Jenike, M. A., Baer, L., & Ballantine, H. T. (1991). Cingulotomy for refractory obsessive-compulsive disorder: A long-term follow-up of 33 patients. *Arch. Gen. Psychiat., 48*, 548–555.

Jenike, M. A. & Rauch, S. L. (1994). Managing the patient with treatment resistant obsessive-compulsive disorder: Current strategies. *J. Clin. Psychiat., 55*, 11–17.

Jeste, D. V. & Lohr, J. B. (1989). Hippocampal pathologic findings in schizophrenia. *Arch. Gen. Psychiat., 46*, 1019–1024.

Jimerson, D. C., Lesem, M. D., Kaye, W. H., & Brewerton, T. D. (1992). Low serotonin and dopamine metabolic concentrations in cerebrospinal fluid from bulimic patients with frequent binge episodes. *Arch. Gen. Psychiat., 49*, 132–138.

Johnson, A. M. (1949). Sanctions for superego lacunae of adolescents. In K. Eissler (Ed.), *Searchlights on delinquency* (pp. 225–245). New York: International Univ. Press.

Johnson, J., Weissman, M. M., & Klerman, G. L. (1990). Panic disorder, comorbidity, and suicide attempts. *Arch. Gen. Psychiat., 47*, 805–808.

Johnston, M. H. & Holzman, P. (1979). *Assessing schizophrenic thinking*. San Francisco: Jossey-Bass.

Jung, C. G. (1935). *Über den Archtypus der kollektiven Unbewußten* [On the archetype of the collective unconscious]. Eranos-Jahrbuch.

Kächele, H. (1988). Clinical and scientific aspects of the Ulm process model of psychoanalysis. *Internat. J. Psychoan., 69*, 65–73.

Kächele, H. & Thomä, H. (1995). Psychoanalytic process research. In T. Shapiro & R. N. Emde (Eds.), *Research in psychoanalysis: Process, development, outcome* (pp. 109–129). Madison, CT: International Univ. Press.

Kallmann, F. (1938). *The genetics of schizophrenia*. New York: Augustin.

Kandel, E. R. & Hawkins, R. D. (1992). The biological basis of learning and individuality. *Scient. Am., 267*, 79–86.

Kane, J., Honigfeld, G., Singer, J., & Meltzer, H. (1988). Clozapine for the treatment-resistant schizophrenic. *Arch. Gen. Psychiat., 45*, 789–796.

Kanner, L. (1935). *Child psychiatry*. Springfield, IL: Thomas.

Kaplan, H. I. & Sadock, B. J. (Eds.) (1967). *Comprehensive textbook of psychiatry*. Baltimore: Williams & Wilkins.

Karasu, T. B. (Ed.) (1989). *Treatment of psychiatric disorders* (vols.1–3). Washington, DC: American Psychiatric Association.

Kasanin, J. (1933). Acute schizoaffective psychoses. *Am. J. Psychiat., 97*, 97–120.

Kaye, W. H., Ebert, M.H., Raleigh, M., & Lake, R. (1984). Abnormalities in CNS monoamine metabolism in anorexia nervosa. *Arch. Gen. Psychiat., 41*, 350–355.

Keck, P. E., Jr., McElroy, S. L., & Bennett, J. A. (1994). Pharmacology and pharmacokinetics of valproic acid. In R. T. Joffe & J. R. Calabrese (Eds) *Anticonvulsants in mood disorders* (pp. 27–42). New York: Dekker.

Kelsoe, J. R., Cadet, J. L., Pickar, D., & Weinberger, D. R. (1988). Quantitative neuroanatomy in schizophrenia. *Arch. Gen. Psychiat., 45*, 533–541.

Kendell, R. E. (1975). *The role of diagnoses in psychiatry*. Oxford: Blackwell.

Kendell, R. E. & Gourlay, J. (1970). The clinical distinctions between the affective psychoses and schizophrenia. *Brit. J. Psychiat., 117*, 261–266.

Kendler, K. S. (1980). The nosologic validity of paranoia (simple delusional disorder). *Arch. Gen. Psychiat., 37*, 699–706.

Kendler, K. S., Gruenberg, A. M., & Tsuang, M. T. (1985). Psychiatric illness in first-degree relatives of schizophrenic and surgical control patients. *Arch. Gen. Psychiat., 42*, 770–779.

Kendler, K. S. & Hayes, P. (1981). Paranoid psychosis (delusional disorder) & schizophrenia. *Arch. Gen. Psychiat., 38*, 547–551.

Kendler, K. S., Masterson, C. C. & Davis, K. L. (1985). Psychiatric illness in first-degree relatives of patients with paranoid psychosis, schizophrenia and medical illness. *Brit. J. Psychiat., 147*, 524–531.

Kendler, K. S., McGuire, M., Gruenberg, A. M., O'Hare, A., Spellman, M., & Walsh, D. (1993). The Roscommon family study, III: Schizophrenia-related personality disorders in relatives. *Arch. Gen. Psychiat., 50*, 781–788.

Kennedy, S. H., Garfinkel, P. E., Parienti, V., Costa, D., & Brown, G. M. (1989). Changes in melatonin levels but not cortisol levels are associated with depression in patients with eating disorders. *Arch. Gen. Psychiat., 46,* 73–78.

Kernberg, O. F. (1967). Borderline personality organization. *J. Am. Psychoan. Assoc., 15,* 641–685.

Kernberg, O. F. (1975). *Borderline conditions and pathological narcissism.* New York: Aronson.

Kernberg, O. F., Burnstein, E., Coyne, L., Applebaum, A., Horwitz, L., & Voth, H. (1972). Final report of the Menninger Foundation's psychotherapy research project. *Bull. Menn. Clin., 36,* 1–275.

Kernberg, O. F., Selzer, M., Koenigsberg, H. W., Carr, A., & Applebaum, A. (1989). *Psychodynamic psychotherapy of borderline patients.* New York: Basic.

Kernberg, P. (1983). Borderline conditions: Childhood and adolescent aspects. In K. S. Robson (Ed.), *The borderline child: Approaches to etiology, diagnosis, & treatment* (pp. 101–119). New York: McGraw Hill.

Kernberg, P. (1988). Children with borderline personality organization. In C. J. Kestenbaum & D. T. Williams (Eds.), *Handbook of clinical assessment of children and adolescents* (pp. 604–625). New York: N.Y.U. Press.

Kernberg, P. (1989). Narcissistic personality disorder in childhood. *Psychiat. Clin. N. Am., 12,* 671–694.

Kernberg, P. & Chazan, S.E. (1991). *Children with conduct disorders: A psychotherapy manual.* New York: Basic.

Kestenbaum, C. J. (1994). Psychotic and prepsychotic disorders. In J. M. Oldham & M. B. Riba (Eds.), *Annual review* (vol. 13, pp. 571–588). Washington, DC: American Psychiatric Association.

Kestenbaum, C. J. & Bird, H. R. (1978). A reliability study of the Mental Health Assessment Form for school-age children. *J. Am. Acad. Child Psychiat., 17,* 338–347.

Kestenbaum, C. J. & Kron, L. (1987). Psychoanalytic intervention with children and adolescents with affective disorders: A combined treatment approach. *J. Am. Acad. Psychoan., 15,* 153–174.

Kety, S. S. (1975). Genetics of schizophrenia. In E. Gershon, R. Belmaker, S. Kety, & M. Rosenbaum (Eds.), *The impact of biology on modern psychiatry* (pp. 195–206). New York: Plenum.

Kety, S. S., Rosenthal, D., & Wender, P. (1968). *Transmission of schizophrenia.* Oxford: Pergamon.

Kidd, K. K. (1975). On the possible magnitude of selective forces maintaining schizophrenia in the population. In R. R. Fieve, D. Rosenthal, & H. Brill (Eds.), *Genetic research in psychiatry* (pp. 135–145). Baltimore: Johns Hopkins Press.

Kim, L. I. (1993). Psychiatric care of Korean Americans. In A. C. Gaw (Ed.), *Culture, ethnicity, & mental illness* (pp. 347–375). Washington, DC: American Psychiatric Association.

Kimura, D. (1964). Left-right differences in the perception of melodies. *Q. J. Experim. Psychol., 16,* 355–358.

King, R. A. & Cohen, D. J. (1994). The neuropsychiatric disorders: ADHD, OCD and Tourette's syndrome. In J. M. Oldham & M. B. Riba (Eds.), *Annual review* (vol. 13, pp. 519–539). Washington, DC: American Psychiatric Association.

Kinsey, A. C., Pomeroy, W. B., & Martin, C. F. (1948). *Sexual behavior in the human male.* Philadelphia: Saunders.

Kirby, J. S., Chu, J. A., & Dill, D. L. (1993). Correlates of dissociative symptomatology in patients with physical and sexual abuse histories. *Compr. Psychiat., 34,* 258–263.

Kirkpatrick, M. & Ryan, M. J. (1991). The evolution of mating prefences and the paradox of lek. *Nature, 350,* 33–38.

Kleiman, D. (1988). *A deadly silence: The ordeal of Cheryl Pierson, a case of incest and murder.* New York: Atlantic Monthly Press.

Klein, D. F. (1974). Endognomorphic depression: A conceptual and terminological revision. *Arch. Gen. Psychiat., 31,* 337–454.

Klein, D. F., Gittleman, R., Quitkin, F. & Rifkin, A. (1980). *Diagnosis & drug treatment of psychiatric disorders: Adults & children.* Baltimore: William & Wilkins.

Klein, M. (1952/1975). Some theoretical conclusions regarding the emotional life of the infant. In M. Klein (Ed.), *Envy and gratitude and other works 1964–1963*(pp. 61–91). New York: Delta.

Klein, M. (1975). *Collected papers: Guilt and reparation and other works, 1921–1945* (vol. 1). *Envy and gratitude and other works, 1946–1963* (vol. 2). New York: Delta.

Kleinman, C. C. (1990). Forensic issues arising from the use of anabolic steroids. *Psychiat. Annals, 20,* 219–221.

Kline, N. (1959). Uses of reserpine, the newer phenothiazines, and iproniazid. *Res. Publ. Assoc. for Res. in Nerv. & Ment. Dis., 37,* 218–244.

Kluft, R. P. (1985). Childhood multiple personality: Predictors, clinical findings, & treatment results. In R. P. Kluft (Ed.), *Childhood antecedants of multiple personality disorder* (pp. 167–196). Washington, DC: American Psychiatric Association.

Klüver, H. & Bucy, P.C. (1937). "Psychic blindness" and other symptoms following bilateral temporal lobectomy in rhesus monkeys. *Am. J. Physiol., 119*, 352–353.

Klüver, H. & Bucy, P. C. (1938). An analysis of certain effects of bilateral temporal lobectomy in the rhesus monkey. *J. Physiol., 5*, 33–54.

Klüver, H. & Bucy, P. C. (1939). Preliminary analysis of function of the temporal lobes in monkeys. *Arch. Neurol. Psychiat., 42*, 979–1000.

Knight, R. P. (1953). Borderline states in psychoanalytic psychiatry and psychology. *Bull. Menn. Clin., 17*, 1–12.

Kobayashi, J. S. (1989). Depathologizing dependency: The perspectives. *Psychiatric Annals, 19*, 653–658.

Kohlberg, L. (1976). Moral stages and moralization: The cognitive-developmental approach. In Lickona (Ed.), *Moral development & behavior*. New York: Holt, Rinehart, & Winston.

Kohlberg, L. (1971). Moral stages and moralization: The cognitive developmental appraoch. In T. Lakona (Ed.), *Moral development and epistemology*. New York: Academic Press.

Kohlberg, L., Levine, C., & Hewer, A. (1983). *Moral stages: A current formulation and a response to critics*. Basel: Karger.

Kohon, G. (1986). *The British school of psychoanalysis: The Independent tradition*. New Haven, CT: Yale Univ. Press.

Kohut, H. (1959). Introspection, empathy, and psychoanalysis. *J. Am. Psychoan. Assoc., 7*, 459–483.

Kohut, H. (1966). Forms and transformations of narcissism. *J. Am. Psychoan. Assoc., 14*, 243–272.

Kohut, H. (1971). *The analysis of the self.* New York: International Univ. Press.

Kohut, H. (1977). *The restoration of the self.* New York: International Univ. Press.

Kolb, L. (1963). *Modern clinical psychiatry.* Philadelphia: Saunders.

Kolodny, R. C., Masters, W. H., & Johnson, V. E. (1979). *Textbook of sexual medicine.* Boston: Little, Brown.

Kolvin, I. (1971). Studies in childhood psychoses, 1: Diagnostic criteria and classification. *Brit. J. Psychiat., 118*, 381–384.

Kornhuber, H. H. & Deecke, L. (1965). Hirnpotential-änderungen bei Wilkurbewegungen und passiven Bewegungen des Menschen: Bereit-schaftspotential und reafferente Potentials. *Pfleugers Archiv., 284*, 1–17.

Kotrla, K. J., Chacko, R. C., Haper, R. G., Jhingran, S., & Doody, R. (1995). SPECT findings on psychosis in Alzheimer's Disease. *Amer J. Psychiat., 152*, 1470–1475.

Kovacs, M. & Beck, A. (1977). An empirical clinical approach toward a definition of childhood depression. In J. G. Schulterbrandt & A. Raskin (Eds.), *Depression in childhood: Diagnosis, treatment, and conceptual models* (pp. 1–25). New York: Raven.

Kraepelin, E. (1909–1915). *Psychiatrie, 8th ed.* (vols. 1–4). Leipzig: Barth.

Kraepelin, E. (1921). *Manic-depressive insanity and paranoia.* Edinburgh: Livingstone.

Kringlen, E. (1968). An epidemiological/clinical study on schizophrenia. In D. Rosenthal, S. Kety, & P. Wender (Eds.), *Transmission of schizophrenia* (pp. 49–63). Oxford: Pergamon.

Kringlen, E. & Cramer, G. (1989). Offspring of monozygotic twins disordant for schizophrenia. *Arch. Gen. Psychiat., 46*, 873–877.

Kroll, J. (1988). *The challenge of the borderline patient.* New York: Norton.

Kroll, J., Carey, K. S., & Sines, L. K. (1985). Twenty year follow-up of borderline personality disorder. In C. Shagass (Ed.), *World congress of biological psychiatry* (vol. 7, pp. 577–579). New York: Elsevier.

Kruesi, M. J. (1989). Cruelty to animals and CSF 5–HIAA. *Psychiatric Research, 28*, 115–116.

Kuhn, R. (1958). The treatment of depressive states with G22355 (imipramine hydrochloride). *Am. J. Psychiat., 115*, 459–464.

Kumar, A. M., Sevush, S., Kumar, M., Ruiz, J., & Eisdorfer, C. (1995). Peripheral serotonin in Alzheimer's Disease. *Neuropsychobiol., 32*, 9–12.

Kupfer, D. J., Frank, E., Grochocinski, V. J., Gregor, M., & McEachran, A. B. (1988). Electroencephalographic sleep profiles in recurrent depression. *Arch. Gen. Psychiat., 45*, 678–681.

Kupfer, D. J., Frank, E., & Perel, J. M. (1989). The advantage of early treatment intervention in recurrent depression. *Arch. Gen. Psychiat., 46*, 771–775.

Kupferman, I. (1985). Learning. In E. Kandel & J. Schwartz (Eds.), *Principles of neural science, 2nd ed.* (pp. 805–815). New York: Elsevier.

Kutas, M. & Hillyard, S. A. (1990). Event-related potentials and psychopathology. In R. Michels (Ed.), *Psychiatry* (vol. 3, ch. 62). Philadelphia: Lippincott.

Kutscher, S. P., Blackwood, D. H. R., St. Clair, D., Gaskell, D. F., & Muir, W. J. (1987). Auditory P300 in borderline personality disorder and schizophrenia. *Arch. Gen. Psychiat., 44*, 645–650.

Laborit, H., Huguenard, P., & Alluaume, R. (1952). Un nouveau stabilisateur végétatif. *La Presse Méd., 60*, 206–208.

Lacan, J. (1973). *Les quatre concepts fondamentaux de la psychanalyse.* Paris: Editions du Seuil.

Lambert, P. A. (1966). Action neuropsychotropique d'un nouvel anti-épileptique: Le Depamide. *Ann. Méd. Psychol., 1*, 707–710.

Lanczik, M. & Keil, G. (1991). Carl Wernicke's localization theory and its significance for the development of scientific psychiatry. *History of Psychiatry, 2*, 171–180.

Lane, B. & Gregg, W. (1992). *The encyclopedia of serial killers.* New York: Diamond.

Lang, J. (1995, April 29). *Self-psychology with suicidal patients.* Paper presented at the Cutting Edge Conference, San Diego, CA.

Langfeldt, G. (1937). The prognosis in schizophrenia and the factors influencing the course of the disease. *Acta Psychiat. Scand., 13.*

Lasch, C. (1978). *The culture of narcissism.* New York: Norton.

Leckman, J. F., Goodman, W. K., North, W. G., Chappell, P. B., Price, L. H., Pauls, D. L., Anderson, G. M., Riddle, M. A., McSwiggin-Hardin, M., McDougle, C. J., Barr, L. C., & Cohen, D. J. (1994). Elevated cerebrospinal fluid levels of oxytocin in obsessive-compulsive disorder. *Arch. Gen. Psychiat., 51*, 782–792.

LeGoff, J. (1988). *Medieval civilization 400–1500.* Oxford: Basil Blackwell.

Leonhard, K. (1963). Die Temperamente in den Familien der monopolaren euphorischen Psychosen. *Psychiat. Neurol. und Med. Psychol., 15*, 203–206.

Leonhard, K., Korff, I., & Schulz, H. (1962). Die Temperamente in den Familien der monopolaren und bipolaren phasischen Psychosen. *Psychiat. Neurol., 143*, 416–434.

Lester, D. (1990). The availability of firearms and the use of firearms for suicide: A study of 20 countries. *Acta Scand. Psychiat., 81*, 146–147.

Leuner, H. (1962). *Die experimentelle Psychose.* Berlin: Springer Verlag.

Leung, P. W. L. (1995). Psychotherapy with the Chinese. In M. H. Bond (Ed.), *Handbook of Chinese psychology.* New York: Oxford Univ. Press.

LeVay, S. (1991). A difference in hypothalamic structure between heterosexual and homosexual men. *Science, 253*, 1034–1037.

Levin, H. S., Eisenberg, H. M., & Benton, A. L. (Eds.) (1991). *Frontal lobe function and dysfunction.* New York: Oxford.

Lévi-Strauss, C. (1974). *Anthropologie structurale.* Paris: Plon.

Levy, D. M. (1941). Maternal overprotection. *Psychiatry, 4*, 393–438.

Lewis, O. & Chatoor, I. (1994). Eating disorders. In J. M. Oldham & M. B. Riba (Eds.), *Review of psychiatry* (vol. 13, pp. 541–570). Washington, DC: American Psychiatric Association.

Liberman, R. P. (1994). Biobehavioral treatment & rehabilitation of the seriously mentally ill. In *UCLA School of Medicine Manual.* Los Angeles: UCLA Press.

Lidberg, L. (1992, September 9). *Platelet monamine oxidase activity in mentally disordered violent offenders.* Paper presented at the First European Symposium on Aggression in Clinical Psychiatric Practice, Stockholm, Sweden.

Lidz, T., Fleck, S., & Cornelison, A. R. (1965). *Schizophrenia and the family.* New York: International Univ. Press.

Lieber, A. L. (1978). Human aggression and the lunar synodic cycle. *J. Clin. Psychiat., 39*, 385–393.

Lieber, A. L. & Sherin, C. R. (1972). Homicide and the lunar cycle: Toward a theory of lunar influence on human emotional disturbance. *Am. J. Psychiat., 129*, 69–74.

Linehan, M. M. (1981). A social-behavioral assessment of suicide and parasuicide. In J. F. Clarkin, & H. I. Glazer (Eds.), *Depression* (pp. 229–294). New York: Garland.

Linehan, M. M. (1993). *Cognitive-behavioral therapy of borderline personality disorder.* New York: Guilford.

Linehan, M. M., Armstrong, H. E., Suarez, A., Allmon, D., & Heard, H. L. (1991). Cognitive-behavioral treatment of chronically parasuicidal borderline patients. *Arch. Gen. Psychiat., 48*, 1060–1064.

Linkowski, P., van Cauter, E., L'Hermite-Baleriaux, M., Kerkhofs, M., Hubain, P., L'Hermite, M., & Mendlewicz, J. (1989). The 24–hour profile of plasma prolactin in men with major endogenous depressive illness. *Arch. Gen. Psychiat., 46*, 813–819.

Linnoila, M. (1995, May 12). *Serotonin, impulsivity, & alcoholism.* Paper presented at the New York State Psychiatric Institute, Grand Rounds, NY.

Linnoila, M., Virkkunen, M., Scheinen, M., Nuutila, A., Rimon, R., & Goodwin, F. K. (1983). Low cerebrospinal fluid 5–HIAA concentration differentiates impulsive from nonimpulsive violent behavior. *Life Sciences, 33*, 2609–2614.

Linzen, D. H., Dingemans, P. M., & Lenior, M. E. (1994). Cannabis abuse and the course of recent-onset schizophrenic disorders. *Arch. Gen. Psychiat., 51*, 273–279.

Lish, J. D., Meyer-Bahlburg, H. F. L., Ehrhardt, A. A., Travis, B. G., & Veridiano, N. P. (1992). Prenatal exposure to diethylstilbestrol: Childhood play and adult gender-role behavior in women. *Arch. Sex. Behav., 21*, 423–441.

Livesley, W. J. & Schroeder, M. L. (1990). Dimensions of personality disorder: The *DSM-III-R* Cluster A diagnoses. *J. Nerv. & Ment. Dis., 178*, 627–635.

Loeber, R. & Stouthamer-Loeber, M. (1987). Prediction. In H. C. Quay (Ed.), *Handbook of juvenile delinquency* (pp. 325–382). New York: Wiley.

Loewenstein, R. (Ed.) (1991). Multiple personality disorder. *Psychiat. Clin. N. Am., 14*(3).

Loewenstein, R., Hamilton, J., Alagna, S., Reid, N. & deVries, M. (1987). Experiential sampling in the study of multiple personality disorder. *Am. J. Psychiat., 144*, 19–24.

Loewenstein, R. M. (1957). A contribution to the psychoanalytic theory of masochism. *J. Am. Psychoan. Assoc., 5*, 197–234.

Loftus, E. & Ketchum, K. (1991). *Witness for the defense.* New York: St. Martin's Press.

Lonie, I. (1993). Borderline disorder and posttraumatic stress disorder: An equivalence? *Austral. & New Zeal. J. Psychiat., 27*, 233–245.

Loranger, A. W., Oldham, J. M., Susman, V. L., & Russakoff, L. M. (1987). The Personality Disorder Exam: A preliminary report. *J. Personal. Dis., 1*, 1–13.

Loranger, A. W., Sartorius, N., Andreoli, A., Berger, P., Buchheim, P., Channabasavanna, S. M., Coid, B., Dahl, A., Diekstra, R. F. W., Ferguson, B., Jacobsberg, L. B., Mombour, W., Pull, C., Ono, Y., & Regier, D. A. (1994). International Personality Disorder Examination. *Arch. Gen. Psychiat., 51*, 215–224.

Lorenz, K. (1965). *Evolution and modification of behavior.* Chicago: Univ. of Chicago Press.

Lothane, Z. (1983). Cultist phenomena in psychoanalysis. In D.A. Halperin (Ed.), *Psychodynamic perspectives on religion, sect, & cult* (pp. 199–221). Boston: J. Wright.

Luborsky, L. (1962). Clinicians' judgments of mental health. *Arch. Gen. Psychiat., 7*, 404–417.

Lucas, P. B., Gardner, D. L., Cowdry, R. W., & Pickar, D. (1989). Cerebral structure in borderline personality disorder. *Psychiat. Research, 27*, 111–115.

Lucas, R. A. (1990). Hypnosis. In R. Michels (Ed.), *Psychiatry* (vol. 2, ch. 112). Philadelphia: Lippincott.

Luxenburger, H. (1928). Vorlaeufiger Bericht ueber psychiatrische Serienuntersuchungen an Zwillingen. *Z. Ges. Neurol. Psychiat., 116*, 297–326.

Lykken, D. (1995). *The antisocial personalities.* Hillsdale, NJ: Erlbaum.

MacKinnon, I. L., MacKinnon, P. C. B., & Thomas, A. D. (1956). Lethal hazards of the luteal phase of the menstrual cycle. *Brit. Med. J., 1*, 1015–1017.

MacLean, P. D. (1952). Some psychiatric implications of physiological studies on frontotemporal portion of limbic system (visceral brain). *Electroenceph. Clin. Neurophysiol., 4*, 407–418.

MacLean, P. D. (1970). The triune brain, emotion, & scientific bias. In F. O. Schmitt (Ed.), *The neurosciences: Second study program* (pp. 336–349). New York: Rockefeller Univ. Press.

Maeder, A. (1910). Psychologische Untersuchungen an Dementia-praecox-kranken. *Jahrbuch fuer Psychoanal., 2*, 234–245.

Maher, B. (1991). Deception, rational man, and other rocks on the road to a personality psychology of real people. In W. M. Moore & D. Cicchetti (Eds.), *Thinking clearly about psychology: Personality & psychopathology* (vol. 2, pp. 72–88). Minneapolis: Univ. of Minn. Press.

Mahler, M. S. (1952). On child psychosis and schizophrenia (autistic and symbiotic infantile psychosis). *Psychoan. Study of the Child, 7*.

Mahler, M. S. (1968). *On human symbiosis and the vicissitudes of individuation.* New York: International Univ. Press.

Maier, G. J. (1990). Psychopathic disorders: Beyond counter-transference. *Current Opin. in Psychiat., 3*, 766–769.

Main, T. (1957). The ailment. *Brit. J. Med. Psychol., 30*, 129–145.

Mainzer, K. (1994). *Thinking in complexity: The complex dynamics of matter, mind, & mankind.* New York: Springer.

Malmquist, C. (1971). Depression in childhood & adolescence. *New Engl. J. Med., 284*, 887–893.

Mandell, A. J. (1980). Toward a psychobiology of transcendence: God in the brain. In J. M. Davidson & R. J. Davidson (Eds.), *Psychobiol-*

ogy of consciousness (pp.379–464). New York: Plenum.

Mann, J. (1973). *Time-limited psychotherapy.* Cambridge, MA: Harvard Univ. Press.

Mannuzza, S., Gittelman-Klein, R., Konig, P. H., & Giampino, T. L. (1989). Hyperactive boys almost grown up. *Arch. Gen. Psychiat., 46,* 1073–1079.

Marazziti, D., Rotondo, A., Palego, L., & Conti, L. (1992, September 10). *The role of serotonin in aggression abnormalities.* Paper presented at the First European Symposium on Aggression in Clinical Psychiatric Practice, Stockholm, Sweden.

Marks, I. (1969). *Fears and phobias.* New York: Academic.

Marks, I. M. (1986). Genetics of fear and anxiety disorders. *Brit. J. Psychiat., 149,* 406–418.

Marmer, S. S. (1991). Multiple personality disorder: A psychoanalytic perspective. *Psychiat. Clin. N. Am., 14,* 677–693.

Marmor, J. (Ed.) (1965). *Sexual inversion.* New York: Basic.

Marohn, R. C., Offer, D., & Ostrov, E. (1979). Four psychodynamic types of hospitalized juvenile delinquents. *Adolesc. Psychiat., 7,* 466–483.

Martin, R. L., Gerteis, G., & Gabrielli, W. F., Jr. (1988). A family-genetic study of dementia of Alzheimer type. *Arch. Gen. Psychiat., 45,* 894–900.

Marx, O. M. (1990). German Romantic psychiatry, part I. *History of Psychiatry 1,* 351–381.

Marx, O. M. (1991). German Romantic psychiatry, part II. *History of Psychiatry, 2,* 1–25.

Masters, B. (1985). *Killing for company: The case of Dennis Nilsen.* New York: Stein & Day.

Masters, W. H. & Johnson, V. E. (1966). *Human sexual experience.* Boston: Little, Brown.

Masterson, J. (1981). *The narcissistic and borderline disorders.* New York: Brunner/Mazel.

Matthysse, S. W. & Kidd, K. (1976). Estimating the genetic contribution to schizophrenia. *Am. J. Psychiat., 133,* 185–191.

May, P. R. A. (1968). *Treatment of schizophrenia.* New York: Science House.

Maynard-Smith, J. (1974). The theory of games & the evolution of animal conflict. *J. Theoret. Biol., 47,* 209–221.

Maynard-Smith, J. (1975). *The theory of evolution.* London: Penguin.

Maynard-Smith, J. & Price, J. R. (1973). The logic of animal conflicts. *Nature, 246,* 15–18.

Maziade, M., Caron, C., Coté, R., Boutin, P., & Thivierge, J. (1990). Extreme temperament and diagnosis. *Arch. Gen. Psychiat., 47,* 477–484.

Maziade, M., Roy, M. A., Martinez, M., Cliche, D., Fournier, J. P., Garneau, Y., Nicole, L., Montgrain, N., Dion, C., Ponton, A. M., Potvin, A., Lavallee, J. C., Pires, A., Bouchard, S., Boutin, P., Brisebois, F., & Mérette, C. (1995). Negative, psychoticism, and disorganized dimensions in patients with familial schizophrenia or bipolar disorder: Continuity and discontinuity between the major psychoses. *Am. J. Psychiat., 152,* 1458–1463.

McCabe, M. S., Fowler, R. W., Cadoret, R. J., & Winokur, G. (1971). Familial differences in schizophrenics with good and poor prognoses. *Psychosom. Med., 33,* 326–332.

McEwen, B. S. (1983). Gonadal steroid influences on brain development and sexual differentiation. In R. Greep (Ed.), *International Review of Physiology, 27,* 99–145. Baltimore: Univ. Park.

McFarlane, W. R. (Ed.) (1983). *Family therapy in schizophrenia.* New York: Guilford.

McGaugh, J. L., Introini-Collison, I. B., Nagahara, A. H., & Cahill, L. (1989). Involvement of the amygdala in hormonal and neurotransmitter interactions in the modulation of memory. In T. Archer & L. G. Nilsson (Eds.), *Aversion, avoidance, & anxiety* (pp. 231–249). Hillsdale, NJ: Erlbaum.

McGlashan, T. H. (1986a). Chestnut Lodge follow-up study 3: Long-term outcome of borderline patients. *Arch. Gen. Psychiat., 43,* 20–30.

McGlashan, T. H. (1986b). Chestnut Lodge follow-up study 4: The prediction of outcome in chronic schizophrenia. *Arch. Gen. Psychiat., 43,* 167–176.

McNeil, T. F. & Kaij, L. (1984). Offspring of women with non-organic psychoses. In N. F. Watt, E. J. Anthony, L. C. Wynne, & J. E. Rolf (Eds.), *Children at risk for schizophrenia: A longitudinal perspective* (pp. 465–514). Cambridge: Cambridge Univ. Press.

Mednick, S. A. (1960). The early and advanced schizophrenic. In S. A. Mednick & J. Higgins (Eds.), *Current research in schizophrenia.* Ann Arbor, MI: Edwards.

Mednick, S. A., Cudeck, R., Griffith, J. J., Talovic, S. A., & Schulsinger, F. (1984). The Danish high risk project: Recent methods and findings. In N. F. Watts, E. J. Anthony, L. C. Wynne, & J. E. Rolf (Eds.), *Children at high risk for schizophrenia* (pp. 21–78). Cambridge: Cambridge Univ. Press.

Meehl, P. E. (1962). Schizotaxia, schizotypy and schizophrenia. *Am. Psychol., 17,* 827–838.

Meloy, J. R. (in press). A clinical investigation of the obsessional follower. In L. Schlesinger (Ed.),

Explorations in criminal psychopathology. Springfield, IL: Thomas.

Meloy, J. R., Gacono, C. B., & Kenney, L. (1994). A Rorschach investigation of sexual homicide. *J. Personality Assess., 62*, 58–67.

Meltzer, H. Y., Sachar, E. J., & Frantz, A. G. (1974). Serum prolactin levels in unmedicated schizophrenic patients. *Arch. Gen. Psychiat., 31*, 564–569.

Mendelson, W., Johnson, N., & Stewart, M. A. (1971). Hyperactive children as teenagers: A follow-up study. *J. Nerv. & Ment. Dis., 153*, 273–279.

Merikangas, J. R. (1981). The neurology of violence. In J. R. Merikangas (Ed.), *Brain-behavior relationships* (pp. 155–185). Lexington, MA: Lexington.

Merikangas, K. J. & Weissman, M. M. (1986). Epidemiology of *DSM-III* axis-II personality disorders. *Annual Rev. of Psychiatry, V* (pp. 258–278). Washington, DC: American Psychiatric Press.

Mettler, C. C. & Mettler, F. A. (1947). *History of medicine*. Philadelphia: Blackiston.

Meyer, J. K. (1987). A case of hysteria with a note on biology. *J. Am. Psychoan. Assoc., 35*, 319–346.

Mezzich, J. (1988, August 18). *Personality conditions and the International Classification of Diseases (ICD)*. Paper presented at the First International Congress on Disorders of Personality, Copenhagen.

Michels, R. (1994). Psychoanalysis enters the 21st century. *Ann. Rev. of Psychoanalysis, 22*, 37–45.

Miller, K. B. & Nelson, J. C. (1987). Does dexamethasone suppression test relate to subtypes, factors, symptoms, or severity? *Arch. Gen. Psychiat., 44*, 769–774.

Millon, T. (1977). *Millon Multiaxial Inventory manual*. Minneapolis, MN: National Computer Systems.

Minsky, M. (1985). *The society of mind*. New York: Simon & Schuster.

Mirsky, I. A. (1958). Physiologic, psychological and social determinants in the etiology of duodenal ulcer. *Am. J. Digestive Dis., 3*, 285–314.

Mishkin, M., Malamut, B., & Bachvalier, J. (1984). Memories and habits: The neural system. In G. Lynch, J. McGaugh, & N. M. Weinberger (Eds.), *Neurobiology of learning & memory* (pp. 65–77). New York: Guilford.

Mitscherlich, A. (1982). *Die Idee des Friedens und die menschliche Aggresivität*. Baden-Baden: Nomos/Suhrkamp.

Mitsuda, H. (1967). *Clinical genetics in psychiatry*. Tokyo: Igaku-Shoin.

Mitsuda, H. (1979). Clinical-genetic view of the biology of the schizophrenias. In T. Fukuda & H. Mitsuda (Eds.), *World issues in the problem of schizophrenic psychoses* (pp.121–124). Tokyo: Igaku-Shoin.

Money, J. (1990). Paraphilic serial rape (biastophilia) and lust murder (erotophonophilia). *Am. J. Psychother., 44*, 26–36.

Money, J. & Ehrhardt, A. A. (1972). *Man & woman, boy & girl*. Baltimore: Johns Hopkins Univ. Press.

Moniz, E. (1936). *Tentatives opératoires dans le traitement de certaines psychoses*. Paris: Masson.

Moore, K. & Reed, D. (1988). *Deadly medicine*. New York: St. Martin's Press.

Moran, C. & Andrews, G. (1985). The familial occurrence of agoraphobia. *Brit. J. Psychiat., 146*, 262–267.

Morris, J. N. (1975). *Uses of epidemiology*. Edinburgh: Churchill Livingstone.

Morrison, J. J. R. & Minkoff, K. (1975). Explosive personality as a sequel to the hyperactive-child syndrome. *Compr. Psychiat., 16*, 343–348.

Mukerjee, M. (1995). Hidden scars: Sexual and other abuse may alter a brain region. *Scientific Am., 273*, 14–20.

Mundt, C. & Sass, H. (Eds.) (1992). *Für und wieder die Einheitspsychose*. Stuttgart: Georg Thieme.

Myerson, A. (1939). Theory and principles of the "Total Push" method of treatment of chronic psychophrenia. *Amer. J. Psychiat., 95*, 1197–1204.

Myslobodsky, M. S. (Ed.) (1983). *Hemisyndromes*. New York: Academic.

Nacht, S. (1963). The non-verbal relationship in psycho-analytic treatment. *Internat. J. Psychoan., 44*, 328–333.

Nacht, S. (1965). *Le masochisme*. Paris: Payot & Rivages.

Nellist, C. C. (1994). Study suggests multiple forms of obsessive-compulsive disorder. *Clin. Psychiat. News, 22*(9), 1, 22.

Nelson, R. J., Demas, G. E., Huang, P. L., Fishman, M. C., Dawson, V. L., Dawson, T. M., & Snyder, S. H. (1995). Behavioral abnormalities in male mice lacking neuronal nitric oxide synthase. *Nature, 378*, 383–386.

Nofziger, E. A. & Wettstein, R. M. (1995). Homicidal behavior and sleep apnea: A case report and medicolegal discussion. *Sleep, 18*, 776–782.

Nordström, A. L., Farde, L., Nyberg, S., Karlsson, P., Halldin, C., & Sedvall, G. (1995). D-1, D-2, and 5–HT-2 receptor occupancy in relation to clozapine serum concentration: A PET study of schizophrenic patients. *Am. J. Psychiat., 152*, 1444–1449.

Noshpitz, J. D. (1995). *History of childhood and child psychiatry*. Unpublished manuscript.

Noshpitz, J. D. & Coddington, R. D. (Eds.) (1990). *Stressors and the adjustment disorders*. New York: Wiley Interscience.

Nowack, M. A., May, R. M., & Sigmund, K. (1995) The arithmetic of mutual help. *Scientific American, 272*, 76–81.

Noyes, R., Jr., Reich, J., Christiansen, J., Suelzer, M., Pfohl, B., & Coryell, W. A. (1990). Outcome of panic disorder. *Arch. Gen. Psychiat., 47*, 809–818.

Nussbaum, M. (1994). *The therapy of desire: Theory and practice in Hellenistic ethics*. Princeton, NJ: Princeton Univ. Press.

Oberndorf, C. P. (1930). The psychoanalysis of borderline cases. *NY State J. Med., 30*, 648–651.

O'Brien, D. (1985). *Two of a kind: The Hillside stranglers*. New York: New American Library.

Ødegaard, O. (1963). The psychiatric disease entities in the light of genetic investigation. *Acta Psychiat. Scand., 169*, 94–104.

O'Dell, T. J., Huang, P. L., Dawson, T. M., Dinerman, J. L., Synder, S. H., Kandel, E. R., & Fishman, M. C. (1994). Endothelial NOS and the blockade of long-term potentiation (LTP) by nitric oxide synthase (NOS) inhibitors in mice lacking neuronal NOS. *Science, 265*, 542–546.

Ogata, S. N., Silk, K. R., Goodrich, S., Lohr, N., E. Westen, D., & Hill, E. M. (1988). Childhood sexual and physical abuse in adult patients with borderline personality disorder. *Am. J. Psychiat., 147*, 1008–1013.

Okuma, T., Kishimoto, A., Inoue, K., Matsumoto, H., Ogura, A., Matsushita, T., Naklao, T., & Ogura, C. (1973). Antimanic and prophylactic effects of carbamazepine on manic depressive psychosis. *Folia Psychiat. Neurol. Japonica, 27*, 283–297.

Oldham, J. M., Skodol, A. E., Hyler, S. E., Rosnick, L., & Davies, M. (1992). Diagnosis of *DSM-III-R* personality disorders by two structured interviews: Patterns of comorbidity. *Am. J. Psychiat., 149*, 213–220.

Olinick, S. (1964). The negative therapeutic reaction. *Internat. J. Psychoan., 45*, 540–548.

Olsen, G. (1995). *Mockingbird: A mother, a child, a tragedy*. New York: Time-Warner.

Ono, Y. & Okonogi, K. (1988). Borderline personality disorder in Japan: A comparative study of three diagnostic criteria. *J. Pers. Dis., 2*, 212–220.

Orton, S. T. (1928). Specific reading disability: Strephosymbolia. *J. Am. Med. Assoc., 90*, 1095.

Orton, S. T. (1937). *Reading, writing, and speech problems in children*. London: Chapman and Hall.

Ovesey, L. (1955). The pseudohomosexual anxiety. *Psychiatry, 18*, 17–25.

Ovesey, L. (1966). The phobic patient. In G. D. Goldman & D. Shapiro (Eds.), *Developments in psychoanalysis at Columbia University*. New York: Hafner.

Ovesey, L. (1969). *Homosexuality & pseudo-homosexuality*. New York: Science House.

Padesky, C. (1995, April 28). *Brief cognitive therapy*. Paper presented at the Cutting Edge Symposium on the Difficult Patient, San Diego, CA.

Pagels, E. (1988). *Adam, Eve, and the serpent*. New York: Random House.

Papez, J. (1937). A proposed mechanism of emotion. *Arch. Neurol. & Psychiat., 38*, 725–743.

Pappenheim, E. & Sweeney, M. (1953). Separation anxiety in mother and child. *Psychoan. Study of the Child, 7*, 95–114.

Paris, J., Brown, R., & Nowlis, D. (1987). Long-term follow-up of borderline patients in a general hospital. *Compr. Psychiat., 28*, 530–535.

Parker, G., Johnston, P., & Hayward, L. (1988). Parental "expressed emotion" as a predictor of schizophrenic relapse. *Arch. Gen. Psychiat., 45*, 806–813.

Parry, B. L., Berga, S. L., Kripke, D. F., Klauber, M. R., Laughlin, G. A, Yen, S. S. C., & Gillin, J. C. (1990). Altered waveform of plasma nocturnal melatonin secretion in premenstrual depression. *Arch. Gen. Psychiat., 47*, 1139–1146.

Pauls, D. L., Raymond, C. L., & Leckman, J. F. (1991). A family study of Tourette's syndrome. *Am. J. Human Genetics, 48*, 154–163.

Pearl, D., Vanderkamp, H., Olsen, A. L., Greenberg, P. D., & Armitage, S. G. (1956). The effects of reserpine in schizophrenic patients. *Am. J. Psychiat., 112*, 936.

Peele, S. (1990). Does addiction excuse thieves and killers from criminal responsibility? *Internat. J. Law & Psychiat., 13*, 95–101.

Penrose, R. (1994). *Shadows of the mind: A search for the missing science of consciousness*. New York: Oxford Univ. Press.

Perrett, D. I., May, K. A., & Yoshikawa, S. (1994). Facial shape and judgment of female attractiveness. *Nature, 368*, 239–242.

Perris, C. (1973). The genetics of affective disorder. In J. Mendels (Ed.), *Biologic psychiatry*. New York: Wiley.

Petty, L. K., Ornitz, E. M., Michelman, J. D., & Zimmerman, E. G. (1984). Autistic children who become schizophrenic. *Arch. Gen. Psychiat., 41*, 129–135.

Pfeffer, C. R. (1986). *The suicidal child*. New York: Guilford.

Phoenix, C. H., Goy, R. W., Gerall, A. A., & Young, W. C. (1959). Organizing action of prenatally administered testosterone proprionate on the tissues mediating mating behavior in the female guinea pig. *Endocrinology, 65*, 369–382.

Piaget, J. (1932). *The moral judgement of the child*. New York: Free Press.

Piaget, J. (1941). *Introduction à l'epistemologie génétique* (vols. 1–3). Paris: Maradan.

Piaget, J. (1972). *The moral judgment of the child*. New York: Free.

Pichot, P. (1990). History of the treatment of anxiety. In R. Noyes, Jr., M. Roth, & G. D. Burrows (Eds.), *Handbook of anxiety* (vol. 4, pp. 4–25). New York: Elsevier.

Pichot, P. (1995). The birth of the bipolar disorder. *Euro. Psychiat., 10*, 1–10.

Pies, R. (1996, March). The neurobiology of schizophrenia. *Psychiatric Times*.

Pilkonis, P. A., Imber, S. D., Lewis, P., & Rubinsky, P. (1984). A comparative outcome study of individual, group & conjoint psychotherapy. *Arch. Gen. Psychiat., 41*, 431–437.

Piper, A., Jr. (1994). Multiple personality disorder. *Brit. J. Psychiat., 164*, 600–612.

Pitman, R. K. (1993). Posttraumatic obsessive-compulsive disorder: A case study. *Compr. Psychiat., 34*, 102–107.

Pitts, F. N. & McClure, J. N. (1967). Lactate metabolism in anxiety neurosis. *New Eng. J. Med., 277*, 1329–1336.

Plakun, E. M., Burkhardt, P. E., & Muller, J. P. (1985). Fourteen year follow-up of borderline and schizotypal personality disorders. *Compr. Psychiat., 26*, 448–455.

Plomin, R. & Daniels, D. (1987). Why are children in the same family so different from one another? *Behav. & Brain Sci., 10*, 1–60.

Plutshik, R., van Praag, H., & Conte, H. (1985). Suicide and violence risk in psychiatric patients. *Biol. Psychiat., 20*, 762–763.

Post, R. M. (1980). Biochemical theories of mania. In R. H. Belmaker & H. van Praag (Eds.), *Mania: An evolving concept* (pp. 217–265). New York: Spectrum.

Post, R. M., Lake, C. R., Jimerson, D.C., Bunney, W. E., Jr., Wood, J. H., Ziegler, M. G., & Goodwin, F. K. (1978). Norepinephrine in affective illness. *Am. J. Psychiat., 135*, 907–912.

Noshpitz, J. D. (1995). *History of childhood and child psychiatry*. Unpublished manuscript.

Poznanski, E., Cook, S. C., & Carroll, B. J. (1979). A depression rating scale for children. *Pediatrics, 64*, 442–450.

Poznanski, E. & Zrull, J. P. (1970). Childhood depression: Clinical characteristics of overtly depressed children. *Arch. Gen. Psychiat., 23*, 8–15.

Prendergast, A. (1986). *The poison tree*. New York: Putnam.

Price, J. S. (1972). Genetic and phylogenetic aspects of mood variation. *Internat. J. Ment. Health, 1*, 124–144.

Prins, H. (1994). Psychiatry and the concept of evil. *Brit. J. Psychiat., 165*, 297–302.

Putnam, F. W. (1989). Diagnosis & treatment of multiple personality disorder. New York: Guilford.

Putnam, F. W. & Trickett, P. K. (1993). Child sexual abuse: A model of chronic trauma. *Psychiatry, 56*, 82–95.

Racamier, P. C. (1973). *Le psychanalyste sans divan*. Paris: Payot.

Raine, A. (1993). *The psychopathology of crime*. New York: Academic.

Raine, A., Lencz, T., & Scerbo, A. (1995). Antisocial behavior: Neuroimaging, neuropsychology, neurochemistry, and psychophysiology. In J. J. Ratey (Ed.), *Neuropsychiatry of personality disorders* (pp. 50–78). Cambridge, MA: Blackwell Science.

Raine, A. & Venables, P. H. (1988). Enhanced P-3 evoked potentials and longer P-3 recovery times in psychopaths. *Psychophysiol., 25*, 30–38.

Raine, A., Venables, P. H., & Williams, M. (1990). Relationships between central and autonomic measures of arousal at age 15 years and criminality at age 24 years. *Arch. Gen. Psychiat., 47*, 1003–1007.

Rank, O. (1924). *Das Trauma der Gerburt und seine Bedeutung für die Psychanalyse*. Leipzig: Internat. Psychoan.

Raphael, B. (1986). *When disaster strikes*. New York: Basic.

Rapoport, J. (1989). The biology of obsessions and compulsions. *Sci. American, 262*, 83–89.

Rauch, S. L., Jenike, M. A., Alpert, N. M., Baer, L. Breiter, H. C. R., Savage, C. R., & Fischman, A. J. (1994). Regional cerebral blood flow measured during symptom provocation in obsessive-compulsive disorder using oxygen-15–labeled carbon dioxide and positron emission tomography. *Arch. Gen. Psychiat., 51,* 62–70.

Rawls, J. (1971). *A theory of justice.* Cambridge, MA: Harvard University Press.

Regier, D. A., Boyd, J. H., Burke, J. D., Rae, D. S., Myers, J. K., Kramer, M., Robins, L. N., Geiorge, L. K., Karno, M., & Locke, B. Z. (1988). One-month prevalence of mental disorders in the United States. *Arch. Gen. Psychiat., 45,* 977–986.

Regier, D. A. & Robins, L. N. (1991). *Psychiatric disorders in America.* New York: Free Press.

Reich, A. (1951). On countertransference. *Internat. J. Psychoanal., 3,* 25–31.

Reinherz, H. Z., Giaconia, R. M., Silverman, A. B., Friedman, A., Pakiz, B., Frost, A. K., & Cohen, E. (1995). Early psychosocial risks for adolescent suicidal ideation and attempts. *J. Am. Acad. Child Adol. Psychiat., 34,* 599–611.

Reiser, M. F. (1984). *Mind, brain, body: Toward a convergence of psychoanalysis & neurobiology.* New York: Basic.

Ressler, R. K., Burgess, A. W., & Douglas, J. E. (1988). *Sexual homicide: Patterns and motives.* New York: Macmillan.

Reveley, M. A., Reveley, A. M., & Baldy, R. (1987). Left cerebral hemisphere hypodensity in discordant schizophrenic twins. *Arch. Gen. Psychiat., 44,* 625–632.

Ribble, M. A. (1945). Anxiety in infants and its disorganizing effects. In N. D. C. Lewis (Ed.), *Modern trends in child psychiatry* (pp. 11–25). New York: International Univ. Press.

Rice, M. E., Harris, G. T., & Quinsey, V. L. (1990). A follow-up of rapists assessed in a maximum-security psychiatric facility. *J. Interpers. Violence, 5,* 435–438.

Ridley, M. (1993). *The red queen: Sex and the evolution of human nature.* New York: Macmillan.

Rifkin, L., Lewis, S., Toone, B., & Murray, R. (1994). Low birth weight and schizophrenia. *Brit. J. Psychiat., 165,* 357–362.

Ritchie, J. (1994). *Stalkers: How harmless devotion turns into sinister obsession.* New York: Harper Collins.

Robson, F. (1989, Oct. 28/29). The Collosus of Boggo Road. *The Australia Magazine.*

Robson, K. S. (1983). *The borderline child: Approaches to etiology, diagnosis, & treatment.* New York: McGraw Hill.

Rocha, A. F., Theoto, M., Oliveira, C. A. C., & Gomide, F. (1992). Approximate reasoning in diagnosis, therapy, and prognosis. In L. A. Zadeh & J. Kacprzyk (Eds.), *Fuzzy logic for the management of uncertainty* (pp. 437–446). New York: Wiley.

Rockland, L. (1989). *Supportive psychotherapy: A psychodynamic approach.* New York: Basic.

Rodnick, E. H., Goldstein, M.J ., Lewis, J. M., & Doane, J. A. (1984). Parental communication style, affect, & role as precursors of offspring schizophrenia-spectrum disorders. In N. F. Watts, E. J. Anthony, L. C. Wynne, & J. E. Rolf (Eds.), *Children at risk for schizophrenia* (pp. 81–92). Cambridge: Cambridge Univ. Press.

Roffwarg, H. P., Muzio, J. N., & Fisher, C. (1962). Dream imagery: Relationship to rapid eye movements of sleep. *Arch. Gen. Psychiat., 7,* 235–258.

Rogers, A. (1996, March 4). The weight of words: Can writing style predict dementia? *Newsweek.*

Rohde-Dachser, C. (1983). *Das Borderline Syndrom, 3rd ed.* Bern: Hans Huber.

Roland, A. (1980). Psychoanalytic perspectives on personality development in India. *Internat. Rev. Psychoan., 7,* 73–87.

Rorschach, H. (1921) *Psychodiagnostik.* Bern und Berlin: Hans Huber.

Rose, S. (1992). *The making of memory: From molecules to mind.* New York: Doubleday/Anchor.

Rosen, J. N. (1947). The treatment of schizophrenic psychosis by direct analytic therapy. *Psychiat. Q., 21,* 3–37.

Rosen, V. (1955). Strephosymbolia: An intra-systemic disturbance of the synthetic function of the ego. *Psychoan. Study of the Child, 10,* 83–99.

Rosenhan, D. L. (1973). On being sane in insane places. *Science, 179,* 250–258.

Rosenthal, N. E., Sack, D. A., Gillin, J. C., Lewy, A. J., Goodwin, F. K., Davenport, Y., Mueller, P. S., Newsome, D. A., & Wehr, T. A. (1984). Seasonal affective disorder: A description of the syndrome and preliminary findings with light therapy. *Arch. Gen. Psychiat., 41,* 72–80.

Ross, C. (1989). *Multiple personality disorder: Diagnosis, clinical features, & treatment.* New York: Wiley.

Roy, A., DeJong, J., & Linnoila, M. (1989). Extraversion in pathological gamblers. *Arch. Gen. Psychiat., 46,* 679–681.

Roy, A., Segal, N. L., Centerwall, B. S., & Roninette, D. (1991). Suicide in twins. *Arch. Gen. Psychiat., 48,* 29–32.

Rule, A. (1987). *Small sacrifices.* New York: New American Library.

Rumelhart, D. E. & McClelland, J. L. (1986). *Parallel distributed processing: Explorations in the microstructure of cognition*. Cambridge, MA: M.I.T. Press.

Runeson, B. & Blakow, J. (1991). Borderline personality disorder in young Swedish suicides. *J. Nerv. & Ment. Dis., 179*, 153–156.

Rushton, J. P., Fulker, D. W., Neale, M. C., Nias, D. K., & Eysenck, H. J. (1986). Altruism and aggression. *J. Pers.& Soc. Psychol., 50*, 1192–1198.

Russ, M. J., Shearin, E. N., Clarkin, J. F., Harrison, K., & Hull, J. W. (1993). Subtypes of self-injurious patients with borderline personality disorder. *Am. J. Psychiat., 150*, 1869–1871.

Russell, D. (1986). *The secret trauma*. New York: Basic.

Russell, G. F. M. (1979). Bulimia nervosa: An ominous variant of anorexia nervosa. *Psychol. Med., 9*: 429–448.

Rusten, J. (1993) *Theophrastus: Characters*. Cambridge, MA: Harvard University Press.

Rutter, M. (1972). Childhood schizophrenia reconsidered. *J. Autism & Childhood Schiz., 2*, 315–338.

Rutter, M. & Giller, H. (1983). *Juvenile delinquency*. New York: Guilford.

Rutter, M., Schaffer, D., & Shepherd, M. (1975). *A multi-axial classification of child psychiatric disorders*. Geneva: World Health Organization.

Sack, R. L., Lewy, A. J., White, D. M., Singer, C. M., Fireman, M. J., & Vandiver, R. (1990). Morning vs. evening light treatment for winter depression. *Arch. Gen. Psychiat., 47*, 343–351.

Sackheim, H. A., Prohovnik, I., Moeller, J. R., Brown, R. P., Apter, S., Prudic, J., Devanand, D. P., & Mukherjee, S. (1990). Regional cerebral blood flow in mood disorders. *Arch. Gen. Psychiat., 47*, 60–70.

Salkovskis, P. M., Richards, H. C., & Forrester, E. (1995). The relationship between obsessional problems and intrusive thoughts. *Behav. & Cogn. Psychother., 23*, 281–299.

Salvador-Carulla, L. (1995). Images in psychiatry: Santiago Ramón y Cajal. *Am. J. Psychiat., 152*, 914.

Sand, R. (1988). Early nineteenth century anticipation of Freudian theory. *Internat. Rev. Psychoan., 15*, 465–479.

Sandler, J. (1962). The Hampstead Index as an instrument of psychoanalytic research. *Internat. J. Psychoan., 43*, 287–291.

Sandler, J. & Hazari, A. (1960). The "obsessional": On the psychological classification of obsessional character traits and symptoms. *Brit. J. Med. Psychol., 33*, 113–122.

Sargeant, W. (1979). *The Bhagavad Gita*. New York: Doubleday.

Schafer, R. (1976). *A new language for psychoanalysis*. New Haven: Yale Univ. Press.

Schenck, C. H. & Mahowald, M. W. (1995). A polysomnographically documented case of adult somnambulism with long-distance automobile driving and frequent nocturnal violence: Parasomnia with continuing danger as a noninsane automatism? *Sleep, 18*, 765–772.

Schiffer, F., Teicher, M. H., & Papanicolau, A. C. (1995). Evoked potential evidence for right brain activity during the recall of traumatic memories. *J. Neuropsych. & Clin. Neurosci., 7*, 169–175.

Schildkraut, J. J. (1965). The catecholamine hypothesis of affective disorders. *Am. J. Psychiat., 122*, 509–522.

Schildkraut, J. J., Orsulak, P. J., & LaBrie, R. A. (1978). Toward a biochemical classification of depressive disorders. *Arch. Gen. Psychiat., 35*, 1436–1439.

Schmideberg, M. (1947). The treatment of psychopaths and borderline patients. *Am. J. Psychother., 1*, 45–70.

Schmideberg, M. (1958). Treating the unwilling patient. *Brit. J. Delinq., 9*, 117–122.

Schmideberg, M. (1971). A contribution to the history of the psychoanalytic movement in Britain. *Brit. J. Psychiat., 118*, 61–68.

Schmideberg, M. & Orr, D. (1959). Psychiatric treatment of offenders. *Mental Hygiene, 43*, 407–411.

Schneider, K. (1923). *Psychopathische Personnlichkeiten*. Leipzig: F. Deutcke.

Schneider, K. (1923/1950). *Psychopathic personalities*. London: Cassell.

Schoeman, F. (1994). Alcohol addiction and responsibility attribution. In G. Graham & G. L. Stephens (Eds.), *Philosophical psychopathology* (pp. 183–204). Cambridge, MA: M.I.T. Press.

Scholem, G. G. (1946). *Major trends in Jewish mysticism*. New York: Schocken.

Schou, M. (1957). Biology and pharmacology of the lithium ion. *Pharmacol. Rev., 9*, 17–58.

Schou, M. (1968). Lithium in psychiatric therapy & prophylaxis. *J. Psychiat. Research, 6*, 67–95.

Schwartz, A. (1992). *The man who could not kill enough: The secret murders of Milwaukee's Jeffrey Dahmer*. New York: Carol.

Seagraves, R. T. (1989). Effects of psychotropic drugs on human erection and ejaculation. *Arch. Gen. Psychiat., 46*, 275–284.

Searle, J. R. (1980). Minds, brains, & programs. *Behav. & Brain Sci., 3*, 417–424.

Searle, J. R. (1992). *The rediscovery of the mind.* Cambridge, MA: M.I.T. Press.

Searles, H. F. (1960). *The nonhuman envorinment in normal development and in schizophrenia.* New York: International Univ. Press.

Searles, H. F. (1964). *Collected papers on schizophrenia and related subjects.* New York: International Univ. Press.

Šebek, M. (1994, January 19). *Psychoanalysis in the Czech Republic during the communist regime.* Lecture presented at the American Academy of Psychoanalysis, New York.

Seccombe, T. (Ed.) (1927). *The surprising adventures of Baron Munchausen.* New York: Boni.

Sechèhaye, M. (1951). *Autobiography of a schizophrenic girl.* New York: Grune & Stratton.

Sechèhaye, M. (1956). *A new psychotherapy in schizophrenia: Relief of frustration by symbolic realization.* New York: Grune & Stratton.

Sedvall, G., Bjerkenstedt, P., Enroth, B., Fyro, C., Harnryd, C., & Wode-Helgodt, B. (1975). Prolactin levels in plasma & cerebrospinal fluid of psychiatric patients in relations to psychoactive drugs. *Euro. J. Clin. Pharmacol., 115,* 121.

Sedvall, G., Fyro, B., Gullberg, B., Nybaeck, H., Wiesel, F. A., & Wode-Helgodt, B. (1980). Relationships in healthy volunteers between concentrations of monoamine metabolites in cerebrospinal fluid and family history of psychiatric morbidity. *Brit. J. Psychiat., 136,* 366–374.

Seivewright, N. (1987). Relationships between life events and personality disorders. *Stress Med., 3,* 163–168.

Selemon, L. D., Rajkowska, G., & Goldman-Rakič, P. S. (1995). Abnormally high neuronal density in the schizophrenic cortex. *Arch. Gen. Psychiat., 52,* 805–818.

Selikoff, I. J., Robitzek, E. H., & Ornstein, G. G. (1952). Toxicity of hydrazine derivatives of isonicotinic acid in the chemotherapy of human tuberculosis. *Q. Bull. Sea View Hosp., 13,* 17.

Semelaigne, R. (1930). *Les pionniers de la psychiatrie française.* Paris: Baillière.

Sen, G. & Bose, K. C. (1931). Rauwolfia serpentina: A new drug for insanity and high blood pressure. *Indian Med. World, 2,* 194–201.

Serban, G. & Siegel, S. (1984). Responses of borderline and schizotypal patients to small doses of thiothixene and haloperidol. *Am. J. Psychiat., 141,* 1455–1458.

Sereny, G. (1995). *Albert Speer: His battle with the truth.* New York: A. Knopf.

Sérieux, P. & Capgras, J. (1909). *Les folies raisonnantes.* Paris: F. Alcan.

Shagass, C. (1968). Averaged somatosensory evoked responses in various psychiatric disorders. In J. Wortis (Ed.), *Recent advances in biological psychiatry* (pp. 205–219). New York: Plenum.

Shagass, C., Amadeo, M., & Overtaon, D. A. (1974). Eyetracking performance in psychiatric patients. *Biol. Psychiat., 9,* 245–260.

Shagass, C., Roemer, R. A., & Straumanis, J. J. (1978). Evoked potential correlates of psychosis. *Biol. Psychiat., 13,* 163–184.

Shagass, C. & Schwartz, M. (1962). Cerebral cortical reactivity in psychotic depression. *Arch. Gen. Psychiat., 6,* 235–242.

Shagass, C., Straumanis, J. J., & Roemer, R. A. (1977). Evoked potentials of schizophrenics in several sensory modalities. *Biol. Psychiat., 12,* 221–235.

Shannon, C. E. & Weaver, W. (1948, July & October). The mathematical theory of communication. In *Bell System Technical Journal.*

Shapiro, E., Shapiro, A. K., Fulop, G., Hubbard, M., Mandeli, J., Nordlie, J., & Phillips, R. A. (1989). Controlled study of haloperidol, pimozide, and placebo for the treatment of Gilles de la Tourette's syndrome. *Arch. Gen. Psychiat., 46,* 722–726.

Shapiro, T. (1983). The borderline syndrome in children: A critique. In K. S. Robson (Ed.), *The borderline child: Approaches to etiology, diagnosis, & treatment* (pp. 11–29). New York: McGraw Hill.

Sharpe, E. F. (1947). The psychoanalyst. *Internat. J. Psychoan., 28,* 1–6.

Shaywitz, B. A., Shaywitz, S. E., Pugh, K. R., Constable, R. T., Skudlarski, P., Fulbright, R. M., Bronen, R. A., Fletcher, J. M., Shankweller, D. P., Katz, L., & Gore, J. C. (1995). Sex differences in the functional organization of the brain for language. *Nature, 373,* 607–609.

Sheehy, G. (1976). *Passages.* New York: Dutton.

Sheldon, W. H. (1940). *The varieties of human physique.* New York: Harper.

Sherfey, M. J. (1966). The evolution and nature of female sexuality in relation to psychoanalytic theory. *J. Am. Psychoan. Assoc., 14,* 28–128.

Sherman, B., Pfohl, B., & Winokur, G. (1984). Circadian analysis of plasma cortisol levels before and after dexamethasone administration in depressed patients. *Arch. Gen. Psychiat., 41,* 271–275.

Siever, L. J., Coursey, R. D., & Alterman, I. S. (1984). Impaired smooth pursuit eye movements: Vulnerability marker for schizotypal personality disorder in a normal volunteer population. *Am. J. Psychiat., 141*, 1560–1566.

Siever, L. J., Silverman, J. M., Horvath, T. B., Klar, H., Coccaro, E., Keefe, R. S. E., Pinkham, L., Rinaldi, P., Mohs, R. C., & Davis, K. L. (1990). Increased morbid risk for schizophrenia-related disorders in relatives of schizotypal personality disordered patients. *Arch. Gen. Psychiat., 47*, 634–640.

Sifneos, P. E. (1981). Short-term anxiety-provoking psychotherapy. In S. H. Budman (Ed.), *Forms of brief therapy* (pp. 45–80). New York: Guilford.

Simeon, D., Stanley, B., Frances, A., Mann, J. J., Winchel, R., & Stanley, M. (1992). Self-mutilation in personality disorders: Psychological and biological correlates. *Am. J. Psychiat., 149*, 221–226.

Simmel, E. (1929). Psychoanalytic treatment in a sanatorium. *Internat. J. Psychoan., 10*: 70–89.

Simon, B. (1978). *Mind and madness in Ancient Greece: The classical roots of modern psychiatry.* Ithaca: Cornell Univ. Press.

Simon, H. A. (1967). Motivational and emotional controls of cognition. *Psychol. Review, 74*, 29–39.

Singer, L. T., Ambuel, B., & Wade, S. (1992). Cognitive-behavioral treatment of health-impairing food phobias in children. *J. Am. Acad. Child & Adol. Psychiat., 31*, 847–852.

Singer, M. T. & Ofshe, R. (1990). Thought reform programs and the production of psychiatric casualties. *Psychiat. Annals, 20*, 188–193.

Sinha, T. (1966). Development of psychoanalysis of India. *Internat. J. Psychoan., 47*, 427–439.

Sjöbring, H. (1914). *Den individualpsykologiska fragestalilningen inom psykiatrien.* Dissertation: Uppsala Univ.

Skinner, B. F. (1930). On the conditions of elicitation of certain eating reflexes. *Proc. Nat. Acad. Sci., 16*, 433–438.

Skinner, B. F. (1938). *The behavior of organisms: An experimental analysis.* New York: Appleton-Century.

Slater, E. (1938). Zur Erbpathologie des manisch-depressiven Irreseins: Die Eltern und die Kinder von Manisch Depressiven. *Z. Gesamt. Neurol. Psychiat., 163*, 1–47.

Slater, E. (1953). *Psychotic and neurotic illnesses in twins* (Medical Research Council Special Report No. 278). London: Her Majesty's Stationery Office.

Slovenko, R. (1995). *Psychiatry and criminal responsibility.* New York: Wiley Interscience.

Smirnoff, V. (1969/1995). The masochistic contract. In M. A. F. Hanly (Ed.), *Essential papers on masochism* (pp. 62–73). New York: N.Y.U. Press.

Smith, D. J. (1994). *Fatal innocence: The crime that shocked the world.* New York: St. Martin's Press.

Smith, M. L., Glass, C. V., & Miller, T. I. (1980). *The benefits of psychotherapy.* Baltimore: Johns Hopkins Univ. Press.

Snyder, S. H. (1976). The dopamine hypothesis of schizophrenia: Focus on the dopamine receptor. *Am. J. Psychiat., 133*, 197–202.

Snyder, S. H. (1978). The opiate receptor & morphine-like peptides in the brain. *Am. J. Psychiat., 135*, 645–652.

Snyder, S. H. (1985). Basic science of psychopharmacology. In H. S. Kaplan & B. J. Sadock (Eds.), *Comprehensive textbook of psychiatry, 4th ed.* (pp. 42–55). Baltimore: Williams & Wilkins.

Snyder, S. H. (1988). *The neurobiology of mood.* New York: Roerig-Pfizer.

Snyder, S. H., Banerjee, S. P., Yamamura, H. I., & Greenburg, D. (1974). Drugs, neurotransmitters & schizophrenia. *Science, 184*, 1243–1253.

Sobin, C., Sackheim, H. A., Prudic, J., Devanand, D. P., Moody, B. J., & McElhiney, M. C. (1995). Predictors of retrograde amnesia following ECT. *Am. J. Psychiat., 152*, 995–1001.

Solomon, M. I. & Murphy, G. E. (1984). Cohort studies of suicide. In H. S. Sudak, A. B. Ford, & N. B. Rushforth (Eds.), *Suicide in the young* (pp. 1–14). Boston: John Wright.

Solyom, L. (1987). A case of self-inflicted leucotomy. *Brit. J. Psychiat., 151*, 855–857.

Sperry, R. W. (1966). Hemispheric interaction and the mind-brain problem. In J. C. Eccles (Ed.), *Brain and conscious experience.* Berlin: Springer.

Spiegel, H. & Spiegel, D. (1978). *Trance & treatment: Clinical uses of hypnosis.* New York: Basic.

Spitz, R. (1946). Anaclitic depression. *Psychoan. Study of the Child, 2*, 313–342.

Spitz, R. (1951). The psychogenic diseases of infancy: An attempt at their etiologic classification. *Psychoan. Study of the Child, 6*, 255–278.

Spitzer, R. L. (1994, May 6). *The Changing Diagnostic & Statistical Manual of Mental Disorders.* Lecture presented at the American College of Forensic Psychiatry XII Annual Meeting, Montreal, Quebec.

Spitzer, R. L., Endicott, J., & Gibbons, M. (1975). Research diagnostic criteria. *Psychopharm. Bull., 11*, 22–24.

Spitzer, R. L., Endicott, J., & Gibbon, M. (1978). Research diagnostic criteria: Rationale and reliability. *Arch. Gen. Psychiat., 35,* 773–782.

Spitzer, R. L. & Fleiss, J. L. (1974). A reanalysis of the reliability of psychiatric diagnosis. *Brit. J. Psychiat., 125,* 341–347.

Sprague, R. L. & Sleator, E. K. (1977). Methylphenidate in hyperkinetic children. *Science, 198,* 1274–1276.

Srole, L. Langner, T. S., Michael, S. T., Opler, M. K., & Rennie, T. A. C. (1962). *Mental health in the metropolis.* New York: McGraw Hill.

Stanton, A. H. & Schwartz, M. S. (1954). *The mental hospital.* New York: Basic.

Steiger, H. & Zanko, M. (1990). Sexual traumata among eating disordered psychiatric and normal female groups. *J. Interpers. Viol., 5,* 74–86.

Stein, D. & Hollander, E. (1993). The spectrum of obsessive-compulsive related disorders. In E. Hollander (Ed.), *Obsessive-compulsive related disorders* (pp. 241–271). Washington, DC: American Psychiatric Association.

Stein, D. J. (1992). Clinical cognitive science: Possibilities and limitations. In D. J. Stein & J. E. Young (Eds.), *Cognitive science and clinical disorders* (pp. 3–17). New York: Academic.

Stein, D. J. & Young, J. F. (1992). *Cognitive science and clinical disorders.* New York: Academic.

Stein, M., Miller, A. H., & Trestman, R. L. (1991). Depression, the immune system, and health & illness. *Arch. Gen. Psychiat., 48,* 171–177.

Stern, A. (1938). Psychoanalytic investigation of and therapy in the border land group of neuroses. *Psychoan. Q., 7,* 467–489.

Stern, D. N. (1995). *The motherhood constellation: A unified view of parent-infant psychotherapy.* New York: Basic.

Sternbach, L. H. (1973). Chemistry of 1.5–benzodiazepines and some aspects of the structure-activity relationship. In S. Garattini, E. Mussini, & L. O. Randall (Eds.), *The benzodiazepines* (pp. 1–26). New York: Raven.

Still, G. F. (1902, April 12, 19, & 26). Some abnormal physical conditions in children. *Lancet,* 1008–1012, 1077–1082, 1163–1168.

Stolorow, R. D., Atwood, G. E., & Brandchaft, B. (1988). Masochism and its treatment. *Bull. Menn. Clin., 52,* 504–509.

Stone, M. H. (1973). Child psychiatry before the 20th century. *Internat. J. Child Psychiat., 2,* 264–308.

Stone, M. H. (1976). Possible influences of the full moon in a case of atypical mania. *Psychiat. Annals, 6,* 47–50.

Stone, M. H. (1977a). Dreams, free association, and the non-dominant hemisphere: An integration of psychoanalytic, neurophysiological, and historical data. *J. Am. Acad. Psychoan., 5,* 255–284.

Stone, M. H. (1977b). The borderline syndrome: Evolution of the term, genetic aspects, and prognosis. *Am. J. Psychother., 31,* 345–365.

Stone, M. H. (1979). Dreams of fragmentation and of the death of the dream. *Psychopharmacol. Bull., 15,* 12–14.

Stone, M. H. (1980). Modern concepts of emotion as prefigured in Descartes' "Passions of the Soul." *J. Am. Acad. Psychoan., 8,* 473–495.

Stone, M. H. (1981). Borderline syndromes: A consideration of subtypes and an overview, directions for research. *Psychiat. Clin. N. Am., 4,* 3–24.

Stone, M. H. (1990). *The fate of borderline patients.* New York: Guilford.

Stone, M. H. (1992). Incest, Freud's seduction theory, and borderline personality. *J. Am. Acad. Psychoan., 20,* 167–181.

Stone, M. H. (1993a). *Abnormalities of personality.* New York: Norton.

Stone, M. H. (1993b). Outcome of personality disorders. *Brit. J. Psychiat., 162,* 299–313.

Stone, M. H. (1994). Early traumatic factors in the lives of serial murderers. *Am. J. Forensic Psychiat., 15,* 5–26.

Stoudemire, J. (1973). Behavioral treatment of voyeurism and possible symptom substitution. *Psychother., 10,* 328–330.

Straus, M. A. & Gelles, R. J. (1990). *Physical violence in American families and adaptations to violence in 8,145 families.* New Brunswick, NJ: Transaction.

Strömgren, L. S. (1973). Unilateral vs. bilateral electro-convulsive therapy: Investigations into the therapeutic effect in endogenous depression. *Acta Psychiat. Scand., 240,* 8–65.

Sue, S. & McKinney, H. (1975). Asian Ameican in the community mental health care system. *Am. J. Orthopsychiat., 45,* 111–118.

Sullivan, H. S. (1953). *The interpersonal theory of psychiatry.* New York: Norton.

Sullivan, H. S. (1962). *Schizophrenia as a human process.* New York: Norton.

Sutton, S., Braren, M., & Zubin, J. (1965). Evoked potential correlates of stimulus uncertainty. *Science, 150,* 1187–1188.

Swanson, J. W., Holzer, C. E., Ganju, V. K., & Jonjo, R. T. (1990). Violence and psychiatric disorders in the community: Evidence from the Epidemiological Catchment Area surveys. *Hosp. & Commun. Psychiat., 41,* 761–770.

Swedo, S. E., Rapoport, J. L., Leonard, H., Lenane, M., & Cheslow, D. (1989). Obsessive-compulsive disorder in children and adolescents. *Arch. Gen. Psychiat., 46*, 335–341.

Takeuchi, M., Yoshino, A., Katoh, M., Ono, Y., & Kitamura, T. (1993). Reliability and validity of the Japanese version of the Tridimensional Personality Questionnaire among university students. *Comprehen. Psychiat., 34*, 273–279.

Tallal, P. (1992, November 20). *Language disorders of children.* Paper presented at the New York State Psychiatric Institute, Grand Rounds, NY.

Tallal, P. & Stark, R. E. (1982). Perceptual/motor profiles of reading impaired children with or without concomitant oral language deficits. *Ann. Dyslexia, 32*, 163–176.

Tancredi, L. (1990). Psychiatric malpractice. In R. Michels (Ed.), *Psychiatry* (vol. 3, ch. 29). Philadelphia: Lippincott.

Tandon, R. & Greden, J. F. (1989). Cholinergic hyperactivity and negative schizophrenic symptoms. *Arch. Gen. Psychiat., 46*, 745–753.

Tanzi, R. E. (1995, August 18). Third gene tied to early onset Alzheimer's. *New York Times.*

Taubman, B. (1988). *The "preppy" murder.* New York: St. Martin's Press.

Taubman, B. (1992). *Hell hath no fury: A true story of wealth and passion, love and envy, and a woman driven to the ultimate act of revenge.* New York: St. Martin's Press.

Tausk, V. (1919). Über den Beeinflußingsapparat in der Schizophrenia. *Internat. Zeitschr. für Psychoan., 5*, 1–33.

Taylor, M. A. & Abrams, R. (1975). A critique of the St. Louis Psychiatric Research criteria for schizophrenia. *Am. J. Psychiat., 132*, 1276–1280.

Taylor, P. J. & Hodgins, S. (1994). Violence and psychosis: Critical timings. *Crim. Behav. & Ment. Health, 4*, 267–289.

Taylor, P. J., Mullen, P., & Wessely, S. (1993). Psychosis, violence, & crime. In J. Gunn & P. J. Taylor (Eds.), *Forensic psychiatry: Clinical, legal, and ethical issues* (pp. 329–372). Oxford: Butterworth-Heinemann.

Terman, J. S., Terman, M., & Schlager, D. (1989). Efficacy of brief intense light exposure for treatment of winter depression. *Psychopharmacol. Bull., 26*, 3–11.

Theander, S. (1983). Research on outcome and prognosis of anorexia nervosa and some results of a Swedish long-term study. *Internat. J. Eating Dis., 2*, 167–174.

Theophrastus (1993). *Characters* J. Rusten, J. C. Cunningham, & A. D. Knox (Eds. and Trans.). Cambridge, MA: Harvard Univ. Press/Loeb Classical Library.

Thigpen, H. & Cleckley, H. M. (1950). A case of multiple personalty. *J. Abnorm. & Soc. Psychol., 49*, 135–151.

Thomas, A. & Chess, S. (1977). *Temperament & development.* New York: Brunner/Mazel.

Thomas, A., Chess, S., Birch, H., Hertzig, M., & Korn, S. (1963). *Behavioral individuality in early childhood.* New York: N.Y.U. Press.

Thorndike, E. L. (1911). *Animal intelligence.* New York: Macmillan.

Tienari, P. (1963). Psychiatric illnesses in identical twins. *Acta Scand. Psychiat., 171*, 1–195.

Tinbergen, N. (1948). Social releasers and the experimental method required for their study. *Wissenschaft. Bull., 60*, 6–52.

Tinbergen, N. (1951). *The study of instinct.* London: Oxford Univ. Press.

Toran-Allerand, D. (1984). On the genesis of sexual differentiation of the central nervous system: Morphogenetic consequences of steroidal exposure and possible role of alpha-fetoprotein. In G. J. DeVries, J. P. C. DeBruin, H. B. M. Uylings, & M. A. Corner (Eds.), *Sex differences in the brain: Progress in brain research* (pp. 63–98). New York: Elsevier.

Träksman-Bendz, L., Asberg, M., & Schalling, D. (1986). Serotonergic function and suicidal behavior in personality disorders. In J. J. Mann & M. S. Stanley (Eds.), *Psychobiology of suicidal behavior* (pp. 168–174). New York: NY Academy of Science.

Tremblay, R. E., Pihl, R. O., Vitaro, F., & Dobkin, P. L. (1994). Predicting early onset of male antisocial behavior from preschool behavior. *Arch. Gen. Psychiat., 51*, 732–739.

Trivers, R. L. (1974). Parent-offspring conflict. *Am. Zool., 14*, 249–264.

Tseng, W. S., Lu, Q. Y., & Yin, P. Y. (1995). Psychotherapy for the Chinese: Cultural considerations. In T. Y. Lin, W. S. Tseng, & E. K. Yeh (Eds.), *Chinese societies and mental health* (pp. 281–294). New York: Oxford.

Tsuang, M. T., Dempsey, G. M., & Rauscher, F. (1976). A study of atypical schizophrenia: Comparison with schizophrenia and affective disorder. *Arch. Gen. Psychiat., 33*, 1157–1160.

Tsuang, M. T., Lyons, M. J., & Faraone, S. V. (1990). Heterogeneity of schizophrenia: Conceptual models and analysis strategies. *Brit. J. Psychiat., 156*, 17–26.

Tsuang, M. T., Tohen, M., & Zahner, G. E. P. (Eds.)

(1995). *Textbook in psychiatric epidemiology*. New York: Wiley.

Tupes, E. C. & Christal, R. E. (1961–2). Recurrent personality factors based on trait ratings. *J. Personality, 60*, 225–251.

Tyrer, P. & Alexander, J. (1988). Personality asssessment schedule. In P. Tyrer (Ed.), *Personality disorders: Diagnosis, management, and course* (pp. 43–62). London: Wright.

Tyrer, P., Alexander, J., Cicchetti, D., Cohen, M.S., & Remington, M. (1979). Reliability of a schedule for rating personality disorders. *Brit. J. Psychiat., 135*, 168–174.

Vaillant, G. E. (1963). Natural history of remitting schizophrenia. *Am. J. Psychiat., 120*, 367–375.

Valzelli, L. (1970). Variazioni biochimiche cerebrali nel ratto muricida. In *Atti de IIdo Riunione Nazionale della Societa Italiana di Neuropsicofarmacologia* (pp. 20–25). Pisa: Pacini-Mariotti.

Valzelli, L. (1977). About a "specific" neurochemistry of aggressive behavior. In J. Delgado & F. DeFeudis (Eds.), *Behavioral neurochemistry* (pp. 113–132). New York: Spectrum.

Valzelli, L. (1978). Human & animal studies on the neurophysiology of aggression. *Prog. Neuropsychopharmacol., 2*, 591–611.

Valzelli, L. (1981). *Psychobiology of aggression*. New York: Raven.

Valzelli, L., Bernasconi, C., & Cusumano, G. (1977). Annual and daily changes in brain serotonin content in differently housed mice. *Neuropsychobiol., 3*, 35–41.

van der Kolk, B. A. (1989). Compulsion to repeat the trauma: Reenactment, revictimization, and masochism. *Psychiat. Clin. N. Am., 12*, 389–411.

van der Kolk, B. A. (1995, July 8). *Trauma in adolescents*. Paper presented at the Fourth International Society of Adolescent Psychiatry Congress. Athens, Greece.

van der Kolk, B. A., Greenberg, M. S., & Boyd, H. (1985). Inescapable shock, neurotransmitters, and addiction to trauma. *Biol. Psychiat., 20*, 314–325.

van Praag, H. M. & Kort, J. (1971). Endogenous depression with and without disturbances in 5–hydroxy-tryptamine metabolism: A biochemical classification? *Psychopharmacol., 19*, 148–152.

Vanggaard, T. (1989). *Panic*. New York: Norton.

Vaughn, C. E. & Leff, J. P. (1976a). The influence of family and social factors on the course of psychiatric illness. *Brit. J. Psychiat., 129*, 125–137.

Vaughn, C. E. & Leff, J. P. (1976b). The measurement of experienced emotion in the families of psychiatric patients. *Brit. J. Soc. & Clin. Psychol., 15*, 157–164.

Vela, R., Gottlieb, H., & Gottlieb, E. (1983). Borderline syndromes in childhood: A critical review. In K. S. Robson (Ed.), *The borderline child: Approaches to etiology, diagnosis, and treatment* (pp. 31–48). New York: McGraw Hill.

Virkkunen, M., DeJong, J., Bartko, J., Goodwin, F. K., & Linnoila, M. (1989). Relationship of psychological variables to recidivism in violent offenders and impulsive fire-setters. *Arch. Gen. Psychiat., 46*, 600–603.

Virkkunen, M. & Linnoila, M. (1992, September 10). *CSF 5–HIAA and testosterone in violence*. Paper presented at the First European Symposium on Aggression in Clinical Psychiatric Practice, Stockholm, Sweden.

von Bertalanffy, L. (1968). *General system theory*. New York: George Braziller.

von Neumann, J. & Morgenstern, O. (1944). *Theory of games and economic behavior*. Princeton, NJ: Princeton Univ. Press.

Walk, A. (1969). The pre-history of child psychiatry. *Brit. J. Psychiat., 110*, 754–767.

Walker, N. (1991). Dangerous mistakes. *Brit. J. Psychiat., 158*: 752–757.

Waller, G. (1991). Sexual abuse as a factor in eating disorders. *Brit. J. Psychiat., 159*, 664–671.

Waller, G. (1992). Sexual abuse and the severity of bulimic symptoms. *Brit. J. Psychiat., 161*, 90–93.

Wallerstein, R. (1986). *Forty-two lives*. New York: Guilford.

Wallerstein, R. S. (1995). The effectiveness of psychoanalysis and psychotherapy: Conceptual issues and empirical work. In T. Shapiro & R. N. Emde (Eds.), *Research in psychoanalysis: Process, development, outcome* (pp. 299–312). Madison, CT: International Univ. Press.

Walter, W. G., Cooper, R., & Aldridge, A. (1964). Contingent negative variation: An electric sign of the sensorimotor association and expectancy in the human brain. *Nature, 203*, 380–384.

Watson, J. B. & Raynor, R. (1920). Conditioned emotional reactions. *J. Experiment. Psychol., 3*, 1–14.

Wechsler, D. (1938). *The measurement of adult intelligence*. Baltimore: Williams & Wilkins.

Wehr, T. (1989). Seasonal affective disorder: A historical overview. In N. E. Rosenthal & M. C. Blehar (Eds.), *Seasonal affective disorder and phototherapy* (pp. 11–32). New York: Guilford.

Weil-Malherbe, H. & Bone, A. D. (1959). The effect of reserpine on the intracellular distribution of catechol-amines in the brain stem of the rabbit. *J. Neurochem., 4,* 251–263.

Weiner, D. B. (1992). Philippe Pinel's "Memoir on Madness" of December 11, 1794: A fundamental test of modern psychiatry. *Am. J. Psychiat., 149,* 725–732.

Weiner, H. (1969). *Nine and a half mystics: The Kabbalah today.* New York: Collier.

Weinrich, J. D. (1987). A new sociobiological theory of homosexuality applicable to societies with universal marriage. *Ethol. & Sociobiol., 8,* 37–47.

Weintraub, S. & Neale, J. M. (1978). The Stony Brook high risk project. In B. Feinsilver & C. Bank (Eds.), *Developmental disabilities of early childhood.* Springfield, IL: C. Thomas.

Weintraub, S. & Neale, J. M. (1984). Social behavior of children at high risk for schizophrenia. In N. F. Watts, E. J. Anthony, L. C. Wynne, & J. E. Rolf (Eds.), *Children at risk for schizophrenia: A longitudinal perspective* (pp. 279–285). Cambridge: Cambridge Univ. Press.

Weiss, J. (1990). Unconscious mental functioning. *Scientific Am., 262,* 103–109.

Weissberg, M. (1992). *The first sin of Ross Michael Carlson: A psychiatrist's personal account of murder, multiple personality disorder, and modern justice.* New York: Delacorte.

Weissman, M. M. (1979). The psychological treatment of depression: Evidence for the efficacy of psychotherapy alone, in comparison with pharmacotherapy. *Arch. Gen. Psychiat., 36,* 1261–1269.

Weissman, M. M., Kidd, K. K., & Prusoff, B. A. (1982). Variability of rates of affective disorders of depressed and normal probands. *Arch. Gen. Psychiat., 39,* 1397–1403.

Weissman, M. M., Meyers, J. K,. & Harding, P. S. (1978). Psychiatric disrders in a U. S. urban community. *Am. J. Psychiat., 135,* 459–462.

Wen, J. K. (1995). Sexual beliefs and problems in contemporary Taiwan. In T. Y. Lin, W. S. Tseng, & E. K. Yeh (Eds.), *Chinese societies and mental health* (pp. 219–230). New York: Oxford.

Wender, P. H. (1971). *Minimal brain dysfunction in children.* New York: Wiley Interscience.

Wender, P. H., Reimherr, F. W., & Wood, D. R. (1981). Attention deficit disorder in adults. *Arch. Gen. Psychiat., 38,* 449–456.

Werry, J. S. & Aman, M. G. (1993). *Practitioners' guide to psychoactive drugs for children and adolescents.* New York: Plenum.

Whatley S. A. & Owen, M. J. (1989). Molecular genetics and its application to the study of psychi-atric disorders. *Internat. Rev. Psychiat., 1,* 219–230.

Whitam, F. L., Diamond, M., & Martin, J. (1993). Homosexual orientation in twins: A report on 61 pairs and 3 triplet sets. *Arch. Sexual Behav., 22,* 187–206.

Whitman, R., Torsman, H., & Koenig, R. (1954). Clinical assessment of passive aggressive personality. *Arch. Neurol. Psychiat., 72,* 540–549.

Widiger, T. A. & Rogers, J. H. (1989). Prevalence and comorbidity of personality disorders. *Psychait. Ann., 19,* 132–136.

Widiger, T. A. & Trull, T. J. (1992). Personality and psychopathology: An application of the Five-Factor Model. *J. Personality, 60,* 353–393.

Wiener, N. (1948). *Cybernetics, or, Control and communication in the animal and the machine.* New York: Wiley.

Willerman, L. (1973). Activity level and hyperactivity in twins. *Child Develop., 44,* 288–293.

Willi, J. & Grossman, S. (1983). Epidemiology of anorexia nervosa in a defined region of Switzerland. *Am. J. Psychiat., 140,* 564–567.

Wilson, A., Brown, A., & Matheny, A. (1971). Emergence and persistence of behavioral differences in twins. *Child Develop., 42,* 1381–1398.

Wilson, B. (1938). *As Bill sees it: The A .A. way of life. Selected writings of A. A.'s co-founder.* New York: Alcoholics Anonymous World Services.

Wilson, C. (1984). *A criminal history of mankind.* New York: Putnam.

Wilson, C. & Seaman, D. (1992). *The serial killers: A study in the psychology of violence.* New York: Carol.

Wilson, E. O. (1971). *The insect societies.* Cambridge, MA: Harvard Univ. Press.

Wilson, E. O. (1975). *Sociobiology: The new synthesis.* Cambridge, MA: Harvard Univ. Press.

Wilson, E. O. (1978). Altruism. *Harvard Mag. Nerv. Dev.,* 23–28.

Wilson, J. Q. & Herrnstein, R. J. (1985). *Crime & human nature.* New York: Simon & Schuster.

Wilson, J. Q. (1993). *The moral sense.* New York: Macmillan/Free.

Winnicott, D. W. (1949). Hate in the countertransference. *Internat. J. Psychoan., 30,* 69–74.

Winnicott, D. W. (1965). *The maturational process and the facilitating environment.* New York: International Univ. Press.

Winokur, G. (1975). The Iowa 500: Heterogeneity and course of manic-depressive illness (bipolar). *Compr. Psychiat., 16,* 125–131.

Winokur, G., Clayton, P., & Reich, T. (1969) *Manic depressive illness.* St. Louis: Mosby.

Winokur, G. & Tanna, V. I. (1969). Possible role of X-linked dominant factor in manic-depressive disease. *Dis. Nerv. System, 30*, 89.

Winson, J. (1985). *Brain & psyche: The biology of the unconscious*. Garden City, NJ: Doubleday.

Winson, J. (1990). The meaning of dreams. *Scient. Am., 263*, 86–96.

Winston, A. & Laikin, M. (1994). Short term dynamic psychotherapy of personality disorders. *Am. J. Psychiat., 151*: 190–194.

Wise, S. P. & Rapoport, J. L. (1989). Obsessive-compulsive disorder: Is it basal ganglia dysfunction? In J. L. Rapoport (Ed.), *Obsessive-compulsive disorders in children and adolescents* (pp.327–344). Washington, DC: American Psychiatric Association.

Wolf, E. (1980). On the developmental line of selfobject relations. In A. Goldberg (Ed.), *Advances in self psychology* (pp. 117–135). New York: International Univ. Press.

Wolff, L. (1988). *Postcards from the end of the world: Child abuse in Freud's Vienna*. New York: Atheneum.

Wolpe, J. (1969). *The practice of behavior therapy*. New York: Penguin.

Wright, R. (1994). *The moral animal: The new science of evolutionary psychology*. New York: Pantheon.

Wurtman, R. J. (1985) Alzheimer's disease. *Scient. Am., 252*, 62–74.

Wurtman, R. J. & Wurtman, J. J. (1989). Carbohydrates and depression. *Scient. Am., 260*, 68–75.

Wynne, L. C. (1958). Pseudomutuality in the family relations of schizophrenia. *Psychiatry, 21*, 215–220.

Wynne, L. C., Singer, M. T., Bartko, J. J., & Toohey, M. L. (1977). Schizophrenics and their families. In J. M. Tanner (Ed.), *Developments in psychiatric research* (pp. 254–286). London: Hodden Stoughton.

Yang, K. S. & Lee, P. H. (1989). Likeability, meaningfulness, and familiarity of 557 Chinese adjectives for personality trait descriptions. *Acta Psychol. Taiwanica, 13*, 36–37.

Yeh, E. K., Hwu, H. G., & Lin, T. Y. (1995). Mental disorders in Taiwan: Epidemiological studies of community population. In T. Y. Lin, W. S. Tseng, & E. K. Yeh (Eds.), *Chinese societies and mental health* (pp. 247–265). New York: Oxford.

Yudofsky, S. C., Silver, J. M., & Hales, R. E. (1993). Cocaine and aggressive behavior: Neurobiological and clinical perspectives. *Bull. Menn. Clinic, 57*, 218–226.

Yudofsky, Silver, J. M., Jackson, W., Endicott, J., & Williams, D. (1986). The Overt Aggression Scale for the objective rating of verbal and physical aggression. *Am. J. Psychiat., 143*, 35–39.

Yudofsky, S. C., Silver, J. M., & Schneider, S. E. (1987). Pharmacological treatment of aggression. *Psychiat. Annals, 17*, 397–407.

Zadeh, L. (1965). Fuzzy sets. *Information & Control, 8*, 338–353.

Zanarini, M. & Gunderson, J. G. (1990). Childhood experiences of borderline patients. *Comprehen. Psychiat., 30*, 18–25.

Zanarini, M., Gunderson, J. G., Marino, M. F., Schwartz, E. O., & Frankenberg, F. R. (1989). Childhood experiences of borderline patients. *Compr. Psychiat., 30*, 18–25.

Zilboorg, G. (1941). *A history of medical psychology*. New York: Norton.

Zubin, J. & Spring, B. (1977) Vulnerability: A new view of schizophrenia. *J. Abnorm. Psychol., 86*, 103–126.

Zuckerman, M. (1991). *Psychobiology of personality*. New York: Cambridge Univ. Press.

Zung, W.K. (1971). A rating instrument for anxiety disorders. *Psychosomatics, 12*, 371–379.

INDEX